CONTENTS

Summary of Contents

Chapter 1:   Distributing Objects
Distributed computing fundamentals and a comparison of available distributed systems, including Sockets, Inferno, Java, CORBA and COM.

Chapter 2:   Distributed Objects on Windows
An examination of traditional methods of sharing code and data on Windows. Examples include a simple remote server. Builds up the concepts to provide you with a deeper understanding of COM.

Chapter 3:   The Component Object Model
The structure of COM. Examines object creation, interfaces, Automation, marshaling and monikers.

Chapter 4:   Distributed Component Object Model
Covers the essentials of DCOM — its relationship with RPC, relevant registry entries, its APIs and interfaces.

Chapter 5:   Writing DCOM Clients and Servers
Microsoft's Interface Definition Language (MIDL) in detail. Looks at proxy-stub and type library marshaling, and connection points.

Chapter 6:   DCOM under the Hood
An investigation of DCOM internals and a comparison of DCOM with raw RPC.

Chapter 7:   Security
A detailed breakdown of NT's security model and its application to DCOM.

Chapter 8:   DCOM Servers as NT Services
Creating DCOM servers as NT services. An examination of the APIs and ATL services. Also shows event logging.

Chapter 9:   Multithreading
An examination of threading with Win32, synchronization issues, multithreading techniques and DCOM's threading models.

Chapter 10: Microsoft Transaction Server
An overview of Microsoft Transaction Server. Examines MTS components and packages, security, threading and transactions.

Appendix A: Debugging Tips

Professional
DCOM
Programming

Dr Richard Grimes

Wrox Press Ltd.®

Professional DCOM Programming

Published by Wrox Press Ltd, 30 Lincoln Road, Olton, Birmingham B27 6PA , UK.
Printed in Canada
5 TRI 99 98

ISBN 1-861000-60-X

Trademark Acknowledgements

Credits

Authors
Richard Grimes

Technical Editors
Alex Stockton

Technical Reviewers
Saud Alshibani
Glenn DeWysockie
Dave Gristwood
Magus Gudmundsson
Charlie Kindell
Claus Loud

Technical Reviewers
Anil Peres-da-Silva
Marc Simpkin
Michael Tracy

Development Editor
John Franklin

Cover/Design/Layout
Andrew Guillaume
Graham Butler

Copy Edit/Index
Dominic Shakeshaft

Cover photo by Ken Fisher
Supplied by Tony Stone/Hulton Getty Images

About the Author

Richard Grimes first learnt to program at school using an aged teletype terminal with remote access to a local University's HP 2000 – after that he was totally infected by the programming bug. He honed his skills writing instrument control and data analysis software while studying for a PhD in semiconductor physics. After leaving the relative safety of academia, he was thrust into the commercial world and took up residence as an instructor and course writer for a programming training company.

Richard now works for Parallax Solutions designing and writing distributed object based applications for the retail automotive industry. Parallax is a Sun Object Reality Center and Richard's primary task is to compare Microsoft's object model with other available technologies and apply his conclusions to actual application development.

Richard can be contacted via email at dcom.dev@grimes.demon.co.uk

Dedication

To my wife Ellinor, and children, Jennifer and Thomas, for their patience and support while I wrote this book.

Thanks

I would like to thank several people at Wrox Press: Dave Maclean, who originally persuaded me to write this book; John Franklin, for his support when I was having doubts, but particularly Alex Stockton, whose considerable efforts have made sure that this book flows well, and that the technical details are right. I would also like to thank my colleagues at Parallax for the numerous conversations about COM.

Thanks also to the numerous reviewers who put things in perspective.

Of course, the text would never have been written without the support of my family, particularly my wife Ellinor, who always believed in me, even in those dark times when I felt that the book wasn't possible.

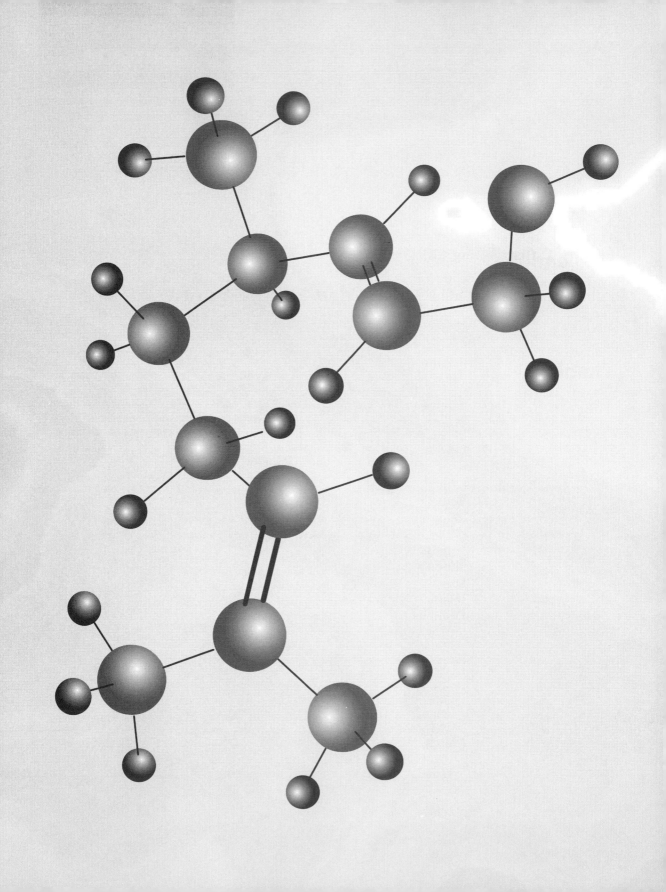

CONTENTS

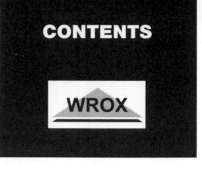

Table of Contents

Introduction   **1**

Chapter 1: Distributing Objects   **9**

  Introduction   9
  Distributed Objects and Distributed Data   9
    Distributed Data   10
    Distributed Objects   11
    Handling Heterogeneous Systems   12
  Distribution   13
    Network Protocols   13
      Connection-Based Protocols   13
      Connectionless Protocols   13
    Properties of Systems of Distribution   14
      Object Locator   14
      Communication   14
        Data Typing   14
        Data Representation   15
        Synchronous and Asynchronous Communication   15
      State Persistence   15
      Security   15
      Reliability and Availability   16
      Load Balancing   16
  Methods of Distribution   16
    Sockets   17
    Inferno   17
    Distributed Computing Environment RPC   19
      The RPC Mechanism   19
      Comparing Microsoft RPC and DCE   20
        DCE Directory Service and the Microsoft Locator   20
        Security   22
      Using Mixed DCE and Microsoft RPC   23
      Multithreading   24
      Objects and Interfaces   24
      Server Activation   25
    CORBA   25
      CORBA Architecture   25
      Interface Invocation   30
        Static Invocation Interface 30
        Dynamic Interface Invocation 30
      Object Adapters   31

OMA - The Wider Picture	31
ORB Interoperability	32
Security	32
CORBA Platforms	32
Multithreading	33
Server Activation	33
Java Distributed Objects	33
Java and Sockets	34
RMI	35
Server Activation	40
Java IDL	40
Multithreading	43
Server Activation	43
COM	43
COM Architecture	43
Dynamic and Static Invocation	44
Multithreading	45
Server Activation	45
OLE Interfaces	45
Other Services	46
Remote Automation	46
Summary	47

Chapter 2: Distributed Objects on Windows — **49**

Dynamic Link Libraries	50
Sharing Code	50
Dynamic Linking	50
Interfaces	51
Exporting Functions	52
Language Issues	54
Runtime Linking	55
Defining Interfaces	56
Example: Window Enumerator Library	59
Putting It All Together	62
Visible and Hidden Windows	64
Enhancing the Interface	64
Problems with DLLs	65
DLLs - Summary	65
Sharing Data	66
DLL Data Sections	67
Memory Mapped Files	68
MMF Pitfalls	70
Listening Executables	72
Running the Server	72
The Interactive User	72
The Startup Folder	72
NT Services	73
Windows 95 PseudoServices	73

COM Servers 73
Listening Methods 73
TCP 74
UDP 74
Windows Messages 74
DDE 75
Named Pipes 75
DCE RPC 75
COM 76
Example: TCP Server 76
WinSock 77
TCPServer and TCPClient 77
Protocol 77
Initializing the Server 81
Threads 81
Connection Objects 82
ClientSocket 83
Putting It All together 83
Issues 84
Multithreading 84
Data Formats and Transmission 84
Calling Functions 85
Pinging 86
Exceptions 86
How Does This Relate to DCOM? 86
Summary 87

Chapter 3: The Component Object Model   89

Introduction 89
COM Milestones 91
The Clipboard 91
DDE 92
16-bit OLE 1.0 92
16-bit OLE 2.0 94
OLE Controls 95
32-bit OLE 95
ActiveX 96
Standards 96
COM Basics 97
Memory Allocation 98
IUnknown 99
Reference Counting 99
QueryInterface() 101
Standard Error Reporting and Status Codes 102
Identifiers 103
Registry 104

File Extensions	104
ProgIDs	104
GUIDs	105
COM Information	106
Initializing COM	106
Creating COM Objects	107
CoGetClassObject()	108
CoCreateInstance()	109
COM Servers	110
Inproc Servers	111
Creation Sequence	111
DLL Management	113
Local Servers	113
Remote Servers	116
Inproc Handlers	116
Interfaces	117
Implementing Interfaces	120
Multiple Inheritance	120
Nested Classes	122
Object Server Lifetime	124
Automation	126
Object Description Language	127
IDispatch	128
BSTR	130
SAFEARRAY	130
Data Type Coercion	132
Late and Early Binding	132
Using Automation	133
Dual Interfaces	133
Interface Marshaling	134
Standard	135
TypeLib	136
Custom	136
Monikers	138
Persistent State	138
Running Object Table	138
COM and Object Orientation	139
Objects	140
Classes	140
Encapsulation	140
Inheritance	140
Interface Inheritance	140
Implementation Inheritance	141
Containment/Delegation	141
Aggregation	141
Polymorphism	141
Summary	141

Chapter 4: Distributed Component Object Model   **143**

What is DCOM?   143
DCOM and DCE   143
DCOM on Windows   144
How Does DCOM Work?   144
Protocols   145
Object Lifetimes   146
Reference Counting   146
Pinging   146
Delta-Pinging   148
Configuring Legacy Components   150
Registry Settings   152
ActivateAtStorage   154
Surrogates   156
Surrogate Registry Entries   157
Activating Inproc Objects in a Surrogate   157
Writing a Surrogate   158
Limitations   159
DCOM Applications   160
Client Code   160
Locating Servers   160
Optimizations   161
Querying for Multiple Interfaces   161
Security   163
Server Code   165
Threading Issues   165
Security   167
Writing DCOM Code   167
Working Code   168
Time Server   168
The Proxy-Stub   172
Time Client   173
Testing the Code   179
The Tests   179
Summary   182

Chapter 5: Writing DCOM Clients and Servers   **185**

Introduction   185
Interface Definition Language   185
MIDL   186
Files Created by MIDL   187
MIDL Variable Types   187
Base Types   188
Automation Types   189
Typedefs, Constants and Enumerations   189
Structs and Unions   190

Discriminated Unions	191
Non-encapsulated Unions	192
Arrays	192
Fixed Arrays	193
Conformant Arrays	194
Varying Arrays	195
Open Arrays	196
Enumerators	196
Strings	197
BSTRs	198
Exceptions	198
Help File Support in MIDL	198
Interfaces	200
dispinterface	202
dispinterface syntax	203
Dual Interfaces	204
oleautomation	205
Defining Objects	206
Type Libraries	206
Interface Definition Inside Library Block	207
Modules	209
Mappings for Other Languages	210
Type Library Marshaling	210
Environment Server	211
Environment Client	215
Testing the Code	219
Local Testing	219
Remote Testing	220
Connection Points	222
Making Connections	223
IConnectionPoint Interface	223
IConnectionPointContainer Interface	225
Enumeration Interfaces	226
IEnumConnectionPoints	227
IEnumConnections	227
Type Information	227
Implementing Connection Points	228
AlarmServer	230
Creating the Project	230
Editing CRemoteAlarm	232
Adding Thread Structure	233
Implementing Incoming Methods	234
AlarmClient	237
CAlarm	244
Accessing ATL from MFC projects	245
Testing the Code	246
Remote Test	247
Summary	248

Chapter 6: DCOM Under the Hood   **251**

   Introduction   251
   The Test Interface   251
   The DCOM Test Application   252
      The Client   266
      Hidden Windows   268
     Remote Testing   269
   Experiments on the DCOM Application   269
     Tests on the Local Machine   269
      IExternalConnection   272
      IStdIdentity   272
     Tests with a Remote Machine - Apartment Model   274
     Tests with a Remote Machine - Free Threading Model   278
   The Microsoft RPC Test Application   279
      RPC Client   283
     Tests on the Local Machine   284
     Tests with a Remote Machine   285
   Network Tests   285
     Network Monitor   285
     RPC   285
     DCOM   287
      Start of the Conversation   287
      CoCreateInstance   288
      Server Identifies its Security   290
      Client Sends its Security Context   290
      Server Acknowledgement   291
      Reverse   295
      The Final Death Throes   297
     Analysis   298
   Service Control Manager and the OXID Resolver   299
     The OXID Resolver   299
     The Service Control Manager   300
   Optimizations   301
     MultiTest   302
     MultiClient   307
     Results   313
      Local Calls   314
      Remote Calls   314
     Conclusion   315
   Summary   316

Chapter 7: Security   **319**

   Introduction   319
   The Need for Security   321
     The Catalogue Project   322

Client	326
Protecting Servers from Users	328
Protecting Users from Servers	328
Protecting Users from Themselves	328
Ringing Alarm Bells	328
The NT Security Model	**329**
Accounts	329
Workgroups	330
Domains	330
Trusted Domains	330
Domain Account != Local Account	331
Groups	332
Security IDs	334
Privileges and User Rights	336
AccessTokens	337
Impersonation	338
NT Objects	338
Security Descriptors	340
Summary	343
Accessing Objects	344
Security Programming	**344**
Getting Information	344
SIDs	345
Trustees	346
Access Tokens	347
Privileges and Rights	349
Security Descriptors	352
Access Control Lists	354
Impersonation	356
Services	356
Window Stations and Desktops	358
Using Window Stations	360
COM Security	**361**
Registry	361
DCOMCnfg	361
OLEView	363
EnableDCOM	364
Activation Security	365
Call Security	366
AccessPermission	367
DefaultAccessPermission	367
Impersonation	367
LegacyAuthenticationLevel	369
LegacyImpersonationLevel	369
LegacySecureReferences	370
Experiments	370
Coding Security	376
Initializing Security	376
Process-wide Basis	376

Interface-Wide Client-Side	379
Interface-Wide Server-Side	381
Experiments	382
Summary	389

Chapter 8: DCOM Servers as NT Services — 391

Introduction	391
NT Services	391
Utilities	393
Control Panel	394
Winmsd	397
SC	398
Registry	399
Writing an NT Service	400
Executable Entry Point	400
ServiceMain()	401
ServiceCtrlHandler	405
Logging Errors	407
Communication with SCM	409
Service Database	409
Multithreading	411
Worker Threads	411
IO Completion Ports	411
Registry Settings	412
Global Settings	412
Security	413
Debugging Services	413
DCOM Services	414
Cons	414
Pros	415
Code	415
ATL Support for Services	415
EnumWinSvr	419
Client	429
Creation	429
Tests	434
Event Log	435
The Event Viewer	436
Event Sources	440
Message Resource Files	441
Registry Entries	444
Reporting Events	445
Reading Events	446
Example: Adding an Event Resource File	447
Adding a New Event Log	449
Summary	450

Chapter 9: Multithreading   **453**

Multithreaded Win32 Applications   453
   Thread Handling Functions   454
     Lifetime of a Thread   454
     Creating Threads   455
     Terminating a Thread   458
     Threads and Windows   458
     Fibers   459
   Thread Data   459
     Synchronization   460
     Reentrancy   462
     Synchronizing Thread Actions   464
       Event Object   464
     Thread Local Storage   464
       Thread Local Storage   466
   Thread Models   467
     Worker Threads   467
     Improving the Server Model   470
       Threads In MFC   471
       Thread Pool   472
       IO Completion Ports   480
Multithreaded DCOM Servers   481
   Apartment Models   481
     Single Threaded Apartment   483
     Multithreaded Apartment   486
     Choosing Between STA and MTA Models   487
     Mixed Model   488
     InProc Servers   489
       Single Threaded Server and Multiple-STA Client   489
       Single Threaded Server and MTA Client   489
       MTA Server and STA client   489
   Examples   490
     LoggerSvr   490
     ATL Threading Models   491
     CLogger   493
       s_mutex   494
       Message()   495
       FinalConstruct()/FinalRelease()   496
       LogMessage()   496
       VB Client   497
     ReverseLoggerSvr   498
       _tWinMain()   500
       ReverseThread()   501
       FinalConstruct()/FinalRelease()   503
       LogMessage()   504
       Running the code   506
Summary   508

Chapter 10: Microsoft Transaction Server   **511**

  Introduction   511
    Transactions   511
      Threading   511
      Security   512
      Installation   512
      JIT Activation and Object Pooling   512
  What is MTS?   512
    Surrogate Exe   513
    Distributed Transaction Coordinator   514
      Resource Provision   514
    MTS Explorer   514
  MTS Components   516
    Registration   517
    The Context Object   519
    Passing Interface Pointers   520
    Component Location   520
  Packages   521
    MTS Packages   522
    Creating Packages   522
  Base Clients and Activities   522
  Transactions   523
    Resource Managers   524
      SQL Server 6.5   524
    Resource Dispensers   524
      ODBC Resource Dispenser   524
      Shared Property Manager   525
    Transaction Requirements   526
    Distributed Transactions   528
    DTC and Transactions   528
  Threading   529
    Main   530
    Apartment   530
    Rental   530
  Security   530
    Declarative Access Control   532
    Programmatic Access Control   532
  Activating Objects   533
    Just in Time Activation   533
    Instance Pooling   534
  ATL Components   534
  Programming Paradigm   536
  MTS and DCOM   537
  Summary   537

Appendix A: Debugging Tips **539**

  Debugging DCOM Servers 539
    Starting a Server from Developer Studio 539
    Attaching to a Running Server 539
    Starting the Debugger from a Command Line 540
    Debugging an Object Server from the Client 541
    Running an Object under an Appropriate Account 542
  COM Tips 542
    CoCreateInstance() fails 542
    Method Calls Fail 543
    Casting Interface Pointers 543
    Using OLEView 544
    Writing VB Clients 545
      Creating Objects in VB 546

Index **549**

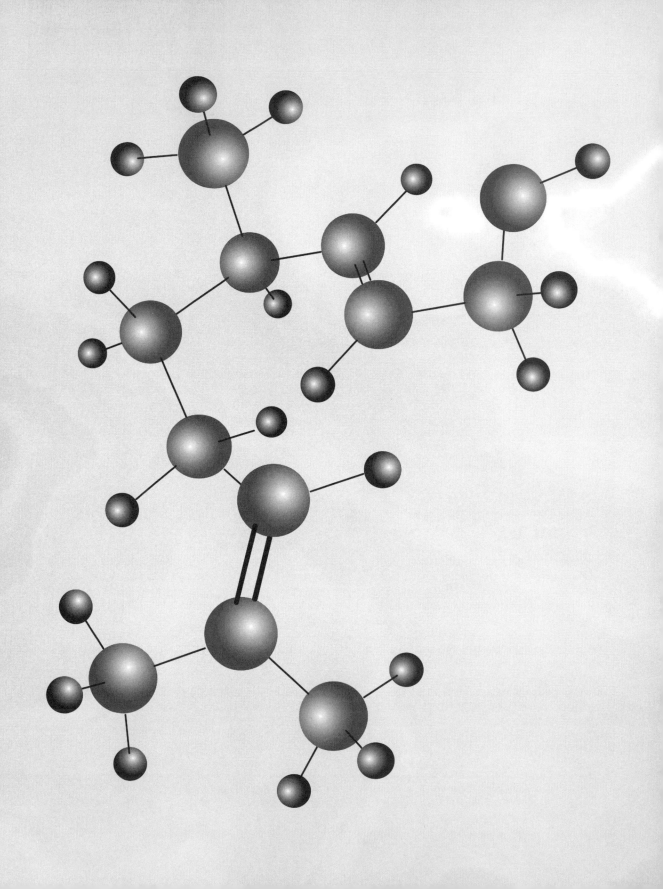

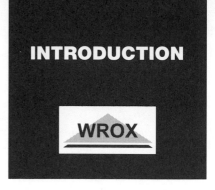

I know a lot of people tend to skip the introduction to books, but if you keep reading, you'll find it worthwhile. You'll discover what DCOM is (if you don't already know), you'll find a neat summary of the contents of the book, and you'll see what you need in the way of software and prior experience to get the most out of this book.

Welcome to *Professional DCOM Programming*. As I hope the title suggests to you, we're going to be looking at DCOM programming! DCOM is the Distributed Component Object Model, a language-independent binary standard for distributing objects across a network.

DCOM started life as plain old COM, which first gained acceptance as the plumbing under OLE. If you know anything about COM, you've probably heard DCOM referred to as 'COM with a longer wire'. This is certainly true to an extent, in that it allows COM objects to be activated on remote machines. However, DCOM is more than just 'COM with a longer wire'. It introduces programming, security, and threading issues not present before the release of DCOM. Those issues form the main subject of this book.

Whether or not you've programmed for COM before, if you're an experienced C++ Windows programmer who wants to understand DCOM, this is the book for you.

Book Structure

Chapter 1

In Chapter 1, we'll look at distributed systems in general. I start by explaining the differences between distributed data, remote objects and distributed objects, then move on to the mechanisms that are necessary for distribution. Firstly, I'll be describing the fundamentals of connection-based and connectionless protocols, then looking at the facilities that a good distribution mechanism should provide.

The majority of the chapter consists of an examination of the various systems of distribution currently available. You'll see the benefits and shortcomings of Sockets, Inferno, DCE RPC, CORBA, Java and COM.

Whether you're familiar with traditional systems of distribution like Sockets or RPC with no support for objects, or you're from a CORBA or Java background, you'll see the difference that DCOM makes.

Chapter 2

In Chapter 2, we examine how data and code can be shared between executables in Windows. Throughout the chapter, we build up the concepts to provide you with a deeper understanding of COM. You'll see some of the fundamental problems with traditional methods of sharing code that COM helps to solve.

We start by looking at dynamic link libraries (DLLs) and how they can be used to share code between processes. While showing how useful DLLs can be, I also show the difficulties in managing different versions. We'll engage COM to solve those difficulties.

Next we examine the most popular ways of sharing data between Windows processes: using data sections and using memory mapped files. COM does not allow you to directly access data (in OO parlance, this is data hiding).

Then we launch into true servers. If you're running code on a remote machine, the server must, in some way, be started. It must also accept a client request, dispatch the request to the appropriate code and then return data back to the client. Sounds simple, but we'll be going through the pitfalls and solutions in detail.

Finally, we'll develop a real remote server, using WinSock. By studying the code, you'll get an idea of the problems involved in marshaling data and dispatching method calls. If you were to use Sockets to write such a server yourself, you would have to solve these problems too, but if you use COM, all this (and more) has been solved for you.

Chapter 3

Here we move on to a real introduction to COM. We start with a brief history of COM in Windows, then move swiftly on to key aspects of COM programming. You'll see how a client creates an object, what COM interfaces are, and how they are used to handle reference counting on objects. I'll explain how the system registry is used to hold information about objects and how this ties in with various methods of activation. We'll examine the various server types, their implementation and usage.

After that, we're ready for a little Automation. Objects that provide Automation interfaces (dispinterfaces) can be called by scripting languages and are self-describing through a resource called a type library. Automation is extremely flexible in that it allows a client to create an object that it initially knows nothing about, but it also imposes some discipline on the server developer.

At this stage, you'll need to refine your understanding, so we'll cover marshaling (how clients and servers pass data and method requests to each other over the network) and monikers (a method of naming objects) before deciding whether COM is object oriented or not.

Chapter 4

As more and more people use distributed objects, you'll find that the distinction between COM and DCOM will fade away. Indeed there should be no difference between a COM and a DCOM object, since a COM object *should* be written to be remotely activated. However, the arrival of DCOM is still relatively recent, so this chapter outlines the new features that DCOM introduces.

I'll explain how DCOM relates to Microsoft RPC (and DCE) and what additional infrastructure is necessary to allow an object to be activated on a remote machine. I'll explain how you can configure your legacy components to be remotely activated without any code and we'll examine the code you'll need to write to make your objects and clients DCOM-aware. We'll step through a simple example to illustrate this.

Along the way, you'll have the opportunity to play with two of the most useful tools in DCOM development: **DCOMCnfg** and **OLEView**.

Chapter 5

Now we've put together a simple object, we'll have to refine that object for robust DCOM use. We explore marshaling and the definition of an interface in depth, before we can use type libraries in earnest.

In this chapter, I'll show how DCOM interfaces are described using Microsoft's extensions to the DCE Interface Definition Language (IDL). I'll show you how to use IDL to create efficient marshaling code and type libraries. I'll also show you how to use connection points and outgoing interfaces to provide asynchronous-like calls.

Chapter 6

Chapter 6 takes a look at how DCOM applies its magic. The chapter is essentially split into two. In the first half, we develop two applications with the same interface: one a DCOM server, and the other a Microsoft RPC server. I have used these two servers to show you that DCOM is essentially an extension of Microsoft RPC and the results allow me to explain some of the infrastructure that Microsoft has provided to allow the client and server to find and then talk to each other.

In the second half of the chapter, we develop a DCOM server that is used to investigate the overhead that DCOM applies to method calls. In particular I use this example to compare making many small method calls to making a single, big method call.

Chapters 7, 8 and 9 cover DCOM-specific issues: security, NT services and threading. In each of these chapters, I spend the first half of the chapter explaining how the subject is handled in Win32 and the second half explaining how this is applied to DCOM.

Chapter 7

Chapter 7 is concerned with security. I start by explaining the benefits of a consistent security system. After that, I go through how NT security works and give a simple example to show the privileges held by the logged on user.

In the second half, I show you how DCOM uses security. I start by explaining how security information is stored and how to apply security to legacy COM applications written before DCOM. Then I show how to use the security interfaces and APIs in your new clients and servers.

Chapter 8

In Chapter 8, I'll show you how to create DCOM servers as NT services (and why you would want to). Services are NT processes that can be started automatically by the system when a machine is rebooted and, unlike other processes, they remain even when the interactive user logs out. Although DCOM has an activation mechanism, there are times when it makes sense for the object server to be running before a client attempts to create an object. In such a situation, the server should be put into a service.

The example developed in this chapter allows you to experiment with security as well as services and, in the final section of this chapter, I explain how the NT Event Log is used.

Chapter 9

Chapter 9 starts by explaining how you can create threads in Win32 and how you can control what a thread can do. Threading, however, carries with it many pitfalls, and these are covered in depth. I explain the differences between, and provide code for, two popular threading techniques: worker threads and thread pooling.

The second half of the chapter covers threading in DCOM. Put simply, a DCOM server can be single threaded or it can be multithreaded; and if it is multithreaded it can use a threading model compatible with legacy single threaded objects (apartment model) or it can use a new threading model (free threaded model), that is potentially more efficient, but needs more code from the developer. In this Chapter I develop a simple example that uses an object in a second thread, run as either an apartment threaded object or as a free threaded object. I use log files to indicate the threads that are used.

Chapter 10

The final chapter introduces the Microsoft Transaction Server. MTS provides a wrapper for COM components that allows objects to be distributed across a network, running under a specified security context and threading model, without requiring extra code to be written to handle security and threading. Oh, and MTS can also run the object under a distributed transaction. MTS uses DCOM as its underlying plumbing, so MTS gives you all the advantages of DCOM without the complexity.

What You Need to Use This Book

Minimum Requirements

As the bare minimum, you need a computer with an operating system that supports DCOM and a C++ compiler that supports MFC 4.x and ATL 2.x.

Operating System

Currently, DCOM has been officially released on Windows NT 4.0 and Windows 95. Beta versions are available for Solaris 2.5 and Digital UNIX 4.0. DCOM development on other platforms is continuing rapidly and releases, most notably for MacOS and Linux, should be available soon.

If you are running Windows NT 4.0, you already have access to most of the features of DCOM, but you should also get Service Pack 2 (or later). This service pack features bug fixes and enhancements to DCOM on Windows NT and is freely downloadable from Microsoft's web site (http://www.microsoft.com).

If you are running Windows 95, you will need to obtain DCOM for Windows 95 by downloading it from Microsoft's web site.

If you are interested in DCOM on other platforms, you should check out Software AG's web site (http://www.sagus.com). Software AG is working closely with Microsoft to port DCOM to non-Windows platforms. The beta versions of DCOM for Solaris and Digital UNIX are currently available for free download from the Software AG site. Also keep an eye on the Active Group's web site for further up-to-the-minute information (http://www.activex.org/).

Compiler

MFC and ATL are supported by a number of different compiler vendors in various versions and at various prices. ATL 2.0 (which seems to be identical to ATL 2.1, which ships with Visual C++ 5.0) is available for free download from Microsoft's web site and is aimed at users of Visual C++ 4.*x*.

Recommended System

To get the most out of this book, you should have access to Visual C++ 5.0 and a network of two or more computers, at least one of which is running Windows NT 4.0.

Visual C++ 5.0

All of the DCOM servers in this book have been developed with Visual C++ 5.0. Most of the servers have been written using ATL 2.1 and the remaining servers call on the COM API directly using C++. The DCOM clients are almost all written in MFC.

Although, you should have no trouble recreating the servers and clients to run under Visual C++ 4.*x* (or another compiler) with ATL 2.0, I do refer to a few features that are specific to the Visual C++ 5.0 development environment to make things easier for users of Visual C++ 5.0. The source code on the web site is also provided for users of Visual C++ 5.0 only.

Windows NT 4.0

Most of the book is as useful to Windows 95 developers as it is to Windows NT developers, but Windows 95 lacks the security features of Windows NT. In Chapter 7, I talk specifically about the security features of Windows NT.

Two Computers

DCOM is about *distributed* computing. Although you can run both the client and the server on a single machine to see them in action, you will be missing some of the point of DCOM development!

Additional Tools

Although the vast majority of the clients are MFC applications, a few are written using Visual Basic 5.0 for variety. Source and executables for these projects will be provided on the Wrox Press web site.

The final chapter is on Microsoft Transaction Server (MTS). Microsoft Transaction Server is part of the Enterprise editions of Visual Studio and Visual C++. An evaluation version of MTS is available by download or by requesting a CD from Microsoft's web site.

The only other software I use is in Chapter 1 where I outline some of the more popular distribution methods. The Java examples have been written using the Sun JDK 1.1, the RMI beta and the JavaIDL alpha2 release. You can find out more information about Java and download the latest tools from http://java.sun.com/.

Of course, Internet access is one of the most important tools for modern developers. Nothing in this book specifically requires you to have it, but if you do have Internet access, it will benefit you greatly. If nothing else, maybe the quantity of URLs in this introduction will convince you of that! The most important URL to remember is for the Wrox Press web site at http://www.wrox.com/. You can download all the source code for this book, and find clarifications and corrections there.

Conventions Used

We use a number of different styles of text and layout in the book to help differentiate between the different kinds of information. Here are examples of the styles we use and an explanation of what they mean:

> **These boxes hold important, not-to-be forgotten, mission critical details which are directly relevant to the surrounding text.**

Background information, asides and references appear in text like this.

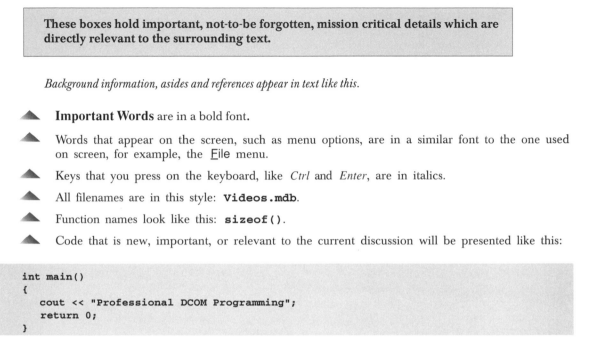

▲ **Important Words** are in a bold font.

▲ Words that appear on the screen, such as menu options, are in a similar font to the one used on screen, for example, the File menu.

▲ Keys that you press on the keyboard, like *Ctrl* and *Enter*, are in italics.

▲ All filenames are in this style: **Videos.mdb**.

▲ Function names look like this: **sizeof()**.

▲ Code that is new, important, or relevant to the current discussion will be presented like this:

```
int main()
{
   cout << "Professional DCOM Programming";
   return 0;
}
```

▲ Code you've seen before, or isn't directly relevant to the matter at hand, looks like this:

```
int main()
{
   cout << "Professional DCOM Programming";
   return 0;
}
```

The Wrox Press Web Site

Our desire to see you succeed doesn't stop once you've purchased a Wrox Press book. We believe that you've entered into a partnership with us, and as such, it's our responsibility to provide you with the latest information available to us to help you succeed.

The Wrox Press web site is the medium we use to provide this information to you. The web site provides:

▲ Extensive information on our latest titles

▲ A wealth of links to relevant web sites around the world

- Errata sheets for current Wrox Press titles
- Useful tools, add-ins and tips

If you have any suggestions regarding the Wrox Press web site, then please email the Webmaster at **webmaster@wrox.com**. The web site is as much your resource as it is ours.

Finally, we have two identical sites:

For Europe, on a 64K line: http://www.wrox.co.uk/
For the US, on a 256K line: http://www.wrox.com/

We recommend that you use a version 3.0 (or later) web browser.

Tell Us What You Think

We've tried to make this book as accurate and enjoyable for you as possible, but what really matters is what the book actually does for you. Please let us know your views, whether positive or negative, either by returning the reply card in the back of the book or by contacting us at Wrox Press using either of the following methods:

email:	**feedback@wrox.com**
Internet:	http://www.wrox.com/contact.stm
	http://www.wrox.co.uk/contact.stm

Source Code

All the relevant code is included in the book, but for those who have better things to do than type in reams of code, the full programs are available from our web sites:

http://www.wrox.com/scripts/bookcode.idc?Code=060X
http://www.wrox.co.uk/scripts/bookcode.idc?Code=060X

Errors

While we have made every effort to make sure the information contained within this book is accurate, we're only human. If you're having difficulty with some aspect of the book, or have found a genuine error, then please check the errata sheet for this book on our web site:

http://www.wrox.com/scripts/errata.idc?Code=060X
http://www.wrox.co.uk/scripts/errata.idc?Code=060X

If the answer to your problem isn't there, please feel free to fill out the form at the bottom of the web page with your question and we'll do our best to sort it out for you.

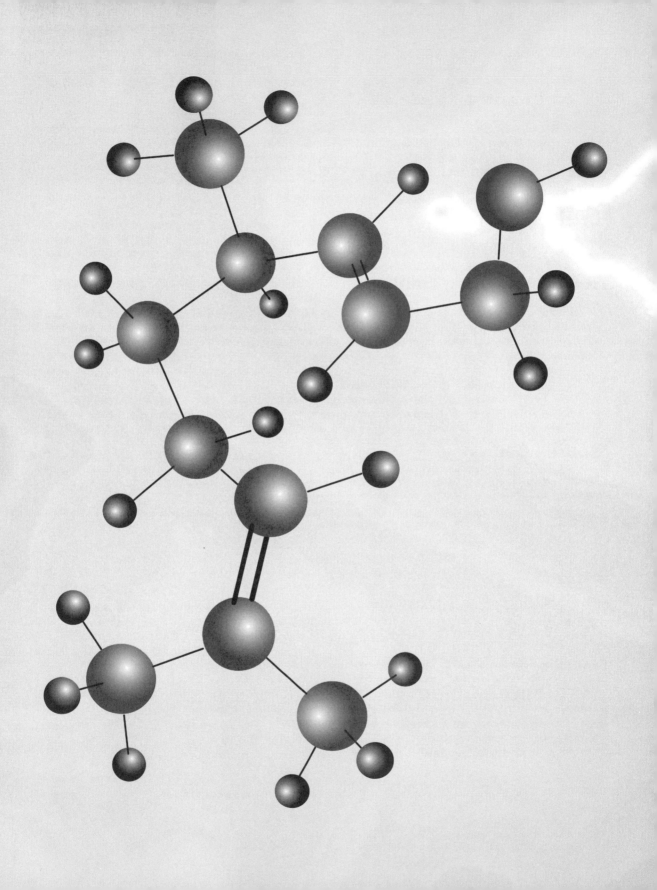

Distributing Objects

Introduction

Objects are everywhere: you can't avoid them. If you have anything to do with software, whether as a user or as a programmer, you will be using objects all the time. Indeed, most of the software you've installed on your PC will have 'object' in its name, or will have been created using the latest object technology.

Undoubtedly, objects make life much easier for the developer. Using object-based techniques focuses the developer's mind on the overall functionality rather than the minutiae of the implementation. You could argue that languages like C++ have become popular because of the desire to make software more object oriented (OO), but I would argue the converse: more software is OO now, because it has been made easy through languages like C++.

Whatever the reason, everyone seems to be using objects these days. However, until recently, these objects have suffered from one great restriction: they could be used only within the process in which they were created.

This book is about extending an object's use beyond the confines of a single process by distributing the object across the network. Distribution has a specific meaning here. It does not necessarily mean dispatching the object out from a central position in an unsolicited manner, as a mail order catalogue company may distribute their catalogues as inserts in a Sunday newspaper. Distribution means that a process can find, and have access to, objects across the network. These objects are created upon request, either via a central controller (or **broker**), or directly to the object server itself.

In this first chapter, we'll cover what a distributed object is, and look at some methods of providing distributed objects using current technology. My intention is to point out the strengths and weaknesses of the various methods, and to present a general introduction to the facilities offered by the **Distributed Component Object Model** (**DCOM**), which is the main subject of this book. As such, I have tried to make this chapter as fair-minded as I can, although the other chapters in this book are unashamedly biased towards DCOM. Hopefully, by the end of this chapter, you'll agree with me that DCOM is the easiest and most effective method of deploying distributed objects at the current time.

Distributed Objects and Distributed Data

Distribution seems to be the great buzzword, much as client-server was five years ago. In fact, the two are essentially the same: under the client-server model, the server will be an autonomous piece of code, separate from the client, and usually available on a machine other than the client.

Although distributed computing has been around for many years, the recent increase in interest undoubtedly comes from the phenomenal increase in the popularity of the Internet (particularly the use of the World Wide Web). People have come to realize that it's possible to distribute code across a network with apparent ease. Although you may not know it, many of the pages that you access on the web are actually programs that run on a remote machine; such pages have extensions like **asp**, **dll** or **cgi**.

But distribution has been around for many years. My first exposure to computers was in the mid-seventies, when my school had a connection to the computer of a local University. The connection was via a dedicated telephone wire, and access was through a terminal with a VDU. Programs were run on the mainframe computer, and data input and program output was through the terminal.

There was distribution of functionality here: the terminal had a processor and firmware (code on ROM) that handled the translation of control codes from the mainframe into a form that could be used by the VDU's electronics, and translation of the keyboard codes into a form that could be transmitted to the computer. So, conceptually, you could view the situation as being a small program at the terminal accessing a more complex and powerful program on the mainframe.

Furthermore, the terminal's program initiated the program at the remote computer: you pressed *Enter* twice and the terminal dialed the remote computer, set up the connection, and presented the login screen; pressing *Ctrl+* closed the connection. There is no difference between this and a C++ program I write today that connects to a remote computer to get, say, the latest stock prices, and then shuts down the connection. Even in those days the code could be widely distributed: once I had connected to a remote computer, it could run a program on another machine, sending my commands to this second machine and then directing its output back to me.

Distributed Data

In the early days of computing, the sheer cost of machines meant that connections to the computer had to be via remote terminals, and the bulk of the code ran on the mainframe. The only way to execute a program was to run it on the remote computer. Although functionality was important, **information** had the real power.

By centralizing the data in one place (or at least, providing methods of accessing all the relevant data), you could perform analysis on the data that was impossible to do when the data was held on paper. It meant that trends could be identified, and predictions could be made, with far greater accuracy than before. This was important for industries such as insurance and finance, where large amounts of money can be made just by guessing which way the market will go.

These repositories of data were, of course, databases. The data had to be accessed via a program on the central mainframe. This would need to accept a client connection, identify the data that the client requested, and return this data. However, database management systems could do more than that: to speed up data retrieval, they implemented indexing; to prevent huge amounts of data being sent to the client, they implemented aggregation and other data analysis functions; and to protect the data, they implemented transactions and constraints (or integrity checks).

The database management systems became quite sophisticated, but the main point was that they held data that was shared amongst many users. Although the data was held centrally, the data access was distributed.

In the early days, the terminal connected through to the database and the requested data was typically returned as rows. Then electronics became cheaper and terminals began to offer more functionality. With the advent of the personal computer (with the likes of the IBM PC and the Apple II), the terminal itself was a fully-fledged computer. In fact, the emphasis was the other way round: these were personal computers that could be used as terminals. Now a program on the local computer could make the connection to the remote computer, query the database, and present the results on screen without the user knowing about the database at all.

These were typically 2-tier systems; that is, there was a client and a server portion, each running on a different machine. A client could have several servers, but usually it just had one. Although the server was a program, its main purpose was to get hold of the data on behalf of the client. Most of the logic of the application lay in the client: it would ask the server for the data that it required, and the client would perform the necessary manipulation and presentation.

Distributed Objects

As object orientation became more popular, developers started to use objects, since it made the programming easier. Developers would often simplify the presentation of data by using an object to wrap up the code and data required to access a window on the terminal. In a similar vein, they would use an object in the client to wrap up the access to the database. To the client, all access to the database was through this object. This meant that a *local* object represented the database, and although objects could be used in the server (*remote* objects), the client knew nothing about them.

This architecture was still rather constrained, because the client still held the **business logic** necessary to manipulate the data from the database. If the developer needed to change this logic, while still keeping the same presentation, every client that had been distributed to the users would have to be changed. In a large organization, this could mean *thousands* of clients.

In fact, it need not have been so. The client viewed the database as a data source, so it didn't matter if that source was the actual database, or another server application. This led to a three-tier approach where the data presentation, business logic, and database became three separate layers.

The business logic could now be provided in its own object, and it could decide the source of its data. The client could talk to the business object without needing to know where the raw data came from. So if the schema of the database changed, causing queries on the database to be modified, only the business object would need to be changed; the client would remain the same. Indeed, if the developer decided to use a totally different database, only the business object would be changed.

Although the model is useful, there is still something missing from this description: the communications mechanism between the objects. Communications between client programs and databases are well established, and there is a plethora of network protocols and APIs that allow two programs to talk to each other. So if one program implements some functionality, it's possible for another program to use that functionality. Therefore, since object methods are the functionality of the object, it should be possible to access them across the network.

To do this, the object server has to make the object public, so that any remote client can access it; the object server also has to listen for client requests on the object, and dispatch those calls to the object. Furthermore, the client has to make the network calls to connect to the object, and must pass the method requests in a fashion that the object understands.

If we look at this from the client side, the client needs to know how to create the remote object, how exactly to talk to the object to call its methods, and how to extract the results from the reply sent by the object. This requires lots of network API calls, and is not the sort of programming that the client developer wants to do: he is just concerned with getting the data and presenting it. The programming is messy and counter-intuitive.

To ease this problem, the object developer could encapsulate all these network calls in a 'shadow' (or **proxy**) object that looks like the server object, in terms of the methods it implements. However, its implementation of the object methods would carry out the network calls to forward them to the remote object. The object developer could then write the necessary code in the server program to accept the calls and pass them to the object.

Now the client developer can create an object and use it without worrying about any network programming issues. The developer just creates the object and calls its methods. The object is more than just remote: it is *distributed*.

Distributed objects are used for several reasons: they could, for example, perform complex calculations that require a high specification machine; or maybe, for licensing reasons, only one copy of the code can be run. But since one remote object could easily become the client of another object, these remote objects (and the functionality that they provide) can be distributed across the network.

Handling Heterogeneous Systems

One problem with distributed objects is that of implementing and using objects from heterogeneous operating systems. In a truly distributed system, there may be Intel x86 machines running Windows (3.1x, 95, NT) or MS-DOS. There may be Intel x86s running Unix (SCO, Linux), or NT on other CPUs (Alpha for current versions of NT, or MIPs and PowerPC for older versions). There may be MacOS machines (Motorola, or PowerPC), various flavors of Unix running on various CPUs (Alpha, MIPs, SPARC etc.) and even larger machines (e.g. AS400). The problem is how to connect the various operating systems together, and to define standards on data types, sizes and byte order.

The DOS/Windows family of operating systems can be connected together with Microsoft RPC or named pipes (although for pipes only NT machines can act as the server), and to widen the network further, TCP/IP can be used. TCP/IP is hosted by most operating systems, either for the client or the server, and is thus the lowest common denominator for all platforms.

However, writing the object and object-user at one time may be difficult; there are methods of defining what an object can do (via an Interface Definition Language), but the client and the object still have to be coded, possibly using different platform-specific tools. In a heterogeneous network with different operating systems, using a particular method of object distribution may allow for a similar API to be used for the object framework on the client and server; but other services, such as file access and character or graphical output, may be totally different.

Restricting object distribution to a particular API helps (e.g. Win32 platforms: Intel x86 Windows 95 or NT, or NT on Alpha, MIPs, or PowerPC), but this restricts the usefulness of the distribution.

Distribution

In this section, we'll take a look at some of the items that you'll need to consider when choosing an object distribution system. We'll begin by examining the two fundamental types of network protocol: connection-based and connectionless. Then we'll move on to the fundamental services that should be provided by all good object distribution systems.

Network Protocols

To distribute anything across a network (be it an object or some other form of code), the client and server must agree on the distribution method and, in particular, how data is carried across the network. This is defined by the network protocol. In general, there are two types of protocol: connection-based and connectionless.

In both cases, the client end must resolve the address of the server. In other words, the client must find out the machine name of the server and any endpoint information to identify the right process on the server machine. At the server end, there must be some listening process to determine when a client is making a request.

Connection-Based Protocols

With **connection-based protocols** (also called **stream protocols**), the client makes some kind of connection to the server, and this connection remains in force until either the client or server terminates it. The advantage of this approach is that once the connection is made, the client and server can talk directly to each other. When either the client or the server needs to communicate, it doesn't need to do any extra work to find the other, since the connection still exists.

A connection-based protocol is a bit like making a telephone call: there is some overhead in making the connection (looking up the telephone number and dialing it), but once the connection is made, it remains for the length of the conversation and does not require any servicing by the callers.

The problem with connection-based protocols is that, although using the connection seems effortless once it has been established, it is constantly being maintained behind the scenes. This takes up system resources. That's fine as long as the connection is being used almost constantly, but it's wasteful when there are long periods of time between transfers of data. Suppose you phone a colleague and ask for an estimate that will take 20 minutes for them to calculate; if you keep the phone connection open, this will cost you in telecom charges. It's better to hang up and wait for your colleague to return the call.

TCP and SPX are connection-based protocols.

Connectionless Protocols

Connectionless protocols (also called **datagram protocols**) pass data across a network without enforcing a connection between each end of the conversation. Each time the client, or server, needs to communicate, it must find out where the target of the message is and how to talk to it. Data sent across a connectionless protocol is similar to a conversation carried out via mail: each part of the conversation requires the letter to be addressed and sent off. In addition, connectionless protocols, like the mail, do not guarantee the order of delivery or even that a message will get to its destination. The advantage of connectionless protocols is that requests are sent off and forgotten. No effort or resources are expended to maintain the connection, because there isn't one. When you send a letter, once the letter is in the post box, it's out of your control. The reply may be immediate, or it may come after some time, but in either case, no resources are wasted keeping a connection alive unnecessarily.

UDP and IPX are examples of connectionless protocols.

Properties of Systems of Distribution

Every system of distribution must provide certain core facilities to allow objects to be distributed. Here is a list of properties that every good distributed system must possess.

Object Locator

All systems must provide a mechanism by which objects can be located and activated. Object users must be able to find the objects that they wish to use. If a server machine agrees that it can activate the object, it must be able to select the right executable, and the right object implemented in that executable.

Some schemes use machine addresses and port numbers, but such schemes are inflexible and can lead to collisions between objects. Better systems, such as COM, allow for a locally maintained object locator on the server machine using object names. Other systems, such as CORBA 2 and Microsoft Transaction Server, centralize the locator on a single (or perhaps a few) domain machines that can identify object servers in the domain.

In a heterogeneous environment, there may be several native naming systems; the object user must either settle on one standard or agree to follow several standards in its quest for an object.

If objects are replicated over several machines, to provide for greater availability or fault tolerance, some kind of object locator is required to make the selection of the most appropriate object.

Communication

Of course, once an object has been located and activated, the client will need to be able to communicate with it. There are, at least, three areas of communication that you need to consider when choosing a system of distribution:

 Data typing

Data representation

Synchronous or asynchronous communication

Data Typing

Strong data typing is extremely important for any distributed system. I'm sure that you understand how strong data typing can help you write complex and robust code in the language of your choice. Why should you have to give that up just to distribute your objects across a network?

Many traditional systems of distribution require you to pass all data across the network as streams of bytes, but this seems like a step back into the dark days of computing. Any good object system should allow you to declare contracts between your objects and their clients using specific data types. These contracts are known as **interfaces**.

Although strong and predetermined data typing is extremely important, it is also nice to enjoy the flexibility of slightly looser typing of the sort important to interpreted scripting languages. The major distributed object systems allow for this by providing dynamic querying of objects for the functionality that they support. CORBA provides this through its DII (dynamic interface invocation) mechanism, and COM through its dispatch interface. In essence, these are predetermined typed interfaces that allow a dynamic interface to be queried.

Data Representation

Objects will be distributed across many machines, and there is no guarantee that the same method of data representation will be used on all the machines even if a single operating system like NT is used on these machines. This gives rise to definitions of network data types for the marshaling and unmarshaling of data.

DCE RPC defines NDR, the Network Data Representation, that allows data to be transmitted between machines in a manner that's independent of the actual data transmitted. DCOM is based upon RPC (either Microsoft or DCE), so it uses NDR for its data transmission.

Synchronous and Asynchronous Communication

Put bluntly, synchronous communication means that when the client makes a request from the object, the client process is blocked until the object replies. Usually, this is not a problem, since the requests from the client are made because the continuing action of the client depends on the data returned from the server. However, there are situations when the object request may take a large amount of time or when the data returned is not required immediately (for example, during initialization). In these situations, asynchronous communications are used. This may complicate the client code if it requires some callback mechanism from the object to indicate when the request has been serviced.

At present, DCOM is synchronous; however, it does allow for callback mechanisms, such as connection points, to be implemented.

State Persistence

Objects, by their nature, represent both functionality and data. A client wishing to access an object would typically create the object, access its services, and then destroy it. The object server will need to be able to associate a client connection with a particular object, since each client will have some assumption about the state of the object when it last accessed it.

For connection-based transports, this is not a great problem, since a connection is maintained between the client and the object. The object server (or the system services maintaining the object) can assume that once the connection has been broken, the object can be destroyed.

However, for connectionless transports, state persistence is a problem. Firstly, the system must be able to associate an object with a client so that, when a client requests service from the object, the correct object is accessed. Secondly, the system must be able to determine whether or not long periods without accesses from the client mean that the client has died. This will allow the server to release the object's resources.

Security

When a client activates a remote object, it is running code on another machine. Such an action becomes worrying if the administrator of the remote machine has no control over how or when this code is run. The administrator will also want some means of auditing the object's use and identifying who has been using, or attempting to use, the object.

A secure distribution mechanism would require that the client use some account name and password that the system can authenticate, with a trusted security authority, before it allows the client to activate the object. The system could also ensure that the authentication is carried out each time the client calls an individual method on the object. This way, the system can be assured that the client is allowed to perform that action and the auditing system can log the call.

DCOM has been designed with security built in. Security is such an important subject that I have dedicated the whole of Chapter 7 to it.

Reliability and Availability

Distributed objects should offer transparency for the client, and part of this transparency is the guarantee that the object connection will be reliable throughout the client's use of the object. In the optimum case, the remote object must be as reliable as a local object. Many systems allow location transparency. COM is particularly good at this, because it allows objects to be activated in the process' address space, or in a separate address space either on the same machine or on another machine. The client doesn't need to behave differently between these three types of activation.

Reliability can be achieved by using a **transaction monitor**, like the OMG Transaction Service, or Microsoft's Transaction Server. A system can replicate objects around the network to produce better reliability. In such a system, some controlling object makes sure that all the replicated objects are kept up to date. If a machine failure occurs, there will be at least one copy of the object that could be used to replicate others when the failed machine is brought online again.

Fault tolerance is supported by such systems as Isis RDO, and hence the CORBA implementation in Orbix + Isis.

Load Balancing

Load balancing is an area that has little available support in the mainstream distribution frameworks at present, but intensive development is currently underway. A server machine may provide several object servers, and each of these may provide several object types. The server machine may become a bottleneck in the distribution of objects, and this leads to the need for load balancing.

In essence, the server employs some mechanism to allow the objects to be distributed across the network to other servers, so that the load is spread. The load balancing service determines the servers' load, and when an object request is made, it will choose the server with the least loading. This facility is not offered in DCOM.

Methods of Distribution

So, you've decided that you want to create objects on one or more machines and access them from a client. How should you do this?

There are several ways that you can distribute objects. In the rest of the chapter, we'll look at a few of the systems available to PC and UNIX users. We'll start with systems that have very little direct support for objects and keep going until we arrive at DCOM, which has excellent facilities for distributing objects built-in.

Sockets

Sockets is a method of allowing applications to communicate, handling the details of the communication through a data structure known as a socket. Sockets can be connection-based or connectionless, and can run over one of several protocols. The most popular is the Internet Protocol (IP). If the application requires a connection-based protocol, TCP/IP is used. If a connectionless protocol is required then UDP/IP is used.

Sockets allows a common API to be used, whatever protocol is selected. It defines a mechanism for the client to find and pass data to the server, and also for the server to listen on an endpoint for the client request. However, sockets has no inherent support for objects. There is no mechanism to activate an object (that is, run an executable), no support for interfaces, fault tolerance, or load balancing. There is limited support for binary exchange, since Sockets defines a **network order** and a **host order** for primitive types and provides functions to convert between the two.

Winsock, the implementation of Sockets on Windows, is covered in the next chapter.

Inferno

Inferno is included here because it's an operating system designed to distribute code across the heterogeneous network.

Inferno is the latest operating system to come out of Lucent Technologies, formerly known as Bell Labs, who, I'm sure you're aware, are responsible for Unix and the C programming language. With a pedigree like that, we must at least look at what is possible with Inferno.

Inferno is the name of the operating system, and the facilities of Inferno all take names from Dante: the programming language is called **Limbo**, the programs are run in a virtual machine called **Dis**, and the communication between programs is done via a protocol called **Styx**.

At the time of writing, Inferno was in beta and hence available for free.

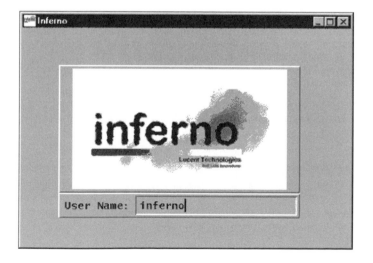

Inferno was designed so that it could be implemented as an operating system in its own right, or supported in emulation mode by other operating systems. For example, Inferno can already be run under Windows on Intel machines.

Inferno takes a high-level view of the network: it has a single namespace with every resource on the network appearing within this hierarchical file system. To Inferno, this is important: any resource type can be accessed through the same API, and accessing a resource on another machine just requires specifying the appropriate path.

Programs for Inferno are written in Limbo, which is a procedural C-like language. This is significant: Limbo is *not* object orientated; it does not support objects like C++ does. However, Inferno does support distribution across a network, and the portability of the operating system means that other Inferno systems will exist across the network to support distributed code; or at least, that is the hope of Lucent.

Note that Limbo requires Dis: Limbo is an interpreted language. In this sense, Inferno takes the same line as Java RMI, which we'll discuss later in the chapter. Inferno lets code talk across a network, but it requires each end of the communication to use the same protocol *and* be implemented with the same language. This is both an advantage and a disadvantage.

The advantage is obvious: if you're writing a distributed system, it makes sense that you write both the server and the client code that will use it. However adaptable you are, you will have a language with which you are most familiar, so it makes sense to use this language. But what if the client and server are on different machine types and different operating systems? Well, an environment like Inferno helps here, since the code can be used whatever emulation operating system or CPU is used.

The disadvantage comes when you are required to write a distributed system using code written by a third party. If the server does not run under Inferno, is it possible to communicate to it from Inferno? Actually, the answer is yes, because Inferno supports the TCP/IP protocol through its unified namespace. Talking to a TCP/IP server just requires using the API to send data to the 'file' that represents the server in the 'file system'.

The Inferno namespace is flexible because it is hierarchical and extensible. So assuming, for example, that the necessary steps are taken to give the server access to the client machine, a server can mount and then bind part of the client's namespace on to its own. The Styx protocol carries messages across the network between the two machines. This enables the client to register itself for callbacks and notifications.

Once the two machines have bound parts of their namespaces together, clients and servers communicate using the namespace file I/O API. To open a TCP connection, a client would use the **open()** Limbo command, send data and read replies with **write()** and **read()**, respectively, and then finally close the connection with **close()**. Like DCE RPC, the Limbo language does not support objects. Unlike DCE RPC, Limbo allows connections to be made and maintained between machines very simply, without complicated API calls.

Distributed Computing Environment RPC

The Open Software Foundation (OSF) has defined the Distributed Computing Environment (DCE). DCE provides many facilities, such as **security**, **directory services**, **time services**, **threads**, and **remote procedure calls** (**RPC**). These are provided as multivendor APIs running over some network protocol (like TCP/IP, or pipes). The *multi* part is key to DCE, since the APIs have been defined and standardized by a number of companies. This allows for connectivity between RPC implementations from many vendors.

DCE RPC defines an API to remote function calls from a client to a server running on a remote machine. The programmer defines what functions can be called through the RPC mechanism using the DCE **Interface Definition Language** (IDL). IDL groups these functions together for convenience into **interfaces**. The server program on the server machine implements these functions. Through IDL, both the client and server know what functions are in an interface, and what the parameters of those functions are.

> *Microsoft IDL, based on DCE IDL and used extensively in DCOM, is covered in Chapter 5.*

When a client wishes to use a server's interface, it has to identify which interface to use. DCE defines Universally Unique IDs (UUIDs), 128-bit numbers, to identify interfaces. Since a UUID is unique, when a client requests a server that implements an interface with a particular UUID, the client can guarantee that the server presents the interface *exactly* as it expects. This means that the interface implemented in the server will have the methods and parameters expected by the client.

UUIDs also allow for versioning: a server can extend the functionality of its previous version by implementing a new interface with a new UUID, while also implementing the old interface. Older clients request the old interface without knowing about the new interface, but new clients that know about the new interface can use either.

The RPC Mechanism

The actual remoting of the function calls is carried out via sections of code called **stub code** that are created by the IDL compiler. The stub code could be statically bound into the executables or, in an operating system like Windows, the stub code could be compiled into a separate dynamic link library. In either case, the functions that are implemented in the stub code on the client-side look just like the functions that are implemented on the server. The client is largely unaware that the code is implemented on another machine.

> *DCE calls this code a stub in both the client and server. COM uses the term proxy on the client side and stub on the server side.*

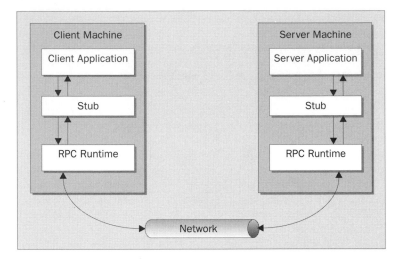

The client-side stub packages up the function requests and the method parameters and, through the RPC runtime library, sends the request via the network to the server machine. On the server machine, the RPC server is already running and waiting for client connections. If the server is not running, the client cannot call its methods, since there is no remote activation mechanism in RPC. Once a connection is made, the RPC runtime calls the server-side stub, which unpackages the request from the client and calls the method in the server.

Any replies from the server code are packaged up and returned to the client. During this time, the client thread that made the call is effectively blocked: RPC calls are **synchronous**.

Comparing Microsoft RPC and DCE

As mentioned above, DCE is supported on many platforms and by many vendors. Microsoft has taken DCE RPC and implemented it in its own operating systems. Microsoft RPC is compliant with DCE RPC. This means that although Microsoft RPC provides (almost) all the facilities of DCE RPC, it is necessary to use some additional software to allow Microsoft RPC programs to communicate with DCE RPC programs. This is because Microsoft has its own way of handling security and naming services.

Note that the DCE RPC functions that have been implemented by Microsoft have been renamed to use Microsoft's capitalization standards and eliminate embedded underscores. However, there is a direct one-to-one mapping. You can compile standard DCE programs on Microsoft platforms using a header file to map DCE function names to Microsoft names (unfortunately, such a header file is not supplied by Microsoft).

Note, also, that with a few exceptions (such as attributes like **[async]**), Microsoft's IDL compiler, **MIDL**, supports all the functionality of the DCE IDL compiler. **MIDL** compiles IDL to produce the client and server side stub code, as well as a header to describe the interface. We'll look at an example of Microsoft RPC using **MIDL** in Chapter 6, where you will see how DCOM is built upon RPC.

DCE Directory Service and the Microsoft Locator

Directory services is the mechanism by which a server can be found on the network. DCE uses the **Cell Directory Service** (CDS) to section up a network into administrative units and provide a hierarchical naming system. These units hold security information about the users who can log on, and a central repository (the Directory Service) where the current servers can register themselves. NT administers groups of computers through **domains**, which are analogous to DCE cells. The domain has logon facilities, and defines groups so that particular users can be given access to particular resources.

DCE provides a naming service so that when a DCE client requests a server, the service can find the server machine and the running server. This is carried out via an intermediate program on the local machine called a **CDS clerk**. When the client wants to find the server, it makes a request to the clerk which looks in its local cache. If the clerk cannot find the name, it will query the CDS server on a networked machine. The CDS server uses its database of named servers, which is called a **clearinghouse**.

If the CDS server can find the server, it returns this information to the CDS clerk, which caches the result, and returns the data to the client. A CDS cell can have more than one clearinghouse, and individual clearinghouses can hold information about locations of the other clearinghouses. The CDS clerk can use this to extend its search further if it can't find the server on its first attempt.

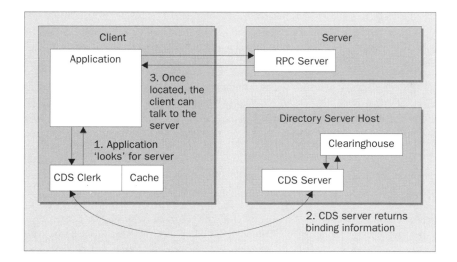

The situation is similar under NT. Microsoft RPC uses a service called the **locator** to provide this functionality. The locator uses a dynamic database of running servers, and when a request is made for a particular server, the locator first looks in its own database. If the server cannot be found, it will then forward the request, via RPC, to a designated master locator. If the master locator fails to find the RPC server, it will send a mailslot broadcast to all computers in the domain. If one of these computers finds the server, it replies to the master locator via a directed mailslot. All the replies are collated, and the server's location is returned via RPC to the client locator, which passes this back to the client.

CDS is based upon a hierarchical namespace, as opposed to NT's UNC. CDS also provides a flexible approach, allowing clearinghouses to refer to other clearinghouses in the same cell or, via a **Global Directory Agent**, in another cell. Although Microsoft RPC on NT can search around the domain, the search does not extend further.

> *Note that UNC will give way, in the near future, to Microsoft Directory Services. Directory Services will be available on all Microsoft's 32-bit operating systems, and will be able to handle a number of naming systems, including X.500 addresses, which are used by CDS.*

Security

Another difference between DCE and Microsoft RPC can be found in their security models.

DCE security is part of the DCE environment, which is implemented on top of whatever operating system is being used. DCE security uses the Kerberos Version 5 authentication system, which was developed as part of the Athena project at MIT. Under this model, the RPC client and server can agree to use authenticated RPCs. The client and server use encrypted data structures, called **tickets**, that can pass authentication information from the client to the server, and can even be used to encrypt the RPC packets themselves.

Kerberos version 5.5 is currently in beta.

Authentication allows the server to know that the request came from a known client, and it assures the client that the responses have come from the requested server. This prevents 'spoofing', where a rogue server can pretend to be an authentic server and pass bogus data to unsuspecting clients.

Security requires another facility: authority. When a client makes a request, even if the server agrees that the client is who he says he is, the question remains: does this client have the necessary authority to use particular resources on the server machine?

To answer this question, resources used by the DCE RPC server have **Access Control Lists** that specify the users or groups that have access to the resource. The ticket that is used in the authenticated RPC has a structure called a **Privilege Attribute Certificate**. This structure can give the RPC server the group information of the client user, and so determine if the server can access the particular resource.

Microsoft RPC security is part of the operating system that uses it. MS-DOS, 16-bit Windows and Windows 95 have no built-in security, so Microsoft RPC on these platforms has no security (although Windows 95 can do pass-through security). However, Windows NT has security built in as part of the operating system. System objects such as files, processes, and threads, can take a security descriptor that determines the **access control list** of the object as well as the **security identifier** (SID) of the current owner (for more details, see Chapter 7 on security). Microsoft RPC can use named pipes as its transport mechanism, and since pipes are part of the file system (which uses the Microsoft security model), Microsoft RPC can support security.

However, named pipes restricts RPC to Microsoft operating systems. In fact, although any Microsoft operating system can be on the client end of a named pipe, only an NT process can be a named pipe server. Of all these platforms, only NT uses security; the result is that secure RPC is restricted to clients that are NT processes.

The other transport mechanism that is used in Microsoft RPC is TCP/IP. TCP/IP has the advantage that it is ubiquitous: most platforms, including Microsoft's, support it. The raw Sockets API is generic and has no support for security. Although it is possible for clients to use TCP/IP to set up a secure channel to a server using the Secure Sockets Layer, applications have to be written specifically for SSL. SSL defines a protocol on top of TCP/IP that defines how clients and servers authenticate each other's security certificates and then set up a secure channel.

Thus, to allow heterogeneous RPC systems where one part is implemented upon a Microsoft OS, TCP/IP must be used as the transport; the result is that security cannot be used. To use security on Microsoft RPC, you must use named pipes; and in this case, the security is implemented by the OS and not by the RPC mechanism.

Note that it isn't strictly true that RPC over TCP/IP cannot use security. Microsoft RPC actually provides two APIs related to security: `RpcImpersonateClient()` and `RpcRevertToSelf()`. The former allows the server to use the NT security context of the client user, and hence get the same access, or restrictions, to system objects as the client. The latter gives the server its own security context back again. These functions are particularly useful if the RPC server is running as a service under NT, where the server doesn't necessarily have the security of an interactive user.

Using Mixed DCE and Microsoft RPC

The differences between DCE and Microsoft RPC that were outlined in the last section have no bearing when using Microsoft RPC on a Microsoft-only network, but the problems do appear when using mixed DCE and Microsoft clients and servers.

To get over the naming and location problem, steps must be taken to allow Microsoft RPC clients and servers to use the DCE CDS naming service. This is done with a product called the **name service interface daemon** (**nsid**).

To enable a Microsoft RPC client to use a DCE server, the DCE machine must be running the nsid to translate the Microsoft RPC client's name service requests into the DCE name service requests. To the Microsoft RPC client, nsid looks like the locator; to the DCE CDS server, nsid looks like a CDS name service client (**CDS clerk**).

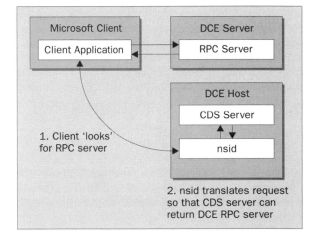

Looking at the problem from the other perspective: to enable a DCE client to use services provided by an NT RPC server, the RPC server must register itself with a CDS server somewhere on the network. To do this, the NT machine must direct the RPC server registration from the NT locator to the DCE nsid on a DCE host. This redirection is carried out by the NT administrator. In NT 3.x, the administrator had to change some configuration values in the NT registry using RegEdit. However, under NT 4, there is a page in the Network control panel applet to do this (Services tab, RPC Configurations).

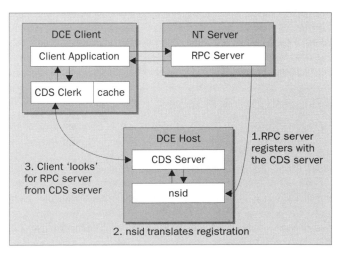

DCE servers cannot use Microsoft named pipes, hence the only transport possible is TCP/IP. This rules out any possibility of mixed DCE and Microsoft RPC systems using authenticated RPCs. A DCE client sending requests via an authenticated RPC won't be accepted by a Microsoft RPC server: the client will pass RPCs with some or all of the packets encrypted, and the Microsoft server will not be able to interpret these packets. On the other hand, the RPCs from a Microsoft client will never have security (since it will need to be sent over TCP/IP), so this will be accepted by a DCE server as an unauthenticated RPC.

DCE servers will have been administered to provide default ACLs for the resources they use. These ACLs include access from unauthenticated requests; therefore, requests from a Microsoft client to a DCE server would be possible, if restricted.

Multithreading

Although you can write multithreaded RPC servers, using worker threads to perform tasks, you don't need to worry about creating threads to handle the RPC connections: the RPC runtime does this for you. When you call DCE's **rpc_server_listen()** (**RpcServerListen()** under Microsoft RPC) in your server to listen for client requests, the process goes into a listening state waiting for a connection. Upon a client request, the RPC runtime creates a thread and calls the RPC function within the context of this thread. If you have other client connections active at this point in time, the code they are executing will still be run, since they will be executing within different threads.

As with all multithreaded processes, you must be careful about using global and static data. In particular, if you wish to retain data from one RPC call to another, you cannot do it using persistent variables, and certainly not using thread local storage, since you can't guarantee which thread will be used on the follow-up call.

To preserve data between calls, you can use a **context handle**. This handle is essentially a token that's passed to the client from the server. This token uniquely identifies the state information from the RPC call (it could be a pointer to a structure in the server's memory space, for example). On follow-up calls, the client passes back this token so that it can be dereferenced into the state information again. In this respect, a context handle can be viewed as similar to the **this** pointer in C++, which gives access to an object's state.

Using context handles does not require a large amount of code: they simply need to be declared in the IDL and then initialized by the server just before returning from the method call. However, since context handles can represent allocated resources on the server, some method must be used in the event of a client unexpectedly closing down while holding an active context handle. To account for this situation, the server must implement a **_rundown()** routine. This routine is used to clean up any resources that are held by the context handle.

Objects and Interfaces

So far, we've only considered interfaces: collections of functions logically grouped together. This book is about objects, so you may well ask: does RPC support objects?

Well, what you do with RPC is your own concern. If you wish to write your client and servers in, say, C++, and match your interface to the methods of a class, then you can do that. Microsoft RPC does support the object orientated principles of **encapsulation** (where an object exposes functionality, but not its underlying data), and **polymorphism** (whereby the same method can be called on two different objects; something provided for by interfaces), but DCE RPC, and hence Microsoft RPC, does not support inheritance.

DCE RPC does offer resource objects. The idea here is that a server may export an interface to act upon a particular generic type of data, and the server could have several instances of specific data that the interface can act upon. These specific interfaces are resources and are exported as objects. An example could be a server that has an interface for customer information, and this could act upon a database of both business customers and perhaps employee customers using an employee discount. The two databases are two different resources; they are exported from the server as separate entities so that the client can select the most appropriate one.

Resource objects, however, hardly fit the category of objects that you'll be familiar with from your experience of C++. There is no mapping, as yet, from RPC into an object oriented language such as C++, although some extensions to DCE RPC, like Hewlett Packard's OODCE, do provide C++ class libraries. Resource objects are not used by DCOM.

Server Activation

One final point needs to be made. The RPC server 'listens' for connections. This is apparent in the description of the RPC mechanism above, whereby the RPC server registers itself with the naming service (DCE CDS server or the NT locator). The RPC server calls **rpc_server_listen()** (or **RpcServerListen()**) to indicate that the server has finished initialization and is ready to service requests. Therefore a server must already be running before any client can make requests of it.

The advantage of this approach is that any server initialization has already been carried out, so client requests can be processed almost immediately. It does assume, however, that some mechanism is employed to ensure that the RPC servers are started when the host machine is booted. This is particularly important in the event of a machine crash, which should cause the machine to reboot automatically, without any administrator attendance. NT provides such a mechanism by allowing you to define certain processes as **services**. A service requires a little extra code to start up: in particular, it must register itself as a service and take part in a conversation with the **service control manager** as it starts up. We cover services from a DCOM perspective in Chapter 8.

However, the big problem with this approach is that the administrator needs to know in advance what servers are going to be used, and must therefore identify which services to automatically start. This can only be done by monitoring the network to find out what service requests are made. If a client requests a method from a service that isn't running, the request will fail: there's no way that the service control manager will kick-in and start up the service. On the other hand, if you start all possible services, regardless of whether they will be used or not, valuable resources may be used needlessly.

CORBA

Whenever distribution is mentioned in any conversation, CORBA will appear at some point. There are good reasons for this: the Object Management Group (OMG) has embarked on an ambitious project to provide a specification for a distributed object system through the **Common Object Request Broker Architecture** (**CORBA**). By no means have all the facilities in the latest CORBA specification been implemented, but robust commercial implementations are available and are in use.

CORBA Architecture

CORBA defines an environment where clients can make requests upon an object and the object can send responses back to the client. It's a distributed system, so the clients and objects are not necessarily in the same address space, or on the same machine. As we have seen, if an object runs in a different address space than the client, there must be some mechanism to connect the two together. In CORBA, this is the responsibility of the ORB (the **object request broker**; hence the name Common Object Request Broker Architecture). Since the object interaction occurs through the ORB, it's often referred to as an **object bus**. The ORB provides a software bus that connects objects in much the same way that a computer provides a hardware bus to channel the communications between pieces of hardware in the machine.

However, CORBA is a *specification*. It defines an interface for how clients can get objects via the ORB, but it does not define the implementation; so vendors are free to implement their ORBs in whatever way they wish. An ORB can be implemented upon DCE RPC, for example; but according to the specification, the object client and server would be oblivious to this.

As for programming, CORBA works in a similar fashion to DCE RPC. The programmer defines the object's interface using CORBA's interface description language (IDL), and then compiles this with the vendor-supplied IDL compiler. Note that CORBA's IDL is different to the DCE or Microsoft IDL.

The IDL compiler produces **stub** code, which sits on the client machine, and **skeleton** code, which sits on the server machine. Depending on the vendor and the operating system, the stubs and skeletons could be in C, C++, Smalltalk, or even Java. The implementation language is not important, as long as it can conform to the standards that allow the code to interact between the ORB and the client (or object).

> *Although the interface between the client application and ORB is well defined, the interface between the ORB and object is not so well agreed upon, and is the subject of ongoing work by OMG.*

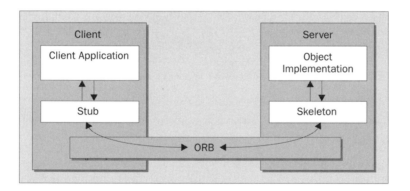

The client application uses the CORBA API to request the object through a process known as **binding**. Binding maps the object's interface into the language that is used in the client. This may be a class in C++ or Java, or a set of functions in C.

Realistically, these language mappings must provide a mechanism for the client to specify the particular object on a specific machine. This is done through **object references**. An object reference is an ID that uniquely identifies the object across the network. It's the responsibility of the ORB to provide the object reference, and this is held by the stub implementation, to be passed back to the ORB whenever the object is accessed.

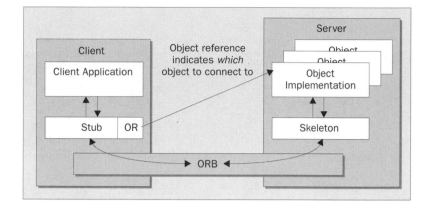

Think of the object reference as a token that's given to the client by the ORB when the client requests access to an object. This a bit like the way RPC uses context handles. Since there may be several objects instantiated by the object server, this token must uniquely identify the object that the client requires. Whenever the client accesses the methods of the object, the token (object reference) is passed to the ORB, and this is used to identify the object on the server. The programmer, however, does not see the object reference: the details of obtaining, storing, and passing around object references are all hidden by the stub and skeleton code.

Note that prior to CORBA 2, an object reference could be in whatever format the vendor chose. CORBA 2 defines **Interoperable Object References** that ORBs must use to pass object references in a heterogeneous system. In addition, there are APIs that can be used by programmers to manipulate object references. For example, you may wish to make the reference persistent, saving it in a file for later use. CORBA defines **object_to_string()** to convert an object reference into a format that can be saved, and **string_to_object()** to convert an object reference back again.

On the programming side, the call to the object is through a C++ object pointer (or whatever the equivalent is in the language mapping). After the binding process has been performed, the programmer does not see any CORBA-specific code. This even stretches as far as exceptions: when an exception occurs in a CORBA object, it is propagated back to the client, where it can be caught with the normal C++ exception handling mechanisms.

Suppose we define an interface like this using CORBA IDL:

```
interface Ticker
{
   exception InvalidStock {};

   void GetQuote(in string StockName, out double StockPrice)
        raises (InvalidStock);
};
```

The first thing of interest in the IDL is the definition of an **exception**, **InvalidStock**, and the declaration that **GetQuote()** throws this exception. This is one major difference between DCE IDL and CORBA IDL: DCE (and also DCOM) does not support exceptions. If the **StockName** is invalid or cannot be found, the **GetQuote()** method will throw the exception. When this IDL is compiled to give a C++ language mapping, we can catch this exception with a standard **try-catch** block:

```
double price;
try
{
   pticker->GetQuote("MSFT", &price);
}
catch(...)
{
   cerr << "Call failed" << endl;
}
```

Let's look deeper into the code generated by the IDL compiler. The IDL shown above, when compiled with Iona's Orbix IDL compiler, gives the class:

```
class Ticker: public virtual CORBA::Object
{
public:
// Constructors...
// ...
   static Ticker* _bind (CORBA::Environment &IT_env);
// ...
   virtual void GetQuote (const char * StockName,
      double& StockPrice,
      CORBA::Environment IT_env=CORBA_default_environment);
};
```

This class contains many methods that are not important here; but there are some points to note. The class is derived from **CORBA::Object**, which has the necessary methods to handle the object references. Note that the base class is inherited using **virtual** inheritance; this is because CORBA allows interfaces to inherit from other interfaces.

Here is another important difference between CORBA and DCOM: DCOM allows interface inheritance, whereas CORBA allows *implementation* inheritance. Interface inheritance means that when one interface is derived from another, the derived interface must supply an implementation for the methods of the base interface; all it inherits is the responsibility to supply the interface. Implementation inheritance means that a derived interface inherits the interface and an implementation. COM provides a similar mechanism using *aggregation*.

If a CORBA interface inherits from another interface, these other interfaces would also inherit from **CORBA::Object**; therefore, we need **virtual** inheritance to solve the age-old C++ multiple inheritance problems.

In the case of the Orbix compiler, there's a **static** function in the class called **_bind()**. This is one of several methods that can be used to create the object. This function creates the client C++ object and uses the **CORBA::Object** methods to use the ORB to create the remote object. The ORB returns an object reference to the **Ticker** object, which the class caches. If the compiler doesn't support exceptions, a standard work-around can be used: an extra parameter is passed that has a reference to a **CORBA::Environment** object. Macros can be used to test the values of this object after the method has returned.

Using this class definition, the Orbix client could call the object with code like:

```
#include "ticker.h"
void main()
{
```

```
    Ticker* pticker;
    char host[] = "Ticker_Server";
    IT_TRY
    {
       pticker = Ticker::_bind("", host, IT_X);
    }
    IT_CATCHANY
    {
       cerr << "Cannot create Ticker object" << endl;
       exit(1);
    }
    IT_ENDTRY

    double price;
    IT_TRY
    {
       pticker->GetQuote("MSFT", &price, IT_X);
    }
    IT_CATCHANY
    {
       cerr << "Call failed" << endl;
    }
    IT_ENDTRY

    cout << "Stock price is: " << price << endl;
    delete pticker;
}
```

In this example, the calls to **_bind()**, and to the object methods, are enclosed by **IT_TRY**, **IT_CATCHANY** and **IT_ENDTRY**. This is to simulate exception handling for compilers that don't support exceptions directly, such as Visual C++ 2.0. For compilers that use exception handling, the normal **try-catch()** blocks can be used.

The IDL compiler generates a **cpp** file with the stub code, which is linked into the client project. This code provides implementations of the **Ticker::GetQuote()** method to marshal the parameters to the server, the **_bind()** methods, and the methods inherited from **CORBA::Object**.

On the server-side, the same header file is used. The IDL compiler provides **.cpp** files for the object factories that are needed to create the object. Such a factory will use a **Basic Object Adapter** implementation to create the object. The programmer is not required to create this class, merely to put the object implementation in a class derived from the BOA implementation (**TickerBOAImpl**, in this case, which is provided by the compiler):

```
    class TickerBOAImpl : public virtual Ticker
    {
    public:
       TickerBOAImpl (const char *m="",
         CORBA_LoaderClass *l=NULL);
       virtual void GetQuote (const char * StockName,
         double& StockPrice,
         CORBA_Environment &IT_env = CORBA_default_environment)
         = 0;
    };
```

The IDL compiler also produces the skeleton code that should be linked to the server project. This provides dispatching code that tests the request from the ORB and calls the appropriate object method, as well as implementing the constructor for the **TickerBOAImpl**.

The actual CORBA object is an instance of a class derived from **TickerBOAImpl**. The server code written by the programmer should therefore implement the inherited pure virtual function **GetQuote()**. The programmer also has to implement the server **main()** function, which is called when the server is started. This function should create an object and tell the ORB that the object is ready to be used.

Interface Invocation

The code above defines one method of invoking the methods on an object. With CORBA there are, in fact, two ways to do this: static and dynamic. The reason for the two methods is largely historical: when OMG requested submissions on how to invoke objects, it received two: HyperDesk and Digital preferred the dynamic approach, Sun and HP preferred the static approach. So now every ORB has to handle both methods. This is what gave us the C (Common) in CORBA.

Note that the difference is only on the client-side. On the server-side they translate to the same calls: an object doesn't know if it was invoked statically or dynamically. So what's the difference between these two?

Static Interface Invocation

In this case, all methods are specified in advance and are known to the client and server. This is the primary aim of the stubs and skeletons that are produced by the IDL compiler. The code used in the client and the server uses object definitions provided by the IDL compiler (in C++, these are **class** declarations). The client creates the object, which in effect it calls through the stub code.

On the server side, the request to create the object comes through the skeleton. Since these two pieces of code exist all the time (the client cannot call the object methods without the stub code for the specific object, and the object on the server can only be called via the specific skeleton code), this method is called **static interface invocation**.

Dynamic Interface Invocation

Dynamic Interface Invocation (DII) allows the information about objects to be determined at runtime; hence the name. In this case, the client does not have to compile with the stub for a particular object, because the client can use a generic object which has methods that allow the parameter lists of methods to be built up and then the method to be invoked.

This generic object can gain information about the requested object by looking at data stored in the **Interface Repository**. The ORB remotes this call to the server, which ends up in a call through the skeleton code, produced by the IDL compiler. The Interface Repository holds information about the IDL interface declarations; it also holds information about any object's interface hierarchy, since CORBA allows interfaces to be derived from each other.

One advantage of DII is that it allows for deferred synchronous requests. This allows the method to be called with a call to **send()**, and the results to be obtained, at a later stage, with a call to **get_response()**.

Note that the flexibility of DII is offset by the cost of the DII calls. DII requires calls to query for the interface of the object (through an **InterfaceDef** object and its method **describe_interface()**); further, it requires the creation of a **Request** object, and then a call on this object to **add_arg()** for every parameter of the method, before a call to **invoke()** can be made. Using SII, this could be done in a single call.

Object Adapters

An object adapter provides a mechanism through which objects can access an ORB's services. An object could be written in one of many languages. It could be written specifically to be invoked by the ORB, or it could implement legacy code written well before the ORB was available. The object adapter sits between the object and the ORB. Objects should support the **Basic Object Adapter** (BOA). Usually, this is done by the IDL compiler providing BOA code that the server code can use. In the example above, Orbix provides the BOA in the **TickerBOAImpl** base class. The BOA supports the following facilities:

- Generation and interpretation of object references
- Activation and deactivation of object implementations
- Activation and deactivation of individual object
- Method invocations via skeletons

The BOA must activate the object from some code, and these code modules may implement more than one object type. BOA supports the following object activation modes:

- *Shared*: one process, one host
- *Unshared*: each object has its own server
- *Per-method Call*: each method call gets its own process
- *Persistent*: the server is launched 'manually' (i.e. other than BOA)

Note that if the object server is not running when the request is made, the ORB will start the server. To do this it needs to know how to start the server, and what invocation method to use. This requires that the server be registered in the **Implementation Repository**. This repository holds information about the server location and the command line to start it.

OMA - The Wider Picture

CORBA, as described above, provides the basic mechanisms to use objects on remote machines. However, applications require more than this: they require certain stock services to be implemented which perform distinct tasks.

OMG has defined the **Object Management Architecture** (**OMA**). This is a collection of services and facilities that are provided by an ORB to a CORBA object. These are split into two: the lower-level CORBAservices and the higher-level **CORBAfacilities**.

CORBAservices defines such object services as object lifetimes, naming, and persistence. CORBAfacilities defines collections of facilities that processes may use through CORBA objects; such facilities include compound documents, user interface, and system management. The basic CORBAservices have been defined, and are implemented, by several CORBA vendors. CORBAfacilities, at the time of writing, have been defined but not implemented.

ORB Interoperability

There are two ways that ORBs can talk to each other: either all ORBs must talk the same protocol, or they can talk different protocols and a **bridge** is used to translate from one protocol to another. The first solution requires all ORBs to talk IIOP (Internet Inter-ORB Protocol). Any ORB that wishes to be CORBA 2 compliant must understand IIOP. A bridge is software specifically written to translate from one ORB to another. IIOP is flexible in that any ORB can talk to any other ORB, but it is unlikely to be optimized for any particular situation. Bridges allow for non-generic, and hence optimized, code to be used.

IIOP is, in fact, an implementation of GIOP (General Inter-ORB Protocol) that specifies the inter-ORB messaging protocol. IIOP implements GIOP over TCP/IP, hence the *Internet* in the name.

Security

Although the Security CORBAservice was published in November 1996, security has yet to be implemented in any major commercial CORBA implementation. However, CORBA objects can implement their own security mechanisms for the platform on which they are implemented. For example in NT, the object methods could take a user name and then impersonate this user to get that user's security.

CORBA Platforms

The strength of CORBA is that it's available over a wide range of operating systems, and for a wide range of languages. This, however, is also its weakness, since there are many operating systems, and many languages: the choice to target one in priority to another is difficult. Of course, OMG is a collective of several software vendors, so the work can be split between the members. However, as in any committee, some members get the more interesting and important jobs, and others get the less exciting jobs. So it is with CORBA. The vast majority of personal computers are PCs and this, as far as CORBA is concerned, is the real make or break.

The key players in CORBA on the PC are: IBM, with **SOM** (**System Object Model**); and Iona, which has developed **Orbix**. The interesting thing about Orbix is that Iona has written their IDL compiler so that, if the appropriate switch is used, code is produced for an ActiveX control that connects to the CORBA object. This means that a programmer can write code in 16-bit Windows using, say, Visual Basic 4 to connect to an object on a remote machine. Such a facility is quite powerful.

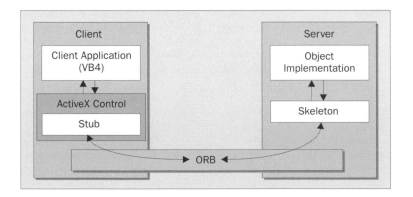

Distributed System Object Model (DSOM) is IBM's CORBA ORB. The present implementation, which is part of OS/2 Warp, and the MacOS, and is also available for Windows and AIX, is based upon CORBA 1.2. SOM is essentially a collection of class libraries used to abstract objects in a language-neutral way.

Multithreading

Just as with DCE RPC, CORBA object servers can be multithreaded. Just as with RPC, they need not be: issues such as whether an object is created in a new process or in a new thread, for example, are handled by the ORB through the object adapter.

Server Activation

Server activation is handled by the object adapter. If the client makes a request for an object that isn't running, but the object has been defined as being, say unshared, then the object adapter will find the server and launch it to create the object.

Java Distributed Objects

Java has been written for the Internet, and when you hear people talking about programming for the Internet, Java is always mentioned. Java code is written in such a way as to make it easily distributed around the network; but note: it is the Java code that is distributed, and not necessarily the data that the code uses.

Java's great strength is that when it's compiled, it produces **bytecode**. This bytecode can be interpreted by any computer that has a Java **virtual machine** (VM). This is also the approach taken by the Inferno language, Limbo, which produces bytecode to be run under the Dis VM. However, Java has huge support from software vendors, and Java is supported on most platforms, usually with VMs available from different vendors. (The Microsoft Java VM will become part of the Windows 95 operating system with the introduction of Memphis a.k.a. Windows 97.)

This is fine for animating penguins in a web page, but it has little to do with distributing objects. This mechanism *copies* the code between machines in a form that allows it to be run on the machine that it is copied to. What we want to do, however, is use distributed objects where the code *running on a server* machine is accessed by a client. This is an entirely different concept altogether.

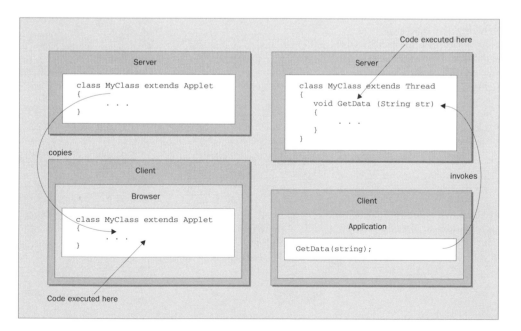

The difference, of course, is in the location of the code. In the first case, the code is copied to the client, as a file, and it is executed there. The client applications have access to the locally executing code. In the second case, the code is executed on the server, but the client code can still access the server's functionality.

In the following sections, I outline three ways in which we can use Java to distribute code: sockets, Remote Method Invocation, and IDL. The examples are written using the Sun JDK 1.1, and for IDL, you also need the latest IDL release; the example uses the alpha 2.2 release. All this software can be downloaded from the Javasoft web site.

> *A fourth way to implement remote Java objects is to use Microsoft Visual J++. This has a tool to convert a type library to Java classes that will call methods on an object. This method is not covered here.*

Java and Sockets

Java has networking built in: you can write Java applications that open a TCP socket to a remote server, and use this to request services from the server. (Java Applets, however, require security clearance from the browser that they are launched in; generally, browsers don't allow TCP connections to machines other than the machine from which the Applet was downloaded.)

The API is quite straightforward. The server creates a listening socket of the class **java.net.ServerSocket** and then calls **accept()**. When the client makes a request, **accept()** returns a socket (**java.net.Socket**) . The server can then read from this through its **java.io.InputStream**, obtained by calling **getInputStream()**, and it can write to the client through the socket's **java.io.OutputStream**, obtained by calling **getOutputStream()**.

The client makes the connection to the server by creating a new instance of the **java.net.Socket** class, and then writing to the server via the socket's **OutputStream**; replies are read via the socket's **InputStream**.

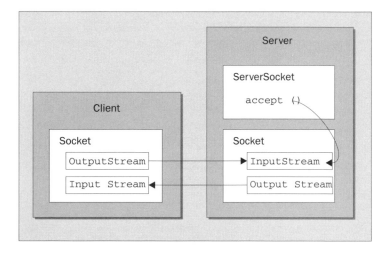

The server has to determine what command has been sent, and then dispatch it to an appropriate function in its class. This is more effort than DCE RPC! We'll see an example of the sort of effort involved in the next chapter (although that example will actually use C++ and WinSock on Windows). Alternatively, you can download some Java code from the Wrox Press web site that demonstrates a simple client and server. The screenshot below shows the server running with Windows Telnet as a client.

There are two ways to improve on this. The first is to write your own classes that handle the TCP connections to the server and dispatch the calls to the server classes functions. This approach has produced several Java class libraries, for example **Horb** and **Black Widow**, and Sun's own RMI. The other method is to use Sun's IDL compiler, **idlgen**, to create CORBA stubs and skeletons in Java.

RMI

Remote Method Invocation (RMI) is a mechanism to access the methods of a remote Java class. The remote object has to be Java because RMI depends on Java serialization, which allows objects and primitive data types to be marshaled (transmitted) as a stream. Java serialization is specific to Java, so both the client and server have to be written in Java.

RMI depends on three components. The first of these components involves defining an interface extending the **Remote** interface. The **Remote** interface has the method definitions that allow an object to be accessed outside of the current VM and, if necessary, on another machine. Your extended interface should also include the methods that you want accessible from the remote machine.

The second component that RMI depends on is an actual implementation of the Java **interface**. RMI provides a class, **java.rmi.server.UnicastRemoteObject**, that provides this code, so the next task is to extend this class with a class of your own. Your class must provide the actual implementation of the methods you declared.

The third component that RMI depends on is a naming mechanism. For the client to locate the object, it requires a naming mechanism for the server to publicize itself so that the client can find it. This is done by having a **registry** running on the server machine that holds information about the available objects. The server registers the object by calling the **bind()** (or **rebind()**) method of **java.rmi.Naming**. This associates a running object with a name that the client knows about, so your server code should create an instance of the object in its **main()** function and call **bind()** on this object.

Java remote objects are named using URLs, so the call to **bind()** should also have the URL of the object, as you would with a URL to a HTML page. In the following example, the URL is

DataRetrievalImpl, and the client would bind to it using the URL **rmi://host:port/ DataRetrievalImpl**, where **host** is the name of the machine that implements the object (defaults to the current machine) and **port** is the port number of the registry (defaults to 1099):

```
DataRetrieval data = new DataRetrieval();
Naming.bind("DataRetrievalImpl",data);
```

For the client to be able to find the object, it calls the **lookup()** method of **java.rmi.Naming** with the full URL to the object. For example:

```
DataRetrieval data = null;
String name = "rmi://remotehost/DataRetrieval";
data = (DataRetrieval)Naming.lookup(name);
```

This method returns the **Remote** interface of the object, and to call our remote method, this needs to be cast to the remote object's **Remote**-derived interface. **lookup()** finds the binding information to get to the server. This information is saved in the RMI registry (and is entered with the **bind()** method), so the remote host must run the **rmiregistry** executable.

Once the client has the object's interface, it can call the remote method.

Finally, to allow the client and server to marshal data to each other, the stubs and skeletons must be generated. This step is like the IDL compilation step in CORBA or DCE RPC. The **rmic** tool is run with the name of the object's implementation file; that is, the server file that extends the **java.rmi.server.UnicastRemoteObject** class. Before you do this, you must compile that class. This tool will generate a stub class that's used by the client, and a skeleton class that's used by the server.

Now the registry and the server class can be run on the server machine. The client class and stub can be distributed to the client machine and run to connect to the server.

As an example, let's describe an interface:

```
import DataRetrieval;
import java.rmi.Remote;
import java.rmi.RemoteException;

public interface DataRetrieval extends Remote
{
    String GetData()
            throws RemoteException;
}
```

This defines the interface to be used by both client and server. Note that this is *not* written in an IDL, it is written in Java. The method returns the data, and if a connection isn't possible to the remote object, an exception of class **RemoteException** is thrown.

The client must now get a remote object, and then call its methods:

```
import DataRetrieval;
import java.rmi.Naming;

public class DataRetrievalClient
{
```

```
    public static void main(String[] args)
    {
       if (args.length != 1)
       {
          System.out.println("Please give server name");
          return;
       }
       try
       {
          DataRetrieval data = null;
          String name = "rmi://" + args[0]
                      + "/DataRetrieval";
          data = (DataRetrieval)Naming.lookup(name);
          String reply;
          reply = data.GetData();
          System.out.println("Got "+reply);
       }
       catch(Exception e)
       {
          System.out.println("Exception "+e);
       }
       System.exit(0);
    }
}
```

This is a typical Java application: it implements a **main()** method that's executed when the application is run. The unusual part is that the application uses an object of type **DataRetrieval**, which it does not instantiate. Instead, it accesses the remote registry with a call to **lookup()**.

So what about the server?

```
import DataRetrieval;
import java.rmi.Naming;
import java.rmi.RemoteException;
import java.rmi.RMISecurityManager;
import java.rmi.server.UnicastRemoteObject;
import java.net.InetAddress;

public class DataRetrievalImpl
        extends UnicastRemoteObject
        implements DataRetrieval
{
   private int call;

   public DataRetrievalImpl()
        throws RemoteException
   {
      super();
      call = 0;
   }

   public String GetData()
                    throws RemoteException
   {
      String client = null;
```

```
      try
      {
         client = getClientHost();
      }
      catch(Exception e)
      {
         System.out.println("exception: " + e);
         client = "unknown";
      }

      call++;
      System.out.println(client + " request, data is:"
                              + call);
      return "data is:" + call;
   }

   public static void main(String args[])
   {
      System.out.println("Started server...");
      try
      {
         InetAddress host = InetAddress.getLocalHost();
         String name = "//" + host.getHostName()
                    + "/DataRetrieval";
         System.out.println("binding to " + name);
         System.setSecurityManager(
                              new RMISecurityManager());
         DataRetrievalImpl data = new DataRetrievalImpl();
         Naming.rebind(name,data);
      }
      catch(Exception e)
      {
         System.out.println("exception: " + e);
      }
   }
}
```

Note that the **DataRetrievalImpl** class *implements* the **DataRetrieval** interface, and thus provides the code for **GetData()**. It also *extends* the **UnicastRemoteServer** class. In Java this is how you can provide for implementation inheritance. In other words, **UnicastRemoteServer** (which extends the **RemoteObject** class) provides the code to remote the object.

A couple of tips here. For this class to compile, it *must* have a public default constructor. Also notice that I am catching the generic **Exception** object in the **try-catch()** block around **rebind()**. If you want to catch the specific exception (**UnknownHostException**), you need to specify its full name, including the package. This is because there are two definitions of this exception: one is in **java.net**, and the other is in **java.rmi**. It is the second of these that we want to catch.

Notice that the implementation of **GetData()** increments a static variable. As in C++ this is a class variable: there is just one variable for all objects, and its value is persistent over repeated calls. I have also used **getClientHost()** from **RemoteObject** (the base class of **DataRetrievalImpl**) to get the name of the client machine that made the call.

In this code, the **main()** function gets the host name with the **InetAddress** object. You don't have to do this if you don't want to; I've only done it here to allow me to print out the full binding string. After that, it creates a security manager from the class **RMISecurityManager** and registers it with a call to **setSecurityManager()**. It must do this to ensure that the client calling the object's methods doesn't try to call any sensitive methods. If you don't register a security manager, the remote object won't be created.

After this, we create a new object of the **DataRetrievalImpl** class, and bind it to a particular name. Now that the name is bound, the client can access it. Note that for the **rebind()** operation to work, the registry must be running. The command lines to run this example are:

On the server (in two CMD boxes):

```
rmiregistry
java DataRetrievalImpl
```

This starts the registry and then starts the server, which registers itself.

You have to copy the **DataRetrievalClient.class**, **DataRetrieval.class**, and **DataRetrievalImpl_Stub.class**, to the client machine, and then you can run the client with:

```
java DataRetrievalClient host
```

where **host** is the name of the server machine. The client application queries the registry on the server machine, which returns the object requested.

This shows the results of running the server on a machine called **zeus**, with two clients: one on **zeus** and the other on **hera**.

Server Activation

Since the server is a Java application, and RMI requires the RMI registry to be active, this presupposes that at least one Java VM is running on the server machine. The RMI server can only be run in a Java VM, so to dynamically activate a RMI server would require some method of launching a Java VM with the appropriate Java class. This is too much to expect, so RMI servers must be started on the server machine that is waiting for connections from clients.

Java IDL

Sun has provided a series of Java classes that are CORBA-compliant, along with an IDL compiler (called **idlgen**) that creates CORBA stubs and skeletons in Java. (At the time of writing, Sun had produced an interim light-weight ORB called **Door ORB** that is implemented over TCP/IP; this should soon be replaced, or augmented, with modules that implement IIOP and connectivity to Sun's NEO ORB.)

The Java CORBA system looks like this:

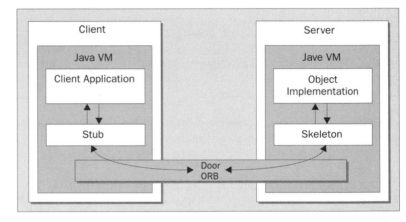

Notice the inherent problem with Java: the Java VM has to be used to interpret the Java bytecodes. Of course, when the IIOP module is implemented, either end may be implemented in another language and may use a different ORB; but this is not the situation at present.

Using the example given above, we can define the interface:

```
interface IDataRetrieval
{
   string GetData();
};
```

This is then compiled with **idlgen**, using the following command line:

```
idlgen -fclient -fserver -fno -cpp IdataRetrieval.idl
```

The compiler produces a new directory, in the current directory, called **idlGlobal**; it also creates Java source files for the stubs and skeletons:

IDataRetrievalHolder.java
IDataRetrievalOperations.java
IDataRetrievalRef.java   A reference to the server object

`IDataRetrievalServant.java`	Interface implemented by the server
`IDataRetrievalSkeleton.java`	Used by the server to create references
`IDataRetrievalStub.java`	Used by the client to create references

Note that if your IDL has more interfaces, **idlgen** will produce more classes, and your **idlGlobal** directory can fill quite quickly! You'll need to build these with:

javac idlGlobal*.java

(and fill the directory with more files).

The server implements the **Servant** interface on the actual object. This is exposed by the server through the creation of a reference to the interface and the subsequent publication of that reference:

```
import idlGlobal.*;
import sunw.door.*;

public class DataRetrievalImpl
        implements IDataRetrievalServant
{
   private int call;

   public DataRetrievalImpl()
   {
      super();
      call = 0;
   }

   public String GetData()
         throws sunw.corba.SystemException
   {
      call++;
      System.out.println("request, data is:" + call);
      return "data is:" + call;
   }

   public static void main(String args[])
   {
      System.out.println("Started server...");
      DataRetrievalImpl server = new DataRetrievalImpl();
      try
      {
         Orb.initialize(6000);
         IDataRetrievalRef ref =
                 IDataRetrievalSkeleton.createRef(server);
         String name = "DataRetrieval";
         System.out.println("binding to " + name);
         Orb.publish(name, ref);
      }
      catch(Exception e)
      {
         System.out.println("exception: " + e);
      }
   }
}
```

This code implements the object on the port 6000. This is referenced by the client using the following URL:

```
idl:sunw.door://host:6000/DataRetrieval
```

where *host* is the name of the server machine. The Door ORB is actually implemented in the classes that the server imports from **sunw.door**, so you don't need to run a separate registry (as in the RMI case) or a daemon (as is the case with Orbix, for example).

The client code is:

```
import idlGlobal.*;
import sunw.corba.*;

public class DataRetrievalClient
{
   public static void main(String[] args)
   {
      if (args.length != 1)
      {
         System.out.println("Please give server name");
         return;
      }
      try
      {
         IDataRetrievalRef ref =
                         IDataRetrievalStub.createRef();
         String name = "idl:sunw.door://" + args[0]
                         + ":6000/DataRetrieval";
         Orb.resolve(name, ref);
         String reply;
         reply = ref.GetData();
         System.out.println("Got "+reply);
      }
      catch(Exception e)
      {
         System.out.println("Exception "+e);
      }
      System.exit(0);
   }
}
```

This gets a reference to the remote object using the **Orb.resolve()** method; it then calls the remote object method on this reference. Note that, since the stub implements the same methods as the remote object (that's why it's there), you don't have to cast the reference, as you did in the RMI example.

You need to copy the following files to the client machine:

```
DataRetrievalClient.class
idlGlobal\DataRetrievalOperations.class
idlGlobal\DataRetrievalRef.class
idlGlobal\DataRetrievalStub.class
```

and the client also needs the **sunw.corba** classes in its **CLASSPATH**.

The server machine should have:

```
DataRetrievalImpl.class
idlGlobal\DataRetrievalOperations.class
idlGlobal\DataRetrievalRef.class
idlGlobal\DataRetrievalStub.class
idlGlobal\DataRetrievalSkeleton.class
idlGlobal\DataRetrievalServant.class
```

The surprising thing is that the server needs the stub class as well as the skeleton class. Note, however, that these examples have been taken from the alpha 2.2 release, so the classes are likely to change before the release.

To run the server you just use:

```
java DataRetrievalImpl
```

This implements the ORB and the server object. On the client, use:

```
java DataRetrievalClient host
```

where **host** is the name of the machine that implements the object.

Multithreading

The Java servers invoked via the Java Door ORB can use Java threads.

Server Activation

As with other CORBA ORBs, the Door ORB can start up a Java class. However, the Door ORB is implemented in Java, so at least one Java VM must be running on the server machine.

COM

The Component Object Model is covered in Chapter 3, and distribution of objects using COM (DCOM) is the main subject of this book. COM is Microsoft's binary standard, defining how objects can interact. COM is available on all Microsoft Windows platforms, starting with Windows 3.1. It's available in both a 16-bit version (OLE 2.0) and a 32-bit version. COM is also available on MacOS and various Unix platforms.

DCOM is COM distributed across the network. The client of a DCOM object sees that object as if it's in its own address space, whether it's on a local machine or a remote machine. In addition to distributing objects, DCOM also brings security to COM and multithreading. Security is a welcome addition, although using the security facilities to their full potential demands a thorough understanding of the security model. This is why we devote Chapter 7 to security. Multithreading is covered in Chapter 9.

COM Architecture

I offer, below, a simple view of the COM architecture. The client uses COM objects through interfaces, much as a DCE RPC client does. The client requests that an object is activated on the server, and is passed back an interface on that object. This interface may be the generic interface that all COM objects support, **IUnknown**, or it may be another interface that the client requested.

The client accesses this interface through a piece of code called a **proxy** (in RPC terminology, a stub). The proxy appears to the client as the interface that it requested, but the proxy may be code generated by the Microsoft IDL compiler to marshal the request to the server. The server itself may or may not be on the same machine as the client.

The interface method invocations are sent, via the channel, to the stub code on the server machine. The channel may be Windows messages, if the server is on the local machine, or it may be some RPC mechanism, like Microsoft RPC. The stub unmarshals the request, and invokes the method in the interface of the server object.

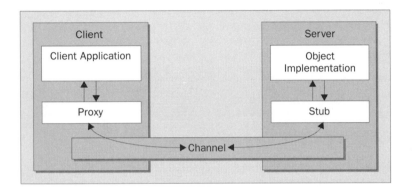

To enable clients to find the objects that they require, all objects are registered in the local system registry. This can mean that a machine's registry gets rather full of registrations. To get around this (and to centralize the administration of remote objects), NT 5.0 will have a registry of objects in the domain; each machine's registry will act as a local cache for the objects that it uses or implements.

As with DCE, interfaces and COM classes have UUIDs that are called IIDs (interface IDs) and CLSIDs (class IDs) respectively; and GUIDs in general. This enables object classes to be uniquely identified. The registry allows information to be saved about the executable code that implements an object, where it resides, and what code implements the proxies for the interfaces. This builds in flexibility that allows alternatives to be present.

For example, an object can be implemented as an in-process object, or as a remote object on another machine. The client can explicitly choose one of these implementations, or it can leave it to COM to choose.

Dynamic and Static Invocation

COM supports a dynamic and a static method of invoking methods on objects. However, it is slightly different to the way that CORBA does it. The static method has already been explained: the programmer defines the object, and its interfaces in IDL and MIDL create the proxy and stub code. These are registered in the system registry to allow greater flexibility of their use. Due to the way that the static invocation is implemented, this is often referred to as the vtable method.

One standard interface that COM defines is the **IDispatch** interface. This is the dynamic technique of invoking object methods. As with CORBA, to allow for dynamic invocation, there has to be some way to describe the methods implemented by an object and the parameters that these methods require. In COM, this is done with a **type library**. Type libraries are files that describe the object, and COM provides interfaces, obtained through the **IDispatch** interface, to query an object's type library.

In COM, an object whose methods are dynamically invoked must be written to support **IDispatch**; this is unlike CORBA, where any object can be invoked with DII (as long as the object's information is in the implementation repository). In COM, if the object has just the **IDispatch** interface then it can only be invoked in this way. However, COM also allows for an object to implement **dual interfaces**, where an interface is implemented both through **IDispatch** and through the vtable method.

However, since the methods must be supported by the dispatch interface, it means that the methods can only support particular data types. The great advantage of this is that there's no need to use MIDL to create specific proxy-stub code, since COM will use the default **IDispatch** proxy and stub. This method can even be used without implementing a dispatch interface, in which case it is referred to as **type library marshaling**. This offers a performance near to that obtained with a custom interface, and it requires fewer files to install. There's no way to do type library marshaling in CORBA.

Multithreading

COM supports multithreaded servers, but it requires that the COM libraries be initialized in the threads that use them. This leads to two main models. The first of these is the apartment model, where every thread should initialize the COM libraries, and any interaction between objects in these threads, even in the same process, should be marshaled. The second model is the free threading model, which relaxes this requirement, but places restrictions on the data that a thread can use.

A third model, still to be released, is called the rental model. This will be used by the Microsoft Transaction Server, where one thread 'helps' another, in a fashion that still behaves as if the object is single threaded. The first two models are explored in Chapter 9.

Why so many models? The free threading model allows developers to write multithreaded clients and servers. However, as with any multiple threaded application, using many threads in a COM client or server means that the developer must be careful to prevent multiple threads changing the same data value at the same time. This is a technique called synchronization, and it can lead to some complicated code.

Prior to DCOM, COM didn't allow multithreading: a single thread was used in the server, and all access to the objects was synchronized through a Windows message queue. This is used as the synchronization method in the DCOM apartment model and is adequate in most cases. However, if you're willing to write the extra code, free threading allows for better performance.

Server Activation

COM has several ways that servers can be activated. The bottom line is that a COM object server need not be running when a client request is made to instantiate an object. COM will locate the server code through the registry, and will start the server (it does this with a service called the Service Control Manager). COM also allows access to servers that are already running when the client request is made. Running objects can register themselves with a dynamic system table called the **running object table**.

OLE Interfaces

OLE, object linking and embedding, describes the interfaces required by desktop COM objects. These interfaces describe facilities like compound documents, in-place activation, and inter-application drag-and-drop. These are the same facilities that are described by the (as yet, unimplemented) CORBAfacilities interfaces. Although SOM does have such facilities on OS/2 and the MacOS through OpenDoc, and although SOM is a CORBA API, OpenDoc is not part of the official CORBA standard.

Other Services

Other object services like naming, persistence, object lifetimes, and the facilities that are implemented in CORBAservices, are part of the COM specification.

Remote Automation

I only mention Remote Automation, here, as an attempt to dispel some myths. Remote Automation was introduced in VB4 as a method to allow a VB automation client to use an Automation server (implementing an **IDispatch** interface) on another machine. Remote Automation is completely and utterly redundant on 32-bit Windows systems with DCOM, since these systems support the distribution of the **IDispatch** interface.

Remote Automation works by replacing the usual dispatch interface's proxy with a proxy that remotes the call to the server machine. On the server machine, a process called the **Remote Automation Manager** dispatches the automation calls to the object via the standard dispatch stub.

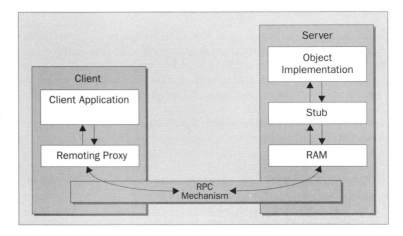

The proxy reads information that is stored in the registry for the required interface and uses this to determine information like the server machine and the transport mechanism that is used to talk to the server. Rather than allowing COM to dispatch the method calls from client to server, remote automation handles the remoting from the proxy, through the transport to the Remote Automation Manager, which does the actual method invocation. It's here that COM takes over again, calling the dispatch interface on the object.

In effect, the client of the object is the Remote Automation Manager and not the client application. This means that even after an object has been activated, every method call has to go through the Manager. Remote Automation is *not* DCOM; it is a method of remoting automation calls, using an inferior method to that used by DCOM.

DCOM makes Remote Automation redundant in all but one sense: DCOM will not be available on 16-bit Windows, whereas Remote Automation is. I mentioned above that Remote Automation became available with VB4; but it is not confined to VB objects. Indeed, any client can use Remote Automation, and any server may be activated using it.

Summary

This chapter has introduced you to some of the more popular (and some less popular, but interesting) methods of distributing code across a network. When you decide to write a distributed application you have a tough choice to make. Should you use a method that has no support for objects like Sockets and RPC, or should you use a method that supports objects implicitly, like DCOM and CORBA?

In general, the higher level methods (DCOM and CORBA) require the developer to write less code and add functionality, such as object persistence, remote activation, and dynamic invocation, that the lower level methods lack. As to the choice between DCOM and CORBA, you have to look at the current implementations to make your choice. There are many vendors producing CORBA ORBs, because there are many platforms supported, particularly Unix, which as a 'standard' appears to have many different implementations. CORBA appears to have taken the strategy of supporting the most platforms possible to the detriment of the actual common functionality between all the versions.

Microsoft took a different approach: they got most of the facilities of COM *right* on Intel Windows machines first, and then started porting it to other platforms. Since the majority of personal computers are PCs using Windows, this was a shrewd decision.

Apart from that, DCOM is more manageable to use than CORBA. The examples in this chapter have shown that CORBA IDL compilers produce many source files and require that the object and the client developer write their code around some strange CORBA structures. As you'll see in the rest of this book, MIDL does not produce piles of generated code, and the DCOM API is simple to use and the objects are straightforward to implement. This, and the fact that there are many excellent 'visual' tools to enable you to develop (D)COM objects, makes this the right choice for PCs; and once the ports have been completed, for all the other platforms too.

This chapter gave the general methods of distributing objects on a heterogeneous network; the next chapter narrows the platform to Windows, in order to explore the methods of sharing data and code on a Windows machine.

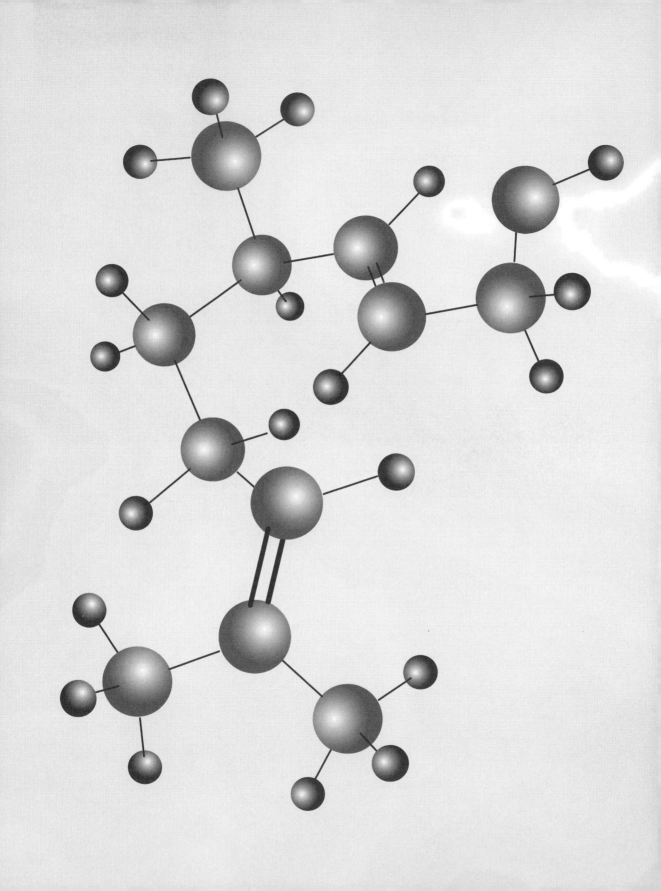

Distributed Objects on Windows

CHAPTER 2

COM allows you to create objects on Windows; DCOM extends this, allowing you to create objects on other machines across the network. However, before we venture into COM and DCOM, let's gain a deeper understanding by taking a look at the alternatives for a Windows programmer.

In this chapter, we'll look at a few of the problems that COM and DCOM solve by looking at how we can provide some of their functionality using other methods. The chapter starts by looking at DLLs. Dynamic Link Libraries allow code (and data) to be shared between applications on a single machine. The main point of this section is to introduce to you, by devious means, two important aspects of COM: interfaces and DLL maintenance.

Interfaces are important because they define the apparent functionality of the code module (be it a DLL or a COM object). Defining an interface is not as straightforward as it may appear. This chapter will outline some of the problems that you're likely to come across.

The maintenance and loading of DLLs is vital to efficient and robust code. Dynamic loading of DLLs allows functionality to be available when you need it, without imposing a huge overhead; dynamic loading also opens the possibility of using libraries provided by different vendors, without having to recompile the client code. Using multiple DLLs in your application can, however, be a maintenance nightmare. In this chapter, you'll see one simple solution that I provide for this; and by following me through, you'll achieve a greater understanding of the work that COM does on your behalf.

We finish the chapter with an application that uses TCP/IP sockets to remote functionality over a network. You'll come face to face with such concepts as marshaling data, dispatching method calls, pinging, and exception handling. These are all issues that you'll need to confront when you write your own distributed applications and, as you'll see from the example, they do require quite a lot of code. The good news is that you'll be seeing the facilities that COM and DCOM offer to solve these problems.

Dynamic Link Libraries

Sharing Code

Perhaps the best example of memory being wasted through code duplication is when applications statically link functions in the C runtime library (CRT). Imagine that you have a data analysis application that needs to format a string and print it on a window; this application could use the C runtime library function **sprintf()**. Another application, say a resource watcher, could also use **sprintf()**. Since the function is statically linked into both applications, and they are likely to be running at the same time, the code is replicated, and memory is allocated twice for this function.

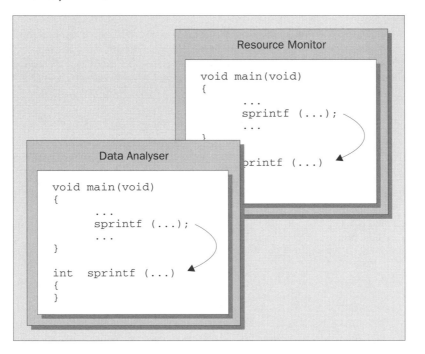

Of course, the problem isn't confined to the CRT. Any API that's used by a single application which can have several instances loaded at one time (or an API that will be used by several different applications which will be loaded at the same time) suffers from this problem. How do we allow a number of applications, that are running concurrently, to use the same library functions?

Dynamic Linking

The answer lies in **dynamic link libraries** (**DLLs**). Windows allows the programmer to dynamically link to functions at runtime rather than statically link at compile time. This makes the application's executable file smaller, since the code for the library functions is in another file; furthermore, it allows the functions to be distributed separately from the applications that use them.

The dynamic linking process maps the DLL into the address space of the executable that uses it; calling the function is, therefore, no different than calling a statically linked function. However, the functions in a DLL take up a fixed amount of memory, regardless of the number of applications using them.

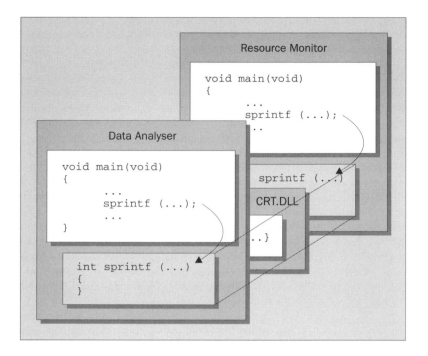

In this picture, the DLL is mapped into the address space of two applications at the same time. There is just *one* copy of the DLL: the two applications share this code, but through the technique of memory mapping, both applications think that they have a separate copy.

Thus, the call to **sprintf()** in one application will execute the same piece of code as the call made from the other application. The data used by the code, however, is specific to the application in which the DLL is mapped. Sharing data through a DLL requires some extra work, and is covered later in this chapter.

Note that the DLL is *mapped* into the address space of each executable; in other words, there is just *one* copy of the code in memory for all the executables using the DLL. The mapping may put the DLL in different virtual memory positions for the different executables that use the DLL, but this doesn't matter: the system ensures that the applications have the right address for the functions.

These statements may seem a little strange, if you consider how a debugger sets breakpoints; that is, by altering the code of the application to indicate where the debugger should stop. If you set breakpoints in a memory-mapped DLL, you might imagine that all applications using this DLL would receive the modified code. In fact, the system has been designed to take this possibility into account: when a debugger attempts to write to the DLL's code, the system makes a copy, and it's this copy that is altered.

Interfaces

In the previous example, we have two applications sharing a piece of code. Both applications know the format of the shared code, and how to call it, because the prototype of the code has been widely publicized. The function has a public **interface**.

The interface specifies the function name, its parameters, and its return type. In this case the interface refers to a single function, but it may be applied to a collection of related functions. For example, you could think of the interface to the system registry as being the set of **Reg...()** Win32 functions (**RegOpenKey()**, **RegCloseKey()**, etc.) exported from **Advapi32.dll**.

One immediate advantage of using DLLs with predefined interfaces is that the DLL can be distributed and updated separately from the applications that use it. If a new version of a DLL becomes available, an existing EXE could use the new DLL without recompilation.

This is a powerful feature, but it does impose some discipline on the developer. In particular, the developer of a DLL must think carefully about what functions the DLL will export, and the parameters that these functions will use. Once the interface has been defined, it's very difficult to change it.

> *An interesting example of interface design is the COM function* **CoGetClassObject()**. *The designer of this code was foresighted enough to ensure that when this function was provided in the OLE DLLs on 16-bit Windows 3.1, the third parameter was a* **void** *pointer reserved for future use. The programmer was told to pass* **NULL** *in this parameter. This prototype persisted right up to 32-bit COM on NT 3.51; for DCOM, however, this parameter is now a pointer to a* **COSERVERINFO** *structure that determines, among other things, the name of the remote server machine. Code written for early 32-bit OLE will still work on NT 4.0 with DCOM.*

Another problem with DLLs, pertinent here, is that although tools exist to list the functions exported from a DLL (such as Microsoft's **Exehdr** for 16-bit DLLs, or **Dumpbin** for 32-bit DLLs), the tool only gives the name (or the ordinal) of the function and not the parameters. This means that a DLL developer must distribute the DLL with associated header files and documentation. A DLL is *not* self-documenting.

Looking at this from another perspective, a programmer could use a tool to find out the functions implemented in a DLL, and make guesses about the use of that DLL. The developer of the DLL may not want this, the developer may decide to hide the functions that are implemented. One method is to export functions just by ordinal; another, more cryptic, way is to group function pointers into tables and export these tables through a single DLL function. Such a method is particularly important to COM, as you'll see in the next chapter.

We see the benefits of a consistent interface in the DLLs of the Win32 API. For example, if you take a function like **wsprintf()** in Win32, you don't know whether the implementation in NT 4.0 is the same as in Windows 95. Only the Microsoft developers know, or care. All we're interested in, as developers, is that my Win32 application running under NT gets the same result from calling **wsprintf()** as it did when it ran under Windows 95. To do this, the DLL must preserve the interface of the function, but there's actually no real requirement to provide the same implementation. Interfaces are important, so we'll return to this concept many times in the chapters to come.

Exporting Functions

The 16-bit Windows method of marking a function to be shared in a DLL is to include the function name in the **EXPORTS** section of the DEF file. This is used by the linker when it generates the name tables of the DLL.

```
LIBRARY COOLFUNCTIONS
EXPORTS
    GetRichQuickFromFiveDollars    @1
    FoolYourTaxmanYouHaveNoMoney   @2
```

This method works for 32-bit Windows too, but better performance can be achieved with the **__declspec(dllexport)** and **__declspec(dllimport)** storage class modifiers, which can be applied to function definitions and prototypes in the source and header files.

To export a function (or data) the function is marked with the `__declspec(dllexport)` modifier.

```
__declspec(dllexport) LONGLONG GetRichQuickFromFiveDollars(short outlay);
__declspec(dllexport) short FoolYourTaxmanYouHaveNoMoney(LONGLONG bankbalance);
```

This is fine, as long as the user of the interface has the same C++ compiler as the implementor, because C++ 'decorates' function names to allow the overloading of methods. If a function is exported as a C++ function, it will be exported with the C++ decorated name. An application importing a C++ function must import it with this decorated name. The complicating factor is that there's no standard method to decorate C++ functions; so different C++ compilers decorate in different ways, and one compiler will export a function with a different name than another would expect to import.

Name decoration is a perennial problem with implementing DLLs with C++, and so there exists a method to alleviate the problem: turn off decoration by prototyping the functions with **extern "C"**. You can assume that the prototypes given above, and those in the rest of this section, are using the **extern "C"** modifier, although this won't be stated explicitly, because of space constraints.

The code that imports these functions will have to prototype them with the `__declspec(dllimport)` modifier:

```
__declspec(dllimport) LONGLONG  GetRichQuickFromFiveDollars(short outlay);
__declspec(dllimport) short FoolYourTaxmanYouHaveNoMoney(LONGLONG bankbalance);
```

A function marked this way will load faster than a function exported through the **EXPORTS** section of the DEF file, because the modifiers give a software pledge that the function does exist in the DLL. This results in the linker reducing the function-calling code by one level of indirection. You can find out more information about this in Win32 Knowledge Base article Q132044. All of this does not, of course, render the DEF file redundant, because a DEF file still allows the programmer to control the exported name and ordinal.

These mechanisms allow us to export a function, or a collection of functions, from a DLL. Using a header file with the function prototype is not enough, of course, to import the function. The programmer must use some method of accessing the library. There are two ways we can do this: we can indicate to the linker that a particular DLL will be used (known as **implicit linking**), or we can dynamically load the DLL at runtime (known as **explicit linking**).

In the first case, the linker links to an **import library** that's generated by the linker that created the DLL. This static linked library essentially consists of stub functions that forward the call on to the DLL. The loading of the DLL is done when the EXE is loaded, and the function calls are carried out via the static library. **Code fixups** are done when the DLL is loaded.

> *Code (and static data) fixups are required because the DLL is not always loaded into a process' address space at the same place for every process that uses the DLL, since there may be a DLL already loaded into that address. In this situation, the operation will relocate the DLL to a free address, and change (or 'fixup') the addresses of functions, absolute jumps, and static data, to reflect the new address.*

In the second case (explicitly linking to a DLL), the client code doesn't need the import library; all that's required is the header file for the DLL interface, so that function type-checking can be performed by the compiler. The programmer is responsible for loading the DLL and getting the addresses of the functions in the DLL interface before calling those functions.

Loading the DLL is straightforward, with a call to **LoadLibrary()**; and getting the address of a function is trivial: you call **GetProcAddress()** with the loaded DLL's instance handle and either the name of the function or its ordinal. The address that's returned is valid in your application's address space, and you can cast this to the function pointer of the function that you want to call. Of course, the address is in the address space of your process because that's where the DLL has been mapped.

Each of these methods has its strengths and weaknesses. Implicit linking through an import library is used for the functions in the Win32 API via the **Kernel32.lib** and **User32.lib** import libraries, and through this the functions are called in the appropriate system DLL. The advantage of this is that the DLLs are loaded, and the function addresses are resolved, at initialization time. This may slow the loading of the application, but it is at a time when users will expect to wait. On the downside, implicit linking loads *all* of the specified DLLs, even if a DLL is used for only a short amount of time, at a single point in the application. Such a situation is wasteful in terms of the memory taken to hold the DLL, and in the time spent loading it.

Explicit linking is more flexible, but can be complicated. To get access to a function whose DLL is loaded with **LoadLibrary()**, the application will need to get the function address. If there are many functions, this means multiple calls to **GetProcAddress()** and the problems of managing many function pointers. However, it allows DLLs to be loaded only when (and *if*) they are needed and the application can make a decision as to what particular DLL to load.

Finally, DLLs may seem like a great idea, but there are some pitfalls. One temptation is to provide many small DLLs, each holding interfaces with associated functions. This will provide flexibility, in that an application requiring just one interface would not need to load the superfluous code of other interfaces. However, applications that require many interfaces of functions would have to load many DLLs, and this would slow the application load up (implicit linking), or make the application pause during execution (for explicit linking). The current conventional wisdom is to reduce the number of DLLs that are loaded by putting many interfaces in a single DLL.

This final point is just as important when designing COM servers as when designing standard DLLs. COM places no limits on the number of functions, interfaces, or classes that you can place in a single DLL, so you'll need to decide how to manage these tradeoffs yourself.

Language Issues

Note that there is a language issue here. Functions exported from a DLL are generally C functions, albeit C functions that use the Pascal method of passing parameters and cleaning up the stack frame. You can use other languages to produce DLLs, but they should provide DLL interfaces that are C-like to ensure compatibility. DLLs exist to share code, so many applications must be able to import the DLL functions. The only way to do this is to define a standard and then stick by it; the standard is C.

With this said, a designer still needs to be careful to use C data types that can be used by other languages. One situation where this is particularly important is when a C/C++ developer creates a DLL to be used from Visual Basic 4.0. VB4 does not have pointers, and in particular, it does not have function pointers. This means that a DLL cannot expect a VB program to provide callback functions; for example, Win32's **EnumWindows()** function, which we'll use in an example later in this chapter, cannot be called from VB4.

As in C, you can export C++ functions from a DLL. Moreover, you can export an entire class from a DLL by prototyping the class like this:

```
class __declspec(dllexport) CMyClass {...};
```

However, methods in a class are passed an implicit **this** pointer as a parameter, and class methods and global functions can be overloaded (i.e. several functions have the same name but take different parameters). To allow for this, the C name is not sufficient; therefore, C++ compilers **mangle** or **decorate** function names to include information about the class that a method belongs to and the parameters that the method takes.

As mentioned in the last section, different C++ compilers have different name decoration schemes, which makes exporting classes and overloaded functions difficult. If **CMyClass** was exported by a DLL compiled by a Microsoft C++ compiler, it could be unusable in an application compiled with another compiler.

This is not to say that exporting classes is a bad thing. If you're designing your own suite of programs written in C++ and compiled with a single compiler, you may decide to create a utility DLL. Exporting classes would probably be a good idea in this case. Indeed, MFC allows you to create MFC extension DLLs that are designed specifically to augment the MFC classes and must, therefore, export MFC classes. However, for maximum usage of your library (so that programs written in Visual Basic, VBA, Delphi, C, C++, etc., can use it), the interface must be C. Therefore, you should not export classes, and your functions should be prototyped with **extern "C"**.

This is a major problem, since it means that functions are often associated to form interfaces by artificial and ungainly means, such as giving the function names special prefixes. (An instance of this occurs later in the chapter, when we create an interface with a set of functions prefixed with **EnumerateWindows_**.)

Runtime Linking

Let's return to the issue of loading the DLL. If the client statically links to the DLL's import library, then the DLL is loaded as soon as the EXE is loaded. The system does some searching to find the required DLL (searching the current directory, the Windows directory, the Windows System directory, and the directories in the **PATH**). If the system can't find the DLL, the user will be presented with a dialog that indicates this fact and the application loading is aborted.

The programmer can gain greater flexibility by explicitly loading the DLL at runtime. This allows the application to determine, at runtime, where the DLL is kept, rather than allowing the system to determine its location. It means that if a call to **LoadLibrary()** fails, the application can take some evasive action, either disabling the functionality that requires the DLL, or attempting to find another DLL.

For example, an application could link to a **CoolFunctions.lib** import library and allow the system to find **CoolFunctions.dll**, or it could specify the path of the DLL at runtime:

```
HINSTANCE coollibrary;
coollibrary = LoadLibrary(_T("C:\\CoolLibs\\CoolFunctions.DLL"));
// Function pointer
LPFYTYHNM FoolYourTaxman;
FoolYourTaxman = (LPFYTYHNM)GetProcAdddress(coollibrary,
  _T("FoolYourTaxmanYouHaveNoMoney"));
short taxreturn;
LONGLONG salary = 100000;
taxreturn = (FoolYourTaxman)(salary);
FreeLibrary(coollibrary);
```

(The usual disclaimers apply about not having put any error detection in the above code and how you *really* should do when you write your own code.) In this code, **FoolYourTaxman** is a function pointer of type **LPFYTMYHNM**, which is defined as:

```
typedef short (LPFYTMYHNM*)(LONGLONG);
```

By explicitly linking to a DLL, the application writer can decide not only the location of the DLL, but also the name of the DLL. This could, potentially, allow for several versions of a particular DLL to reside on a hard disk, using the name and location as a crude versioning mechanism.

Defining Interfaces

Imagine the situation where I have a **CoolLibs** directory, as outlined in the code above, and then my dodgy accountant gives me a version of the functions in **CoolFunctions.dll** in a new DLL called **DodgyFunctions.dll**. The new functions make the taxman ask for even less money from me (using a none-too-legal method that I do not want to use too frequently), so I alter the code in my application as shown:

```
HINSTANCE coollibrary;
if (poorthismonth)
    coollibrary =
        LoadLibrary(_T("C:\\Dodgy\\DodgyFunctions.dll"));
else
    coollibrary =
        LoadLibrary(_T("C:\\CoolLibs\\CoolFunctions.dll"));
LPFYTYHNM FoolYourTaxman;
FoolYourTaxman = (LPFYTYHNM)GetProcAdddress(coollibrary,
    _T("FoolYourTaxmanYouHaveNoMoney"));
short taxreturn;
LONGLONG salary = 100000;
taxreturn = (FoolYourTaxman)(salary);
FreeLibrary(coollibrary);
```

This code will only work if the prototype of **FoolYourTaxmanYouHaveNoMoney()** is the same in **DodgyFunctions.dll** as it is in **CoolFunctions.dll**. The interface must be the same, even though the implementation is different. Of course, the big problem with this code is that I have to code into my application the locations of the DLLs. One solution would be to put these addresses in the registry under some well known key.

```
├─ Taxman
│      ├──── Dodgy
│      │        └──── DLL = C:\Dodgy\DodgyFunctions.dll
│      └──── Accurate
│               └──── DLL = C:\CoolLibs\CoolFunctions.dll
```

We could now use code like this:

```
HINSTANCE coollibrary;
HKEY hkey;
TCHAR regkey[MAX_PATH];
TCHAR library[MAX_PATH];
LONG size = MAX_PATH;

lstrcpy(regkey,_T("\\SOFTWARE\\MyApps\\Taxman\\"));
if (poorthismonth)
   lstrcat(regkey, _T("Dodgy"));
else
   lstrcat(regkey, _T("Accurate"));
RegOpenKey(HKEY_LOCAL_MACHINE, regkey, &hkey);
RegQueryValue(hkey, _T("DLL"), library, &size);
RegCloseKey(hkey);
coollibrary = LoadLibrary(library);

LPFYTYHNM FoolYourTaxman;
FoolYourTaxman = (LPFYTYHNM)GetProcAdddress(coollibrary,
   _T("FoolYourTaxmanYouHaveNoMoney"));
short taxreturn;
LONGLONG salary = 100000;
taxreturn = (FoolYourTaxman)(salary);
FreeLibrary(coollibrary);
```

To load the DLL that I require, I query the registry for **TaxMan\Dodgy** or **TaxMan\Accurate** and read the **DLL** value in that key. This value has the path to the DLL that I want to load, which I do with a call to **LoadLibrary()**.

At this point, the interface of the DLLs is fixed, so I cannot change the names of the functions or their prototypes. Indeed, if the parameter list of **FoolYourTaxmanYouHaveNoMoney()** changes, multitudes of applications that rely on this function (well, in this case, *one* application) will break, since the client of the DLL is expecting to call a specific function with particular parameter types and a particular return type. In essence, the header file of the DLL is a contract defining what the DLL can do. And remember, once you've signed a contract it takes lots of effort (and money, since lawyers' time is like gold) to break the contract. The message is: don't do it.

Using a register of installed DLLs has some disadvantages. How should the DLLs be categorized? I've used a scheme of interface, then vendor, and then a key called **DLL**, but this may not be the best scheme. The other main headache is keeping the register up to date, making sure that, as new DLLs supersede older ones, the register entries are modified or removed when the DLLs are removed entirely.

However, there are also some advantages. Firstly, the DLLs can reside anywhere on the disk (indeed anywhere in the namespace of the machine). All I have to do is make sure that the registry has the correct path. The implementation of the application using the DLL does not have to change if the position of the DLL changes. Secondly, an application can enumerate the implementations of this interface and thus give the user a choice of implementation to use; it can be assumed that all keys in the **TaxMan** key refer to functions that follow the same interface.

Now let's say that I want to extend my library. To the existing functions of my **CoolFunctions.dll** I want to add functions that are used to calculate, say, the day of the week for a particular date. These functions are not applicable to the **TaxMan** category, so they need a new category:

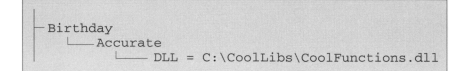

```
├─Birthday
│   └────Accurate
│            └──── DLL = C:\CoolLibs\CoolFunctions.dll
```

This has a function with the following prototype:

```
typedef enum {Mon, Tues, Wed, Thurs, Fri, Sat, Sun} DOTW;
__declspec(dllexport) DOTW DayOfTheWeek(SYSTEMTIME time);
```

Since we have only one DLL implementing the **Birthday** API, it would seem that the extra level of keys (**Accurate**) in the registry is unnecessary (and we come back to the question of whether this registration scheme is the most appropriate). However, we'll keep it for the sake of compatibility with the **TaxMan** API.

Now we can find out the day of the week for our birthday with:

```
HINSTANCE coollibrary;
HKEY hkey;
TCHAR regkey[MAX_PATH];
TCHAR library[MAX_PATH];
LONG size = MAX_PATH;

lstrcpy(regkey, _T("\\SOFTWARE\\MyApps\\Birthday\\Accurate"));
RegOpenKey(Hkey_LOCAL_MACHINE, regkey, &hkey);
RegQueryValue(hkey, _T("DLL"), library, &size);
RegCloseKey(hkey);
coollibrary = LoadLibrary(library);

LPDOTW DayOfTheWeek;
DayOfTheWeek = (LPDOTW)GetProcAddress(coollibrary, _T("DayOfTheWeek"));

SYSTEMTIME mybirthday = {1964, 9, 0, 8, 0, 0, 0, 0};
DOTW dotw = (DayOfTheWeek)(mybirthday);
FreeLibrary(coollibrary);
```

There's nothing wrong with this implementation having two dissimilar interfaces in the same DLL. The interface definitions should keep the interfaces separate:
In **Taxman.h** we have

```
__declspec(dllimport) LONGLONG
    GetRichQuickFromFiveDollars(short outlay);
__declspec(dllimport) short
    FoolYourTaxmanYouHaveNoMoney(LONGLONG bankbalance);
```

whereas in **Birthday.h** we have:

```
__declspec(dllimport) DOTW DayOfTheWeek(SYSTEMTIME time);
```

If, at a later stage, we decide to move the Birthday API to its own DLL, we can do this by supplying the new DLL and changing the registry setting. (Note that the **CoolFunctions.dll** could remain the same;

the **Birthday** functions will never be called, since the code references the DLL name through the registry key, which would point to the new DLL.)

This scheme of putting more than one interface into a single DLL is more efficient than using a DLL for every interface in those cases where an application requires more than one interface of functions.

Example: Window Enumerator Library

Now let's look at some real code, which we'll elaborate upon in the rest of this chapter.
The Windows API provides a function called **EnumWindows()** that will enumerate through all the windows on the current desktop, returning the window handle for each one. It does this by calling a user-provided callback function (of type **WNDENUMPROC**) for each window. One of the parameters of the callback is used to pass the window's handle.

Let's define a new API that is a little easier to use. We'll have three functions:

```
BOOL EnumerateWindows_Reset();
BOOL EnumerateWindows_Next(ULONG num, HWND* array, ULONG* pnumFetched);
BOOL EnumerateWindows_Skip(ULONG items);
```

EnumerateWindows_Reset() resets the enumerator to the beginning of the list of windows. **EnumerateWindows_Next()** will return the next **num** (or less) **HWND**s in the **array** buffer, and **EnumerateWindows_Skip()** will skip over the next **items** number of **HWND**s. The **array** buffer is allocated by the caller, the actual number of **HWND**s returned is supplied by **pnumFetched**.

Before we can use these functions, however, we need to construct the list of window handles, and when we have finished using the library, we need to carry out some cleanup on the resources previously allocated. We define two other functions to do this: **EnumerateWindows_Start()** and **EnumerateWindows_Finish()**.

Since the functions are implemented in a DLL, we could do the resource allocation and cleanup in response to a process (or thread) attaching to, or detaching from, the DLL. We could determine which event is taking place by using the **fdwReason** parameter of **DllMain()**. However, that would mean that the library could only be used once by a single thread, because the *only* time the resource allocation takes place is when a thread attaches to the DLL, and the freeing of the resources is only carried out when the thread detaches. This would be too restrictive, so we'll provide functions that the user of our library can use to explicitly initialize and clean up the DLL. The problem with this approach (and it's a problem with most of the C Win32 API) is that we can't guarantee that the library is initialized before it's used: that is left to the discipline of individual programmers.

The complete interface is:

```
// EnumWindows.h - used by both client and server

#ifdef IMPLEMENT_DLL_INTERFACE
#define DLLFUNCTION _declspec(dllexport)
#else
#define DLLFUNCTION _declspec(dllimport)
#endif

// DLL interface function prototypes are "C" for maximum compatability
```

```
extern "C"
{
DLLFUNCTION BOOL EnumerateWindows_Start();
DLLFUNCTION BOOL EnumerateWindows_Next(ULONG num,
                                       HWND* array,
                                       ULONG* pnumFetched);
DLLFUNCTION BOOL EnumerateWindows_Reset();
DLLFUNCTION BOOL EnumerateWindows_Skip(ULONG items);
DLLFUNCTION BOOL EnumerateWindows_Finish();
}
```

Here, I've defined the macro **DLLFUNCTION** according to whether the header file is being used in the server (when **IMPLEMENT_DLL_INTERFACE** is defined) or in a client. Note, also, that the functions are marked **extern "C"** to turn off name-mangling if a C++ compiler is used.

The actual implementation of this example (which, like all of the examples in this book, you can download from the Wrox Press web site at http://www.wrox.com/) is a Visual C++ AppWizard-generated regular DLL, which uses the DLL version of MFC. This allows us to use MFC classes without requiring the full integration with MFC that extension DLLs require. In this case, we make very little use of MFC, just using it to provide **DllMain()**. In fact, we could just as easily have created a non-MFC application and written our own **DllMain()**.

The implementation defines a class **CEnumData** (declared in **EnumData.h**), which holds a linked list of **CHwndNode** objects. Each of these objects has a data member used to hold an **HWND**. This library may be used by several threads in an application; therefore, to prevent the situation of **EnumerateWindows_Start()** being called by more than one thread (and causing damage to the (single) **CEnumData** object) we allocate a separate object per thread and keep a pointer to the object in **thread local storage** (TLS).

TLS allows code that may be executed by multiple threads at any one time to keep static or global data in a fashion that makes the data specific to just a single thread. Protecting data from corruption by multiple threads is very important, so we cover this in much more detail from a DCOM perspective in Chapter 9.

The Win32 TLS API maintains an array of 32-bit values for each thread used by the application. To use TLS you call **TlsAlloc()**, which returns an index into this array. You are guaranteed that successive calls to **TlsAlloc()** will return a different value, so you can call this function for each index that you require. This identifies a 'slot' in the array. Whatever you put into the slot is specific to this thread.

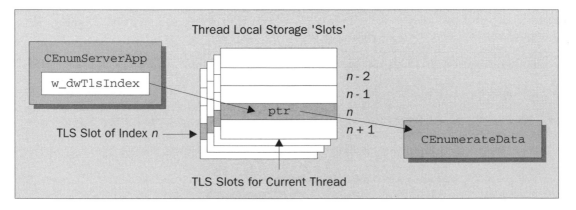

So in this diagram, the **CEnumServerApp::InitInstance()** gets an index; further on in the server code, a **CEnumerateData** object is created, and the pointer to this object is put into the slot with **TlsSetValue()**. The value can always be obtained by calling **TlsGetValue()**, but the value returned is the one that is specific to this thread; therefore, the object that the pointer points to is the one that was created in the current thread's context.

The code in **EnumServer.cpp** uses the **InitInstance()** function of the application class to allocate a TLS index with **TlsAlloc()**, and this index is released in **ExitInstance()** with a call to **TlsFree()**.

```
BOOL CEnumServerApp::InitInstance()
{
   m_dwTlsIndex = TlsAlloc();
   return CWinApp::InitInstance();
}

int CEnumServerApp::ExitInstance()
{
   TlsFree(m_dwTlsIndex);
   return CWinApp::ExitInstance();
}
```

This TLS index is held as a data member of the **CWinApp**-derived class, and the data in this TLS data slot is accessed with **GetEnumerationObject()** and **SetEnumerationObject()** to get and set the value.

SetEnumerationObject() is called by **EnumerateWindows_Start()**, which creates a new **CEnumData** object and passes the pointer to this object to the **SetEnumerationObject()** function. Now, whenever we want to access the object, we call **GetEnumerationObject()** in the application object.

```
inline CEnumData* CEnumServerApp::GetEnumerationObject()
{
   return (CEnumData*)TlsGetValue(m_dwTlsIndex);
}

inline void CEnumServerApp::SetEnumerationObject(CEnumData* pEnumObject)
{
   TlsSetValue(m_dwTlsIndex, pEnumObject);
}
```

Note that I used the **Tls...()** API and not **__declspec(thread)**, which you may have read as being another method of making static data thread local.

You can use **__declspec(thread)**, but it requires the application loader to be supplied with information about how much thread local storage to allocate when a thread is created. This is not a problem if the DLL is statically loaded, since the DLL's TLS requirement can be read and, as new threads attach to the DLL, the resource can be allocated. If the DLL is dynamically loaded, the TLS data can't be allocated for the loading thread; the net effect of this is that variables marked with **__declspec(thread)** will most likely end up overwriting the memory of other variables. To be safe, we don't use **__declspec(thread)**; instead, we let Win32 allocate the TLS slots for us.

The **CEnumData** class has the following members:

```
class CEnumData
{

public:
   CEnumData();
   virtual ~CEnumData();

   void Add(HWND hwnd);
   BOOL GetNext(HWND* phwnd);
   void Reset();

private:
   // Implementation Detail: windows hwnds are held as a
   // linked list of CHwndNode structures
   struct CHwndNode
   {
      CHwndNode* pNext;
      HWND hwndData;
      CHwndNode(HWND hwnd) : pNext(NULL), hwndData(hwnd) {}
   };

   CHwndNode* m_pPosition;
   CHwndNode* m_pHead;
};
```

The **HWND**s are held in a linked list of **CHwndNode**s, in this implementation, because it is not possible to determine the number of windows before the code is run. A simple array could have been used, but this would have needed code to check that enough space is available in the array when a new **HWND** is added. If there were not enough space, we'd have to write code to allocate a new array and copy the previous data into the new buffer.

In this implementation I've chosen to use a linked list. To maintain this list, we have two pointers in **CEnumData**: **m_pHead**, to point to the head of the list, and **m_pPosition**, to point to the current position.

With this defined, I can now create the enumeration object. **EnumerateWindows_Start()** creates the **CEnumData** object and calls **EnumWindows()**, passing **AddToList()** as the callback. This callback is called once for every window on the desktop with the **HWND** of the window. This handle is then added to the enumeration object with a call to **CEnumData::Add()**.

For the client application to gain access to this data, it calls **EnumerateWindows_Next()** to get some values from the object. Each call to this function requires the address of a caller-allocated buffer (to hold the data), the size of the buffer, and a pointer to a variable to take the number of data items that the server returns. All of this code is implemented in the **EnumServer.dll** library.

Putting It All Together

The client application is an MFC dialog-based application. It has the minimal interface of a list box and a couple of push buttons. The DLL in this application is statically linked by including the **EnumServer.lib** in the Object Library/Modules list in the Link tab of the Build|Settings dialog box. We could have dynamically loaded the DLL, but this would have required writing three more lines of code: first, to load the DLL; then, to get the address of the function; and finally, to unload it at an appropriate point. Like most programmers I want to make my life easy, and since there's no particular reason to use explicit linking, I've decided to use implicit linking instead.

When the user clicks on the Refresh button, the **CEnumClientDlg::OnRefresh()** handler function is called. This calls the DLL functions to create the list of window handles, read them, and then free the DLL resources. Each **HWND** obtained is then used to get the window title, which is put into a list box. If the window does not have a title, the value of the window's handle is given instead:

The static control at the bottom left has a count of all the entries in the list box.

The list box is filled when the Refresh button is clicked; this is handled by the following code in the dialog class:

```
void CEnumClientDlg::OnRefresh()
{
   DWORD dwFetched;
   HWND array[ARRAY_SIZE];
   UINT uCount = 0;

    EnumerateWindows_Start();
    EnumerateWindows_Reset();

   CListBox* pList = (CListBox*)GetDlgItem(IDC_WINDOWS);
   ASSERT(pList);

   pList->ResetContent();

   do
   {
      EnumerateWindows_Next(ARRAY_SIZE, array, &dwFetched);
      uCount += dwFetched;

      DWORD dwIndex;
      for (dwIndex = 0; dwIndex < dwFetched; dwIndex++)
      {
         int nTextLength;
         nTextLength = ::GetWindowTextLength(array[dwIndex]) + 1;
         CString strWindowName;
         if (nTextLength > 1)
         {
            ::GetWindowText(array[dwIndex],
                  strWindowName.GetBufferSetLength(nTextLength + 1),nTextLength);
            strWindowName.ReleaseBuffer();
         }
         else
            strWindowName.Format(_T("[%08x]"),array[dwIndex]);
```

```
            pList->AddString(strWindowName);
        }
    }
    while (dwFetched > 0);

    EnumerateWindows_Finish();

    CWnd* pwndCount = GetDlgItem(IDC_COUNT);
    ASSERT(pwndCount);

    CString strCount;
    strCount.Format(_T("%ld windows"), uCount);

    pwndCount->SetWindowText(strCount);
}
```

Here, the enumerator in the DLL is first initialized with **EnumerateWindows_Start()**, which creates the list of the current windows on the desktop. Then **EnumerateWindows_Next()** is called, repeatedly, to get the window **HWND**s in batches of **ARRAY_SIZE** until the enumerator is exhausted. For every **HWND**, the code calls **GetWindowText()** to get the window title, and then adds this to the list box. Finally, the DLL resources are released with a call to **EnumerateWindows_Finish()**.

Visible and Hidden Windows

As an aside, it's interesting to look at how many windows exist on the desktop at any one time. In the screenshot above, **EnumClient** is reporting 59 windows, yet only Word, a command prompt, and Developer Studio are running. Of course, many of these reported windows are controls that are part of the applications. (For example, any application that was written with MFC will have a window for both the frame *and* what appears to be the client area of this frame; this extra window is, of course, the **CView** object of the application.) Conversely, some controls are not windows: although toolbars are windows, the buttons on a toolbar are not: they are bitmaps that are animated when the user clicks on them.

It is interesting to search a desktop with *Spy++* and look at what is and what is not a window. However, more relevant to this book are the extra windows that are created to handle interprocess communication. The screenshot above shows three windows that are involved in DDE and OLE calls. We'll investigate the OLE windows later in the book.

You may also try running more than one copy of **EnumClient** to convince yourself that the code in the DLL is shared. Deft manipulations with your mouse cursor (on a desktop with many windows), can be used to show that the list of windows in one instance of **EnumClient** is independent of the list shown in another instance. Here's the giveaway: when one instance calls **EnumerateWindows_Finish()** before another instance has finished filling the list box, the second instance would crash if the lists were indeed dependent.

Enhancing the Interface

The **EnumServer** returns the handles of the windows that it enumerates; **EnumClient** gets the titles of those windows. Now, to show that we can enhance the interface and change the underlying implementation of the DLL without breaking older applications based on it, let's add a new function to that interface:

```
DLLFUNCTION BOOL EnumerateWindows_NextNames(ULONG num,
    LPTSTR array, ULONG* pnumFetched);
```

This works like **EnumerateWindows_Next()**, except that it returns the **pnumFetched** window names in the **LPTSTR** buffer **array**. Now, each time **AddToList()** is called, we not only save the window's **HWND** but also its title. If you're interested, you can review the code, but basically the **CHwndNode** has been altered to have a data member of type **TCHAR[ITEM_SIZE]**, and the access function **GetNext()** gets the **HWND** and this string. **EnumerateWindows_NextNames()** takes the number of items in the array, and assumes that every item is **ITEM_SIZE** characters or less; if the addition of a title would exceed the passed buffer then the enumeration stops.

> *Note that I have used **TCHAR** and **LPTSTR**. This means that, depending on whether or not **UNICODE** is defined, you will create a UNICODE or an ANSI DLL. It should be stressed that the UNICODE DLL cannot be used with an ANSI client.*

The result is **EnumServer2.dll**, which supports the same interface as **EnumServer**, as well as the new function. **EnumClient2** uses the new function to add the windows' names to its list box; but, since the DLL supports the **EnumServer** interface, you can use this DLL with the older **EnumClient**. (Just rename **EnumServer2.dll** as **Enumserver.dll**, copy it into the same directory as **EnumClient**, and then run the client.) The point of this exercise is to show that it's the interface that is important and not the implementation.

This new function also returns the names of the windows without the client having to determine this from the handles. This means that, if we could remote the calls, the client could be on a different machine (where the **HWND**s would be meaningless anyway). We will return to this idea later in the chapter.

Problems with DLLs

The server DLL in this example doesn't do anything too complicated, but it could do! Any code can contain bugs, however careful the developer, and however thorough the quality control process.

DLLs are loaded into the address space of an application. This means that the DLL has access to the memory used by the application. If a badly written DLL decides to overwrite memory, you can bet that the memory it will trash will be used to hold critical data in your application, rather than the DLL's own variables. This problem is worse if the DLL is written by a third party over which you have no control.

Other than corrupting your data, the DLL may generate other exceptions: an access violation, or a divide by zero, for example. Since the DLL is running in your address space, it is effectively part of your application, so the exception will appear (to the casual user) to come from your code. If you're careful, you can use structured exception handling to catch the exception and prevent the nasty Windows 95 or NT exception dialog box appearing; you may even be able to recover from the exception, but that's a lot of work to get round someone else's bad code.

DLLs - Summary

DLLs enable us to share code between processes by exporting functions from the module. To enable the widest use of a DLL, it must export its functions as C functions, either with readable names, or just an ordinal; the designer is also required to use data types that can be used by all the languages and applications that will use the DLL.

The DLL can be used by clients either by loading the DLL implicitly when the application loads (in which case an import library is used to resolve the function names) or by explicitly loading the DLL at runtime. The second method is particularly flexible, because the application has a choice as to where on the hard disk the DLL lives. Also, through dynamic loading and unloading of DLLs, an application could be updated with new functionality without having to restart the application. However, both uses of a DLL presuppose that the interface of the DLL remains constant.

Exporting interfaces of functions from a DLL provides an efficient way of sharing code. In the implicitly linked case, once the DLL has been loaded, and any address fixups performed, calling a DLL function is just about as efficient as calling a function imported by linking to a static library. The same is true for the explicitly linked case, except it is the programmer's responsibility to get the address of the function.

We've also looked at a simple method of handling different versions of DLLs by registering the DLLs' functionality in the system registry and using **LoadLibrary()** and explicit linking to load the required library and execute the appropriate code. This method is widely used in Windows; perhaps the most widely known example is ODBC drivers.

Sharing Data

In the previous example, we deliberately isolated the data from different threads: if a single application has more than one thread of execution, and each uses the **EnumServer** API to enumerate the windows on the desktop, the data they receive will have been generated for the individual thread. Similarly, if two applications use the DLL simultaneously, they will each generate a new list of window handles. The *data* is thread-specific, despite the fact that the *code* is shared between the processes by memory mapping.

However, we may decide that we really want to share data between applications. This data could be static (read-only) or dynamic (read-write).

Resource-only DLLs are an excellent example of sharing static data. For example, Windows 95 has a DLL called **Moricons.dll** that has extra icons that you can use for DOS programs. NT uses resource DLLs to hold format strings of messages in the Event Log; such a resource DLL is loaded, for example, by the Event Viewer. Fonts are another example: the (hidden) **.fon** files in the **Fonts** directory are actually DLLs whose sole purpose is to share a font resource.

You may have static data that you want to provide for use by other applications as resources. However, the real power of sharing data is when that data is dynamic. There are two ways to share dynamic data. The first way is to have an executable that holds the data, which it alone can access. This executable then accepts requests from other applications, returning or changing the data on their command. We'll cover this approach in the latter half of this chapter.

The second method is to make the data truly shareable, and therefore directly accessible by other applications. This could be done by putting the data into a shared memory area. Windows 95, because of its compatibility with 16-bit Windows, automatically provides areas of memory that are shared between all processes. Of the 4Gb addressable memory, the top 2Gb has the system DLLs, and is shared. The bottom 4Mb holds system data (trying to look like Windows 3.1 for legacy applications that directly manipulated this data) and is also shared. It is only the memory in between these addresses that is private to each application. NT has totally protected memory spaces: the memory used by one application is not usually accessible by another application.

However, in both operating systems, it is possible to make some areas of memory shareable. There are two ways to do this; the first is to use **shared data sections** in a DLL, and the second is to use **memory mapped files** (**MMFs**).

DLL Data Sections

We can define a data section in a Win32 DLL with the **data_seg** pragma.

```
#pragma data_seg(".shared")
    DWORD dwSharedData = 0;
#pragma data_seg()
```

Initialized global variables can be declared between the two **pragma**s. Note that the variable *must* be initialized: uninitialized variables are always put into the **.bss** data segment by the compiler. Also note that the length of the data section name, including the period, must be eight characters or less. The convention is to precede the segment name with a period, but you can use more or less any name you choose (however, you should avoid any section names used by the Visual C++ compiler: **.bss**, **.data**, **.idata**, **.rdata**, **.reloc**, **.rsrc** and **.text** are some of the common ones).

This data section is made sharable by mentioning the section with the **-SECTION** linker switch, or by placing a reference to the section in the **SECTIONS** section of the DEF file:

```
SECTIONS
    .shared    READ WRITE SHARED
```

This data is now shared between every instance of the DLL. Of course, the data will need to be exported in some way, and one method is to export a pair of functions that behave as Get/Set methods on this data:

```
__declspec(dllexport) DWORD GetSharedData();
__declspec(dllexport) void SetSharedData(DWORD dwNewValue);
```

The problem here is a matter of data access synchronization. If one thread is writing to the shared data area, we'll want it to complete the operation before another thread tries to read the data. We can do this by surrounding all accesses to the data with a mutex.

The **DllServer** example shares a **DWORD** via a data segment called **.shared**, exactly as we have just described. The DLL is used by **SDClient**. This application also demonstrates sharing data with memory mapped files, which we'll describe in the next section. The application has two edit boxes for the DLL shared data. The first is the data entered by the user. The second, which is read-only, is the data obtained from the DLL.

The data in the first box is copied to the shared data area by clicking on the Update button, which corresponds to a call to **CSDClientDlg::OnUpdatedata()**. One of the responsibilities of this function is to read from the top edit box and write the data to the shared area in the DLL with a call to **SetSharedData()**.

On initialization, the application creates a timer with an elapse time of 100ms. This means that, ten times a second, the **CSDClientDlg::OnTimer()** handler function is called. One of its responsibilities is to call the **GetSharedData()** function and put the data from the DLL into the read-only edit box.

The implementation of the DLL is fairly trivial. A data segment called **.shared** is declared, as well as a variable **dwSharedData**, exactly as you've just seen. To ensure that only one thread has access to the data at any one time, we declare a global **CMutex** object called **"_DLLDATA"**. Any access to **dwSharedData** must be bracketed by calls to the mutex's **Lock()** and **Unlock()** member functions.

```
CMutex g_hSharedDataMutex(FALSE, "_DLLDATA");

DLLFUNCTION DWORD GetSharedData()
{
   DWORD dwData;

   // Lock the mutex before trying to access the shared
   // data. We are prepared to wait for ever if the mutex
   // is already locked
   g_hSharedDataMutex.Lock(INFINITE);
   dwData = dwSharedData;
   g_hSharedDataMutex.Unlock();

   return dwData;
}

DLLFUNCTION void SetSharedData(DWORD dwNewValue)
{
   // Lock the mutex before trying to access the shared
   // data. We are prepared to wait for ever if the mutex
   // is already locked
   g_hSharedDataMutex.Lock(INFINITE);
   dwSharedData = dwNewValue;
   g_hSharedDataMutex.Unlock();
}
```

Note that when using **CMutex** you need to explicitly **#include** the header file **<Afxmt.h>**: the AppWizard-produced **Stdafx.h** will not do this for you. This reinforces the idea that MFC is inherently a non-multithreaded class library (as you'll already know if you have ever tried to use multiple threads in a Document/View MFC application). With the phenomenal success of Windows 95 as *the* operating system of choice for the desktop, and with NT becoming the operating system for power users and network servers, you might have thought that the preferred class library for Win32 would be written with multithreading in mind. Well, you can only hope for the future.

Memory Mapped Files

The other method of sharing data is to create a **memory mapped file** (**MMF**). MMFs are usually attached to user-specified files, although it is possible to base an MMF on a system-supplied paging file:

```
HANDLE hmap = CreateFileMapping((HANDLE)0xFFFFFFFF,
          NULL, PAGE_READWRITE, dwSizeHigh, dwSizeLow,
          _T("Map_Object"));
LPVOID pmem = MapViewOfFile(hmap, FILE_MAP_ALL_ACCESS,
          0, 0, 0);
```

The first parameter to **CreateFileMapping()** usually takes a handle to an open file from
CreateFile(). However, the special handle value **0xFFFFFFFF** specifies that a system paging file should
be used instead. The parameters **dwSizeHigh** and **dwSizeLow** indicate how big the memory mapped file
is (and the first two zeros in **MapViewOfFile()** are the offset of the mapping into this MMF).

This example passes **NULL** as the security parameter; you may not want to do this on NT, particularly if
different processes using this MMF have been created with different levels of security. One particular
problem to look out for is when an MMF is created by an NT service running under the System account.
If an interactive user attempts to access the MMF then that access will fail, because the user will more
than likely have fewer rights than the System. (See Chapter 7 for more information on security)

The final parameter to **CreateFileMapping()** is a name to associate with the MMF. This is the main
way of sharing the MMF with other processes. A process can test to see if it is the first instance to use the
MMF by checking the return value of **GetLastError()** immediately after the call to
CreateFileMapping(). If **ERROR_ALREADY_EXISTS** is returned, the handle is valid, but the MMF has
been created by another process. Your code can use this to determine if it should initialize the memory in
the MMF or not. Alternatively, the code could call **OpenFileMapping()** and if this fails, it indicates that
the MMF hasn't been created.

The MMF is a raw buffer of memory. It is up to the user of the MMF to organize this memory into some
useable chunks, perhaps by casting the **pmem** pointer to a **struct** pointer or by using the memory as a
memory pool in a class.

The example program **SDClient** creates an MMF in the constructor of the **CSDClientDlg** class, and
then creates a view on to this MMF. The application uses the MMF as a **char** buffer, which it displays in
an edit box. If this is the first instance of the application to use the MMF, it initializes the first character to
be a null character.

```
CSDClientDlg::CSDClientDlg(CWnd* pParent /*=NULL*/)
  : CDialog(CSDClientDlg::IDD, pParent),
    m_MMFMutex(FALSE, _T("_MMFDATA"))
{
  //{{AFX_DATA_INIT(CSDClientDlg)
  //}}AFX_DATA_INIT
  m_hIcon = AfxGetApp()->LoadIcon(IDR_MAINFRAME);

  // Create a file mapping with a system supplied file
  m_hMMF = CreateFileMapping((HANDLE)-1, NULL,
                             PAGE_READWRITE,
                             0, 4 * 1024,
                             _T("_MMFDataFile"));

  // GetLastError and save it for later use...
  // Should be either ERROR_SUCCESS (if it's the first
  // access to the MMF) or ERROR_ALREADY_EXISTS (for
  // subsequent accesses)
  DWORD err = GetLastError();
```

```
        // Map the file mapping into the address space of this
        //application
        m_szdata = (LPTSTR)MapViewOfFile(m_hMMF, FILE_MAP_ALL_ACCESS, 0, 0, 0);

        if (err == ERROR_SUCCESS)
        {
            // Creating the MMF was successful, and this is the
            // first access to the MMF so initialize it.
            m_MMFMutex.Lock(INFINITE);
            m_szdata[0] = 0;
            m_MMFMutex.Unlock();
        }
    }
```

The user writes data by typing characters into the top edit box in the Memory Mapped File Data frame, and then clicking on the Update button. The second responsibility of the **OnUpdatedata()** handler (other than reading the data shared by the DLL, which we've already discussed) is to read the data in the edit control and copy this data into the MMF. It does this by calling the **Lock()** member function of the **m_MMFMutex** object to ensure that this thread is the only one accessing the data. Once the writing action has finished, the function calls the **Unlock()** function to release the mutex.

Similarly, in the **OnTimer()** handler function (which is called every 100ms), the code reads from the MMF and writes the data into the read-only edit box; once again, it is protected by the **m_MMFMutex** object. You can run several instances of this application and confirm that, when you press Update, the data is replicated to the other instances.

MMF Pitfalls

In this code, we've used the MMF as a simple string data buffer. We could devise some scheme where the MMF holds many different data types, casting the pointer from **MapViewOfFile()** to a **struct** pointer, for example. However, it must be pointed out that this function can return an address anywhere in your address space, and each client using the MMF may not get the same address (although they do point to the same address in physical memory). This means that you cannot freely put pointers in your data, even if the pointers are to memory locations within the MMF.

Suppose you have a **struct** like this:

```
struct Customer
{
    LPTSTR szForeName;
    LPTSTR szLastName;
};
```

You could then have the following memory arrangement.

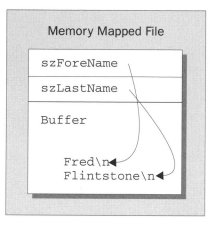

However, this is only likely to work in one instance of the server. For other instances, the pointers could point outside of the MMF. A solution to this would be to store offsets from the start of the buffer in the pointers. So, to access the forename, you would now use:

```
typedef struct TAG_Customer
{
    int szForeName;
    int szLastName;
    LPTSTR lpBuffer;
} Customer,*LPCustomer;

LPCustomer pMMF = (LPCustomer) pmem;

wsprintf(szName, _T("ForeName is %s"), pMMF->ForeName + pMMF->lpBuffer);
```

However, this is getting messy. A serious problem is that the data shared by the MMF can only be used by applications with the same character sets as created it. In other words, if the creator application was compiled as a UNICODE application then the MMF could only be used by other UNICODE applications.

Another solution to this problem would be to use **MapViewOfFileEx()**. This function has one more parameter than **MapViewOfFile()**, and this parameter happens to be an address that suggests a base address for the MMF (which is a multiple of the system's memory allocation granularity). This poses two questions: what value do you use for the base memory and what happens if the function cannot map the MMF to the suggested address?

To decide what value to use for the base memory, the first instance should call **MapViewOfFile()**, and get the system to assign an address; this address could be saved in the MMF itself. Other applications could call **MapViewOfFile()**, read the address and then call **UnmapViewOfFile()** to close the MMF. A view on the MMF could then be created with **MapViewOfFileEx()**, passing the address read earlier. Of course, the first application to use the MMF would need to set up the address, and subsequent applications would just read it, but we've already established a method to determine if an application is the first to use an MMF.

If the function cannot map the MMF to the suggested address, the application won't be able to use it, so it will fail.

One other strategy to allow the use of pointers in an MMF is to create the view of the MMF with `MapViewOfFile()`, and then save the address in some position in the MMF. Other applications would need to create the view with `MapViewOfFile()`, read the saved address and compare this with the address that `MapViewOfFile()` returned. They could then fix up any addresses of pointers in the MMF. Of course, the fix up will have to be on a copy of these pointers, and not in the MMF itself, otherwise other applications would get the fixed-up address thinking it was the original!

As you can see, sharing data via an MMF is not as straightforward as it may appear, although a carefully written class library could hide all this complexity from the developer.

Listening Executables

Now we come on to *processes* written to share code and data. In the previous sections, we looked at DLLs as a method to share code (and data) between applications. The major disadvantage (and also the major advantage) of DLLs is that they are mapped into the address space of the executable using the DLL. The disadvantage is that a badly written DLL could trash the memory used by the executable, causing all sorts of problems. The overwhelming advantage of a DLL is that the functions are called directly, with no need for context switching.

We've also seen that sharing data via DLLs' data segments and via MMFs is not straightforward; so rather than sharing the data directly, we'll look at another method, where data is owned by a single process that provides some mechanism to accept and return data on request.

In Chapter 1, we established that some distribution mechanisms are connection-based and that others are connectionless. That chapter also outlined some strategies for handling multiple requests for service. In this section, we'll look at some of the common methods for providing servers, and we'll implement the window enumeration example using two of these methods.

Running the Server

Since the server is a process, it must be running before any requests can be serviced. One upshot of this is that the interactive user, or the system, must start the server. Here are some ways to do that.

The Interactive User

There are several ways for a user to start a server process under Windows. The user could double-click on a shortcut to the executable, double-click the icon for the executable itself in Explorer, or even click on an entry in the Start menu. Alternatively, they could type the application name in the Run... box, or after `start` at a command prompt. The server runs on the desktop.

What happens if the server, or even the system, dies? Nothing. The interactive user started the server originally, and must do so again. Any attempts by a client to communicate with the server will fail.

The Startup Folder

Windows 3.1 introduced the Startup group in Program Manager. Later versions of Windows retain this facility, although Windows 95 and NT 4.0 now call it the Startup folder. The idea is that any application in this folder is run whenever the Explorer starts up. This is usually when an interactive user logs on, but it is possible to close and restart Explorer under Windows 95 and NT4.0 by using the Task Manager: a method (not recommended!) that obviously doesn't involve logging off and back on again.

What happens if your server dies? Nothing. The system will only restart your server when Explorer starts. If the system dies, your server will start when Explorer restarts. If the server is not running, and a client tries to communicate with it, the call will fail.

NT Services

NT has a process called the Service Control Manager. Applications can be written as **Services** which are run under the control of the SCM. Services are covered in greater depth in Chapter 8, but the registry entry for a service indicates whether a service is run when the system starts.

If the system dies and restarts, your server will restart if it was configured to do so. If the server dies, the SCM will not automatically restart the server. Again, if the server isn't running and a client tries to communicate with it, the call will fail.

Windows 95 PseudoServices

Windows 95 doesn't have the Service Control Manager; instead, it simulates its behavior by running servers mentioned in the registry. Under
HKEY_LOCAL_MACHINE\Software\Microsoft\Windows\CurrentVersion, there are two keys, **RunServices** and **RunServicesOnce**. The values under these keys determine the applications that are run when the system starts (and before a user has logged on).

As far as restarting a server when it dies, and communication to a server that is not running, the notes in the section on the Startup folder apply.

COM Servers

Component Object Model (COM) servers can be implemented as NT Services (as you'll see in Chapter 8), and the notes under NT Services apply for the process start up.

However, a COM server can also be started by the COM system when a request is made to access an object in the server. This is a distinct advantage over the other methods of activation since we can ensure that, even if something catastrophic occurs in the server, the services that it provides will always be available.

Note that if the COM server is implemented as an NT Service, and then somehow the service dies, and a client attempts to communicate with it, then the system will see that the object is marked as a **LocalService** and will restart it as a service.

Listening Methods

Whether the server is run interactively or as a service, it must get requests from the client. As mentioned in Chapter 1, the server must implement some strategy to handle multiple requests. The simplest strategy is to create a worker thread for every request; a more sophisticated strategy would be to implement some form of thread pool and use a queuing system to stack requests until a worker thread is available. The NT 3.51 **IOCompletionPort()** API was designed as such a strategy. Multithreading for a server really only becomes important for multiprocessor machines. These issues are covered in Chapter 9.

Chapter 1 also covered the issues concerning connection-based and connectionless protocols. With a connection-based protocol (like the TCP side of the WinSock API), the connection remains open until either the client or server closes it. This means that after the server has serviced the request, it can return any results immediately, without having to find the client. However, this also means that resources are used to keep the connection open. With a connectionless protocol, the server does not have to keep open a connection to the client, but when it wants to send results back to the client, it needs to find out where the client is and then send the data.

The sections below cover some of the more popular methods of getting client requests.

TCP

TCP is a connection-based method. The Windows implementation is covered by the WinSock API. This defines the API for accessing sockets over the Internet Protocol Suite, otherwise known as TCP/IP. The API also works over the SPX protocol used on NetWare networks. The advantage of TCP/IP is that it is available on a wide range of platforms, including MS-DOS, all forms of Windows, MacOS, and all forms of UNIX. If your server talks TCP/IP then you can almost guarantee that you can write a client for just about any useful OS. (Of course, although TCP/IP may be implemented on a wide range of platforms, it may not be the preferred protocol.)

You can use the raw WinSock API to define an entry point for client requests, and the programming is not too difficult. However, it is basic: there's no support for objects or data types more complex than byte streams, and the programmer must implement some mechanism to keep the client and server informed that the other is still alive. TCP/IP is usually used as a transport by other higher-level interprocess communications methods.

A TCP server needs to listen on a well known port for connections from a client. Once a client has made a connection, a socket is returned through which all client-server communications occur. The socket is basically a byte stream communication channel between the client and server, and the two need to decide how they will talk along this stream. When you pass data via TCP packets, the protocol makes sure that the packets arrive at the destination in the same order that they were sent, but it has no control over what is sent or how that data is represented.

The Internet Protocol Suite, as the name suggests, can be used to connect applications running on remote machines; indeed, the code to use TCP between applications local to each other on one machine is exactly the same as the code for the applications on two different machines.

MFC provides the **CSocket** and **CAsyncSocket** classes that allow for communication via TCP packets.

UDP

UDP or datagram packets are the connectionless version of TCP. The WinSock API and MFC **CSocket**-based classes can be used to program for UDP. UDP does not guarantee that the packets arrive at the destination in the same order as they were sent. However, if you decide to manage packet ordering yourself, UDP provides a low bandwidth version of the socket protocol. (As an interesting aside, DCOM uses UDP as its preferred protocol, managing the packets to guarantee their arrival and order.)

UDP, like TCP, can be used to send messages between applications on different machines.

Windows Messages

Windows carries out most of its own interprocess communications via Windows messages. Every window has a message queue and a window procedure for handling messages obtained and then dispatched from the queue. Threads can also have a message queue and implement message handling routines. A console (non-GUI application) can also implement a message queue, either through a thread or via a hidden window.

There is a well established API for handling Windows messages and the messages themselves are accepted: there is no confusion as to what a particular message means. The main disadvantage of using Windows messages is that they are restricted to communication between applications on a single machine. On the upside, this method of communication is efficient. (In fact, it is *the* most efficient method, probably because it's the most important Windows communications method and has, therefore, been highly tuned.)

DDE

Dynamic Data Exchange is a Windows message-based mechanism used to allow applications to dynamically share data. The specification defines a distinct protocol of messages to request data and a defined sequence of acknowledgment messages. Although DDE is based on Windows messages, it is a connection-based protocol.

Since DDE is message-based, the handler routines are part of a Windows procedure. To allow servers to handle multiple connections, the mechanism is usually performed through invisible utility windows. The main reason for inclusion here is that there is an extension to DDE, called NetDDE. This provides a mechanism for distributing functionality on a network of Windows (for Workgroups, 95 or NT) machines. However, it cannot be used with machines running other operating systems.

Named Pipes

Pipes are a connection-based mechanism of communication between applications on one local machine or on separate machines. With named pipes the server (which *must* be an NT machine) can create the end point of a pipe and wait for a connection. The client, which could be an MS-DOS or a Windows machine, uses the ordinary file access API to connect to the named pipe. The two applications can then talk via file API functions: the Win32 `ReadFile()` and `WriteFile()`; the Windows 3.1 `_lread()` and `_lwrite()`; or the C runtime library `fread()` and `fwrite()`; and because of this, they are simple to use with IO Completion Ports.

As with sockets, the pipe transmits a raw stream of bytes between the applications, so a data format must be agreed between the two to make the data useable.

Named pipes are restricted to Microsoft networks, which limits them to the LAN.

DCE RPC

Microsoft have implemented their own version of the OSF (Open Software Foundation) DCE (Distributed Computing Environment) RPC (Remote Procedure Call) mechanism.
MS-RPC is compliant with the OSF DCE standard which means that, to a large extent, machines running DCE RPC on operating systems other than Windows can talk to machines running MS-RPC (including Mac and Windows 3.1 machines).

> *OSF has merged with X/Open to form The Open Group. The Open Group is now custodian of the core ActiveX technologies, including COM and DCOM.*

RPC is a higher level IPC mechanism than those covered so far, in that it allows the client to call functions in its own address space that are remoted by RPC to the function implementation in the server. The two halves of the conversation don't need to worry about how the data gets to the other side of the conversation since this is carried out by the RPC runtime.

The 'magic' of RPC is carried out by the RPC runtime and the **Interface Definition Language** (**IDL**) compiler (for Microsoft operating systems, 'MIDL'). The IDL compiler takes a programming language independent description of the interface and writes stub code to call the RPC runtime code that will remote function calls to the server and also remote the results back to the client.

RPC can be a connectionless mechanism, but the API is so rich that the server can retain context data between RPC calls. RPC can run over a variety of protocols, including TCP/IP and named pipes. RPC servers, like TCP/IP servers, can be beyond the LAN. Chapter 6 compares DCOM and Microsoft RPC at a low level; the results show that DCOM is essentially an extension to RPC.

COM

COM is a connection-based mechanism that is, in programming terms, at the highest level of the mechanisms that we've covered so far. Unlike the other mechanisms, which are used to pass data or function calls between applications, COM is used to distribute *objects*. This is its *raison d'être*. COM defines how the objects are implemented and how long they survive. COM is also designed to be language-independent. At present, COM has been released for 32-bit Windows, but even as I write, versions are being written (or are in beta release) for other operating systems, including Solaris and the MacOS.

COM can be distributed, allowing machines to talk over many protocols, including UDP, TCP, IPX, SPX and, in the future, Internet protocols like HTTP. COM is covered in more depth in the next chapter and, of course, throughout the rest of the book.

Example: TCP Server

One question I often get asked by COM novices is: Why use DCOM to remote functionality when TCP/IP sockets could be used instead?. This example implements a TCP client and server, allowing for methods to be remoted across a network. As you go through the code, you'll see how involved it is. The example gives one solution to packaging data to be transmitted and then unpackaged at the other end, and it gives a rudimentary method of dispatching the method call at the server end.

TCP/IP is a widespread method of communicating between applications. It's also the protocol of the Internet, so an application that can talk TCP/IP can potentially talk across the Internet to any machine around the world.

Programming the WinSock API is not as onerous as it may sound. The functions may look very Unix-like, and they may behave in a non-Windows way, but once you've got over the different capitalization, the commands appear quite straightforward. Indeed, once you've written one TCP/IP application and generated the boilerplate code for making and maintaining connections, using those connections is quite easy.

MFC provides two classes to provide this boilerplate code: **CAsyncSocket**, and its derivative **CSocket**. Indeed, the developers of MFC have added support for the **CArchive** class, which allows you to treat a socket as a method to provide object persistence through the serialization support.

This section is not meant to be an in-depth discussion of how to use these classes, and it certainly is not a tutorial on socket programming (enough books have been written about that!). This section is about the issues raised from supporting a communication between two applications, and the lessons to be learned are equally important whether sockets, named pipes, MMFs, or Window messages are used.

WinSock

WinSock is the Windows implementation of the BSD 4.3 standard of sockets. As explained before, sockets can be stream (TCP), or datagram (UDP); whichever you use, they're created with the same API.

The first action the server does is to create a listening socket. This will listen for connections. When a client connects, it will perform some action to handle the connection in an orderly manner, like spawning a worker thread to service the request, or queuing the request until a thread in a thread pool is free. To handle the request, the server socket calls **accept()**, which returns a socket to talk to the client. All communication with the client is through this connection socket. The client and server use **send()** and **recv()** to pass data to the other end of the socket. To end the conversation, both ends must close the connection socket.

When making a connection, the client must be able to identify the server machine and the service on the machine. It does this by specifying the server machine's IP address and a **port** number. To facilitate administration of ports, you can give them a name by adding an entry in the **SERVICES** file (in the **System32\Drivers\Etc** folder in the NT directory, or in the **Windows** folder on a Windows 95 machine) that maps a string to a port number. The WinSock API provides functions to manipulate port names and numbers. Every TCP service on the server machine has a port number; there may be more than one TCP service in a process.

TCPServer and TCPClient

We'll now look at how the MFC sockets classes work through an example. **TCPServer** is a single-threaded dialog-based MFC application that provides an enumeration of the windows on a desktop. To do this it uses the **EnumServer2.dll** developed earlier in this chapter, and presents the DLL's functionality through a TCP interface. The enumerated windows' names are displayed by **TCPClient**, another dialog-based MFC application.

Protocol

TCPServer provides an interface for the following functions (as shown in **PacketTypes.h**):

```
#define VERB_ACK                0L
#define VERB_GETWINDOWS_START   1L
#define VERB_GETWINDOWS_NEXT    2L
#define VERB_GETWINDOWS_FINISH  3L
#define VERB_DISCONNECT         4L
```

The first one is an acknowledgment, the last one disconnects a client from the server, and the other three are the enumeration functions.

As mentioned above, to talk to each other the two applications must agree on some protocol, since the socket is simply a conduit for raw data. In this application, the client and server agree to talk in packets. Each packet has the following format:

The verb is the action that the application will perform, and it's followed by a variable number of parameters. Notice that since TCP is connection based, once a socket has been created, there's a fixed conduit between the client and server. In a connectionless protocol the packet

would need to have an identifier to indicate where the packet should be sent. Also, since the server only has one interface implementing these verbs, the server need not have any more information about what code to call.

This may not always be the case: the server could have several interfaces that respond to a **VERB_INITIALIZE** verb, so the package would need to identify which interface the verb is destined for. These are problems that exist in distributing functionality with DCOM and RPC. Chapter 6 shows how this is actually done.

The verb given in the packet defines the parameter list that is sent. The server understands the last four verbs listed above. Every reply from the server is sent back as a **VERB_ACK** reply, and this is the only verb that the client recognizes. The actual values are transmitted in a fashion to identify the data type:

The type is a **long** that identifies the data; the size is present for the string and binary (raw data) types, and identifies how big the data is (it is omitted for other data types because it's unnecessary); the final item is the actual data itself. This is a binary value of the data. No attempt is made to take into account different data representations on different machines: it is assumed that the client and server will run on the same machine type.

The data types are declared in **PacketTypes.h**:

```
#define DEF_CHAR    17L    // VT_UI1
#define DEF_WORD    2L     // VT_I2
#define DEF_INT     3L     // VT_I4
#define DEF_DOUBLE  5L     // VT_R8
#define DEF_STRING  8L     // VT_BSTR
#define DEF_BINARY  24L    // VT_VOID
```

As long as the client and server agree on the values, it doesn't matter what they are. I have decided to use the values used for the Automation-compatible types as the value of the discriminator in the **VARIANT** type. For simplicity's sake, the string type is ANSI, not UNICODE; to save the code from excessive **#ifdef**s, I have made no provision for UNICODE.

TCPServer has a class, **Packet**, which makes the use of these data packets more straightforward; selected members are shown here:

```
class Packet
{
public:
    Packet(UINT size);
    Packet(LPVOID pdata, UINT size);
//...
    void Reset();
    UINT GetSize();
    LPBYTE GetData();
//...
```

```
    Packet& operator>>(DWORD& dword);
    Packet& operator>>(LPSTR& str);
//...
    Packet& operator<<(DWORD dword);
    Packet& operator<<(LPSTR str);

    void AddData(LPVOID lp,int size);
//...
};
```

The packet is constructed either by specifying a buffer size that it will use, or by passing a pre-formatted buffer. You can use the first method if you want to construct a packet to send data to the server, and the second method if you want to extract data from a packet sent by a client. Insertion operators are provided to put data into the packet, and a few are shown here. Corresponding extraction operators take the data out of the packet. (**AddData()** exists so that raw binary data can be sent.)

The data can be accessed directly by calling the **GetData()** member, and the number of bytes written to the packet can be obtained by calling **GetSize()**. Once a packet is constructed, the data pointer is obtained and the whole data is sent to the client as one binary block.

The server manipulates packets like this:

```
DWORD dwNumFetched;
DWORD dwGetWindows;

packet >> dwGetWindows;
LPSTR parray = new char[dwGetWindows * ITEM_SIZE];
EnumerateWindows_NextNames(dwGetWindows, parray, &dwNumFetched);
packet.Reset();
packet << VERB_ACK << (DWORD)dwNumFetched;

LPSTR ptr = parray;
for (DWORD dwIndex = 0; dwIndex < dwNumFetched; dwIndex++)
{
    packet << (LPCSTR)ptr;
    plist->AddString(ptr);
    ptr += lstrlen(ptr) + 1;
}

(*this) << packet;
delete [] parray;
```

This is taken from the **Connection::OnReceive()** handler. The code has already extracted the verb from the packet **(VERB_GETWINDOWS_NEXT)**; it then extracts the number of windows to return, and calls **EnumerateWindows_NextNames()** to fill an array with the names.

To send this data back to the client, it resets the packet, and inserts a **VERB_ACK** verb followed by the number of windows obtained and then the window names themselves. This is then sent to the client with a call to **Connection::operator<<()**.

The client has a class called **ClientSocket** that is derived from **CSocket**. This has similar functionality to **Packet**, but it also encapsulates the data with the ability to use the **CSocket** functionality to send the data. The client request to get window names is made by:

```
void CTCPClientDlg::OnRefresh()
{
    ClientSocket* psocket = new ClientSocket;

    CListBox* pListBox = (CListBox*)GetDlgItem(IDC_DATA);
    ASSERT(pListBox);

    pListBox->ResetContent();

    psocket->Create();
    psocket->Connect(m_server, 8000);

    DWORD reply;

    // Reset the socket
    psocket->Reset();
    // Initialise the Window list on the server
    (*psocket) << (DWORD)VERB_GETWINDOWS_START;
    // Send the command and receive the reply
    psocket->Send();
    // Get the reply from the socket
    (*psocket) >> reply;
    // Make sure that the command was executed OK
    if (reply != VERB_ACK)
    {
        // it wasn't, so exit
        delete psocket;
        return;
    }

    DWORD noWindows = 0;
    do
    {
        // Now get all the windows
        char name[256];
        noWindows = 0;

        // Reset the buffer
        psocket->Reset();
        // Ask for windows from the list
        (*psocket) << (DWORD)VERB_GETWINDOWS_NEXT;
        (*psocket) << (DWORD)MAX_WINDOWS;
        // Send the command and get the reply
        psocket->Send();

        // Check that the command completed successfully
        (*psocket) >> reply;
        if (reply != VERB_ACK)
            break;

        // Read the number of items in the packet
        (*psocket) >> noWindows;
        // For each one, extract the name and add it
        // to the list box
        for (DWORD i = 0; i < noWindows; i++)
        {
            (*psocket) >> (LPSTR)name;
```

```
                pListBox->AddString(name);
        }
    }
    while (noWindows > 0);

    // Now need to clean up
    psocket->Reset();
    (*psocket) << (DWORD)VERB_GETWINDOWS_FINISH;
    // Send the data
    psocket->Send();
    // Reply should be just VERB_ACK, but don't bother
    // to check
    (*psocket) >> reply;

    // Clean up the socket
    psocket->Close();

    delete psocket;
}
```

This code, in **TCPClientDlg.cpp**, constructs a packet with the request and the number of windows to return. The return packet should have a reply of **VERB_ACK** followed by the number of windows that were obtained and then the names themselves.

Initializing the Server

Now we need to set up the code for passing data between the two applications. In the code for **TCPServer**, I have derived a class called **ListeningSocket** from **CSocket**. An object of this class is created in the dialog's **OnInitDialog()**, and is deleted in the **OnOK()** handler. I keep a pointer to this object as a data member of the dialog object.

This socket needs to specify what port it is listening on, and this is done by passing the port number as a parameter to the **Create()** method, which is called just before the socket is told to listen.

```
// Start the listener
pListSock = new ListeningSocket(this);
if (pListSock->Create(8000))
{
  pListSock->Listen();
}
```

The port number is hard coded to 8000, so you should check in your machine's **SERVICES** file to make sure that this port isn't used by any other process.

After the socket has been initialized, it is told to listen. When a connection is requested, the socket object calls its **OnAccept()** member function, in which you should place the code to handle the connection. After the **OnAccept()** returns, the socket goes into a listening mode waiting for another connection.

Threads

The server in this example is single-threaded. For a server, this isn't a particularly good design choice, but since this is only a test application, it simplifies the code to avoid any worries about multithreaded issues. Changing this application to work as a multithreaded application is possible (and, in time-honored fashion, this is left to the reader); unfortunately, as you start to make threads to handle connections, you'll come up against the inherent single-threadedness of MFC.

In particular, any API that has anything to do with **CWnd*** pointers is likely to cause you grief with threads. This is because the mapping of window handles to **CWnd**s is done using thread local storage from the thread that created the **CWnd**. Generally, this is the primary thread, but it needn't be. The upshot of this is that any access to the window handle of the **CWnd** must be done in the thread that created it; otherwise, a totally random (and completely invalid) value will be returned, and your carefully crafted code will crumble before you eyes.

You may understand how such problems can manifest themselves with code that's written to write to windows, but why should it affect the **CSocket** classes?

The WinSock API provides a facility to use callbacks into your code that allow asynchronous socket reading and writing. These callbacks are handled by sending a message to a designated window in the application when the action has completed. Since this message needs to be handled by the application's GUI thread, other GUI messages are blocked by your thread; this will result in poor user interface responsiveness. And, you've guessed it, **CSocket** holds a **CWnd** pointer to the handler window.

The bottom line is that although multithreaded TCP applications are possible and desirable, the only way to do this without some serious hacking into MFC is to write directly to the WinSock API.

Connection Objects

The **OnAccept()** handler of **ListeningThread** is called when a connection is made. **TCPServer** implements this by creating a **Connection** object (which is derived from **CSocket**) and then calling the **Accept()** method to complete the connection between the client and server.

```
Connection* pconnection = new Connection(m_parent);
if (Accept(*pconnection))
{
   pconnection->Init();
}
else
   delete pconnection;
```

The **Init()** function allows for any initialization that may be necessary before handling the connection. It is not used in this example.

The effect of calling **Accept()** is that the class sets up the code so that the **Connection::OnReceive()** function will be called whenever the client sends data to the server. It is in this function that you put the code to handle client requests. I do this with a **switch**:

```
int size, sizesize = sizeof(int);
GetSockOpt(SO_RCVBUF, &size,&sizesize);
LPBYTE buffer = new BYTE[size];
int nobytes = Receive(buffer, size);
Packet packet((LPVOID)buffer, size);
int verb;
packet >> verb;
switch(verb)
{
   case VERB_GETWINDOWS_START:
//...
   case VERB_GETWINDOWS_NEXT:
//...
   case VERB_GETWINDOWS_FINISH:
```

```
//...
   case VERB_DISCONNECT:
//...
   default:
//...
}

delete [] buffer;
```

Here, I call **GetSockOpt()** with **SO_RCVBUF** as the first parameter to determine how big the receiving buffer should be. Then I use the **CAsyncSocket::Receive()** member to fill the buffer with the client request. A **Packet** is constructed on this buffer and the items in the packet can be obtained by using the extraction operators.

When the client sends a **VERB_DISCONNECT** message, the **Connection** object deletes itself and the destructor closes the connection.

ClientSocket

The client end is very similar. Since the client does not need to dispatch service requests as the server does, the **ClientSocket** class is written to encapsulate the data formatting of the server's **Packet** class and the socket communications of the **Connection** class.

The client knows that every call it makes to the server will result in a reply, so the **Send()** method both sends the request and waits for the reply.

Putting It All Together

Compile both the client and server. Now copy the executables into some convenient directory and copy the **EnumServer2.dll** into this directory. Run **TCPServer** and then run **TCPClient**. **TCPClient** will show a dialog box like this

This is asking for the name of the server on which **TCPServer** is running. In the edit box, type either the domain name, or the dotted IP address of the server. Since, for this first test, you are running both applications on the same machine, just press Cancel.

> *If you're running this on Windows 95 with Dial Up Networking, you'll get the dial up connection box.*
> *For this first test, just press Cancel on the connection box to connect to the server on your own machine.*

The client will now make the TCP calls to the server, and the list box will show the window names:

The server window also shows the messages sent by the client; in this example, 16 bytes have been sent and the first 14 can be seen. This is a request for the server to execute **VERB_GETWINDOWS_NEXT** for 10 windows; 3 is the type of data (**DWORD**) which follows, the 2 is the verb, then there is another 3 to indicate that another **DWORD** follows, and then there is the value 10 (**0A** in hex).

Now the fun begins. Close down the client and copy the executable to another machine. You may need to copy various MFC DLLs too, but you can use **dumpbin/imports** to determine which the example uses.

Now run the client: you'll be asked for the server name, so type it in. You'll then get a list of the windows on the remote machine!

Issues

There are a number of issues that this example raises...

Multithreading

The first is multithreading. This example was single-threaded, for the reasons explained above (although even on a LAN the updates are too fast to have an effect on the UI). To protect the data, the server should be multithreaded.

However, a sophisticated server will use a pool of threads to service client connections in order to limit the total number of threads in the process. This is a reasonable strategy because using extra threads in a process can only improve performance when the process is running on a multiprocessor machine, and even in this situation, only if the number of threads equals (or is less than) the number of CPUs in the system. In a system where the number of threads exceeds the number of processors, threads only improve the apparent *responsiveness* of the server, particularly with GUI applications. The overall performance is not improved.

In NT, a programmer can use IO Completion Ports as an implementation of a thread pool. This API allows connections (via sockets, named pipes, or overlapped file access) to be queued and then serviced by one of a few designated worker threads.

Data Formats and Transmission

Another issue raised in the example is the transmission of data between the applications. The thread servicing the request will need to determine the service that was requested. In other words, the client must convey to the server information about the service that it requires and any parameters that will be needed by that service. We say that this information is **marshaled** to the server, and that the server will need to **unmarshal** the data before it can decide what to do.

TCP/IP is only concerned with making sure that data reaches its destination. It will split up data into discrete packets, if necessary, to pass the data along the wire, but as far as the applications at either end of the wire are concerned, the data appears as a simple stream of bytes.

This was why I devised the **Packet** class, and the following rules:

- ▲ Data is identified by a data type, and some types also have a length
- ▲ Requests consist of a verb followed by zero or more parameters
- ▲ The server always acknowledges requests
- ▲ The data format is the same on the client and server machine

One concern here is that since the data is passed in the internal format of the processor of the machine sending the data, it restricts us to one machine type. This means that we really should define a network data type. TCP/IP does define a *network order*, which is the purpose of the socket functions **htonl()** and **htons()**, which convert **long**s and **short**s from the byte order of the local ('host') machine to the network byte order (**h**ost **to n**etwork **l**ong, **h**ost **to n**etwork **s**hort). The network byte order is an order that has been agreed to be standard across the network. The corresponding **ntohl()** (and **ntohs()**) do the reverse conversion back to host byte order. Depending on the host CPU and the agreed network order, these functions may reverse the byte order or they may just do nothing. Whatever happens, they allow numbers to be transmitted as binary data.

We also have to determine common formats for **float**s and **double**s (the IEEE have standards for these) and determine how pointers are handled. In the previous example, **LPSTR** is handled by making a copy of the buffer and sending this buffer to the server. However, if a buffer should be altered by the server then the client code needs to copy data out of the returned packet and into its own buffer.

This is all very messy: both the client and server code need to implement buffers to hold data, and they need to copy data out of the buffer and into locally held buffers. In addition to simple **char** buffers, what about **structs** and **unions**? This is looking like lots of code for the overworked programmer to write.

Calling Functions

The TCP client code had to package up the calls to the server by inserting the verb and parameters into the **ClientSocket** object. The reply from the server is then extracted from the object. This code could be packaged up into a function call, for example:

```
BOOL GetWindows_Next(DWORD num, LPSTR parray, LPDWORD returned)
{
    // Some global ClientSocket object
    g_psocket->Reset();
    (*g_psocket) << (DWORD)VERB_GETWINDOWS_NEXT << num;
    g_psocket->Send();
    DWORD reply;
    (*g_psocket) >> reply;
    if (reply != VERB_ACK)
        return FALSE;
    (*g_socket) >> *returned;
    LPSTR ptr = parray;
    for (DWORD i = 0; i < *returned; i++)
    {
        (*psocket) >> pstr;
        pstr += lstrlen(pstr) + 1;
    }
    return TRUE;
}
```

Now, although it is possible to implement code in this way, it does become tedious to do it for every function.

Similarly, at the server end, the code to handle the requests is done in a **switch**. The code gets the data out of the **Packet**, does the action, and then puts the data back into the **Packet**. The code looks very much like a Windows procedure, and you may ask if there's some way to package this up into MFC-like message handlers.

Well, if you write for a distribution method like DCE RPC, CORBA 2, ILU and, of course DCOM, then you'll use an **interface description language** (**IDL**) and an IDL compiler, which will generate stub code that does all this for you. The Microsoft IDL compiler, MIDL, will be used throughout the remainder of this book, and will be described more fully in the next chapter.

Pinging

When you run the client and server on a single machine, you can see them both. If one dies, or hangs, you can close down the other and start again. If the applications are on different machines, you don't know if the remote end is alive, and this can be a problem with blocking calls. If a call to **recv()** blocks, is this because a large amount of data is being read, because the remote socket is not yet ready, or because the remote application has died?

To a certain extent, you can determine some of this by calls such as **select()**. You can also determine whether an application is alive by setting up a pinging mechanism. A ping is a small piece of data sent between applications; when the server gets the ping, it echoes it back to the client. This way the client knows that the server is still alive.

If the ping is sent at a regular interval, both ends of the wire will know when to expect the ping and can use this information to decide whether the other end has died. If one end decides that the other is dead, it can then close down the connection, and possibly take some action. The ping would require a socket of its own so as not to interfere with the data transmission.

Exceptions

The data manipulation code in the example is fairly basic. If data is read past the end of the internal buffer in **Packet** or **ClientSocket**, a zero is returned. Similarly, if an attempt is made to write past the end of the internal buffers, the attempt quietly fails.

The data manipulation routines should handle these situations by throwing some kind of exception. This way, the application at the other end of the wire knows that something is amiss and can take corrective action.

How Does This Relate to DCOM?

It's a nice example, but where is the relevance to DCOM? As a method of implementing distributed functionality, it succeeds, but a lot of code has been written. As the final section of this chapter, let's compare the code of the last example with what you can get for free in DCOM.

First, let's look at the interface. In our example, I decided on the verbs that I wanted to support, and the client and server had to be coded to those verbs. So that the client knows about the server functionality, a header file is common to both. DCOM uses IDL to define the interface, and this also creates a header that can be used by both the client and server. However, DCOM allows interfaces to be written, using **IDispatch** or Automation-compatible data types, that can describe themselves; therefore, no header has to be generated for the client. This 'self description' is carried out using type libraries.

To describe the verb parameters, I had to create my own protocol. The client and server were responsible for packaging up the data for transmission and then unpackaging the data on receipt. Further, the server had to recognize the verb being requested and then explicitly call the corresponding method.

In DCOM, you define the interface with IDL. When you compile this code, the compiler will create marshaling code for you that does all the packaging and unpackaging. You don't need to implement any code to do this: all you do is implement the method, and the runtime will unpackage the data and call the method. If you implement the code as a dispatch interface, the system will already know how to marshal your method calls, otherwise you associate the interface with the MIDL-generated marshaling code.

As I mentioned above, I haven't implemented any pinging mechanism: it was just too much work for this example. If I wrote the example with DCOM, I wouldn't have to worry, because DCOM has a sophisticated and efficient mechanism to ensure that if a client dies, a server is not running needlessly on a server machine.

The TCP server has to be started on the server machine. This requires user intervention (although you could put the server in the Startup folder, or change the code so that it runs as a service). However, DCOM (on NT, *not* Windows 95) allows a server to be started remotely when it's needed. This means that a server machine only runs the servers that are actually needed at any point in time.

This example has no security, so anyone could call my server and get information about the windows on the server desktop; anyone could create a server and supply bogus information to the client, and anyone could monitor packets on the network and look at my client-server interaction. To remedy this, I would need to make sure that the client and server identify each the other, and that the client can make the calls on the server. I would also have to encrypt the packets to make sure that no one can eavesdrop on my transmissions. This is a lot of code. DCOM does all of this and more, as you'll see in Chapter 7.

Finally, and most importantly, the server can *only* be used by this client. The interface and data transmission protocol are proprietary, so there's a steep learning curve for other programmers to learn how to use my interface. DCOM is open. It's available on many platforms, and you can use many different languages to write or use interfaces. Indeed, many languages have class libraries to make COM interfaces easier to use (MFC and ATL for Visual C++, and OCF for Borland).

So the moral is this: distributing data across a network in an effective, efficient, and secure manner, requires a lot of code. DCOM provides that code for you. It's already been written, tested, and debugged; it frees you to work on the actual functionality that you need distributed, rather than the distribution method itself.

Summary

Now I hope I've whetted your appetite for DCOM. But before we get into the specifics of distributing functionality between machines, it's useful to see what COM has to offer for objects on a single machine. (Remember that just about everything that you can do with COM, you can do with DCOM.) In the next chapter, I'll introduce you to the what and the why of COM, and we'll see how ubiquitous it really is.

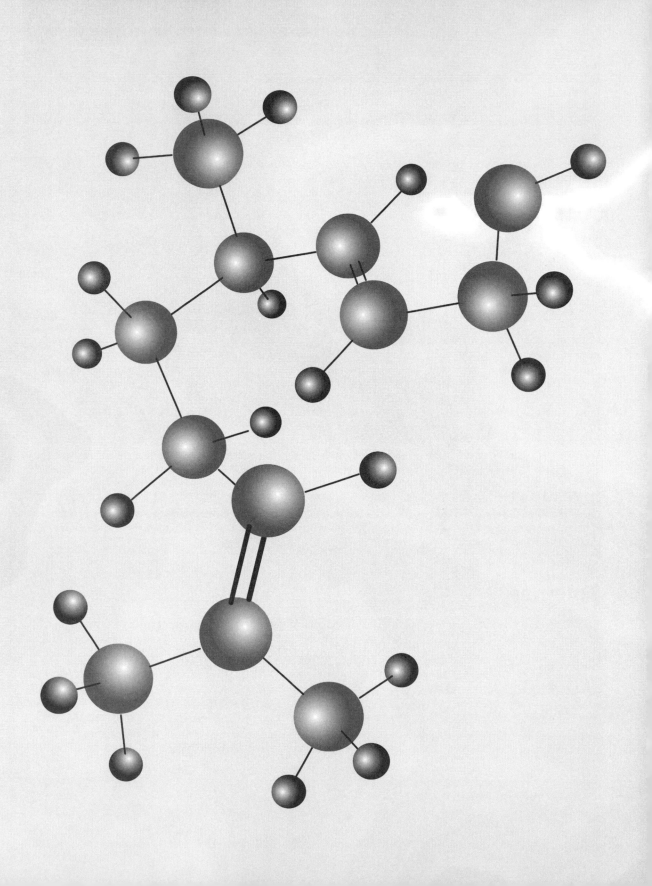

The Component Object Model

CHAPTER 3

Introduction

A long time ago I used to write scientific reports. These documents presented the results of the experiments that I carried out as a young scientist; they contained graphs of the data, and text containing the analysis of what I had done.

To acquire the data, I wrote a DOS program that collected data from my experiment and saved it as comma-separated (x, y) pairs in a text file (CSV file). To analyze the data, I used a spreadsheet application. This could load and manipulate large amounts of data, but the graphs that it exported were not too hot, so I exported the manipulated data as another CSV text file. I had a graphing application that had good graphing support: it allowed me to use scientific symbols, and to make careful adjustments of the axes and labeling, but it had limited spreadsheet support. This wasn't a problem since the graphing application could import CSV files from the spreadsheet. Finally, I had a word processor that could import the pictures produced by the graphing program and place them within the document. All these programs were DOS on a VGA system.

My routine was this: I would do an experiment, and save the data as a CSV text file; I would then manipulate (or sometimes 'enhance') the data in the spreadsheet. Normally, this would be to remove glitches caused by colleagues powering up heavy equipment nearby; or maybe, to remove excessive noise with some digital smoothing (but not too much, since, as my research supervisor remarked, no one would believe the traces if they were perfectly smooth). When I was satisfied with the data, I would export the results into another comma-separated text file.

This file would be imported into the graphing application, and I would carefully adjust the scales and axes, sometimes adding annotations. Once satisfied with the result, I would export this as an HPGL file, since other than talking directly to plotter or printer, this was the only way to export the result. Finally, I would import the HPGL file into a graphics box in the document that I was preparing in my word processor.

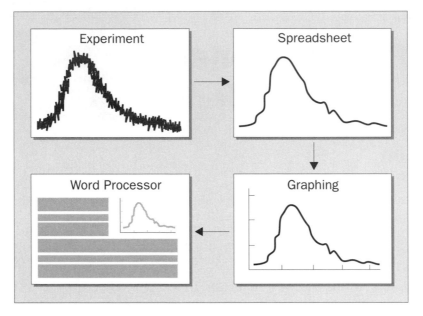

At every stage in this process, I would have to execute a program, load data, manipulate it, save the data, and close the application. The output of one fed the input of the other, and I had to make sure that I named the raw data files carefully (with the annoying 8.3 DOS filenames) to distinguish not only the experimental details, but also the application for which the data was an input.

Finally the report would be finished and the results would look quite good. I would seek approval from my research supervisor who would inevitably say, 'It's fine, but couldn't you add the results of yesterday's experiment on to this graph?'. Dutifully, I would go back to my office and do it: run the spreadsheet, load the raw data file from experiments of the existing graph and of the new data, manipulate the data, save the results; then run the graphics program, manipulate the graph, export the result as HPGL, and finally import the data into my word processor document.

By the time I showed the results to my research supervisor, two days later, he was likely to say, 'It's fine, but couldn't you add a new line to this graph comparing it with these other results?'. It is a surprise that I got anything published at all! But these were the days of DOS and, despite all this, the results were better than using pen and ink.

Object Linking & Embedding was invented to solve this kind of problem. OLE 1.0 is the forebear of the technology that we now call ActiveX, and it is historically important for a complete understanding of DCOM; so let's take a brief look at the family history.

COM Milestones

The Clipboard

If we really want to start at the beginning, I guess we should start with the Windows clipboard. This was the fundamental method of sharing data between applications on Windows. The user at the PC would copy data from one application and then switch to another one and paste in that data. To make this work, the application that was the data provider had to copy the data, with some indication of its type, to the clipboard. The application that was the data consumer would check that it could use the data, and if so, it would then read it and incorporate the data into its document.

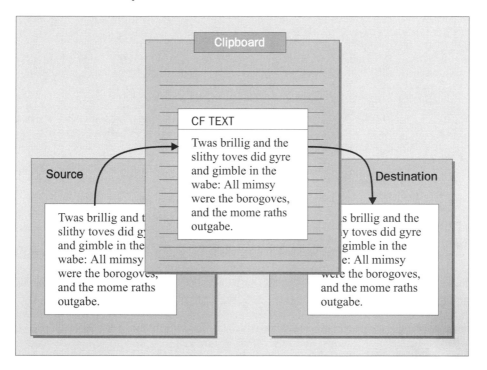

Let's reiterate this: the data provider described the data, which the data consumer used. This is essentially all there was to the clipboard. OK, there were some other fancy things you could do, like delayed rendering, but the bottom line was one application copied the data to the clipboard, and later on some other application pasted from it.

The data consumer could integrate clipboard data, as part of a document, which it could then manipulate. Before it copied data from the clipboard, it read the data type; but this was the only information that was saved in the clipboard. The upshot of this was that the data consumer couldn't know who created the data, or what raw data was used to create the clipboard data. Since the data consumer could not get access to this data, it could not associate the data it added to its document with the source of that data. Consequently, when the data had to be edited, the *user* would have to start up the editor that generated the data, retrieve the original raw data from disk somewhere, edit it, copy it to the clipboard, and finally paste it into the data consumer again.

DDE

Next came **dynamic data exchange**. This was a protocol for two applications to link pieces of data together *dynamically*, so that when one item of data in the source document changed, the linked item in the destination document would also change: DDE magic!

DDE was a pain to program (although life was made slightly easier with the DDE Management Library), and the protocol was designed for data that was *expected* to change rather than data that *might* change. This meant that the DDE server always had to be running at the same time as the DDE client.

DDE was completely based upon the Windows messaging system. This is one of the reasons it was a pain to program: packing all that information and semantics in to **WPARAM**s and **LPARAM**s isn't easy. In addition, the protocol was never really defined all that well, which made it very difficult to actually interoperate with a large number of other applications.

DDE is still used today, mainly because it can be relied upon as a lowest common denominator. Microsoft Office applications support it, and for a long while it was the only method that one Office application could use to talk to another. DDE has also been used by Internet browsers to support 'plug-ins'. Until recently, both Netscape Navigator and Microsoft Internet Explorer supported the Mosaic DDE interface; however, both browsers now support Automation, and plug-ins are being superseded by Java Applets and ActiveX Controls.

16-bit OLE 1.0

At around the same time that DDE was introduced, there came **Object Linking & Embedding 1.0** (**OLE 1.0**). OLE 1.0 utilized the clipboard to copy not only the data, but also information about the data source and the application that provided the data. If a user copied a graph to the clipboard, the application would actually copy three pieces of information to the clipboard: **presentation data**, which was a metafile of the graph that the destination application would show in its document; **class information**, which was an identifier of the application used to provide or edit the data; and either the raw data itself (**native data**), or a reference to the file containing the raw data.

Copying the raw data created an **embedded object**, and copying a file reference created a **linked object**. These were *objects*, because the class information associated the code that generated the data with the data that was linked or embedded. Thus there was OLE: Object Linking & Embedding version 1.0.

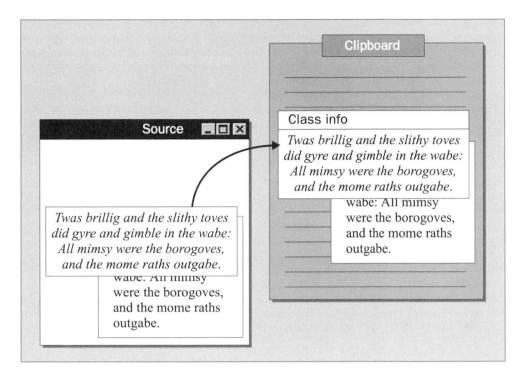

This was clever, but required developers to support the new method of sharing data. Since OLE objects were created in applications other than those that used them, the documents were known as **compound documents** (the classic example is a word processor document containing a spreadsheet graph).

OLE 1.0 used DDE as it's interprocess communications mechanism. OLE 1.0 provided support for loading and printing these compound documents by associating the document's three-letter extension with the application that created it. Information was saved by the system that indicated the command line arguments or DDE commands to do this loading or printing.

OLE 1.0 introduced the desktop user to a whole new way of sharing data in Windows. It is a method that is still used today. It could be argued that, today, the majority of COM objects in use are the OLE objects that are linked or embedded into compound documents. So most of the features of OLE 1.0 objects that I'll describe here are as valid for 32-bit OLE objects now as they were for 16-bit OLE 1.0 objects five years ago.

Perhaps the biggest advantage with OLE 1.0 over raw data pasted from the clipboard, was its support for **activating** objects. When you clicked on an object in a compound file it was selected; when you double-clicked on the object it was activated and the primary verb of the object was executed. The object server determined what the primary verb was: usually, to edit the object.

Editing an object in this way involved the OLE subsystem determining the class name and, from the information stored in the system, the name and location of the application that was to edit the data. This application, the object server, was then invoked and loaded either with the file that contained the raw data of the object (for linked objects), or a new document with the native data from the compound file (for embedded objects).

The user could then edit the object in the editor, which ran as a separate window to the compound document editor. When the user closed down the object editor, the presentation data of the edited object was copied, and either the data was saved to the file (linking), or the native data was copied onto the clipboard. The object editor was then shut down, and the object in the compound document was updated with the new data.

This was great, and led to a hurried proliferation of Write documents containing, well, **.wav** files. You see the big problem, initially, was that not that many applications used OLE 1.0. To help users think that OLE was a *good idea*, Microsoft even supplied an application that converted non-OLE data into OLE objects, which was called the Object Packager. This really had a very limited use.

However, OLE 1.0 did catch on. I guess the first time I thought OLE was a useful facility was when someone sent me a message via MS Mail that had an embedded Word document. By just double-clicking on the object, I could launch Word to view and edit the document. This may seem trivial, now, but back then it seemed wonderful that the small icon in the message was, in fact, a document, and I would not have to explicitly search through the network with File Manager to load it.

A short while after OLE 1.0 was released, Windows NT 3.1 emerged and it (as well as Windows for Workgroups) had **Network DDE**. This was essentially DDE that allowed one side of the link to be on another machine across the network. It was a nice idea, and applications were developed to use it, but the most common use seemed to be to share bitmaps with other users using the clipboard viewer. (Following in this tradition, the first 'real' DCOM application is NetClip. This distributes clipboard data over the network using DCOM.)

16-bit OLE 2.0

Then came a huge leap. OLE 1.0 became 16-bit OLE 2.0. The technology was still called Object Linking & Embedding, but it meant far more than that. It was first released in Visual Basic 3.0 and later in Microsoft Office 4 (specifically Word 6.0 and Excel 5.0).

For a start, OLE 2.0 was based upon completely new underpinnings. Gone was the dependency on DDE as the interprocess communication mechanism; gone was the primarily message-based programming model. At the core of OLE 2.0 was the **Component Object Model**, a binary standard of how you talk to an object, how that object handles its own lifetime, and how it tells the world what it can do. COM was designed with some foresight: it was designed to allow objects to be called across machine (not just process) boundaries, even though, at the time of its release, this was just a fantasy in a developer's eye.

COM also gave us a standard error reporting scheme, and a coherent memory management mechanism. OLE 2.0 defined compound files, an implementation of structured storage; it gave us inter-application drag and drop, in-place editing, and OLE Automation (now known simply as Automation).

However, anyone who used OLE 2.0 on 16-bit Windows will have noticed that although it was a good idea, it was a good idea for another operating system. The problem that plagued 16-bit Windows users after its release was that of limited system resources. In Windows 3.1, if you loaded Word then you'd get down to about 70% resources; if you loaded Excel too, you'd get down to maybe 40%; load any more applications and you'd soon get near to that disastrous 0% resources limit.

If you reached 0%, it did not matter how much virtual memory (or indeed physical memory) you had, Windows would not launch any more applications. System resources were extremely valuable, and applications that had lots of menu items, loads of windows, and used excessive amounts of GDI objects, were the worst for eating system resources. The first major applications to use OLE 2.0 were Word and

Excel, and these were terrible for using resources. (The system resource problem eased a little with Windows for Workgroups 3.11 which doubled the size of the USER heap, but the problem still remained.)

What OLE 2.0 needed was an operating system that had no resource problems, and where you could load almost limitless numbers of processes (well, more than two). NT was a likely candidate, but NT 3.1 only had 16-bit OLE 1.0, for compatibility with Windows 3.1. Although you could install Microsoft Office on NT, it was the 16-bit version (and hence used 16-bit OLE 2.0) and it ran in the Windows on Windows (WOW) 16-bit VDM (Virtual DOS Machine) environment. This meant that OLE was only applicable to other applications running in the same VDM.

To the user, 16-bit OLE gave exciting UI features. For example, it gave inter-application drag and drop, so that objects could be dragged from one application on the desktop and dropped into the document of another application; and it gave in-place activation, so that when an object was activated, the UI of the object server would be integrated with the UI of the object container. These features depended upon the OLE features of Universal Data Transfer (UDT), which allowed for data to be shared between different processes, and structured storage, which allowed objects to be embedded within compound documents.

OLE Controls

While we waited for other operating systems to emerge, OLE developed further and we got OLE Controls. These appeared initially with Access 2.0, but they really came into force with the release, 9 months later, of Visual Basic version 4 (VB4). The previous version, VB3, extended itself with VBXs: DLLs that contained controls with methods and properties and could respond to a limited number of stock events. VB4 needed a more extensible architecture that could be used by other applications, and this gave us OLE Controls (OCXs).

An OCX could not be used on its own: it had to be loaded in a container. The OCX knew how to talk to the container and the container knew how to talk to the OCX. The way they did this was with COM interfaces. An OCX is implemented in a DLL, and it exports COM interfaces that it uses to support methods and properties; the container exports COM interfaces so that it can handle events from the OCX.

VBXs at that time were a thriving industry, and it appeared that OCXs would do the same for 32-bit platforms. Indeed, some commentators speculated that OCXs would herald the new component age in Windows software.

32-bit OLE

The next milestone was the release of NT 3.51: this had 32-bit OLE. Now, protected 32-bit applications could share data with other processes via OLE. 32-bit OLE used some NT features like Unicode strings, but it lacked others, like NT security.

It was also around this time that the version number was being dropped. The whole idea of COM was that the architecture allowed for it to be extended: you just added more interfaces as you needed them. The 2.0 served its purpose in distinguishing it from 16-bit OLE 1.0, but it suggested that there would be an OLE 3.0 in the future and there wasn't going to be, so the 2.0 was dropped.

Windows 95 was released shortly after Windows NT 3.51 went out the door. The 32-bit OLE implementation on Windows 95 was delivered by the same team that delivered the Windows NT 3.51 code, and was basically equivalent in functionality.

The COM infrastructure in 32-bit OLE was firmed up and layered completely on top of Microsoft's RPC (Remote Procedure Call) system, a compatible implementation of the Open Software Foundation's DCE RPC. On Windows NT 3.51 and Windows 95, cross-process COM calls were delivered using MS-RPC.

With the 2.0 dropped, we found that the term 'Object Linking & Embedding' also started to be dropped. We were told it was just OLE (pronounced *olay*), and that the initials had no significance. Microsoft did this in an attempt to counter the arguments that OLE was only desktop-based; that it was primarily concerned with sharing objects between compound documents of Windows applications. With 16-bit OLE 2.0 this was not the case, and it was certainly not the case with 32-bit OLE.

ActiveX

Rumors started to circulate about a future version of NT, code-named **Cairo**. One of its features was to be a distributed version of OLE. This was initially called **Network OLE**. Network OLE was what we know now as Distributed COM, and it had been released well ahead of Cairo.

Network OLE still had the 'OLE' name in it, and the result was that it, too, suffered from the versioning problem; indeed, some parts of the press called it OLE 3. To counter this, the technology briefly became just COM, but not long enough for it to stick, because Microsoft suddenly went 'Internet' in a big way. They announced their new strategy for the Internet on 'Internet Day' (December 7, 1995), and this strategy included a new term: **ActiveX Controls**.

ActiveX Controls, it turned out, were what we used to call OLE Controls; or, at least, they were a near replacement. (ActiveX Controls are lightweight COM objects without the need to carry all the baggage of OLE Controls. The mapping is one way: an OLE Control is an ActiveX control, but an ActiveX Control is not necessarily an OLE Control.) The term ActiveX became ubiquitous: we had ActiveX Controls, ActiveX Documents, ActiveX Data Objects and the ActiveX Server. Everything COM, it seemed, was really ActiveX.

On one level, ActiveX was active content, a way of making web pages do more than just text and pictures. However, Microsoft was trying to get ActiveX everywhere. In a way, this was acceptable, since we then had just one term to cover everything based on COM.

Standards

Distributed computing will become extremely important over the next few years. The growth of the Internet, and the ease with which a user on one side of the world can execute a CGI script on a server on the other side of the world, has shown that not only is distributed computing *possible*, but it is also *desirable*.

This means that the operating systems that will be successful in the next millennium will be those that make distributed computing easy, either as a client platform, a server platform, or as both. But however technically superior a distribution technology is, it's only useful if it is widespread. To a certain extent DCOM already has a head start over other distribution technologies, because Windows is by far the most popular desktop platform.

However, although NT is becoming more and more popular as a server platform, there are many more servers that do not run NT than do! Those other servers run Unix of some kind or another. If you, as a developer, are charged with designing a distributed application in a heterogeneous enterprise of Windows and MacOS clients, and NT and Unix servers, then your natural reaction would be to use a distribution technology that covers all those platforms. Chapter 1 has covered the main candidates and, briefly, these include Sockets, DCE RPC or even CORBA. The pros and cons of these methods have been discussed already, and if every developer decided to use a technology other than DCOM, Microsoft would still sell Windows operating systems in large quantities.

However, if the majority of the clients are using COM as the glue between local objects, it seems odd to use different glue to talk to remote objects. It complicates the code and does not present a fully integrated solution. However, if Windows (95 and NT) were the only platforms that used DCOM then all those other servers would be wasted resources.

So Microsoft decided early on to port DCOM to as many platforms as possible. This is a project that they started with DEC and Software AG, but now they are including many more vendors through the Open Group. The strategy is called 'The ActiveX Core technology/DCE Integration Pre-Structured Technology' or ACD PST for short. It is a double-pronged strategy. Both prongs will lead to code that can be licensed from the Open Group.

On the one hand is the ActiveX technology based on Microsoft RPC. This is, effectively, a port of the NT 4.0 source code to Unix. Software AG has been active in this project and, as I write this, the technology, ported to Solaris, is in a late beta stage. The emphasis of this project is to target server platforms where there isn't already a heavy investment in DCE RPC.

For platforms where DCE RPC is prevalent, the Open Group strategy is to develop DCOM based on DCE. This is the second prong of ACD PST. The main platform targeted here is DEC Unix.

The Solaris version of DCOM is expected by mid-1997 and the DEC version is expected by the end of 1997. Meanwhile, DCOM is already available on Windows 95 and NT 4.0, and with COM recently released on the MacOS, DCOM will be expected soon. The ubiquity of DCOM is imminent!

COM Basics

After that history lesson, let's find out what COM is really all about.

The Component Object Model is a specification describing what an object is, how an object can manage its own lifetime, and how it tells the outside world what it can do. Note that COM is a binary specification: it is not a language, and it does not require the use of a particular language. Any language that has support for arrays of function pointers, and can call functions through those pointers, can be used directly. This includes languages like C, C++ and Pascal. Other languages that do not have direct support for function pointers, like VB and J++ (Microsoft's Java implementation), have extensions that allow them to call or create COM objects. J++ has classes that use native code to access COM objects, whereas VB has evolved a syntax that hides function pointers from the user.

COM allows you to group together associated functions into an **interface**, which you can name and register. A COM interface consists only of function prototypes and a protocol for their use. It doesn't imply a particular implementation.

A **COM class** defines the implementation of one or more interfaces and acts as a template or recipe by which COM objects can be produced. **COM objects** are instantiated from COM classes, and combine the implementation defined by the class, with instance data specific to that object. This is very similar to the relationship between classes and objects in any object-oriented programming language, but remember that COM is a language-independent binary standard.

All COM objects must implement the interface called **IUnknown**, as this is the key to lifetime management and the ability to query objects for functionality. A client can ask a COM object whether it supports a particular interface; if the object can, it will return an interface pointer to the client.

This mechanism has a number of advantages over traditional methods of sharing functionality. Remember that in the last chapter we developed a DLL that enumerated the handles of the windows on a desktop? In that example, the list of windows had to be initialized before use and the resources it used had to be freed when the list was no longer needed. We did this by defining two functions: one that indicated that we wanted to create a new list, and another that indicated that the list could be freed. I designed the enumeration functions only to be called after the initialization function was called. However, there was nothing to prevent the user of our DLL from accessing an uninitialized list, and this error would only come to light at runtime.

COM can prevent the use of uninitialized objects because the only way for the client to access the functions in a COM object's interface is by first requesting a pointer to that interface. This means that the object can ensure that any data the interface relies upon is initialized before the interface pointer is returned. In addition, the COM specification also requires a client to tell the object when it has finished using an interface. This allows the object to release any resources used by the interface.

Memory Allocation

16-bit Windows had little memory protection, and tasks could allocate global memory and pass data to other applications through this memory. COM was designed with protected memory systems in mind and, in particular, passing data between applications on different machines.

The last chapter introduced some of the problems associated with marshaling data, passing data between different processes. I gave one method of packaging up standard data types (**int**s, **long**s) for transmission, and I also made an attempt at transmitting variable length strings. It is the word *variable* that is important here. If you create a buffer in the client, fill the buffer with data, and transmit that data to the server, then the server will have to create a buffer large enough to take the data. Similarly, if the client expects a server to create some data, it will need to make a buffer big enough to take that data. So how is all this handled in COM?

COM uses the DCE RPC definitions of **[in]** and **[out]** parameters of methods on an interface. **[in]** parameters are parameters that pass data from the client to the server. **[out]** parameters pass data from the server to the client. Both of these are one way, but **[in, out]** parameters pass data from the client to the server and from the server to the client. All parameters, whether standard data types or buffer pointers, must be marked as one of these three.

By declaring parameters like this, the code that's needed to transmit data between client and server can determine what data to copy and hence what buffers to create. Further, it gives a commitment as to who is responsible for creating and freeing buffers.

For example, if a client calls an object method with an **[in]** and an **[out]** parameter, the marshaling code knows that it can copy the **[in]** data and transmit it to the server. It also knows that, when the method returns, it must copy the data from the **[out]** buffer into a process-specified buffer. If the parameters are standard data types, the marshaling code knows how much memory to allocate. The fun begins when the parameters are pointers to buffers, as, for example, with strings.

Chapter 5 explains the details of how to pass variable length buffers as parameters and explores IDL in greater depth.

This manipulation of memory, and the passing of buffers between protected memory processes, means that COM has to copy data between buffers allocated in different processes. To enable this (and the subsequent freeing of these buffers), COM uses memory allocators to allocate and free process memory. The rules of parameter memory allocations for memory buffers are:

> **[in]** parameters are allocated and freed by the client
>
> **[out]** parameters are allocated by the server and freed by the client
>
> **[in, out]** parameters are allocated and freed by the client, although during the method call, the server may free and reallocate memory for the buffer

These rules apply to data that is not passed by value. Data passed by value does not require memory to be allocated by the user, as the marshaler will do this. When you program using COM interfaces (and using the COM library functions), pay careful attention to whether the parameters are **[in]** or **[out]** so that you can avoid memory leaks.

> *When the COM runtime is initialized for your process, it will create a memory allocator for you. You can register an object with COM called a **MallocSpy**, and COM will call methods of this object when memory allocations and frees are performed through the process allocator. A MallocSpy could be used to add debugging messages to track memory usage. However, it should only be used in debug builds, because it degrades performance.*

IUnknown

Let's take a closer look at **IUnknown**. Remember that this is the interface that *all* COM objects must implement, without exception, and thus it is the basis of all other interfaces. In other words, all interfaces must derive from **IUnknown** and all interface pointers are polymorphic with **IUnknown**.

The **IUnknown** interface has the following functions:

```
HRESULT QueryInterface(REFIID iid, void** ppvObject);
ULONG AddRef(void);
ULONG Release(void);
```

Let's examine the role of the last two functions first.

Reference Counting

An object that implements **IUnknown**, or any interface based upon it, must keep a reference count on that interface. How the object implements this depends on the language being used. In C++, for example, you would use a class to represent the interface and associate a reference count with that class. The **AddRef()** function increments the reference count and the **Release()** function decrements it. Both functions return the new value of the reference counter, but because the return value may be unreliable in some circumstances, this should only ever be used for diagnostic purposes.

This mechanism allows the object to keep track of whether each interface is in use or not. When an interface is no longer being used, the reference count drops to zero and the object can clean up any resources associated with that interface. When reference counts of every interface implemented by an object become zero, the object is not being used by anyone, so it can happily die. If just one interface has a non-zero reference count, that interface is in use, so the data that the interface uses cannot be released and the object must still live.

> *This principle is fundamental to the lifetime of a raw COM object. Although this principle may seem to get blurred a little in some particular cases, such as objects managed by the Microsoft Transaction Server (MTS), it is never actually broken. MTS is the subject of the final chapter of this book.*

To ensure that reference counts are maintained correctly, you should make sure that your client code follows a couple of simple principles:

▲ Whenever you make a copy of an interface pointer, you must increment the reference count on the interface

▲ Whenever you have finished with an interface, you must decrement the reference count

If you copy an interface pointer, you're saying that the interface will be used by another part of your program (or if it is a COM application, it could pass this pointer to another application) and therefore the reference count must be incremented to make sure that the pointer is still valid and pointing to an existing interface of an existing object. The user of that pointer will know that the function that gave it the pointer will have already incremented the reference count, so it does not need to do this; but when this user has finished with the pointer, it must signal this by decrementing the reference count.

```
PINTERFACE GetInterface(void)
{
    PINTERFACE pInterface = NULL;
    // Get the interface pointer as an [out] parameter
    GoGetIt(&pInterface);
    // Pass it as an [in] parameter
    UseInterface(pInterface);
    // Release it
    pInterface->Release();
}

void UseInterface(PINTERFACE pInterface)
{
    // Use the interface pointer

    // Now save it for later use
    pInterface->AddRef();
    g_pInterface  = pInterface;
}
```

In this code, we have a function **GetInterface()** that obtains an interface pointer from a function called **GoGetIt()**. It passes this on to some other function (**UseInterface()**) before using it itself. Since the interface pointer is obtained from another function, it is an **[out]** parameter; that is, it's allocated by **GoGetIt()**, but it's the responsibility of the **GetInterface()** function to release the pointer when it's no longer needed.

The interface pointer is passed to another function (**UseInterface()**) as an **[in]** parameter, so that function need not manage the interface reference counting. In this example, however, the

UseInterface() function makes a copy of the interface pointer in some global variable, so it must **AddRef()** the interface before returning. If the code did not do this, some other part of the application could call **Release()**, the reference count would drop to zero, the object would die, and the global pointer would end up pointing to an invalid address.

QueryInterface()

The remaining function in **IUnknown** is **QueryInterface()**. This function is used by an object to hand out pointers to its interfaces.

```
HRESULT QueryInterface(REFIID riid, void** ppvObject);
```

riid is an identifier of the interface that the client wants to use. If the object implements that interface, it returns a pointer to the interface in the pointer referenced by **ppvObject**. If the object doesn't implement the interface, the function returns an error value (**E_NOINTERFACE**) and a **NULL** pointer is passed in the interface pointer.

The **ppvObject** parameter is an **[out]** parameter, so it's the responsibility of the caller to release the interface pointer returned. As a rule of thumb, for every successful call to **QueryInterface()**, there must also be a call to **Release()**.

An example of **QueryInterface()** could be:

```
HRESULT IMyInterface::QueryInterface(REFIID iid,
        void** ppvObject)
{
   *ppvObject = NULL;
   HRESULT hr = S_OK;
   if (riid == IID_IUnknown)
      *ppvObject = (IUnknown*)this;
   else if (riid == IID_IMyInterface)
      *ppvObject = (IMyInterface*)this;
   else
      hr = E_NOINTERFACE;

   if (SUCCEEDED(hr))
      ((IUnknown*) *ppvObject)->AddRef();
   return hr;
}
```

This is the implementation of **QueryInterface()** for the interface called **IMyInterface**. (Remember that every interface is based upon **IUnknown** and so must implement its functions.) It tests to see if the ID of the interface requested is one that the object supports (**IMyInterface** or **IUnknown**) and, if so, it returns a pointer to that interface. If the request was for an unsupported interface, an error value is returned (**E_NOINTERFACE**). The **SUCCEEDED()** macro tests to see if the status code, **hr**, is a success code (those starting with **S_**) or failure code (starting with **E_**); if a valid interface pointer is returned, the reference count on the interface is incremented. Status codes are covered a little later in this chapter.

Note that to find out what an object can do using only **IUnknown**, you would need to query for all the interfaces that it supports. **IUnknown** does not support any enumeration of the interfaces supported by an object, so the only way to get such a list is to separately compile a list of all possible interfaces and to go through this list one by one asking the object if it supports the interface.

*This is how **OLEView** lists the interfaces used by objects. **OLEView** is the OLE/COM Object Viewer, a
utility supplied with Visual C++ (or it can be obtained separately from **www.microsoft.com**). It is used
to list all the classes and interfaces registered on a machine.*

You may have 200 interfaces registered on your machine, so it may seem a little excessive to call
QueryInterface() 200 times to determine what the object will do. This is true, and the only way
around this problem is for the object to describe itself. The standard way to do this is for the object to
provide the **ITypeInfo** interface. The client still has to call **QueryInterface()** for this interface, but
once obtained, it can ask the object what methods it supports. The information that **ITypeInfo** returns
allows the client to determine what methods the server supports through its **IDispatch** interface, so that
it can only be used on automation objects.

Standard Error Reporting and Status Codes

COM set a standard for status and error codes which was based upon the Win32 error codes system.
Status codes are 32-bit and are made up of a 16-bit status (bits 0 to 15), a 12-bit facility (bits 16 to 27), and
a single bit success indicator (the other three bits are reserved). The success-bit (the most significant bit)
determines if the status code represents a success or failure. It is this bit that is tested by the **SUCCEEDED()**
and **FAILED()** macros. The facility describes what part of the system generated the codes. Finally, the 16-
bit status (the least significant 16 bits) specifies what actually happened.

Win32 error codes, however, also have a 16-bit status code, but in the top **WORD** Win32 error codes have a
category code, a severity code, a customer bit and a reserved bit. These last three bits correspond to the
reserved COM error code bits. The customer bit can be used to indicate that the code is defined by you
rather than by Microsoft. Win32 and COM codes are listed in the **Winerror.h** header files in the Win32
SDK.

The table shows the defined values for the facility. Microsoft recommends that if you wish to create your
own error codes you use the **FACILITY_ITF** facility. This is used for interface specific error codes (hence
the name) and thus they can have different meanings for different interfaces. Although you can use all the
codes from 0x0000 to 0xffff in this facility, the range 0x0000 to 0x1fff contain error codes for the OLE
interfaces and so should be avoided.

Note that this is in contrast to Win32 error codes, where
you can define whatever catagory you like, and as long as
the customer bit is set there will be no clash with the
system defined codes.

Facility	Value
NULL	0
RPC	1
Dispatch	2
Structured Storage	3
Interface	4
Win32	7
Windows	8
SSPI	9

Identifiers

We have established that an object can specify whether it supports a requested interface. However, there must be some mechanism to identify the interface that we are interested in. This is done with an **IID** or **Interface ID**. IIDs are just **GUIDs** used to identify interfaces. GUID stands for **G**lobally **U**nique **ID**entifier and each GUID is a 128-bit number. GUIDs are exactly the same as the OSF DCE **UUID** (**U**niversally **U**nique **ID**); there's some bizarre historical reason why Microsoft invented another acronym for the same thing, but no one seems to remember it.

GUIDs really are very unique! Thousands of machines can be generating GUIDs 10 million times a second and there will not be a duplicate generated until sometime after the year 5770 AD (or so they say!). GUIDs are generated by calling the **UuidCreate()** API in MS-RPC, or **CoCreateGuid()** which calls the same function. This function combines numerous pieces of information, including the time and date, to create a statistically unique 128-bit number. You can easily create GUIDs for yourself using the **Guidgen** utility that's part of the Win32 SDK and also comes as a component with Visual C++.

GUIDs are used extensively in COM for Interface IDs and **Class IDs** (**CLSIDs**) which identify COM classes. Here you can see an example of a pair of IIDs:

```
{00000000-0000-0000-C000-000000000046}
{00020400-0000-0000-C000-000000000046}
```

The first is the IID for **IUnknown**, the second is for the **IDispatch** interface used for Automation. They look nice and ordered, don't they? That's because these interfaces are defined by Microsoft, and Microsoft has already allocated these 'neater' IIDs for the more important interfaces. Here's an IID for one of my interfaces; it looks much messier:

```
{98397522-4458-11D0-9A62-0060973044A8}
```

However, this is a GUID that I know is unique. Now I can use this GUID as the IID for my very own interface called **IRemoteTime**. Although I can't guarantee that there isn't another interface in use, somewhere, that the designers have called **IRemoteTime**, I *can* guarantee that it doesn't use the same IID as mine–and it's the IID that needs to be unique. (You'll see this interface used in the next chapter.)

But how does a client know about my interface? The Microsoft interfaces are well known because they are documented in the Win32 SDK documentation, and the prototypes are in the Win32 header files. My interface is unique, but how will anyone find out what it can do? The only way is through publicity; for my interface to be used (whether implemented by servers or used by clients), I will have to make my interface public. One good way is to publish it in a book like this!

So, the interfaces that an object implements are identified by IIDs, and you can ask an activated object if it supports a particular interface by passing the IID to the **QueryInterface()** of the object. An object class is identified by a CLSID and this can be used to tell COM from which class to create an object. That's fine, but where do you get the CLSID from? Even if you can get a CLSID from somewhere, it's a string of numbers and not at all easy to remember; it's error-prone to type, and definitely user unfriendly and most unsuitable for user friendly macro languages like VBA. There must be an easier way to identify a class than this:

```
{98397522-4458-11D0-9A62-0060973044A8}
```

How about a string like **"RemoteTime.RemoteTime"**? This is much easier to remember and is the type of name that VBA uses when creating objects. This string is called a ProgID. Of course, it's the CLSID that COM uses, so there must be some mapping from ProgIDs to CLSIDs, and this mapping must be readily available. The obvious place for this mapping, and other information about COM classes and interfaces, is the system registry.

Registry

The system registry has a hive devoted to COM information called **HKEY_CLASSES_ROOT**. On a well used NT or Windows 95 machine, this hive will be packed full of entries, but there are essentially just three types of information.

File Extensions

The first is information that maps file extensions to the executables that use the files. When you double-click on a data file in Explorer, the system will launch the server that plays (or edits) the data file, and loads the file into that server. This does not necessarily use COM.

Every file type (i.e. persistent data associated with an object) is registered under the file extension in the root of **HKEY_CLASSES_ROOT**. For example, Excel spreadsheets are registered under **.xls**. If you run the registry editor (**Regedit**) and scroll down to the **.xls** entry, you will see something like this:

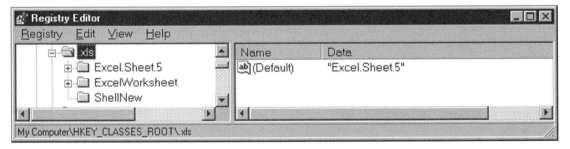

This shows that files of the extension **.xls** are Excel objects of the type **Excel.Sheet.5**.

ProgIDs

The second type of information in the registry is ProgIDs. Again, these are held in the root of **HKEY_CLASSES_ROOT**. Following from the example above, if you scroll to the entry for **Excel.Sheet.5**, you'll see something like this:

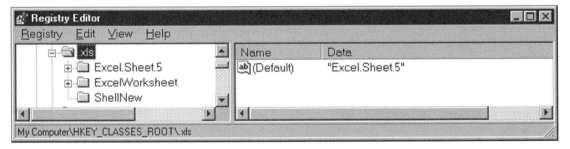

Among other things, this is saying that the object represented by the ProgID **Excel.Sheet.5** (which we know is represented by files with extension **.xls**) has a CLSID of **{00020810-0000-0000-C0000-000000000046}**.

GUIDs

File extensions and ProgIDs make up the bulk of the clutter in **HKEY_CLASSES_ROOT**. It would have been nicer if they had been put into separate keys (say **\Ext** and **\ProgID**), since this would have left us with a better organized hive. However, that was not done from the start, and we have the clutter that exists now.

The rest of the information that we're interested in is in the following keys:

Key	Contents
AppID	Application IDs.
CLSID	Class IDs.
Interface	Interface IDs.
TypeLib	Type library IDs.

These keys contain information about items identified by GUIDs. So, from the last example, move up the hive to the **CLSID** key, and look for the CLSID of this object:

Now we have the information about our **.xls** object. There's a lot of information here, and we'll cover at least some of it in the following pages; but at this point in time, the most important is the key **LocalServer32**. On my machine, this key has a value of:

```
C:\Msoffice\Excel\Excel.exe
```

In other words, this is the path to where Excel is installed on my machine. Now COM can find the process that it must use to handle the objects held in the files with extensions of **.xls**. Note that interfaces are also registered; we'll see why in a moment.

COM Information

The previous examples have shown how Explorer associates a file type with a server. It also shows how to map between a ProgID and a CLSID and how, from a CLSID, the COM system determines which module to load. I say module, here, because COM servers can be processes or DLLs. In this example, the **LocalServer32** key gives the path to a process; but the CLSID could have an **InprocServer32** key which specifies the path to a DLL that contains the object.

Normally, these two keys give paths to the actual server that will create or handle the object. However, the value in the key could give an executable that will do some extra work for you to find the object server; all COM does is launch the specified process in the case of **LocalServer32**, or call **LoadLibrary()** if **InprocServer32** is used.

Initializing COM

So how do you, as a developer, use COM objects? We'll go through the various steps here. The first step is to initialize COM. The main point of this is to load up the COM DLLs and to carry out initializations.

There are three functions that can be used to initialize COM:

```
HRESULT CoInitialize(LPVOID pvReserved);
HRESULT CoInitializeEx(void* pvReserved, DWORD dwCoInit);
WINOLEAPI OleInitialize(LPVOID pvReserved);
```

The first initializes COM; this has been extended for DCOM to give the second version; and the third initializes the *OLE* libraries, so that an application can use compound documents. Notice the difference – the **Co** functions initialize COM, and a call to one of these is required for any COM code; the **Ole** function is used if your application uses OLE features (mostly the UI features and compound document features; things like drag and drop and in-place activation). Internally, this calls **CoInitialize()**, since OLE uses COM.

All three functions have a reserved parameter which should be **NULL**. This parameter is left over from the 16-bit OLE 2.0 days when you could create a memory allocator and pass this as the parameter. You can no longer do this.

CoInitializeEx() has an additional parameter that specifies the threading model to be used. This affects the process whether it is a client or a server. **CoInitialize()** simply calls **CoInitializeEx()**, passing the parameter **COINIT_APARTMENTTHREADED**, which was the only threading model used in 32-bit COM prior to the arrival of DCOM. We cover threading models in more detail in Chapter 9.

The implication here is that since **OleInitialize()** calls **CoInitialize()**, which in turn calls **CoInitializeEx(NULL, COINIT_APARTMENTTHREADED)**, OLE applications follow an apartment model. You'll see the implications of this in Chapter 9.

Before the process terminates, there must be a corresponding uninitialize call to either **CoUninitialize()** (if you called **CoInitialize()** or **CoInitializeEx()**), or **OleUninitialize()** (if you called **OleInitialize()**).

Creating COM Objects

Once COM has been initialized, you can create objects and then call methods on them. So how do you do this?

Suppose we have a client application that wants to use an object because it thinks that object can provide a service for it. The client must somehow create an instance of the object, ask the object if it supports the required interface, and then, if it does, use the interface pointer that is returned. We've already seen that once we have one interface pointer on an object, we can use **QueryInterface()** to get to any other interface supported by that object; but how do we create objects and get that interface pointer in the first place?

COM objects are actually created by a particular type of object called a **class factory**. A class factory is a COM object that implements the **IClassFactory** (or **IClassFactory2**) interface. There may be several objects implemented in a server, and each object will have a particular class factory to create it.

This is quite an important point. The temptation with COM is to create a single object type in each code module. However, this is not the most efficient way to create objects, especially if your application requires many different types of objects. A single code module for each object would mean that **CreateProcess()** or **LoadLibrary()** would have to be called for each object. However, if a single code module implements the class factories for several objects, and several objects from these class factories are created, then **CreateProcess()** (or **LoadLibrary()**) would be called only a single time.

Why have class factory objects? Why don't the code modules just create objects directly when asked? There are several reasons. The first is that class factories are just that: *factories*. They exist to create multiple objects of a single type, so they can be used to perform initializations necessary for the object type.

In addition to providing the link between the client and object, class factories also provide a link between the client and the code module. Through a class factory, a client application can tell the executable that, even if there are no reference counts on any interfaces on any object implemented by the server, the client still wants the server to remain in memory. Without this facility, a server could unload itself from memory as soon as it finds that all reference counts are zero. However, with this facility, a client may decide, for performance reasons, to keep a server in memory so that it can create objects very quickly without the overhead of loading up the server.

I mentioned that class factories could implement the **IClassFactory2** interface. This interface implements methods to allow a client to create an object that can only be used when licensed. This feature usually applies to ActiveX (OLE) Controls and is particularly prevalent among OCXs used by VB. This interface is designed to stop the use of controls in applications that haven't paid a fee to the creators of those controls. It features the same methods as **IClassFactory** plus some further methods specific to licensing.

Now, how exactly does a client create an object? It does it by calling one of these functions:

```
STDAPI CoGetClassObject(REFCLSID rclsid,
    DWORD dwClsContext, COSERVERINFO* pServerInfo,
    REFIID riid, LPVOID* ppvObject);

STDAPI CoCreateInstance(REFCLSID rclsid,
    LPUNKNOWN pUnkOuter, DWORD dwClsContext,
    REFIID riid, LPVOID* ppvObject);

HRESULT CoCreateInstanceEx(REFCLSID rclsid,
    IUnknown* pUnkOuter, DWORD dwClsContext,
    COSERVERINFO* pServerInfo,
    ULONG cmq, MULTI_QI rgmqResults);

HRESULT CoGetInstanceFromFile(COSERVERINFO* pServerInfo,
    CLSID* pclsid, IUnknown* punkOuter, DWORD dwClsCtx,
    OLECHAR* szName, ULONG cmq, MULTI_QI* rgmqResults);

CoGetInstanceFromIStorage(COSERVERINFO* pServerInfo,
    CLSID* pclsid, IUnknown* punkOuter, DWORD dwClsCtx,
    IStorage* pstg, ULONG cmq, MULTI_QI* rgmqResults);
```

The last three functions were introduced with DCOM and they allow objects to be created on remote machines. We'll leave these until a later chapter, where they can be studied in greater depth. The first two, **CoGetClassObject()** and **CoCreateInstance()**, will be covered here.

CoGetClassObject()

Of these two functions, **CoGetClassObject()** can be considered the lower level of the two. In fact **CoGetClassObject()** will only create objects of one type: it gets the class factory of a particular object and does not create the object at all.

rclsid is used to specify the object class factory that we wish to create. This is actually the CLSID of the object we ultimately want to create. Since a class factory can have one of two class factory interfaces (**IClassFactory** and **IClassFactory2**), **riid** is used to specify which one to get. In most cases this will be the **IClassFactory** interface.

dwClsContext and **pServerInfo** are used to determine where the object will be created. The first is the context of the server (which we'll look at shortly), and **pServerInfo** is a parameter that was reserved for pre-DCOM Windows, but is now used to specify the machine on which the server will run.

So now COM can use the CLSID to find the path to the object server (using the entries under the **CLSID** key in the registry). It will launch the server and then create a class factory object. If this object creation is successful and it has the requested interface, a pointer to the interface is returned in the pointer pointed to by **ppvObject**.

In the case just outlined, the interface pointer returned is an interface of the class factory. We now need to ask this class factory to make us the object that we really require. We can do this by calling the **IClassFactory::CreateInstance()** function to get an interface pointer on the object.

```
HRESULT IClassFactory::CreateInstance(IUnknown* pUnkOuter,
    REFIID riid, void** ppvObject);
```

The parameters to this function are used in the same way as their equivalents in **CoCreateInstance()**, which we'll examine next. Note that this is a two stage process: call **CoGetClassObject()** to get a class factory interface and then **CreateInstance()** to get an interface pointer on the object.

CoCreateInstance()

CoCreateInstance() does both of the tasks outlined above: it creates a class factory on the object **rclsid** and queries for the interface referenced by **riid**; it then releases the class factory. If you only want to create one instance of an object, this is the simplest way to do it; however, if you want to create many instances of an object then it may be best to hang on to the class factory. Such a strategy is important if the class factory is on a remote machine, since it will reduce the number of network calls.

You may have noticed that **CoCreateInstance()** has a parameter that takes an **IUnknown** interface pointer (**pUnkOuter**). This is used when the object is being created as part of another object, in a process called **aggregation**. This pointer allows the object being created to know about the **IUnknown** interface of the aggregating object, so that it can pass on any calls to its **IUnknown** interface to that interface.

For example, imagine that you have an object that implements the **ISpellChecker** interface, which you use in your word processor. Now you are writing an email application and you want to reuse the spell checker code. One way to do this is through containment, where the email object hides the **ISpellChecker** from the client, exposing its own **IEmailSpeller** instead. Calls to this interface are handled internally by calls to the methods on the spell checker's **ISpellChecker**.

Another way to do this is to aggregate the spell checker object as part of the email object and so expose the **ISpellChecker** interface directly from the spell checker. This means that when a client of the email object wants to check a spelling, it **QueryInterface()**'s for **ISpellChecker** and gets the interface pointer from the aggregated object. Now, according to the COM rules, the client could call **QueryInterface()** on this interface pointer for one of the email object's interfaces (say, **ISendMail**), but because the spell checker is a separate object, it knows nothing of the email object. This is where the **pUnkOuter** pointer is used.

When the email object creates the spell checker object, it passes its **IUnknown** pointer to the aggregated object. If, at a later stage, a client calls **QueryInterface()** for an interface on the spell checker object, the email object can forward the call to the spell checker object's **IUnknown**. If an object is not being created for aggregation, **NULL** is passed for this parameter. Note that you can only aggregate on in-process servers

The **dwClsContext** parameter can be one (or a combination) of the following:

```
CLSCTX_INPROC_SERVER
CLSCTX_INPROC_HANDLER
CLSCTX_LOCAL_SERVER
CLSCTX_REMOTE_SERVER
```

This determines the type of server to be used. An inproc server is a DLL; a local server is an EXE or a DLL (loaded into a surrogate process); and a remote server is either an EXE or a DLL (loaded into a surrogate process) on a remote machine. An inproc handler is a DLL that is used to implement custom marshaling.

COM uses this parameter to determine whether it should read the **LocalServer32**, the **InprocHandler32,** or the **InprocServer32** keys for this object to find the server code. If you specify a combination of all these context flags, COM will look for a server in order of least remoteness. In other words, inproc handler first, then inproc server, then local server, and finally remote server. The client provides this parameter to specify what sort of server is acceptable. Normally you would prefer an inproc server, since calls to an object are quicker. However, if you know that the object will always be created on a remote machine then you could specify **CLSCTX_REMOTE_SERVER** to prevent unnecessary registry reads.

One slight complication to this order is if the server is installed as an NT service, as outlined in Chapter 8. In this situation, the local machine has a service process that contains the server for the object. When the service is registered a **LocalService**, a value will be added under the **AppID** key for the server's CLSID. This named value is used to identify the name of the service that contains the object server. COM will look for an object server in a service before checking for a local server.

The following diagram summarizes this:

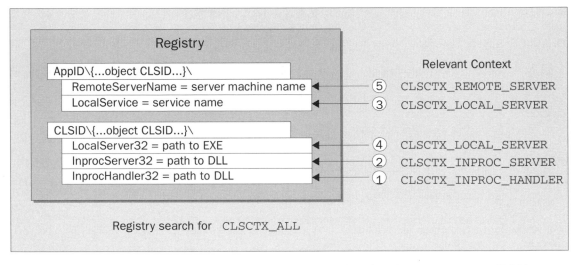

Let's look, in more depth, at what is required for a local server (EXE) and an inproc server (DLL).

COM Servers

COM servers are executables that implement one or more COM objects; COM objects implement one or more interfaces. The great thing about COM objects is that they share functionality between various client applications. In other words, somewhere there is code that can be used by several processes at one time. In the last chapter, we explored several ways to do this: we looked at putting code in a DLL that can be loaded by several applications at any one time; we saw that we could put code in a separate process (as long as we could have some method of communicating a request and getting a reply from that process); and we saw that if the process used a suitable communications protocol, we could situate the client and server on separate machines. So how does COM do this?

Inproc Servers

Inproc means **in-process**. In other words, the object is executed in the same process space as the client and hence the server code must be implemented in a DLL. In-process servers are fast and efficient, but the downside, as always with a DLL, is that the 'foreign' object is run in the protected memory space of the client, with the same privileges as any other client code.

This means that the object must execute in a way that is compatible with the client. In particular, it must have the same threading model as the client, something that we'll be covering in Chapter 9. Also, since the object has complete access to the client's memory, an errant object can wreak havoc and crash the entire process. The process must be extremely trusting of the inproc server and careful about how it calls it. If you do not want to trust an object like this, you'll need to call an object as a local server, if one exists, or call the inproc object through a surrogate.

To make shared code useful, we must somehow provide a public entry point so that a client can create an object. In terms of an inproc server, this entry point is the DLL-exported function `DllGetClassObject()`.

```
STDAPI DllGetClassObject(REFCLSID rclsid, REFIID riid, LPVOID* ppv);
```

Although you'll need to implement this function in COM servers that you write, you'll never need to directly call this function from client code. This function will be called for you when you call `CoCreateInstance()` or one of the other creation functions to create an object from an inproc server.

The object must also registered in the registry as being implemented in a DLL:

```
HKEY_CLASSES_ROOT\{Some CLSID}\
    InprocServer32 = "c:\some_path\my_server.dll"
```

Since the object is in a DLL, the creation of the object is quite fast. Calls to the object's methods are also swift, because they are essentially calls to functions in a standard DLL (albeit with an extra level of indirection).

Creation Sequence

In this picture, the client calls `CoGetClassObject()` to get a pointer to the class factory of the object. This results in the COM system querying the registry, calling `CoLoadLibrary()` to load the DLL, and then calling `DllGetClassObject()` to get a pointer to the object's class factory. Since the server is a DLL, this pointer is to memory in the address space of the client.

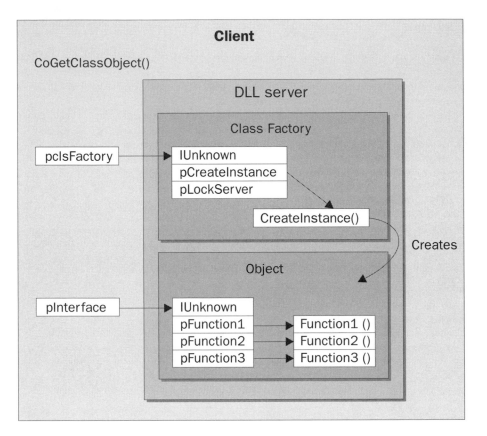

Now the client calls **`IClassFactory::CreateInstance()`** to get an interface pointer on the object. Again, this interface pointer points to memory that is in-process, and the function pointers in the interface point to the actual functions themselves, within the address space of the process.

As always, the object is released by the client calling **`Release()`** on the interfaces on which it has a reference. Once all reference counts on all interfaces of the object(s) in the server reach zero, the server DLL can be unloaded. Notice that the object server was loaded *dynamically* as a DLL. It also makes sense that the DLL could be unloaded dynamically, too. To be able to do this, COM (which originally loaded the DLL) must be able to know when all reference counts on objects in that DLL are zero. COM can determine if all reference counts are zero by calling the DLL's exported **`DllCanUnloadNow()`** function. A return value of **`S_OK`** indicates that COM can unload the DLL, which it will do by calling **`CoFreeLibrary()`**.

When a client releases all objects in a DLL, it can tell COM about this as a hint that it should think about unloading the DLL. The client does this in one of two ways: by calling **`CoFreeUnusedLibraries()`** or by calling **`CoUninitialize()`**. You'll normally want to call **`CoFreeUnusedLibraries()`** in your client's idle processing loop and **`CoUninitialize()`** when your client has finished using COM completely.

If a server DLL that you write relies on another DLL, you can use an import library to make sure that the DLL is loaded, or you can load it explicitly with a call to **`CoLoadLibrary()`**.

```
HINSTANCE CoLoadLibrary(LPOLESTR lpszLibName, BOOL bAutoFree);
```

This function has two parameters, the first is the DLL name and is the same as you would use in a call to `LoadLibrary()`. The second parameter determines whether the DLL should be auto-unloaded, which is the mechanism initiated by `CoFreeUnusedLibraries()`.

DLL Management

To a certain extent, COM behaves as a sophisticated DLL manager. As a developer, you must have come across the situation where you wished to provide an extensible framework through dynamically loaded DLLs. Indeed, in the last chapter we showed such a contrived situation with the `CoolFunctions` interface example.

Think again about the work that COM is doing here. You are saying, by specifying `CLSCTX_INPROC_SERVER` as `dwClsContext` in the `CoGetClassObject()` or `CoCreateInstance()` call, that you want a DLL to be loaded. (Ignore, for a moment, the idea of specifying other server contexts as well.) COM, on your behalf, will find that DLL, load it, and get the entry point that you've requested. If you had to implement that code yourself, it would require quite a bit of effort: you'd need to determine some way of registering the DLL, define a common entry point for DLLs of that type, then load the DLL, get the entry point, and provide a method of determining whether the DLL could safely be unloaded. It makes you breathless just thinking about it!

Local Servers

Local servers are implemented as EXEs. When a client requests an object from a local server, the object that COM returns is implemented in another process. The advantage of this approach is that in 32-bit operating systems like NT (and to some extent, systems like Windows 95), the memory of one process is protected from other processes.

The processes containing the client and server are separate, their memory is separate (a memory pointer in one process means nothing in the other process), and yet the clever thing is that the client can call the functions of the object 'directly' through an interface pointer. Furthermore, the client can call the object's methods, passing pointers to buffers in it's own memory, and the server can access the data, and even change it. To the client, it's as if the object is in the address space of the client, just as it would be if the object were implemented in-process.

Let's look at the mechanics of this from the server's point of view. Firstly, we must publicize that the server process implements the particular class. As in life, publicity is easy: you just shout loudly somewhere public. In terms of Windows, the publicity is created by putting the information somewhere everyone can get it: the registry. The `LocalServer32` key contains the path to the local server:

```
HKEY_CLASSES_ROOT\{Some CLSID}\
    LocalServer32 = "c:\some_path\my_server.exe"
```

Now, we must export the functionality, rather like a DLL does. Under Win32, we could actually export functionality in exactly the same way as a DLL by using `_declspec(dllexport)`, but in 16-bit Windows this wasn't possible. COM was released originally on 16-bit Windows, so another method had to be devised to register the class factories that a server implemented.

Windows applications used a well established mechanism of providing callbacks, pointers to code in the task's memory (`EnumWindows()`, which we saw in the last chapter, is an example of this). So by placing the address of an interface of an object's class factory in some central place, the EXE server allows COM to allow access to the object from other EXEs.

This is done with a call to **CoRegisterClassObject()** during the initialization of the server process. This function takes a pointer to a class factory object, so the server must create all the class factories of all the object types it manages, and call this function for each one. To specify that the class factory is for a particular object type, the CLSID is passed as another parameter.

We have now provided a callback, or entry point, that a suitable piece of code can call. When a client makes a call on an EXE server, the registry identifies the server to load. If the server is not already running, COM will load it and the server will then register the class factories that it implements. The server has been loaded to create a particular object, so COM waits for the server to initialize itself and then it picks the right entry point from the functions registered by the server. Thus it gets the class factory and finally the object.

You might think this a little strange. Even if the server EXE exports some function pointers, they are still only valid in the address space of the server process. If another process called the entry point, the code at that memory address would be meaningless. However, we are moving in the right direction. What we need is some code that translates the method calls from one process space to another.

The most obvious way to do this is to implement it in a DLL which can be loaded as part of the server process that has all the necessary code to accept calls from other processes and translate them into calls on the object. A DLL loaded as part of a process can call functions in the process' address space, so if a process publicizes where these functions are, the only problem is loading the DLL into the process in the first place.

Of course, this is what COM is for. COM loads a **stub** DLL into the address space of the server process. The stub can resolve the addresses in the server's interface and call the object's methods. However, the stub does need to talk to the client.

Let's look at the client again. When a client calls **CoGetClassObject()** it expects to get an interface pointer and it expects to be able to call the interface's methods through this pointer. So we need another DLL, this time one that can be loaded into the client's address space to provide usable pointers for each interface and method in the server. This DLL will provide code that looks just like the interface of the server, but exists only to transmit the requests to call an interface's methods to the stub in the object's address space. Such a piece of code is called a **proxy**.

All proxies are bits of code that take method calls, package them up along with any parameters, and send the packages off via some inter-process communication method. At the other end, the stub unpackages the request, calls the object method, and then packages up any results to transmit them back to the client.

This packaging and unpackaging is called **marshaling** and **unmarshaling**, and is one of the most important parts of COM. There are several ways to carry out marshaling and these are covered later on in this chapter, but if the interface methods use prescribed data types, the proxy and stub code can be automatically generated by the Microsoft IDL compiler (**MIDL**).

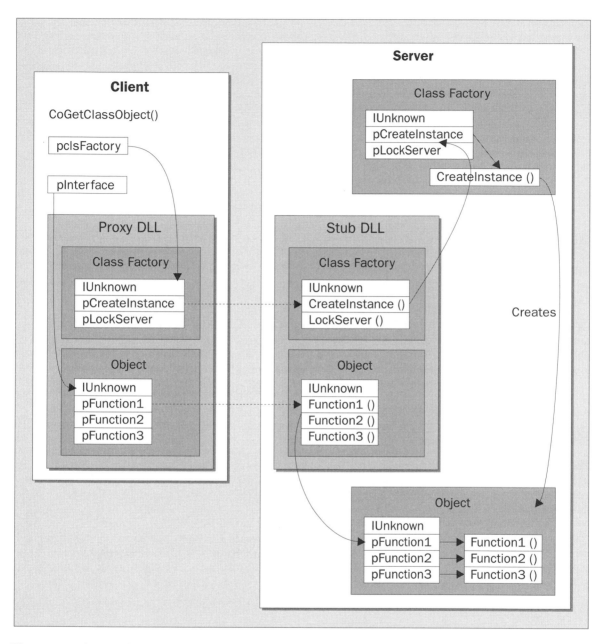

This picture shows a local server in action. The client calls **CoGetClassObject()** to get a class factory pointer. The actual class factory lives in another process, so we can't access it directly. Instead, the proxy DLL is loaded and the client gets a pointer to the proxy class factory. The functions in the proxy remote the function calls (via some RPC mechanism or other; it doesn't really matter what's used) to the stub DLL.

The stub DLL provides handler functions for these method calls, but since the stub is loaded into the address space of the server, it can activate the object's class factory and gain access to the class factory's interface pointer. Now the stub can create the object and return an acknowledgment of this back to the proxy in the client. The client calls methods on the object interface pointer that it holds, which is in fact an interface pointer on the proxy. The proxy remotes these calls through to the stub on the server where handler functions translate these calls, through the actual object's interface pointer, as method calls on the object.

I've been deliberately vague about the RPC mechanism used to remote the marshaled packets between the proxy and stub. As far as the client and stub are concerned, it doesn't really matter what method is used: Windows messages; DCE RPC; or direct TCP/IP (even a mechanism of having a little man writing the requests on a piece of paper and running back and forth between the proxy and stub!). The point is that the client has an interface pointer; it makes calls on this, and somehow the server gets the requests through its interface.

Once we've established some reliable and efficient mechanism to handle the communication between the client and server (a little man with a notepad would be rather slow), it matters little to the programmer of either client or server where they are situated. They could be on the same machine, but they don't have to be. As long as the inter-process communication mechanism used by the proxy and stub is network-capable, the location of client and server is irrelevant. This is a principle called *location transparency*.

Of course, if the last few paragraphs were completely true, there would be no need for a book like this, since writing a remote server would be the same as writing a local server. However, DCOM is more than just remote objects. DCOM represents the first stage in integrating COM objects as part of the NT architecture and, as such, it provides additional facilities not previously available in COM. These facilities include security, multithreading, and implementing servers in NT services. All these topics will be covered in later chapters of this book.

Remote Servers

There are two reasons why a section on remote servers really isn't necessary here: firstly, the rest of the book is about remote servers; secondly, on the surface, remote servers are no different from local servers as far as the client is concerned. The same API is used to activate the object. The only difference is that the piece of wire between the client and server is longer.

Although you can launch remote objects from pre-DCOM code (as you'll see in the next chapter), to get the full benefit of the new facilities provided with DCOM, you need to call DCOM-specific functions or the older COM functions with DCOM-specific parameters. This means that the client would have to be written specifically for DCOM.

Inproc Handlers

Inproc handlers are supplied to implement **custom marshaling**. Marshaling is the process of packaging up object method requests into a transmittable packet and then sending it to the server. Usually, COM does this using **standard marshaling**, but for greater control over this process (in particular, to improve efficiency), you can implement the marshaling process yourself. We will see more of this later in this chapter.

If an object uses custom marshaling, it should implement the **IMarshal** interface and register itself with the **InprocHandler32** value in the registry.

```
HKEY_CLASSES_ROOT\{Some CLSID}\
    InprocHandler32 = "c:\some_path\my_handler.dll"
```

Interfaces

Objects share out their functionality through interfaces. An interface is a contract; a server says I support this interface, and a client knows *exactly* the format of the interface. In fact, the client is so sure of the interface that it calls functions on that interface as if it had created the object. For the client to be able to do this, it must be able to prototype the interface and the functions.

Although any language that supports function pointers can be used, we'll use C++ because an interface is like a C++ vtable. The interface **IUnknown** has three functions, and is defined in IDL (interface definition language) as:

```
interface IUnknown
{
    HRESULT QueryInterface([in] REFIID riid, [out] void **ppvObject);
    ULONG AddRef();
    ULONG Release();
}
```

IDL is programming language independent, and is used to describe interfaces used by clients and implemented by servers. There are many IDLs around; CORBA and DCE have their own IDLs, while COM borrows its syntax from DCE. (DCOM is based upon Microsoft RPC, which is an implementation of DCE RPC). We'll cover IDL in greater depth in Chapter 5, but the syntax is C++ like so I won't spend much time here describing how to use it.

The only points that should be made are that interfaces are a little like C++ classes in that one interface can be derived from another. Deriving an interface from another means that the derived interface must implement the functions of the base interface. Unlike C++ classes, you only declare methods and cannot declare data members. This makes sense, since you call object methods and have no access to the internal state of an object. (Objects that have 'properties' expose these through get/put methods.)

Since the interface could be on an object in a different process, or machine, you need to specify in the IDL what the parameters are used for, so that memory can be allocated or freed appropriately. Parameters must be marked as either **[in]**, **[out]** or **[in, out]**.

So, getting back to **IUnknown**, an object that implements this interface would have the following memory implementation:

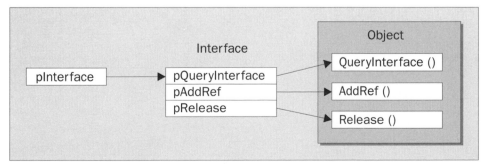

Here we can see that the interface methods are implemented in the object, and this gives access to the methods by constructing a table with function pointers to these methods. The interface pointer that is returned by calls to **QueryInterface()** is a pointer to this table.

When you compile the IDL with the Microsoft IDL compiler (**MIDL**), prototypes are created for a C++ class for the interfaces described in the IDL. For example, **IUnknown** can be implemented as a C++ class with:

```
class IUnknown
{
// Private data members etc
public:
   virtual HRESULT QueryInterface(REFIID riid, void **ppvObject);
   virtual ULONG AddRef();
   virtual ULONG Release();
};
```

Making the functions **virtual** means that when a C++ object of this class is created, the compiler creates a vtable, which has pointers to the functions. (This does assume that the C++ compiler will create the vtable with the functions in the same order as they are in the **class**.)

To create an object with this interface, we create a C++ object:

```
IUnknown obj;
```

To get an interface pointer, we just get a pointer to the object:

```
IUnknown* pobj = &obj;
```

We can pass this pointer between functions, even make copies of it; and as long as the object exists, the function pointers in the interface are valid.

An object implementing just **IUnknown** would be pretty boring, since all it could do is implement its own lifetime and tell you that that it implements **IUnknown**. For an object to export some functionality it would need to export some other interface.

Let's say we have an object that can hold a data buffer though some interface called **IName** with an IDL definition like this:

```
interface IName : IUnknown
{
   HRESULT SetName([in] BSTR bstrName);
   HRESULT GetName([out] BSTR* bstrName);
}
```

There are two methods. One sets the name by passing in a string, and the other returns the name. Thus, the **SetName()** method has an **[in]** parameter of type **BSTR**, which is an automation data type. A **BSTR** is essentially a pointer to a **WCHAR** array, although it's a bit special because it has a **long** *before* the address pointed at, which contains the size of the string. The **[in]** tells the marshaler that the buffer contains data and that data goes in the one direction: from client to server. The marshaler finds out how big the buffer held by the parameter is, and hence it can determine how much data to send to the server.

The **GetName()** receives data from the server, so the parameter is a **BSTR***. That is, the client calls the method with an address of a **BSTR**, which the method fills with the **BSTR** pointing to the data marshaled from the server. This is a general principle of interfaces. **[in]** parameters are generally passed by value, **[out]** parameters are passed by reference and, as we have already seen, memory pointers passed out in **[out]** parameters must be freed by the client. (If you attempt to pass an **[out]** parameter by value, **MIDL** will complain.)

Here we can see an example of interface inheritance. The interface must be derived from **IUnknown**, because the **IName** interface, like all interfaces, must support reference counting and **QueryInterface**ing. Note that the object must also support the **IUnknown** interface itself.

Now imagine that the same object could also support an **ITime** interface that returns the current time:

```
interface ITime : IUnknown
{
    HRESULT GetTime([out] long* time);
}
```

The object thus has three interfaces:

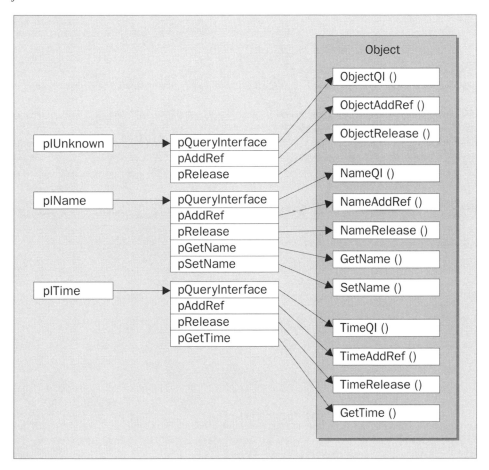

Objects and interfaces are conventionally
illustrated as lollipop diagrams, as shown here.

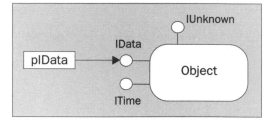

Implementing Interfaces

If you look at the diagram above, you'll see a problem: we need to construct three vtables, one for the
IUnknown interface and one each for the **IName** and **ITime** interfaces. There are two ways that we can
implement this object in C++, through containment and through inheritance.

Let's look at these two methods:

Multiple Inheritance

Using multiple inheritance we construct a C++ class that inherits from two other classes which have the
vtables that we need:

```
class IName : public IUnknown
{
public:
   virtual HRESULT SetName(BSTR bstrName) = 0;
   virtual HRESULT GetName(BSTR* bstrName) = 0;
};

class ITime : public IUnknown
{
public:
   virtual HRESULT GetTime(long* time) = 0;
};

class Time_and_Name_Object : public IName, ITime
{
public:
   HRESULT QueryInterface(REFIID riid, void **ppvObject);
   ULONG AddRef();
   ULONG Release();
   HRESULT SetName(BSTR bstrName);
   HRESULT GetName(BSTR* bstrName);
   HRESULT GetTime(long* time);
private:
   ULONG m_cRefs;
};
```

I've written out the methods, here, as they actually appear in C++. Normally when you use **MIDL** to
compile an interface definition, you'll find that **MIDL** gives interface definitions for C and C++. These days
you can largely ignore the C definitions: there may be people writing COM objects in C, just as there are
people who insist on rowing single-handed across the Atlantic. It may be good for the soul, but there are
quicker ways to do it!

Some of the older books on COM will go to great pains to explain the macros used in the implementations of interface methods; for example, the methods that return **HRESULT** are defined with the **STDMETHOD()** macro, and the methods that return **ULONG** are defined with the **STDMETHOD_()** macro:

```
class Time_and_Name_Object : public IName, public ITime
{
public:
    STDMETHOD(QueryInterface)(REFIID riid, void **ppvObject);
    STDMETHOD_(ULONG, AddRef)();
    STDMETHOD_(ULONG, Release)();
    STDMETHOD(SetName)(BSTR bstrName);
    STDMETHOD(GetName)(BSTR* bstrName);
    STDMETHOD(GetTime)(long* time);
private:
    ULONG m_cRefs;
};
```

I find this difficult to read as it introduces what is essentially another language to understand (that of the COM macros). From my C++ background, I prefer the more direct definition so that I don't have to convert to a C++ method in my head. However, it is a personal preference and you can decide which you prefer. The main reason for the macros is, of course, that it simplifies the interface definitions in C, making them seem a little more like the C++ version.

Now, back to the object. Since we've inherited from two abstract classes, casting a **Time_and_Name_Object** pointer to one of the base classes will give us the appropriate vtable.

```
Time_and_Name_Object* pObj = new Time_and_Name_Object;
// Get IUnknown
IUnknown* pUnk = (IUnknown*)pObj;
// Get IName
IName* pName = (IName*)pObj;
// Get ITime
ITime* pTime = (ITime*)pObj;
// Call interface methods
BSTR bstrName = SysAllocString(L"Richard");
pName->SetName(bstrName);
SysFreeString(bstrName);
LONG lTime;
pTime->GetTime(&lTime);
// Finished using the object
delete pObj;
```

All this is occurring within the server code. However, although the casts are valid and this code will work most of the time, you're actually very unlikely to see code like this in your server, since you're more likely to use **QueryInterface()** on an interface to get another interface, rather than casting like this. This ensures that reference counting issues and threading issues are addressed. However, you are likely to see casts like this in the implementation of **QueryInterface()** itself.

Implementing the reference counting is trivial in this case: the **Time_and_Name_Object** class has a **private** data member called **m_cRefs**, which can be used to hold the reference count. A call on **IData::AddRef()** or **ITime::AddRef()** will result in a call to **Time_and_Name_Object::AddRef()**, so the reference count for the object can easily be maintained.

Note that the reference counting, here, is applied on an object level and not an interface level. This isn't too much of a problem, but if you want to use the return from **AddRef()** and **Release()** to learn about how many clients have reference counts on a specific interface, or to free the resources for a specific interface when its reference count has dropped to zero, then this implementation clearly won't do.

In a similar vein, the single **Time_and_Name_Object** implementation for **QueryInterface()** will be called whichever interface is used. This is almost always beneficial, since it helps to ensure that COM's rules for **QueryInterface()** are not broken.

As we discussed, you can return a pointer to the desired interface by casting the **this** pointer of the object and getting the compiler to do the work:

```
HRESULT Time_and_Name_Object::QueryInterface(REFIID riid, void** ppv)
{
    *ppv = NULL;
    if (riid == IID_IName)
        *ppv = (IName*)this;
    else if (riid == IID_ITime)
        *ppv = (ITime*)this;
    else if (riid == IID_IUnknown)
        *ppv = (IName*)this;
    if (*ppv)
    {
        ((IUnknown*)*ppv)->AddRef();
        return S_OK;
    }
    else
        return E_NOINTERFACE;
}
```

This is relatively painless, but it does require the use of multiple inheritance (MI). This method is not used in MFC to implement multiple interfaces because the design of the class library means that MI can't be used.

The Active Template Library (ATL), on the other hand, uses MI in its implementation of COM and, by implication, this means that reference counting is applied on an object level and not an interface level.

Nested Classes

In this method, the vtables are provided by objects of the interface classes contained in the class object. These interface classes are derived from the abstract classes declared above, but they will need to share the same implementation of the **IUnknown** interface as the other interfaces. The simplest way to do this is to nest the class within the object class:

```
class Time_and_Name_Object : public IUnknown
{
public:
    HRESULT QueryInterface(REFIID riid, void **ppvObject);
    ULONG AddRef();
    ULONG Release();
    class XName : IName
    {
    public:
        Time_and_Name_Object* m_pParent;
```

```
        HRESULT SetName(BSTR bstrName);
        HRESULT GetName(BSTR* bstrName);
    };
    class XTime : ITime
    {
    public:
        Time_and_Name_Object* m_pParent;
        HRESULT GetTime(LONG* lTime);
    };
    XName m_name;
    XTime m_time;
};
```

The two nested classes need to delegate all calls to their **IUnknown** interfaces to the implementation in the containing class; hence each class has a pointer to the containing object. The constructor of the **Time_and_Name_Object** class should initialize the **m_pParent** member of the two contained objects to the value of its **this** pointer; the **IUnknown** functions of these objects can use this pointer to get at the parent **IUnknown** functions.

The **QueryInterface()** of the methods can be delegated to the object's implementation:

```
HRESULT Time_and_Name_Object::IName::QueryInterface( REFIID riid, void** ppv)
{
    return m_pParent->QueryInterface(riid, ppv);
}
```

and this is implemented as:

```
HRESULT Time_and_Name_Object::QueryInterface(REFIID riid, void** ppv)
{
    *ppv = NULL;
    if (riid == IID_IName)
        *ppv = (IName*)&m_name;
    else if (riid == IID_ITime)
        *ppv = (ITime*)&m_time;
    else if (riid == IID_IUnknown)
        *ppv = (IUnknown*)this;
    if (*ppv)
    {
        (IUnknown*(*ppv))->AddRef();
        return S_OK;
    }
    else
        return E_NOINTERFACE;
}
```

If the interface is for **IName** (or **ITime**), the address of the appropriate object is returned; otherwise the **this** pointer is returned.

For the reference counting methods, we have a choice. To implement reference counting on an object level, we can redirect calls from **AddRef()** and **Release()** on the **ITime** and **IName** interfaces to the object via the **m_pParent** pointer. However, because these functions are called on pointers that point to actual objects, these objects could equally well implement their own versions of these two methods. Thus we can have reference counting on an interface level.

Interface level reference counting is useful if you want to use the reference returned by these methods as debugging aids. It is also useful to allow the object to use **tear-off interfaces**. These are interfaces which contain code (and/or data) that is expensive to load and initialize; for performance reasons it may be undesirable to load the interface whenever the object is created. Instead, such an interface can be loaded only when it is actually referenced. This implies that the interface code could also be unloaded when the interface is no longer needed, which requires the interface to have its own reference count separate from the object.

> *ATL allows you to define tear-off interfaces, but because its default reference counting model uses per-object reference counting, tear-off interfaces are created in a different manner to normal interfaces.*

However, there is one big problem with tear-off interfaces: when an interface has a non-zero reference, the object is being used, and so the object server cannot be released. Thus any check made to see if the object is in use would have to check the references on all interfaces. This complicates the code.

Object Server Lifetime

There is one final issue before we move to the next section. We know that the **IUnknown** members allow us to keep a reference count on the object. An object server (in- or out-of-process), can implement one or more objects and should keep a count of all the objects currently activated. This is a job for the class factory of the objects. But what happens when the number of objects falls to zero? In this situation, the object server is allowed to remove itself from memory. So how can we do this?

The usual implementation of **Release()** is:

```
ULONG ISomeInterface::Release()
{
   m_uRef--;
   if (m_uRef == 0)
   {
      delete this;
      return 0;
   }
   return m_uRef;
}
```

This code will delete the object when the reference count becomes zero. If the **return 0** was omitted the code would still compile and, in most cases, it would execute. This is because, even after the object has been deleted, the stack frame still exists, and so the code will be able to run. However, at this point the object will have been deleted and so you cannot call any of its methods or access any data members. Returning **m_uRef** in such a situation would return some random value, and any code dependent upon the return value of **Release()** would fail.

> *This code uses the C++ decrement operator (--) to reduce the reference count. In 16-bit COM (and pre-DCOM code), this is fine, since the code is single-threaded and synchronized. However, if the object is running in one thread of a multithreaded server, and another thread also has access to the object, there could be the situation when two threads make a call to **Release()** at the same time. Since the -- operator is not atomic, one thread could be pre-empted when it is half way through the operation and so the reference count would be corrupted. We'll see how to deal with this issue in Chapter 9 on multithreading.*

Although this code will remove the C++ object from memory when the reference count reaches zero, there is no check here to determine whether the object server needs to remain in memory.

To remedy this, we can implement an object count as a global variable. This can be incremented by the **CreateInstance()** of the class factories of each of the objects, and decremented in the **Release()** method of the object when the object reference count falls to zero.

When the object is implemented as a local server, the executable can unload the server by posting a **WM_CLOSE** message to its main window. This code should be called in **Release()** when the global object count reaches zero. However, this is not the whole story, since the object class factory could have a lock on the server specifically to keep the server in memory. Thus both **Release()** *and* **LockServer()** should test the global lock count and the global object count; and if both are zero, unload the server:

```
ULONG ISomeInterface::Release()
{
   m_uRef--;
   if (m_uRef == 0)
   {
      // Going to destroy an object
      g_objcount--;
      // Next lines for out-of-process server
      if (g_objcount == 0 && g_lockcount == 0)
         PostMessage(...,WM_CLOSE,...);
      delete this;
      return 0;
   }
   return m_uRef;
}

HRESULT ObjClassFactory::LockServer(BOOL fLock)
{
   if (fLock)
      g_lockcount++;
   else
   {
      g_lockcount--;
      // Next lines for out-of-process server
      if (g_objcount == 0 && g_lockcount == 0)
         PostMessage(...,WM_CLOSE,...);
   }
   return S_OK;
}
```

If the server is in-process, in other words implemented as a DLL, we cannot unload the DLL from its own code. We need COM to do this, as described earlier in this chapter when the return value of **DllCanUnloadNow()** returns **S_OK**.

So, the implementation of the code for **Release()** and **LockServer()** is as in the EXE case, except for the checks on the global counts

```
ULONG ISomeInterface::Release()

{
   m_uRef--;
   if (m_uRef == 0)
```

```
    {
        // Going to destroy an object
        g_objcount--;
        delete this;
        return 0;
    }
    return m_uRef;
}

HRESULT ObjClassFactory::LockServer(BOOL fLock)
{
    if (fLock)
        g_lockcount++;
    else
        g_lockcount--;
    return S_OK;
}
```

The code that checks whether the server can unload goes in the **DllCanUnloadNow()** function:

```
HRESULT DllCanUnloadNow()
{
    if (g_objcount == 0 && g_lockcount == 0)
        return S_OK;
    else return S_FALSE;
}
```

Automation

When you design a COM server, you have to decide what interfaces the server will implement. If you decide to define your own interfaces, you may be restricting your object to be used just by your own clients. This is because the client will still need a header file that describes the interface, and the client will need a declaration of the IIDs.

There are two ways round this. The first solution, which is the most complete, is to use an interface that has already been defined. Microsoft have done this with many OLE interfaces which you can find in the Win32 SDK. Most of these interfaces are declared in **objidl.h**, which is created from **objidl.idl** and is included when you include **Windows.h**. The IIDs for these 'standard' interfaces are made available to a project by linking with **uuid.lib**; you'll find that, by default, Developer Studio will do this for you for a non-MFC application, and MFC links to this library via a **pragma**.

This now means that multiple vendors could create objects to do the same action and your client could choose which ever it wanted in the belief that it knows exactly how to talk to the server. The problem with this is that to cover all the possibilities would require the definition and registration of many thousands of interfaces. This is not practical.

Another solution would be for Microsoft to define a generic interface that is flexible enough for a server to use to provide all the methods that it requires, but being a Microsoft defined interface it will be widely known. Such an interface is the automation interface, **IDispatch**.

COM interfaces are strongly typed: the interface is a binding contract between the server and client. The client can ask the server if it supports an interface, but the client must know *everything* about the interface. It must know what functions the interface has, what order they are in the interface, and what parameters the functions take.

Automation interfaces (called **dispinterfaces**), on the other hand, do not have to be so well known. The client has to know about **IDispatch** and its methods, but once it knows this, the client can call the **IDispatch** methods to find out about the server: the methods it provides, their names and parameters. The server may implement one or one hundred methods and they can all be called through a single **IDispatch** method, as we'll see in a moment.

Object Description Language

ODL is yet another language used by OLE and, specifically, it is used to describe dispinterfaces. Originally, the 16-bit OLE 2.0 SDK provided a tool called **MkTypLib** to compile ODL into a type library. Today, **MIDL** will do this. **MkTypLib** was a little odd in that it was a UI-less Windows program: you had to run it directly from Program Manager (or another program like Visual C++) and not from a DOS box (which, on Windows 3.1, ran as a DOS virtual machine).

Because **MkTypLib** did not have a UI, it meant that output had to be redirected to files for later inspection. To compile the ODL for each dispinterface I was using in a project, I had to create Program Manager icons for each on my development machine that would run **MkTypLib** with the appropriate input and output file. The things we endured to use 16-bit OLE!

These days **MkTypLib** (even the 32-bit version) is no longer needed, as a dispinterface can be described in IDL, as you'll see in Chapter 5. However, to allow you to use ODL created with older tools, **MIDL** will compile ODL as well as IDL.

If you create automation objects with MFC, the Visual C++ AppWizard will create an ODL file and the ClassWizard OLE Automation tab will write data into this file. ATL, on the other hand, will allow you to create dual interfaces using IDL. (Dual interfaces are a 'better' version of **IDispatch** interfaces, as you'll see near the end of this chapter.) ATL is more suited to creating automation servers than MFC, and this is perhaps the death knell of ODL.

So **MIDL** will take ODL or IDL and compile it and create a type library. **MIDL** will also, by default, create the header files and C files needed to create a proxy-stub DLL, and the header file necessary to describe any interfaces in the file. (**MkTypLib**, as its name suggested, only created a type library.)

A word of caution here. The type library format is different for NT 4.0 and NT 3.51. **MIDL** can detect the version of the NT operating system that it is being run on and will create the appropriate format (because ultimately **MIDL** uses COM to create the library). However, although COM on NT 4.0 can read a type library generated for NT 3.51, COM on NT 3.51 will not read a type library created on NT 4.0.

There's no switch on the COM function used to create a type library to tell it the type library format to create, so there is no switch to tell **MIDL** what format to generate. A type library created on NT 4.0 can only be used on NT 4.0. If you create an ATL server, the build process will add the type library as a resource; this means that you must compile that server on the platform on which it will be used.

IDispatch

`IDispatch` looks like this in IDL.

```
interface IDispatch : IUnknown
{
    HRESULT GetTypeInfoCount([out] UINT *pctinfo);
    HRESULT GetTypeInfo([in] UINT itinfo, [in] LCID lcid,
            [out] ITypeInfo ** pptinfo);
    HRESULT GetIDsOfNames([in] REFIID riid,
            [in, size_is(cNames)] LPOLESTR *rgszNames,
            [in] UINT cNames, [in] LCID lcid,
            [in, out, size_is(cNames)] DISPID *rgdispid);
    HRESULT Invoke([in] DISPID dispidMember,
            [in] REFIID riid, [in] LCID lcid,
            [in] WORD wFlags,
            [in, unique] DISPPARAMS *pdispparams,
            [in, out, unique] VARIANT *pvarResult,
            [out] EXCEPINFO *pexcepinfo,
            [out] UINT *puArgErr);
}
```

The full details of IDL are left for Chapter 5, but even with the knowledge you have now, you should be able to get an idea about what these methods indicate.

`IDispatch` is a sort of 'gateway' interface to many more interfaces. The most important is the interface of methods that export the functionality of the server. It also gives access to interfaces that allow the server to describe what it will do. This information is called **type information**, and the binary representation is called a **type library**, which can either be bound into the server as a resource, or provided as a separate file.

`GetTypeInfoCount()` determines if the object supports type information and if it does, a client can call `GetTypeInfo()` to get a pointer to an `ITypeInfo` interface. The `ITypeInfo` interface can be used to find out what methods and properties the server supports. The client can query for the method name and parameters, get a short description of the method, and get a help file context for the method. This information is particularly useful for scripting languages like Visual Basic.

Although the type information will return the name of the function as a string, the method is invoked via its dispatch ID, which is a numeric identifier. Every method in the interface has a unique ID (and every parameter has an ID too), and the client can get the ID for a particular method by calling `GetIDsOfNames()` (this function does not require the object to support type information). Once the client knows the dispatch ID of the method, and the values of the parameters that the method takes, it can call the method through the `Invoke()` function.

To enable this to happen, the client must be able to pass many parameters of many different types. This requires the `IDispatch` interface to be very flexible. `Invoke()` passes parameters to the server, and any return values back to the client, by using **VARIANT**s. A **VARIANT** is a discriminated union that accepts a set of standard types (known as the Automation types) and pointers to these types. Since a method may take many parameters, these must be packaged together in an array. This is done by constructing and then passing a pointer to a **DISPPARAMS** structure to `Invoke()`.

This structure is defined as:

```
typedef struct  tagDISPPARAMS
{
   VARIANTARG FAR* rgvarg;
   DISPID FAR* rgdispidNamedArgs;
   unsigned int cArgs;
   unsigned int cNamedArgs;
} DISPPARAMS;
```

rgvarg and **rgdispidNamedArgs** are arrays. The first one contains **cArgs** members, and each member contains a parameter for the method. If these parameters are not named, they are inserted into the array in reverse order to which the parameters are defined in the type information. The client can, however, pass data for particular, named, parameters of the method. It does this by putting the ID of the parameters in **rgdispidNamedArgs**, and the number of items in **cNamedArgs**. The ID refers to the data in the corresponding position in **rgvarg**.

The great advantage of this is that scripting languages can send data for only some of the parameters, and it can pass the values in a different order to that defined in the type information. However, to allow generic code to be used, the **IDispatch** interface must be quite inflexible in the data types that can be sent to the server. **IDispatch** restricts the user to these particular data types:

Type	Variant Type	Description
short	VT_I2	16-bit integer
long	VT_I4	32-bit integer
boolean	VT_BOOL	Boolean
char	VT_UI1	Single char
float	VT_R4	Single precision floating point
double	VT_R8	Double precision floating point
IUnknown*	VT_UNKNOWN	**IUnknown** pointer
IDispatch*	VT_DISPATCH	**IDispatch** pointer
CY	VT_CY	Currency
DATE	VT_DATE	Date
BSTR	VT_BSTR	String
VARIANT	VT_VARIANT	Variant
NULL	VT_NULL	**NULL**
SCODE	VT_ERROR	Status Code
SAFEARRAY	VT_ARRAY	Safe Array

These types are those that can be put into a **VARIANT**. Pointers to these types are also permissible and this is done by a bitwise OR with **VT_BYREF**, but such types are only allowed in a **VARIANTARG**. The other difference between **VARIANT** and **VARIANTARG** is that a **VARIANT** can be passed by value but a **VARIANTARG** cannot.

Two of the automation types of particular interest are **BSTR** and **SAFEARRAY**.

BSTR

BSTR is defined as:

```
typedef WCHAR OLECHAR;
typedef OLECHAR __RPC_FAR *BSTR;
```

which makes it look like a pointer of type **WCHAR***. However, **BSTR**s are more than this. They are created using the COM function **SysAllocString()** and its variants, which allocate a buffer for the **WCHAR** array, and also precede the buffer with a 32-bit value that is the count of the characters in the array. So when you create a **BSTR** you get something like the following hypothetical **struct**:

```
typedef struct real_BSTR
{
   DWORD size;
   OLECHAR* buffer;   ← Pointer returned
} BSTR;
```

The **size** part is hidden from the user and is used by the COM automation data type manipulation functions. This data type looks suspiciously like the Visual Basic **String** type, which is exactly what it is.

The advantage of **BSTR**s is that, since they are transmitted with their lengths (the marshaling ensures this), the proxy/stub code can allocate the correct buffer sizes. It also means that you can embed nulls in the string, so you must be careful how you use such strings.

Because **BSTR**s are more than just an array of **WCHAR**s, you should create and destroy them by using the COM functions provided for that purpose: **SysAllocString()** and **SysFreeString()**, or a class that wraps these functions, such as **CComBSTR** (from ATL) or **CString** (from MFC). Do not create a **BSTR** any other way, since marshaling code will need the 'hidden' length.

One final point about **BSTR**s is that, on 32-bit systems, they are arrays of wide chars (Unicode). To convert them to single byte **char** strings, you'll need to call the Win32 **WideCharToMultiByte()** or an equivalent C Runtime Library function. On 16-bit systems **OLECHAR** is **typedef**ed as **char**, so no conversion is necessary.

SAFEARRAY

The other particularly interesting **VARIANT** data type is **SAFEARRAY**. This is another type with a background from Visual Basic. First let's look at the definition of the type:

```
typedef struct FARSTRUCT tagSAFEARRAY
{
   unsigned short cDims;
   unsigned short fFeatures;
#if defined(WIN32)
   unsigned long cbElements;
   unsigned long cLocks;
#else
   unsigned short cbElements;
   unsigned short cLocks;
```

```
      unsigned long handle;
#endif
   void HUGEP* pvData;
   SAFEARRAYBOUND rgsabound[1];
} SAFEARRAY;
```

There are some slight differences between the 16-bit and 32-bit versions, mainly due to the different data type sizes and how memory is allocated. In this book we'll only use Win32, since DCOM is not available on 16-bit systems.

The **SAFEARRAYBOUND** is declared as:

```
typedef struct tagSAFEARRAYBOUND
{
   unsigned long cElements;
   long lLbound;
} SAFEARRAYBOUND;
```

A **SAFEARRAY** can have one or more dimensions; this is given in **cDims**, and each dimension, **n**, can specify its size, **rgsabound[n].cElements**, and the index of the lower bound, **rgsabound[n].lLbound**. This is used in Visual Basic to declare arrays such as this 11 x 11 array:

```
Dim Values(-5 To 5, 5 To 15) as Integer
```

The **rgsabound** member has as many elements as there are dimensions (and the first element is the leftmost dimension of the array, **rgsabound[0]** is the **-5 To 5** dimension in our example). The dimension information in **rgsabound** determines how many elements there are in the array; the actual size of each element is given in **cbElements**. The actual array is held in **pvData,** which is just an untyped buffer.

When you come to implement a **SAFEARRAY** in C++, you'll see how allowing for such flexibility in VB requires some convoluted code. For example, the 11 x 11 array is declared with:

```
SAFEARRAYBOUND rgb [] = {{11, -5}, {11, 5}};
SAFEARRAY *psa = SafeArrayCreate(VT_I4, 2, rgb);
```

Several functions could be using a **SAFEARRAY** at any time, so **cLocks** exists as a reference count to make sure that the **SAFEARRAY** is only deleted when everyone has finished using it. Finally, the **fFeatures** member is mainly used to indicate how the buffer **pvData** was allocated:

Symbol	Meaning
FADF_AUTO	Array is allocated on the stack
FADF_STATIC	Array is statically allocated
FADF_EMBEDDED	Array is embedded in a structure
FADF_FIXEDSIZE	Array may not be resized or reallocated
FADF_BSTR	An array of **BSTR**s
FADF_UNKNOWN	An array of **IUnknown***

Table Continued on Following Page

Symbol	Meaning
FADF_DISPATCH	An array of **IDispatch***
FADF_VARIANT	An array of **VARIANT**s
FADF_RESERVED	Bits reserved for future use

You should only ever access the data within a **SAFEARRAY** with the COM functions provided. (These functions are all of the form **SafeArrayxxx()**, so you should be able to find them easily in the SDK documentation.) This ensures that the correct reference counting is applied. Also note that although **MIDL** will allow methods to pass **SAFEARRAY**s as parameters, to make a method compatible with Visual Basic, the method should pass a **VARIANT** whose data type is **VT_ARRAY**.

If you decide that you want to pass data to an interface method as a structure then you will find that there's no obvious way to do this in IDL. However, you can simulate a C **struct** using a **SAFEARRAY** of **VARIANT**s. In fact, this is more flexible than a **struct**, because a **VARIANT** is self-describing.

Data Type Coercion

Interpreted languages like VBA use very loose typing of parameters. After all, to a VB programmer, if you're using an integer as an index in a loop, it hardly matters whether the integer is 16- or 32-bit or whether it's signed or unsigned. The language will change the type of the variable to the type that it requires. Moreover, Visual Basic allows variables to be used without first declaring them, and the language has no idea, other than the context in which the variable is used, as to what type to use. In this situation, it will make the variable a **VARIANT** type.

However, as we've seen above, there are variants and there are variants. The **VARIANT** data type is a discriminated union; the actual type of the data is held in the structure. It may be necessary to be able to convert between the possible **VARIANT** data types. This is done using the data coercion function, **VariantChangeType()**.

The method is quite straightforward. Initialize a **VARIANTARG** with **VariantInit()** and then fill it with the appropriate data. Take this **VARIANTARG** and pass a pointer to it to **VariantChangeType()** along with a pointer to another **VARIANTARG** that will accept the result. Another parameter specifies the type to convert to.

Data coercion is useful if the interface is being used with mixed language code modules. If you are writing both your clients and servers in C++, you'll rarely see these COM functions.

Late and Early Binding

When clients call automation servers, they do so in one of two ways. The client can query the server as to what it can do; if the client finds what it wants, it can then query for the **DISPID** of the method and parameters with calls to **GetIDsOfNames()**. Further calls to the type information can then be used to get information about the number and types of the method, so as to construct the **DISPARAMS** parameter to send to **Invoke()**. This has total flexibility, but suffers badly in performance, since it involves so many calls to the server. This method is called **late binding**.

There is another way to do this: if the client knows in advance what the server can do, it can hard-code the dispatch IDs of the methods that it will use, and then use non-generic code to construct the

DISPARAMS to be passed to the **Invoke()** function. This is known as **early binding**, since the decision has been made by the programmer about which method to call. It has the advantage that it is reasonably fast, but it does lack flexibility. It may seem to be quite an effort to hard-code parameters (and hence removing any options) into what is meant to be a flexible method of calling functions.

It may seem even stranger to do this when calling the method is slower than calling it via a vtable. However, one major advantage of this method is that no marshaling code needs to be generated, because the proxy and stub code for **IDispatch** already exists.

Note that calling methods directly on a standard COM or dual interface is sometimes known as **vtable binding** or **very early binding**. All three forms of binding are supported by Visual Basic.

Using Automation

Writing dispinterfaces, and calling methods on them, is a pain if you do it in C or C++ and use the dispatch interfaces directly. For example, writing an **IDispatch** interface requires writing quite a lot of code: you have to map names to dispatch IDs for all the methods in the dispatch interface and all their parameters (**GetIDsOfNames()**), and you have to implement a function to dispatch method invocation to the actual method code (**Invoke()**). However, there are ways to make this easier.

For a start, the COM library has a function called **CreateStdDispatch()** that, from a pointer to an object and a pointer to a type library, will create a standard implementation of a dispatch interface. However, it will only support certain default error codes and it will allow the dispinterface to use only one locale (Automation allows you to have different names for the methods depending on the language of the country where the code is called; the same code is called because it is called using the dispatch ID: it's just the mapping of strings to **DISPID**s that is different).

Calling methods on a dispinterface is also a pain, because once the **IDispatch** interface has been obtained, we must get the **DISPID** of the method and then create a **DISPPARAMS** array with all the parameters to pass to the method. Once the function is called, and it is successful, we then need to get any returned data out of the **DISPPARAMS** array and free any previously allocated memory. Remember that with other COM interfaces, the proxy/stub code does this for you, but to get the additional flexibility of the dispatch interface, you have to endure this tedium yourself.

The easy way to implement and use dispinterfaces in C++ is to use MFC. If you're creating an automation server, the Visual C++ ClassWizard allows you to add dispatch methods (and properties) to a **CCmdTarget**-derived object. ClassWizard will alter the ODL file (which will be compiled into a type library in the build process) and will put stub code in the class for you to fill with the actual method code. Calling a dispinterface is even easier, since the ClassWizard allows you to specify a type library and, from this information, it will generate a **COleDispatchDriver**-derived class with member functions for each dispatch method. You just call the member function to call the method on the dispinterface.

Dual Interfaces

As outlined above, a dispinterface can be used to provide early or late binding to objects. Which is used depends upon how much information you know, as the client programmer, about the dispatch interface; it also depends upon whether you will acknowledge that the dispatch interface may change.

Early binding, by hardcoding **DISPID**s and constructing **DISPARAMS** parameters, gains over late binding in terms of speed, but is nowhere near the performance of vtable binding (calling COM interface methods directly)particularly with in-process scenarios. Dual interfaces were created to overcome this problem. A dual interface combines a user-defined COM interface with a dispatch interface. Scripting languages (and others that require late binding) can use the dispatch interface and the type information. However, the server will also export the automation methods as functions in a COM interface, giving direct access to these functions to clients that want the best performance.

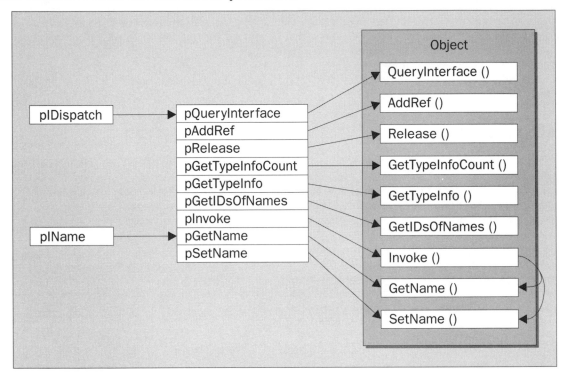

In this picture, we have a hypothetical dispinterface that has two methods, **GetName()** and **SetName()**. A client can either **QueryInterface()** for the **IDispatch** interface and then call these methods though the **Invoke()** method, or it could **QueryInterface()** for the **IName** interface and call them directly. The *dual* dispinterface behaves both like a custom interface and an **IDispatch** interface.

But hold on. If you create a custom interface, don't you also have to create the proxy-stub pairs so that out-of-process clients and servers can talk to each other? Yes. But the proxy-stub marshaling objects have already been written for the Microsoft-defined interfaces, and **IDipatch** is one such interface. The methods called using **Invoke()** have to pass particular data types for the **IDispatch** proxy and stub to handle the method calls. Since the methods in the vtable part of the dual interface are clones of the **Invoke**able methods, they must conform to these same rules, so the **IDispatch** proxy-stubs can be used on them too. This does away with any need for **MIDL** to be invoked to create proxy-stubs.

Interface Marshaling

By now you should be familiar with marshaling, which is the packaging of data that is carried out by proxy and stub code so that it can be sent cross-process via some communications mechanism. However, in the previous discussion, I was a little vague on how the code was actually used. For example, what decides the communications mechanism to be used, what is it that actually loads the proxy and stub? We know that the client calls the proxy code, thinking that it is the object that it needs, but what calls the stub code?

All these questions will be answered in this section, where we look into the marshaling process in a little more depth.

When you define your own interfaces, you first need to ask the same question that you should ask yourself whenever you write a new piece of code: 'Do I really need to do this?'. The question is important, because if the interface is to be used on an out-of-process object then you'll need to create proxy and stub DLLs. If you choose to use standard marshaling, you use **MIDL** which generates the code for you. However, if you choose to use custom marshaling, you need to write extra code. Microsoft has defined many interfaces to do most of the actions that you'll need, and for every interface, marshaling code exists.

Think a little about the work that occurs during the marshaling process. When a method is called on an inproc server, the call is just like any call on a function in your process or a DLL loaded by your process. The only complicating factor is that an interface pointer is used, so we have an extra level of indirection (but unlike dynamically loading a DLL and using its functions, in COM you don't have to call **GetProcAddress()**).

So you call a function and the C/C++ compiler creates a stack frame for the call, putting on it things like the return address within the calling function. Significantly, it also pushes the function parameters on to the stack. The called function pops off these parameters, does its work, and then pushes any return value back on to the stack and returns. The return address is now used to return to the calling function and the return value popped off the stack (somewhere in this process a certain amount of cleaning up of the stack occurs, but this is unimportant here).

Somehow the object, sitting in one address space, will have calls on its methods that came from another address space. So, if your object will be called across a process boundary, marshaling will always be used (and, as you'll see in Chapter 9, there are many cases where the object is called across a *thread* boundary and marshaling is used).

What do you have to do to provide marshaling? Well, probably not much. There are three ways you can marshal an interface: standard marshaling; custom marshaling; and type library marshaling.

Standard

Once you're determined to write your own interface, you need to write IDL for that interface. Here is the IDL for the **IName** interface:

```
interface IName : IUnknown
{
    import "unknwn.idl";
    HRESULT SetName([in] BSTR bstrName);
    HRESULT GetName([out] BSTR* bstrName);
}
```

This is compiled with the **MIDL** compiler, as we've already seen. However, in addition to the C header files that prototype the interface, this tool also generates C code to create the proxy and stub code in a DLL. From the **IName.idl** file, **MIDL** produces the following files:

IName.h	Header file for the interface definitions
IName_i.c	Definitions of the IID constant for the interface
IName_p.c	Proxy and stub code
DLLData.c	DLL entry points for the proxy and stub.

IName.h is included in the server implementation files and in any client files that will use the interface. The **IName_I.c** contains constants for the interface IIDs and the object CLSID. The other files are used to create the proxy-stub DLL. All we need to do is compile these C files, which will create a DLL to marshal the method calls to an object implementing this interface.

To use this DLL as the marshaler, it has to be registered. The **MIDL**-generated files export the **DllRegisterServer()** and **DllUnregisterServer()** functions, so you can use **RegSvr32** (provided with Developer Studio) to register the proxy-stub DLL. **RegSvr32** calls **DllRegisterServer()**, which adds an entry to the **Interface** key of **HKEY_CLASSES_ROOT** for the interface IID and, in this key, adds a key called **ProxyStubClsid32**. The default value of this key has the CLSID of the proxy and stub objects defined in the DLL that perform the marshaling.

Standard marshaling uses the code generated by **MIDL**. The advantage of standard marshaling is that the programmer just has to write an IDL and compile it with **MIDL**, and let the IDL compiler handle the marshaling. To create the proxy-stub DLL, the programmer just has to compile the **MIDL**-generated files and link with **Rpcrt4.lib**. The programmer does have to register the proxy-stub, but as outlined above, this is quite straightforward.

TypeLib

This type of marshaling uses the Automation (**IDispatch**) marshaler. The advantages here are that the programmer doesn't have to create a proxy-stub DLL, as with standard marshaling, since every system that has NT 4.0 or Windows 95 already has such a DLL for the **IDispatch** interface.

The marshaling process takes method parameters and packages them up for transmission. Standard and custom marshaling have code that is specific to a particular interface. Type library marshaling, however, uses a generic marshaler. For this marshaler to be able to package a method call, it has to know what types the parameters are, and this is where the type library comes in: it is used to describe the interface so that the marshaler knows how to package the parameters.

Again the process is fairly painless, although the one main restriction is that TypeLib marshaling restricts the programmer to the data types permitted by Automation (i.e. the types that can be put in a **VARIANT**).

Although the term may be new to you, the effects are ubiquitous. VB and J++ code can call any interface as long as it is described by a type library. This is a powerful example of how important type library marshaling is. Of course, there is a slight performance hit, because the marshaler must consult the type library. However, the great flexibility of this method means that more and more interfaces will use it.

Custom

This allows for complete flexibility. Custom marshaling allows the object to determine how the data packets are formed. The first requirement of custom marshaling is that the object supports the **IMarshal** interface:

```
interface IMarshal : IUnknown
{
   HRESULT GetUnmarshalClass([in] REFIID riid,
                [in, unique] void* pv,
                [in] DWORD dwDestContext,
                [in, unique] void* pvDestContext,
                [in] DWORD mshlflags,
                [out] CLSID* pCid);
```

```
        HRESULT GetMarshalSizeMax([in] REFIID riid,
                       [in, unique] void* pv,
                       [in] DWORD dwDestContext,
                       [in, unique] void* pvDestContext,
                       [in] DWORD mshlflags,
                       [out] DWORD* pSize);
        HRESULT MarshalInterface([in, unique] IStream* pStm,
                       [in] REFIID riid,
                       [in, unique] void* pv,
                       [in] DWORD dwDestContext,
                       [in, unique] void* pvDestContext,
                       [in] DWORD mshlflags);
        HRESULT UnmarshalInterface(
                       [in, unique] IStream* pStm,
                       [in] REFIID riid,
                       [out] void** ppv);
        HRESULT ReleaseMarshalData([in, unique] IStream* pStm);
        HRESULT DisconnectObject([in] DWORD dwReserved);
    }
```

The great advantage of using **IMarshal** is that you can use whatever inter-process communications method you wish. Standard marshaling uses Microsoft RPC to send the marshaled packets to the stub, but through custom marshaling, you can choose to use another marshaling mechanism, named pipes, raw TCP/IP streams or datagrams, or you can even go on top of another protocol like HTTP.

Every object has a chance to use custom marshaling. When an object is first created (by a call to **CoGetClassObject()**), COM will always **QueryInterface()** for **IMarshal**. If your object does not support this interface, COM will use standard marshaling instead (and thus look for a **ProxyStubClsid32** entry as described above). If the object supports custom marshaling, it does not necessarily call your custom marshaler; rather, the choice of marshaler is made at runtime on an interface-by-interface basis, and so the object can decide to marshal one interface with a custom marshaler and another with the standard marshaler. The only restriction is that once a marshaler is chosen for a particular interface, it remains for the object lifetime.

The actual marshaling occurs with a call to **CoMarshalInterface()**:

```
    STDAPI CoMarshalInterface(IStream *pStm, REFIID riid, IUnknown *pUnk,
                    DWORD dwDestContext, void *pvDestContext, DWORD mshlflags);
```

The **riid** is the IID of the interface that is to be marshaled, which is passed in **pUnk**. The other parameters determine the context of the marshaling and how the marshaling is to occur. The stream parameter is used to pass the data of the marshaling process.

The first part of the process is a call to **CoGetStandardMarshal()**, which is called by COM as part of the object creation process and creates the stub side of the call. This stub has an identifier, and this is put in the stream to enable the client to identify the stub that it will connect to. Then the function call results in a call to the object's **QueryInterface()** for an **IMarshal** interface. If the object returns a valid pointer, the caller calls **IMarshal::GetUnmarshalClass()**, which returns the CLSID of the proxy. This CLSID is then written to the stream and the interface is marshaled by calling **IMarshal::MarshalInterface()**.

The marshaled packet, represented by the **pStm** parameter, is unmarshaled in the proxy with a call to **CoUnmarshalInterface()**:

```
STDAPI CoUnmarshalInterface(IStream* pStm, REFIID riid, void** ppv);
```

Here the marshaling packet is the **pStm** parameter, and the **riid** parameter determines the interface to be returned in the **ppv** parameter. The stream contains the CLSID of the proxy to be used, so that the client can call **CoCreateInstance()** to obtain the proxy. The remainder of the stream has the stub identifier that is used in subsequent calls.

Monikers

A moniker is a name. In COM, a moniker is an intelligent name and, as such, monikers are described by an interface. There are several types of moniker that can be implemented (memory and file monikers are the two most popular). In this chapter, we'll just cover two aspects of monikers.

Persistent State

OK, you know that you can create an object and that object can have some internal state. From the introduction, you also know that the internal state can be saved in a fashion that allows the object to be de-activated and activated later using that saved state. So how is this done?

If the object is embedded in a compound document, the internal state is saved into a storage that is part of the compound document's structured storage. Activating an embedded object requires launching the object server, passing it the dumped state, and saying 'create me an object from this'. But what happens if the object is linked into the compound document?

In this case, information is saved that allows the client to obtain the internal state of the object at some later stage. However, that state may not be saved in its own dedicated file. It could be a field in a database, or it could be just part of a larger file. So to help find the raw data, COM uses another object, a moniker object, to find the object and then re-activate the object from this raw data. The compound document has data that allows the moniker to find this raw data, and the moniker does the hard work of activating the object.

The process of finding the object server, launching it and loading the appropriate data into it to activate an object, is called **binding**. Monikers know how to bind to objects. All monikers look the same to a container, so it doesn't matter what type of moniker is used to store a link in a compound document: the container just tells the moniker to bind to the object.

An application can call **CreateFileMoniker()** to create a moniker based upon an object in a file (e.g. an Excel spreadsheet). This can then be activated with a call to **BindMoniker()**. This function is a wrapper function to a call on the moniker's **BindToObject()** method. This method requires a bind context, which is provided as part of the wrapper. The bind context is used to store information about the binding process specific to this moniker.

Monikers are useful for holding information for inactive objects that are held in some persistent state. They are also good for identifying a running object stored in some temporary storage.

Running Object Table

Such a temporary storage is the **Running Object Table** (**ROT**). There is only one ROT on every machine, but when you query the ROT for the current objects, it will filter out the objects that aren't relevant to your **Window Station**. The effect of this filtering is that running objects put in the ROT by one user are not accessible by another user logged on to the same machine.

Window Stations are security objects that NT creates to separate the UI objects accessible by one logged on user from those accessible to another logged on user. They are covered in greater depth in Chapter 7.

Why would you use the ROT? Well, many objects add themselves to the ROT when they are created. This is so that a potential client can get access to a particular object quickly. It is also useful as a temporary method of persisting an object. For example, one project with which I was involved distributed functionality via an HTTP server. This allowed COM objects to be executed on the server machine, but since HTTP is a connectionless protocol, it meant that any COM objects created from one call would have to be released when the call finished. The solution was to put the COM object into the ROT, using a moniker that was used as a 'cookie' on the web page.

Of course, we couldn't guarantee that the client would call back again, and so we had to implement a mechanism for the running object to time out, but that's another story....

COM and Object Orientation

There have been many heated arguments on the Usenet newsgroups about whether COM is object oriented or not. The discussions involved some quite heavy-weight names in the distributed objects world, and some classic object orientation texts were quoted *ad nauseam*. However, as always in such discussions, the bottom line of the argument always returned to something along the lines of "COM is not OO, so it sucks. CORBA is OO, so it reigns supreme" (from one side -you guess who); and "COM implements enough of the OO paradigm" from the other.

I am not an OO academic, so far be it for me to give an in-depth discussion of object orientation. After all, as pragmatists you want to know what COM can do, not whether it conforms to some idealized object model created by an academic in his ivory tower. So, in this section, we'll go through the general features of object orientation and see how COM does (or doesn't) support them. If you want a long and detailed description of operating systems that follow OO to the letter, I suggest you find your local CORBA fanatic and whisper the single word 'COM' in their ear. That fanatic will suddenly spring into life and give you the stock monologue. You can finish the argument at any stage by comparing the number of computers that use CORBA to those that use COM!

Below, I will go through some of the common terms used to characterize object orientation. These are encapsulation, polymorphism and re-use. Typically, inheritance is mentioned instead of re-use, but inheritance (particularly implementation inheritance) is just one method of re-use. It is this point that seems to cause the most argument, but the bottom line is that re-use will save your company money and, to a certain extent, it is irrelevant if that re-use is achieved through subclassing a Windows control or deriving a C++ class. Both methods re-use some code that does not have to be re-written and re-tested.

This does bring out another point. COM's idea of re-use is from the binary perspective and not from a language perspective. You can reuse a COM object through aggregation or containment, and it does not matter if the object was written with C, C++, Delphi, Java or VB. You can contrast this to the approach that DSOM takes: although you can derive from a DSOM object, you must use the same language.

So, without getting too academic about it, let's look at a few object orientation issues and see how COM handles them.

Objects

There are many definitions of what an object is, especially in the realm of computers. Every language and technology has its own definition. One common theme is that an object has **attributes** and **methods**. Attributes represent the state or the data of the object, and methods are what the object can do.

COM objects fit this specification. COM objects have interfaces of methods, which the client can call. These methods affect the data of the object. For example, one item of data that all COM objects should have is a reference count, and calling **AddRef()** and **Release()** will affect this data. This is an example of the principle of abstraction, where the user is insulated from the underlying data model.

Classes

Generally, in object orientation we talk about **classes**. A class is a type and an object is an instance of that type. In COM, we also have the idea of a class. A class is a particular implementation of several interfaces. A class is unique, and to prove it, every class has a unique CLSID.

Two classes may support the same interfaces. For example, two automation servers, without dual interfaces, will support **IUnknown** and **IDispatch**. However, the automation methods provided, and hence the implementation of **IDispatch**, will be totally different for the two. If the implementation is different, they are different classes.

This is quite an important aspect of COM and shows an example of polymorphism: by having the same interface, but a different implementation, a single client can access a variety of functionality. For example, the widespread use of the **IDispatch** interface allows VBA clients to use a huge range of objects.

Encapsulation

Encapsulation is where the attributes of an object are totally hidden from the users of the object. This is enforced by COM, because COM objects can only export methods. These methods may give direct access to the data of the object, but the client does not know this, since all the client knows is that it is calling another method.

Inheritance

Inheritance comes in many flavors and the two that we'll look at here are interface inheritance and implementation inheritance. Inheritance is a mechanism for specifying a relationship between two classes.

Interface Inheritance

Interface inheritance means that a class or interface inherits a specification, but not an implementation. COM supports interface inheritance, as you can see from the following IDL code:

```
interface IDispatch : IUnknown
{
    ...
}
```

IDispatch inherits the **IUnknown** interface, so it must support **QueryInterface()**, **AddRef()** and **Release()**. How these methods are implemented will depend upon the class that implements **IDispatch**.

Implementation Inheritance

Implementation inheritance means that one class can inherit the implementation of a particular function or interface from another class. The problem here is that to inherit the implementation, there must be some access to the inherited class' data from the base class. COM does not allow this.

However, implementation inheritance is really a code re-use issue. It's unlikely that programmers want to use implementation inheritance because they have a religious attachment to it: they just want a method whereby they can re-use the implementation of an existing COM class. COM offers two ways to do this:

Containment/Delegation

In containment, a COM object activates another object and provides functionality by calling the contained object's methods. The outside user, the client, does not know that the object is using another object to provide its functionality. The contained object is created in the usual way, but is isolated from the outside world.

Aggregation

This method presents interfaces of the aggregated object as interfaces of the aggregating object. When the client accesses the interfaces of the aggregated object, the use is direct, so there are speed advantages to using aggregation. However, any calls on the aggregated object's **IUnknown** methods must have knowledge of the aggregator's **IUnknown** methods, and this means that objects must be written in such a way as to allow them to be aggregated. Aggregation is currently only supported for in-process servers.

Polymorphism

Put simply, polymorphism means that, to a particular client, objects of different classes all look the same. COM's usage of interfaces guarantees this. For example, if a client can talk to an **IDispatch** interface, it knows what that interface can do and so it can talk to *any* object that implements that interface.

So is COM object orientated? Well, it doesn't support implementation inheritance, so I guess it has failed there, but in all other respects it is object orientated; besides, the end result of OO is achieved with COM just as well as with other OO techniques.

Summary

In this chapter, we've covered a lot of ground: in just a few pages, I have attempted to summarize what has become the most widespread object technology. The rest of this book is devoted to the distribution of COM over networks and to the advanced features of COM relevant to distributed applications.

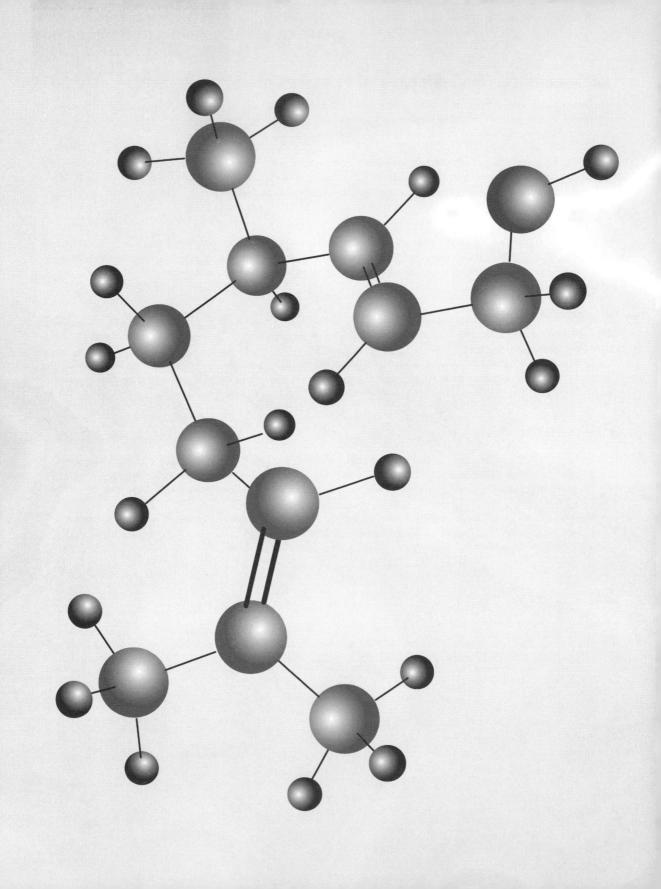

Distributed Component Object Model

We've looked at COM and seen some of the things that it can do. We have seen how it allows you to define objects that export functionality in groups of associated methods called interfaces, and we've looked at how these interfaces are defined and used. We've also mentioned that COM objects can be mapped into the memory space of the calling process, or exist in a totally different address space. Before DCOM, this meant that the object was in a server process on the same machine as the client; DCOM allows the object to be on a totally different machine.

So what do you need to do to make your existing object a DCOM object? Well the short answer is very little, since DCOM is just COM, and any COM object or client can be used with DCOM without the need for recompilation.

However, the long answer is that DCOM introduces a number of new issues that your objects need to deal with, which go along with the new facilities of which you can take advantage. If you want to make your client-object interactions efficient and secure then you do need to write some extra code. We'll look at precisely what you need to do throughout the rest of this book.

What is DCOM?

DCOM and DCE

In the first chapter, I mentioned the Open Software Foundation's Distributed Computing Environment in terms of RPC (Remote Procedure Calls). I dismissed DCE for distributed objects for the simple reason that the DCE spec has little support for objects: DCE is very much a method to remote C functions.

Although DCE RPC does not provide support for objects, it can be used as the underlying mechanism for distributing objects. On Windows and Solaris, DCOM basically sits on Microsoft RPC, which is a compliant implementation of DCE RPC. The Open Group is currently developing DCOM to run on top of true DCE RPC for other platforms, particularly DEC Unix. This means that features of DCE, if not already in DCOM, will appear at some time. Such features include DCE security (Kerberos) and DCE authentication. If you read through the DCOM specification you'll see how apparent its DCE pedigree is. DCOM is effectively Microsoft RPC version 2, even to the point of the names of the structures used: the main structure in a DCOM packet is called an ORPC, for **O**bject **RPC**.

As for COM object orientation, DCE RPC adapts well to it. Both COM and RPC associate methods together as interfaces. Each interface can be described with IDL and identified by a UUID. This gives us a language-independent way to define interfaces, and a method of accessing those interfaces as well as providing versioning. Objects, of course, associate instance data with their methods. In C, you can associate data with methods by passing every function a pointer to the instance data (in C++, the pointer is called the **this** pointer and the compiler does all the work). With DCE, a context handle can be used and passed as a parameter to every interface method.

COM, unlike CORBA, is not complicated by the semantics of implementation inheritance, so there are no problems with this approach. Indeed, DCOM handles multiple instances of objects well, marking each with (yet another) ID, called a causality ID, as you'll see in Chapter 6.

DCOM on Windows

DCOM is currently available for both Windows NT 4.0 and Windows 95. However, to get the most out of DCOM, you're going to need more than just the basic packages. Although NT 4.0 (Workstation and Server) shipped with DCOM in the box, Service Pack 2 for NT 4.0 saw a number of new features added. The most important of these are the support for launching an object under the guest account (a facility that you'll appreciate in Chapter 7) and the support for launching DLL-based objects remotely via a surrogate (which will be explained more fully later in the chapter). You can download NT Service Packs from Microsoft's web site or find them on the MSDN (Microsoft Developer Network) CDs if you're a subscriber.

DCOM for Windows 95 was first released in January of 1997 as a free download from Microsoft's web site. DCOM for Windows 95 is more limited than its relative on Windows NT. Although it allows both DCOM clients and servers to run on Windows 95, it doesn't allow automatic launching of DCOM servers running on Windows 95.

This is because Microsoft has taken the attitude (quite rightly) that if your client wants to launch a server on an other machine, the client must have the right authority, but once the server has been launched, the server can enforce security checks on any client. Windows 95 has no intrinsic security, so the system cannot test a user for its security context; however, once launched a server program could make network calls to an NT security authority to authenticate a user, or even provide its own custom security checks.

DCOM is also, or will shortly be, available on a number of other platforms.

How Does DCOM Work?

DCOM has been widely described as COM with a longer wire. This means that it offers implementation transparency: it should not matter, in terms of your client and server code, whether the object is on the same machine as the client or across the network. In fact, this is true for largely trivial cases, but as you'll see through the rest of this book, life isn't always that simple. The major effort comes when you have to deal with security, as you'll see in Chapter 7.

In the previous chapter, we saw that when interfaces are accessed across process boundaries, the method calls are handled via objects called proxies and stubs. The following picture shows how this looks on a network.

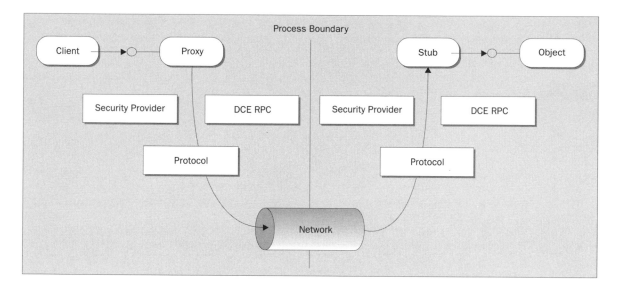

Here we have a client in one process space accessing an interface on an object in another process space. When the client activates the object, COM loads the proxy in the client's address space and a stub object in the object's address space. The proxy talks to the stub, marshaling the method calls across the network.

Protocols

The method calls are made over RPC, and the protocol used is the one used by the RPC mechanism. You can view the available protocols by looking at the registry key **HKEY_LOCAL_MACHINE\SOFTWARE\Microsoft\Rpc**. There, you'll find the named value **DCOM Protocols**, which lists the protocols available to DCOM. My NT machine lists these:

Value	Description
ncadg_ip_udp	UDP/IP connectionless protocol
ncacn_ip_tcp	TCP/IP connection-based protocol
ncacn_nb_nb	Connection-based NetBIOS over NetBEUI
ncacn_nb_tcp	Connection-based NetBIOS over TCP
ncacn_np	Connection-based over named pipes

COM chooses which protocol to use based on the order in this registry value. The first value (on NT) is usually **ncadg_ip_udp**, which specifies that DCOM will use UDP to talk between objects. Raw UDP is defined as connectionless and doesn't guarantee packets ordering or even arrival at their destination. However, the DCOM runtime adds functionality to UDP to guarantee the delivery of packets, and the pinging mechanism (described below) overcomes any problems with a connectionless protocol. You are free to change the **DCOM Protocols** value to suggest to DCOM to choose another protocol, but it is worth pointing out here that Windows 95 (as the poor cousin of NT) only uses TCP.

Although DCOM runs over RPC, the programmer doesn't have to worry about RPC or DCE when writing DCOM applications. The only DCE aspect that the programmer will see is IDL. A COM programmer should be familiar with IDL anyway, so this isn't really extra knowledge required to use DCOM. We'll cover IDL in detail in the next chapter.

Object Lifetimes

When a client creates an object it has a conceptual connection to that object. If the object is inproc, the connection is more than a concept, it is real: the interface pointer that the client holds on the object interface is a pointer to code in its own address space. In this situation, when the client finishes and is unloaded, so is the object. If the object is out of process on the local machine or on a remote machine, the connection is not so straightforward.

In the out-of-process cases, it is the proxy and stub objects that are the key to the connection between the client and object. A proxy in the address space of one process refers to a specific stub in another address space, so the client remains 'connected' to the specific object. (Although the two processes are conceptually connected, the underlying wire protocol used could be connectionless, like UDP. It's up to DCOM to maintain the semblance of a connection.)

Reference Counting

We've already seen how important reference counting is to standard COM objects as it allows them to manage their own lifetimes. Reference counting is no less important when we consider DCOM in a networked environment. However, there are some interesting differences introduced by DCOM in this area, the most important of which is the concept of local and remote reference counts. Here the terms 'local' and 'remote' are relative to the location of a client.

The local reference count of an object is increased whenever a client calls **QueryInterface()** or **AddRef()** on an object's interface (via the proxy, of course). The remote reference count is increased when an object's **QueryInterface()** or **AddRef()** are called (via the stub). Although it may seem that the local and remote reference counts should be the same, they don't have to be. In fact, a single remote reference count can be used to service multiple local ones.

The distinction between local and remote reference counts leads to the ability to optimize the amount of calls across the network. This is apparent when you consider the way DCOM caches calls to **Release()**. When the client has finished using an interface, it calls **Release()** on that interface. However, DCOM does not immediately call **Release()** on the remote object. The proxy caches the calls to **Release()** and it is only when all interfaces on this object held by this client have been released that a single **Release()** will be made across the network. This call indicates to COM on the server machine that the client on this particular machine has finished with the object, and so the remote COM stub will make all the necessary local calls to **Release()** to match all the **AddRef()**s from this client.

Although this means that interface reference counts are kept artificially high for longer than they would be in the local case, there are few repercussions, since all object usage is tracked and the correct reference handling is maintained. However, caching reference counts like this does mean that reference counting is effectively applied on a per-object basis rather than a per-interface basis; but, as we mentioned in the last chapter, for most interfaces that you write with ATL, reference counting will be per-object anyway.

Pinging

If the object server dies, the client must get some indication that this has occurred and it must be able to adapt to this condition. Conversely, if the client dies without releasing the object, and hence the connection has not been officially broken, the object could remain running on the server indefinitely. The action for the first case is quite easy: the client can call an object method and if the proxy fails to get a reply, the object must be dead. If this happens, your method call will return one of the **RPC_** status codes, usually **RPC_S_UNKNOWN_IF** (**0x800706b5**). Remember that, when you are checking for this in **Winerror.h**, the facility is **7,** so you should look for the decimal of **0x6b5** (i.e. message **1717**). Alternatively, you can use the error lookup tool provided with Visual C++ 5. The real problem is on the server-side, where the server must determine if the clients are still active.

If the server is in-proc and dies, your application will know about this immediately (most likely you'll get an exception, which will be caught by your application's exception handling). If the server is a local server (on the same machine) or a remote server, it is not the client that is connected to the object, but the stub. The stub manages the connection to the proxy in the client's address space. If the client dies, so does the proxy. The stub, therefore, must be able to know when this happens.

The mechanism to do this is called **pinging**. Pinging is a well-established method in other areas of networking, whereby a process sends a small packet of data (a **ping**) to another process to indicate that it is alive, and the receiving process replies to the ping to indicate this it is also alive (a **pong**). The ping is continually repeated with a predetermined interval. Since the ping is a small amount of data, it can be argued that it is not much of a demand on the network.

If the ping originator finds that it does not get a reply to the ping then this may not necessarily mean that the other process is dead. Network capacity may vary between pings, so the absence of one ping reply may simply indicate that the network is overloaded, delaying the packet. For this reason, several unsuccessful pings must be sent (or several ping intervals must elapse) before it can be assumed that the process at the end of the connection has died.

The following picture shows a hypothetical ping mechanism:

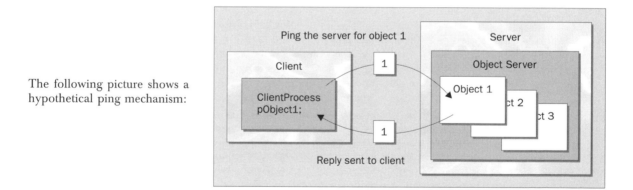

Here, a client process on one machine obtains a pointer to an object on another machine. To check that the object is alive (and to indicate that it is alive), the client can periodically ping the server with the ID of the object that it requires. If you were to write a client and server using raw TCP/IP, you would have to implement such a mechanism.

Such a mechanism would work like this: first the process would need to create a separate pinging thread and this would use some inter-thread communication method to tell the thread that uses the object when the ping fails and therefore the object is assumed to have died. On the server end, there must be some mechanism that measures the time between pings. If several ping periods have elapsed without a ping, it can assume that the connection to the client has been broken and hence decrement the appropriate object reference count.

This sounds like quite a bit of work, but it gets worse. If there were several client processes using the object, the pinging mechanism could get quite complicated:

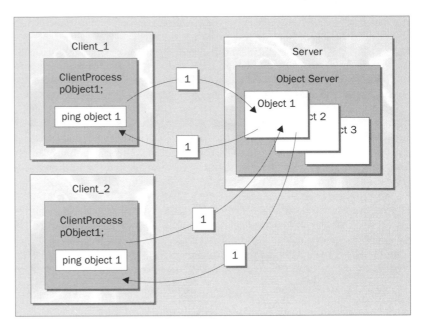

Now the object would have to reply to both clients. Similarly, if the client process had references to several objects, it would have to ping every object. This is obviously something that should be carried out by the RPC mechanism, and thankfully it is, freeing you from the task of implementing this in your client and server.

The ping mechanism is essentially between the proxy and stub, and it's generated by the RPC runtime, so the client and server code need know nothing about pings. By getting the system to generate the pings, a further optimization on the hypothetical ping mechanism can be carried out. The system can group together pings and send them off on a machine-by-machine basis. So if a client has proxies to objects **1** and **2,** then after each ping period, a ping packet containing the IDs of objects **1** and **2** is sent to the server.

Now, if pings were generated for every object in this way, this could potentially mean a large amount of data sent between the client and server just to confirm that the connection still exists. Imagine the case of many object references on a client machine to objects that are relatively stable, accessed over a reliable network. Passing such large ping packets is unnecessary, so DCOM uses a concept called **delta-pinging**.

Delta-Pinging

In this situation, DCOM finds out the objects that the client wishes to ping and creates a **ping-set** with a unique ID. It then tells the server about this ping set and, whenever it needs to send a ping, it just sends the ID of the ping-set. If an object gets released, or a process on the client machine activates an object on the server machine, DCOM handles this by adding to the ping any changes in the ping-set.

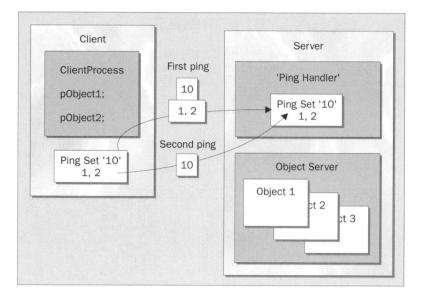

Here, ping-set '**10**' refers to objects **1** and **2** on the server. The first time this ping set is used, it carries the ping-set ID and the IDs of the objects that it contains; on subsequent pings this is unnecessary, so just the ping-set ID is sent. This mechanism is on a per-computer basis, with delta-pings from one client PC being sent to all the server PCs that the processes on the client PC has references to. As a further optimization, the delta pings are 'piggy-backed' on to other DCOM packets between the client and server PC. If the client PC is idle (making no calls to the server), but still has references to remote objects, DCOM will create ping packets every 2 minutes.

The ping handler is a DCE object called the **OXID Resolver** that runs on the server. This object is in the front line. It resolves the **object exporter IDs** (**OXID**) that are used to identify objects on a machine, to provide the bindings to the object that they refer to. The OXID Resolver exports its functionality via a DCE RPC interface, and *not* a COM interface (which makes sense since it is the mapping between RPC calls and the object stub). You will see OXIDs mentioned again in Chapter 6, where the DCOM packets sent between the client and server are investigated.

The DCOM runtime decides when it should release the object. If it does not receive pings from the client over a predetermined number of ping periods, it will assume that the client is dead. At present, this is fixed at a ping period of 2 minutes and a timeout of three ping periods. The object exporter interface does have a method that can change this period, but it is not exposed to the user. When DCOM believes that a client has died, it will go through the objects in the client machine's ping set and if this client holds the only references on an object, DCOM will release it. If there are references held on the object by another client then DCOM will do nothing. This means that if, at a later stage, the first client recovers (perhaps someone replaced the network cable that was causing the problem in the first place) then the client will be in the same situation as before.

Configuring Legacy Components

In the introduction, I said that you did not need to change the code of a client or server to allow it to make use of DCOM. This is certainly true, and it has been allowed specifically to enable legacy applications to be distributed around the network. Although there are shortcomings with this approach (security concerns and lack of programmatic control over which remote server machine is used), there are so many legacy components that it would have been foolish of Microsoft not to provide this.

DCOM allows existing clients and servers to be used by introducing a number of new registry settings. We'll be examining these settings and their effects shortly in terms of the registry keys and values. This will allow you to edit the information using nothing more than **Regedit**.

However, you'll usually want to use one of two main tools for configuring these settings. The first tool, **DCOMCnfg**, is provided with Windows NT 4.0 as standard and is also part of the DCOM for Windows 95 package. You can find the executable in your **System32** (NT) or **System** (95) directory. This tool is covered in more depth in Chapter 7, when security is discussed.

The second, more versatile, tool is **OLEView**, the OLE-COM Object Viewer. This is supplied with Visual C++ and the Win32 SDK; you can also download it from the Microsoft web site. **OLEView** is more versatile for two main reasons: the first is that it presents the registered objects in a tree view, in a way that associates objects of particular types together; the second reason is that it allows you to get the interfaces that an object supports.

When you select an object in the tree control, and open the branch, **OLEView** will create an instance of that object and call **QueryInterface()** with every IID registered on your machine. When it gets a positive reply from the object, it adds the interface name to the lower right-hand box:

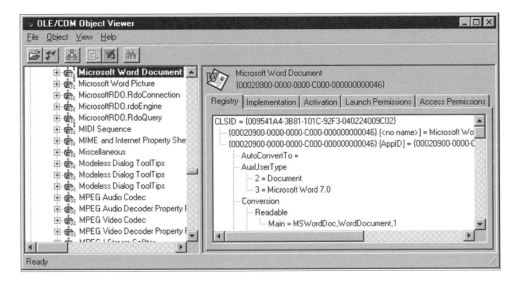

*If your **OLEView** does not have the tree control in the left-hand pane, you probably have an old version (most likely the one that comes with Visual C++ 4.x). You should download the latest version from Microsoft's web site.*

The really neat thing about **OLEView** is that it can install interface viewers that are written to call appropriate methods on an interface and present information about them to the user.

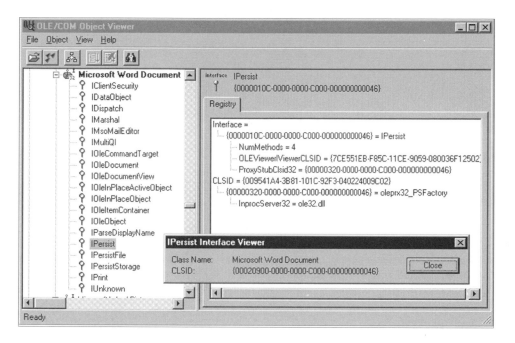

This viewer, for example, calls **IPersist::GetClassID()** and prints the CLSID in the dialog. Other more complex viewers are the **IDataObject** viewer (which lists all the formats supported by the interface) and the Type Library viewer, which you'll see used throughout this book. You can write your own interface viewers, and an SDK is available on the Microsoft Web site (**http://www.microsoft.com/oledev**).

In addition, **OLEView** is invaluable for browsing the registry settings for a class, and this information is presented in the right-hand pane when you first select a class (see the first screenshot, above). The first tab shows all the registry entries, and these are presented in a more readable, and editable, manner in the other tabs. The registry settings are covered in detail in the following sections, but the tabs are summarized here:

Tab	Description
Implementation	How the object is implemented: inproc, local, via a surrogate, etc.
Activation	Is the object activated on this machine or a remote machine?
Launch Permissions	Who is able to launch the object
Access Permissions	Who can call methods on an activated object

Registry Settings

Prior to DCOM, objects were generally created with one of two functions:

```
STDAPI CoCreateInstance(REFCLSID rclsid,
                        LPUNKNOWN pUnkOuter,
                        DWORD dwClsContext, REFIID riid,
                        LPVOID* ppv);
STDAPI CoGetClassObject(REFCLSID rclsid,
                        DWORD dwClsContext,
                        LPVOID lpReserved, REFIID riid,
                        LPVOID* ppv);
```

As explained in the previous chapter, **CoCreateInstance()** is really a helper function that calls **CoGetClassObject()**, so we'll just consider the second function. The client can specify which object to create (with **rclsid**) and which interface on that object should be returned (with **riid**). The interface pointer comes back in the **[out]** pointer, **ppv**.

The second parameter, **dwClsContext**, specifies the context of the object: it identifies whether the object should be instantiated in-process, though a handler, or out-of-process as a local server (or a combination of these). DCOM introduces an additional context for a *remote* server. When asked to launch a server, the COM subsystem will search under the indicated CLSID for this class in the **HKEY_CLASSES_ROOT\CLSID** key of the registry for a key or named value associated with the context:

Description	Context	Key/Value
In-process	**CLSCTX_INPROC_SERVER**	**InprocServer32**
In-process Handler	**CLSCTX_INPROC_HANDLER**	**InprocHandler32**
Local out-of-process	**CLSCTX_LOCAL_SERVER**	**LocalServer32**
Remote out-of-process	**CLSCTX_REMOTE_SERVER**	**AppID**

In the first three cases, COM searches for a key and the default value of this key contains the path and name of the server. In the local case, this includes any command line parameters that are required to launch the server. If the server has the **AppID** set (you can use **OLEView** to set an AppID for a pre-DCOM server), COM will use the GUID in this value to find the entry for the server in the **HKEY_CLASSES_ROOT\AppID** part of the registry. This key is used for DCOM servers too, but some of its functionality can be determined by programmatic means in the client. It is most useful with a pre-DCOM process.

> Don't get confused over what an AppID actually is. The Windows documentation refers to two types of AppID. The other type of AppID is an identifier for a user interface application that is mentioned in the registry under the **HKEY_CLASSES_ROOT** hive. This is used to associate an application with a document extension so that the Windows Explorer can identify the specific icon for this document, determine the actions to perform to print or edit the document, and perform particular shell features (shell extensions). The documentation uses the phrase AppID as a placeholder for the actual application ID, which can be any string of characters.

This shows the settings for the RemoteTime example, which we'll create later in this chapter. You can see that it has a **LocalServer32** key, to indicate the server that will be loaded, but it also has a **AppID** named value. Searching through the registry gives this for the ID gets us this:

In this case, it just shows the description for the class.

The **AppID** key is used for a different purpose, depending on whether this machine holds the object server or client. If this is the machine on which the client is running then the key holds information about *where* the object server will be activated. If the machine has the server then this key holds information about *how* the object server is activated and by *whom*. First, the values relevant to the server machine:

Value	Description
LocalService	Specifies that the server is running as an NT Service. This is covered in more depth in Chapter 8.
ServiceParameters	If the server is a Win32 Service, this value is passed on the command line of the service when it is started.
RunAs	This specifies the username of the security context under which the server is run.
LaunchPermission	This is the access control list of users and groups that can launch the server. Security is covered in Chapter 7.
AccessPermission	This is the access control list of the users and groups that can access the methods of running objects.

Now here are the values relevant to the client machine:

Value	Description
`RemoteServerName`	This is an identifier for the remote machine that an object will be run on. This can be a UNC name, or a DNS name (either a domain name or a dotted IP address).
`ActivateAtStorage`	This indicates that the persistent object that the client is activating should be activated on the server where it is held rather than on the client machine. This has a value of `"Y"` or `"N"`.

We'll be looking at the issues surrounding the server values later in this book in the chapters on Security (Chapter 7) and NT Services (Chapter 8). Of the client-relevant values, the second item, `ActivateAtStorage`, is particularly interesting.

ActivateAtStorage

You can access a persistent object using the `IMoniker` method, `BindToObject()`. This method can be called through a moniker created with `CreateFileMoniker()`, and the file mentioned in this function can be on a remote machine by specifying either its UNC name or its path via a drive mapping.

Prior to DCOM, even if you specified a remote file, the object would still be activated on the *local* machine. In other words, the data in the file would be copied across the network to the local machine and the server would be run there. With the `ActivateAtStorage` value in DCOM, the user can specify that when remote objects are activated, it is done on the machine where the persistent data is stored, even if this isn't the same machine doing the activation.

Suppose you have an application that does this:

```
LPMONIKER pMon;
HRESULT hr;
hr = CreateFileMoniker(L"\\\\Zeus\\Shopping Lists"
                        "\\Groceries\\13-Oct-96.xls",
                        &pMon);
if (SUCCEEDED(hr))
{
   IOleItemContainer* pCont;
   hr = pMon->BindToObject(pBndCtx, NULL,
                        IID_IOleItemContainer, &pCont);
   // ...Use pCont

   pCont->Release();
   pMon->Release();
}
```

With `ActivateAtStorage` set to `"N"`, Excel will be launched on the local machine, and the file `13-Oct-96.xls` from the `Groceries` directory of the `Shopping Lists` share on `Zeus` would be dragged across the network. With the value set to `"Y"`, Excel is launched on `Zeus` and loaded with this file.

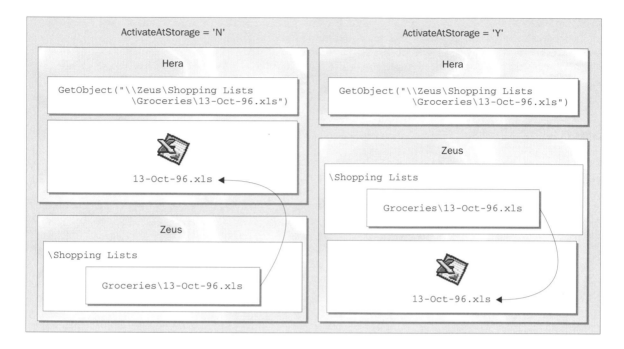

The use of the **AppID** key allows for legacy applications to launch objects and to be launched via DCOM. As the last example suggests, for a non-DCOM application like Excel 7.0 to be activated remotely, it just takes a small adjustment to the registry settings.

This does allow for some flexibility, since the application can be written without any regard to the absolute name of the server. The details, to adjust the object so that documents of the selected type are activated at storage, can be added to the registry at installation, or set up by a user with **OLEView**.

Note that, like most of the entries in the **AppID** key, the **ActivateAtStorage** value is used as a default when no other value is specified. So, for example, the new DCOM functions **CoGetInstanceFromFile()** and **CoGetInstanceFromIStorage()** have a parameter that takes a **COSERVERINFO** structure to specify the remote machine, and the **ActivateAtStorage** values are used as a default if this parameter is **NULL**. It also applies to **IMoniker::BindToObject()**, because the binding context passed to this method has a **COSERVERINFO** which could be **NULL**.

Surrogates

The last chapter showed that an object can be created in one of three contexts: inproc, local, or remote. So far, we've seen that legacy local (EXE) servers can be remotely activated by putting appropriate values in the registry. DCOM uses these values to determine the machine on which the object should be activated and the security settings to use as part of the DCOM security blanket. DCOM will then create the object on the remote machine, setting up the default (or object-specific) security context. The object server is an executable, so it can initialize COM, register its class factories, and wait for DCOM to create an object.

But what about inproc servers? If you run **DCOMCnfg**, you'll see that the classes that can be activated are all local servers. This is because a DLL cannot be launched remotely and it cannot have its own security context. Inproc servers are DLLs and so they can only be executed in the context of a process. A process that provides a wrapper for in-process servers so that they can be used out of process is known as a surrogate. DCOM supplies a standard surrogate that you can use to remote your in-process servers.

In addition to allowing you to launch an inproc server on a remote machine, there are other important uses for a surrogate: code isolation and security. One problem with inproc objects is that they are created in the address space of the client process. If an inproc server decides to write over memory maintained by the client, it is quite free to do so, even if this will cause the client to crash. A surrogate will isolate the DLL server from the client, and provides benefits even in the local case. If an errant in-process object overwrites any memory, it will be in the surrogate process. The surrogate may die, but the client will just get an error **HRESULT** when it attempts to access the object.

Another problem with loading a DLL into a process is that the inproc server DLL is loaded into the security context of the process. To get around this, you could write a surrogate that uses a specific security context for the object, or you can use **DCOMCnfg** to mark the surrogate's security in the registry.

It's worth pointing out that the Microsoft Transaction Server is a kind of value-added surrogate in that it supports all these features and more. MTS allows inproc servers to be remotely activated within a transaction and a security context. The transaction context protects data from a badly written inproc object crashing the process, and the security context allows the administrator to determine in what security context the object is activated. MTS is covered in Chapter 10.

Of course, the inproc server DLL and client must be written so that neither makes assumptions about where the object is activated. For example, the object and client cannot assume that the object is running in the process space of the client. A client should never pass the unmarshaled address of a callback function, for instance, and the object cannot implement a global variable and assume that the client can access it. If the inproc server does this, you should write a custom surrogate.

Although a surrogate isolates an object from the process space of the client, it may be desirable for several inproc servers to be activated in the same surrogate (for example, to allow them to have the same security context). The default surrogate handles this (and the threading models of such objects), but again, if you want special handling you can also write your own surrogate.

Surrogate Registry Entries

So how is an object launched in a surrogate rather than in-process? The key to this in the registry.

The registry entries relevant to remote objects are found under the **AppID** key in **HKEY_LOCAL_MACHINE**. For pre-service pack 2 DCOM objects, this just had the CLSIDs for EXE servers with named values that specified things like the name of server machine and the account under which the server should run. Now, with service pack 2, a new named value is supported: **DllSurrogate**. This specifies that if the CLSID is for an inproc server, the path given is for the surrogate server that will launch the inproc object. If this value is empty, the default surrogate (**DllHost.exe**) is used. To launch an inproc server remotely on another machine, the **DllSurrogate** should be present on the remote machine, but not on the local machine, which should have the **RemoteServerName** value instead.

The CLSIDs keys for EXE servers must reference the GUID of the AppID for the server. The same is now true of inproc servers that use surrogates. So under the CLSID entry for a class that uses an inproc server, there should be a named value called **AppID**.

Activating Inproc Objects in a Surrogate

To activate an inproc object, the object class must be registered to use a surrogate. Thus the object's CLSID must have an AppID value and there must be an **AppID** key with the **DllSurrogate** value. The convenient way to do this is to use **OLEView**:

Here is the entry for a class that I've created and called **EventLog**, implemented as an inproc server. This can be activated through a custom surrogate called **EVSurrogate.exe**. **OLEView** adds the value **AppID** under the objects CLSID:

and the appropriate key under **AppID**:

The object can now be viewed and manipulated in **DCOMCnfg** as if it were a local (or remote) object.

There are two ways to create an inproc server in a surrogate: either with the surrogate running on the local machine (so the surrogate provides the protection described above) or on a remote machine.

The client can activate the server by calling **CoCreateInstanceEx()** or **CoGetClassObject()** with the **CLSCTX_LOCAL_SERVER** context (yes, *local* server), but the **CLSID** key for the class has neither a **LocalServer32** or **LocalService** key. Instead, it has the **InprocServer32** key and the **AppID** value. COM will look under the **AppID** key for the object's CLSID for either the **DllSurrogate** or **RemoteServerName** key. If the former exists, the object is activated locally in the surrogate. If the latter exists, the remote machine mentioned is used to launch the server. This server must, however, have a **DllSurrogate** value. Remember, in order to use the system provided surrogate, the **DllSurrogate** value must exist, but it must be empty.

Writing a Surrogate

The default surrogate can be used to host several DLL servers. The first call to create an object will make COM load the surrogate and pass the CLSID of the object on the command line; the surrogate then registers a generic class factory that is called by COM to create subsequent objects. The objects activated in the host are activated using the threading model specified in the object's registry entry. For example, if there are several free threaded objects then these are launched in the same Multi Threaded Apartment (MTA), whereas apartment threaded objects are each launched in their own Single Threaded Apartment (STA). These terms are explained in Chapter 9.

The default surrogate is adequate for most objects: it handles DLL loading and unloading, and will even unload itself when all the objects have been released. However, there are situations when you may decide to write your own surrogate. For example, the inproc server that you wish to remote may have been written in a way that makes it unsuitable for the default surrogate (perhaps it uses global variables that it assumes exist in the client, or it could require specific security settings other than those supported by the values set in the registry).

The surrogate is fairly straightforward to implement. Essentially, it is a COM server that registers itself as a surrogate by calling **CoRegisterSurrogate()**:

```
HRESULT CoRegisterSurrogate(ISurrogate* pSurrogate);
```

This function takes an **[in]** parameter to the **ISurrogate** interface that must be implemented by your surrogate. This interface has these methods:

```
[
  uuid(00000022-0000-0000-C000-000000000046),
  version(1.0),
  pointer_default(unique),
  object
]
interface ISurrogate : IUnknown
{
  HRESULT LoadDllServer([in] REFCLSID Clsid);
  HRESULT FreeSurrogate();
}
```

COM calls the surrogate's **LoadDllServer()** method when it wants it to load a server. The surrogate must create a class factory and then register it with a call to **CoRegisterClassObject()**, passing **REGCLS_SURROGATE** for the class factory's flags. COM will create an instance of this class factory. In the implementation of this class factory, you should create the object with a call to **CoGetClassObject()** and then **CreateInstance()** to create the actual object.

Now the client can use the object, and when it is finished, call **Release()** to release it. As with all inproc servers, the DLL is only unloaded when **CoFreeUnusedLibraries()** is called. Therefore, the surrogate must call this function periodically to catch the occasions when a DLL is no longer needed. Once all the inproc server DLLs have been released, COM will call the **FreeSurrogate()** method. At this point, the surrogate must revoke any class factories that it has registered.

The class factories registered by the surrogate must implement a generic class factory that delegates the **CreateInstance()** call to the actual class factory. In addition to **IClassFactory** (and **IUnknown**), the class factory must also implement the **IMarshal** interface. The reason for this is that a client is not constrained to requesting just the **IClassFactory** and **IUnknown** interfaces, so by implementing the **IMarshal** interface, it provides a method for a proxy object for another interface to be created.

Surrogates allow you to create remote objects implemented in an inproc server. This now completes the list of all possible types of objects that you will want to create: inproc and local servers on the local machine; and inproc and local servers on a remote machine.

Limitations

Note that DCOM is not a universal panacea. It is restricted in the facilities that it can remote. The major restriction is that DCOM can only be used to remote non-UI interfaces. In these days of graphical user interfaces, this is quite a big restriction. In Windows, all graphics are carried out on windows (each with an associated **HWND** handle) in a graphics context specific to the adapter card (or indeed, some other device) called a device context (with an associated **HDC** handle).

A **HWND** or **HDC** handle is a reference to a data structure describing the window or DC. These are dependent on the hardware used on a particular machine, and are thus meaningless to another machine. The corollary of this is that any interfaces that are associated with device contexts cannot be remoted; in particular, in-place activation and drag-and-drop will not work across machine boundaries. (Although it would be fun to see someone drag an Excel cell from one machine and drop it on to a Word document on another machine!)

It is interesting to look in the **Wtypes.idl** file of the NT 4.0 SDK, to find that many GUI types have been defined in terms of IDL; it is therefore possible to define interfaces using these types. You can pass an **HWND** to another machine, but your server will have to know what it means.

DCOM Applications

The last section implies that to remote an object across the network, you need not change the client or server code: remoting across the network can be enabled by changing values in the registry. This is true, but there are situations where you will want the code to specify the server. More importantly, originally COM understood nothing about security, so legacy COM clients won't use any security when trying to launch or access a server (as opposed to DCOM clients, which can). Such a situation is only tolerable in a few cases, where the server object is either not accessing any resource or the resource is trivial and not sensitive. Most applications will want to protect their resources in some way. This section will outline changes that need to be done to make your client and server code DCOM-aware.

Client Code

The COM API has been enhanced for the additional features of server location and security in DCOM. In the last chapter I said that there would be no OLE 3.0, since the COM architecture is extensible, allowing you to enhance the system by adding new objects and new interfaces. This is true, in part, for the DCOM enhancements: the security object is accessed through the new interfaces **IClientSecurity** and **IServerSecurity**, for example. However, other enhancements, like the ability to specify the server location, require new API functions, replacing those that exist in COM.

Locating Servers

Under plain old COM, it was not possible for a client to specify through code the machine on which the server was run. This made sense, since a server could only be run on the same machine as the client. However, Microsoft reserved the third parameter to **CoGetClassObject()** so that it could be used to specify this information when DCOM arrived. The reserved parameter is now of type **COSERVERINFO***. You can also pass a **COSERVERINFO*** to a new helper function, **CoCreateInstanceEx()**, which replaces **CoCreateInstance()**.

The prototype for **CoGetClassObject()is**:

```
STDAPI CoGetClassObject(REFCLSID rclsid,
         DWORD dwClsContext,
         COSERVERINFO* pServerInfo, REFIID riid,
         LPVOID* ppv);
```

COSERVERINFO is a structure with the following members:

```
typedef struct COSERVERINFO
{
    DWORD dwReserved1;
    LPWSTR pwszName;
    COAUTHINFO *pAuthInfo;
    DWORD dwReserved2;
} COSERVERINFO;
```

Here are those reserved items again: Microsoft is hedging its bets. The second element, **pwszName**, is the name of the machine on which the object server is running or will be launched. This can be a UNC name (**\\Zeus**), an IP domain name (**zeus.testdevl.com**), or a dotted IP address (**123.123.123.123**). Note that the name is a string of wide characters; **TCHAR** is not used. This fits in with the rest of the COM API, where all strings are wide.

This means that the client process could hardcode the address of the server machine. This may not be the most ideal solution, but may be useful if the server is known and will not change. Alternatively, the client process could ask the user to provide a server name, and possibly save this in a persistent store and then use this in the future as the default server name. Indeed, if the value of **pServerInfo** is **NULL** then the values under the **AppID** key are used anyway.

This may not seem like much of an improvement over using the registry keys explained above, but the real power in this new API is the third member of the **COSERVERINFO** structure: **pAuthInfo**.

This is a pointer to a **COAUTHINFO** structure that holds information about the authentication used in the activation of the object. This is partly covered by the settings in the **LaunchPermissions** registry key for an object, but **COAUTHINFO** allows for more flexibility. These values will be covered in more detail later in this chapter, as well as in Chapter 7.

Optimizations

Querying for Multiple Interfaces

Imagine that we have a client that requires access to a particular remote object, and this object has *lots* of interfaces to which the client needs pointers. This is not as silly as it seems, especially if you consider functionality like OLE documents where the specification requires many interfaces to be supported.

A client, when accessing a local object, can make a call to **CoCreateInstance()** (or **CoGetClassObject()**) and then make multiple **QueryInterface()** (**QI()**) calls until it has all the interfaces it requires. However, if the client accesses the object across the network, every **QI()** will involve a new RPC call, and this could be costly in resources.

Remember that **CoCreateInstance()** is the combination of a call to **CoGetClassobject()** followed by **IClassFactory::CreateInstance()** on the class factory and then **IClassFactory::Release()**.

To optimize on the number of RPC calls, a replacement for the **CoCreateInstance()** helper function has been devised that can **QueryInterface()** for more than one interface at a time. The enhancement involves passing the function a structure containing all the IIDs of the interfaces required. The prototype is:

```
HRESULT CoCreateInstanceEx(REFCLSID rclsid,
                    IUnknown* punkOuter, DWORD dwClsCtx,
                    COSERVERINFO* pServerInfo,
                    ULONG cmq, MULTI_QI rgmqResults[]);
```

The **rclsid** is a reference to the CLSID of the object that we are interested in; **punkOuter** is the controlling interface if aggregation is being used; and **dwClsCtx** is the context for the object that will be instantiated. These parameters are the same as their equivalent in **CoCreateInstance()**. **pServerInfo** holds information about the server machine to use.

rgmqResults is an array of **MULTI_QI** structures that hold information about the interfaces to **QI()** for and have **[out]** parameters for the interface pointers and the results of the **QI()**. The number of entries in this array is passed in **cmq**.

The **MULTI_QI** structure has this prototype:

```
typedef struct _MULTI_QI
{
    const IID*    pIID;
    IUnknown *    pItf;
    HRESULT       hr;
} MULTI_QI;
```

pIID is a pointer to the IID of the interface to query for, **pItf** is an **[out]** parameter and if the **QI()** is successful, it holds the pointer to the interface, and **hr** is an **[out]** parameter that holds the **HRESULT** of the **QueryInterface()**.

The programmer can create an array of **MULTI_QI** structures, filling each **pIID** with the IIDs of the interfaces that the client will use on the object. After the call to **CoCreateInstanceEx()** it can then obtain the interfaces through the pointers in the **pItf** members. For example:

```
HRESULT hr;
COSERVERINFO ServerInfo;
IRemoteTime* pTimerServer = NULL;
IAnotherInterface* pAnotherInterface = NULL

// Create the server info
ServerInfo.dwReserved1 = 0;
ServerInfo.dwReserved2 = 0;
ServerInfo.pwszName = L"Zeus";
ServerInfo.pAuthInfo = NULL;

MULTI_QI qi[2] = {{&IID_IRemoteTime, NULL, 0},
                  {&IID_IAnotherInterface, NULL, 0}};

hr = CoCreateInstanceEx(CLSID_RemoteTime, NULL,
            CLSCTX_LOCAL_SERVER | CLSCTX_REMOTE_SERVER,
            &ServerInfo, 2, qi);

if (SUCCEEDED(hr))
{
    // Now get the interfaces
    if (SUCCEEDED(qi[0].hr))
        pTimeServer = (IRemoteTime*)qi[0].pItf;
```

```
      else
         printf("Cannot get IRemoteTime interface\n");
      if (SUCCEEDED(qi[1].hr))
         pAnotherInterface = (IAnotherInterface*)qi[1].pItf;
      else
         printf("Cannot get IAnotherInterface interface\n");
   }
   else
   {
      printf("Cannot get either interface\n");
   }
```

Security

Security is covered in greater depth in Chapter 7. In this section, we'll just outline a little about security to whet your appetite. There are essentially two ways of setting security in a client. You can set per-process level security values, and you can set the security that will be used when accessing a particular object.

Process-level security is handled by a call to **CoInitializeSecurity()**. If the client does not make a call to this function then COM will do so on its behalf, using the default values in the registry (which you can set using **DCOMCnfg** or **OLEView**). This function is dual purpose: you can call it in both clients *and* servers. It has these parameters:

```
HRESULT CoInitializeSecurity(PSECURITY_DESCRIPTOR pVoid,
                DWORD    cAuthSvc,
                SOLE_AUTHENTICATION_SERVICE* asAuthSvc,
                void* pReserved1,
                DWORD dwAuthnLevel, DWORD dwImpLevel,
                RPC_AUTH_IDENTITY_HANDLE pAuthInfo,
                DWORD dwCapabilities,
                void* pvReserved2);
```

Several of these parameters (**pvReserved1**, **pvReserved2** and **pAuthInfo**) are reserved for later use and so must be **NULL** or **0**. The first parameter, **pVoid**, is a pointer to an **access control list** (ACL) or is **NULL**. If it is non-**NULL** then this ACL is used to check that the user has access to the object; if it is **NULL** then no checking is done. The **asAuthSvc** is only relevant to a server as it identifies the authentication services to use. **cAuthSvc** specifies how many entries there are in **asAuthSvc**.

dwAuthnLevel determines the authentication level, and this must the same level or greater than that expected by the server. The **dwImpLevel** determines the impersonation level. Authentication and impersonation are covered later in this section. **dwCapabilities** is a parameter to hold general flags about security. Currently, the only values that it can hold are these:

Value	Description
EOAC_MUTUAL_AUTH	Mutual authentication
EOAC_SECURE_REFS	Secure references
EOAC_NONE	None

The object level security is handled when the client creates the object with a call to
`CoGetClassObject()` or `CoCreateInstanceEx()`. Security information is passed via the `pAuthInfo`
member of the `COSERVERINFO` structure. This is a pointer to a `COAUTHINFO` structure that holds
information about the authentication of the object launch. This structure has these members:

```
typedef struct _COAUTHINFO
{
    DWORD           dwAuthnSvc;
    DWORD           dwAuthzSvc;
    WCHAR*          pwszServerPrincName;
    DWORD           dwAuthnLevel;
    DWORD           dwImpersonationLevel;
    AUTH_IDENTITY*  pAuthIdentityData;
    DWORD           dwCapabilities;
} COAUTHINFO;
```

The first member is the authentication server that will be used. It can be one of:

Value	Description
`RPC_C_AUTHN_NONE`	No Authentication
`RPC_C_AUTHN_DCE_PRIVATE`	DCE private key
`RPC_C_AUTHN_DCE_PUBLIC`	DCE public key
`RPC_C_AUTHN_DEC_PUBLIC`	DEC public key
`RPC_C_AUTHN_WINNT`	NT LM security
`RPC_C_AUTHN_DEFAULT`	System Default (`RPC_C_AUTHN_DCE_PRIVATE` for NT 4.0)

Of the six possible values, only `RPC_C_AUTHN_WINNT` is currently supported by NT 4.0, but others may
be supported by third party add-ons, or may even be supplied in future versions of NT. The authentication
authority may need to have a username and if so, this is given in the third parameter,
`pwszServerPrincName`. For NT authentication this should be `NULL`.

The authentication service may need additional information about the client to be able to authenticate the
call. This is provided by the sixth element, `pAuthIdentityData`, which has data specific to the particular
authentication service used. For `RPC_C_AUTHN_WINNT`, it is in the form of Windows NT's
`SEC_WINNT_AUTH_IDENTITY` structure. This structure holds information about the client username, the
domain and the user password.

The level of authentication is given in the fourth member, `dwAuthnLevel`, and this determines features
such as whether authentication is carried out when the client connects initially, when it makes a method
call, or whether the packets are encrypted.

Once the client is *authenticated* (it is who it says it is), the server still needs to see if the client is *authorized*
to make the call (i.e. whether the client has the right authority or permissions to make the call). This is the
purpose of the second member of the `COAUTHINFO` structure. At present, for an NT (or Windows 95)
server, the value should be `RPC_C_AUTHZ_NONE`.

Now that the server is reassured that the client is who it says it is and can do what it has asked to be done, the server still must know how to make the calls. This is an issue for many reasons; the two most important are the launch status of the server, and auditing.

To cover the first point: the server may be already running or it may need activating. If it is running and has been activated as an NT service, it may not have all the necessary permissions to carry out the task requested. (NT services usually run under a special NT account that has super permissions in some respects, and lousy permissions in others. See Chapters 7 and 8 for more information). If the server is not running, it will need to be activated and it will need to have a username to do this.

The second point raises the subject of auditing. If the server uses some default account when running a COM object, this will show in the audit trail in the NT event log. The server should use a user name that more accurately reflects the client so that the audit trail shows that the action was performed on behalf of a client and not the server.

These two important actions are carried out by the server *impersonating* a user, and the level of impersonation is indicated by the fifth member, `dwImpersonationLevel`.

Value	Description
`RPC_C_IMP_LEVEL_ANONYMOUS`	The client is anonymous to the server
`RPC_C_IMP_LEVEL_IDENTITY`	The server can obtain the client's identity
`RPC_C_IMP_LEVEL_IMPERSONATE`	The server can impersonate the client
`RPC_C_IMP_LEVEL_DELEGATE`	The server can behave as the client

Currently, NT 4.0 only supports `RPC_C_IMP_LEVEL_IDENTIFY` and `RPC_C_IMP_LEVEL_IMPERSONATE`, which means that the server can impersonate the user to determine if the user has the correct permissions to perform the action, or it can impersonate the user to actually do the action.

The impersonation level can be viewed as the client telling the server how much it trusts it. If the client passes a low value of impersonation then it is telling the server that it doesn't really trust it. If a client were to pass `RPC_C_IMP_LEVEL_ANONYMOUS` (in a future version of DCOM) then this is saying, 'I don't trust you, so I won't let you know who I am'. Higher levels of impersonation indicate to the server that the client trusts it more, to the extent of `RPC_C_IMP_LEVEL_DELEGATE`, where the client will be saying (in the future) 'I trust you so much that you can do anything in my name'.

The final member of **COAUTHINFO**, `dwCapabilities`, determines the capabilities of the proxy used to remote the call. This flag is not used at present.

Server Code

Threading Issues

This section really just introduces the fact that DCOM introduces a new threading model in addition to that offered in previous versions of COM (i.e. the apartment model). Multithreaded servers will be covered thoroughly in Chapter 9.

In early, non-threaded versions of Windows, a process had to call **CoInitialize()** before making any calls to COM. If your process needed to use things like compound files then you had to call **OleInitialize()** instead, which called **CoInitialize()** for you. The purpose of these functions is to initialize the COM libraries. OLE 2.0 in Windows 3.x even allowed you to pass a pointer to a memory allocator if you wanted to use your own.

COM clients naturally have to call **Co/OleInitialize()** to be able to use COM. This is also true of out-of-process servers, the other end of the COM connection. Inproc servers do not call this, because they will run in the address space of a process that has already initialized the COM libraries. These clients and servers are single threaded.

Windows NT 3.51 and Windows 95 introduced a new threading model. In these operating systems you could create multithreaded servers. If the server was a local server then **Co/Oleinitialize()** had to be called in every thread that the server would use COM. Inproc servers do not initialize COM like this, since they are loaded as DLLs and rely on the loading process to have already initialized COM.

However, as you'll see in Chapter 9, the different thread models synchronize access to instance data in different ways, and because of this, the client must be written for a compatible threading model. The client indicates its threading model in the call to **CoInitializeEx()**, but since inproc servers do not call this, the server must mark its threading model using the **ThreadingModel** named value in its CLSID key. COM can check this value when it wants to launch the server and determine if the server's threading model is compatible with that of the client. The full details of this are given in Chapter 9.

In the apartment model, each thread is isolated, since the COM libraries are initialized separately in each. This causes some difficulties in passing objects between threads in a single process. This is because, to COM, each thread is separate; so the object has to be marshaled between the threads, just as an object would be marshaled if it were passed to another process.

NT 4.0 came with the free threading model, which relaxes these restrictions, but makes the programmer more disciplined as far as thread safe data and synchronization of COM calls.

To specify that an out-of-process server is free threaded, the process calls **CoInitializeEx()**. This has the following prototype:

```
HRESULT CoInitializeEx(void* pvReserved, DWORD dwCoInit);
```

The first parameter must be **NULL**, and the second parameter should be one of the **COINIT** enumerated values:

```
typedef enum tagCOINIT
{
   COINIT_APARTMENTTHREADED   = 0x2,
   COINIT_MULTITHREADED       = 0x0,
   COINIT_DISABLE_OLE1DDE     = 0x4,
   COINIT_SPEED_OVER_MEMORY   = 0x8
} COINIT;
```

The important values are the first two that specify that the server is apartment model or free-threaded. If you call **CoInitialize()** then this just maps to a call to **CoInitializeEx()** with the second parameter of **COINIT_APARTMENTTHREADED**.

Security

On the server side, the object can implement per server, per object, or per method security. These are all covered in Chapter 7, where we also cover authentication and authorization.

Writing DCOM Code

If you want to write a COM server, you have three main options. The first is to write using the Win32 SDK, the second is to use MFC, and the third is to use ATL. Writing at the SDK level will involve you writing large amounts of code and, inevitably, you will end up writing your own library to take the drudgery out of the process. Because you have to write so much code, SDK-level programs are prone to bugs; but, they give you the finest level of control, and if you're concerned about such things, you can ensure that the code produced is compact.

MFC is really designed for UI programs, but since there are COM features in the UI, COM has been added to key MFC classes. Every window class derives from **CCmdTarget**, and this has the necessary methods to support COM interfaces. In addition, there are other helper classes (like **COleDispatchDriver** for Automation, and **COleDocument** to provide compound document support) that allow you to access most of the UI COM interfaces of other objects, and provide implementations of your own.

MFC is great for providing an Automation interface on your application: you just click the appropriate box in the AppWizard and then add the methods into your **CCmdTarget**-derived class with ClassWizard. You don't need to know anything about **IDispatch** interfaces to do this. Similarly, if you want to add embedded or linked objects in your documents, provide in-place activation, support for copy-and-paste or drag-and-drop, all the functionality is provided in the MFC classes. All you have to do is follow the recipes given in the documentation and implement a few methods in your derived classes. Again, you don't need to know anything at all about COM to do this.

This sounds wonderful, doesn't it? But there is a downside. The first is application size. The MFC classes bloat your applications to quite a ridiculous level, especially if you statically link the libraries. Even if you choose to dynamically link to the MFC DLL, the applications are still large, and you need to ship the DLL with your application. This can be irritating if you want to ship it on a 1.44Mb floppy, but becomes a major headache if you want to distribute it via the Internet (whether your code is merely for download or is intended for live use as an ActiveX control on a web page).

The other major problem with MFC is that it is hard to extend the number of interfaces that are supported. MFC has great support for interfaces like **IDispatch**, which is backed up by code in **CCmdTarget** and **COleDispatchDriver**, or **IViewObject**, **IDropTarget**, **IDropSource** and **IDataObject**, but if you wish to add other COM interfaces into your class, or even provide custom interfaces, you will have a struggle. MFC does some pretty hairy things with C++, messing around with vtables and even dropping into assembler at some points, all to make the programming 'easier'. This can cause problems.

MFC also provides some COM macros that look, in many ways, like the MFC message map macros. If you come from a COM background, the MFC macros do seem an unnecessary complication, especially since Microsoft keeps telling us that COM is easy to implement in C++ and all the text books say that an interface is just a C++ vtable. If you come from an MFC background, they appear a little more familiar, but their actions can seem like black magic.

Although useful, MFC is not exactly a satisfactory solution. My best advice is: if you're writing a UI client that uses COM then, by all means, use MFC; that's what it is designed for. If you're writing a UI OLE server that's providing the desktop OLE interfaces, then also use MFC, because it takes all the hard work away from you. For all other COM servers (like ActiveX controls and UI-less servers), avoid MFC.

If the SDK is too involved and potentially error-prone, and MFC is too heavy-weight, what are we left with? The answer is ATL. Since it is a template library you use as much, or as little, as you need; so the servers are lean. ATL is designed for just one purpose: writing COM servers, so you don't have the baggage of fitting COM into some other model or class library like MFC does.

ATL has a Visual C++ AppWizard that generates all the starting files: it will allow you to write COM inproc servers, local servers, and servers as NT services. There is also an ATL Object Wizard that allows you to quickly create the skeleton code for a number of different types of object. ATL allows you to write standard, dispatch, dual, or custom interfaces, and marshal the parameters via a type library or proxy-stub.

There are some fundamental differences between ATL and MFC, particularly in how they handle reference counting. MFC handles interfaces through nested C++ classes and, because of this, it can apply reference counting on a per-interface level. ATL, however, for the most part handles interfaces through multiple inheritance and, as such, can only apply reference counting on a per-object level. The full implications have been covered in the last chapter, but it's worth noting that per-interface reference counting is more flexible than the per-object method. It is possible to use interfaces that have per-interface reference counting in ATL (the so-called 'tear-off' interfaces), but it does require a little more work.

ATL 2.1 comes as part of Visual C++ 5.0, and an identical version called ATL 2.0 is available on Microsoft's web site for users of previous versions of Visual C++.

Working Code

Now on to the working code. The server is very simple, all it does is provide a custom COM interface to remote a method called **GetTime()** that returns the time on the server machine. The client program will show this next to the local time to compare any differences in the clocks of the two machines. Such an object could be used to synchronize machines on a network for example.

The server is written with the Active Template Library (ATL 2.1). The client will be written using MFC, because it needs to provide a UI interface. Since I dislike the MFC COM macros (in this case they're more effort than they're worth), the COM access will be carried out directly using SDK calls.

Time Server

The first thing to do is to run Developer Studio and create a new workspace for a project called TimeServer, using the ATL COM AppWizard. On the first and only step of the AppWizard, you should choose to make a server of type Executable (EXE).

In addition to the files for the server project, the ATL COM AppWizard will also create a make file called **TimeServerps.mk** for the proxy-stub DLL, and the associated **.def** file to export functions from this DLL. MIDL will generate an implementation of this DLL (called **dlldata.c**) when you compile the IDL file.

Once the project has been created, right-click on the TimeServer classes icon in ClassView and select New ATL Object... from the context menu. Use the resulting ATL Object Wizard to add a new Simple Object to the project. Give the object a short name of RemoteTime and leave all the other names with their defaults.

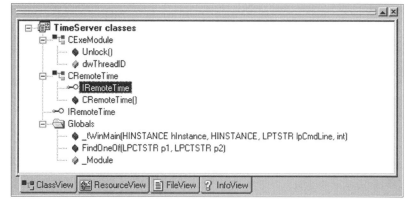

Now go to the **Attributes** tab and change the interface type to **C**ustom. Although the interface that we'll create could be a **D**ual interface, since it only uses standard Automation types, we will treat this example as if it were a genuine custom interface.

Now click **OK** to add the simple custom interface COM component, represented by the class **CRemoteTime**, to the project. Your ClassView should now look like this:

Now add the single method **GetTime()** into the definition for **IRemoteTime**. The **GetTime()** method should be specified as:

```
HRESULT GetTime([out, retval] DATE* date);
```

To do this, right-click on the **IRemoteTime** interface in ClassView and choose Add **M**ethod... then fill in the dialog as shown.

The **IRemoteTime** interface in **TimeServer.idl** will now look like this:

```
[

    uuid(4BAFEEFC-803F-11D0-BB98-002018349816),

    helpstring("IRemoteTime Interface"),
    pointer_default(unique)
]
interface IRemoteTime : IUnknown
{
    [helpstring("method GetTime")] HRESULT GetTime(
            [out, retval] DATE* date);
};
```

Now we need to add the implementation of the method into the **RemoteTime.cpp** file:

```
STDMETHODIMP CRemoteTime::GetTime(DATE * date)
{
    SYSTEMTIME st;
    GetSystemTime(&st);

    if (SystemTimeToVariantTime(&st, date))
    {
        return S_OK;
    }
    else
    {
        *date = 0;
        return E_FAIL;
    }
}
```

This just gets the local machine's system time, converts it to an Automation **DATE** type, and returns it to the client.

The next step is to build then register the component. Visual C++ 5.0 will register the components as part of its build process, but if your development tool will not do this for you then you can just run the server with the **/RegServer** switch. The component base class **CComModule** provides all the functionality to actually complete the registration.

The Proxy-Stub

Since **IRemoteTime** is a custom interface, and we have defined a local server, we need to have a proxy-stub DLL.

When you compile the **.idl** file, MIDL will produce the necessary files (**DllData.c**, **TimeServer_i.c** and **TimeServer_p.c**) to build into the proxy-stub DLL. The ATL COM AppWizard will also have made a make file, **TimeServerps.mk**, which will build these files into a proxy-stub DLL when you run **nmake** on this file.

Once the proxy-stub has been built, it also needs to be registered. Since it's a DLL that exports the **DllRegisterServer()** function, you can register it by running the **RegSvr32** utility. The DLL is the proxy for the *interface* that's used by the object, so to see if the registration has been successful, you need to search through the registry with **RegEdit** or **OLEView** for the entry for the **IRemoteTime** interface.

You should see a CLSID under the key **ProxyStubClsid32**, and in the entry for this CLSID, under **CLSID**, you should find a key called **InProcServer32** that will have the proxy-stub DLL. On my machine, I have these values:

Both building and registering the proxy-stub can be done from the command line, but you may well find it more convenient to add the lines to do this to the project's Post-build step.

Note that, for VC++ 4.x, there's a slight mistake in the Wizard-produced proxy-stub make file: if you run **nmake** on it, you will get an error:

```
LIBC.lib(crt0.obj) : error LNK2001: unresolved external symbol _main
```

The reason for this is that the linker directives in the makefile define the entry point as **DllMain()**. On the surface this may appear to be true; after all, this is the entry point that MIDL has written for you. The problem is that if you are using the C Runtime Library, you need to initialize it first (the CRT needs to allocate some thread local storage for some of its static variables, and perform other initializations), so the CRT defines a function called **_DllMainCRTStartup()**, which does this initialization and then calls your

DllMain(); thus your function is not the real entry point. If you specify **DllMain()** as the entry point then the CRT will not be initialized. If you do not specify an entry point to the linker, it will use the one defined by the CRT. Thus you need to edit **TimeServerps.mak**, and on the **link** line remove the following:

```
/entry:DllMain
```

The DLL will now link correctly, although you may get some warnings about certain functions not being specified as **PRIVATE** in the **.def** file. You can safely ignore these warnings.

Once the server has been built, you can use **OLEView** to browse the type library for the server as shown below:

Time Client

The client is written using MFC and Visual C++ 5. If you're using an earlier version of Visual C++, you should still be able to follow along with the example, but you should make sure that you have the most up to date versions of the Win32 header files. Note that Microsoft released a patch for users of Visual C++ 4.2 that upgrades the product to version 4.2b. You will certainly need this patch if you are to write DCOM applications successfully using that version. In addition, new Win32 header files are occasionally released (such as the NT 4.0 service pack 2 SDK update), so check Microsoft's web site for any files you may need.

The client will present a dialog asking the user to enter the machine that it should connect to for the time. It will then display a second dialog showing both the local time and the time on the machine that the user specified. The time displayed on the dialog will be updated every second in response to a **WM_TIMER** message.

The first step is to create an MFC dialog-based project, using MFC AppWizard (exe), called TimeClient. Apart from choosing a dialog-based application, all the options can be left at their default settings. Once the files have been generated, you need to define the preprocessor directive **_WIN32_DCOM** so that you can access all the features introduced with DCOM (such as **CoCreateInstanceEx()**, for example). You can do this by adding the symbol to the list of Preprocessor definitions for all configurations on the C/C++ tab of the Project Settings dialog.

Now create a dialog resource and give it an ID of **IDD_SERVERNAME**. Add an edit box to this dialog as shown. This will be used to receive the name of the server to connect to.

Ctrl-double-click on the dialog to create a new class for it called **CServerNameDlg**; then use ClassWizard to add a new **CString** member variable called **m_strServerName** for the edit box. We'll be using this dialog class in **TimeClientDlg.cpp**, so add **#include "ServerNameDlg"** to the top of that file. That's all you need to do to use the server name dialog. We'll be using this dialog again in future projects, so it would be a good idea to add it to the Component Gallery, which makes it easy to reuse.

Now add some controls to the main dialog: **IDD_TIMECLIENT_DIALOG**, to act as the user interface for the client; remove the OK button; relabel the Cancel button as Finish; and add two frames (**IDC_REMFRAME** and **IDC_LOCFRAME**), two read-only edit boxes (**IDC_REMOTE** and **IDC_LOCAL**) and a static text control (**IDC_ERRORS**), as shown below.

The top edit box will contain the remote machine's time and the bottom will hold the local time. The text of the frames will be changed at runtime to reflect the actual name of the server and the local machine. The static control, selected in the picture, will be used to relay any errors, which is useful if you forgot to register the object.

The first thing that our application needs to do is initialize the COM libraries. We could have had the code to do this added to our application by the AppWizard if we'd selected the Automation check box on Step 2, but this would also have introduced a lot of extra code in our client to allow it to act as an Automation server. Since we didn't want that, it's just as easy to add the code by hand. Add the following code to the top of the application class' **InitInstance()** function (you'll also need to add an entry to the string table for the **IDP_OLE_INIT_FAILED** error message).

```
// Initialize OLE libraries
if (!AfxOleInit())
{
   AfxMessageBox(IDP_OLE_INIT_FAILED);
   return FALSE;
}
```

Because we're using **AfxOleInit()**, we don't need to worry about uninitializing the libraries; that's all handled for us by MFC.

Since the code in the main dialog class, **CTimeClientDlg**, needs to know about the timeserver and its interface, you need to include the header file **TimeServer.h** from the time server directory at the top of the **TimeClientDlg.cpp**. This will include the prototype of the **IRemoteTime** interface.

```
// TimeClientDlg.cpp : implementation file
//

#include "stdafx.h"
#include "TimeClient.h"
#include "..\TimeServer\TimeServer.h"
#include "TimeClientDlg.h"
```

TimeClientDlg.h is also included in **TimeClient.cpp**, so you'll also have to add an include for
TimeServer.h just before that too.

Now add declarations for the IID and the CLSID of the **IRemoteTime** interface and **RemoteTime**
coclass near the top of the same file.

```
const IID IID_IRemoteTime = {0x4BAFEEFC,0x803F,0x11D0,{0xBB,0x98,0x00,0x20,0x18,0x34,
    0x98,0x16}};
const CLSID CLSID_RemoteTime =
{0x79FF7302,0x802D,0x11D0,{0xBB,0x98,0x00,0x20,0x18,0x34,
    0x98,0x16}};
```

You can copy these declarations straight out of the MIDL-generated **TimeServer_i.c** file in the
timeserver's directory. You could query the registry using the COM APIs or use the type library to get
these values, but this is easiest and I'm lazy.

At this point, you need to add a few member variables to **CTimeClientDlg**.

```
// Implementation
protected:
// The name of the server machine
CString m_strServerName;
// The interface on the remote object
IRemoteTime* m_pTimeServer;
// The ID of the timer
UINT m_nTimerID;
```

Hopefully these variables are self-explanatory. You could also define a function to easily display messages
in the dialog's static text control.

```
void CTimeClientDlg::Message(const CString& strMessage)
{
   CWnd* pTextCtrl = GetDlgItem(IDC_ERRORS);
   ASSERT(pTextCtrl);

   pTextCtrl->SetWindowText(strMessage);
}
```

Another helper function will allow you to set the frame names with a single call using the information
stored in **m_strServerName** and the **GetComputerName()** API.

```
void CTimeClientDlg::SetUpFrameNames()
{
   // Set up the names on the frames
   TCHAR szLocalName[MAX_COMPUTERNAME_LENGTH + 1];
   DWORD dwSize = MAX_COMPUTERNAME_LENGTH + 1;
   if (GetComputerName(szLocalName, &dwSize))
   {
      CWnd* pFrame = GetDlgItem(IDC_LOCFRAME);
      ASSERT(pFrame);

      pFrame->SetWindowText(szLocalName);

      pFrame = GetDlgItem(IDC_REMFRAME);
      ASSERT(pFrame);
```

```
      if (m_strServerName.IsEmpty())
         pFrame->SetWindowText(szLocalName);
      else
         pFrame->SetWindowText(m_strServerName);
   }

}
```

The major code for the client goes in **CTimeClientDlg::OnInitDialog()**.

```
BOOL CTimeClientDlg::OnInitDialog()
{
   // ...Standard initialization
```

```
   CServerNameDlg dlg;

   // Get the name of the server to use
   if (dlg.DoModal() == IDOK
              && !dlg.m_strServerName.IsEmpty())
      m_strServerName = dlg.m_strServerName;
   else
      m_strServerName.Empty();

   SetUpFrameNames();

   // Create the server and get the time
   m_pTimeServer = NULL;

   HRESULT hr;
   COSERVERINFO serverinfo;
   COSERVERINFO* pServerInfo;

   // Create the server info
   // Note that we use CString to convert to wide chars
   serverinfo.dwReserved1 = 0;
   serverinfo.dwReserved2 = 0;
   serverinfo.pwszName = m_strServerName.AllocSysString();
   serverinfo.pAuthInfo = NULL;

   if (m_strServerName.IsEmpty())
      pServerInfo = NULL;
   else
      pServerInfo = &serverinfo;

   MULTI_QI qi = {&IID_IRemoteTime, NULL, 0};

   hr = CoCreateInstanceEx(CLSID_RemoteTime, NULL,
           CLSCTX_LOCAL_SERVER | CLSCTX_REMOTE_SERVER,
           pServerInfo, 1, &qi);

   if (SUCCEEDED(hr) && SUCCEEDED(qi.hr))
   {
      // Now get the interface
      m_pTimeServer = (IRemoteTime*)qi.pItf;
      m_nTimerID = SetTimer(ID_TIMER, 1000, NULL);
   }
   else
```

```
      {
        m_pTimeServer = NULL;
        CString str;
        str.Format("Cannot get object: 0x%x and QI: 0x%x",
                   hr, qi.hr);
        Message(str);
      }

      // Free the buffer previous allocated
      ::SysFreeString(serverinfo.pwszName);

    return TRUE;  // return TRUE  unless you set the
                  // focus to a control
  }
```

To make things easy (and because the subject has its own chapter), we'll use default security; so we let COM call **CoInitializeSecurity()**. The object creation is done in the **WM_INITDIALOG** handler.

Right at the beginning, the code creates a **CServerNameDlg** dialog to prompt for the server name. If the user clicks OK without typing a name, or clicks on Cancel, then no name is used. This indicates that the client is working on the same machine as the server. Next, the client machine name is obtained and, along with the server name, it is used to initialize the titles of the frames on the dialog box.

The **COSERVERINFO** structure is initialized with the server name, if one was supplied. I have done this by using the **CString** method **AllocSysString()**; this will create a **BSTR**, initialize it with the contents of the **CString** and return a pointer to it. Although a **BSTR** implicitly has a 16-bit length associated with it (and appended to the front of the string), the pointer is to the wide char string itself. It is fine to use a **BSTR** in this situation as long as **::SysFreeString()** is used to free the **BSTR**.

The **pServerInfo** variable is initialized here depending on whether a server name was given. Again, if the user did not give a server name, it's assumed to be the same as the client machine name; so **pServerInfo** is set to **NULL**.

The function now needs to obtain a pointer to the **IRemoteTime** interface on the **TimeServer** object. It does this with a call to **CoCreateInstanceEx()** passing the **pServerInfo** variable, initialized earlier, and a pointer to a **MULTI_QI** structure that has the IID of the interface that we require. This structure returns the pointer to the interface and an **HRESULT**. If the call is successful, we save the pointer in an instance variable, and create a timer.

You need to use ClassWizard to add a handler to the dialog for the **WM_TIMER** message. When the dialog gets a **WM_TIMER** message we need to query the server for the time:

```
void CTimeClientDlg::OnTimer(UINT nIDEvent)
{
    // We will assume that all timer messages are from
    // our timer
    CWnd* pRemote = GetDlgItem(IDC_REMOTE);
    ASSERT(pRemote);
    CWnd* pLocal = GetDlgItem(IDC_LOCAL);
    ASSERT(pLocal);

    SYSTEMTIME st;
    DATE theDate;
    HRESULT hr;
```

```
        CString strTime;
        CString strError;

        if (m_pTimeServer)
        {
           hr = m_pTimeServer->GetTime(&theDate);

           if (SUCCEEDED(hr))
           {
              VariantTimeToSystemTime(theDate, &st);
              strTime.Format("%02d:%02d:%02d",
                              st.wHour, st.wMinute, st.wSecond);
           }
           else
           {
              strError.Format("Cannot get time: %x", hr);
           }
        }
        else
           strError = "No object";

        pRemote->SetWindowText(strTime);
        Message(strError);

        // Now get the local time
        GetSystemTime(&st);
        strTime.Format("%02d:%02d:%02d",
                        st.wHour, st.wMinute, st.wSecond);
        pLocal->SetWindowText(strTime);

        CDialog::OnTimer(nIDEvent);
     }
```

This code gets pointers to the controls and then calls **GetTime()** on the cached interface pointer. Remember that **GetTime()** returns a **DATE** value, so this is first converted to a **SYSTEMTIME** type and then used to initialize a **CString**, which is sent to the edit box to display the remote time. After this, we get the local time and display that in the dialog. If any error occurs, the problem is written to the dialog's static control for display.

The final part is clean up; the timer is killed and the server released in response to a **WM_DESTROY** method. You'll need to add a handler for **WM_DESTROY** using ClassWizard. The cleanup is best done here because the window that the timer is attached to has to exist when the timer is killed. The more logical place may be in the class destructor, but, by that point, the window would already have been destroyed.

```
  void CTimeClientDlg::Destroy()
  {
     CDialog::OnDestroy();

     // Destroy the timer
     if (m_nTimerID)
        KillTimer(m_nTimerID);
     // Release the server
     if (m_pTimeServer)
        m_pTimeServer->Release();
  }
```

Testing the Code

The tests that follow were carried out with NT 4.0 as the operating system for both the client and the server machines. However, you can also run this code quite happily on Windows 95. Make sure that you follow the instructions for setting up DCOM for Windows 95 carefully, and remember that if you are using a Windows 95 machine as a server, you will need to manually start the server before you can connect to it.

Also note that, at the time of writing, Microsoft had identified a bug with **Rpcss.exe** on Windows 95. This process is the executable that contains the Service Control Manager (SCM) that launches DCOM objects. Under NT, **Rpcss.exe** is run as a service; but, under Windows 95, it's launched by the COM libraries when the first COM object is registered (i.e. when the server is run and calls **CoRegisterClassObject()**). The bug is that the **Rpcss** is *not* launched if the first server is a Single Threaded Apartment model (see Chapter 9 for an explanation of this term) and a client on a remote machine attempts to create an object.

Until Microsoft fixes this bug, the best work around is to pre-launch **Rpcss.exe** using the Windows 95 'pseudo service' feature, as described in Chapter 2; in other words, add it to **HKEY_LOCAL_MACHINE\Software\Microsoft\Windows\CurrentVersion\RunServices**. Alternatively, you can launch **Rpcss.exe** manually whenever you need it.

The Tests

The first test is on a local machine running NT 4.0. Make sure that the server and the proxy-stub DLL are registered on a local (*not* a network) drive. If one of these components is on a network drive then the path to the module will give a mapped driver letter or a UNC name. However, the Service Control Manager that launches COM objects runs under the SYSTEM account, which cannot access network drives, so the creation will fail.

Now run the client. You will get a dialog asking for a server name:

Click on **OK** without typing a name, or click on **Cancel**, and the main dialog will show:

My machine is called **ZEUS**, and the code has queried for its name and used it for the titles of both boxes. In this case, the **pServerInfo** variable would have been **NULL**. Notice that the times are the same in the two edit boxes.

Now press Finish and run the client again, this time typing the name of the machine that the client is running on. You should get the same effect as before, but this time an initialized **COSERVERINFO** pointer was passed to **CoCreateInstanceEx()**. In this screenshot, I typed the machine name in lowercase:

Now we need to test this on a remote NT machine. Copy **TimeClient.exe** and **TimeServerps.dll** to the client machine. Don't copy **TimeServer.exe**. Register the proxy-stub DLL so that the **GetTime()** method can be marshaled, and then run **TimeClient** on the client machine. Enter the name of the server and press OK.

Here I have a client machine **Hera** that is connected to **Zeus**. The times are slightly different, as you would expect. Note that **Hera** knows nothing about the **TimerServer** class: it only knows about the **IRemoteTime** interface, because we registered the proxy-stub since it has got to have information about how to marshal the **GetTime()** method. It is DCOM that marshals the object ID to the remote machine where the ID is relevant. To show this, run **TimeClient** on the server machine and try to connect to the client machine:

The error codes correspond to **REGDB_E_CLASSNOTREG**. In other words, the CLSID has not been registered, so the object is not available on **Hera**.

Earlier on in this chapter we looked at pinging as a mechanism of maintaining the connection between the client and object. To see pinging working, run the NT Task Manager on the server machine, and **TimeClient** on the client machine. From the Task Manager View | Update Speed menu, make sure that High or Normal is selected (Normal is an update interval of about 2 seconds). You will see something like this on the server:

Here, the Task Manager shows that the **TimeServer** is running on the server machine, with a process ID of 152. Since this process has no UI component (and is run non-interactively), you won't see it on the desktop. Now click Finish on the **TimeClient** and watch Task Manager. The entry in Task Manager for **TimeServer** remains for a few seconds after **TimeClient** has apparently released it. This is because the effect of the call to **Release()** in the client is not immediate: the object is released when the delta ping set (which should now contain the **IRemoteTime** ID) is received.

Now let's try this experiment from a different perspective: run **TimeClient** on the client and Task Manager on the server. In Task Manager, select **TimeServer** and click on the End Process button and then click on Yes on the resulting dialog. It takes about 35 seconds until an error is generated on **TimeClient**; this delay is caused by **GetTime()** blocking and eventually returning with a value of **0x800706B5**. Since **TimeClient** is a single threaded application, the UI is frozen during this time.

> *If you get an Access Denied error from Task Manager, your account does not have enough privileges to kill the server. There are several ways round this; the first is to get the right privileges (as will be explained in Chapter 7); the second method is to debug the server by clicking on Debug in Task Manager's right-click context menu and then stopping the server; the final method is to use a utility like **kill.exe** from the NT3.51 resource kit.*

If you look at the implementation of **GetTime()**, you'll see that it only returns **S_OK** or **E_FAIL**. The error generated is not even a COM error: it is **RPC_S_UNKNOWN_IF**, a Microsoft RPC error, complaining that an interface does not exist. Notice, also, that once this error has been generated, subsequent calls to **GetTime()** return immediately with this error, and the UI becomes responsive again.

When the COM server starts up, part of the COM runtime registers the UUID of the object's interface with the RPC runtime. This maintains a *dynamic* table of interface UUIDs (as opposed to the *static* registry of IIDs used by COM). When the server dies, the table is updated; so when the RPC runtime queries for the interface on the object, **RPC_S_UNKNOWN_IF** will be returned, since the interface is no longer in the table.

One final test to try on NT is that of running several **TimeClient**s on the client machine and monitoring the NT Task Manager. However many clients you start on the client machine, you will only ever have one server running. If you run **PView**, the Process Viewer utility provided with the Windows SDK (and Visual C++), you can monitor how many threads the server has running. The following table indicates my results:

Number of Clients	Number of Threads in the Server
1	4
2	4
3	5
4	5
5	6
6	6
7	6
8	6
9	6
10	6

The server starts with 4 threads and has a maximum (in this situation) of 6 threads. This application has been written without any threading in mind. Inspection of the ATL-generated code shows that it uses the apartment model.

The threads created on the server's behalf have been created by DCOM out of the pool of threads that it maintains. In this situation, the server uses up to 6 threads. There's no way for the system administrator to change this. However, DCOM has been built with flexibility and scalability in mind: if the server is heavily used, DCOM may dynamically create more threads to handle the requests and make the clients more responsive. Threading will be covered more thoroughly in Chapter 9

Summary

This chapter has presented the rudiments of writing a DCOM client and server. You should have found that the process is fairly painless, especially if you're already familiar with writing COM code. The basic point to note is that if the client or server has not been written specifically for DCOM, all is not lost: default values for the security, along with information indicating where the server should run, are stored in the registry.

If you're writing a client or server from scratch, you should use the new API functions to initialize COM and create objects, even if you think the objects will only be created on the same machine as the client. This way, you can change your mind in the future without too many changes to your code!

The next chapter will take us into the real depths of writing code using DCOM, starting with the important topic of how we write interface definitions using IDL.

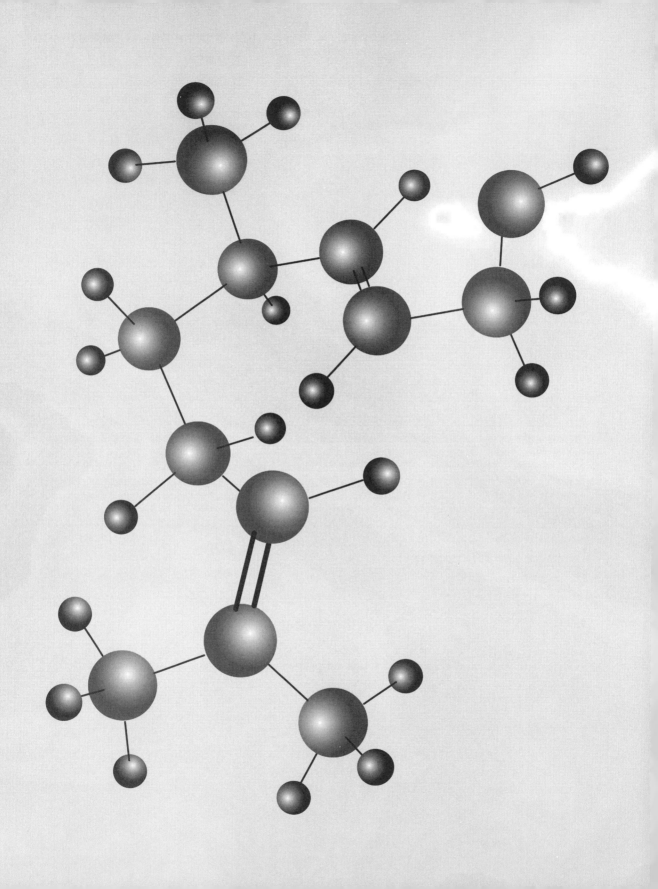

Writing DCOM Clients and Servers

Introduction

This chapter is concerned with the real problems with writing applications to use DCOM. We've already established that legacy applications can remote calls across the network with DCOM. This chapter will concentrate on writing applications specifically for DCOM.

In the first section, I'll describe the use of the **Microsoft Interface Definition Language** (**MIDL**) which is the programming language-independent shorthand for defining COM (and RPC) interfaces. In particular, I show the language mapping of MIDL to C++, since C++ is the natural language of COM.

MIDL will lead on to a description of dispatch interfaces and type libraries, and this neatly brings us to a method of marshaling data that doesn't require interface-specific proxy or stub objects: type library marshaling.

Since this chapter is concerned with writing interfaces, it's an ideal opportunity to introduce the concept of a client and server calling interfaces on each other. To do this, the client and server have to support interfaces called sources and sinks, and support a mechanism called connection points.

The majority of this chapter is reserved for examples. First is an example of type library marshaling, using a custom interface to pass environment variables from a remote server to a client without the use of a dual interface or a proxy and stub. We finish with an example of connection points that extends the remote time server developed in the last chapter. We'll get it to call back to the client when a particular time has been reached – a remote alarm clock.

Interface Definition Language

With any distribution method, the client and server processes may be running on totally different operating systems. Indeed, the two machines may have totally different methods of handling data. One may treat integers as big-endian (the most significant byte stored first) and the other as little-endian. With DCOM, the two processes may even be written in totally different languages.

To enable these different languages, with different data types, on different machines, to talk to each other, they need to talk a common language. That's answered by IDL, the **interface definition language**.

With IDL, the interface designer can write the interface, including prototypes of the interface methods and then compile the IDL with a language-specific compiler. The compiler produces source code for a particular language on a particular machine type. Thus Microsoft's IDL compiler (**MIDL**) produces C and C++ code for Intel machines, or for Alpha and PPC.

To use an object from a client on a particular platform, the client writer will need the interface description of the server's interfaces in the language, and for the processor type, that the designer intends to use for the client. If the **MIDL** compilation for the server is not satisfactory, the designer can just recompile the interface definition with the appropriate IDL compiler.

> *An alternative way of describing interfaces is to use a type library. Type libraries describe interface methods in terms of known data types and are particularly useful for clients written in a scripting language such as Visual Basic. We'll cover type libraries later in the chapter.*

MIDL

The Microsoft IDL compiler (**MIDL.exe**) is provided as part of the Win32 SDK and with Visual C++. **MIDL** provides a mapping between IDL and C or C++.

IDL is similar to C and C++ and allows you to use preprocessor definitions and macros in the same way. Because of this, **MIDL** requires a C/C++ compiler/preprocessor that it can access. You can either allow **MIDL** to use the default compiler, **cl.exe**, (which works just fine if you're using Visual C++, for example), or you can explicitly specify one on the **MIDL** command line with the **/cpp_cmd** switch.

The C preprocessor is used to parse the IDL file to expand any macros that you have entered. However, since **MIDL** can create (among other things) a header file, you may want to use your IDL file to add preprocessor definitions or, other C++ code, that will appear in the header file. To prevent the preprocessor expanding these preprocessor commands (or the MIDL compiler complaining about C++ code), you can wrap the code up in the special MIDL directive **cpp_quote()**. Anything within the parentheses will appear in the final C/C++ header unscathed (e.g. **cpp_quote("#define NO_ITEMS 10")**).

MIDL is a combination of the previous version of **MIDL**, used to generate code for Microsoft RPC (and hence DCE IDL), and **MkTypeLib** which was used to compile ODL (**object description language**) files into type libraries for automation. Microsoft IDL has now subsumed ODL, but, the Visual C++ MFC AppWizard and ClassWizard still produce and maintain ODL files for automation objects. Therefore it's important that you understand the differences between IDL and ODL.

The structure of an IDL file is determined by what you intend to use the IDL for. Generally the items contain descriptive blocks in braces **{}** to which are attached **attributes** given in square brackets **[]**. The **entities** that can be described are given in the following table:

Entity	Description
interface	COM or DCE RPC interfaces. COM interfaces can be custom interfaces derived from **IUnknown** or any COM interface. Or it may be a dispatch or dual interface derived from **IDispatch**
dispinterface	COM interface derived from **IDispatch**
module	A DLL of exported functions
library	A type library
coclass	A component object

We are only concerned with COM here so we will not cover DCE **interface**s. The statements in the IDL file have the following format:

[attributes] statement name {statement_block};

 statement is one of the five entities given in the table above. Each must have a name, which **MIDL** uses to generate the appropriate named structure in the generated C/C++ files. For example: the **interface** name is used as the name of a **class** in a **MIDL**-generated C++ header file).

 The *statement_block* contains other statements, data definitions and **typedef**s for the structure being described. Each *statement* is preceded by a list of *attributes*.

In the following sections, I will identify the important attributes used in IDL when describing COM items.

Files Created by MIDL

There are two main reasons for using **MIDL**. The first is to provide a language-specific mapping for the interface. The second is to provide code for proxy-stub marshaling (creating type libraries can be considered part of marshaling).

In the case of C/C++ (the languages generated by **MIDL**), the interface is described by C and C++ definitions in a header file. The C mappings are a combination of functions and macros (including a definition of a vtable in C). The C++ mappings describe the interface as an abstract class.

The proxy and stub code is created as several C files that can be compiled to produce a self-registering DLL. The proxy and stub are described by a file that has the form *name_p.c*, where *name* is the name of the IDL file. These **MIDL**-generated files contain code that implements marshaling. This is carried out by proxy and stub objects that implement the COM interfaces **IProxyInterface** and **IStubInterface**.

The proxy-stub C source files produced by **MIDL** make quite an interesting read, especially if you are keen to learn about how method calls are marshaled. Much of the boilerplate code is implemented with macros defined in **rpcproxy.h** (from the Win32 SDK), calling on functions in the **rpcrt4.lib** library. The necessary code to provide class factories for the proxy-stub, as well as the default exported DLL functions, is provided in the file **Dlldata.c**. If you look in **Dlldata.c**, you will see that these functions are actually defined in **rpcproxy.h** and accessed through the macro **DLLDATA_ROUTINES()**.

To be able to use the object (and its interfaces) in a client, or to implement the server, two more files must be generated:

 The header that has the C/C++ definitions of the interface. The header file has the name *name.h*, where *name* is the name of the IDL file.

 A declaration of the UUIDs of the object classes (**CLSID**s) and their interfaces (**IID**s) so that references can be taken as parameters in the COM API. These UUIDs are declared in the file *name_i.c*.

MIDL Variable Types

COM must be able to transfer data from the client to the server and back to the client. This may require the proxy and stub to create and maintain separate memory buffers and, if a parameter is an interface pointer, it may require additional proxies and stubs to be loaded.

Since proxies and stubs must create packets of data to be sent along the wire, they need to know the data type and the size of the parameters. As a consequence, the programmer is restricted to particular types in describing methods and properties. MIDL does allow the programmer to define complex data types like **struct**s and **union**s from these basic types, but they require some extra work in addition to the C equivalents.

We'll look at these later in the chapter. Let's run through a description of the types that can be marshaled:

Base Types

IDL defines base types, which you can use as parameters for your methods or as members in **struct**s or **union**s. You can also use these types as the return values for methods.

For remoted interfaces, and interfaces that are going to be accessed from Visual Basic, the method return type can only be **HRESULT**. You saw this in the last chapter, where the underlying RPC remoting layer can substitute its own status codes if the remote (or local) object is temporarily or permanently unavailable.

Remember that the COM IDL is based upon DCE IDL, which has no support for objects or advanced features like exceptions and interface inheritance. Contrast this with CORBA IDL that was designed for objects and has support for both of these.

The base types that MIDL handles are:

Base type	Default sign	Description
boolean	unsigned	8-bit data item
byte	-	8-bit data item
char	unsigned	8-bit unsigned data item
double	-	64-bit floating-point number
float	-	32-bit floating-point number
handle_t	-	Primitive handle type
hyper	signed	64-bit signed integer
int	signed	32-bit (platform-dependent) signed integer
long	signed	32-bit signed integer
short	signed	16-bit signed integer
small	signed	8-bit signed integer
void *	-	32-bit context handle pointer type
wchar_t	unsigned	16-bit unsigned data item

In addition, the **signed** and **unsigned** modifiers can be used.

Automation Types

Methods that are part of a **dispinterface**, a **dual** interface or an interface that will be marshaled using type library marshaling, will use the automation proxy and stubs.

They can only marshal data types (or pointers to those data types) supported by those objects. The data types supported are:

Type	Description
boolean	This is an **unsigned char** that is either **TRUE** or **FALSE**.
unsigned char	8-bit unsigned data item.
double	64-bit IEEE floating-point number.
float	32-bit IEEE floating-point number.
int	Integer whose size is system dependent. On 32-bit platforms, **int** is a 32-bit signed integer.
long	32-bit signed integer.
short	16-bit signed integer.
BSTR	Length-prefixed string.
CY	8-byte fixed-point number used to pass currency values.
DATE	64-bit floating-point fractional number of days since December 30, 1899.
HRESULT	Built-in error type.
enum	Signed integer, whose size is system-dependent. By default, when transmitted over a network, **enum** objects are **unsigned short**. By applying the **v1_enum** attribute, you can force an **enum** type to be transmitted as a 32-bit entity.
IDispatch*	Pointer to **IDispatch** interface.
IUnknown*	Pointer to interface that is not derived from **IDispatch** (**VT_UNKNOWN**).

In addition to these, a parameter can be declared as **SAFEARRAY** or **VARIANT**.

- A **VARIANT** is a discriminated union of the types described in the table. This allows methods to be called from languages that are not typed, or do not enforce variable typing.

- **SAFEARRAY**s are a method of passing variable sized arrays of data without having to use the semantics of DCE arrays. A parameter which is an array of a data type: **type**, is declared as being of type **SAFEARRAY(type)**.

- We'll look at **SAFEARRAY**s in more detail later in the chapter.

Typedefs, Constants and Enumerations

An IDL statement can contain **typedef**s for other types. The **typedef** statement works like the C equivalent, allowing you to use one symbol in your code in place of another. The statement also allows attributes to be used. Examples of **typedef**s from the Win32 **Wtypes.idl** are:

```
typedef unsigned short WORD;
typedef [string] char *LPSTR;
```

These provide mappings from IDL types to Win32 types. The first is straightforward, declaring the symbol **WORD** to mean an **unsigned short**. In the second case, we also have an attribute. This is declaring that the symbol **LPSTR** can be used for **[string] char***. **[string]** declares a null terminated string type. You'll see how and when to use the **[string]** attribute later in this chapter.

You can also use IDL statements to declare constants, which can be of integer, character, string or Boolean types. As in C++, the constant is declared as an initialized value modified with **const**. This modifier can also be used to declare the **const**ness of method parameters, just as C++ does. Examples are:

```
typedef [string] const char *LPCSTR;
const DISPID DISPID_UNKNOWN = -1;
```

The first example is from **Wtypes.h** and declares that a **LPCSTR** is a pointer to a constant string type. The second example, from **Oaidl.idl**, defines a constant called **DISPID_UNKNOWN** that has a value of **-1**. Thus, wherever you use the symbol **DISPID_UNKNOWN** in your code, the value **-1** is used. DCE IDL does not support **const**, so this is mapped to the C **#define** preprocessor directive.

As in C, constants are fine when used singly, but when you wish to declare a series of constants or if you want to pass an integer from a limited list of values, then an enumeration is more appropriate. In IDL you use the **enum** statement to declare an enumeration in the same way as you would in C.

Here's an example from **Wtypes.idl** :

```
typedef enum tagCLSCTX
{
    CLSCTX_INPROC_SERVER = 0x01,
    CLSCTX_INPROC_HANDLER = 0x02,
    CLSCTX_LOCAL_SERVER = 0x04,
    CLSCTX_INPROC_SERVER16 = 0x08,
    CLSCTX_REMOTE_SERVER = 0x10,
    CLSCTX_INPROC_HANDLER16 = 0x20,
    CLSCTX_INPROC_SERVERX86 = 0x40,
    CLSCTX_INPROC_HANDLERX86 = 0x80
} CLSCTX;
```

Here the IDL defines the **CLSCTX** enumeration that is used to specify the object server type in **CoCreateInstance()**. By default **enum**s are transmitted as 16-bit **unsigned short**. To force an **enum** to be transmitted as a 32-bit value, use the **[v1_enum]** attribute:

```
typedef [v1_enum] enum tagTAPTYPE {TAP_HOT, TAP_COLD} TAPTYPE;
```

Structs and Unions

As in C, IDL has the **struct** statement. This works in much the same way as C, except you cannot use bit fields or function pointers. Another section of **Wtypes.idl** :

```
typedef struct _SYSTEMTIME {
    WORD wYear;
    WORD wMonth;
```

```
    WORD wDayOfWeek;
    WORD wDay;
    WORD wHour;
    WORD wMinute;
    WORD wSecond;
    WORD wMilliseconds;
} SYSTEMTIME, *PSYSTEMTIME, *LPSYSTEMTIME;
```

structs are not supported in automation, so you can't pass a **struct** as a parameter of a method in a **dual** interface, a **dispinterface**, or any typelib marshaled interface. The two main solutions to this problem are to define an interface for the structure, and hence pass the **struct** as a COM object, or to use a **SAFEARRAY** of **VARIANT**s.

An interface for the **SYSTEMTIME struct** could be:

```
interface ISystemTime : IDispatch
{
    [propput, id(1)] HRESULT wYear([in] short sVal);
    [propget, id(1)] HRESULT wYear([out, retval]
                                   short* psVal);
    [propput, id(2)] HRESULT wMonth([in] short sVal);
    [propget, id(2)] HRESULT wMonth([out, retval]
                                    short* psVal);
    [propput, id(3)] HRESULT wDayOfWeek([in] short sVal);
    [propget, id(3)] HRESULT wDayOfWeek([out, retval]
                                        short* psVal);
    [propput, id(4)] HRESULT wDay([in] short sVal);
    [propget, id(4)] HRESULT wDay([out, retval]
                                  short* psVal);
    [propput, id(5)] HRESULT wHour([in] short sVal);
    [propget, id(5)] HRESULT wHour([out, retval]
                                   short* psVal);
    [propput, id(6)] HRESULT wMinute([in] short sVal);
    [propget, id(6)] HRESULT wMinute([out, retval]
                                     short* psVal);
    [propput, id(7)] HRESULT wSecond([in] short sVal);
    [propget, id(7)] HRESULT wSecond([out, retval]
                                     short* psVal);
    [propput, id(8)] HRESULT wMilliseconds([in] short sVal);
    [propget, id(8)] HRESULT wMilliseconds([out, retval]
                                           short* psVal);
};

typedef ISystemTime* LPSYSTEMTIME;
```

This defines an interface that has property accessor methods for each of the members of the structure.

Since the **SYSTEMTIME struct** only contains **WORD**s, we could use a **SAFEARRAY(WORD)** to pass the data to a method. However, for a structure with elements of multiple types, the safest way to pass the data is to use a **SAFEARRAY** of **VARIANT**s which allows each member of the array to specify its own data type.

Discriminated Unions

Discriminated unions are declared with the **union** keyword. MIDL supports two types of discriminated unions, **encapsulated unions** and **non-encapsulated unions**. In the first case the discriminator is declared with the **switch()** keyword. An example from **oaidl.idl** is:

```
typedef union _wireSAFEARRAY_UNION switch(ULONG sfType) u
{
    case SF_BSTR:         SAFEARR_BSTR       BstrStr;
    case SF_UNKNOWN:      SAFEARR_UNKNOWN    UnknownStr;
    case SF_DISPATCH:     SAFEARR_DISPATCH   DispatchStr;
    case SF_VARIANT:      SAFEARR_VARIANT    VariantStr;
    case SF_I1:           BYTE_SIZEDARR      ByteStr;
    case SF_I2:           WORD_SIZEDARR      WordStr;
    case SF_I4:           DWORD_SIZEDARR     LongStr;
    case SF_I8:           HYPER_SIZEDARR     HyperStr;
    default:              ;                  // error
} SAFEARRAYUNION;
```

Here the discriminator **sfType**, is declared of type **ULONG** and, depending on the value of **u**, the data in the **union** is treated as a **BSTR**, a **VARIANT** or any of the other members declared. The discriminator and the **union** are *encapsulated* in a **struct**, hence the name. This requires the discriminator to be set when the value of the **union** is got or set. It would be nice to use a discriminator outside of the **union** and this is the purpose of non-encapsulated **union**s.

Non-encapsulated Unions

In this case, the **union** is declared with the **[switch_type()]** attribute to specify the type that is used to switch the **union** members on. When a **union** is declared, the discriminator is declared with the **[switch_is()]** attribute:

```
typedef struct tagTYPEDESC
{
   [switch_type(VARTYPE), switch_is(vt)]
   union
   {
     [case(VT_PTR, VT_SAFEARRAY)]
     struct tagTYPEDESC * lptdesc;
     [case(VT_CARRAY)]
     struct tagARRAYDESC * lpadesc;
     [case(VT_USERDEFINED)]
     HREFTYPE hreftype;
     [default] ;
   };
   VARTYPE vt;
} TYPEDESC;
```

This was taken from **oaidl.idl**. Here the **struct TYPEDESC** has a **union** and the discriminator of the **union** is declared outside as the member **vt**.

Arrays

When you pass a pointer to a function in C, it is up to the function to determine exactly what the pointer means. The problem with C (and hence C++) is that pointers and arrays are interchangeable. In fact, the pointer syntax and array syntax are just two different ways of saying the same thing. So both lines of code shown below are equivalent:

```
void PassData(UINT* pInts);
void PassData(UINT pInts[]);
```

To a programmer, the second form implies that the parameter is passing an array of **UINT**s, and the first implies that the parameter is either a pointer to a single **UINT** or the start of an array. Neither gives any indication of the size of the array.

Convention has it that strings, arrays of **char**s or **wchar_t**s, specify their length by making the last member a **NULL**. The string user can then use a runtime library function like **lstrlen()** to test every member of the array until a **NULL** is reached and then return the running character count.

For other data types, or if the parameter is an **[out]** value, such a convention cannot be used (after all, it would be an unreasonable overhead for the caller to fill the whole of the buffer for an **[out]** value with non-**NULL** values except for the last member). In these cases, there is no option but to give the actual size of the array buffer when passing it to a function.

Consider the Win32 function, **RegQueryValue()**:

```
LONG RegQueryValue(HKEY hKey, LPCTSTR lpSubKey,
        LPTSTR lpValue, PLONG lpcbValue);
```

This gets the data of a value in the registry in the subkey named by **lpSubKey** (**[in]** parameter) of the opened key with the handle **hKey** (**[in]** parameter). The data is written to the buffer pointed to by **lpValue** (**[out]** parameter) and the size of this buffer is held in a variable that is pointed to by **lpcbValue** (**[in, out]** parameter). If the buffer is too small, the function can return an error value (**ERROR_MORE_DATA**) and specify the required size of the buffer via the **[in, out]** parameter.

This is a technique used quite often in Win32, and allows the programmer to determine how big a buffer to allocate with the first call, and then get the data with a second call.

The Win32 function to set a value is

```
LONG RegSetValue(HKEY hKey, LPCTSTR lpSubKey, DWORD dwType,
            LPCTSTR lpData, DWORD cbData);
```

Which passes the buffer size by value, since the buffer is an **[in]** parameter.

IDL is used to prepare methods for transmission across the network and thus the proxy must create a data packet with the method parameters. To do this it will have to copy the parameters, so it must be able to determine how big any variable length buffers are. It may look simple in the case of **[in]** parameters (for example functions like **RegSetValue()**) where a separate parameter determines the size of the buffer. However, this masks the fact that the proxy and stub are generated from the IDL and must indicate the parameter to which the buffer size actually refers.

In the case of **[out]** buffers (in functions like **RegQueryValue()**), the technique of calling the method twice may be unacceptable since every call must go over the network.

IDL manages passing arrays of data though arrays known as **fixed**, **conformant**, or **varying**. The array type that you use will be determined by whether the caller or callee knows the size of the buffer and/or the expected size of the returned data and how much overhead you are willing to tolerate.

Fixed Arrays

This is the simplest case; here the interface designer knows in advance how big the array needs to be and can hardcode the size of the buffer in the IDL. The simplest case is for a single value to be sent:

```
HRESULT SetLongValue([in] long value);
```

If we need to send an array, the IDL should specify the array's length:

```
HRESULT SetLongArray([in] long array[10]);
```

Here we are specifying that 10 **long**s are being passed to the method. The proxy will copy the 40 bytes following the address pointed to by **array** into the marshaled packet, and the stub knows that it needs to allocate 40 bytes to hold the passed data.

Conformant Arrays

It is not always possible for the programmer to know in advance the size of the array that needs to be sent, so he or she will need to pass an extra parameter with the size of the data. As mentioned above, there must be an indication as to which parameter has the size, and this is done with the **size_is()** attribute:

```
HRESULT SetLongArray([in] long nSize,
            [in, size_is(nSize)] long array[]);
```

Now since the size of the array is passed in **nSize**, the size of the array is not specified in the **array** parameter. Since this is, after all, just a pointer, we can write:

```
HRESULT SetLongArray([in] long nSize,
            [in, size_is(nSize)] long* array);
```

The array passed is called a **conformant** array and the parameter to **size_is()** is the **conformance**. The conformance need not be a single parameter of the method; it could be an arithmetic expression involving other parameters of the method.

> *There's another IDL attribute called* **max_is()** *that specifies the maximum index of the array. Since both attributes assume the start index is 0, this means that* **size_is(n)** *is equivalent to* **max_is(n - 1)**.

So far we have just looked at **[in]** buffers, but what about **[out]** buffers? This is equivalent to the **RegQueryValue()** above, where the caller allocates a buffer and sends the address of the buffer and its size to the server, for example:

```
HRESULT GetLongArray([in, out] long* pSize,
                [out, size_is(*pSize)] long* array);
```

The method can test the data that the object holds and if there are too many values to fill the array (i.e. ***pSize** is too small), the function can fail. This will require the caller to make another attempt with a larger array. If the size of the array is an **[in, out]** parameter, then the function can return the required size of the buffer in that parameter. However, this is expensive in terms of RPC calls.

Conformant arrays are great, but they don't solve all possible problems that you may encounter. Consider a function that allows a client to ask a server to fill part of an array with certain values. The client could pass the array, the first element in the array that it wants the server to change and a pointer to a variable to receive the total number of elements that the server changed:

```
HRESULT GetNextLong([in] long nSize, [in] long start,
                    [out] long* count,
                    [in, out, size_is(nSize)] long* buffer);
```

The client could call this with:

```
long* value = (long*)CoTaskMemAlloc(10 * sizeof(long));
long count = 1;
long offset = 0;
while (count > 0)
{
   pobj->GetNextLong(10, offset, &count, value);
   offset += count;
}
CoTaskMemFree(value);
```

And the server could implement the function like this:

```
HRESULT CObjServerImpl:: GetNextLong(long nSize,
                                     long start,
                                     long* count, long* buffer)
{
   *count = 0;
   while (start <= nSize - 1 && *count != 2)
   {
      buffer[start] = start;
      *count = *count + 1;
      start++;
   }
   return S_OK;
}
```

This rather contrived method returns an array in portions. The client creates an array of **long**s and passes this along with the start of the items to change in the array. When the method is called, a buffer of **nSize long**s is passed to the server, **count** elements are changed and then the entire buffer, **nSize long**s, is transmitted back to the client. This is clearly inefficient. The greater the disparity between the size of the buffer (**nSize**) and the number of elements that are changed (**count**), the greater the inefficiency of the method.

Varying Arrays

To make methods like **GetNextLong()** more efficient, IDL allows you to use the **first_is()** and **length_is()** attributes to mark parameters as indicating how much of the buffer was altered and hence must be passed across the network. To increase efficiency, the IDL for **GetNextLong()** could be changed to this:

```
#define SIZE 1024
HRESULT GetNextLong([in] long start, [out] long* count,
   [in, out, first_is(start), length_is(*count)]
   long buffer[SIZE]);
```

Notice that the size of the buffer is specified. This is necessary since the stub code will need to know how much memory *in total* the buffer requires. The other attributes specify the elements that are changed, and hence allow the marshaler to transmit only those items that have changed. This is just as expensive as the original in terms of memory. This is because the stub on the server will still need to create a buffer of **SIZE long**s on the server side, even if only **count** items are actually returned - but it reduces the amount of network traffic.

There is one slight variation on this. Instead of **length_is()** you can use **last_is()**, where **last_is()** gives the index of the last element transmitted in the array. The main disadvantage of a varying array, for the programmer, is that the largest size of the array has to be known when the IDL is written. In the above example the programmer must define a value for **SIZE**. For a conformant array this is not an issue since the maximum size of the array is passed as a parameter, what we need is the network efficiency of varying arrays and the flexibility of conformant arrays.

Open Arrays

A variant on varying arrays is when the size of the array is passed as a parameter:

```
HRESULT GetNextLong([in] long start, [out] long* count,
        [in] long nSize,
        [in, out, first_is(start),
           length_is(*count), size_is(nSize)]
        long* buffer);
```

This is a combination of conformant and varying arrays and is known as an **open array**. Now we can determine both the maximum size of the array and the number of elements to transmit both at runtime.

Enumerators

The previous three sections have concentrated on passing an array as one whole entity. This requires the source of the array to tell the marshaler how big the array is, so that the marshaler at the client end can transmit the required number of bytes across the network. The marshaler at the other end can allocate a buffer large enough to take the data.

This is fine for relatively small amounts of data, but if the method could pass a huge amount of data, this would result in the creation of large temporary buffers. This would result in a corresponding performance hit.

A solution to this problem would be to allow the client to ask for a part of the data at a time. This could be like the Win32 file find functions. Remember, **FindFirstFile()** is called first to initialize the internal data, then **FindNextFile()** is called repeatedly to get information about the requested files. This continues until the function indicates that there is no more data. Finally, **FindClose()** is called to clear up any data held by the system.

COM has a standard way to do this using an **enumeration interface**. The enumeration interface consists of four methods:

- ▲ **Next()** - User calls **Next()** to get the next element from the enumerator
- ▲ **Skip()** - To ignore a specified number of elements
- ▲ **Reset()** - To set the enumerator's marker back to the start of the list
- ▲ **Clone()** - To get a copy of the enumerator

COM defines some standard enumeration interfaces (including **IEnumConnectionPoints**, which we'll look at later in the chapter), but there are as many potential enumeration interfaces as there are data types. This because each interface is specific to one data type. Enumeration interfaces are named **IEnum** followed by the type of data that they enumerate, thus a generic enumeration interface is often written as **IEnumXXXX**, although no such interface exists.

The advantage of using an enumerator is that the client can ask for just a few members of the array and can stop enumerating at any point. Since the enumerator is an object, the enumerator data can be initialized when the object is created and the data can be released when the object is released. Thus the **GetlongArray()** function could be:

```
HRESULT GetLongArray([out] IEnumLONG** ppEnum);
```

Where **IEnumLONG** is an interface that supports the methods of the **IEnumXXXX** interface. The enumerator interface provides a method called **Next()** that a client can call to obtain data from the enumerator. This method allows the client to ask for as many or, as few data items as it wants. The server can then either return all the requested data items or, if the data is not available, fewer.

Strings

Strings, of course, are arrays of **char**s or **wchar_t**s, so the information in the previous section is as applicable to strings as to any other type of array. However, strings are special in that the convention is to mark the end of an array with a **NULL** and thus it is unnecessary to specify the length of a string since you could call a function like **lstrlen()** to find out how long it is. Although you can perform simple arithmetic in a **size_is()**, you can't call a function in IDL, so the following 'IDL' code will not work:

```
HRESULT PassString([in, size_is(lstrlen(str) + 1)]
                        const char* str);
```

Instead, IDL has a **[string]** attribute that ensures that the appropriate function is called to determine the length of the string in the generated C code:

```
HRESULT PassString([in, string] const char* str);
```

If the method returns the string as an **[out]** parameter then we have the problem of the client knowing how big the buffer should be. This brings us back to the example with **RegQueryValue()** again. IDL offers no magic solution: you could pass a string buffer in with a **size_is()**, check to see if it's large enough, and reallocate the buffer if necessary. Unfortunately this would require at least two calls of the method.

The solution lies in COM. COM defines a task allocator for the server, and any memory allocated with the task allocator in the server is marshaled across to the client process. Thus a method could allocate a buffer with the task allocator and pass this buffer back as an **[out]** parameter. The client then would have to free the memory using its task allocator (*not* **delete** or **free()**!).

So a method that returns a string could be defined and implemented like this:

```
HRESULT GetString([out, string] char** str);
```

```
HRESULT CObj::GetString(char** str)
{
    *str = CoTaskMemAlloc(lstrlen("Reply"));
```

```
    // ... assign a useful value to str
      return S_OK;
    }
```

The client would call the method with:

```
    LPSTR str;
    pObj->GetString(&str);
    printf(str);
    CoTaskMemFree(str);
```

BSTRs

In addition to using standard arrays of **char** or **wchar_t** as strings, you could use **BSTR**s, as we mentioned in the last chapter. **BSTR**s are length-prefixed arrays of wide characters. The marshaler can read this hidden length to determine how big an array to create and how many characters to transmit, so there's no need to specify the **[string]** attribute for **BSTR** parameters. Because of the hidden length, you should create and free **BSTR**s with the **SysAllocString()** and **SysFreeString()** functions. These functions are actually just helpers that call **CoTaskMemAlloc()** and **CoTaskMemFree()**, but they take the hidden length into account.

Exceptions

You can throw exceptions *within* a process. You can do this by either using the C++ **throw** statement or the NT, structured exception handling function **RaiseException()**. However, you cannot throw exceptions out of a process. So, if your COM object's method fails in some way, this is propagated back to the client via the method's status code. This is in contrast to CORBA where methods can throw exceptions and the exceptions can be marked in the CORBA IDL.

Help File Support in MIDL

The original aim of type libraries was to allow a client to dynamically query a server for the methods it supported and thus to construct the method call at runtime from the information it received. This is the reason for the **ITypeInfo** interface, which allows a client to query for a method's signature in terms of its parameters and return type. This is fine for browsers like Visual Basic, which query the type library to syntax check VB code that calls on an object. However, a function prototype is not usually enough for a human reader to know what a function does. Therefore, it makes sense to add more descriptive information into the type library.

IDL has three attributes to add help information. A Windows help file is a series of topics that can be accessed via hyperlink jumps that are marked with identifiers called context IDs. Thus to allow a user to get access to the help text for an item in a type library, you need to specify the name of the help file and the context ID for the help text. This is done by specifying two attributes, **[helpfile]** and **[helpcontext]**. The first is applied to the **library** statement and specifies the help file for the entire library. The second attribute can be applied to **library** and any other element that you can mention in the **library** block. The attribute specifies the context ID of the text for this particular item:

```
    // Helptest.idl
    import "oaidl.idl";

    [ uuid(FC540109-48A7-11d0-9A73-0060973044A8),object ]
    interface ITest1 : IUnknown
```

```
{
   [helpcontext(0x100005)]
   HRESULT Method2([in] UINT param1);
};

[ uuid(FC540107-48A7-11d0-9A73-0060973044A8),
  helpfile("Testhelp.hlp"), helpcontext(0x100001)]
library test
{
   [helpcontext(0x100002)] interface ITest1;
   [uuid(FC540108-48A7-11d0-9A73-0060973044A8)]
   interface ITest2 : IUnknown
   {
      [helpcontext(0x100004)]
      HRESULT Method1([in] UINT param1);
   };
};
```

This IDL specifies that the library is associated with the help file **Testhelp.hlp**.

▲ General help can be found under the context **0x100001**

▲ Help on interface **ITest1** can be found under index **0x100002**

▲ Help on **Method1** and **Method2** at **0x100004** and **0x100005**, respectively

A browser can use **ITypeInfo::GetDocumentation()** to get the help file name and the context ID and then use the Win32 **WinHelp()** function, passing this information. This will launch the Windows help file viewer, which will load the help file and display the specified topic.

> *The path to a type library's help file should be stored in the registry under*
> **HKEY_CLASSES_ROOT\TypeLib\{typelib}\version\HELPDIR** *where* **{typelib}** *is the*
> *GUID of the type library (eg* **{FC540107-48A7-11d0-9A73-0060973044A8}** *in the* **test**
> *example above) and* **version** *is the version of the library*

While these two attributes are helpful for getting help from a help file, there are also cases when a single line of help text would be useful.

For example in the Visual Basic Object Browser:

This shows the methods in the VBA type library **Vbaen32.olb**. The module **Math** has been selected in the left-hand box, and its methods are listed in the right hand box. The method **Randomize()** has been selected and the object browser has given a short piece of help text at the bottom of the dialog. The first piece of information, the method prototype, is obtained by calling the **ITypeInfo::GetFuncDesc()** method on the type library. The second line gives a description of the method.

This description has not been obtained from the type library help file (you cannot query a help file for a piece of text, you can only tell WinHelp to display a particular topic). This help text has been read directly from the type library. You attach a piece of help text to an item with the **[helpstring()]** attribute, and it can be read using the **ITypeInfo::GetDocumentation()** method.

OLEView gives the following IDL for the **Randomize()** method:

```
[
  uuid(000204F3-0000-0000-C000-000000000046),
  version(1.0),
  helpstring("Visual Basic For Applications"),
  helpfile("VBA.HLP"),
  helpcontext(0x000f6791)
]
library VBA
{
    // other entries
    [
        dllname("VBA32.DLL"),
        uuid(39D67E60-2BCC-1069-82DB-00DD010EDFAA),
        helpstring("Procedures used to perform mathematical
                        operations"),
        helpcontext(0x000f6ec3)
    ]
    module Math
    {
    // other entries
      [
          entry(0x60000004),
          helpstring("Initializes the random-number
                        generator"),
          helpcontext(0x000f6566)
      ]
      void _stdcall Randomize([in] VARIANT* Number);
    };
};
```

Math is a **module**, which is a DLL of exported functions. The functions in the DLL are not part of an interface and so are not accessed through an object. However, the type library provides a convenient way of managing DLLs.

Interfaces

We know that an object exposes its functionality through groups of associated methods called *interfaces*. Before you can write an object, you must determine which interfaces it supports. A client of the object can tell if the object supports a particular interface by calling **QueryInterface()** on an interface pointer that it already holds, passing the IID of the interface to query for.

If the object just supports standard OLE interfaces (like **IDataObject**, or **IDropTarget**) then the object writer knows what methods the interface supports. It also knows parameter lists from the headers in the Win32 SDK. Since the interfaces are standard interfaces, the proxy-stub objects will be supplied with the system, and information about them will already be held in the registry. The client will also know about the interface and thus won't need any further information to call the interface methods. Therefore a type library, for example, is not required.

If the object has a custom interface, or it is an automation object with a dual interface, the object writer must define the interface before it can be implemented. There are several reasons for this:

- The interface must have an IID so that it can be uniquely identified.
- It must have proxy-stub objects to marshal the calls across process (and machine) boundaries.
- There must be a language-dependent description of the interface so that both the client and server can use the interface (in C/C++ this is a header file).

As with the other entries in an IDL file, interfaces have the following format:

[*attributes*] interface *name* **{***interface_definition***};**

This defines the interface called *name*; the statement block has the types and method definitions for the interface. Interfaces may be based upon other interfaces. In fact, *all* interfaces must support the functionality of the **IUnknown** interface. This is done by deriving from another interface:

[*attributes*] interface IMyInterface : IUnknown {*interface_definition***};**

This specifies that the interface supports the **IUnknown** methods, the object writer must implement the methods defined in the interface block and the **IUnknown** methods **QueryInterface()**, **AddRef()** and **Release()**.

There are several attributes that are important for an interface. The most important is the **[uuid()]** which identifies the interface's IID. MIDL can be used to define both COM and DCE interfaces (for Microsoft RPC) and to distinguish between the two you must use the **[object]** attribute.

For example, the following excerpt from **Objidl.idl** defines the **IPersist** interface:

```
[
    object,
    uuid(0000010c-0000-0000-C000-000000000046)
]

interface IPersist : IUnknown
{
    typedef [unique] IPersist *LPPERSIST;

    HRESULT GetClassID
    (
        [out] CLSID *pClassID
    );
}
```

Note that the [odl] attribute, which served a similar purpose to [object] and was used by MkTypeLib, is now obsolete.

All interfaces ultimately derive from an interface defined by an **interface** statement. Quite often there may be many layers of derivation involved. **MIDL** is a code generator and so we might as well get it to carry out this work of derivation.

dispinterface

Automation objects provide methods that are marshaled by the automation marshaler, so they don't need a separate proxy-stub DLL. So that a scripting client can call methods dynamically, the automation methods are called through a single, well known, dispatch method called **IDispatch::Invoke()**. The client informs this method which automation method it's actually invoking, by passing an ID called a DISPID. Of course, the automation method will require parameters and return types - these will also need to be marshaled. One effect of this is that types that can be used must be recognized, i.e. the automation types.

We discussed in Chapter 3 how a client needs to determine the IDs of the methods and parameters before building up a structure that can be passed to **Invoke()**.The client can find out about the available methods and get IDs from method names. It uses the information provided through the server's **IDispatch** interface or the type library provided by the server.

The server must implement **Invoke()** so that it can perform the correct action. This may mean simply that it checks which method was invoked, then passes the **DISPPARAMS** parameter to an internal function that corresponds to that particular method. The called function can then check the validity of the parameters and, if possible, perform the task. This is rather messy, as it involves each function corresponding to a dispatch method having to interpret the values in the **DISPPARAMS** parameter.

A better implementation of **Invoke()** would do this parameter checking and extraction from the **DISPPARAMS** structure on behalf of the dispatch methods. This would enable the server programmer to write the dispatch methods to take typed parameters instead of a general pointer to a **DISPARAMS** structure. Such an implementation would know about the dispatch method parameter lists, since the methods are implemented in the same code module.

A further refinement could be to make the **IDispatch** implementation more generic so that the parameter lists of the dispatch methods are not hard-coded, but extracted from a type library. Thus **GetIDsOfNames()** could be implemented by calling **ITypeInfo::GetIDsOfNames()**, which does all the work. Similarly, since the **ITypeInfo** interface implements an **Invoke()** function, it should call the appropriate dispatch method. To wrap this up even further, we can call the generic dispatch implementation: **CreateStdDispatch()**. This takes a pointer to an **ITypeInfo** and to an interface in the **dispinterface** and does all the work that we would have done if we implemented the **IDispatch** interface methods ourselves.

In other words, if we create a type library and use the facilities available to us, we can save ourselves a lot of work when it comes to implementing **IDispatch**, and we can make it particularly easy for clients to find out about the abilities of our servers.

So how does MIDL let us define dispinterfaces so that they can be compiled into a type library? Well, MIDL provides the **dispinterface** statement for a start.

dispinterface syntax

The **dispinterface** statement has two syntaxes. The first lists the **interface** whose methods are exposed through automation:

```
[uuid(FC54010A-48A7-11d0-9A73-0060973044A8)]
dispinterface DispTime
{
    interface ITime;
};
```

By declaring the **dispinterface**, **DispTime**, we're specifying that the interface is derived from **IDispatch** and that it uses the interface **ITime**. This is enough for the **ITypeInfo** implementation to match the DISPIDs in the type library to the methods in the interface implementations. However we still need to delegate the **IDispatch** methods to the appropriate methods in **ITypeInfo**.

The other syntax of the **dispinterface** is to list all the methods and properties that the interface will expose. This allows anyone using the type library to easily get the dispatch IDs from the names of the methods, or vice versa.

```
// Timeanddate.idl
import "oaidl.idl";

[uuid(FC54010A-48A7-11d0-9A73-0060973044A8)]
dispinterface ITimeAndDate
{
    properties:
        [id(1)]  WORD Year;
        [id(2)]  WORD Month;
        [id(3)]  WORD Day;
        [id(4)]  WORD Hour;
        [id(5)]  WORD Minute;
        [id(6)]  WORD Second;
    methods:
        [id(7)]  HRESULT DayOfTheWeek([out,retval] BSTR* dotw);
};

[uuid(FC54010B-48A7-11d0-9A73-0060973044A8)]
library TimeAndDateLib
{
    dispinterface ITimeAndDate;
};
```

This syntax is reminiscent of ODL. In this example the properties are declared under the **properties** section, as you would in ODL (the property is read and write unless the **[readonly]** attribute is used).

To be more like IDL they can be declared in the **methods** section, in which case the accessor method should be given and these are marked with one of **[propput]**, **[propputref]** or **[propget]**. You can specify whether the property is read/write, read-only or write-only by specifying both accessor methods or just one. This also allows you to control how the parameters are sent to the object: **[propput]** has the data sent by value, **[propputref]** has the data sent by reference. Thus, the above interface can be given as:

```
// Timeanddate.idl
import "oaidl.idl";
```

```
[uuid(FC54010A-48A7-11d0-9A73-0060973044A8)]
dispinterface ITimeAndDate
{
properties:
methods:
    [id(1),  propput] HRESULT Year([in] WORD wYear);
    [id(1),  propget] HRESULT Year([out, retval]
                                        WORD* pwYear);
    [id(2),  propput] HRESULT Month([in] WORD wMonth);
    [id(2),  propget] HRESULT Month([out, retval]
                                        WORD* pwMonth);
    [id(3),  propput] HRESULT Day([in] WORD wDay);
    [id(3),  propget] HRESULT Day([out, retval]
                                        WORD* pwDay);
    [id(4),  propput] HRESULT Hour([in] WORD wHour);
    [id(4),  propget] HRESULT Hour([out, retval]
                                        WORD* pwHour);
    [id(5),  propput] HRESULT Minute([in] WORD wMinute);
    [id(5),  propget] HRESULT Minute([out, retval]
                                        WORD* pwMinute);
    [id(6),  propput] HRESULT Second([in] WORD wSecond);
    [id(6),  propget] HRESULT Second([out, retval]
                                        WORD* pwSecond);
    [id(7)] HRESULT DayOfTheWeek([out, retval] BSTR* dotw);
};

[uuid(FC54010B-48A7-11d0-9A73-0060973044A8)]
library TimeAndDateLib
{
    dispinterface ITimeAndDate;
};
```

Dual Interfaces

The automation described so far is *late binding*. This means that the address of the method is not known at compile time and is only known at runtime via the information in the type library. If the client developer is willing to hard code DISPIDs into the code then calls to **GetIDsOfNames()** are not necessary – this is called *early binding*.

The problem with late binding is that querying a type library is a slow process and early binding still requires parameters to be packaged and unpackaged. This makes the code slower than calling through the vtable, but it also makes it more complicated and therefore error prone.

Contrast calling a method through a vtable with the following process: passing a name of a method to **ITypeInfo::GetIDsOfNames()**; getting a DISPID; calling **ITypeInfo::GetFuncDesc()** to find out the parameters of a method; creating a **DISPARAMS** with the parameters we want to use; and, finally, calling **IDispatch::Invoke()**. In the second case, we have many method calls on the server (potentially across a network). In the first, the client just calls the method through an interface pointer as if the method was implemented in the address space of the client.

If the automation client knows at compile time which interface it will call and the class of the object, there is no need for the client to go through the process of querying the type library – it should be able to call the method directly through a vtable. However, if the client doesn't know these things, it should still be able to use the same interface through **IDispatch::Invoke()** if it decides it needs to at runtime.

A dual interface exposes its methods through a vtable and through **IDispatch::Invoke()**. This means that clients have the option of calling **Invoke()** (and therefore using late binding or early binding), or calling the methods in the vtable directly, which is known as *very early binding*. You can specify that an interface is dual by using the **[dual]** attribute in IDL:

```
// Dualdate.idl
import "oaidl.idl";

[uuid(FC54010C-48A7-11d0-9A73-0060973044A8), dual]
interface IDualDate : IDispatch
{
    [id(1), propput] HRESULT Year(WORD wYear);
    [id(2), propput] HRESULT Month(WORD wMonth);
    [id(3), propput] HRESULT Day(WORD wDay);
    [id(4)] HRESULT DayOfTheWeek([out,retval] BSTR* dotw);
};

[uuid(FC54010D-48A7-11d0-9A73-0060973044A8)]
library DualDateLib
{
    interface IDualDate;
};
```

For example here we have an automation object that supports the automation method **DayOfTheWeek()** and the properties **Year**, **Month** and **Day**. Without a dual interface, these would have to be accessed via **Invoke()**, whether late binding or early binding is used. With the dual interface, the object now supports two vtable interfaces, **IDispatch** as before, and the **DualDate** methods that support the automation methods and properties.

By marking the interface as **[dual]**, you are stating that all its methods are accessible via **Invoke()** *and* via the vtable, so you need to implement this in any classes that expose this interface. Dual interfaces are a bit of a pain to implement in MFC, but in ATL, dual interfaces are a breeze. In fact all simple controls produced by the ATL Object Wizard have dual interfaces by default.

oleautomation

The **[oleautomation]** attribute is used to identify that an interface is compatible with automation. An interface is automation compatible if it meets these criteria:

 Each parameter of its methods is one of the automation types, a pointer to an automation type, or a **SAFEARRAY** of automation types.

 The return type of each of its methods is an **HRESULT**, **SCODE** or **void**. (**MIDL** will only allow the first two, presumably because the RPC runtime needs to be able to return status codes using the return value).

 It's derived from **IDispatch**, **IUnknown**, or any other interface that is automation compatible.

 It declares itself as automation compatible with the **[oleautomation]** attribute.

> Note that **dispinterface**s are implicitly **[oleautomation]**, so if you create an interface as a **dispinterface**, you should not use the **[oleautomation]** attribute.

Defining Objects

Objects use interfaces so, before you can define an object, you must define the interfaces it will use. Once the interfaces have been defined, (which can be done in the same file or in a separate IDL file and imported), you must define your class. The class declares all the interfaces that objects of this class will expose and, of course, associates a CLSID with the class. Classes are declared with the **coclass** statement.

As with the other statements in IDL, **coclass** has a **[uuid()]** attribute that specifies the CLSID. The client can use this CLSID with **CoCreateInstanceEx()** or **CoGetClassObject()** to create an instance of the class. If the **coclass** is marked with the **[licensed]** attribute then **CoGetClassObject()** will query for **IClassFactory2** rather than **IClassFactory**.

To fool some browsers, **coclass**es can be marked **[hidden]**, or they may be named in such a way that is illegal to the browser. The usual way is to make the first character an underscore. These will allow the method to be called, but object browsers (like those in VB and the Office applications) will not list these methods. This attribute can also be applied to **interface**s, **dispinterface**s, properties and methods. Another way of restricting access to an item in a type library is to mark it as **[restricted]**, which means that a scripting language cannot call the method or use the interface.

The flip side is when you explicitly want to specify that the methods of the type library or class refer to a visual control. You do this by marking the **library** or **coclass** with the **[control]** attribute.

If the **coclass** object is to be used by a language like Visual Basic, it is useful to define an interface as being **[default]**. VB can force a **QI()** on an object reference, by (effectively) casting the return from **CreateObject()** to the interface required. However, this is a pain to do every time, so to help VB, the interface that is returned from the call to **CreateObject()** is the one marked **[default]**.

A default interface should be the most commonly used interface, and in general a **coclass** has two **[default]** interfaces. One that is incoming and one outgoing. Outgoing interfaces are marked by **[source]** and this indicates that the **interface** or **dispinterface** has a method or property that is the source of an event.

Sources and sinks are used for connecting objects. Clients provide *sink* interfaces and pass a pointer to this interface to the *source* interface of a connection point object on the server. When the event occurs, the source calls the sink. This allows client objects to provide callbacks for server objects. This is an interesting subject and it is covered (together with an example) later in this chapter.

Type Libraries

Type libraries have become much more important since they were first used in 16-bit OLE 2.0. In those days, a type library was used simply to list the methods and properties supported by a dispatch interface. Other interfaces did not use type libraries, and suffered from the additional build step of creating proxy and stub objects.

More recently, type library marshaling has become available whereby a non-dispatch interface can use the standard dispatch proxy and stub objects to marshal method parameters. For the dispatch marshaler to be able to marshal parameters, it must know what the parameter types are, hence the importance of type libraries. We'll look more closely at type library marshaling a little later in the chapter.

Before we go any further, it is worth pointing out that a type library is a binary file that is CPU specific. These days a type library is typically bound as a resource into the module that implements it, so you can be sure that it will only be read on the platform that it is meant for. The only departure from this is the difference between type libraries for NT 3.51 and NT 4.0.

NT 3.51 could be described as NT 4.0 without the Win95 interface (or DCOM), and it certainly deserved more than a 0.01 update on NT 3.5. NT 3.51 had the ability to run Win95 programs although it did not have the UI. It even supported things like shell links, even though they were meaningless without the Explorer desktop.

However, in the context of this discussion, an important difference between NT 3.51 and the later version is in the format of the type library. Type libraries created on NT 3.51 can be used on NT 4.0, but not the other way around. If your target platform is NT 3.51 then you must compile the type library on an NT 3.51 machine. There is no switch on **MIDL** to produce a platform-specific type library, since **MIDL** just calls on the current version of COM to compile the library. If your target is NT 3.51, your final build must be made on that platform.

A type library block can contain **typedef**s, constants, **coclasse**s and **module**s, but should include some declarations of interfaces, or a reference to one: the interfaces can be standard, **[dual]**, or **dispinterface**.

> Note that the statements outside a library block are treated as normal IDL. In other words, **MIDL** will use the IDL outside a library block to generate C code. However, the code within the library block is treated as ODL and is used for the purpose of generating the type library. (If the interfaces are **[dual]** then this code is also used to create appropriate C code.)

Lets look at the different ways you can define your interfaces and libraries to find out exactly what gets generated:

Interface Definition Inside Library Block

```
// Typelib01.idl
[
    uuid(FC540100-48A7-11d0-9A73-0060973044A8)
]
library typelib01
{
    import "unknwn.idl";

    [uuid(FC540101-48A7-11d0-9A73-0060973044A8)]
    interface interface01_01 : IUnknown
    {
        [id(0)] HRESULT Method01([in] BSTR string);
    };
};
```

This type library contains only the definition of the interface **interface01_01**. Because the definition is inside the **library** block, the IDL allows us to produce a library for type library marshaling of the interface. The more usual case is for the library to contain interfaces derived from **IDispatch** so that they can be used by an automation controller like Visual Basic, but this isn't a necessity.

We can get **MIDL** to compile this file with the following command line:

```
midl Typelib01.idl
```

MIDL creates a type library called **Typelib01.tlb**, which you can view with **OLEView**. **OLEView** is quite helpful in that it decompiles the type library into IDL again, adding the parts that we missed out (or decided were unimportant at this stage):

```
// Generated .IDL file (by the OLE/COM Object Viewer)
//
// typelib filename: <could not determine filename>
// Forward declare all types defined in this typelib
interface interface01_01;
interface IUnknown;

[
  uuid(FC540100-48A7-11D0-9A73-0060973044A8),
  version(0.0)
]
library typelib01
{
    [
      odl,
      uuid(FC540101-48A7-11D0-9A73-0060973044A8)
    ]
    interface interface01_01 : IUnknown {
        HRESULT _stdcall Method01([in] BSTR string);
    };

    [
      odl,
      uuid(00000000-0000-0000-C000-000000000046)
    ]
    interface IUnknown {
        HRESULT _stdcall QueryInterface(
                        [in] _GUID* riid,
                        [out] void** ppvObject);
        unsigned long _stdcall AddRef();
        unsigned long _stdcall Release();
    };

    typedef struct tag_GUID {

unsigned long Data1;

unsigned short Data2;

unsigned short Data3;

unsigned char Data4[8];
    } _GUID;
};
```

Since the interface was defined inside the library block, no C files, or header files are generated automatically for the interface. In the past, if a C or C++ client wanted to use this interface, it would need to load the type library and use the **ITypeLib** interface to find out the format of the functions, negating much of the convenience of type library marshaling. However, because **OLEView** can decompile type libraries into IDL, it's a simple matter to copy the IDL and run it through MIDL with the right command line to generate the header file. Visual C++ 5 can also generate headers from type libraries using its **import** keyword.

This type library should really have an object, so let's add a **coclass** and move the interface out of the library block to see what difference that makes to the files that MIDL generates when no command line switches are used:

```
// Typelib02.idl
interface IUnknown;
interface interface02_01;

[
    uuid(FC540102-48A7-11d0-9A73-0060973044A8)
]
library typelib02
{
    import "unknwn.idl";

    [uuid(FC540103-48A7-11d0-9A73-0060973044A8)]
    interface interface02_01 : IUnknown
    {
        [id(0)] HRESULT Method01([in] BSTR string);
    };

    [uuid(FC540104-48A7-11d0-9A73-0060973044A8)]
    coclass CClass01
    {
        interface interface02_01;
    };
};
```

Notice that "moving the interface out" simply means adding a forward reference for the **IUnknown** and **interface02_01** interfaces outside the **library** block. This has the same effect as moving the entire interface definition outside of the **library** block. Now **MIDL** generates the type library, the C file containing the UUIDs and the interface header file automatically. The interface is still defined in the **library**, so **MIDL** doesn't know whether to generate proxy-stub code for it, so it doesn't. This is fine, since the whole idea of type library marshaling is that we don't need separately generated proxy-stub objects.

Modules

Finally, a **module** defines methods exported from a DLL. The DLL described is not necessarily an inproc COM server, it can just be a standard DLL. Using **module**s, allows you to describe the methods in a DLL in a way that allows browsers that are designed to browse automation information to give information about the DLL.

modules themselves group together similar functions. For example the VBA object library, **Vbaen32.olb**, describes the following **module**s:

Each module in a type library is marked with the **[dll()]** attribute to specify the name of the DLL that the module describes. Within the **module** block, the functions are listed and each is marked with the **[entry()]** attribute that gives the entry point of the method in the DLL. The entry point is either the name or the ordinal of the DLL function.

Mappings for Other Languages

One of the goals of COM is to allow COM objects to be language independent. That is, an object could be written in one language, but called by a client written in another language. So far in this discussion of **MIDL**, the languages that have been mentioned are C and C++, with a passing reference to VB.

It is true that **MIDL** produces headers and proxy-stub code in C (C++), but this does not mean that only clients of these languages can use the object. One method would be to convert the C header to an appropriate version for the language being used (perhaps possible in the case of Delphi), but it's hardly satisfactory. The real language independence comes when the object provides a type library, since all mainstream languages can access type libraries and the objects they describe (either directly or transparently).

So, for example, in VB, you have to specify the type libraries that you are going to use in a particular project by selecting them in the References dialog. Once you've done that you are free to use the objects described in those libraries without really thinking about it. On the other hand, J++ (Microsoft's Java implementation) takes the same line as MFC and provides a tool that generates a class from a type library description that provides mappings to the method DISPIDs.

Type Library Marshaling

If your object uses a standard interface you do not have to worry about providing a separate proxy-stub DLL to marshal the interface across process (and machine) boundaries. These already exist (most of them are in **Ole32.dll**, but also in **Oleaut32.dll**). This is one of the reasons to use standard interfaces on your object: every other COM object knows about the interface that your object supports.

However, not all objects can expose their functionality using standard interfaces, so there are two ways that we can get round the problem of supplying proxy-stubs. The first solution is to use **MIDL**-generated proxy-stubs. These can be generated for custom COM interfaces, which allows us to define whatever functionality and pass any data types we want. The only problem is that these objects must be registered on the client machine before the interface can be used. (Remember the **IRemoteTime** interface from the last chapter? Before you could use the **TimeClient**, you had to register the **Remotetimeps.dll** proxy-stub DLL.)

The other way is to use a flexible, but standard, OLE interface. **IDispatch** is such an interface. If you write a **dispinterface**, you can call methods on your object without having to register any other objects. All that is needed is for the client to know exactly what the methods and the parameters of the methods are, and a type library is the most convenient way to do this. The downside is that automation is often very slow, especially if late binding is used.

What we need is a method that has the flexibility and speed of custom interfaces with the added bonus of not requiring a new proxy-stub DLL. If you don't want to provide separate proxy and stub objects for your object then you need to use existing ones, and the automation proxy and stubs are the obvious candidate. This is type library marshaling.

Environment Server

Type library marshaling is quite straightforward and the best way to illustrate it is to give an example. The Environment Server allows the client to request the value of an environment variable on the server. The server is an ATL process, let's break it down:

First, create a new project called **Environment** using the ATL COM AppWizard and set the server type to be Executable (EXE). Add a Simple Object to the project using the Insert | New ATL Object... menu item, and set its Short Name to **EnvVar**. Make sure that Custom interface is selected on the Attributes tab of the ATL Object Wizard Properties dialog. This will give you an interface, **IEnvVar**, and a class, **CEnvVar**.

Once you've finished with the Wizard, you can add a single method to the **IEnvVar** interface:

```
HRESULT GetVariable([in] BSTR variable,
                    [out, retval] BSTR* value);
```

The easiest way to add this is to right-click on the interface name in ClassView and select Add Method... from the context menu, then fill in the dialog. If you add the IDL by hand, you'll also need to add the declaration and implementation stub for **GetVariable()** to **CEnvVar**, but if you use the dialog, this is handled for you.

The next step is to implement the method in **EnvVar.cpp**:

```
STDMETHODIMP CEnvVar::GetVariable(BSTR variable,
                                  BSTR * value)
{
    DWORD dwSize;
    LPTSTR pVar;
    LPTSTR pVal;
    HRESULT hr = S_OK;

    // This indicates that we wish to use ATL string
    // conversion macros
    USES_CONVERSION;
```

```
   // May need to convert to ANSI if UNICODE is not defined
   pVar = OLE2T(variable);

   // First get the size of the variable value
   dwSize = GetEnvironmentVariable(pVar, NULL, 0);

   if (0 == dwSize)
   {
      // No environment variable
      *value = NULL;
      hr = E_FAIL;
   }
   else
   {
      // Allocate a buffer to take the data
      pVal = new TCHAR[dwSize];

      // and get the value
      GetEnvironmentVariable(pVar, pVal, dwSize);

      // May need to convert to wide char
      *value = SysAllocString(T2OLE(pVal));

      if (NULL == *value)
         hr = E_OUTOFMEMORY;

      // and clean up
      delete [] pVal;
   }

   return hr;
}
```

The code simply gets the indicated environment variable by calling the Win32 **GetEnvironmentVariable()** function. Since we don't know how big the environment variable will be, the function is called once with the size of the **[out]** buffer (the last parameter) set to zero. The function will return the size of the variable, or zero if the variable does not exist. We can then allocate a temporary buffer and call **GetEnvironmentVariable()** again to actually get the value. Once a value has been obtained, a **BSTR** is allocated for it, and this is returned in the **[out]** parameter, **value**.

In the code, I have tried to take into account the fact that the programmer may be using Unicode or ANSI strings, so the code uses **LPTSTR**s and the **OLE2T()** and **T2OLE()** text conversion macros. If **UNICODE** is defined, the Win32 functions take **LPWSTR** parameters, so you can use a **BSTR** directly. If **UNICODE** is not defined then the **variable** parameter must be converted to a **LPSTR** using the conversion macros and the data returned from **GetEnvironmentVariable()** must be converted to an **OLESTR** before allocating a **BSTR**. To use the ATL macros, you must place the **USES_CONVERSION** macro in the method before using them.

Now, open the IDL file and add the **[oleautomation]** attribute to the interface definition for **IEnvVar**. Since this interface uses automation *types*, it is marked with the **[oleautomation]** attribute. This does not necessarily mean that it is a dispatch interface. Your IDL file should now look something like this:

```
import "oaidl.idl";
import "ocidl.idl";
```

```
    [
       uuid(E8B5BB2E-88D3-11D0-BBAC-002018349816),
       oleautomation,
       helpstring("IEnvVar Interface"),
       pointer_default(unique)
    ]
    interface IEnvVar : IUnknown
    {
       [helpstring("method GetVariable")]
       HRESULT GetVariable([in] BSTR variable,
                           [out, retval] BSTR* value);
    };
[
   uuid(E8B5BB21-88D3-11D0-BBAC-002018349816),
   version(1.0),
   helpstring("Environment 1.0 Type Library")
]
library ENVIRONMENTLib
{
   importlib("stdole32.tlb");

   [
      uuid(E8B5BB2F-88D3-11D0-BBAC-002018349816),
      helpstring("EnvVar Class")
   ]
   coclass EnvVar
   {
      [default] interface IEnvVar;
   };
};
```

You can now compile the whole project. The server will be registered at the same time because the ATL COM AppWizard generates a Custom Build Step to do just that.

Let's consider this registration in a little more detail. If you select View | Resource Includes..., you'll see that there is a compile-time directive for the type library, 1 TYPELIB "Environment.tlb". In other words, the type library generated by **MIDL** is bound into the executable as a resource. When you run the server with the **-RegServer** switch, this calls the ATL function **CComModule::RegisterServer()** which in turn calls **AtlModuleRegisterTypeLib()**, shown here:

```
ATLAPI AtlModuleRegisterTypeLib(_ATL_MODULE* pM,
                                LPCOLESTR lpszIndex)
{
   _ASSERTE(pM != NULL);
   USES_CONVERSION;
   _ASSERTE(pM->m_hInstTypeLib != NULL);
   TCHAR szModule[_MAX_PATH+10];
   OLECHAR szDir[_MAX_PATH];
   GetModuleFileName(pM->m_hInstTypeLib, szModule,
                     _MAX_PATH);
   if (lpszIndex != NULL)
      lstrcat(szModule, OLE2CT(lpszIndex));
   ITypeLib* pTypeLib;
   LPOLESTR lpszModule = T2OLE(szModule);
   HRESULT hr = LoadTypeLib(lpszModule, &pTypeLib);
   if (!SUCCEEDED(hr))
```

```
   {
      // typelib not in module, try <module>.tlb instead
      LPTSTR lpszExt = NULL;
      LPTSTR lpsz;
      for (lpsz = szModule; *lpsz != NULL;
                              lpsz = CharNext(lpsz))
      {
         if (*lpsz == _T('.'))
             lpszExt = lpsz;
      }
      if (lpszExt == NULL)
          lpszExt = lpsz;
      lstrcpy(lpszExt, _T(".tlb"));
      lpszModule = T2OLE(szModule);
      hr = LoadTypeLib(lpszModule, &pTypeLib);
   }
   if (SUCCEEDED(hr))
   {
      ocscpy(szDir, lpszModule);
      szDir[AtlGetDirLen(szDir)] = 0;
      hr = ::RegisterTypeLib(pTypeLib, lpszModule, szDir);
   }
   if (pTypeLib != NULL)
      pTypeLib->Release();
   return hr;
}
```

This tries to load the type library from the executable, and if this fails, it tries to load the **.tlb** file. Whichever method is successful leads to the same result: the type library and the **interface**s and **coclass**es it uses are registered with a call to the Win32 **RegisterTypeLib()**. (The **ProgID** for the **coclass** is registered via another method, the **DECLARE_REGISTRY_RESOURCEID()** macro in the declaration of the **CEnvVar** class.)

Let's just review what we have: we have a server that has a custom interface that uses automation types but is not a **dispinterface** (that is, it is not based on **IDispatch**). The interface is described by a type library. We have not created proxy-stub code with **MIDL**, since the interface only uses types that the automation marshaler can handle (although these files will be generated for you).

```
ITypeLib Viewer                                                  _ □ ×
File  View
┌──┐ ┌─┐
│  │ │?│
└──┘ └─┘
⊟ ✦ ENVIRONMENTLib (Environment 1.0 Type Library)   [
  ⊞ coclass EnvVar                                      odl,
  ⊞ ? interface IEnvVar                                 uuid(E8B5BB2E-88D3-11D0-BBAC-002018349816),
                                                        helpstring("IEnvVar Interface"),
                                                        oleautomation
                                                      ]
                                                      interface IEnvVar : IUnknown {
                                                          [helpstring("method GetVariable")]
                                                          HRESULT _stdcall GetVariable(
                                                                          [in] BSTR variable,
                                                                          [out, retval] BSTR* value);
                                                      };
Ready
```

Next you need a client to test the server.

Environment Client

For the client, we will use the same format as before: an MFC dialog-based application with an extra dialog to get the name of the server. Use MFC AppWizard (exe) to create a new project called **EnvClient**. You'll need to set the option on Step 1 to create a dialog-based application, but you can leave the other steps with their default settings. Once the project's been created, add the **_WIN32_DCOM** preprocessor definition to the project settings for all configurations.

Add the following code to the top of the application class' **InitInstance()** function (you'll also need to add an entry to the string table for the **IDP_OLE_INIT_FAILED** error message).

```
// Initialize OLE libraries
if (!AfxOleInit())
{
  AfxMessageBox(IDP_OLE_INIT_FAILED);
  return FALSE;
}
```

Because we are using **AfxOleInit()**, we don't need to worry about uninitializing the libraries; that's all handled for us by MFC

Now edit the main dialog, **IDD_ENVCLIENT_DIALOG**, to add a couple of edit boxes and a couple of static controls as shown:

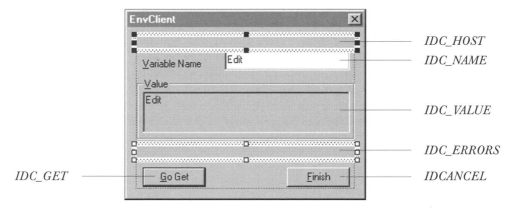

The static controls are highlighted here. The top one will show the server name and the bottom one will display any error messages that are generated. I have deleted the OK button and renamed the Cancel button as Finish.

Now we need to make the **IEnvVar** interface and the **EnvVar** coclass usable from our dialog. Copy the UUIDs from **Environment_i.c** in the server directory into the top of the **cpp** file for the dialog class, **EnvClientDlg.cpp**.

```
const IID IID_IEnvVar = {0xE8B5BB2E,0x88D3,0x11D0,
     {0xBB,0xAC,0x00,0x20,0x18,0x34,0x98,0x16}};
const IID LIBID_ENVIRONMENTLib = {0xE8B5BB21,0x88D3,0x11D0,
     {0xBB,0xAC,0x00,0x20,0x18,0x34,0x98,0x16}};
```

```
const CLSID CLSID_EnvVar = {0xE8B5BB2F,0x88D3,0x11D0,
    {0xBB,0xAC,0x00,0x20,0x18,0x34,0x98,0x16}};
```

Whenever you **#include** the dialog class header, you will need to precede it with a **#include**
"..\Environment\Environment.h". In other words, you'll need to add this line to
EnvClientDlg.cpp and **EnvClient.cpp**. With this done, you can add a pointer to the **IEnvVar**
interface as a **protected** member of the dialog class and also a string member to hold the server's
machine name.

```
// Implementation
protected:
    HICON m_hIcon;
    IEnvVar* m_pEnvServer;
    CString m_strServerName;
```

As with the **TimeClient** example from the previous chapter, you should also add a helper function called
Message() to put a message string into the lower of the static controls, **IDC_ERRORS**. (You can just copy
this from **CTimeClientDlg**.)

```
void CEnvClientDlg::Message(const CString& strMessage)
{
    CWnd* pTextCtrl = GetDlgItem(IDC_ERRORS);
    ASSERT(pTextCtrl);

    pTextCtrl->SetWindowText(strMessage);
}
```

The last resource you need is the server name dialog. Again, this is just like the dialog in the
TimeClient example (and if you added it to the Component Gallery then you can reuse it now).

Now you need to add the code to **CEnvClientDlg::OnInitDialog()** to load the server. This is
almost identical to the code that we had in the **TimeClient**.

```
BOOL CEnvClientDlg::OnInitDialog()
{
    //... Standard Wizard-supplied initialization

    CServerNameDlg dlg;

    // Get the name of the server to use
    if (dlg.DoModal() == IDOK &&
                    !dlg.m_strServerName.IsEmpty())
        m_strServerName = dlg.m_strServerName;
    else
        m_strServerName.Empty();

    // Setup the name on the static
    CWnd* pRemote = GetDlgItem(IDC_HOST);
    ASSERT(pRemote);

    if (m_strServerName.IsEmpty())
    {
        TCHAR szLocalName[MAX_COMPUTERNAME_LENGTH + 1];
        DWORD dwSize = MAX_COMPUTERNAME_LENGTH;
        GetComputerName(szLocalName, &dwSize);
```

```
      pRemote->SetWindowText(szLocalName);
   }
   else
      pRemote->SetWindowText(m_strServerName);

   HRESULT hr;
   COSERVERINFO serverinfo;
   COSERVERINFO* pServerInfo;

   // Create the server info
   // Note that we use CString to convert to wide chars
   serverinfo.dwReserved1 = 0;
   serverinfo.dwReserved2 = 0;
   serverinfo.pwszName = m_strServerName.AllocSysString();
   serverinfo.pAuthInfo = NULL;

   if (m_strServerName.IsEmpty())
      pServerInfo = NULL;
   else
      pServerInfo = &serverinfo;

   m_pEnvServer = NULL;
   CString strError = "Object Created";
   MULTI_QI qi = {&IID_IEnvVar, NULL, 0};

   hr = CoCreateInstanceEx(CLSID_EnvVar, NULL,
             CLSCTX_LOCAL_SERVER | CLSCTX_REMOTE_SERVER,
             pServerInfo, 1, &qi);

   if (SUCCEEDED(hr) && SUCCEEDED(qi.hr))
      m_pEnvServer = (IEnvVar*)qi.pItf;
   else
      strError.Format("Error getting object: 0x%x",hr);

   Message(strError);

   // Free the buffer previous allocated
   ::SysFreeString(serverinfo.pwszName);

   return TRUE;  // return TRUE  unless you set the focus
                 // to a control
}
```

The first action is to create the dialog box to get the server name, and then this is used to initialize a **COSERVERINFO** structure. If a server name was given, a pointer to this structure is passed to **CoCreateInstanceEx()**, otherwise a **NULL** pointer is used (indicating that the server and client are running on the same machine).

The **MULTI_QI** parameter indicates that we want the **IEnvVar** interface on the object. If the object creation is successful, we save the interface pointer for later use and then do some clean up.

The next task is to implement the Go Get button. To do this, you need to create a **BN_CLICKED** handler with ClassWizard and then add the following code:

```
void CEnvClientDlg::OnGet()
{
```

```
      BSTR var;
      BSTR retvar;
      CString str;

      if (NULL == m_pEnvServer)
      {
         Message(CString("No object!"));
         return;
      }

      CWnd* pEdit = GetDlgItem(IDC_NAME);
      ASSERT(pEdit);

      pEdit->GetWindowText(str);
      pEdit = GetDlgItem(IDC_VALUE);
      ASSERT(pEdit);
      pEdit->SetWindowText("");

      var = str.AllocSysString();

      HRESULT hr;
      hr = m_pEnvServer->GetVariable(var, &retvar);
      if (SUCCEEDED(hr))
      {
         str = retvar;
         pEdit->SetWindowText(str);
         Message(CString(""));
         ::SysFreeString(retvar);
      }
      else
      {
         if (hr == E_FAIL)
            Message(CString("No environment variable"));
         else
            Message(CString("Unspecified error"));
      }

      ::SysFreeString(var);
   }
```

The code first checks that an object exists and then gets the requested environment variable name from the **IDC_NAME** edit box. Then it creates a **BSTR** from the variable name and calls **GetVariable()** on the interface pointer. If this call is successful, the result is converted from a **BSTR** to a **CString** using **CString::operator=()** and then put into the **IDC_VALUE** edit box. Since the value returned, **retvar**, is an **[out]** variable, we need to free it with a call to **SysFreeString()**.

The final task is to release the **EnvVar** object when it is no longer needed. The dialog can be closed in two ways. The first is by clicking the Finish button and the second is by using Close in the system menu or the close button in the top right corner. We can handle both these cases with a single **WM_DESTROY** message handler in the dialog class. Use ClassWizard to add this handler, then add the following code:

```
void CEnvClientDlg::OnDestroy()
{
   CDialog::OnDestroy();
```

```
    if (m_pEnvServer)
        m_pEnvServer->Release();
}
```

Now all you need to do is compile the code!

Testing the Code

There are two scenarios to test: the local case and the remote case. The easiest is the local case.

Local Testing

Make sure that the server is registered (if necessary type **Environment -RegServer** at the command line in the build directory of the server). Then run **EnvClient**. You will get the following dialog:

Since we're testing the local case, press OK or Cancel without entering a name. **EnvClient** will read the local computer name and put it in the top static control, then it will create a local object. The object is defined in the registry as:

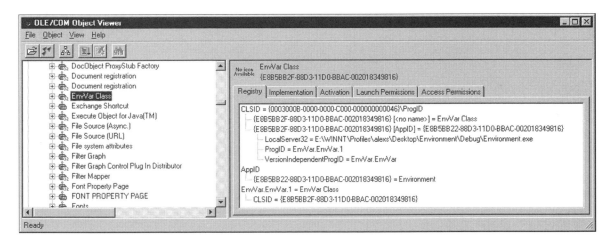

and COM can query for the interface marshaler:

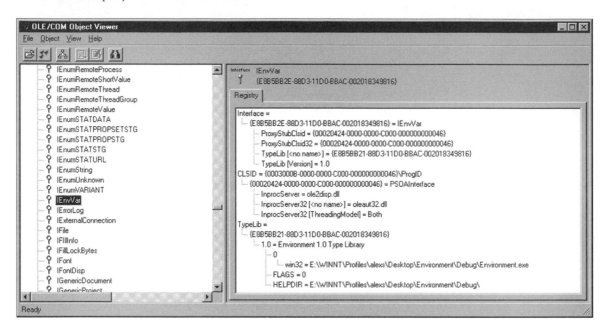

Remember that these are values placed here by the registration of the type library. This shows that the interface uses the automation marshaler (**PSOAInterface**) and it is described by a type library. Once the object has been created, you will see the next dialog:

To test the application, type the name of an environment variable, **COMPUTERNAME**, say, and click on Go Get. The value of the variable will be given in the lower edit box. When you are finished, click on Finish and the object will be released.

Remote Testing

The next test is to run **EnvClient** from another machine. To do this, you need to copy the following files to the client machine:

   **EnvClient.exe**

   **Environment.tlb**

   **EnvClient.reg**

The first is created from compiling the client, the second comes from compiling **Environment.idl** in the server project. But what about **EnvClient.reg**?

This *new* file has information about the server. You see, when you run the client on the same machine as the server, there is information in the registry to indicate how data is marshaled between the client and server. When you run the client on another machine, that machine needs to have its registry updated. In the last chapter, we saw this in action when we ran **TimeServerps.dll** with **RegSrv32** on the client. This updated the client's registry with the information about the interface that we wished to use.

In this project, we are not providing a proxy DLL, we will use the automation marshaler instead, but we still need to indicate that the interface will be marshaled via automation when the client asks for an interface on an object.

The **reg** file is given here:

```
REGEDIT4

[HKEY_CLASSES_ROOT\Interface\
     {E8B5BB2E-88D3-11D0-BBAC-002018349816}]
@="IEnvVar"
[HKEY_CLASSES_ROOT\Interface\
     {E8B5BB2E-88D3-11D0-BBAC-002018349816}
     \ProxyStubClsid32]
@="{00020424-0000-0000-C000-000000000046}"
[HKEY_CLASSES_ROOT\Interface\
     {E8B5BB2E-88D3-11D0-BBAC-002018349816}\TypeLib]
@="{E8B5BB21-88D3-11D0-BBAC-002018349816} "
"Version"="1,0"

[HKEY_CLASSES_ROOT\TypeLib\
     {E8B5BB21-88D3-11D0-BBAC-002018349816}\1.0]
@="EnvVar 1.0 Type Library"
[HKEY_CLASSES_ROOT\TypeLib\
     {E8B5BB21-88D3-11D0-BBAC-002018349816}\1.0\0\Win32]
@="c:\\winnt\\System32\\Environment.tlb"
[HKEY_CLASSES_ROOT\TypeLib\
     {E8B5BB21-88D3-11D0-BBAC-002018349816}\1.0\Flags]
@="0"
[HKEY_CLASSES_ROOT\TypeLib\
     {E8B5BB21-88D3-11D0-BBAC-002018349816}\1.0\HelpDir]
@=""
```

(You can extract this data from the server's registry, using **RegEdit**.)

There are two parts to this. This first part registers the **IEnvVar** interface and the second registers the type library.

The first part is quite straightforward: we indicate the IID and specify the CLSID of the automation marshaler as the **ProxyStubClsid32**. The magic comes in the next entry: the interface associates itself with a type library.

The second half of the **reg** file registers the type library in standard fashion. The example shown here registers the type library as being in the **Winnt\System32** directory, you'll need to change this path to match the path to the library on your client machine.

All you need to do is run RegEdit on the client with this file, copy the type library to the indicated directory and run the client. You will get the dialog asking for the server, enter the server name and then you will get the main dialog. Now ask for **COMPUTERNAME** and you'll get the value from the remote machine. So **EnvClient**, running on **hera**, gives:

Yes, **zeus** thinks that its name is **ZEUS**! Isn't that great? So what have we gained? Well, a small amount of education is a dangerous thing. Some people are unhappy about a separate proxy DLL on the client, in addition to the client code, irrational though it is. This method has no additional proxy DLL to register, but you do have to register the type library. To counter this argument, there is nothing stopping you from putting proxy code into the client executable

The most important reason for using type library marshaling is that if the server changes, only the type library needs to change. In addition, if the type library backwardly supports old methods, you will not need to reregister anything on the client machine to use the new functionality. You'll just need to replace the old type library with the new one.

Hopefully, the use of a custom interface in this example has also dispelled the myth that only dispinterfaces or dual interfaces can use the automation marshaler. As you've seen, any automation compatible interface can use type library marshaling. There's no need to implement any **IDispatch** functionality if you don't want to. Remember also that marshaling is done on a per interface basis. Your coclasses are free to implement interfaces that use a mixture of automation marshaling, MIDL-generated marshaling code, or even your own custom marshaling.

Connection Points

COM is inherently synchronous – when you make a method call on an object, the client thread making the call is blocked. The blocking occurs in the method handler in the proxy which is itself waiting for the stub to return. The client thread can only continue executing once the object method has returned. If the object method takes a long time to complete, the client will have to accommodate this, otherwise the performance of the client would be appalling.

There are two ways to alleviate this problem. One way would be for the client to create a separate thread to make the method call. The other is for the server to create a separate thread to handle the task and then immediately return the method call. In the second case, the client would have to find out when the server had actually finished the task. It could either poll the server, which would be expensive in network calls, or it could pass the server a pointer to a callback that the server can call when it has finished.

This brings up the subject of multithreading, which we cover in detail in Chapter 9. For now you can treat the complexities of multithreading as incidental to the discussion.

This last solution is used throughout Windows, Chapter 2 showed a callback used by the **EnumWindows()** API. Connection points work in a similar manner: when a particular event occurs, the server will call a callback on the client. In COM parlance, we say that the server has an **outgoing** interface. This is an interface that is defined in the server's IDL, but is implemented in the client.

To enable **MIDL** to create this marshaling code, the server IDL declares that it will use this outgoing interface. Since the server calls this interface to indicate to the client that something has happened, and so the server is a **source** of notifications, outgoing interfaces are declared in the server IDL using the **[source]** attribute.

The other interfaces in the IDL that are not marked with **[source]** are known as **incoming** interfaces because the interface will be called by the client. These are the interfaces that the server implements. In the context of connection points, the incoming interface on a client is called a **sink**.

The term connectable object means that a *conceptual* connection can be made between a client and the object. Of course the connection is not as direct as it was in the example of the callback function in **EnumWindows()** where the address of a function is passed, because the actual connection is maintained using proxies and stubs, but this is transparent to you as a programmer.

Making Connections

A client implements a sink interface that will allow it to connect to a specific type of object. When this client wants to make a connection to a connectable object, it must verify that the object will be able to call the client's sink interface (i.e. it has the appropriate outgoing interface). Once it has done this, the client can get a connection to the object and give the object a pointer to the client's sink interface.

The connectable object is connectable because it implements the **IConnectionPoint** interface (and to manage these connections, it must support the **IConnectionPointContainer** interface). This interface has the necessary methods to allow a client to make or break a connection, but to be useful, the object must have some other interface which has functionality that the client wishes to call.

Once the connection is made, the client can make a method call on the object's incoming interface, which will start some processing, in a separate thread. With the processing initiated, the object can return from the method call, which unblocks the thread in the client that called the object. When the processing has completed, the object can call a method on the client sink interface, either to indicate that there is data available or, indeed, to provide the data itself.

IConnectionPoint Interface

Once the client has obtained an interface pointer on an **IConnectionPoint** interface (in a process that will be made clear in the next section), it can call the interface methods to register or unregister its interest in the connectable object:

```
[
    object,
    uuid(B196B286-BAB4-101A-B69C-00AA00341D07),
    pointer_default(unique)
]
interface IConnectionPoint : IUnknown
{
    HRESULT GetConnectionInterface([out] IID* piid);
```

```
       HRESULT GetConnectionPointContainer(
                  [out] IConnectionPointContainer** ppCPC);
       HRESULT Advise([in] IUnknown* pUnkSink,
                  [out] DWORD* pdwCookie);
       HRESULT Unadvise([in] DWORD dwCookie);
       HRESULT EnumConnections(
                  [out] IEnumConnections** ppEnum);
    }
```

The client calls the **Advise()** method to specify that it wants a connection to be made. The client passes a pointer to its sink interface (the one that the server will call back to) and in return it obtains a **DWORD** value, called a cookie. This data has no real meaning other than to identify this client-object connection. The client passes the cookie back to the object when it wishes to break the connection with a call to **Unadvise()**.

The architecture is very flexible: a client can have multiple connections on many connectable objects, and a single connectable object can have connections to many clients.

The one-to-many case is shown here:

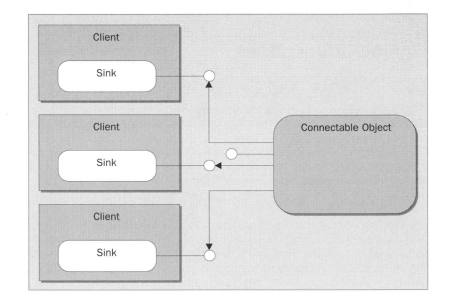

This is the situation described above. The connectable object is a server of some kind providing functionality via an incoming interface. Each client obtains a connection to the object and makes their requests on the incoming interface of the object. When the server needs to notify the clients, it will call back on each client via the sink interface.

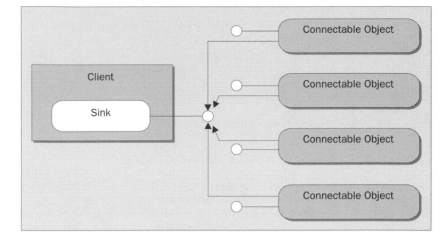

In the many-to-one case, a client's sink can be called by many objects:

This is actually the sort of situation for which connection points were originally devised. This situation is just like an automation controller with multiple ActiveX controls. The client in the picture is the automation controller and the connectable objects are the controls.

One property of controls that makes them useful is their ability to fire events in the controller. A control, for example, may handle a Click event by firing the event in the controller; in other words, when the user clicks on the control, code in the controller will be triggered. To handle this, the controller must give to the control a pointer to a sink interface that it implements.

A server that can handle the one-to-many case can also handle connections in the many-to-one case, thus the following discussion just focuses on the case described first – support for multiple client connections to connectable objects over DCOM.

The other methods in the **IConnectionPoint** interface provide information about the container and the outgoing interface. The client can get the IID of the outgoing interface by calling **GetConnectionInterface()**.

The server may have many connectable objects, so it implements an object with an interface called the **IConnectionPointContainer**, which acts as an interface dispenser, giving access to the **IConnectionPoint** interfaces on the connectable objects. If the client wishes to get information about this container object, perhaps to make a connection to another connectable object, it can get a pointer to it by calling **GetConnectionPointContainer()**.

It may be necessary for a client to determine how many connections have been made to this particular outgoing interface. The client can do this by calling the **EnumConnections()** method. This method returns a pointer to an **IEnumConnection** interface on an enumeration object. **IEnumConnection** interface supports the standard enumeration methods.

IConnectionPointContainer Interface

So far the discussion has alluded to a *container* object, but what is this for? The server may implement many objects each supporting a different outgoing interface, so the server must be able to maintain these connections. It does this through the container object. This object allows the client to ask for a particular interface, or to query for all the interfaces that the server supports. This first capability of the server, to be able to dispense a pointer to an interface, is how the client determines that an object has a particular outgoing interface, and then gets a pointer to that object's interface.

Here is a description of the **IConnectionPointContainer** interface:

```
[
    object,
    uuid(B196B284-BAB4-101A-B69C-00AA00341D07),
    pointer_default(unique)
]
interface IConnectionPointContainer : IUnknown
{
    HRESULT EnumConnectionPoints(
                [out] IEnumConnectionPoints ** ppEnum);
    HRESULT FindConnectionPoint([in] REFIID riid,
                [out] IConnectionPoint ** ppCP);
};
```

There are only two methods here. The first method lets you obtain an interface pointer to an object that allows you to enumerate over all the connectable objects in the server. The second method will return the **IConnectionPoint** interface on the object that handles the specified outgoing interface.

Another way to look at these is to compare **FindConnectionPoint()** with **QueryInterface()**. In the first case, if the container object has an object that handles the specified interface, an interface pointer is returned. In the case of **QI()**, if the object supports the specified interface then **QI()** will return a pointer to that interface.

Enumeration Interfaces

The two connection point interfaces allow the client to obtain an enumerator to determine the connection points implemented on the server, and the current connections on a particular connection point. These enumerators are accessed through interfaces that implement methods of the **IEnumXXXX** interface as described in the Win32 SDK.

The **IEnumXXXX** isn't a real interface, it is a documentation device to indicate the requirements of all enumeration interfaces. Thus, such interfaces are derived from **IUnknown** and not from **IEnumXXXX**. Having said that let us quickly look at this 'interface', using IDL as an aid:

```
interface IEnumXXXX : IUnknown
{
    HRESULT Next([in] ULONG celt, [out] T* rgelt,
                [out] ULONG* pceltFetched);
    HRESULT Skip([in] ULONG celt);
    HRESULT Reset();
    HRESULT Clone([out] IEnumXXXX** ppenum);
};
```

Here, the interface enumerates over items of type **T**. These items can be data passed by value or reference and can be interface pointers to allow an object to provide an enumerator on objects.

This concept should be familiar to you from Chapter 2. There we implemented a DLL interface that enumerated **HWND**s. This COM interface is called in the same way: the client allocates an array to hold the items and passes this to the **Next()** method, together with the size of the array (**celt** - the name, I guess, comes from **c**ount of **el**ements of **T**) and a pointer to a counter variable (**pceltFetched**). The server will attempt to fill the array with the number of items specified and will return the actual number in the counter.

The other methods in the interface allow a client to start the enumeration again from the first item (**Reset()**), miss out a number of items in the enumeration (**Skip()**), and finally, to make a copy of the enumerator object (**Clone()**). To provide an enumerator for an item type, an interface specific to that type must be defined: **IEnumXXXX** is not polymorphic.

Perhaps the most used of these methods is **Next()**, so in the following sections we will only concentrate on that method.

IEnumConnectionPoints

The items that are enumerated in this interface are **IConnectionPoint** pointers:

```
HRESULT Next([in] ULONG cConnections,
             [out] IConnectionPoint** rgpcn,
             [out] ULONG* pcFetched);
```

This enables a client to get **IConnectionPoint** interface pointers on all the connectable objects in a container. Since interface pointers are marshaled, you must call **Release()** on these pointers when you have finished with them.

IEnumConnections

In this interface, it is **CONNECTDATA** structures that are enumerated:

```
typedef struct tagCONNECTDATA
{
   IUnknown*  pUnk;
   DWORD      dwCookie;
} CONNECTDATA;

HRESULT Next([in] ULONG cConnections,
             [out] CONNECTDATA* rgcd,
             [out] ULONG* lpcFetched);
```

The **CONNECTDATA** structure has an **IUnknown** pointer of the sink interface of each client connected to the object, and the cookie that the client holds. As is the case for all interface pointers obtained through **[out]** parameters, you must release the interfaces you get through **CONNECTDATA** when you have finished with them.

Type Information

If the client knows the incoming interfaces that the server supports and the server knows about the sink interface on the client then connection points are relatively easy to use. But what if the client and server are not written by the same developer? Control containers like Visual Basic can access the incoming interfaces of ActiveX controls without knowing about every interface on every control. Such a control container can do this, of course, by looking into the control's type library.

The object's type library has information about the incoming and outgoing interfaces on the object. To get the type information, the client needs access to the object's type library file (**tlb**, **olb**, **oca** or whatever), or it may ask the object for the type information. The client does this by **QI()**ing the object for **IProvideClassInfo**. This interface has a method, **IProvideClassInfo::GetClassInfo()**, that returns the **ITypeInfo** interface of the type library of the entire object.

So far this is pretty standard stuff. Now for the interesting bit: from this **ITypeInfo** interface, the client can call **GetTypeAttr()** to look for an interface with the **[source]** attribute. This method returns a **TYPEATTR** structure:

```
typedef struct tagTYPEATTR
{
    GUID guid;
    LCID lcid;
    DWORD dwReserved;
    MEMBERID memidConstructor;
    MEMBERID memidDestructor;
    LPOLESTR lpstrSchema;
    ULONG cbSizeInstance;
    TYPEKIND typekind;
    WORD cFuncs;
    WORD cVars;
    WORD cImplTypes;
    WORD cbSizeVft;
    WORD cbAlignment;
    WORD wTypeFlags;
    WORD wMajorVerNum;
    WORD wMinorVerNum;
    TYPEDESC tdescAlias;
    IDLDESC idldescType;
} TYPEATTR, * LPTYPEATTR;
```

The **idldescType** parameter has a member, **wIDLFlags**, that is the combination of the IDL flags for the interface. The attributes to check for are **IMPLTYPEFLAG_FSOURCE**, for a source interface and the combination of this and **IMPLTYPEFLAG_FDEFAULT** for the *default* source interface. Once a source interface is identified, the **guid** member gives the IID of the interface. To get information about this interface, you can call **GetRefTypeOfImplType()** or **GetRefTypeInfo()**.

If you do not need all this information, you can just **QI()** for **IProvideClassInfo2**. You can then call **GetGUID()**, which has the following prototype:

```
HRESULT GetGUID([in] DWORD dwGuidKind, [out] GUID * pGUID);
```

The first parameter is one of the **GUIDKIND** enumeration constants (although there are several declared in the Platform SDK, the only member given in the Win32 headers is **GUIDKIND_DEFAULT_SOURCE_DISP_IID**). If **dwGuidKind** is valid, the actual GUID is returned in the **[out]** parameter, **pGUID**.

Implementing Connection Points

Now that we have seen the interfaces used in connection points, how do you use them?
The code to implement the server is quite involved. First, you have to implement an object with an **IConnectionPointContainer** interface. This object must maintain a list of the connectable objects,

provide access to these objects when requested via the **FindConnectionPoint()** method, and allow enumeration of these objects by implementing the **IEnumConnectionPoints** interface.

Every connectable object must implement the **IConnectionPoint** interface as well as its own incoming interface. To do this, the object will have to maintain an array of **CONNECTDATA** structures for the connected clients, which are added with **Advise()**, and removed with the **Unadvise()**. Finally, these structures must be enumerated with the **IEnumConnections** interface.

Much of this code (in fact, all except the connectable object's incoming interface) is boilerplate code. This makes the implementation of connection point servers an ideal use for ATL.

At the other end, the client must provide the sink interface. When it wishes to use the connectable object, it needs take the following actions:

- Find the server.
- **QueryInterface()** for **IConnectionPointContainer**.
- Get the **IConnectionPoint** interface of the connectable object.
- Call **Advise()** with a pointer to its sink interface.
- **QueryInterface()** for the object's incoming interface.
- Call appropriate methods on the object's incoming interface and then wait for notifications.

Again, much of this code is boilerplate. However, unlike the server, where it is unusual to have a user interface, the client process invariably requires one. So far in this book we have used ATL to implement servers and MFC to write the clients. This has worked well since the COM code in the client has usually been quite straightforward.

However, MFC complicates matters when providing support for generic connection points. Support for full ActiveX controls using connection points is good, but that is not what we are doing here (we have no concept of a client-side window to represent the server, unlike full ActiveX controls). ATL has been written specifically for COM, so use it whenever the COM code you want to implement is anything more than trivial. In this case, we will use both ATL and MFC in the client.

Once again, we will use MFC and ATL to create the code. MFC will help us create the user-interface and ATL will be used for the COM code. Much of the example will look familiar to you, since we will base the new code on the TimeServer and TimeClient example from the last chapter. We'll be starting with brand new projects, but you'll be able to reuse much of the code from those projects.

This example will allow the client to set an alarm on the server, and when the alarm time has been reached, the server will use its outgoing interface to notify the client. This example has support for just one connection, but the code is quite straightforward, and it should be a minor task to adapt it to handle multiple connections. However, because of the nature of this example, it does touch slightly on the issues of security and multithreading. To a certain extent, you'll have to take some of the code on trust; alternatively, you could skip ahead to Chapters 7 and 9 where these topics are covered in greater depth.

AlarmServer

The Alarm Server will implement two incoming interfaces, **IRemoteTime** and **IRemoteAlarm**. The first one we have seen already: it is the interface used to ask the server for the current time. The second interface allows a client to ask the server to set an alarm. The AlarmServer also has an outgoing interface called **IRingAlarm**, this must be implemented on the client and is called by the server when the alarm time has been reached.

Creating the Project

First use the ATL COM AppWizard to create a new project for an EXE server called **AlarmServer**. Once the project has been created, use Insert | New ATL Object... to add a new Simple Object with a short name of **RemoteAlarm**. Before adding the object, make sure that Support Connection Points is checked on the Attributes tab of the ATL Object Wizard Properties dialog. This will mean that the Wizard will derive the object's class from the ATL class **IConnectionPointContainerImpl** to provide support for the **IConnectionPointContainer** interface.

Now you've added a COM class with a single incoming interface, **IRemoteAlarm**, to the project. This interface will be responsible for setting or canceling the alarm on the server. The next step is to add the methods to this interface that will make that possible, so right-click on the **IRemoteAlarm** icon in ClassView and select Add Method.... Fill in the dialog as shown for **SetAlarm()** then repeat the procedure for **CancelAlarm()**.

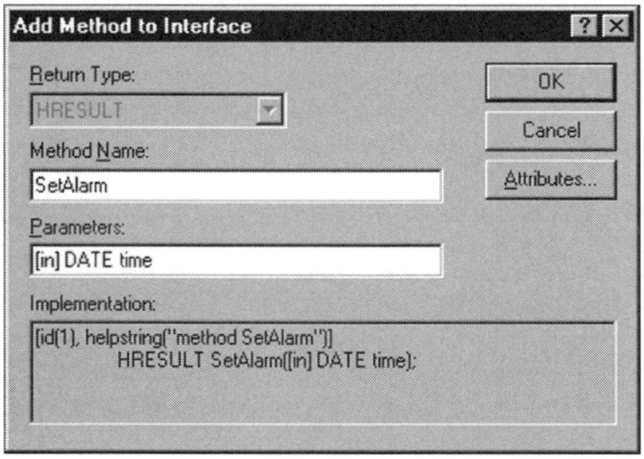

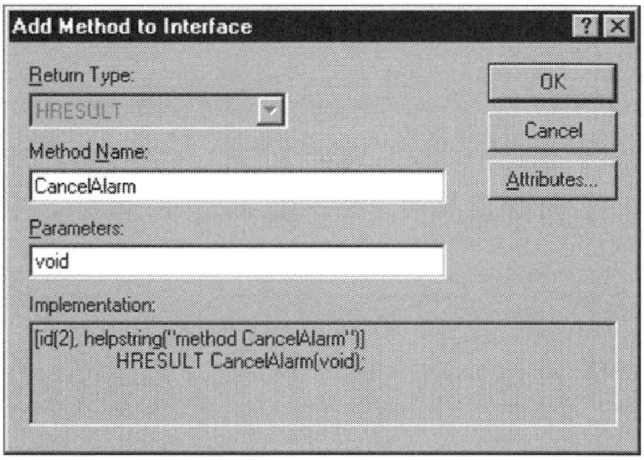

Remember that you can always edit the IDL by hand, but using the dialogs provided by Visual C++ means that function stubs are automatically added to your ATL classes.

Remember, there are no useful dialogs to help with adding an outgoing interface, so that's something that you'll have to do by hand. You'll need to add the code shown below to the **idl** file, just below the definition of the **IRemoteAlarm** interface and before the definition of the type library:

```
[
    object,
    uuid(7A3209E1-8B1C-11d0-BBB7-002018349816),
    dual,
    helpstring("IRingAlarm Interface"),
    pointer_default(unique)
]
interface IRingAlarm : IDispatch
```

```
    {
        [id(1), helpstring("method Brinnnnng")]
        HRESULT Brinnnnng(void);
    };
```

If you were creating your own interface, you'd need to generate a new **uuid** for this interface using the GUID Generator.

Next we need to specify support for the **IRemoteTime** interface. We've already defined this interface in **TimeServer.idl** and compiled it in **TimeServer.tlb** from the example in the last chapter. Copy this type library into the project directory and add an **importlib** line into the **idl** file at the top of the **library** block.

```
    importlib("TimeServer.tlb");
```

The final change to the **idl** is to specify the interfaces that the **coclass** will use:

```
    [
        uuid(8CBA959F-8B1B-11D0-BBB7-002018349816),
        helpstring("RemoteAlarm Class")
    ]
    coclass RemoteAlarm
    {
        [default] interface IRemoteAlarm;
        interface IRemoteTime;
        [default, source] interface IRingAlarm;
    };
```

Notice how the outgoing interface is marked **[source]**. Now compile the **idl** with **MIDL**.

This produces the type library **AlarmServer.tlb**, which, when viewed with **OLEView**, looks like this:

Editing CRemoteAlarm

The next step is to edit the **CRemoteAlarm** class declaration that will support this object. You'll need to do two main things: add support for the incoming interface, **IRemoteTime**, and provide support for the connection points necessary for the outgoing interface, **IRingAlarm**. The **IRemoteAlarm** interface has already been handled by Developer Studio when we created the object and used the dialog to add the interface methods, as far as the class definition goes.

Change the definition for **CRemoteAlarm** so that it matches that shown below. The changes and additions that you need to make have been highlighted.

```
class ATL_NO_VTABLE CRemoteAlarm :
    public CComObjectRootEx<CComSingleThreadModel>,
    public CComCoClass<CRemoteAlarm, &CLSID_RemoteAlarm>,
    public IConnectionPointContainerImpl<CRemoteAlarm>,
    public IDispatchImpl<IRemoteAlarm, &IID_IRemoteAlarm,
                         &LIBID_ALARMSERVERLib>,
    public IDispatchImpl<IRemoteTime, &IID_IRemoteTime,
                         &LIBID_ALARMSERVERLib>,
    public IConnectionPointImpl<CRemoteAlarm,
                                &IID_IRingAlarm>
{
public:
    CRemoteAlarm()
    {
    }

DECLARE_REGISTRY_RESOURCEID(IDR_REMOTEALARM)

BEGIN_COM_MAP(CRemoteAlarm)
    COM_INTERFACE_ENTRY(IRemoteTime)
    COM_INTERFACE_ENTRY(IRemoteAlarm)
    COM_INTERFACE_ENTRY2(IDispatch, IRemoteAlarm)
    COM_INTERFACE_ENTRY_IMPL(IConnectionPointContainer)
END_COM_MAP()

BEGIN_CONNECTION_POINT_MAP(CRemoteAlarm)
    CONNECTION_POINT_ENTRY(IID_IRingAlarm)
END_CONNECTION_POINT_MAP()

// Outgoing interface helpers
    void Brinnnnng();

// IRemoteAlarm
public:
    STDMETHOD(CancelAlarm)(void);
    STDMETHOD(SetAlarm)(/*[in]*/ DATE time);

// IRemoteTime
public:
    STDMETHOD(GetTime)(/*[out]*/ DATE* date);
};
```

First, you'll notice that **CRemoteAlarm** has two new base classes. The first is a dispatch implementation for the **IRemoteTime** interface and the second is a connection point implementation for the **IRingAlarm** interface. This allows the server to call the outgoing interface. This **IConnectionPointImpl** class template takes three parameters, the first is the class we are deriving, and the second is the IID of the outgoing interface. The third indicates the class that will actually handle the list of connections, and in this case we use the default, **CComDynamicUnkArray**.

Further down the definition, you can see that changes have been made to the COM interface map. All exposed incoming interfaces should have an entry here so we've added one for the additional interface that we implement: **IRemoteTime**. We don't need to add an entry to this map for **IRingAlarm** because it's an outgoing interface. The entry for **IDispatch** has been altered to use **COM_INTERFACE_ENTRY2()** to resolve the ambiguity that results from inheriting from two dual interfaces.

The outgoing interface is finally mentioned in the connection point map, reproduced here:

```
BEGIN_CONNECTION_POINT_MAP(CRemoteAlarm)
   CONNECTION_POINT_ENTRY(IID_IRingAlarm)
END_CONNECTION_POINT_MAP()

// Outgoing interface helpers
   void Brinnnnng();
```

The connection point map allows you to specify all the outgoing interfaces. Internally ATL uses this map in its implementation of the connection point container. The purpose of the connection point is for a client to register a sink interface that the server calls when an event occurs. This interface is held by the connection point container. When the event occurs, the server will have to go through the process of getting the connection point from the container, getting the outgoing interface and then calling the notification method. It is better to encapsulate all this in a single function: hence the helper method **Brinnnnng()** which obtains the **IRemoteAlarm** interface and then calls **IRemoteAlarm::Brinnnnng()**.

Finally the **GetTime()** declaration has been added for the method in the **IRemoteTime** interface. Since the code needs to know about the **IRemoteTime** interface, we need to add the C++ prototypes somewhere. The easiest way to do this is to copy **TimeServer.h** from the TimeServer project directory into the current project directory and add the following line after the resource header include in **RemoteAlarm.h**.

```
#include "resource.h"     // main symbols
#include "TimeServer.h"    // definition of IRemoteTime
                           // interface
```

We're also going to need access to the IDs defined in **TimeServer_i.c**, so you should also add this file to your project and alter its build settings so that it doesn't try to make use of the precompiled header.

Adding Thread Structure

Finally we need some instance data members and helper functions to handle the connections. When a client makes a connection with the server, we need to save the time requested for the alarm and then start a thread to check the time. This thread will need to have a thread function. We can either supply a global function to do this, or we can declare a **static** class method. The method has to be **static** to ensure that C++ does not alter the function prototype: for other class methods, C++ will add a hidden **this** parameter, so the function wouldn't have the prototype required for thread functions.

There is one problem with this approach, the **static** function will only be able to access **static** variables. To get over this problem, we introduce the nasty kludge of passing the method a pointer to the current object. This is declared in the **struct ThreadData** as **m_bkptr**. Prior to creating a new thread, we initialize the structure to have the **this** pointer of the current object, as well as providing some other data the thread needs (any other object data, it can get through the **m_bkptr** pointer).

```
// Thread data
protected:
   struct ThreadData
   {
      CRemoteAlarm* m_bkptr;
      HANDLE m_die;
      HANDLE m_dead;
      DATE m_time;
   } m_td;
   static unsigned int _stdcall CheckTime(void* pv);
   HANDLE m_hthread;
```

You should also initialize the thread handle to zero in the constructor's initialization list.

```
CRemoteAlarm(): m_hthread(0)
   {
   }
```

This is the last change to this header.

Implementing Incoming Methods

The next task is to implement the incoming interface methods. **GetTime()** is straightforward, just copy the code from the **TimeServer** project and edit the class name.

```
STDMETHODIMP CRemoteAlarm::GetTime(DATE* date)
{
   SYSTEMTIME st;
   GetSystemTime(&st);

   if (SystemTimeToVariantTime(&st, date))
   {
      return S_OK;
   }
   else
   {
      *date = 0;
      return E_FAIL;
   }
}
```

Now we need to implement the other incoming interface, **IRemoteAlarm**. The first method is **SetAlarm()**, which is called by the client when it wants the server to check for a particular time. The implementation is:

```
STDMETHODIMP CRemoteAlarm::SetAlarm(DATE time)
{
   unsigned threadid;

   if (m_hthread != 0)
      CancelAlarm();
```

```
    m_td.m_time = time;
    m_td.m_die = CreateEvent(NULL, TRUE, FALSE, NULL);
    m_td.m_dead = CreateEvent(NULL, TRUE, FALSE, NULL);
    m_td.m_bkptr = this;

    m_hthread = (HANDLE)_beginthreadex(NULL, 0, CheckTime,
                        &m_td, 0, &threadid);

  return S_OK;
}
```

To simplify the code, the object only allows one connection, so we first check if the thread handle is **0**. The handle is set to zero in the constructor, and again when the worker thread dies. So, if it's non-zero, that means that there is a thread already created, which we need to stop by calling **CancelAlarm()**.

Then we initialize the thread information. **m_time** is the time when the alarm should ring, and **m_bkptr** is the **this** pointer of the object so that the thread can have access to the outgoing interface. The other two members are events that are used to synchronize the death of the thread with the method telling it to die. **m_die** is signaled if another thread wants the worker thread to die, and **m_dead** is signaled when the worker thread has died.

Finally the C runtime function **_beginthreadex()** is called to create the thread and run it. To access this function, you'll need to add an include for **<process.h>** to **RemoteAlarm.cpp** and you'll need to make sure that you're using the multithreaded versions of the run-time libraries. For this second item, you'll need to alter the project settings so that the **/MT** switches are used rather than the **/ML** equivalents. Although you can do this by hand, the easiest way to do it is by opening up the Project Settings dialog (use the Project | Settings... menu), select the project in the left-hand box and the C/C++ tab in the right-hand box. From this tab select Code Generation from the Category box and then select an appropriate multithreaded library from the Use run-time library box.

The thread executes the **CheckTime()** method:

```
unsigned int _stdcall CRemoteAlarm::CheckTime(void* pv)
{
    struct ThreadData* ptd = (struct ThreadData*)pv;
    DWORD dwRet;
    SYSTEMTIME st;
    DATE dt;

    while (TRUE)
    {
        // Check time every second
        dwRet = WaitForSingleObject(ptd->m_die, 1000);

        if (dwRet == WAIT_OBJECT_0)
        {
            SetEvent(ptd->m_dead);
            break;                          // Told to die
        }

        GetSystemTime(&st);
        SystemTimeToVariantTime(&st, &dt);

        if (dt >= ptd->m_time)
        {
```

```
            // Ring alarm bell
            ptd->m_bkptr->Brinnnng();
            CloseHandle(ptd->m_die);
            CloseHandle(ptd->m_dead);
            ptd->m_bkptr->m_hthread = 0;
            _endthreadex(0);
        }
    }

    return 0;
}
```

The thread goes into a loop checking for one of two conditions: either it is told to die or the alarm time has been reached. The first condition is tested for in the **WaitForSingleObject()** call, this is done every second. If the **m_die** event is signaled, it will signal the **m_dead** event and return from the thread function. This situation only occurs when **CancelAlarm()** is called, and this method cleans up the thread data.

The rest of the code checks the time and if it is greater than or equal to the time requested, the **Brinnnng()** helper is called and the thread dies. In its death, the thread cleans up, releasing the event objects and setting the thread handle to zero.

As mentioned before the **Brinnnng()** method is a helper that calls back to the **IRingAlarm** interface in the client.

> *Note that, here, the server is the client of the client. In other words, the client is acting as a COM server. This is an important point particularly when you are considering security*

```
void CRemoteAlarm::Brinnnng()
{
    // m_vec is a member of the IConnectionPointImpl class
    // of type CComDynamicUnkArray. m_vec manages the
    // connection points.
    IUnknown** ppUnk = m_vec.begin();

    if (*ppUnk != NULL)
    {
        IRingAlarm* pIAlarm = (IRingAlarm*)*ppUnk;
        pIAlarm->Brinnnng();
    }
}
```

This code shows you why ATL is so useful. All we need to do is to get the outgoing interface is to obtain the interface pointer out of the **m_vec** list (inherited from **IConnectionPointImpl**) then use this to call the method. Simple!

The final method is the **CancelAlarm()** method. We need to make sure that only one client can set an alarm (and also to cancel an already set alarm).

```
STDMETHODIMP CRemoteAlarm::CancelAlarm()
{
    SetEvent(m_td.m_die);
    WaitForSingleObject(m_td.m_dead, INFINITE);
```

```
        CloseHandle(m_td.m_die);
        CloseHandle(m_td.m_dead);
        CloseHandle(m_hthread);
        m_hthread = 0;
        return S_OK;
    }
```

This must tell the worker thread to die. It does this by signaling the **m_die** event and waiting until the thread has said that it is dead. Once the thread is dead, **m_dead** is signaled and we can clean up the data.

There is one final change to make before we can compile the project. Since this project uses more than one thread, we need to make sure that we handle this correctly. More details are given in Chapter 9, but here we will merely mark the server as free-threaded. If the ATL Object Wizard has not already done this for you, the change is simple: follow the instructions in the function **_tWinMain()** in **AlarmServer.cpp**. and uncomment the line with **CoInitializeEx()** and comment out the line with **CoInitialize()**.

```
    extern "C" int WINAPI _tWinMain(HINSTANCE hInstance,
    HINSTANCE /*hPrevInstance*/, LPTSTR lpCmdLine, int /*nShowCmd*/)
    {
    lpCmdLine = GetCommandLine(); //this line necessary for _ATL_MIN_CRT
    //  HRESULT hRes = CoInitialize(NULL);
    //  If you are running on NT 4.0 or higher you can use the following call
    //  instead to make the EXE free threaded.
    //  This means that calls come in on a random RPC thread
        HRESULT hRes = CoInitializeEx(NULL, COINIT_MULTITHREADED);
```

As usual, you'll need to add **_WIN32_DCOM** to the preprocessor symbols for this project in order to be able to use this function.

Now you should be able to compile the project and register the server. All we need to do now is write a client.

AlarmClient

The **AlarmClient** is a mix of MFC and ATL code. We'll use MFC to provide the user interface and ATL to provide the connection point code.

The first step is to use MFC AppWizard (EXE) to create a dialog-based project called **AlarmClient**. Once the project has been created, add the code to **CAlarmClientApp::InitInstance()** to initialize the OLE libraries, along with the entry in the string table for the error message used when initialization fails:

```
    // Initialize OLE libraries
    if (!AfxOleInit())
    {
        AfxMessageBox(IDP_OLE_INIT_FAILED);
        return FALSE;
    }
```

Now edit the dialog box resource, **ID_ALARMCLIENT_DIALOG**, to look like this:

IDC_REMFRAME — Alarm Client — [Remote Time / Edit] — IDC_REMOTE

IDC_LOCFRAME — [Local Time / Edit] — IDC_LOCAL

IDC_ERRORS

IDC_MINS — Minutes [Edit] Seconds [Edit] — IDC_SECS

IDC_MIN — IDC_SEC

IDC_SETALARM — Set Alarm Cancel — IDCANCEL

This is essentially the **TimeClient** dialog, but with two spin-and-buddy pairs to enter the time that must elapse before the alarm will sound. This time will be added to the remote time and then passed to the server via **SetAlarm()**. As before there is a static text control to relay errors.

Just as you did with the previous clients, add a dialog, **CServerNameDlg**, to get the server name. If you've already added this dialog to the Component Gallery as suggested earlier then this will be particularly easy.

In the main dialog class, **CAlarmClientDlg**, add the following **protected** members:

```
protected:
    CString m_strServerName;      // The name of the server
                                  // machine
    IRemoteTime* m_pTimeServer;   // The interface on the
                                  // remote object
    UINT m_nTimerID;              // The ID of the timer
    IRemoteAlarm* m_pAlarmServer; // The other interface on
                                  // the remote object
    DWORD m_dwCookie;             // Used for Unadvise()

// Helpers
    void Message(const CString& strMessage);
    void SetUpFrameNames();
    void SetUpSpinRanges();
```

A lot of these members will look very familiar to you from the **TimeClient** example:

m_pTimeServer provides the current remote time and this is used in the **WM_TIMER** handler provided for the timer identified by **m_nTimerID**. The name of the server machine is kept in **m_strServerName** as before. **m_pAlarmServer** holds the pointer to the **IRemoteAlarm** interface. When the connection point is **Advise()**'d, the value returned is stored in **m_dwCookie** so that we can use it in a call to **Unadvise()** later. **Message()** provides us with a quick way of displaying error messages on the dialog. **SetUpFrameNames()** displays the names of the local and remote machines. **SetUpSpinRanges()** just sets the ranges of the spin controls for easy input of time values.

The helper functions can be implemented as shown:

```
void CAlarmClientDlg::Message(const CString& strMessage)
{
   CWnd* pTextCtrl = GetDlgItem(IDC_ERRORS);
   ASSERT(pTextCtrl);

   pTextCtrl->SetWindowText(strMessage);
}

void CAlarmClientDlg::SetUpFrameNames()
{
   // Set up the names on the frames
   TCHAR szLocalName[MAX_COMPUTERNAME_LENGTH + 1];
   DWORD dwSize = MAX_COMPUTERNAME_LENGTH;
   if (GetComputerName(szLocalName, &dwSize))
   {
      CWnd* pFrame = GetDlgItem(IDC_LOCFRAME);
      ASSERT(pFrame);

      pFrame->SetWindowText(szLocalName);

      pFrame = GetDlgItem(IDC_REMFRAME);
      ASSERT(pFrame);

      if (m_strServerName.IsEmpty())
         pFrame->SetWindowText(szLocalName);
      else
         pFrame->SetWindowText(m_strServerName);
   }
}

void CAlarmClientDlg::SetUpSpinRanges()
{
   // Set the spin controls' extents
   CSpinButtonCtrl* pSpin;
   pSpin = (CSpinButtonCtrl*)GetDlgItem(IDC_MINS);
   ASSERT(pSpin);
   pSpin->SetRange(0, 59);

   pSpin = (CSpinButtonCtrl*)GetDlgItem(IDC_SECS);
   ASSERT(pSpin);
   pSpin->SetRange(0, 59);
}
```

Since we need access to the interfaces and IDs for **IRemoteTime** and **IRemoteAlarm**, you need to copy the files **TimeServer.h**, **AlarmServer.h**, **TimeServer_i.c** and **AlarmServer_i.c** into the **AlarmClient** project directory. Add **include**s for the first two files to **AlarmClientDlg.h**, and add the second two files to the project, then alter their build settings so that they don't use the precompiled header.

The **OnInitDialog()** handler needs to instantiate the server, much as **TimeClient** does, and then call **Advise()** on the server's **IConnectionPoint** interface:

```
BOOL CAlarmClientDlg::OnInitDialog()
{
   //...Standard wizard-supplied code
```

239

```
         CServerNameDlg dlg;

         // Get the name of the server to use
         if (dlg.DoModal() == IDOK &&
                           !dlg.m_strServerName.IsEmpty())
            m_strServerName = dlg.m_strServerName;
         else
            m_strServerName.Empty();

         SetUpFrameNames();
         SetUpSpinRanges();

         HRESULT hr;
         COSERVERINFO serverinfo;
         COSERVERINFO* pServerInfo = NULL;

         // Create the server info
         // Note that we use CString to convert to wide chars
         serverinfo.dwReserved1 = 0;
         serverinfo.dwReserved2 = 0;
         serverinfo.pwszName = m_strServerName.AllocSysString();
         serverinfo.pAuthInfo = NULL;

         if (m_strServerName.IsEmpty())
            pServerInfo = NULL;
         else
            pServerInfo = &serverinfo;

         MULTI_QI qi[] = { {&IID_IRemoteAlarm, NULL, 0},
                        {&IID_IRemoteTime, NULL, 0} };

         hr = CoCreateInstanceEx(CLSID_RemoteAlarm, NULL,
                    CLSCTX_LOCAL_SERVER | CLSCTX_REMOTE_SERVER,
                    pServerInfo, 2, qi);

         if (SUCCEEDED(qi[0].hr))
         {
            // Now get the remote alarm interface
            m_pAlarmServer = (IRemoteAlarm*)qi[0].pItf;

            CComObject<CAlarm>* pAlarm;
            CComObject<CAlarm>::CreateInstance(&pAlarm);
            m_dwCookie = 99;

            hr = AtlAdvise(m_pAlarmServer, pAlarm->GetUnknown(),
                        IID_IRingAlarm, &m_dwCookie);
         }
         else
         {
            m_pAlarmServer = NULL;
            CString str;
            str.Format("Cannot get alarm interface: 0x%x",
                        qi[0].hr);
            Message(str);
         }

         if (SUCCEEDED(qi[1].hr))
```

```
        {
            // Now get the time interface
            m_nTimerID = SetTimer(ID_TIMER, 1000, NULL);
            m_pTimeServer = (IRemoteTime*)qi[1].pItf;
        }
        else
        {
            m_pTimeServer = NULL;
            CString str;
            str.Format("Cannot get time interface: 0x%x",
                        qi[1].hr);
            Message(str);
        }

        // Free the buffer previous allocated
        ::SysFreeString(serverinfo.pwszName);
```

```
    return TRUE;  // return TRUE  unless you set the focus
                  // to a control
}
```

The first task is to get the name of the server machine from the user using **CServerNameDlg**. This is then used to initialize the text on the dialog's frames. If the user does not enter a machine name, the local machine is used. The dialog uses the spin common control, so we set the maximum value for the control using **SetUpSpinRanges()**.

Now we deviate from the **TimeClient** example. **AlarmClient** uses two interfaces on the server object so we **QI()** for both of them with a single call to **CoCreateInstanceEx()**. (Remember, that you may need to define **_WIN32_DCOM** to be able to use this function). This will return the **HRESULT** for the **QI()** on each interface, as well as the interface pointer in the array passed in, so we need to check each member. If the **QI()** on **IRemoteTime** is successful, we can cache the pointer and start the timer as in the **TimeClient** example.

If the **QI()** on the **IRemoteAlarm** is successful, we need to set up the sink interface and call **Advise()** on the remote object **IConnectionPoint** interface. Our code actually uses the ATL function, **AtlAdvise()**. This gets the **IConnectionPoint** interface on the server as well as calling the **IConnectionPoint::Advise()** method. The **CComObject<>** template class implements a **static** member called **CreateInstance()** that allows you to create an instance of the class of the type given.

We haven't yet defined the **CAlarm** class, but we will shortly...

AtlAdvise() calls through to the remote object's **IConnectionPoint::Advise()**, so we need to pass the IID of the source interface, the **IUnknown** interface of the sink interface, and a cookie value that uniquely identifies this connection. Since this is done through a global function call, we need to specify the **IUnknown** of the remote object on which we will make the call. Thus the function's parameters are the **IUnknown** of the remote object, the **IUnknown** of the sink, the IID, and then the cookie.

We need to implement a **WM_TIMER** handler in the dialog. This is the same as implemented for **TimeClient**.

```
void CAlarmClientDlg::OnTimer(UINT nIDEvent)
{
    // We will assume that all timer messages are from
    // our timer
```

```
        CWnd* pRemote = GetDlgItem(IDC_REMOTE);
        ASSERT(pRemote);
        CWnd* pLocal = GetDlgItem(IDC_LOCAL);
        ASSERT(pLocal);

        SYSTEMTIME st;
        DATE theDate;
        HRESULT hr;
        CString strTime;
        CString strError;

        if (m_pTimeServer)
        {
            hr = m_pTimeServer->GetTime(&theDate);

            if (SUCCEEDED(hr))
            {
                VariantTimeToSystemTime(theDate, &st);
                strTime.Format("%02d:%02d:%02d",
                                st.wHour, st.wMinute, st.wSecond);
            }
            else
            {
                strError.Format("Cannot get time: 0x%x", hr);
            }
        }
        else
            strError = "No object";

        pRemote->SetWindowText(strTime);
        Message(strError);

        // Now get the local time
        GetSystemTime(&st);
        strTime.Format("%02d:%02d:%02d",
                        st.wHour, st.wMinute, st.wSecond);
        pLocal->SetWindowText(strTime);
        CDialog::OnTimer(nIDEvent);
    }
```

Of course, we also need a handler for when the Set Alarm button is clicked:

```
    void CAlarmClientDlg::OnSetAlarm()
    {
        if (NULL == m_pAlarmServer)
            return;

        SYSTEMTIME st;
        DATE dt;
        HRESULT hr;

        if (m_pTimeServer)
        {
            hr = m_pTimeServer->GetTime(&dt);

            if (SUCCEEDED(hr))
            {
```

```
                VariantTimeToSystemTime(dt, &st);
        }
        else
        {
            CString strError;
            strError.Format("Cannot get time: 0x%x", hr);
            Message(strError);
            return;
        }
    }

    // Add the elapse time
    CTime alarm(st);
    int mins, secs;

    CSpinButtonCtrl* pSpin;
    pSpin = (CSpinButtonCtrl*)GetDlgItem(IDC_MINS);
    ASSERT(pSpin);
    mins = pSpin->GetPos();

    pSpin = (CSpinButtonCtrl*)GetDlgItem(IDC_SECS);
    ASSERT(pSpin);
    secs = pSpin->GetPos();

    CTimeSpan howlong(0, 0, mins, secs);

    alarm += howlong;
    st.wYear = (WORD)alarm.GetYear();
    st.wMonth = (WORD)alarm.GetMonth();
    st.wDay = (WORD)alarm.GetDay();
    st.wHour = (WORD)alarm.GetHour();
    st.wMinute = (WORD)alarm.GetMinute();
    st.wSecond = (WORD)alarm.GetSecond();

    SystemTimeToVariantTime(&st, &dt);

    hr = m_pAlarmServer->SetAlarm(dt);

    if (FAILED(hr))
    {
        CString str;
        str.Format("Cannot set time: 0x%x", hr);
        Message(str);
    }
}
```

This reads the values in the spin buddies, and adds the time to the current time on the remote machine. This is obtained by a call to **IRemoteTime::GetTime()**. The new time is sent to the server with a call to **IRemoteAlarm::SetAlarm()**.

When the client closes down, we need to clean up: kill the timer, release the remote object, and call **Unadvise()**. This is done in the **WM_DESTROY** handler.

```
void CAlarmClientDlg::OnDestroy()
{
    CDialog::OnDestroy();
```

```
    if (m_nTimerID)
        KillTimer(m_nTimerID);

    AtlUnadvise(m_pAlarmServer, IID_IRingAlarm, m_dwCookie);
    if (m_pTimeServer)
        m_pTimeServer->Release();
    if (m_pAlarmServer)
        m_pAlarmServer->Release();
}
```

CAlarm

The sink interface is implemented in a class called **CAlarm**. Create two new files in the project directory called **Alarm.h** and **Alarm.cpp**, add **Alarm.cpp** to the project, and add the code shown below.

```
// Alarm.h
class CAlarm :
    public CComObjectRootEx<CComSingleThreadModel>,
    public IDispatchImpl<IRingAlarm, &IID_IRingAlarm, &LIBID_ALARMSERVERLib>
{
public:
    CAlarm() {}

    BEGIN_COM_MAP(CAlarm)
        COM_INTERFACE_ENTRY(IDispatch)
        COM_INTERFACE_ENTRY(IRingAlarm)
    END_COM_MAP()

// IRingAlarm
    STDMETHOD(Brinnnnng)(void);
};
```

```
// Alarm.cpp
#include "StdAfx.h"
#include "AlarmClient.h"
#include "AlarmServer.h"
#include "Alarm.h"
#include "AlarmClientDlg.h"

STDMETHODIMP CAlarm::Brinnnnng()
{
    CAlarmClientApp* pApp = (CAlarmClientApp*)AfxGetApp();
    CAlarmClientDlg* pDlg =
                    (CAlarmClientDlg*)pApp->m_pMainWnd;

    pDlg->OnAlarm();

    return S_OK;
}
```

CAlarm is quite straightforward. The class is derived from **CComObjectRootEx<>**, which handles reference counting on the object, and **IDispatchImpl<>**, which provides dual interface **IDispatch** support. The **COM_MAP** declares the interfaces that the object supports, and further down is the single method in the sink interface: **Brinnnnng()**. The **AlarmServer** calls this function whenever the time that was set has expired. Our implementation just calls an **OnAlarm()** method in the dialog class.

You can implement **OnAlarm()** to give whatever response you need, but we've just used it to display a message box.

```
void CAlarmClientDlg::OnAlarm()
{
    AfxMessageBox("Wake Up!");
}
```

Accessing ATL from MFC projects

ATL defines some global data and functions, for example it defines its own Win32 memory heap for all objects that are created and the handle to this heap is held as a global value. The programming device used is to handle these globals is have a global object called **_Module** of type **CComModule**. The logical place to declare this is in the **AlarmClient.cpp** file:

```
//////////////////////////////////////////////////////////////////////
// The one and only CAlarmClientApp object
CAlarmClientApp theApp;

//////////////////////////////////////////////////////////////////////
// The one and only CComModule object for ATL support
CComModule _Module;
```

The **CComModule** must be initialized and this is done in the **InitInstance()** of the app:

```
BOOL CAlarmClientApp::InitInstance()
{
    _Module.Init(NULL, NULL);

    // Initialize OLE libraries
    if (!AfxOleInit())
    {
      AfxMessageBox(IDP_OLE_INIT_FAILED);
      return FALSE;
    }
```

The parameters to **Init()** are a pointer to the object map implemented by the **CComModule** and the instance handle of the resources used by the server implementation of the class. These are irrelevant here and so are set to **NULL**.

This still isn't enough to use ATL, because we need to include the ATL headers somewhere so that we can use the templates. In this project, we have put these in the **StdAfx.h** header:

```
#include <atlbase.h>
extern CComModule _Module;
#include <atlcom.h>
```

This gives the necessary headers and an **extern** declaration of the global **CComModule** object. ATL implements most of its code in templates, but some is implemented in non-templated code (the **CComModule** class is such a class), so this must be added to a **cpp** file somewhere. We have added it to **StdAfx.cpp**:

```
#include <atlimpl.cpp>
```

Testing the Code

The first test is to run the client on the same machine as the server. Note that you don't need to compile the **MIDL**-produced proxy-stub since the automation marshaler is used. Run **AlarmClient** on the server machine and when you get the dialog box asking for the server name, press OK or Cancel without entering a name, this will make sure that the local machine is used.

You will get a dialog box looking something like this:

Unsurprisingly, the two times should be the same. If you get an error of **0x80080005**, it is probably because you haven't registered the server.

Now change the Seconds box to something like 10 seconds and press Set Alarm. Watch the time and after 10 seconds, you will get the modal message box appearing:

Click on OK and then on Set Alarm again, and you should find that after 10 seconds the message box will appear again. Now launch the NT Task Manager and you should see **AlarmServer.exe** in the list box on the Processes tab. When you click on Cancel on **AlarmClient**, you should see the server disappear immediately.

Remote Test

Now for the remote test. Copy **AlarmClient** to the client machine and run it. When asked for the server machine name, enter it into the dialog. You will see the main dialog appear, and briefly an error message will show:

Then the dialog will show the two times (probably different) on the two machines. So what's happening here? This is indicating that the client cannot get the **IRemoteAlarm** interface, but it's clearly getting the **IRemoteTime** interface, since the error occurs after the application checks for a valid **IRemoteTime** interface. The reason for this error is registration: we have already registered the **IRemoteTime** interface in the last chapter, but we need to do the same for the alarm interface. Otherwise, when COM is asked for this interface, it doesn't know what you're asking for.

We could use type library marshaling, but since one interface already uses a proxy-stub DLL, we might as well create another. Once you've compiled the proxy-stub DLL, copy it to the client and register it.

Now try again. Run the client, select your server machine and you'll find that the client can find the server interfaces. Now set an alarm time and wait for the server to detect it. You'll probably find something like this happening on the server machine:

So what's causing this? Well, we have told the client about the server: the proxy-stub registration added the necessary information in the client's registry. The server knows about the client, since it has registered itself and anyway it has the type library with the client sink interface defined in it. What else is there?

Security! The client has launched the server object and accessed the server object's methods with default security. In the absence of any specified security, DCOM will use the defaults (as explained in the last chapter, and in more detail in Chapter 7). However, with a connection point, the server must call back to the client, so we must allow the server to have the permissions to access the client.

If this seems confusing, don't worry, we'll cover security in Chapter 7. For now, the easiest way to get the application working is to use **DCOMCnfg** to specify the account that will be used to run the server. For this fix to work, there must be an account of the same name on both the client and server (or both must be part of the same domain and a domain account used).

Run **DCOMCnfg** and select the RemoteAlarm Class properties and then the Identity tab:

Select This user (the default is The launching user) and type in the details.

Now restart the client again and set an alarm time, you will find that the server will be able to make the callback to the sink interface.

Summary

The most important problem to surmount when you write distributed objects is to provide a mechanism for the client to call on the methods of the objects and to pass data between the two. This mechanism is known as marshaling and it is provided by proxy and stub objects.

This chapter has described the two most important methods of creating those proxy-stub objects – either use the automation marshaler and tell it what it should be marshaling, or use **MIDL** to create proxy and stub objects that know what they are marshaling. The two examples in this chapter have shown these two marshaling methods.

EnvServer uses type library marshaling. The information in the type library provides the automation marshaler with all the information it needs. **AlarmServer** uses standard marshaling using a proxy-stub DLL created just for the specific interfaces used by the client. This last example also illustrates the important concept of connection points that allow for a client to make a method call that behaves like an asynchronous method call (in the absence of COM supporting asynchronous method call semantics).

Of course, before you can implement an interface, or create the objects to do the interface marshaling, you need to have defined the interface. This is carried out using the COM Interface Definition Language (IDL), which is based upon the standard DCE IDL. That was the focus of the first part of this chapter.

Now, having seen DCOM in action, I hope that you will have many questions in your mind about DCOM and how it works. After the last example, you'll almost certainly want to know more about how security and threading are handled in COM. These subjects are covered in Chapters 7 and 9, respectively.

However, I'm sure you are more than a little bit curious about how the DCOM magic works to connect a client to an object across a network in a way that appears as if the object is in the client's address space. It will all be explained in the next chapter, where I show you how DCOM uses Microsoft's DCE compliant RPC runtime to handle remote objects.

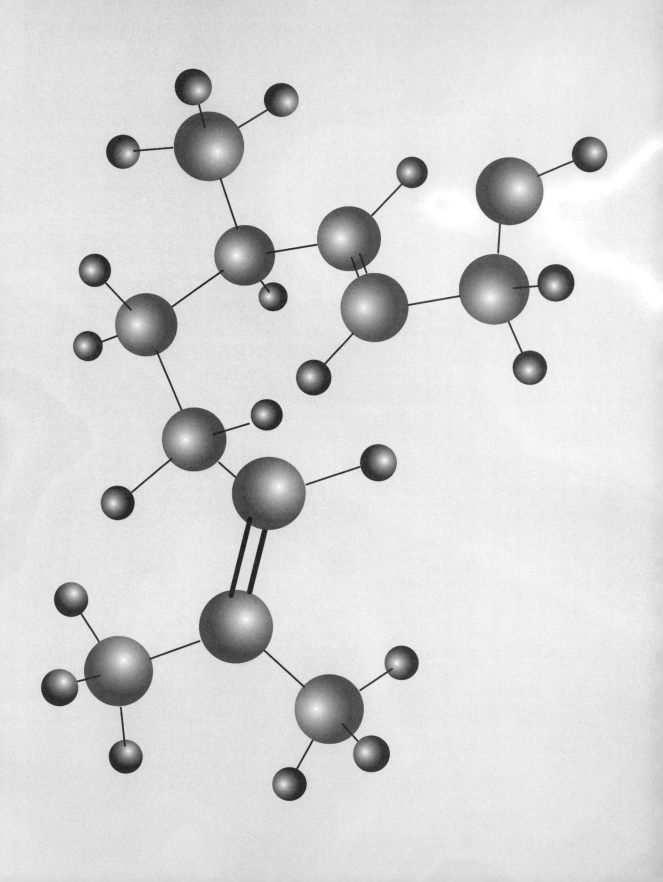

DCOM Under the Hood

Introduction

In this chapter, we will look more closely at how DCOM works and how it uses the underlying RPC mechanism to remote requests across the network. We'll use two methods to investigate this behavior. Firstly, the example programs will save COM system calls to a log file that we can analyze later, and secondly we will use the Microsoft Network Monitor program to analyze the packets that are sent between the machines.

Since DCOM is based upon RPC, we'll also write the DCOM example program using an RPC interface. This will allow us to compare the packets sent by both methods. Armed with this data, and the DCOM and RPC specs, we will be able to view the data that is sent to activate an object and to make a method call. The second half of the chapter will concentrate on DCOM and will center on optimizing method calls.

The Test Interface

To perform the tests in this chapter, we will need to use a simple interface, **IReverse**. The COM definition of this interface is shown below.

```
[
    object,
    uuid(...),
    pointer_default(unique)
]
interface IReverse : IUnknown
{
    import "oaidl.idl";
    HRESULT Reverse([in, string] char* str,
                    [out, string] char** revstr);
};
```

The interface is simple, one function called **Reverse()** that takes the **str** parameter, reverses it and returns the result in the buffer pointed to by **revstr**. This is a COM interface, and moreover it is a *custom* interface so, using **MIDL** to compile this, we will also get the files for a proxy-stub DLL.

DCOM is based on RPC, so it is interesting to compare the servers created for DCOM and Microsoft RPC. The RPC interface is:

```
[
   uuid(...),
   version(1.0),
   pointer_default(unique)
]
interface IReverse
{
   unsigned long Reverse([in, string] char* str,
                         [out, string] char** revstr);
};
```

The interfaces look remarkably similar: the main differences are that the COM interface has the **[object]** attribute, whereas the RPC interface has the **[version()]** attribute, and the COM interface is derived from **IUnknown**, which requires the import of the **oaidl.idl** file. However, this is not the entire story. The RPC IDL file contains only the definition above, but the COM file also requires the definition of the **coclass** and type library.

The DCOM Test Application

The server application could be written with ATL, and creating such a project would be simple with the help of the ATL COM AppWizard and ATL Object Wizard. However, to illustrate some of the messaging that occurs and to allow us to log method calls to a file on disk, we will write the server ourselves as a console application.

First use Visual C++ to create a new Win32 Console Application called ReverseDCOM. Create a new text file and save it in the project directory as **ReverseDCOM.idl**. Add the file to the project and add the following text to it. This is the complete IDL definition necessary for the server.

```
// Interface for reversing strings

import "unknwn.idl";

[
   object,
   uuid(31B5ACC3-552F-11D0-9A90-0060973044A8),
   pointer_default(unique)
]
interface IReverse : IUnknown
{
   HRESULT Reverse([in, string] char* str, [out, string] char** revstr);
};

[
   uuid(31B5ACC1-552F-11D0-9A90-0060973044A8),
   version(1.0)
]
library ReverseDCOMLib
{
   [
      uuid(31B5ACC7-552F-11D0-9A90-0060973044A8)
   ]
```

```
   coclass Reverse
   {
     [default] interface IReverse;
   };
};
```

Now select the Settings for this file and give the file the Custom Build step shown below. This will ensure that the header and C files are created from the IDL file whenever it is compiled.

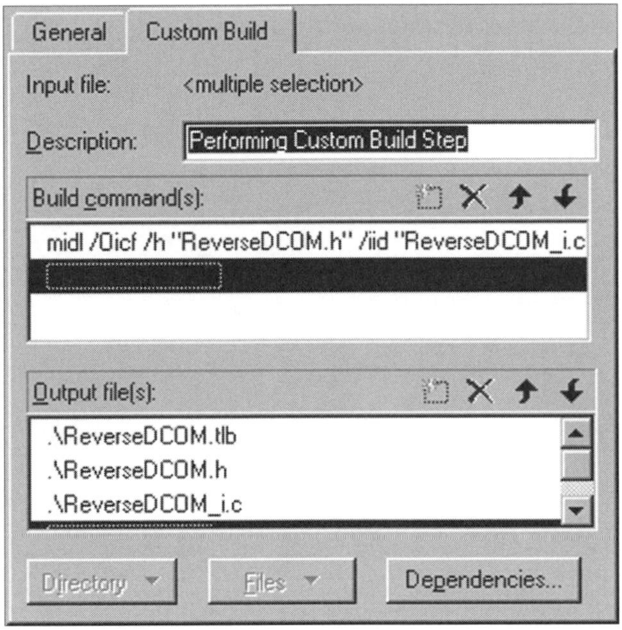

You can use this build step to compile the IDL file. Once **ReverseDCOM_i.c** has been generated, you should also add that file to the project.

The project needs to include several helper functions that will enable us to output chunks of memory or GUIDs to a log file. The first function, **print_guid()**, will convert a GUID into a string, **output()** will print its string parameter to the console and append it to a log file, and **hex_buffer()** will fill a string with the hex dump of a memory location. These functions are used extensively in **ReverseDCOM** so that we can see what is going on as the server is called. The functions need to be implemented in a file called **Utils.cpp** and declared in **Utils.h**, as shown below:

```
// Utils.h
void print_guid(REFGUID guid, LPTSTR strguid);
void output(LPCTSTR str);
void hex_buffer(LPVOID lp, UINT size, LPTSTR str);
TCHAR hex(const TCHAR c);

// Utils.cpp
#include <windows.h>
#include <tchar.h>
#include <stdio.h>

#include "Utils.h"
```

```
void print_guid(REFGUID guid, LPTSTR strguid)
{
   OLECHAR oszClassID[39];
   TCHAR szClassID[39];

   StringFromGUID2(guid, oszClassID, 39);
#ifdef UNICODE
   lstrcpy(szClassID, oszClassID);
#else
   WideCharToMultiByte(CP_ACP, 0, oszClassID, 39, szClassID, 39, NULL, NULL);
#endif
   wsprintf(strguid, _T("%s"), szClassID);
}


void output(LPCTSTR str)
{
   FILE* f = _tfopen(_T("DCOMReverse.log"), _T("a"));
   _fputts(str, f);
   _tprintf(str);
   fclose(f);
}

void hex_buffer(LPVOID lp, UINT size, LPTSTR str)
{
   TCHAR left[25];
   TCHAR right[9];
   TCHAR addr[10];

   CHAR* ptr = (CHAR*)lp;
   str[0] = 0;

   while (ptr < (CHAR*)lp + size)
   {
      lstrcpy(left, _T("                           "));
      lstrcpy(right, _T("          "));

      int x;
      for (x = 0; x < 8 && ptr + x < (CHAR*)lp + size; x++)
      {
         if (ptr[x] > ' ' && ptr[x] < 0x7f)
         {
            char cStr[2] = {0,0};
            cStr[0] = ptr[x];
            right[x] = *cStr;
         }
         else
            right[x] = _T('.');

         left[x * 3] = hex((ptr[x] & 0xf0)/0x10);
         left[(x * 3) + 1] = hex(ptr[x] & 0xf);
      }

      wsprintf(addr, _T("%08x "), ptr);
      lstrcat(str, addr);
      lstrcat(str, left);
      lstrcat(str, right);
      lstrcat(str, _T("\n"));
```

```
        ptr += 8;
    }

}

TCHAR hex(const TCHAR c)
{
    if ((BYTE)c > 9)
        return c + _T('A') - 10;
    else
        return c + _T('0');
}
```

These functions are pretty straightforward, so I won't explain them.

Next we need to implement the object that implements the **IReverse** interface, and its class factory. Here is the header file, **Reverse.h**, for the object and class factory.

```
// Reverse.h

#ifndef _REVERSE_H_
#define _REVERSE_H_

class CReverse : public IReverse
{
public:
    // IUnknown methods
    STDMETHOD(QueryInterface)(REFIID riid, void** ppvObj);
    STDMETHOD_(ULONG, AddRef)(void);
    STDMETHOD_(ULONG, Release)(void);

    // IReverse method
    HRESULT STDMETHODCALLTYPE Reverse(unsigned char* str,
                                      unsigned char** revstr);

    CReverse();
    ~CReverse();

private:
    ULONG m_cRef;
public:
    static ULONG g_objcount;
};

class CReverseCF : public IClassFactory
{
public:
    // IUnknown methods
    STDMETHOD(QueryInterface)(REFIID riid, void ** ppvObj);
    STDMETHOD_(ULONG, AddRef)(void);
    STDMETHOD_(ULONG, Release)(void);

    // IClassFactory methods
    STDMETHOD(CreateInstance)(IUnknown* punkOuter, REFIID riid,
                              void ** ppv);
    STDMETHOD(LockServer)(BOOL fLock);
```

```
        CReverseCF();

private:
    ULONG m_cRef;
public:
    static ULONG g_lockcount;
};

#endif
```

Notice that **MIDL** has created **Reverse()** with **unsigned char*** parameters. Normally you would use **LPOLESTR** or **BSTR**, but we will leave them in here because the RPC example needs a similar interface and it does not have these OLE types.

Here is the code for the class factory, which should go in a new file, **Reverse.cpp**:

```
#include <windows.h>
#include <stdio.h>
#include <tchar.h>

#include "Utils.h"
#include "ReverseDCOM.h"
#include "Reverse.h"

ULONG CReverseCF::g_lockcount = 0;
ULONG CReverse::g_objcount = 0;

CReverseCF::CReverseCF(void)
: m_cRef(0)
{
    output(_T("Class factory: reference count initialised\n"));
}

STDMETHODIMP CReverseCF::QueryInterface(REFIID iid, void ** ppv)
{
    *ppv = NULL;

    TCHAR _buf[1024];
    print_guid(iid, _buf);
    lstrcat(_buf, _T("\n"));
    output(_T("CF: QI "));
    output(_buf);

    if (iid == IID_IUnknown || iid == IID_IClassFactory)
        *ppv = this;
    else
    {
        output(_T("CF: no interface\n"));
        return E_NOINTERFACE;
    }

    AddRef();
    return S_OK;
}

STDMETHODIMP_(ULONG) CReverseCF::AddRef(void)
```

```
{
   TCHAR _buf[1024];
   wsprintf(_buf, _T("CF: AddRef %ld\n"), m_cRef + 1);
   output(_buf);
   return ++m_cRef;
}

STDMETHODIMP_(ULONG) CReverseCF::Release(void)
{
   TCHAR _buf[1024];
   wsprintf(_buf, _T("CF: Release %ld\n"), m_cRef - 1);
   output(_buf);
   if(--m_cRef == 0)
   {
      output(_T("CF: Release, destroy class factory\n"));
      delete this;
      return 0;
   }
   return m_cRef;
}

STDMETHODIMP CReverseCF::CreateInstance(IUnknown* punkOuter, REFIID riid,
         void** ppv)
{
   *ppv = NULL;

   TCHAR _buf[1024];
   print_guid(riid, _buf);
   lstrcat(_buf, _T("\n"));
   output(_T("CF: CI "));
   output(_buf);

   if (punkOuter)
   {
      return CLASS_E_NOAGGREGATION;
   }

   if (riid == IID_IReverse || riid == IID_IUnknown)
   {
      output(_T("CF: create object\n"));
      *ppv = (void*) new CReverse;
      if (*ppv == NULL)
      {
         return E_OUTOFMEMORY;
      }
   }

   ((CReverse*)*ppv)->AddRef();
   CReverse::g_objcount++;

   return S_OK;
}

STDMETHODIMP CReverseCF::LockServer(BOOL fLock)
{
   output(_T("CF: LS "));
   if (fLock)
      output(_T("TRUE\n"));
```

```
      else
         output(_T("FALSE\n"));

      if (fLock)
      {
         g_lockcount++;
      }
      else
      {
         g_lockcount--;
         if (CReverse::g_objcount == 0 && g_lockcount == 0)
         {
            PostQuitMessage(0);
         }
      }
      return NOERROR;
}
```

This is a simple implementation of the class factory. The only interesting part is that it will print out messages as COM makes calls on it. Here's the code for the object itself (also in **Reverse.cpp**):

```
/////////////////////////////////////////////////////////////////////
// Object

CReverse::CReverse()
: m_cRef(0)
{
}

CReverse::~CReverse()
{
}

STDMETHODIMP CReverse::QueryInterface(REFIID iid, void** ppv)
{
   *ppv = NULL;

   TCHAR _buf[1024];
   print_guid(iid, _buf);
   lstrcat(_buf, _T("\n"));
   output(_T("Obj: QI "));
   output(_buf);

   if (iid == IID_IUnknown || iid == IID_IReverse)
      *ppv = this;
   else
   {
      output(_T("Obj: no interface\n"));
      return E_NOINTERFACE;
   }

   AddRef();
   return S_OK;
}

STDMETHODIMP_(ULONG) CReverse::AddRef(void)
```

```
{
    TCHAR _buf[1024];
    wsprintf(_buf, _T("Obj: AddRef %ld\n"), m_cRef + 1);
    output(_buf);
    return ++m_cRef;
}

STDMETHODIMP_(ULONG) CReverse::Release(void)
{
    TCHAR _buf[1024];
    wsprintf(_buf, _T("Obj: Release %ld\n"), m_cRef - 1);
    output(_buf);
    if (--m_cRef == 0)
    {
        g_objcount--;
        delete this;
        if (g_objcount == 0 && CReverseCF::g_lockcount == 0)
        {
            output(_T("Obj: Release closing server\n"));
            PostQuitMessage(0);
        }
        return 0;
    }
    return m_cRef;
}

HRESULT STDMETHODCALLTYPE CReverse::Reverse(unsigned char* str,
                                            unsigned char** revstr)
{
    TCHAR _buf[1024];

    int count = lstrlenA((LPCSTR)str);
    *revstr = (unsigned char*)CoTaskMemAlloc(count + 1);

#ifdef UNICODE
    LPWSTR strTemp = new WCHAR[count + 1];
    MultiByteToWideChar(CP_ACP, 0, (char*)str, -1, strTemp, count + 1);
    wsprintf(_buf, L"%s reversed is ", strTemp);
    delete [] strTemp;
#else
    wsprintf(_buf, "%s reversed is ", (char*)str);
#endif
    output(_buf);

    unsigned char* ptr = *revstr + count;

    *(ptr--) = 0;

    while (ptr >= *revstr)
        *(ptr--) = *(str++);

#ifdef UNICODE
    strTemp = new WCHAR[lstrlenA((LPSTR)*revstr) + 1];
    MultiByteToWideChar(CP_ACP, 0, (LPSTR)*revstr, -1, strTemp,
lstrlenA((LPSTR)*revstr) + 1);
    wsprintf(_buf, L"%s\n", (char*)strTemp);
    delete [] strTemp;
#else
```

```
      wsprintf(_buf, "%s\n", (char*)*revstr);
#endif
   output(_buf);

   return S_OK;
}
```

The code for **Reverse()** is embarrassingly simple, it takes the string, creates an **[out]** buffer and then copies the characters from the **[in]** parameter in reverse order.

Now create a new file called **Main.cpp**. This will hold the entry point for the executable, **_tWinMain()**; two functions to initialize and uninitialize the server, **Initialize()** and **Uninitialize()**; and a function responsible for registering the server in the registry, **RegisterServer()**:

```
#include <windows.h>
#include <stdio.h>
#include <tchar.h>
#include <string.h>
#include <winnls.h>

#include "ReverseDCOM.h"
#include "Reverse.h"
#include "Utils.h"

// Forward declarations
BOOL Initialize(LPDWORD pdwRegisterCF);
void Uninitialize(LPDWORD pdwRegisterCF);
HRESULT RegisterServer(const CLSID& clsid, LPCTSTR progid,
                       LPCTSTR classname);

extern "C" int WINAPI _tWinMain(HINSTANCE hInstance,
    HINSTANCE hPrevInstance, LPTSTR lpCmdLine, int nShowCmd)
{
   DWORD dwRegisterCF = 0;

   TCHAR szTokens[] = _T("-/");
   LPCTSTR lpszToken = _tcstok(lpCmdLine, szTokens);
   while (lpszToken != NULL)
   {
      // Check to see if COM started server
      if (lstrcmpi(lpszToken, _T("Embedding")) == 0)
         break;

      // See if it was started to register the server
      else if (lstrcmpi(lpszToken, _T("RegServer")) == 0 )
      {
         if (SUCCEEDED(RegisterServer(CLSID_Reverse,
                          _T("Reverse.Reverse.1"), _T("Reverse Class"))))
            _tprintf(_T("Server Registration Succeeded\n"));
         else
            _tprintf(_T("Server Registration Failed\n"));
         return 0;
      }
   }

   _tprintf(_T("Running as an OLE server\n"));
```

```
   // Register class factory and initialize COM
   if (!Initialize(&dwRegisterCF))
      return 0;

   // OLE creates a hidden window for this thread
   MSG msg;
   while (GetMessage(&msg, NULL, 0, 0))
   {
      TCHAR _buf[1024];
      wsprintf(_buf, _T("%08x %08x %08x %08x %08x\n"), msg.hwnd,
              msg.message, msg.lParam, msg.wParam, GetCurrentThreadId());
      output(_buf);
      if (msg.wParam == 0xbabe)
         hex_buffer((LPVOID)msg.lParam, *(LPBYTE)(msg.lParam + 2), _buf);
      else
         hex_buffer((LPVOID)msg.lParam, msg.wParam, _buf);
      output(_buf);

      TranslateMessage(&msg);
      DispatchMessage(&msg);
   }

   // Revoke class factory and uininitialize COM
   Uninitialize(&dwRegisterCF);
   return 0;
}
```

Note that our server needs a message loop. This is because COM, whether the call is local or remote, serializes the calls through a windows message queue when you use a single threaded apartment (you'll see exactly what this means in Chapter 9). You can see the window that is created by COM to handle these calls by running the **EnumClient** application from Chapter 2 when the server is running, as we'll see a little later in the chapter.

The **Initialize()** function creates the class factory and registers it, while **Uninitialize()** will revoke the class factory. **RegisterServer()** will put the class entries into the registry.

> *If you're using NT 4.0, build 1381, the path to the server should be quite short, due to a bug in* **DCOMCnfg**. *This bug has been fixed in Service Pack 2 for NT 4.0 and doesn't affect DCOM for Windows 95.*

Initialize(), **Uninitialize()**, and **RegisterServer()** are shown here:

```
// Initializes COM
BOOL Initialize(LPDWORD pdwRegisterCF)
{
   HRESULT hr;

   hr = CoInitialize(NULL);
   if (FAILED(hr))
      return FALSE;

   // Register class factory
   LPCLASSFACTORY pcf = NULL;
   pcf = new CReverseCF;
   if (!pcf)
```

```
        {
            Uninitialize(pdwRegisterCF);
            return FALSE;
        }

        pcf->AddRef();
        hr = CoRegisterClassObject(CLSID_Reverse, pcf,
            CLSCTX_LOCAL_SERVER | CLSCTX_REMOTE_SERVER,
            REGCLS_SINGLEUSE, pdwRegisterCF);
        if (FAILED(hr))
        {
            Uninitialize(pdwRegisterCF);
            return FALSE;
        }

        pcf->Release();

        return TRUE;
    }

    // Cleanup
    void Uninitialize(LPDWORD pdwRegisterCF)
    {
        if (*pdwRegisterCF != 0)
            CoRevokeClassObject(*pdwRegisterCF);

        CoUninitialize();
    }

    HRESULT RegisterServer(const CLSID& clsid, LPCTSTR progid,
                        LPCTSTR classname)
    {
        TCHAR szModule[MAX_PATH];
        GetModuleFileName(NULL, szModule, MAX_PATH);

        // Stringify the clsid
        LPOLESTR oleCLSID;
        TCHAR strCLSID[40];
        TCHAR strkey[256];
        StringFromCLSID(clsid, &oleCLSID);

#ifdef UNICODE
        lstrcpy(strCLSID, oleCLSID);
#else
        WideCharToMultiByte(CP_ACP, 0, oleCLSID, -1, strCLSID, 40, NULL, NULL);
#endif
        CoTaskMemFree(oleCLSID);

        HKEY hclsid;

        // Create the CLSID key
        lstrcpy(strkey, _T("CLSID\\"));
        lstrcat(strkey, strCLSID);
        RegCreateKey(HKEY_CLASSES_ROOT, strkey, &hclsid);

        // Set the default value and then the AppID
        RegSetValueEx(hclsid, NULL, 0, REG_SZ,
            (const BYTE*)classname, (lstrlen(classname) + 1) * sizeof(TCHAR));
```

```
RegSetValueEx(hclsid, _T("AppID"), 0, REG_SZ,
        (const BYTE*)strCLSID, (lstrlen(strCLSID) + 1) * sizeof(TCHAR));

HKEY hsubkey;

// Set the LocalServer32 key
RegCreateKey(hclsid, _T("LocalServer32"), &hsubkey);
RegSetValueEx(hsubkey, NULL, 0, REG_SZ,
        (const BYTE*)szModule, (lstrlen(szModule) + 1) * sizeof(TCHAR));
RegCloseKey(hsubkey);

// Set the ProgID
RegCreateKey(hclsid, _T("ProgID"), &hsubkey);
RegSetValueEx(hsubkey, NULL, 0, REG_SZ,
            (const BYTE*)progid, (lstrlen(progid) + 1) * sizeof(TCHAR));
RegCloseKey(hsubkey);

// Set the VersionIndependentProgID
RegCreateKey(hclsid, _T("VersionIndependentProgID"), &hsubkey);
LPTSTR indprogid = new TCHAR[lstrlen(progid) + 1];
lstrcpy(indprogid, progid);
LPTSTR str = indprogid + lstrlen(indprogid);

while (*str != _T('.') && str > indprogid)
   str--;

if (str > indprogid)
   *str = 0;

RegSetValueEx(hsubkey, NULL, 0, REG_SZ, (const BYTE*)indprogid,
                        (lstrlen(indprogid) + 1) * sizeof(TCHAR));
delete [] indprogid;
RegCloseKey(hsubkey);

RegCloseKey(hclsid);

HKEY hprogid;

// Set the ProgID
RegCreateKey(HKEY_CLASSES_ROOT, progid, &hprogid);
RegSetValueEx(hprogid, NULL, 0, REG_SZ, (const BYTE*)classname,
                        (lstrlen(classname) + 1) * sizeof(TCHAR));
RegCreateKey(hprogid, _T("CLSID"), &hclsid);
RegSetValueEx(hclsid, NULL, 0, REG_SZ, (const BYTE*)strCLSID,
                        (lstrlen(strCLSID) + 1) * sizeof(TCHAR));
RegCloseKey(hclsid);
RegCloseKey(hprogid);

HKEY happid;

// Set the AppID
lstrcpy(strkey, _T("AppID\\"));
lstrcat(strkey, strCLSID);
RegCreateKey(HKEY_CLASSES_ROOT, strkey, &happid);
RegSetValueEx(happid, NULL, 0, REG_SZ, (const BYTE*)classname,
                        (lstrlen(classname) + 1) * sizeof(TCHAR));
RegCloseKey(happid);
```

```
    LPTSTR exename = szModule + lstrlen(szModule);

    while (*exename != _T('\\') && exename > szModule)
        exename--;

    if (exename > szModule)
        exename++;

    lstrcpy(strkey, _T("AppID\\"));
    lstrcat(strkey, exename);
    RegCreateKey(HKEY_CLASSES_ROOT, strkey, &happid);
    RegSetValueEx(happid, _T("AppID"), 0, REG_SZ, (const BYTE*)strCLSID,
                                (lstrlen(strCLSID) + 1) * sizeof(TCHAR));
    RegCloseKey(happid);

    // Now register the type library
    HRESULT hr;

    // Find extension so we can add tlb
    LPTSTR lpszExt = NULL;
    LPTSTR lpsz;

    for (lpsz = szModule; *lpsz != NULL; lpsz++)
    {
        if (*lpsz == _T('.'))
            lpszExt = lpsz;
    }

    // Cannot find '.'
    if (lpszExt == NULL)
        lpszExt = lpsz;

    lstrcpy(lpszExt, _T(".tlb"));

    OLECHAR oleModule[MAX_PATH];

    int size = lstrlen(szModule) + 1;

#ifdef UNICODE
    lstrcpy(oleModule,szModule);
#else
    MultiByteToWideChar(CP_ACP, 0, szModule, -1, oleModule, size);
#endif

    // Load the tlb
    ITypeLib* pTypeLib;
    hr = LoadTypeLib(oleModule, &pTypeLib);

    if (SUCCEEDED(hr))
    {
        // And register it
        hr = RegisterTypeLib(pTypeLib, oleModule, NULL);
    }
    else
    {
        _tprintf(_T("Cannot find %s, copy it to the appropriate directory [0x%08X]\n"),
                szModule, hr);
    }
```

```
    if (pTypeLib != NULL)
        pTypeLib->Release();

    return hr;
}
```

This is all there is to the server. You can compile it and then run it with the **-RegServer** switch, so that it registers. At this point, run **DCOMCnfg** to check if the server is in the list of applications.

The next task is to create the proxy-stub DLL. The easiest way to do this is to copy the proxy stub makefile and **.def** file generated by an ATL project into the current project directory, then open up the files and edit them so that they point to the files in the current project. In this case, the makefile, **ReverseDCOMps.mk** should look like this:

```
ReverseDCOMps.dll: dlldata.obj ReverseDCOM_p.obj ReverseDCOM_i.obj
    link /dll /out:ReverseDCOMps.dll /def:ReverseDCOMps.def /entry:DllMain dlldata.obj
ReverseDCOM_p.obj ReverseDCOM_i.obj kernel32.lib rpcndr.lib rpcns4.lib rpcrt4.lib
oleaut32.lib uuid.lib
```

```
.c.obj:
   cl /c /Ox /DWIN32 /D_WIN32_WINNT=0x0400 /DREGISTER_PROXY_DLL $<

clean:
   @del ReverseDCOMps.dll
   @del ReverseDCOMps.lib
   @del ReverseDCOMps.exp
   @del dlldata.obj
   @del ReverseDCOM_p.obj
   @del ReverseDCOM_i.obj
```

Once you've got the makefile, you can just compile it from the command line with **nmake**.

The Client

Finally you need to create a client. We will keeps things really simple, so the client will be a console application that can take up to two command line parameters: the string to reverse and the name of the machine on which the server should run.

Use Developer Studio to create a console application and add a new file to the project:

```
#include <stdio.h>
#include <windows.h>
#include <tchar.h>
#include <initguid.h>
#include "..\ReverseDCOM\ReverseDCOM.h"

int __cdecl _tmain(int argc, _TCHAR **argv, _TCHAR **envp)
{
   if (argc < 2)
   {
      _tprintf(_T("You must give a string to work on\n"));
      return 0;
   }

   if (FAILED(CoInitialize(NULL)))
   {
      _tprintf(_T("Cannot initialize COM\n"));
      return 0;
   }

   COSERVERINFO serverinfo;
   COSERVERINFO* pServerInfo;
   serverinfo.dwReserved1 = 0;
   serverinfo.dwReserved2 = 0;
   serverinfo.pAuthInfo = NULL;

   if (argc == 3)
   {
#if defined(UNICODE)
      serverinfo.pszName = argv[2];
#else
      int size = lstrlen(argv[2]) + 1;
      serverinfo.pwszName = new WCHAR[size];
      MultiByteToWideChar(CP_ACP, 0, argv[2], -1, serverinfo.pwszName,
                          size);
```

```
#endif
      pServerInfo = &serverinfo;
   }
   else
   {
      pServerInfo = NULL;
   }

   MULTI_QI qi = {&IID_IReverse, NULL, 0};

   HRESULT hRes;

   hRes = CoCreateInstanceEx(CLSID_Reverse, NULL, CLSCTX_SERVER,
                             pServerInfo, 1, &qi);

#if !defined(UNICODE)
   if (pServerInfo)
      delete [] serverinfo.pwszName;
#endif

   if (FAILED(qi.hr))
   {
      printf("Cannot get IReverse interface: 0x%08x\n", qi.hr);
      return 0;
   }

   IReverse* pRev = (IReverse*)qi.pItf;

   LPSTR reversed;

#if !defined(UNICODE)
   hRes = pRev->Reverse((unsigned char*)argv[1],
                        (unsigned char**)&reversed);
   printf("%s reversed is %s\n", argv[1], reversed);
#else
   int count = lstrlen(argv[1] + 1);
   LPSTR strTemp = new char[count];
   WideCharToMultiByte(CP_ACP, 0, argv[1], -1, strTemp, count, NULL, NULL);
   hRes = pRev->Reverse((unsigned char*)strTemp,
                        (unsigned char**)&reversed);
   // I'm cheating here, assuming the return string is the same length
   MultiByteToWideChar(CP_ACP, 0, reversed, -1, strTemp, count);
   _tprintf(_T("%s reversed is %s\n"), argv[1], strTemp);
   delete [] strTemp;
#endif
   Sleep(10000);   // artificial delay, can be removed
   pRev->Release();

   CoTaskMemFree(reversed);

   CoUninitialize();
   return 0;
}
```

The **ReverseDCOM.h**, referred to in the header names, is in the server directory, so you'll need to make sure that the relative path is right for your system.

The first thing to notice about this code is how simple it is. The code initializes COM, creates the structure to identify the server, creates a server instance, calls the function, cleans up, and then uninitializes COM. Without the code for the **COSERVERINFO** structure, this would be even simpler.

Before you compile the project, you'll also need to give your project access to the GUID constants for the IID and CLSID. You can get these by adding **ReverseDCOM_i.c** to the project. As usual, make sure that **_WIN32_DCOM** is defined before you compile the project.

Hidden Windows

Before you can test the client, you need to register the proxy-stub objects for the interface, so run **regsvr32** against **ReverseDCOMps.dll**. Once the interface is registered, you can run the client from the command line on the same machine as the server, giving the string to reverse as the only parameter:

```
D:\WROX\DCOM\CODE\CHAPTER6\REVERSE\DCOM\DCOMClient\DEBUG>dcomclient Test
Test reversed is tseT

D:\WROX\DCOM\CODE\CHAPTER6\REVERSE\DCOM\DCOMClient\DEBUG>
```

Before testing the DCOM aspects, let's just return to the issue we raised earlier – the message loop in the server. You may have noticed the call to **Sleep(10000)** in the client code. This is to add a delay in the client. The code will work just fine without it, but if it's not there, the server will disappear before you've had a chance to look at the windows that are created.

Now run **EnumClient2** from Chapter 2, you'll get something like this:

This reports 25 windows, including the ones for **EnumClient2** and a command window to run the COM client. From this command window, run **DCOMClient** and when it pauses in the **Sleep()** statement, switch to **EnumClient2** and refresh the display:

Two windows have been added. You'll be able to see the first one – it has the output statements from the COM server – but the other window is hidden. It is called OleMainThreadWndName and is used as a means of queuing the DCOM requests sent to the server.

Remote Testing

Now try the client on a remote machine. Copy the client and proxy-stub DLL to another machine, register the proxy-stub, and run the client. This time you will need to give the string *and* the server name. If you omit the server name, you will get an error of **0x80040154**, **REGDB_E_CLASSNOTREG**, because the class hasn't been registered on that machine.

```
C:\Test Files>dcomclient Test
cannot get IReverse interface: 80040154

C:\Test Files>dcomclient Test zeus
Test reversed is tseT

C:\Test Files>_
```

You now have a simple client and server that we can experiment with.

Experiments on the DCOM Application

These first experiments will concentrate on the information produced from the **output()** messages in the DCOM server. The same server and client will be used later when we will investigate the network packets created by DCOM.

Tests on the Local Machine

Running the client on the same machine as the server will give output like the following. This output will appear in the file **DCOMReverse.log**, which will appear in the same directory as the server executable, if you started the server with the **-Embedding** flag, or in the **System32** directory, if COM started it:

```
class factory: reference count initialised
CF: AddRef 1
CF: AddRef 2
CF: Release 1
004802ae 0000054a 00142178 0000babe 00000091
    ...
CF: QI {00000001-0000-0000-C000-000000000046}
CF: AddRef 2
CF: CI {00000000-0000-0000-C000-000000000046}
CF: create object
Obj: AddRef 1
Obj: AddRef 2
Obj: QI {00000003-0000-0000-C000-000000000046}
Obj: no interface
Obj: QI {0000001B-0000-0000-C000-000000000046}
Obj: no interface
Obj: QI {00000000-0000-0000-C000-000000000046}
Obj: AddRef 3
Obj: AddRef 4
Obj: QI {00000018-0000-0000-C000-000000000046}
Obj: no interface
```

```
Obj: QI {00000019-0000-0000-C000-000000000046}
Obj: no interface
Obj: Release 3
Obj: QI {31B5ACC3-552F-11D0-9A90-0060973044A8}
Obj: AddRef 4
Obj: QI {31B5ACC3-552F-11D0-9A90-0060973044A8}
Obj: AddRef 5
Obj: Release 4
Obj: Release 3
CF: Release 1
004802ae 0000054a 001422d0 0000babe 00000091
    . . .
TestString reversed is gnirtStseT
004802ae 0000054a 00142580 0000babe 00000091
    . . .
Obj: Release 2
Obj: Release 1
Obj: Release 0
Obj: Release closing server
CF: QI {00000003-0000-0000-C000-000000000046}
CF: no interface
CF: QI {0000001B-0000-0000-C000-000000000046}
CF: no interface
CF: QI {00000000-0000-0000-C000-000000000046}
CF: AddRef 2
CF: Release 1
CF: Release 0
CF: Release, destroy class factory
```

It is, perhaps, a little unfair on Microsoft to analyze data like this, since Microsoft have made no pronouncements about how the Windows message queue is used. However, it is interesting to look at the messages sent and the interfaces that are requested.

When the server is started, the class factory is created and initialized. One of the **AddRef()**s and the **Release()** are called in the **Initialize()** function, the other **AddRef()** comes from the registration of the class factory. The server then goes into a message loop waiting for requests. This is where the following line comes from:

004802ae 0000054a 00142178 0000babe 00000091

The first number is a handle for the destination window and the second is the message. This is then followed by the parameters of the message and then the thread ID that the server is running in. It is important to point out here that the server is written to the single threaded apartment model, and as you will understand after reading Chapter 9, it needs to be to see any of these Windows messages. This example shows the request with a message number of **0x0000054a** (which is **WM_USER + 0x14a**). It appears that all the COM messages have this message ID, similarly the **wParam** of the COM messages always seems to be **0x0000babe** – the intention seems to be to sweet-talk the server into action!

It is the **lParam** that is important. This appears to be a pointer to a structure in memory. If we look at the dump of this structure, we can guess a few things about it:

```
004802ae 0000054a 00142178 0000babe 00000091
00142178 84 00 9C 00 01 00 00 00 ........
00142180 49 00 00 00 9C 00 00 00 I.......
00142188 27 56 00 00 00 00 00 00 'V......
00142190 01 41 00 01 04 00 00 00 .A......
00142198 01 00 00 00 A0 00 00 00 ........
001421a0 91 00 00 00 01 00 00 00 ........
001421a8 05 00 01 00 01 00 00 00 ........
001421b0 00 00 00 00 B1 75 4A 30 .....uJ0
001421b8 85 56 D0 11 9A 92 00 60 .V.....`
001421c0 97 30 44 A8 00 00 00 00 .0D.....
001421c8 01 00 00 00 7F 00 00 00 ........
001421d0 C7 AC B5 31 2F 55 D0 11 ...1/U..
001421d8 9A 90 00 60 97 30 44 A8 ...`.0D.
001421e0 01 00 00 00 01 00 00 00 ........
001421e8 C3 AC B5 31 2F 55 D0 11 ...1/U..
001421f0 9A 90 00 60 97 30 44 A8 ...`.0D.
001421f8 91 00 00 00 02 00 00 00 ........
00142200 27 00 23 00 08 00 31 00 '.#...1.
00142208 37 00 32 00 2E 00 31 00 7.2...1.
00142210 30 00 2E 00             0...
```

Thread ID	
Interface ID	
CLSID_CReverse	
IID_IReverse	

We can conjecture that the second **WORD** is the structure length and the **0x00000091** at address **0x001421a0** is the thread ID.

Remember that the client has done a **CoCreateInstance()** on the **IID_IReverse** interface on the **CLSID_Reverse** object. These UUIDs appear near the bottom of the packet. In addition to these two UUIDs, there is a third: **{304a75b1-5685-11d0-9a920060973044a8}**. This is the UUID of an interface used to pass the data of the interface that is marshaled.

What's happening here is that the client has created a stream for the data that will be marshaled between the two processes. When the server has identified the object, it will find the stub that will be used in the marshaling. The identifier of this stub is inserted into the stream, followed by data that allows the proxy to connect to the stub. In the case of standard marshaling, this is **CLSID_StdMarshal**. When the client gets the reply, it can extract this information to load the proxy corresponding to the stub.

After the Windows message, the object is created and COM queries for various interfaces:

{00000001-0000-0000-C000-000000000046}	**IClassFactory**
{00000000-0000-0000-C000-000000000046}	**IUnknown**
{00000003-0000-0000-C000-000000000046}	**IMarshal**
{0000001B-0000-0000-C000-000000000046}	**IStdIdentity**
{00000000-0000-0000-C000-000000000046}	**IUnknown**
{00000018-0000-0000-C000-000000000046}	**IStdMarshalInfo**
{00000019-0000-0000-C000-000000000046}	**IExternalConnection**

It needs to find out if the object implements custom marshaling or whether a handler is to be used, and hence queries for **IMarshal**.

IExternalConnection

IExternalConnection is a little known COM interface. The COM documentation specifies that it is used by objects that are embedded in a compound document and allows the object to keep a track of external connections to it. It suggests that the methods in the interface are called whenever a connection is made or broken on the object. This allows the object to make sure that any changed data is saved before the object is finally released.

However, **IExternalConnection** is not just for embedded objects. Ultimately, it is the major method of handling object lifetimes. The stub manager always **QI()**s for this when the object is first created. If you don't implement this interface then the object gets the default behavior – that is, when the last proxy dies, the Stub Manager will kill itself and then release the object. If you implement this interface then you will be notified through the interface methods when the first marshal occurs and when the last proxy has died.

This interface is used to solve the problem of multiple clients creating an object in a server. Imagine this case: two clients create an object of the same class with a call to **CoGetClassObject()**. The first object, through the invocation serialization that occurs for apartment model servers, or by virtue of thread scheduling if the server is free-threaded (see Chapter 9), creates the object and then immediately releases it before the second client can call on the object. Now, the object count falls to zero, so the server will unload itself and the second client will have a pointer to a proxy that is invalid!

Instead, the server can use **IExternalConnection** to lock the server (maybe through the same mechanism as **IClassFactory::LockServer()**) so that when the first client has finished, the server is not shut down. The second client now has a pointer to a valid proxy and so can use the object. When this client has finished with the object and releases it, the proxy is released, and the stub manager informs the object server with a method call on **IExternalConnection**. The server can now unlock itself and die.

As I said, this interface was little used in previous versions of Windows, so in NT 4.0, Microsoft decided to make an implicit call on **IClassFactory::LockServer(TRUE)** when the first interface is marshaled and a call to **IClassFactory::LockServer(FALSE)** when the final proxy has died. This makes **IExternalConnection** a little redundant, but you may still decide to implement this interface if you want to do some once-only server initialization.

IStdIdentity

The **IStdIdentity** interface is not documented in the Win32 SDK and it does not have an entry in the registry, however, it does have an important role. It is used to determine if two objects are the same. One of the rules of COM is that when you **QI()** on an object for **IUnknown**, the address that you obtain should be the same for successive **QI()**'s on the same object. If the object is implemented as a local or remote server then the address will, of course, originate from the proxy.

However, if the object uses custom marshaling, the process gets complicated since interface pointers can be passed around between objects on different machines. If your client obtains interface pointers from more than one object, how can it tell if the interface pointers are ultimately from the same object or not?

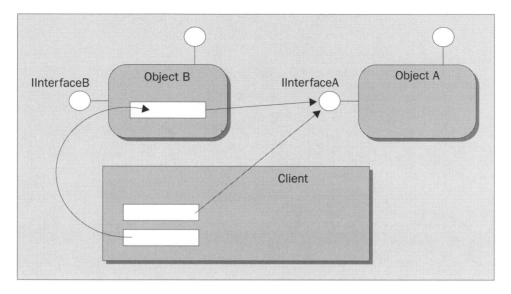

In the picture above, the client obtains an interface pointer on Object A directly, and indirectly via the **IInterfaceB** interface on Object B. How can the client tell if the interface pointers are on the same or different objects? In standard marshaling, this is done by the proxy. In custom marshaling, the programmer has to make sure that the identity is preserved. This is the reason for the **IStdIdentity** interface – it has methods that allow pointers to object interfaces to be marshaled to the objects themselves rather than to the proxy.

Now back to our results. Eventually COM asks for the **IReverse** interface and calls **Reverse()**, which is done in response to another windows message:

```
004802ae 0000054a 001422d0 0000babe 00000091
001422d0 64 00 7C 00 03 00 00 00 d.|.....
001422d8 97 00 00 00 7F 00 00 00 ........
001422e0 58 56 00 00 00 00 00 00 XV......
001422e8 01 01 00 01 03 00 00 00 ........
001422f0 02 00 00 00 A0 00 00 00 ........
001422f8 91 00 00 00 02 00 00 00 ........
00142300 05 00 01 00 01 00 00 00 ........
00142308 00 00 00 00 B1 75 4A 30 .....uJ0
00142310 85 56 D0 11 9A 92 00 60 .V.....`
00142318 97 30 44 A8 00 00 00 00 .0D.....
00142320 00 00 00 00 7F 00 00 00 ........
00142328 0B 00 00 00 00 00 00 00 ........
00142330 0B 00 00 00 54 65 73 74 ....Test
00142338 53 74 72 69 6E 67 00 00 String..
00142340 00 00 00 00 00 00 00 00 ........
00142348 00 00 00 00             ....
```

Thread ID

IStream interface

This makes the call to **Reverse()**, passing the parameter **TestString**. Again we have the marshaling packet UUID. The parameter is passed near the end of the packet, preceded by the length of the string (**0x0B**).

The data is returned and we finally get a **Release()** from the client. This results in a packet sent to the server:

```
004802ae 0000054a 00142580 0000babe 00000091
00142580 64 00 7C 00 03 00 00 00  d.|.....
00142588 97 00 00 00 7F 00 00 00  ........
00142590 62 56 00 00 00 00 00 00  bV......
00142598 01 01 00 01 05 00 00 00  ........
001425a0 00 00 00 00 A0 00 00 00  ........
001425a8 91 00 00 00 00 00 00 00  ........
001425b0 05 00 01 00 01 00 00 00  ........
001425b8 00 00 00 00 B1 75 4A 30  .....uJ0
001425c0 85 56 D0 11 9A 92 00 60  .V.....`
001425c8 97 30 44 A8 00 00 00 00  .0D.....
001425d0 00 00 00 00 7F 00 00 00  ........
001425d8 01 00 00 00 01 00 00 00  ........
001425e0 02 00 00 00 A0 00 00 00  ........
001425e8 91 00 00 00 02 00 00 00  ........
001425f0 05 00 00 00 00 00 00 00  ........
001425f8 00 00 00 00             ....
```

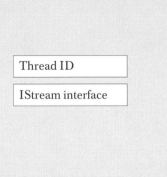

Thread ID

IStream interface

COM then **QI()**s for some other interfaces before releasing the object and the class factory:

```
{00000003-0000-0000-C000-000000000046}    IMarshal
{0000001B-0000-0000-C000-000000000046}    IIdentityUnmarshal
{00000000-0000-0000-C000-000000000046}    IUnknown
```

You can see from these experiments that, even on a local machine, there is a lot going on to create an object and then make a single method call.

Tests with a Remote Machine - Apartment Model

Now let's try the same thing but with a remote client. Run the client with the string to reverse *and* the name of the server machine:

DCOMClient TestString zeus

Here are the results I get:

```
class factory: reference count initialised
CF: AddRef 1
CF: AddRef 2
CF: Release 1
003702c6 0000054a 00142170 0000babe 00000092
    . . .
CF: QI {00000001-0000-0000-C000-000000000046}
CF: AddRef 2
CF: CI {00000000-0000-0000-C000-000000000046}
CF: create object
Obj: AddRef 1
Obj: AddRef 2
Obj: QI {00000003-0000-0000-C000-000000000046}
Obj: no interface
Obj: QI {0000001B-0000-0000-C000-000000000046}
Obj: no interface
```

```
Obj: QI {00000000-0000-0000-C000-000000000046}
Obj: AddRef 3
Obj: AddRef 4
Obj: QI {00000018-0000-0000-C000-000000000046}
Obj: no interface
Obj: QI {00000019-0000-0000-C000-000000000046}
Obj: no interface
Obj: Release 3
Obj: QI {31B5ACC3-552F-11D0-9A90-0060973044A8}
Obj: AddRef 4
Obj: QI {31B5ACC3-552F-11D0-9A90-0060973044A8}
Obj: AddRef 5
Obj: Release 4
Obj: Release 3
CF: Release 1
003702c6 00000400 0180fd78 00000040 00000092
     . . .
TestString reversed is gnirtStseT
003702c6 00000400 00cefd78 00000091 00000092
     . . .
Obj: Release 2
Obj: Release 1
Obj: Release 0
Obj: Release closing server
CF: QI {00000003-0000-0000-C000-000000000046}
CF: no interface
CF: QI {0000001B-0000-0000-C000-000000000046}
CF: no interface
CF: QI {00000000-0000-0000-C000-000000000046}
CF: AddRef 2
CF: Release 1
CF: Release 0
CF: Release, destroy class factory
```

This appears to be the same as the local case, except that when COM calls the **Reverse()** method (the second window message), it sends the server a **WM_USER** message rather than **WM_USER + 0x14a**, and it has stopped sweet-talking it (the **wParam** is no longer **0x0000babe**).

In this case, taking the second **WORD** in the structure as the length does not work. However, the value of the **wParam** in the **WM_USER** messages seems to indicate that it is the length of the structure. So for the length of the structure, we can use the second **WORD** of the buffer (if **wParam** is **0xbabe**), or the value of **wParam**. Let's look at the hex dump of the first message sent to the server:

```
003702c6 0000054a 00142170 0000babe 00000092
00142170 84 00 9C 00 01 00 00 00 ........
00142178 49 00 00 00 90 00 00 00 I.......
00142180 12 6D 00 00 00 00 00 00 .m......
00142188 01 41 00 01 04 00 00 00 .A......
00142190 01 00 00 00 A8 00 00 00 ........
00142198 92 00 00 00 01 00 00 00 ........
001421a0 05 00 01 00 01 00 00 00 ........
001421a8 00 00 00 00 A1 D9 31 A9 ......1.
001421b0 89 56 D0 11 BB 2A 00 C0 .V...*..
001421b8 F0 10 84 5F 00 00 00 00 ..._....
001421c0 01 00 00 00 00 00 00 00 ........
001421c8 C7 AC B5 31 2F 55 D0 11 ...1/U..
001421d0 9A 90 00 60 97 30 44 A8 ...`.0D.
```

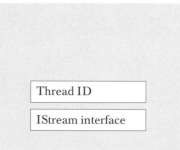

Thread ID

IStream interface

```
001421d8 01 00 00 00 01 00 00 00   ........
001421e0 C3 AC B5 31 2F 55 D0 11   ...1/U..
001421e8 9A 90 00 60 97 30 44 A8   ...`.0D.
001421f0 00 00 00 00 00 00 00 00   ........
001421f8 00 00 00 00 00 00 00 00   ........
00142200 00 00 00 00 00 00 00 00   ........
00142208 00 00 00 00               ....
```

As mentioned before, this is very much like the data received in the local case. The packet contains the CLSID of the object and the IID of the interface that we want as well as the GUID of the marshaling stream.

Later on, the client calls the **Reverse()** method and we get the following dump:

```
003702c6 00000400 0180fd78 00000040 00000092
0180fd78 01 00 00 00 00 00 00 00   ........
0180fd80 00 00 00 00 1E B0 79 96   ......y.
0180fd88 F4 00 00 00 3D D8 A3 0B   ....=...
0180fd90 FC FD 65 80 02 00 00 00   ..e.....
0180fd98 A8 00 00 00 92 00 00 00   ........          Thread ID
0180fda0 02 00 00 00 E0 FE 80 01   ........
0180fda8 BF AC 53 3C 02 00 00 00   ..S<....
0180fdb0 00 00 00 00 00 00 00 00   ........
```

This reveals less information than in the local case. The thread ID is there, but the stream IID is missing and there is no sign of the data. The DCOM packet is obviously not as straightforward as the local COM packet. The structure has a pointer to a nearby area of memory **0x0180fee0**:

```
0180FEE0  C0 43 15 00 10 00 00 00   .C......
0180FEE8  48 48 15 00 48 00 00 00   HH..H...
```

And the third **DWORD** of this gives an address in a totally different area of memory:

```
00154848  05 00 01 00 00 00 00 00   ........
00154850  00 00 00 00 A1 D9 31 A9   ......1.
00154858  89 56 D0 11 BB 2A 00 C0   .V...*..       IStream interface
00154860  F0 10 84 5F 00 00 00 00   ........
00154868  0B 00 00 00 00 00 00 00   ........
00154870  0B 00 00 00 54 65 73 74   ....Test
00154878  53 74 72 69 6E 67 00 00   String..
00154880  00 00 00 00 00 00 00 00   ........
00154888  00 00 00 00 00 00 00 00   ........
00154890  04 00 00 00 01 00 00 00   ........
00154898  60 82 41 F4 A0 EE A3 8B   `,A.....
001548A0  C7 7B 51 71               ..Qq
```

Here, finally, is the parameter of the method and notice also the GUID of the marshaling stream.

I must admit I cheated a little here. I found this memory location by looking at the address of the **str** parameter to **Reverse()** and then searching through the memory pointed to by the Windows message.

If we go back to the original page of data, a little hunting around gives some interesting data:

```
0180F408                 5A 00 45 00        Z.E.
0180F410  55 00 53 00 5C 00 52 00    U.S.\.R.
0180F418  69 00 63 00 68 00 61 00    i.c.h.a.
0180F420  72 00 64 00 47 00 72 00    r.d.G.r.
0180F428  69 00 6D 00 65 00 73 00    i.m.e.s.
0180F430  00 00                      ..
```

This is giving the user that the COM server is logged under, in this case, the name of the interactive user logged on at the time. The reason for this is that the data was taken with **ReverseDCOM** running under the Developer Studio debugger and hence the server was started by the interactive user. Normally the process would be run under the system account or under the account specified under the **RunAs** key. You can find more information on the accounts that a server will run under in the next chapter.

Further on in the memory is:

```
0180F790                 4E 54 4C 4D        NTLM
0180F798  53 53 50 00 03 00 00 00    SSP.....
0180F7A0  18 00 18 00 6A 00 00 00    ....j...
0180F7A8  18 00 18 00 82 00 00 00    ....,...
0180F7B0  08 00 08 00 40 00 00 00    ....@...
0180F7B8  1A 00 1A 00 48 00 00 00    ....H...
0180F7C0  08 00 08 00 62 00 00 00    ....b...
0180F7C8  10 00 10 00 9A 00 00 00    ....š...
0180F7D0  D1 82 10 00 48 00 45 00    Ñ,..H.E.
0180F7D8  52 00 41 00 52 00 69 00    R.A.R.i.
0180F7E0  63 00 68 00 61 00 72 00    c.h.a.r.
0180F7E8  64 00 47 00 72 00 69 00    d.G.r.i.
0180F7F0  6D 00 65 00 73 00 48 00    m.e.s.H.
0180F7F8  45 00 52 00 41 00          E.R.A.
```

This gives the security authority, the machine name of the client, and the user name used in the authentication process that occurs when the server is launched or a server method is accessed (as long as authentication is actually being used).

Finally, if we now look at the page where the method data is held, we find:

```
00154770                 6E 00 63 00        n.c.
00154778  61 00 64 00 67 00 5F 00    a.d.g._.
00154780  69 00 70 00 5F 00 75 00    i.p._.u.
00154788  64 00 70 00 3A 00 31 00    d.p.:.1.
00154790  37 00 32 00 2E 00 31 00    7.2...1.
00154798  30 00 2E 00 31 00 36 00    0...1.6.
001547A0  2E 00 31 00 30 00 5B 00    ..1.0.[.
001547A8  31 00 30 00 38 00 31 00    1.0.8.1.
001547B0  5D 00 00 00                ]...
```

In other words, we find the following string

ncadg_ip_udp:172.10.16.10[1081]

What does this mean? Well, as you will see in the next section, this is the bind string that is used by the client to attach to the server via RPC. The first part is the protocol. **ncadg_ip_udp** says that DCOM is using a datagram protocol and specifically UDP/IP. The next part is the IP address of the server (this is the address of **zeus**) and finally, the last part is a UDP port number. This is proof that DCOM runs over Microsoft RPC.

Now back to the test data again. Once the object method has been called and a value returned, the client makes a call on `Release()` and this results in the following message:

```
003702c6 00000400 00cefd78 00000091 00000092
00cefd78 01 00 00 00 00 00 00 00   ........
00cefd80 00 00 00 00 1E B0 79 96   ......y.
00cefd88 F4 00 00 00 3D D8 A3 0B   ....=...
00cefd90 FC FD 65 80 00 00 00 00   ..e.....
00cefd98 A8 00 00 00 92 00 00 00   ........       Thread ID
00cefda0 00 00 00 00 E0 FE CE 00   ........
00cefda8 BF AC 53 3C 02 00 00 00   ..S<....
00cefdb0 00 00 00 00 00 00 00 00   ........
00cefdb8 00 00 00 00 00 00 00 00   ........
00cefdc0 04 00 00 00 00 00 00 00   ........
00cefdc8 A8 00 00 00 92 00 00 00   ........
00cefdd0 00 00 00 00 04 00 00 00   ........
00cefdd8 02 00 00 00 18 FE CE 00   ........
00cefde0 77 13 E2 77 E0 FE CE 00   w..w....
00cefde8 F0 66 14 00 E0 FE CE 00   .f......
00cefdf0 00 00 00 00 C8 6D 14 00   .....m..
00cefdf8 85 E8 B3 77 00 00 00 00   ...w....
00cefe00 E8 FD CE 00 78 FE CE 00   ....x...
00cefe08 DC                        .
```

This is all horrible stuff, but it does indicate one important point: on Windows platforms, DCOM still uses Window messages to pass information to the server process when the server is running under the apartment model.

However, the moral of this hunting around is that although it gives some interesting insights into how DCOM works, it can get very complicated and messy. Of course, we are looking at the specifics of this implementation of DCOM. It may well be different on other platforms and in later releases of NT.

Tests with a Remote Machine - Free Threading Model

Now make one small change to the `Initialize()` function in `ReverseDCOM`. Change the line

```
        hr = CoInitialize(NULL);
```
to
```
        hr = CoInitializeEx(NULL, COINIT_MULTITHREADED);
```

(You will also need to make sure that **_WIN32_DCOM** is defined). This changes the model of the server from apartment (where the COM runtime ensures that calls to the server from multiple clients are synchronized) to free threading. In the free threading model, it is the responsibility of the programmer to make sure that the method implementations are thread safe (which they most certainly are *not* in this example), so the COM runtime makes no effort at synchronization.

Now when the client is run on a remote machine we get:

```
class factory: reference count initialised
CF: AddRef 1
CF: AddRef 2
CF: Release 1
CF: QI {00000001-0000-0000-C000-000000000046}
CF: AddRef 2
```

```
CF: CI {00000000-0000-0000-C000-000000000046}
CF: create object
Obj: AddRef 1
Obj: AddRef 2
Obj: QI {00000003-0000-0000-C000-000000000046}
Obj: no interface
Obj: QI {0000001B-0000-0000-C000-000000000046}
Obj: no interface
Obj: QI {00000000-0000-0000-C000-000000000046}
Obj: AddRef 3
Obj: AddRef 4
Obj: QI {00000018-0000-0000-C000-000000000046}
Obj: no interface
Obj: QI {00000019-0000-0000-C000-000000000046}
Obj: no interface
Obj: Release 3
Obj: QI {31B5ACC3-552F-11D0-9A90-0060973044A8}
Obj: AddRef 4
Obj: QI {31B5ACC3-552F-11D0-9A90-0060973044A8}
Obj: AddRef 5
Obj: Release 4
Obj: Release 3
CF: Release 1
TestString reversed is gnirtStseT
Obj: Release 2
Obj: Release 1
Obj: Release 0
Obj: Release closing server
```

We have essentially the same calls as in the apartment model case, but there are no Windows messages handled. Furthermore, these results do not show the closing down of the class factory or the unloading of the server. This is because they don't happen, and the server remains in memory. To get rid of the server, use the NT Task Manager.

The reason for this is that in free threading, the COM calls are not serialized via a message queue, so no messages are sent. The console application does not create any windows, so there are none to process Windows messages. This server shuts down by posting a **WM_QUIT** message to the server's message queue with a **PostQuitMessage()** which in the apartment model results in the message loop being broken, allowing the class factory to be released and the process to end. Since this message is not being processed, the message loop continues, consequently **Release()** is not called on the class factory and the **main()** function never returns. Chapter 9 will cover the issues of multithreaded servers.

The Microsoft RPC Test Application

We'll create this RPC test server as a Win32 console application, so use the App Wizard to create one called **ReverseRPC**. Now add a new IDL file to the project called **ReverseRPC.idl**.

The IDL for the RPC interface is:

```
[
    uuid(31B5ACC4-552F-11D0-9A90-0060973044A8),
    version(1.0),
    pointer_default(unique)
]
```

```
interface IReverse
{
   unsigned long Reverse([in, string]char* str,
                         [out, string]char** revstr);
};
```

Since this is an RPC interface, we do not specify the **[object]** attribute, but we do need to use the **[version()]** attribute. Otherwise, the interface is very much like the COM interface. However, DCE does not have a concept of a **coclass**, instead the server registers itself with a dynamic registry. Under NT this is usually the Locator, but it can be a DCE CDS (Cell Directory Service). Thus there is no class factory and no statically registered CLSIDs or IIDs.

To make the binding code simpler, create an application configuration file (ACF) called **ReverseRPC.acf** and add the following code to it:

```
[
   implicit_handle(handle_t hIReverse)
]
interface IReverse
{}
```

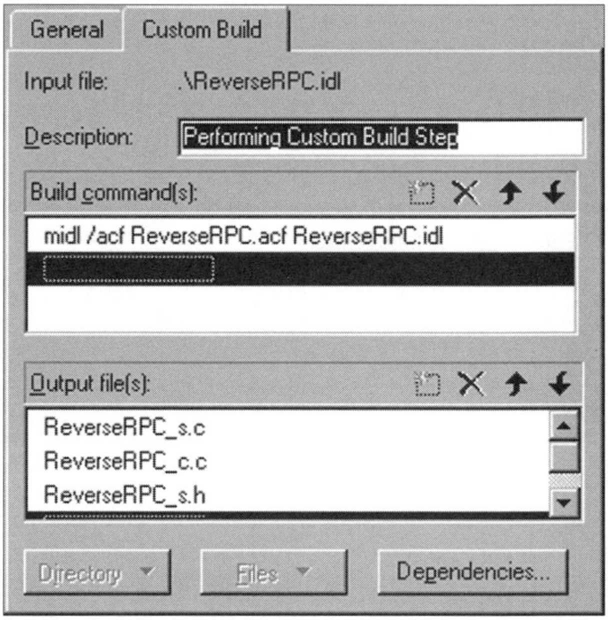

This specifies that the interface **IReverse** uses a handle called **hIReverse** *implicitly* whenever a method call is made, since the method prototypes do not have an *explicit* binding handle. The binding handle is used to maintain the connection between the client and server. If you like, it allows the two to locate each other.

To compile the IDL, you need to specify a custom build setting. To do this, select the **ReverseRPC.idl** in the FileView and choose the Project | Settings... menu. This should open the Project Settings dialog at the Custom Build tab for this file. Add the build command shown here:

General	Custom Build

Input file: .\ReverseRPC.idl

Description: Performing Custom Build Step

Build command(s):

midl /acf ReverseRPC.acf ReverseRPC.idl

Output file(s):

ReverseRPC_s.c
ReverseRPC_c.c
ReverseRPC_s.h

[Directory ▼] [Files ▼] [Dependencies...]

Note that, unlike DCOM, RPC requires the appropriate stub code to be linked into the project, so once you have compiled the **idl**, add the file **ReverseRPC_s.c** to the project.

We now need to implement the RPC function. If you open the header **ReverseRPC.h**, you will find the following prototypes:

```
void __RPC_FAR * __RPC_USER MIDL_user_allocate(size_t);
void __RPC_USER MIDL_user_free( void __RPC_FAR * );
```

```
unsigned long Reverse(
    /* [string][in] */ unsigned char __RPC_FAR *str,
    /* [string][out] */ unsigned char __RPC_FAR *__RPC_FAR
                                                *revstr);

extern handle_t hIReverse;
```

RPC uses **MIDL_user_allocate()** and **MIDL_user_free()** to allocate and free memory that will be used in **[out]** parameters, so you must implement these functions. You can also see here the declarations for the implicit binding handle and the **Reverse()** method.

Create a file, **RevRPC.cpp** for the interface method and add it to the project:

```cpp
#include <stdio.h>
#include "ReverseRPC.h"

unsigned long Reverse(unsigned char *str,
                      unsigned char **revstr)
{
    int count = strlen((char*)str);
    *revstr = (unsigned char*)midl_user_allocate(count + 1);
    printf("%s reversed is ", (char*)str);
    unsigned char* ptr = *revstr + count;

    *(ptr--) = 0;

    while (ptr >= *revstr)
        *(ptr--) = *(str++);

    printf("%s\n",(char*)*revstr);

    return 0;
}
```

This is actually pretty much the same as the implementation of the DCOM **Reverse()** function, since all we need do is reverse the string and return it.

The final file is **main.cpp**, which contains the **main()** function:

```cpp
#include <stdio.h>
#include "ReverseRPC.h"

void _CRTAPI1 main(int argc, char * argv[])
{
    RPC_STATUS status;
    RPC_BINDING_VECTOR* bv;

    status = RpcServerUseProtseq(
                 (unsigned char*)"ncadg_ip_udp",
                 1, NULL);
    if (status)
    {
        printf("RpcServerUseProtseq returned %ld\n", status);
        exit(status);
    }
```

```
      status = RpcServerRegisterIf(IReverse_v1_0_s_ifspec,
                             NULL, NULL);
   if (status)
   {
      printf("RpcServerRegisterIf returned %ld\n", status);
      exit(status);
   }

   status = RpcServerInqBindings(&bv);
   if (status)
   {
      printf("RpcServerInqBindings returned %ld\n",
             status);
      exit(status);
   }

   status = RpcEpRegister(&IReverse_v1_0_s_ifspec,bv,
                       NULL,NULL);
   if (status)
   {
      printf("RpcEpServerRegister returned %ld\n",status);
      exit(status);
   }

   for (unsigned long i=0; i<bv->Count; i++)
   {
      char* bnd;
      RpcBindingToStringBinding(bv->BindingH[i],
                             (unsigned char**)&bnd);
      printf("%s\n",bnd);
   }

   printf("going into listening loop\n");
   status = RpcServerListen(1, 1, 0);
   if (status)
   {
      printf("RpcServerListen returned %ld\n", status);
      exit(status);
   }
}

void __RPC_FAR * __RPC_USER midl_user_allocate(size_t len)
{
   return(malloc(len));
}

void __RPC_USER midl_user_free(void __RPC_FAR * ptr)
{
   free(ptr);
}
```

The exact details of the initialization code need not concern us unduly. Basically the server defines what protocol it will use with a call to **RpcServerUseProtseq()**, then it registers the interface with **RpcServerRegisterIf()**. Next the server needs to set up the binding handles and define the endpoint that identifies this server rather than any other one that implements the same interface. It does this with calls to **RpcServerInqBindings()** and **RpcEpRegister()**.

Since we are not specifying the end point explicitly, we need to get it printed out so that the client can specify it. If this was production code, an end point (UDP port) would be defined specifically for this server, which the client would know about. The call to **RpcBindingToStringBinding()** prints out the binding string that the client should use.

Finally the server goes into a listening loop waiting for requests with a call to **RpcServerListen()**. When a client makes a request, the runtime will call the interface method. The final parameter of zero specifies that the server goes into an infinite loop. If it were non-zero, the function would return after a request.

Before the application can be built, make sure that you are linking to the RPC runtime library: **rpcrt4.lib** (you will want to remove all the other libraries in the link input objects box).

RPC Client

Next you need to create a client. This is even more straightforward than creating the server: create a console application and add the **ReverseRPC_c.c** client stub code from the server directory and create a new **main.cpp** file as shown below:

```cpp
#include <stdio.h>
#include "..\ReverseRPC\ReverseRPC.h"

void main(int argc, char *argv[])
{
   RPC_STATUS status;
   unsigned char* reversed;

   if (argc <= 2)
   {
      printf("You must give the binding string and test "
             "string\n");
      return;
   }

   status = RpcBindingFromStringBinding(
                        (unsigned char*)argv[1],
                        &hIReverse);
   if (status)
   {
      printf("RpcBindingFromStringBinding returned 0x%x\n", status);
       return;
   }

   RpcTryExcept
   {
      Reverse((unsigned char*)argv[2], &reversed);
      printf("%s reversed is %s\n", argv[2], reversed);
   }
   RpcExcept(1)
   {
      unsigned long ulCode;
      ulCode = RpcExceptionCode();
      printf("Runtime reported exception 0x%lx\n", ulCode);
      return;
   }
   RpcEndExcept
}
```

```
void   __RPC_FAR * __RPC_USER midl_user_allocate(size_t len)
{
    return(malloc(len));
}

void __RPC_USER midl_user_free(void __RPC_FAR * ptr)
{
    free(ptr);
}
```

Again, we need to implement **midl_user_allocate()** and **midl_user_free()** for memory allocations. Since we are using implicit handles, the binding process is pretty painless: the binding string from the server is used in **RpcBindingFromStringBinding()** to initialize the implicit handle, and then we can call the interface method.

Now all you need to do is link to **rpcrt4.lib** and compile the project.

Tests on the Local Machine

The first test to make is to run the client and server on the same machine. So from the server directory, run the executable. You should find that the interface registers and a binding string is printed on screen:

```
D:\WROX\DCOM\CODE\CHAPTER6\REVERSE\RPC\ReverseRPC\DEBUG>reverserpc
ncadg_ip_udp:172.10.16.10[1044]
going into listening loop
```

Notice the binding string?

ncadg_ip_udp:172.10.16.10[1044]

All of this (except the port number) is the same as the binding string that DCOM squirreled away that we saw earlier. Now write this down, or copy it to the clipboard and start another command prompt. Start the client using the binding string and the parameter of the method:

```
D:\WROX\DCOM\CODE\CHAPTER6\REVERSE\RPC\RPCClient\DEBUG>rpcclient ncadg_ip_udp:17
2.10.16.10[1044] TestString
TestString reversed is gnirtStseT

D:\WROX\DCOM\CODE\CHAPTER6\REVERSE\RPC\RPCClient\DEBUG>_
```

The server is indeed called, as can be seen from the server console:

```
D:\WROX\DCOM\CODE\CHAPTER6\REVERSE\RPC\ReverseRPC\DEBUG>reverserpc
ncadg_ip_udp:172.10.16.10[1044]
going into listening loop
TestString reversed is gnirtStseT
```

One final test to try with the local case is to run **EnumClient2** before and then after the server is started; this shows that no extra windows are created.

Note that unlike DCOM, the server must be running before a client can make a call, and, unless the server interface has a method specifically implemented to kill the process, it will remain running when the client finishes. If the client is run when there is no server, an error of **RPC_S_SERVER_UNAVAILABLE** will be generated.

Typically, an RPC server will be implemented on NT as a service, so that the server is started automatically when the machine boots. It will usually run under a system account so that it does not require an interactive user to log on. This means that if the machine is rebooted for some reason (there's a hardware fault or a power failure), the server will become available without any user interaction. (See Chapter 8 for more information on DCOM NT Services).

If the server cannot be implemented as a service then it can be started automatically by placing the server in the NT Startup folder. However, this will mean that a user will need to log on.

Tests with a Remote Machine

Now we have ascertained that the RPC server and client work in the local case, we need to check that they work when the client and server are on separate machines. To do this, copy the client to another machine and then run the server as before. Copy the binding string (the port number is likely to be different to the previous test) and then run the client as before, using the binding string and the string to reverse.

We finally have all the software we need to test the network usage of DCOM.

Network Tests

Network Monitor

The NetMon utility is supplied by Microsoft as part of the Developer Network Professional Edition (in the DDK) and also as a utility with NT Server and SMS. NetMon captures the data that flows on the network and performs some analysis on the data. Using this tool, you can view statistics about which computers are making the most use of the network, the protocols that they are using, and the actual data packets that are sent. NetMon can capture all data on the network or you can design filters to reduce the data captured.

In this chapter, NetMon will be used to analyze the packets sent between DCOM clients and servers and between RPC clients and servers. The sample applications and the capture files will be supplied in text form on the Wrox Press web site so that you can view the data yourself even if you do not have access to NetMon.

In the results that follow, the server machine is **zeus**, and is identified by name. The client machine is **hera** and is identified by her network card identifier, **KINGST10845F**.

RPC

The first test is the DCE RPC sample. When this is run over the network, we get the results given in **dce.txt**.

The first packet is from **hera** to **zeus**:

```
00000:   00 60 97 30 44 A8 00 C0 F0 10 84 5F 08 00 45 00    .`.0D......_..E.
00010:   00 83 59 00 00 00 80 11 69 40 AC 0A 10 0B AC 0A    ..Y.....i@......
00020:   10 0A 04 07 04 08 00 6F 03 B1 04 00 08 00 10 00    .......o........
00030:   00 00 00 00 00 00 00 00 00 00 00 00 00 00 00 00    ................
00040:   00 00 C4 AC B5 31 2F 55 D0 11 9A 90 00 60 97 30    .....1/U.....`.0
00050:   44 A8 E0 A6 0E 8A 55 58 D0 11 BB 2C 00 C0 F0 10    D.....UX...,....
00060:   84 5F 00 00 00 00 01 00 00 00 00 00 00 00 00 00    ._.............
00070:   FF FF FF FF 17 00 00 00 00 00 0B 00 00 00 00 00    ................
00080:   00 00 0B 00 00 00 54 65 73 74 53 74 72 69 6E 67    ......TestString
00090:   00                                                 .
```

This is the entire frame sent over the network, so the first part is the protocol header. This consists of the network addresses of the client and server (**0060973044A8** is **hera** and **00C0F010845F** is **zeus**), the protocol type, and other data used by the protocol.

The RPC packet starts at **0x2a**. This is the DCE structure **rpc_dg_pkt_hdr_t**, and is followed by the RPC data. The structure is:

```
typedef struct
{
    u_char _rpc_vers;
    u_char _ptype;
    u_char flags;
    u_char flags2;
    u_char drep[3];
    u_char serial_hi;
    uuid_t object;
    uuid_t if_id;
    uuid_t actuid;
    unsigned32 server_boot;
    unsigned32 if_vers;
    unsigned32 seq;
    unsigned16 opnum;
    unsigned16 ihint;
    unsigned16 ahint;
    unsigned16 len;
    unsigned16 fragnum;
    u_char auth_proto;
    u_char serial_lo;
} rpc_dg_pkt_hdr_t, *rpc_dg_pkt_hdr_p_t;
```

Of the data in this structure, the interesting parts are boxed. The packet type is given as 0, which is a request. The interface UUID is at bytes **0x42** - **0x51**, the interface version is at **0x66**, and the size of the RPC data is at **0x74**. This is then followed by the data itself.

zeus acknowledges this with:

```
00000:   00 C0 F0 10 84 5F 00 60 97 30 44 A8 08 00 45 00    ....._.`.0D...E.
00010:   00 80 CA 01 00 00 80 11 F8 41 AC 0A 10 0A AC 0A    .........A......
00020:   10 0B 04 09 04 07 00 6C FE E0 04 00 28 00 10 00    .......1....(...
00030:   00 00 00 00 00 00 00 00 00 00 00 00 00 00 00 00    ................
00040:   00 00 76 22 3A 33 00 00 00 00 0D 00 00 80 9C 00    ..v":3..........
00050:   00 00 D0 CB D8 84 55 58 D0 11 9A 97 00 60 97 30    ......UX.....`.0
00060:   44 A8 00 00 00 00 03 00 00 00 00 00 00 00 01 00    D...............
```

```
00070:  FF FF FF FF 14 00 00 00 00 00 E0 A6 0E 8A 55 58    .............UX
00080:  D0 11 BB 2C 00 C0 F0 10 84 5F 93 6E B4 32          ...,....._.n.2
```

The RPC interface ID is **{333a2276-00-00-000d-00809c000000}**. This is the Conversion Manager Interface, **conv**, which is implemented by the RPC runtime on the client machine. This type of callback is known as the 'Who Are You' callback (WAY). This is followed by a UUID **{84d8cbd0-5855-11d0-979a-0060973044a8}**.

Then **hera** sends another packet:

```
00000:  00 60 97 30 44 A8 00 C0 F0 10 84 5F 08 00 45 00    .`.0D......_..E.
00010:  00 84 5A 00 00 00 80 11 68 3F AC 0A 10 0B AC 0A    ..Z.....h?......
00020:  10 0A 04 07 04 09 00 70 61 78 04 02 08 00 10 00    .......pax......
00030:  00 00 00 00 00 00 00 00 00 00 00 00 00 00 00 00    ................
00040:  00 00 76 22 3A 33 00 00 00 00 0D 00 00 80 9C 00    ..v":3..........
00050:  00 00 D0 CB D8 84 55 58 D0 11 9A 97 00 60 97 30    ......UX.....`.0
00060:  44 A8 00 00 00 00 03 00 00 00 00 00 00 00 01 00    D...............
00070:  FF FF FF FF 18 00 00 00 00 00 00 00 00 00 E1 A6    ................
00080:  0E 8A 55 58 D0 11 BB 2C 00 C0 F0 10 84 5F 00 00    ..UX...,....._..
00090:  00 00                                              ..
```

Finally **zeus** returns the reply:

```
00000:  00 C0 F0 10 84 5F 00 60 97 30 44 A8 08 00 45 00    ....._.`.0D...E.
00010:  00 8C CB 01 00 00 80 11 F7 35 AC 0A 10 0A AC 0A    .........5......
00020:  10 0B 04 08 04 07 00 78 2E 12 04 02 08 00 10 00    .......x........
00030:  00 00 00 00 00 00 00 00 00 00 00 00 00 00 00 00    ................
00040:  00 00 C4 AC B5 31 2F 55 D0 11 9A 90 00 60 97 30    .....1/U.....`.0
00050:  44 A8 E0 A6 0E 8A 55 58 D0 11 BB 2C 00 C0 F0 10    D.....UX...,....
00060:  84 5F 93 6E B4 32 01 00 00 00 00 00 00 00 00 00    ._.n.2..........
00070:  FF FF 24 00 20 00 00 00 00 00 C0 0B 7E 00 0B 00    ..$. .......~...
00080:  00 00 00 00 00 00 0B 00 00 00 67 6E 69 72 74 53    ..........gnirtS
00090:  74 73 65 54 00 00 00 00 00 00                      tseT......
```

The **_ptype** of this is **0x02**, indicating a response. Now let's compare this to the DCOM network traffic.

DCOM

Again, the client is run on **hera** and the server is run on **zeus**. This time the DCOM client is used. This is an end-to-end test, the results are given in **dcom.txt**, and selected parts are give here. Note that the test is carried out when **ReverseDCOM.exe** is not already running on the server, and the client machine has just been booted. The reason for this caution is that binding information, used for the client to be able to find the interface on the server object, is cached in memory. By running the tests when the machine has just been booted and the server has not been started, we ensure that the whole communication between the client and server is captured.

Start of the Conversation

The client is started with the command line:

DCOMClient TestString zeus

The machine name has to be given so that COM can be told to attach to a particular machine. However, unlike the RPC example, no other binding information is required in this case. In the RPC case, the

287

binding string contained the network protocol, a server identifier and an endpoint identifier. We don't need to supply the protocol and endpoint identifier because the protocol is chosen by the local machine from the registered protocols, and the endpoint is determined by the server and is transferred back to the local machine. You'll see how this is done as we examine the packets sent between the machines.

The first thing is for the client to find the server, so the first two packets are a broadcast from the client, **hera**, and then a reply from the server, **zeus**.

```
From hera: BROADCAST
00000:  FF FF FF FF FF FF 00 C0 F0 10 84 5F 08 00 45 00    ............_..E.
00010:  00 4E 6D 00 00 00 80 11 65 7F AC 0A 10 0B AC 0A    .Nm.....e•......
00020:  FF FF 00 89 00 89 00 3A C9 B6 80 22 01 10 00 01    .......:..."....
00030:  00 00 00 00 00 00 20 46 4B 45 46 46 46 46 44 43    ...... FKEFFFFDC
00040:  41 43 41 43 41 43 41 43 41 43 41 43 41 43 41 43    ACACACACACACACAC
00050:  41 43 41 43 41 41 41 00 00 20 00 01                ACACAAA.. ..

Reply from zeus
00000:  00 C0 F0 10 84 5F 00 60 97 30 44 A8 08 00 45 00    ....._.`.0D...E.
00010:  00 5A 69 01 00 00 80 11 59 68 AC 0A 10 0A AC 0A    .Zi.....Yh......
00020:  10 0B 00 89 00 89 00 46 E5 A4 80 22 85 00 00 00    .......F..."....
00030:  00 01 00 00 00 00 20 46 4B 45 46 46 46 46 44 43    ...... FKEFFFFDC
00040:  41 43 41 43 41 43 41 43 41 43 41 43 41 43 41 43    ACACACACACACACAC
00050:  41 43 41 43 41 41 41 00 00 20 00 01 00 04 93 E0    ACACAAA.. ......
00060:  00 06 00 00 AC 0A 10 0A                            ........
```

CoCreateInstance

Next **DCOMClient** does a **CoCreateInstance()**. This results in the following packet being sent from **hera** to **zeus**:

```
00000:  00 60 97 30 44 A8 00 C0 F0 10 84 5F 08 00 45 00    .`.0D......_..E.
00010:  00 E8 6E 00 00 00 80 11 53 DB AC 0A 10 0B AC 0A    ..n.....S.......
00020:  10 0A 04 08 00 87 00 D4 43 2F 04 00 08 00 10 00    ........C/......
00030:  00 00 00 00 00 00 00 00 00 00 00 00 00 00 00 00    ................
00040:  00 00 B8 4A 9F 4D 1C 7D CF 11 86 1E 00 20 AF 6E    ...J.M.}..... .n
00050:  7C 57 23 66 93 83 BE 5A D0 11 BB 2F 00 C0 F0 10    |W#f...Z.../....
00060:  84 5F 00 00 00 00 00 00 00 00 00 00 00 00 00 00    ._..............
00070:  FF FF FF FF 68 00 00 00 0A 00 05 00 01 00 00 00    ....h...........
00080:  00 00 00 00 00 00 21 65 9D A2 BE 5A D0 11 BB 2F    ......!e...Z.../
00090:  00 C0 F0 10 84 5F 00 00 00 00 C7 AC B5 31 2F 55    ....._.......1/U
000A0:  D0 11 9A 90 00 60 97 30 44 A8 00 00 00 00 00 00    .....`.0D.......
000B0:  00 00 02 00 00 00 00 00 00 00 01 00 00 00 A0 A4    ................
000C0:  14 00 01 00 00 00 C3 AC B5 31 2F 55 D0 11 9A 90    .........1/U....
000D0:  00 60 97 30 44 A8 01 00 00 00 01 00 00 00 08 00    .`.0D...........
000E0:  00 00 04 00 00 00 01 00 00 00 06 BC 2D 8F 06 D1    ............-...
000F0:  D3 11 6A A6 9F 0F                                  ..j...
```

The first thing to notice is that the packet contains the DCE packet header, starting at **0x2a**. This is very much the same as the previous example except now the interface is given as **{4d9f4ab8-7d1c-11cf-1e86-0020af6e7c57}** and the interface version is zero. (The COM spec specifies that the interface version must be zero.)

The data following the DCE packet requires further analysis:

```
00070:                               05 00 01 00 00 00 ⤸      ......
00080:  00 00 00 00 00 00 21 65 9D A2 BE 5A D0 11 BB 2F   ......!e...Z.../
00090:  00 C0 F0 10 84 5F                                 ....._
```

The first two words are the version of DCOM. In this case, it's version 5.1. This version is the first member of the DCOM **ORPCTHIS** structure:

```
typedef struct tagORPCTHIS
{
    COMVERSION              version;
    unsigned long           flags;
    unsigned long           reserved1;
    CID                     cid;
    ORPC_EXTENT_ARRAY*      extensions;
} ORPCTHIS;
```

The **flags** in this structure can be:

Flag	Value	Meaning
ORPCF_NULL	0	Not local
ORPCF_LOCAL	1	The call is local (the client and server are on the same machine)

Our test shows that **flags** is **ORPCF_NULL**, which basically means that the call is remote. After the **flags** and the reserved value is the **Causality ID** (CID), {a29d6521-5abe-11d0-2fbb-00c0f010845f}. This is a UUID that essentially identifies a particular call. Every call a client makes to the server must have a new CID. However, if the server makes a call on another object while processing a client request, it will use the same CID. We identified this UUID in the memory dump for the DCOM Windows messages.

After that are the body extensions, this is the main data of the call:

```
00090:                        00 00 00 00 C7 AC B5 31 2F 55      .......1/U
000A0:  D0 11 9A 90 00 60 97 30 44 A8 00 00 00 00 00 00   .....`.0D.......
000B0:  00 00 02 00 00 00 00 00 00 00 01 00 00 00 A0 A4   ................
000C0:  14 00 01 00 00 00 C3 AC B5 31 2F 55 D0 11 9A 90   .........1/U....
000D0:  00 60 97 30 44 A8 01 00 00 00 01 00 00 00 08 00   .`.0D...m.......
000E0:  00 00 04 00 00 00 01 00 00 00 06 BC 2D 8F 06 D1   ............-...
000F0:  93 11 6A A6 9F 0F                                 ..j...
```

This starts with a structure of type **ORPC_EXTENT_ARRAY**:

```
typedef struct tagORPC_STRUCT_ARRAY
{
    unsigned long    size;
    unsigned long    reserved;
    ORPC_EXTENT**    extent;
} ORPC_EXTENT_ARRAY;
```

In our case **size** is zero. That is then followed by **{31B5ACC7-552F-11D0-9A90-0060973044A8}**, which is **CLSID_Reverse**, the CLSID of the server object. Then there are some flags and then **{31B5ACC3-552F-11D0-9A90-0060973044A8}**, which is **IID_IReverse**. Thus **hera** is saying to **zeus**, "I want interface **IID_IReverse** on an object of class **CLSID_Reverse**".

Server Identifies its Security

At this point, the server knows nothing about the client. No security information has been sent, so the server responds by demanding more information:

```
00000:  00 C0 F0 10 84 5F 00 60 97 30 44 A8 08 00 45 00   ....._.`.0D...E.
00010:  00 B4 6A 01 00 00 80 11 58 0E AC 0A 10 0A AC 0A   ..j.....X.......
00020:  10 0B 04 17 04 08 00 A0 96 BC 04 00 28 00 10 00   ............(...
00030:  00 00 00 00 00 00 00 00 00 00 00 00 00 00 00 00   ................
00040:  00 00 76 22 3A 33 00 00 00 00 0D 00 00 80 9C 00   ..v":3..........
00050:  00 00 4A 05 B7 4C B4 5A D0 11 9A 9C 00 60 97 30   ..J..L.Z.....`.0
00060:  44 A8 00 00 00 00 03 00 00 00 00 00 00 00 03 00   D...............
00070:  FF FF FF FF 48 00 00 00 00 00 23 66 93 83 BE 5A   ....H.....#f...Z
00080:  D0 11 BB 2F 00 C0 F0 10 84 5F 38 69 B8 32 28 00   .../....._8i.2(.
00090:  00 00 4E 54 4C 4D 53 53 50 00 02 00 00 00 00 00   ..NTLMSSP.......
000A0:  00 00 28 00 00 00 F3 82 10 00 6B 4F 5A 2A D3 1A   ..(.......kOZ*..
000B0:  4C DB 00 00 00 00 00 00 00 00 28 00 00 00 00 03   L.........(.....
000C0:  00 00                                             ..
```

This time the DCE interface is **{333a2276-00-00-000d-00809c000000}**, the Conversion Manager DCE Interface, **conv**. It is followed by a UUID **{4cb7054a-5ab4-11d0-9c9a-0060973044a8}**.

The data part starts with a UUID of **{83936623-5abe-11d0-3fbb-00c0f010845f}**, followed by 2 **DWORD**s and the string **NTLMSSP**. This is the server, **zeus**, identifying the security authority that it uses.

Client Sends its Security Context

hera responds to this with:

```
00000:  00 60 97 30 44 A8 00 C0 F0 10 84 5F 08 00 45 00   .`.0D......_..E.
00010:  01 40 6F 00 00 00 80 11 52 83 AC 0A 10 0B AC 0A   .@o.....R.......
00020:  10 0A 04 08 04 17 01 2C 4B DE 04 02 08 00 10 00   .......,K.......
00030:  00 00 00 00 00 00 00 00 00 00 00 00 00 00 00 00   ................
00040:  00 00 76 22 3A 33 00 00 00 00 0D 00 00 80 9C 00   ..v":3..........
00050:  00 00 4A 05 B7 4C B4 5A D0 11 9A 9C 00 60 97 30   ..J..L.Z.....`.0
00060:  44 A8 00 00 00 00 03 00 00 00 00 00 00 00 03 00   D...............
00070:  FF FF FF FF D4 00 00 00 00 00 00 00 00 00 24 66   ..............$f
00080:  93 83 BE 5A D0 11 BB 2F 00 C0 F0 10 84 5F 00 03   ...Z.../....._..
00090:  00 00 00 00 00 00 AA 00 00 00 4E 54 4C 4D 53 53   ..........NTLMSS
000A0:  50 00 03 00 00 00 18 00 18 00 6A 00 00 00 18 00   P.........j.....
000B0:  18 00 82 00 00 00 08 00 08 00 40 00 00 00 1A 00   ..........@.....
000C0:  1A 00 48 00 00 00 08 00 08 00 62 00 00 00 10 00   ..H.......b.....
000D0:  10 00 9A 00 00 00 D1 82 00 00 48 00 45 00 52 00   ..........H.E.R.
000E0:  41 00 52 00 69 00 63 00 68 00 61 00 72 00 64 00   A.R.i.c.h.a.r.d.
000F0:  47 00 72 00 69 00 6D 00 65 00 73 00 48 00 45 00   G.r.i.m.e.s.H.E.
00100:  52 00 41 00 3B 25 7A 0C 6B 05 F7 3C CD 05 E9 D4   R.A.;%z.k..<....
00110:  68 4C AA 57 49 A6 91 8A AD FB 0A 68 78 9C EC D3   hL.WI......hx...
00120:  84 B4 72 DF 95 5C 64 F1 87 8A C8 E8 51 1D 4A 9F   ..r..\d.....Q.J.
00130:  13 BE 1A BF 39 23 B7 79 BA B5 3B 72 05 19 79 43   ....9#.y..;r..yC
00140:  D1 D6 42 45 00 00 AA 00 00 00 00 00 00 00         ..BE..........
```

The DCE portion has the same **conv** interface. The interesting part is further down. **hera** has sent the following string to **zeus**:

NTLMSSP

and then

HERARichardGrimesHERA

This is my username on **hera**. Note that **DCOMClient** does not specifically ask the user for security information, so it uses the security context that it was started under. I logged on as **RichardGrimes**, on **hera**, so this is the principal it uses.

hera also sends another packet:

```
00000:  00 60 97 30 44 A8 00 C0 F0 10 84 5F 08 00 45 00    .`.0D......_..E.
00010:  00 80 70 00 00 00 80 11 52 43 AC 0A 10 0B AC 0A    ..p.....RC......
00020:  10 0A 04 08 00 87 00 6C 1C C1 04 01 20 00 10 00    .......l.... ...
00030:  00 00 00 00 00 00 00 00 00 00 00 00 00 00 00 00    ................
00040:  00 00 B8 4A 9F 4D 1C 7D CF 11 86 1E 00 20 AF 6E    ...J.M.}..... .n
00050:  7C 57 23 66 93 83 BE 5A D0 11 BB 2F 00 C0 F0 10    |W#f...Z.../....
00060:  84 5F 38 69 B8 32 00 00 00 00 00 00 00 00 00 00    ._8i.2..........
00070:  FF FF FF FF 00 00 00 00 0A 01 04 00 00 00 01 00    ................
00080:  00 00 B6 BE AB B7 75 39 E5 B5 6A A6 9F 0F          ......u9..j...
```

This is a DCE packet with the interface **{4d9f4ab8-7d1c-11cf-ie86-0020af6e7c57}**, and **zeus** replies with

```
00000:  00 C0 F0 10 84 5F 00 60 97 30 44 A8 08 00 45 00    ....._.`.0D...E.
00010:  00 80 6B 01 00 00 80 11 57 42 AC 0A 10 0A AC 0A    ..k.....WB......
00020:  10 0B 00 87 04 08 00 6C AA 98 04 04 20 00 10 00    .......l.... ...
00030:  00 00 00 00 00 00 00 00 00 00 00 00 00 00 00 00    ................
00040:  00 00 B8 4A 9F 4D 1C 7D CF 11 86 1E 00 20 AF 6E    ...J.M.}..... .n
00050:  7C 57 23 66 93 83 BE 5A D0 11 BB 2F 00 C0 F0 10    |W#f...Z.../....
00060:  84 5F 38 69 B8 32 00 00 00 00 00 00 00 00 00 00    ._8i.2..........
00070:  FF FF FF FF 00 00 00 00 0A 01 04 00 00 00 01 00    ................
00080:  00 00 77 DB 5C C0 75 39 E5 B5 6A A6 9F 0F          ..w.\.u9..j...
```

This is the first difference between the first call and subsequent runs of **DCOMClient**. In the later runs, these two packets are missing.

Server Acknowledgement

After this, **zeus** replies with a large packet:

```
00000:  00 C0 F0 10 84 5F 00 60 97 30 44 A8 08 00 45 00    ....._.`.0D...E.
00010:  02 58 6C 01 00 00 80 11 54 6A AC 0A 10 0A AC 0A    .Xl.....Tj......
00020:  10 0B 00 87 04 08 02 44 C9 CA 04 02 08 00 10 00    .......D........
00030:  00 00 00 00 00 00 00 00 00 00 00 00 00 00 00 00    ................
00040:  00 00 B8 4A 9F 4D 1C 7D CF 11 86 1E 00 20 AF 6E    ...J.M.}..... .n
00050:  7C 57 23 66 93 83 BE 5A D0 11 BB 2F 00 C0 F0 10    |W#f...Z.../....
00060:  84 5F 38 69 B8 32 00 00 00 00 00 00 00 00 00 00    ._8i.2..........
00070:  FF FF 11 00 D8 01 00 00 0A 00 01 00 00 00 00 00    ................
```

```
00080:   00 00 D4 00 00 00 89 77 EC 1F 50 C9 15 00 76 00    .......w..P...v.
00090:   00 00 76 00 15 00 08 00 31 00 37 00 32 00 2E 00    ..v.....1.7.2...
000A0:   31 00 30 00 2E 00 31 00 36 00 2E 00 31 00 30 00    1.0...1.6...1.0.
000B0:   5B 00 31 00 30 00 34 00 39 00 5D 00 00 00 00 00    [.1.0.4.9.].....
000C0:   0A 00 FF FF 52 00 69 00 63 00 68 00 61 00 72 00    ....R.i.c.h.a.r.
000D0:   64 00 47 00 72 00 69 00 6D 00 65 00 73 00 00 00    d.G.r.i.m.e.s...
000E0:   0C 00 FF FF 52 00 69 00 63 00 68 00 61 00 72 00    ....R.i.c.h.a.r.
000F0:   64 00 47 00 72 00 69 00 6D 00 65 00 73 00 00 00    d.G.r.i.m.e.s...
00100:   0C 00 FF FF 52 00 69 00 63 00 68 00 61 00 72 00    ....R.i.c.h.a.r.
00110:   64 00 47 00 72 00 69 00 6D 00 65 00 73 00 00 00    d.G.r.i.m.e.s...
00120:   0C 00 FF FF 52 00 69 00 63 00 68 00 61 00 72 00    ....R.i.c.h.a.r.
00130:   64 00 47 00 72 00 69 00 6D 00 65 00 73 00 00 00    d.G.r.i.m.e.s...
00140:   0C 00 FF FF 52 00 69 00 63 00 68 00 61 00 72 00    ....R.i.c.h.a.r.
00150:   64 00 47 00 72 00 69 00 6D 00 65 00 73 00 00 00    d.G.r.i.m.e.s...
00160:   0B 00 FF FF 52 00 69 00 63 00 68 00 61 00 72 00    ....R.i.c.h.a.r.
00170:   64 00 47 00 72 00 69 00 6D 00 65 00 73 00 00 00    d.G.r.i.m.e.s...
00180:   00 00 00 00 00 00 8D 00 00 00 86 00 00 00 00 00    ...............
00190:   00 00 02 00 00 00 05 00 01 00 00 00 00 00 01 00    ...............
001A0:   00 00 A8 CA 15 00 92 00 00 00 92 00 00 00 4D 45    ..............ME
001B0:   4F 57 01 00 00 00 C3 AC B5 31 2F 55 D0 11 9A 90    OW.......1/U....
001C0:   00 60 97 30 44 A8 00 00 00 00 05 00 00 00 D4 00    .`.0D..........
001D0:   00 00 89 77 EC 1F DD 00 00 00 89 77 EC 1F 02 00    ...w.......w....
001E0:   00 00 8D 00 00 00 86 00 00 00 02 00 00 00 27 00    ..............'.
001F0:   23 00 08 00 31 00 37 00 32 00 2E 00 31 00 30 00    #...1.7.2...1.0.
00200:   2E 00 31 00 36 00 2E 00 31 00 30 00 00 00 07 00    ..1.6...1.0.....
00210:   31 00 37 00 32 00 2E 00 31 00 30 00 00 00 2E 00 31 00   1.7.2...1.0...1.
00220:   36 00 2E 00 31 00 30 00 00 00 13 00 5A 00 45 00    6...1.0.....Z.E.
00230:   55 00 53 00 00 00 00 00 0A 00 FF FF 00 00 00 00    U.S.............
00240:   00 00 01 00 00 00 00 00 00 00 00 00 00 00 00 00    ...............
00250:   00 00 04 00 00 00 01 00 00 00 2A 40 5A C0 BF 92    .........*@Z...
00260:   B2 E0 6A A6 9F 0F                                  ..j...
```

The server returns back the interface **{4d9f4ab8-7d1c-11cf-1e86-0020af6e7c57}**, which you will remember was the UUID originally sent by the client in the first packet, and then **{83936623-5abe-11d0-2fbb-00c0f010845f}**, which was originally sent by **zeus** in its first reply, forging the links with the previous conversation.

Further on down is the string:

172.10.16.10[1049]

This is the binding information necessary for RPC. The DCOM spec defines **NCADG_IP_UDP** as **0x08**, so presumably this is the purpose of the preceding **WORD**. This is followed by the logon address on **zeus**, also **RichardGrimes**.

However, at **0x01ae** is the identifier **MEOW** (**0x574f454d**) this signifies the start of the **OBJREF** structure:

```
typedef struct tagOBJREF
{
    unsigned long signature;
    unsigned long flags;
    GUID              iid;
    union
    {
      struct
```

```
                {
                    STDOBJREF         std;
                    DUALSTRINGARRAY   saResAddr;
                } u_standard;
                struct
                {
                    STDOBJREF         std;
                    CLSID             clsid;
                    DUALSTRINGARRAY   saResAddr;
                } u_handler;
                struct
                {
                    CLSID             clsid;
                    unsigned long     cbExtension;
                    unsigned long     size;
                    byte              *pData;
                } u_custom;
            } u_objref;
        } OBJREF;
```

This contains a **union** that is switched on the **flags** member. In our case, this is **OBJREF_STANDARD**, which is followed by **IID_IReverse**.

Object references are data types that are marshaled by COM thus the proxy and stub code must understand how to handle a GUID for an object. In DCOM, this is done by defining this data type and it is the only extension to the DCE standard.

The **OBJREF** structure contains information about how the interface is marshaled. There are three alternatives:

> **OBJREF_STANDARD**
>
> **OBJREF_HANDLER**
>
> **OBJREF_CUSTOM**

These are the marshaling methods identified in Chapter 3. Basically, custom marshaling is the most flexible as the programmer decides how the object is marshaled, and to this end there is a **byte** array to hold class-specific data. Handler marshaling uses a proxy object, and the CLSID of this object is passed in the structure.

Finally, standard marshaling uses the DCOM standard methods for marshaling data and makes little effort at optimizing the process. For standard marshaling a standard object reference and a resolver address are sent.

```
001C0:                       00 00 00 00 05 00 00 00 D4 00         ..........
001D0:  00 00 89 77 EC 1F DD 00 00 00 89 77 EC 1F 02 00   ...w.......w....
001E0:  00 00 8D 00 00 00 86 00 00 00 02 00 00 00         ..............
```

STDOBJREF is defined as:

```
typedef struct tagSTDOBJREF
{
    unsigned long flags;
    unsigned long cPublicRefs;
    OXID          oxid;
```

```
        OID             oid;
        IPID            ipid;
    } STDOBJREF;
```

The first member is **SORF_NULL**. The next member is **cPublicRefs**, which is the number of references on the interface. The results show there to be 5 reference counts in this case. The actual reference counting is carried out on the remote object using the **IRemUnknown** interface. This interface is not seen by the user and is used only by the runtime. The reference counting methods of this interface are extended versions of the local version - they can increment or decrement the reference counts on several interfaces at one time, for example.

The local **AddRef()** and **Release()** calls are not immediately translated as calls to the **IRemUnknown** interface methods, the runtime may cache **AddRef()**s and **Release()**s, keeping just one count on the remote object. Such a scheme would only require a single remoted reference increment to hold the object and a single remoted decrement to release it.

After this are several identifiers: two 64 bit and one 128 bit ID:

OXID: D4000000-8977EC1F
OID: DD000000-8977EC1F
IPID: {00000002-008D-0000-0086-000002000000}

The IPID is an identifier of an interface on an object. It is not the IID of the interface. It identifies a particular interface on a particular object on a particular machine. The implementation of the IPID is specific to the machine type and does not contain binding information to the actual object interface.

To resolve the IPID, there is an RPC server called the OXID Resolver. This generates OXIDs, which defines the scope of the IPID and determines if it is machine-wide on the server, or maybe just process-wide. The OXID Resolver will keep a list of all IPIDs exported and imported from other machines.

A client can resolve the OXID into binding information by consulting its locally cached table of bindings. If the OXID is not there, it can ask the server for this information. The OXID Resolver resides on a well-known endpoint, making these confirmation calls easy.

The COM part of the process comes in with a COM object called the OXID object. There is one for every OXID and it is this object that implements the **IRemUnknown** interface for the interface.

The final part of this packet is the resolver address:

```
001E0:                                              27 00              '.
001F0:  23 00 08 00 31 00 37 00 32 00 2E 00 31 00 30 00    #...1.7.2...1.0.
00200:  2E 00 31 00 36 00 2E 00 31 00 30 00 00 00 07 00    ..1.6...1.0.....
00210:  31 00 37 00 32 00 2E 00 31 00 30 00 2E 00 31 00    1.7.2...1.0...1.
00220:  36 00 2E 00 31 00 30 00 00 00 13 00 5A 00 45 00    6...1.0.....Z.E.
00230:  55 00 53 00 00 00 00 00 0A 00 FF FF 00 00 00 00    U.S.............
00240:  00 00 01 00 00 00 00 00 00 00 00 00 00 00 00 00    ................
00250:  00 00 04 00 00 00 01 00 00 00 2A 40 5A C0 BF 92    ..........*@Z...
00260:  B2 E0 6A A6 9F 0F                                  ..j...
```

This is a **DUALSTRINGARRAY** that is made up of some flags and an array of **STRINGBINDING**s and **SECURITYBINDING**s.

```
typedef struct tagSTRINGBINDING
{
   unsigned short  wTowerId;
   unsigned short  aNetworkAddr;
} STRINGBINDING;

typedef struct tagSECURITYBINDING
{
   unsigned short  wAuthnSvc;
   unsigned short  wAuthzSvc;
   unsigned short  aPrincName;
} SECURITYBINDING;

typedef struct tagDUALSTRINGARRAY
{
   unsigned short  wNumEntries;
   unsigned short  wSecurityOffset;
   unsigned short  aStringArray[];
} DUALSTRINGARRAY;
```

In our case, **wNumEntries** is **0x0027** (39), the security offset is **0x23**. After that is the string binding, which starts with the value of **0x0008**, representing UDP, and then the IP address of the server, **172.10.16.10** and the machine name. Finally, this call has default authorization (**0xFFFF**) and authentication (**0x000A**).

Reverse

Now the client makes the method call on the server:

```
00000:  00 60 97 30 44 A8 00 C0 F0 10 84 5F 08 00 45 00   .`.0D......_..E.
00010:  00 C8 71 00 00 00 80 11 50 FB AC 0A 10 0B AC 0A   ..q.....P.......
00020:  10 0A 04 09 04 19 00 B4 7B 07 04 00 08 00 10 00   ........{.......
00030:  00 00 02 00 00 00 8D 00 00 00 86 00 00 00 02 00   ......1/U.....
00040:  00 00 C3 AC B5 31 2F 55 D0 11 9A 90 00 60 97 30   .....1/U.....`.0
00050:  44 A8 22 65 9D A2 BE 5A D0 11 BB 2F 00 C0 F0 10   D."e...Z.../....
00060:  84 5F 00 00 00 00 00 00 00 00 00 00 00 00 03 00   ._..............
00070:  FF FF FF FF 48 00 00 00 0A 00 05 00 01 00 00 00   ....H...........
00080:  00 00 00 00 00 00 21 65 9D A2 BE 5A D0 11 BB 2F   ......!e...Z.../
00090:  00 C0 F0 10 84 5F 00 00 00 00 0B 00 00 00 00 00   ....._..........
000A0:  00 00 0B 00 00 00 54 65 73 74 53 74 72 69 6E 67   ......TestString
000B0:  00 00 00 00 00 00 00 00 00 00 00 00 00 00 00 00   ................
000C0:  00 00 04 00 00 00 01 00 00 00 A3 8D 9F 01 96 68   ...............h
000D0:  B5 04 75 AE 6E AF                                 ..u.n.
```

The interface passed is **IID_IReverse**, and the DCOM data is another **ORPCTHIS**, with the data **TestString** marshaled with its length as the preceding **DWORD**. Again there is no security present, so **hera** sends another packet with this information:

```
00000:  00 60 97 30 44 A8 00 C0 F0 10 84 5F 08 00 45 00   .`.0D......_..E.
00010:  01 40 72 00 00 00 80 11 4F 83 AC 0A 10 0B AC 0A   .@r.....O.......
00020:  10 0A 04 09 04 1A 01 2C 74 77 04 02 08 00 10 00   .......,tw......
00030:  00 00 00 00 00 00 00 00 00 00 00 00 00 00 00 00   ................
00040:  00 00 76 22 3A 33 00 00 00 00 0D 00 00 80 9C 00   ..v":3..........
00050:  00 00 51 2D 95 9D BE 5A D0 11 9A 9C 00 60 97 30   ..Q-...Z.....`.0
00060:  44 A8 00 00 00 00 03 00 00 00 00 00 00 00 03 00   D...............
```

```
00070:   FF FF FF FF D4 00 00 00 00 00 00 00 00 00 23 65    .............#e
00080:   9D A2 BE 5A D0 11 BB 2F 00 C0 F0 10 84 5F 00 03    ...Z.../....._..
00090:   00 00 00 00 00 00 AA 00 00 00 4E 54 4C 4D 53 53    ..........NTLMSS
000A0:   50 00 03 00 00 00 18 00 18 00 6A 00 00 00 18 00    P.........j.....
000B0:   18 00 82 00 00 00 08 00 08 00 40 00 00 00 1A 00    ..........@.....
000C0:   1A 00 48 00 00 00 08 00 08 00 62 00 00 00 10 00    ..H.......b.....
000D0:   10 00 9A 00 00 00 D1 82 10 00 48 00 45 00 52 00    ..........H.E.R.
000E0:   41 00 52 00 69 00 63 00 68 00 61 00 72 00 64 00    A.R.i.c.h.a.r.d.
000F0:   47 00 72 00 69 00 6D 00 65 00 73 00 48 00 45 00    G.r.i.m.e.s.H.E.
00100:   52 00 41 00 E2 0E B5 B3 F1 FA D2 EC 75 0C 08 F9    R.A.........u...
00110:   98 58 4A 5F 00 4F 9D B0 D6 1D 42 81 37 9B 19 48    .XJ_.O....B.7..H
00120:   AC 48 A1 08 08 9D 8A 98 64 9B 4C 0C C8 C7 17 F3    .H......d.L.....
00130:   C3 D0 68 0E 96 BB 25 59 22 E2 4C FB 9E 5E 38 B8    ..h...%Y".L..^8.
00140:   68 85 60 4F 00 00 AA 00 00 00 00 00 00 00          h.`O..........
```

This is remarkably like the previous **conv** packet sent by **hera**. The previous case had a large packet in reply from the server, this time the server returns a smaller packet with its security authority:

```
00000:   00 C0 F0 10 84 5F 00 60 97 30 44 A8 08 00 45 00    ....._.`.0D...E.
00010:   00 B4 6D 01 00 00 80 11 55 0E AC 0A 10 0A AC 0A    ..m.....U.......
00020:   10 0B 04 1A 04 09 00 A0 F4 2B 04 00 28 00 10 00    .........+..(...
00030:   00 00 00 00 00 00 00 00 00 00 00 00 00 00 00 00    ................
00040:   00 00 76 22 3A 33 00 00 00 00 0D 00 00 80 9C 00    ..v":3..........
00050:   00 00 51 2D 95 9D BE 5A D0 11 9A 9C 00 60 97 30    ..Q-...Z.....`.0
00060:   44 A8 00 00 00 00 03 00 00 00 00 00 00 00 03 00    D...............
00070:   FF FF FF FF 48 00 00 00 00 22 65 9D A2 BE 5A    ....H....."e...Z
00080:   D0 11 BB 2F 00 C0 F0 10 84 5F 8A 7A B8 32 28 00    .../....._.z.2(.
00090:   00 00 4E 54 4C 4D 53 53 50 00 02 00 00 00 00 00    ..NTLMSSP.......
000A0:   00 00 28 00 00 00 F3 82 10 00 95 F4 0E DC B4 D8    ..(.............
000B0:   E3 AA 00 00 00 00 00 00 00 00 28 00 00 00 00 03    ..........(.....
000C0:   00 00                                              ..
```

and **hera** replies with:

```
00000:   00 60 97 30 44 A8 00 C0 F0 10 84 5F 08 00 45 00    .`.0D......_..E.
00010:   00 C8 73 00 00 00 80 11 4E FB AC 0A 10 0B AC 0A    ..s.....N.......
00020:   10 0A 04 09 04 19 00 B4 31 56 04 00 08 00 10 00    ........1V......
00030:   00 00 00 00 00 00 8D 00 00 00 86 00 00 00 00 00    ................
00040:   00 00 31 01 00 00 00 00 00 00 C0 00 00 00 00 00    ..1.............
00050:   00 46 22 65 9D A2 BE 5A D0 11 BB 2F 00 C0 F0 10    .F"e...Z.../....
00060:   84 5F 8A 7A B8 32 00 00 00 00 01 00 00 00 05 00    ._.z.2..........
00070:   FF FF 1E 00 48 00 00 00 0A 00 05 00 01 00 00 00    ....H...........
00080:   00 00 00 00 00 00 21 65 9D A2 BE 5A D0 11 BB 2F    ......!e...Z.../
00090:   00 C0 F0 10 84 5F 00 00 00 00 01 00 00 00 01 00    ....._..........
000A0:   00 00 02 00 00 00 8D 00 00 00 86 00 00 00 02 00    ................
000B0:   00 00 05 00 00 00 00 00 00 00 40 00 00 00 1A 00    ..........@.....
000C0:   1A 00 04 00 00 00 01 00 00 00 D6 C3 A6 FE 82 90    ................
000D0:   F6 91 74 AE 6E AF                                  ..t.n.
```

The interface is **{00000131-0000-0000-00c0-000000000046}**, which is the COM interface **IRemUnknown**. This is the interface implemented on the OXID object. The body has the **ORPCTHIS**, which has an **ORPC_EXTENT_ARRAY** with the following data:

size	00000000
reserved	00000001
extent	{00000001-0002-0000-8d00-00000086000000},00000002

Finally, **zeus** replies with:

```
00000:   00 C0 F0 10 84 5F 00 60 97 30 44 A8 08 00 45 00    ....._.`.0D...E.
00010:   00 A8 6E 01 00 00 80 11 54 1A AC 0A 10 0A AC 0A    ..n.....T.......
00020:   10 0B 04 19 04 09 00 94 A4 CB 04 02 08 00 10 00    ................
00030:   00 00 02 00 00 00 8D 00 00 00 86 00 00 00 02 00    ................
00040:   00 00 C3 AC B5 31 2F 55 D0 11 9A 90 00 60 97 30    .....1/U.....`.0
00050:   44 A8 22 65 9D A2 BE 5A D0 11 BB 2F 00 C0 F0 10    D."e...Z.../....
00060:   84 5F 8A 7A B8 32 00 00 00 00 00 00 00 00 03 00    ._.z.2..........
00070:   FF FF 1E 00 28 00 00 00 0A 00 00 00 00 00 00 00    ....(...........
00080:   00 00 18 41 15 00 0B 00 00 00 00 00 00 00 0B 00    ...A..........
00090:   00 00 67 6E 69 72 74 53 74 73 65 54 00 00 00 00    ..gnirtStseT....
000A0:   00 00 04 00 00 00 01 00 00 00 32 EB FB 4E 7F D5    ..........2..N•.
000B0:   A9 6F 75 AE 6E AF                                  .ou.n.
```

This gives the **IID_IReverse** as the DCE interface with an **ORPCTHAT**, which gives the result preceded by its length.

zeus also sends another packet with the **IID_IReverse** in it:

```
00000:   00 C0 F0 10 84 5F 00 60 97 30 44 A8 08 00 45 00    ....._.`.0D...E.
00010:   00 90 6F 01 00 00 80 11 53 32 AC 0A 10 0A AC 0A    ..o.....S2......
00020:   10 0B 04 19 04 09 00 7C 59 EF 04 02 08 00 10 00    .......|Y.......
00030:   00 00 00 00 00 00 8D 00 00 00 86 00 00 00 00 00    ................
00040:   00 00 C3 AC B5 31 2F 55 D0 11 9A 90 00 60 97 30    .....1/U.....`.0
00050:   44 A8 22 65 9D A2 BE 5A D0 11 BB 2F 00 C0 F0 10    D."e...Z.../....
00060:   84 5F 8A 7A B8 32 00 00 00 00 01 00 00 00 03 00    ._.z.2..........
00070:   FF FF 1E 00 10 00 00 00 0A 00 00 00 00 00 00 00    ................
00080:   00 00 00 00 00 00 0B 00 00 00 04 00 00 00 01 00    ................
00090:   00 00 32 EB FB 4E 4C A0 9A EE 74 AE 6E AF          ..2..NL...t.n.
```

The Final Death Throes

When the client has finished, **hera** sends:

```
00000:   00 60 97 30 44 A8 00 C0 F0 10 84 5F 08 00 45 00    .`.0D......._.E.
00010:   00 80 74 00 00 00 80 11 4E 43 AC 0A 10 0B AC 0A    ..t.....NC......
00020:   10 0A 04 08 00 87 00 6C DB 95 04 07 20 00 10 00    .......l.... ...
00030:   00 00 00 00 00 00 00 00 00 00 00 00 00 00 00 00    ................
00040:   00 00 B8 4A 9F 4D 1C 7D CF 11 86 1E 00 20 AF 6E    ...J.M.}..... .n
00050:   7C 57 23 66 93 83 BE 5A D0 11 BB 2F 00 C0 F0 10    |W#f...Z.../....
00060:   84 5F 38 69 B8 32 00 00 00 00 00 00 00 00 00 00    ._8i.2..........
00070:   FF FF 11 00 00 00 01 00 0A 02 04 00 00 00 01 00    ................
00080:   00 00 47 DA 49 C0 75 39 E5 B5 6A A6 9F 0F          ..G.I.u9..j...
```

This has the **{4d9f4ab8-7d1c-11cf-1e86-0020af6e7c57}** interface that was used in the **CoCreateInstance()** call. Then **hera** and **zeus** send a series of packets back and forth. **zeus** starts by sending:

```
00000:   00 C0 F0 10 84 5F 00 60 97 30 44 A8 08 00 45 00    ....._.`.0D...E.
00010:   00 90 70 01 00 00 80 11 52 32 AC 0A 10 0A AC 0A    ..p.....R2......
00020:   10 0B 04 19 04 09 00 7C B1 ED 04 02 00 00 10 00    .......|........
00030:   00 00 00 00 00 00 8D 00 00 00 86 00 00 00 00 00    ................
00040:   00 00 C3 AC B5 31 2F 55 D0 11 9A 90 00 60 97 30    .....1/U.....`.0
00050:   44 A8 22 65 9D A2 BE 5A D0 11 BB 2F 00 C0 F0 10    D."e...Z.../....
00060:   84 5F 8A 7A B8 32 00 00 00 00 01 00 00 00 03 00    ._.z.2..........
```

```
00070:   FF FF 1E 00 10 00 00 00 0A 01 00 00 00 00 00 00   ................
00080:   00 00 00 00 00 00 0B 00 00 00 04 00 00 00 01 00   ................
00090:   00 00 E2 EB FB 4E 4C A0 9A EE 74 AE 6E AF         .....NL...t.n.
```

and **hera** replies:

```
00000:   00 60 97 30 44 A8 00 C0 F0 10 84 5F 08 00 45 00   .`.0D......_..E.
00010:   00 38 76 00 00 00 80 01 4C 9B AC 0A 10 0B AC 0A   .8v.....L.......
00020:   10 0A 03 03 64 37 00 00 00 00 45 00 00 90 71 01   ....d7....E...q.
00030:   00 00 80 11 51 32 AC 0A 10 0A AC 0A 10 0B 04 19   ....Q2..........
00040:   04 09 00 7C 90 27                                 ...|.'
```

The packets are essentially the same each time except one parameter in the server packet is incremented. When it reaches a value of 5, the **ReverseDCOM.exe** server dies. This is the pinging mechanism allowing the server to live for 3 ping intervals before it finally shuts down (the value is 6 because this includes both the ping and the reply).

Analysis

So what can we conclude from all this. Well the first conclusion is that there are twice as many packets in the DCOM conversation than in the DCE case. However, the number of packets involved in making a request from the server and then getting the reply is about the same in both cases.

The other packets in the DCOM case are DCOM trying to get binding and security information from the client and server. As mentioned before, once the server binding information has been obtained, it is cached by the client for later use.

Now look at the conversations from a different angle. The RPC server must be running on the server machine before the client can connect to it: RPC cannot activate the object server. However, COM can activate a server using the Service Control Manager.

In both cases, the server can be shutdown by the client. In the case of RPC, the server will need to implement an RPC that calls **RpcMgmtStopServerListening()**. This function breaks the listening loop created in **RpcServerListen()** in the server's **main()** function, allowing the server to finish. If multiple clients can connect to the server, the RPC runtime will wait until the other connections have finished before the server can close down. Of course, once the server has shutdown, a client will not be able to restart it.

In the case of DCOM, the **IUnknown::Release()** method is called by a client when it has finished with the server. As with the RPC server, if there are no other client connections, the server is closed down. However, unlike the RPC case, if, at a later stage, a client tries to connect to the object, the server will be restarted by the COM runtime.

The next major difference between the two cases is that the DCE client has to be given binding information to be able to connect to the server: in our case, the binding string is given on the command line that invokes the client. In part this is an artifact of this implementation, but the information must come from somewhere; other implementations could have the server listening on an endpoint known to the client and the client can use the RPC runtime functions to generate a binding string. However, the client must know details of the server to be able to generate this string, consequently the protocol and endpoint identifier must be hard coded into the client or, as in our case, passed as a command line parameter.

DCOM takes a different approach. DCOM is built upon RPC so at some point in the conversation, the client must obtain the binding information. The client cannot ask the server what binding string to use since it would need to know it to ask for it! This implies that there must be a separate object that sits on a known endpoint and this object will know about the DCOM server that the client requires. This third party object will, on request, return binding information to the client.

We have already come across this third party object; it is the interface exporter. Since this object maintains COM binding information, it is implicit that it will not have a COM interface. Rather it has a DCE interface: **IOXIDResolver**, and it will usually sit on the DCE RPC Endpoint Mapper server. This interface and the OXID Resolver object are described in the next section.

Service Control Manager and the OXID Resolver

The OXID Resolver

The OXID Resolver has two main responsibilities. The first is to resolve OXIDs to string bindings and the other is to handle pinging. As mentioned above, this object has a DCE interface and usually sits on the DCE RPC Endpoint Mapper endpoint. The **IOXIDResolver** interface is defined as:

```
[
    uuid(99fcfec4-5260-101b-bbcb-00aa0021347a),
    pointer_default(unique)
]
interface IOXIDResolver
{
   import "obase.idl";

   [idempotent] error_status_t ResolveOxid
      (
      [in]         handle_t        hRpc,
      [in]         OXID            *pOxid,
      [in]         unsigned short  cRequestedProtseqs,
      [in,   ref,  size_is(cRequestedProtseqs)]
                   unsigned short  arRequestedProtseqs[],
      [out, ref]   MID             *pmid,
      [out, ref]   STRINGARRAY     **psaOxidBindings,
      [out, ref]   IPID            *pipidRemUnknown
      );

   [idempotent] error_status_t SimplePing
      (
      [in]   handle_t   hRpc,
      [in]   SETID      *pSetId
      );

   [idempotent] error_status_t ComplexPing
      (
      [in]   handle_t        hRpc,
      [in]   SETID           *pSetId,
      [in]   unsigned short  SequenceNum,
```

```
    [in]  unsigned short  SetPingPeriod,
    [in]  unsigned short  SetNumPingsToTimeout,
    [out] unsigned short *pReqSetPingPeriod,
    [out] unsigned short *pReqSetNumPingsToTimeout,
    [in]  unsigned short  cAddToSet,
    [in]  unsigned short  cDelFromSet,
    [in,  unique, size_is(cAddToSet)]   GUID AddToSet[],
    [in,  unique, size_is(cDelFromSet)] GUID DelFromSet[]
    );
}
```

The methods have the **[idempotent]** attribute, this means that calling the method will not affect the state of the object and therefore a method can be called more than once without ill effect (in a way this is similar to labeling a C++ class method as **const**). This is used to signify that if a call to a method fails for any reason, it can be retried with impunity.

With the first method, the client sends an OXID and a list of acceptable protocols, and the server returns the machine ID (**MID**), binding strings and an IPID to the **IRemUnknown** interface on the object. The OXID Resolver knows about all the objects on the server machine and thus can map OXIDs to string bindings. However, it also knows about the OXIDs of objects *imported* to the server machine, in other words OXIDs for which there is a client on this server machine. It knows about these objects because an object running local to this server may activate an object on another machine and pass a reference to this object back to its client.

For the client to resolve this remote object OXID, the server must maintain binding information. The OXID Resolver will retain this information sometime after all references to the object have been released by objects on this machine.

The other two methods concern pinging. Depending on the values used in the **cAddToSet** and **cDelFromSet** parameters, the **ComplexPing()** method will ping a *ping set*, or create, add to or remove items from a ping set. **SimplePing()** will ping a ping set created by **ComplexPing()**.

This interface is used by the COM system, and the programmer does not have direct access to it.

The Service Control Manager

The Service Control Manager (SCM) is the process that is responsible for locating a server and then running it. SCM is part of the RPC service that is implemented in **rpcss.exe**. Under NT this is a service, but under Windows 95 it obviously cannot be run as a service. In that case, it is loaded by COM when the first call to **CoRegisterClassObject()** is made.

When a client requests that an object of a particular CLSID be created, COM contacts the SCM on the local machine. The SCM will then look into its locally held database for information about the object server. Ultimately this information is held in the system registry. It will then launch the server, obtain a class factory from the server and pass this back to the client.

If the server is in-process or local, launching the server is relatively simple (in the case of inproc servers, the SCM need only obtain the path to the server DLL, whereas for local servers, the SCM will have to start the executable).

If the server is on a remote machine, the local SCM will have to contact the SCM on the remote machine that has the object. The remote SCM will then launch the server (or if it is an in-process server and

Service Pack 2 is applied to NT 4.0, a *surrogate* executable will be launched to load the object server's DLL). An RPC connection is then maintained between the client and the server via the OXID Resolver.

The SCM implements the **IRemoteActivation** interface

```
[
  uuid(00000137-0000-0000-C000-000000000046),
  version(1.0),
  pointer_default(unique)
]
interface IRemoteActivation
{
    HRESULT ActivationRequest(
            [in] handle_t                            hRpc,
            [in] ORPCTHIS*                           orpcthis,
            [out] ORPCTHAT*                          orpcthat,
            [in] const GUID*                         rclsid,
            [in, string, unique] WCHAR*              pwszObjectName,
            [in] DWORD                               clsctx,
            [in] DWORD                               grfMode,
            [in] DWORD                               dwCount,
            [in,unique,size_is(Interfaces)] IID*
                                                     pIIDs,
            [out,size_is(Interfaces)] OBJREF**       ppInterfaces,
            [out,size_is(Interfaces)] HRESULT*       pResults
            );
}
```

This interface is essentially three methods in one – it is used to activate an object based solely upon a CLSID, or based on a CLSID and an IID, or based on an object name.

If **pIIDs** is **NULL** and the **rclsid** is non-**NULL** then the object is activated according to the **rclsid**, much as **CoGetClassObject()** works. If the **pIIDs** is non-**NULL** then the object is activated using both the **rclsid** and the **pIIDs**, which behaves like **CoCreateInstanceEx()**. Finally, if the **pwszObjectName** is valid, the method behaves as a call to **CreateFileMoniker()** followed by a call to **IMoniker::BindToObject()**.

Notice that this method allows the caller to query on more than one interface IID by creating an array of IIDs and passing a pointer to this in **pIIDs** and passing the size of the array in **dwCount**.

Optimizations

To illustrate some possible optimizations, we'll use a simple example to show the difference between making multiple method calls for small amounts of data or a single method call for a larger amount of data. The server will return fixed length strings to the client in two different ways. Here is the IDL:

```
[
    object,
    uuid(0070332F-A2C3-11D0-9B40-0060973044A8),
//    dual,
    helpstring("IMultiServer Interface"),
    pointer_default(unique)
]
```

```
interface IMultiServer : IDispatch
{
   [id(1), helpstring("method GetSinglePart")]
   HRESULT GetSinglePart([in] LONG index,
                         [out] BSTR* desc);
   [id(2), helpstring("method GetMultiplePart")]
   HRESULT GetMultiplePart([in] LONG index,
                        [in] LONG count,
                        [out] LONG* got,
                        [out, size_is(, *got)] BSTR** desc);
};
```

The first method gets a single value, passing in the ID of that value in **index**. The second method gets a range of values starting at **index** until **count** values have been got. Notice how I've commented out the **dual** attribute. This is because I am passing out an array of **BSTR** values in **GetMultiplePart()**. The Automation Marshaler does not like passing arrays of parameters like this, it prefers to use a **SAFEARRAY** instead. However, I decided not to use a **SAFEARRAY** so that I could get the two methods as similar as possible. Thus, commenting out **dual** will allow the IDL to compile, but you will need to provide a proxy-stub DLL.

MultiTest

The server is an ATL application. To make the server, you need to run the ATL COM AppWizard to create an EXE server called **MultiTest**. Add a new Simple Object called **MultiServer** to the project, so that the wizard creates the IDL and the class for an object that will implement the **IMultiServer** interface. Once done, right-click on the interface icon in ClassView select Add Method… then add the two methods, **GetSinglePart()** and **GetMultiplePart()** , shown in the interface definition above. Now edit the IDL file directly by commenting out the **[dual]** attribute given to **IMultiServer** by the wizard.

The server object has an embedded object of class **Numbers**. When this object is created, it loads the strings in the specified file (**numbers.dat**) and, to make life fair, it makes each string 80 characters long by adding the appropriate number of dashes to the end of the string. Then it keeps these strings in an array until the data is requested. The data is requested through the member function **GetItem()**. This function allocates system memory for the string at that index and returns it as a **BSTR**.

This class is declared in **Numbers.h**:

```
// Numbers class

class Numbers
{
private:
   LPCTSTR*  m_numbers;
   LONG      m_size;
public:
   Numbers(){}
   ~Numbers();
   void Initialize(LPTSTR filename);
   BSTR GetItem(LONG ID);
};
```

And is implemented in **Numbers.cpp**:

```
// Numbers class
#include "stdafx.h"
#include <winnls.h>
#include "numbers.h"

Numbers::~Numbers()
{
   LONG index;

   for (index = 0; index < m_size; index++)
      HeapFree(GetProcessHeap(), 0, (LPVOID)m_numbers[index]);

   HeapFree(GetProcessHeap(), 0, m_numbers);
}

void Numbers::Initialize(LPTSTR filename)
{
   m_numbers = NULL;
   m_size = 0;
   HANDLE hfile = CreateFile(filename, GENERIC_READ, 0, NULL, OPEN_EXISTING, 0, NULL);

   if (INVALID_HANDLE_VALUE == hfile)
      return;

   HANDLE hmapp = CreateFileMapping(hfile, NULL, PAGE_READONLY, 0, 0, NULL);

   if (NULL == hmapp)
   {
      CloseHandle(hfile);
      return;
   }

   LPTSTR pstr = (LPTSTR)MapViewOfFile(hmapp, FILE_MAP_READ, 0, 0, 0);

   if (NULL == pstr)
   {
      CloseHandle(hmapp);
      CloseHandle(hfile);
      return;
   }

   // Make an educated guess at the number of items
   m_size = 100;
   m_numbers = (LPCTSTR*)HeapAlloc(GetProcessHeap(), 0,
                                   m_size * sizeof(LPCTSTR));
   if (NULL == m_numbers)
   {
      UnmapViewOfFile(pstr);
      CloseHandle(hmapp);
      CloseHandle(hfile);
      return;
   }

   LPTSTR pos = pstr;
   LPTSTR next = pstr;
   DWORD size = GetFileSize(hfile, NULL);
   LONG count = 0;
```

```
    TCHAR padding[] = _T("-------------------------------------------------------------
------------------");

    while (next < pstr+size)
    {
        // Find end of string
        while (*next != _T('\r') && *next != _T('\n') && next < pstr + size)
            next++;

        // End of string, copy data
        LPTSTR temp = (LPTSTR)HeapAlloc(GetProcessHeap(), 0, sizeof(TCHAR) * 160);
        lstrcpyn(temp, pos, next - pos + 1);
        lstrcat(temp, padding);
        temp[80] = _T('\0');
        m_numbers[count] = (LPCTSTR)temp;

        // Move to the next item
        count++;
        next++;
        if (_T('\n') == *next)
            next++;
        pos = next;
    }

    m_size = count;

    UnmapViewOfFile(pstr);
    CloseHandle(hmapp);
    CloseHandle(hfile);
}

BSTR Numbers::GetItem(LONG ID)
{
    if (ID >= m_size)
        return NULL;

    LPWSTR pstr;

#ifndef UNICODE
    pstr = (LPWSTR)HeapAlloc(GetProcessHeap(), 0, sizeof(WCHAR) * 160);
    MultiByteToWideChar(CP_ACP, 0, m_numbers[ID], -1, pstr, 160);
#else
    pstr = m_numbers[ID - 1];
#endif

    BSTR bstr = ::SysAllocString(pstr);

#ifndef UNICODE
    HeapFree(GetProcessHeap(), 0, pstr);
#endif
    return bstr;
}
```

Once you've added these files to the project, the changes that you need to make to the **CMultiServer** are pretty minor:

```
// MultiServer.h : Declaration of the CMultiServer

#ifndef __MULTISERVER_H_
#define __MULTISERVER_H_

#include "resource.h"        // main symbols
#include "numbers.h"

///////////////////////////////////////////////////////////// CMultiServer
class ATL_NO_VTABLE CMultiServer :
      public CComObjectRootEx<CComSingleThreadModel>,
      public CComCoClass<CMultiServer, &CLSID_MultiServer>,
   public IDispatchImpl<IMultiServer, &IID_IMultiServer,
                        &LIBID_MULTITESTLib>
{
public:
   CMultiServer();

DECLARE_REGISTRY_RESOURCEID(IDR_MULTISERVER)

BEGIN_COM_MAP(CMultiServer)
   COM_INTERFACE_ENTRY(IMultiServer)
   COM_INTERFACE_ENTRY(IDispatch)
END_COM_MAP()

// IMultiServer
public:
   STDMETHOD(GetMultiplePart)(/*[in]*/ LONG index,
                              /*[in]*/ LONG count,
                              /*[out]*/LONG* got,
                              /*[out]*/ BSTR** desc);
   STDMETHOD(GetSinglePart)(/*[in]*/ LONG index,
                            /*[out]*/ BSTR* desc);
private:
   Numbers m_list;
};

#endif //__MULTISERVER_H_
```

For the single value case, **GetSinglepart()**, a **BSTR** is generated from the string and passed back to the client. For the multiple case, **GetMultiplePart()**, an array is created and the **BSTR** for each item is placed in the array, then the array and the number of items obtained are returned:

```
// MultiServer.cpp : Implementation of CMultiServer
#include "stdafx.h"
#include "MultiTest.h"
#include "MultiServer.h"

//////////////////////////////////////////////////////////////////////////
// CMultiServer

CMultiServer::CMultiServer()
{
   LPTSTR str[MAX_PATH];
   lstrcpy((LPTSTR)str,_T("numbers.dat"));
   m_list.Initialize((LPTSTR)str);
}
```

```
HRESULT STDMETHODCALLTYPE CMultiServer::GetSinglePart(LONG index,
        BSTR *desc)
{
    *desc = m_list.GetItem(index);

    if (NULL == *desc)
    {
        return S_FALSE;
    }
    else
    {
        return S_OK;
    }
}
```

```
HRESULT STDMETHODCALLTYPE CMultiServer::GetMultiplePart(LONG index,
        LONG count, LONG* got, BSTR** desc)
{
    HRESULT hr = S_OK;
    // Temporary buffer
    BSTR* buf = new BSTR[count];
    *got = count;
    LONG current = index;

    while (current<(index + count))
    {
        buf[current - index] = m_list.GetItem(current);
        if (NULL == buf[current - index])
        {
            *got = current - index;
            hr = S_FALSE;
            break;
        }

        current++;
    }

    *desc = (BSTR*)CoTaskMemAlloc(*got * sizeof(BSTR));

    for (current = 0; current < *got; current++)
        (*desc)[current] = buf[current];

    delete [] buf;
    return hr;
}
```

When you compile this code, Developer Studio will register the server. However, since this code does not use the automation marshaler, you will have to make the proxy-stub DLL by hand and then register it:

nmake /f multitestps.mk
regsvr32 multitestps.dll

MultiClient

To make the client, run MFC AppWizard (exe) and create an MFC dialog-based project called **MultiClient**. Apart from choosing to create a dialog-based application on Step 1, you can leave all the other AppWizard steps alone.

Now add initialization of the COM libraries to **CMultiClientApp::InitInstance()**:

```
BOOL CMultiClientApp::InitInstance()
{
    // Initialize OLE libraries
    if (!AfxOleInit())
    {
        AfxMessageBox("OLE initialization failed.");
        return FALSE;
    }

        AfxEnableControlContainer();
    // Standard initialization
    ...
}
```

Next you need to add the standard server name dialog, **CServerNameDlg**, to the project. If you've already added this to the Component Gallery, as suggested earlier in the book, then your life will be simple. If you haven't, you'll need to knock together a quick dialog that can accept a server name input into a text box, and a **CDialog**-based class called **CServerNameDlg** that represents this dialog and exposes this name as a public member called **m_strServerName**. Once the dialog has been inserted, add **#include "ServerNameDlg.h"** to the top of **MultiClientDlg.h** (below the other **#include**s).

Now add some controls to the main dialog, **IDD_MULTICLIENT_DIALOG**, as shown here.

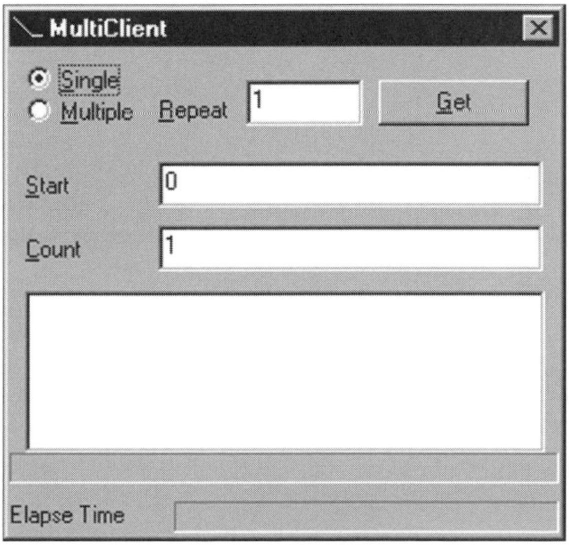

There is a pair of buttons, to determine whether the single or multiple case is used, and two edit boxes to specify the start value and the number of items to get. The values are shown in the list box near the bottom and errors are shown in the first static control, with the average time to make the call in the bottom static control.

307

Now use ClassWizard to add to the dialog class **long** member variables for the Count, Repeat and Start edit boxes, and a member variable for the radio buttons.

While you have the ClassWizard open, add handlers for **WM_DESTROY** and for the click event of the **IDC_GET** button.

Now you need to add some extra **protected** members to the dialog header:

```
// Implementation
protected:
    HICON m_hIcon;
    CString m_strServerName;
    IMultiServer* m_pMultiServer;
    void Message(const CString& strMessage);
```

In order to be able to use the **IMultiServer** interface, you need to copy **MultiTest.h** and **MultiTest_i.c** to the project directory. Add the C file to the project (remember to edit the project settings to turn off pre-compiled headers for this file) and add an **#include** for **MultiTest.h** to the top of **MultiClientDlg.h**.

The **Message()** is just like the helper you've seen in previous examples. It just outputs messages to the static text control on the dialog:

```
void CMultiClientDlg::Message(const CString& strMessage)
{
   CWnd* pTextCtrl = GetDlgItem(IDC_MESSAGE);
   ASSERT(pTextCtrl);

   pTextCtrl->SetWindowText(strMessage);
}
```

Now edit the dialog constructor to give default values for the controls:

```
CMultiClientDlg::CMultiClientDlg(CWnd* pParent /*=NULL*/)
   : CDialog(CMultiClientDlg::IDD, pParent)
{
   //{{AFX_DATA_INIT(CMultiClientDlg)
   m_lCount = 1;
   m_lRepeat = 1;
   m_lStart = 0;
   m_nRadio = 0;
   //}}AFX_DATA_INIT
   m_hIcon = AfxGetApp()->LoadIcon(IDR_MAINFRAME);
   m_strServerName = _T("");
}
```

As before, all the initialization occurs in the **OnInitDialog()** method:

```
BOOL CMultiClientDlg::OnInitDialog()
{
   // ... standard initialization
   CServerNameDlg dlg;

   // Get the name of the server to use
   if (dlg.DoModal() == IDOK &&
                   !dlg.m_strServerName.IsEmpty())
     m_strServerName = dlg.m_strServerName;
   else
     m_strServerName.Empty();

   // Let's create the server and get the time
   m_pMultiServer = NULL;

   HRESULT hr;
   COSERVERINFO serverinfo;
   COSERVERINFO* pServerInfo;

   // Create the server info
   serverinfo.dwReserved1 = 0;
   serverinfo.dwReserved2 = 0;
   serverinfo.pwszName = m_strServerName.AllocSysString();
   serverinfo.pAuthInfo = NULL;

   if (m_strServerName.IsEmpty())
      pServerInfo = NULL;
   else
      pServerInfo = &serverinfo;

   MULTI_QI qi = {&IID_IMultiServer, NULL, 0};
```

```
      hr = CoCreateInstanceEx(CLSID_MultiServer,
              NULL,CLSCTX_LOCAL_SERVER | CLSCTX_REMOTE_SERVER,
              pServerInfo, 1, &qi);

      if (SUCCEEDED(hr) && SUCCEEDED(qi.hr))
      {
          // Now get the interface
          m_pMultiServer = (IMultiServer*)qi.pItf;
      }
      else
      {
          m_pMultiServer = NULL;
          CString str;
          str.Format("Cannot get object: 0x%x and QI: 0x%x",
                      hr, qi.hr);
          Message(str);
      }

      // Free the buffer previous allocated
      ::SysFreeString(serverinfo.pwszName);

      return TRUE;  // return TRUE  unless you set the focus to a control
}
```

The **OnDestroy()** handler merely releases the interface.

```
void CMultiClientDlg::OnDestroy()
{
    CDialog::OnDestroy();

    if (m_pMultiServer)
        m_pMultiServer->Release();
}
```

The main work is carried out in the **OnGet()** handler:

```
void CMultiClientDlg::OnGet()
{
    CListBox* pList = (CListBox*)GetDlgItem(IDC_RESULTS);
    ASSERT(pList);

    pList->ResetContent();

    CWnd* pWnd = GetDlgItem(IDC_ELAPSE);
    ASSERT(pWnd);

    UpdateData();

    if (NULL == m_pMultiServer)
    {
        Message(_T("The server interface pointer is NULL"));
        return;
    }

    if (m_nRadio == 0)
    {
        // Send multiple single requests
```

```
    BSTR* array = new BSTR[m_lCount];

    LONG count;
    LONG loop;
    LONG total = 0;

    for (loop = 0; loop < m_lRepeat; loop++)
    {
        DWORD starttime = GetTickCount();

        for (count = 0; count < m_lCount; count++)
        {
            HRESULT hr;
            hr = m_pMultiServer->GetSinglePart(count +
                                m_lStart, &array[count]);
            if (FAILED(hr) || S_FALSE == hr)
            {
                // Cannot connect, update how many
                // items obtained
                CString str;
                UpdateData();
                if (S_FALSE == hr)
                    str.Format("Cannot get item %ld",
                            count + m_lStart);
                else
                    str.Format("Cannot connect: 0x%08x",hr);
                Message(str);
                break;
            }
        }

        DWORD endtime = GetTickCount();

        total += endtime - starttime;

        for (count = 0; count < m_lCount; count++)
        {
            if (array[count])
            {
                CString str(array[count]);
                ::SysFreeString(array[count]);
                if (loop == 0)
                    pList->AddString(str);
            }
        }
    }

    CString str;
    str.Format("That took %.21f milliseconds",
            total/double(m_lRepeat));

    pWnd->SetWindowText(str);

    delete [] array;
}
else
{
    // Send a single multiple request
```

```
   BSTR* array;
   HRESULT hr;
   LONG got;
   DWORD total = 0;
   LONG loop;

   for (loop = 0; loop < m_lRepeat; loop++)
   {
      DWORD starttime = GetTickCount();

      hr = m_pMultiServer->GetMultiplePart(m_lStart,
                            m_lCount, &got, &array);

      DWORD endtime = GetTickCount();

      total += endtime-starttime;

      if (FAILED(hr))
      {
         // Cannot connect, update how many items
         // obtained
         UpdateData();
         CString str;
         str.Format("Cannot connect: 0x%08x",hr);
         Message(str);
         break;
      }

      LONG index;
      for (index = 0; index<got; index++)
      {
         CString str(array[index]);
         ::SysFreeString(array[index]);
         if (loop == 0)
            pList->AddString(str);
      }

      CoTaskMemFree(array);
   }

   CString str;
   str.Format("Obtained %ld items",got);
   Message(str);

   str.Format("That took %.2lf milliseconds",
            total/double(m_lRepeat));

   pWnd->SetWindowText(str);
}
   }
```

This code first checks to see if this is a single or multiple test. If it is a single test, the **GetSinglePart()** is called. Otherwise the **GetMultiplePart()** method is called. **GetSinglePart()** just gets a single value so it is called for each of the required values (the number of strings is given in Count with the first index given in Start). So that more accurate tests can be made, the texts are repeated the number of times given in Repeat. (All these values are accessed through member values.)

For the multiple case, the readings are repeated, but now the method is called on the object just once. In both cases, the calls to the object are timed and the average for the time to get the requested data is calculated and then added to the status control at the bottom of the dialog. Finally, both cases finish with the returned data in an array and this is used to fill the list box and then all the values are released.

Now all you need do is define the **_WIN32_DCOM** preprocessor symbol. Once done, you can compile and run the project. The server uses a custom interface so you will need to register the proxy-stub DLL on both the client and server machine.

Note that when you run the example, only the results from the first pass are shown, the results from subsequent repeats are ignored. Thus when you run the example with a large repeat count, the results in the list box will come back quite quickly, but you will have to wait until the bottom static control has been updated (with the average time of the calls) until you can do another test.

The client code for the single test repeats this call the number of times in the Count edit box, and the time is the time taken to do this number of calls. The client code has been written to time only the calls to the server, and not any clean up code

Results

In the results given below, I have carried out the tests several times, and have presented the average results. The server machine is a 180MHz Pentium Pro with 32 MB of memory running NT 4.0. The client is a 66MHz Pentium with 16 Mb of memory running NT 4.0.

For these tests to work, the data file, **numbers.dat**, must be in a directory that the server can find. If you are launching the server by DCOM then the current directory will be **%SystemRoot%\System32**. If you start the server under a debugger then the current directory is the directory where the server was launched.

Local Calls

It is to be expected that both calls would be fast, but the measurements show that the single call multiple data case is about 10 times faster than making multiple single calls. Note that the lower end of the graph for the multiple case is unreliable since many of the measurements were returning 0 ms.

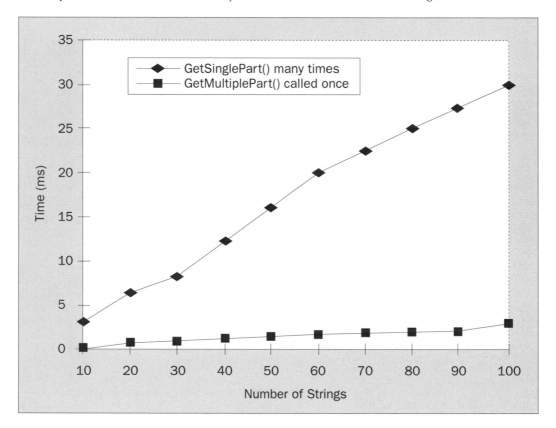

Remote Calls

The following measurements have been taken on a very quiet network. In fact, it was a network of just two machines only running this example software.

As would be expected, the DCOM calls take much longer than the local calls. However, the surprising thing is that the multiple calls of **GetSinglePart()** take about 5 times longer than the **GetMultiplePart()** call, compared to the 10 times achieved in the local case.

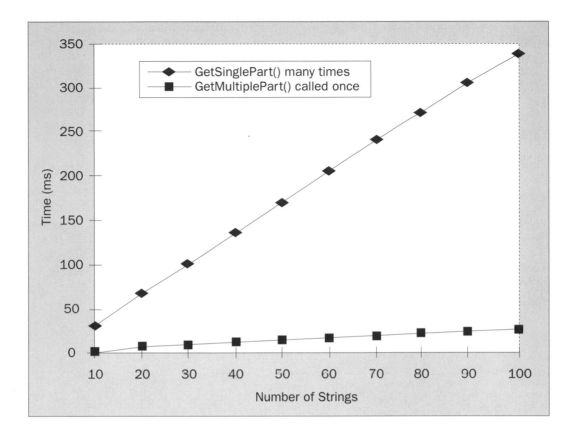

Conclusion

These measurements show that

- DCOM is five to ten times slower than local object calls
- Many single calls are five to ten times slower than a single multiple call.
- The conclusions are that if you want excellent performance then it makes sense to have your objects on the same machine that you want to use them from.

In the example above, the **numbers.dat** data file could be kept on **zeus** in a shared directory and **hera** could have the COM server running locally but accessing the data file remotely. This will get a severe performance hit when the server starts (when it downloads the data from the server) but will give excellent access times to the data. The downside is that such a scheme will assume that the data will be static during the lifetime of the local object.

The second conclusion is that if you are going to have a remote object, design the interface so that the method calls are kept to a minimum. If you look back to the earlier parts of this chapter, you will see that there are many packets involved in making method calls, and a small amount of data will be swamped by the overhead of the DCE packet header and the **ORPCTHAT** DCOM structure. For a method call that returns a large amount of data, the data soon exceeds this overhead.

Another point to bear in mind is that if you are returning *objects* (in effect, pointers to **IUnknown** or **IDispatch** or a custom interface) then each will have a proxy created. There could be an unacceptable overhead involved in the creation of these proxies and in the standard marshaling that they carry out. If possible, use primitive types and if that is not possible, you may have to think about using a custom marshaler.

Summary

This chapter has used several test applications to give you an insight into how DCOM really works. The early tests, where DCOM was compared to DCE RPC, have shown that DCOM really is just an extension to RPC: Microsoft RPC version 2.

The second half of the chapter introduced an interface that allowed you to get many data items as single items through multiple method calls, or as multiple items obtained through a single method call. The results show that the second method is the most efficient in terms of *total* time taken to get all the data, so you should make a careful judgement as to whether you want all the data returned at one time (the multiple item case) or piecemeal over a longer time (the single item case).

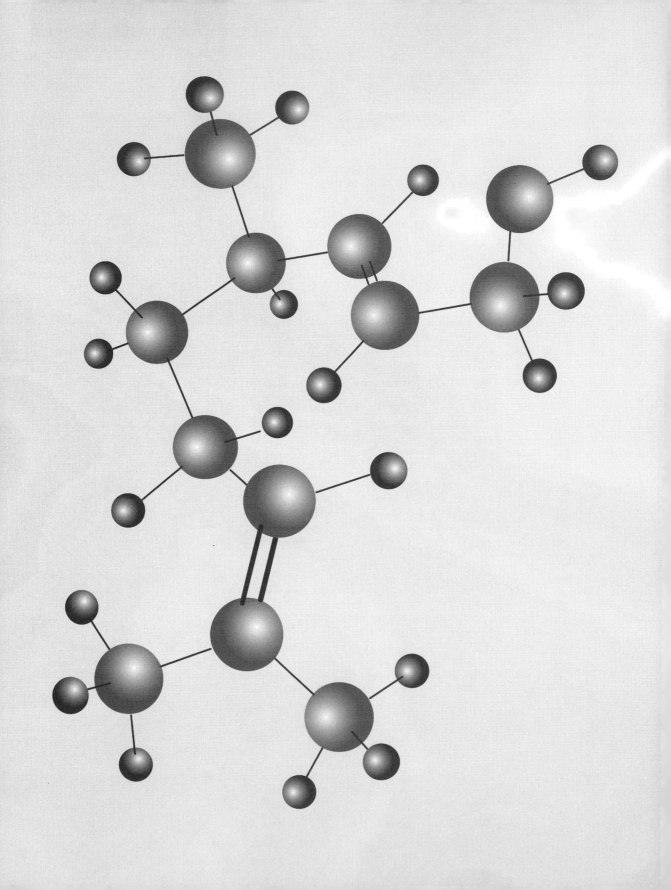

Security

Introduction

Recently a colleague (who will remain nameless to protect his embarrassment) installed NT4. This is usually a fairly painless process and the setup program will make suitable choices for you for most of the process. At one point in the installation, you will be asked to give an administrator's password. My colleague came to me rather timidly (which is unusual for him) and told me that a 'friend' of his had installed NT but had forgotten the administrator's password and so his 'friend' could not log on. Was there a way to change the administrator's password?

My colleague got precisely the answer that he didn't want – *if you forget a password, you cannot get it back, nor can you change it.* Windows NT has the American Department of Defense C2 security clearance and to get this certification it had to pass some stringent criteria. A facility to recover lost administrator's passwords would certainly not allow it to maintain such a security certification!

My colleague was lucky, if he had changed his disk format to NTFS and then saved some files, denying all access to those files except to one user, and then forgotten the user's password, there would be no way to read, write, execute or even delete those files. If you get yourself into this situation and decide to cut your losses and remove the user, you will not be able to recover any data on the disk.

When you run NT for the first time, the biggest difference you will experience between it and other versions of Windows is security. You will be asked to log on and if you do not have an account on the machine or on a **trusted domain**, or if you cannot remember the password of the account then you will not be able to log on. You might as well turn off the machine and read a book, because there is no way that you will get access to that machine.

Under Windows 95 (or even Windows for Workgroups), you will also get a logon box, but if you enter a username and password that is not recognized, the operating system will still happily accept it. The logon box is not used for the operating system, but for the network that the machine is connected to. If you enter a user and an invalid password for that network then you will be denied access to that network's resources, but you will still be able to use the local machine.

Under NT, the logon dialog provides access to the local machine as well as to the network (**domain**) resources. Both logons require a valid user account and password. If you fail to log on to the local machine, you will not be able to use that machine. (Note that NT implements a Guest account that can be enabled on domains to allow logons with an *unknown account* restricted access to domain resources. However, a logon with a recognized account but an invalid password will fail to give access to the domain.)

The security offered by NT protects the local machine from malicious actions: it protects data and software from unauthorized deletion or modification. The selective application of security allows users to manipulate their own files while protecting system or shared files. NT security applied across a Microsoft network extends the concept further, allowing access to resources to some users, while denying it to others.

When you write a DCOM server, the object will run on a machine other than the one on which the client is running. The server will need to access resources on the local machine (or on the domain), so just as an interactive user needs to identify itself as a valid user, so does the DCOM object. Similarly, since the client is accessing the object from another machine, the client must have the correct authority to access the object. Clearly if just anyone was allowed to access objects, there would be a gaping hole in the server machine's security. This implies that both the client and server must implement some form of security.

Originally COM, when implemented as the underlying plumbing for OLE 2.0, had no security. For the single machine case, there appears to be no need. After all, you could argue that this is a single machine, so there can only be one user at a time. When a new process is created, it must be created by that same user, hence if the same user creates the client and server, both processes should have the same security.

However, this argument is flawed: for a start, who actually launches the server? It's not your client. (It is a process called the Service Control Manager, implemented as a service under NT and a Win32 process under Windows 95). In addition, although the client and COM server are on the same machine, the client could easily be a networked server which itself has clients on other machines connected via some other inter-process mechanism (DCE RPC, named pipes or maybe via basic sockets). Imagine for example, a web browser causing a web server to launch a CGI or ISAPI application that, in turn, activates a COM object. Who is the 'client' of the COM object, the web client, the CGI process or something else entirely?

When a client makes a call into a server, the server must be able to verify that the client is who it says it is and it must be able to establish that the client is allowed to issue requests to the server. These two issues, **authenticating** a user and **authorizing** the user's requests, are the responsibility of the security system. DCOM formalizes this; it lays down rules so that you can specify who is the client and thus determine what security is used. Once this is known, the remote client can either specify a username and password, or it can defer to the default username for the server or the system.

Even if we can ensure that the user has access to a particular server, you may decide that not all facilities of the object should be accessible to the user. This is not necessarily because we *distrust* the motives of the user (although sadly, in these paranoid times, it frequently is), but it may be that we wish to *protect* the user from performing actions that they will later regret. Again, this can be achieved through security, allowing system objects to have a list of users that can access them and what these users can do with the object.

Looking at it from the client's perspective, there may also be good reasons why it shouldn't completely trust the server. If the client doesn't trust the server, it may decide that the server should not be able to know who the client is, or if the client trusts the server a little more, it may allow the server to know who it is, but no more. When the client really trusts the server, it will allow the server to use the client's network account to perform actions on its behalf. This level of trust in known as the **impersonation level**.

Just like other objects in NT, administrators will want to keep an eye on how COM objects are being used. A properly written server will keep a log of all the transactions it has performed, this way administrators can determine what the server has been doing, perhaps to tune its performance and identify bottlenecks. The administrator will also want to know who is accessing system objects and, just as important, who has attempted, but *failed*, to access an object. Again this is another task that can be performed by the security subsystem.

Finally, DCOM can be used on many operating systems. Indeed, for it to be useful across a corporate network, it *must* be implemented on many operating systems. This implies that the client and the server machine operating systems may use different security models or one or the other may not use security at all. For distribution to be truly useful, we will require objects to be spread around the network in a manner that makes the users of the objects almost oblivious to the platform that the object is implemented on. Security must be applied in a way that does not depend on a particular operating system.

DCOM uses a replaceable security model whereby a machine exposes its security system to DCOM via a **Security Support Provider Interface** (SSPI). This solves the problem of multiple operating systems with different types and levels of security. NT's default security provider, NTLMSSP, uses SSPI and thus it is replaceable. The Kerberos security system used by DCE RPC is another security provider and is promised in NT 5.0.

This chapter will explain how the operating system's security works with DCOM. Since the most popular operating system will be NT, the main focus will be on NT's security model. The chapter will then follow on with a discussion of how this applies to DCOM.

The Need for Security

In the introduction we saw two terms, **authentication** and **authorization**. In this section we will look at these concepts in more depth and examine ways that we could solve these problems ourselves. This will highlight many problems that have already been overcome by NT security and will give you a greater understanding of the issues we'll be discussing in the following sections.

As an example, suppose we have a server program that gives access to a catalogue information system. The server has direct access to a database with all the catalogue information. The client application makes requests to the server on individual products or groups of products. This current catalogue needs to be made freely available to anyone with the client application. If all potential customers can see all the products in the catalogue, this will encourage them to browse and increase the chance that they will order a product that they were not necessarily intending to buy. Since the server program gives generic access to the database, it is also used by the catalogue compilers to change the information in the catalogue.

The server could be a **PartsCatalogue** coclass with the following interface:

```
interface IPartsCatalogue : IDispatch
{
   [id(1)] HRESULT GetItem([in] LONG itemID,
                           [out] BSTR* itemDescription);
   [id(2)] HRESULT SetItem([in] LONG itemID,
                           [in] BSTR itemDescription);
};
```

However, ordinary customers should be able to view the data, but not have write access to it. Without security, an implementation that relied on just this interface would be disastrous. Anyone would be able to read data from and write data to the database, and a malicious or incompetent user could destroy the database. We could improve on this by only allowing access to the **PartsCatalogue** object through a **SecurePartsCatalogue** object. This object would implement the new interface, **ISecurePartsCatalogue**:

```
interface ISecurePartsCatalogue : IDispatch
{
   [id(1)] HRESULT Logon([in] BSTR userName,
                         [in] BSTR password,
                         [out] IUnknown** ppParts);
};
```

A client would need to call the **Logon()** method with a valid username and password in order to get the **IUnknown** interface to a newly created **PartsCatalogue**. The client could then **QI()** for a pointer to **IPartsCatalogue** to use the methods to read or write data. The **PartsCatalogue** object is made inaccessible by marking its **coclass** in the IDL with the **[restricted]** attribute.

Since the **SecurePartsCatalogue** creates the **PartsCatalogue** object, it can initialize the object with a method **Init()** before returning the object back to the client. Thus the **PartsCatalogue** can obtain the username obtained by **Logon()** and then this can be used when a user calls **GetItem()** to determine the user's access.

The Catalogue Project

I've created a simple project to demonstrate these issues. I will only discuss the interesting code in the sections to come, but you can download the complete project from the Wrox Press web site if you're interested in seeing the whole example working.

The **Catalogue** project was created as an ATL executable project. The only part of the server application that is unusual (compared with the projects created so far) is that it supports two objects, only one of which is createable, and that object is used to create the other one.

To do this, I created an ATL project using the ATL COM AppWizard, and added two simple objects with the Object Wizard, one called **SecurePartsCatalogue** and the other called **PartsCatalogue**. Then using the ClassView in the project workspace window, I added the methods to the **ISecurePartsCatalogue** and **IPartsCatalogue** interfaces according to the IDL given above. The objects have dual interfaces so that we can use them from Visual Basic. To prevent the **PartsCatalogue** object appearing to object browsers I added the **[restricted]** attribute:

```
library CATALOGUELib
{
   importlib("stdole32.tlb");
   importlib("stdole2.tlb");

   [
      uuid(C89F1CDF-9F1F-11D0-9B3A-0060973044A8),
      helpstring("SecurePartsCatalogue Class")
   ]
   coclass SecurePartsCatalogue
   {
      [default] interface ISecurePartsCatalogue;
   };

   [
      uuid(C89F1CE1-9F1F-11D0-9B3A-0060973044A8),
      helpstring("PartsCatalogue Class"),
      restricted
   ]
   coclass PartsCatalogue
   {
      [default] interface IPartsCatalogue;
   };
};
```

CSecurePartsCatalogue looks like this

```
class ATL_NO_VTABLE CSecurePartsCatalogue :
   public CComObjectRootEx<CComSingleThreadModel>,
   public CComCoClass<CSecurePartsCatalogue, &CLSID_SecurePartsCatalogue>,
   public IDispatchImpl<ISecurePartsCatalogue, &IID_ISecurePartsCatalogue,
                    &LIBID_CATALOGUELib>
```

```
{
public:
   CSecurePartsCatalogue() : m_userName(NULL)
   {
   }
   ~CSecurePartsCatalogue()
   {
      if (m_userName)
         ::SysFreeString(m_userName);
   }

   DECLARE_REGISTRY_RESOURCEID(IDR_SECUREPARTSCATALOGUE)

   BEGIN_COM_MAP(CSecurePartsCatalogue)
      COM_INTERFACE_ENTRY(ISecurePartsCatalogue)
      COM_INTERFACE_ENTRY(IDispatch)
   END_COM_MAP()

// ISecurePartsCatalogue
public:
   STDMETHOD(Logon)(/*[in]*/BSTR userName,
                    /*[in]*/BSTR password,
                    /*[out]*/ IUnknown** ppParts);
private:
   BOOL ValidateUser(BSTR userName, BSTR password);
   void Audit(LPWSTR msg);
   BSTR m_userName;
};
```

The **Logon()** method needs to validate the user and, if successful, create a **PartsCatalogue** object. It does this with the following code:

```
STDMETHODIMP CSecurePartsCatalogue::Logon(BSTR userName, BSTR password,
                                          IUnknown * * ppParts)
{
   WCHAR buffer[1024];
   *ppParts = NULL;
   if (userName == NULL || password == 0)
      return E_FAIL;

   if (ValidateUser(userName, password))
   {
      // Now create the object
      if (m_userName)
         ::SysFreeString(m_userName);
      m_userName = ::SysAllocString(userName);
      typedef CComObject<CPartsCatalogue> PartsCat;
      PartsCat* ppcat = new PartsCat();
      if (ppcat == NULL)
         return E_OUTOFMEMORY;
      else
      {
         HRESULT hRes;
         hRes = ppcat->Init(userName, password);
         if (SUCCEEDED(hRes))
            hRes = ppcat->QueryInterface(IID_IUnknown, (void**)ppParts);
         else if (FAILED(hRes))
```

```
        {
            delete ppcat;
            return hRes;
        }
    }
    return S_OK;
}
else
{
    wsprintfW(buffer, L"%s failed to logon: invalid user", userName);
    Audit(buffer);
    return E_FAIL;
}
}
```

First we save the user name, so that it can be used in the **Audit()** method when logging events and then the **ValidateUser()** method is called to check that the user can access the database. In this example, the method **ValidateUser()** will return **TRUE** if the username and password are the same. If the user is valid, the **Logon()** method then creates a new **PartsCatalogue** object by creating a new **CComObject<>** object with our C++ class name as the template parameter. If this is successful, we call its **Init()** method to initialize the object and then get its **IUnknown** interface and pass this back to the client.

CPartsCatalogue::Init() is implemented like this:

```
HRESULT CPartsCatalogue::Init(BSTR userName, BSTR password)
{
    WCHAR buffer[1024];
    // Only allow one user to access the database
    m_onlyUser = CreateMutex(NULL, TRUE, _T("PARTS_CATALOGUE"));
    m_pList = new CPartsList(_T("Parts.dat"));

    if (NULL == m_pList)
    {
        wsprintfW(buffer, L"%s failed to logon: cannot create list",
                userName);
        Audit(buffer);
        return E_FAIL;
    }

    UINT len = SysStringLen(userName);
    m_userName = new WCHAR[len + 1];
    wcscpy(m_userName, userName);

    len = SysStringLen(password);
    m_password = new WCHAR[len + 1];
    wcscpy(m_password, password);

    Audit(L"logged on");

    return S_OK;
}
```

CPartsList is a class that holds a linked list of parts (IDs and descriptions). The parts list is created using the name of the database file. The actual linked list is created in the constructor for **CPartsList** which reads the data from the file. The contents of the list are written back to the file in the destructor of **CPartsList**, and this is called when the **CPartsList** object is destroyed in the **CPartsCatalogue** destructor.

To ensure that only one user can access the database at any one time, a Win32 mutex is created in **Init()** and released in the destructor. That only one user can use the database is very restrictive. This is a design fault of this particular implementation, but it has no bearing on the discussion that follows about security. The point of this example is not how to write a database!

The **GetItem()** method searches the list, calling the **Find()** method on the **m_pList** object and if successful, it returns the description of the part. **SetItem()** calls the **Insert()** method on the list. Since we want everyone to access the database, every user should be able to use the **GetItem()** method. However, only privileged users should be able to change the database. So when the user calls **SetItem()**, a check is made to see whether the user is authorized. In this case, the **AuthorizedUser()** function allows any users whose name begins with **'R'** to add items to the database:

```
STDMETHODIMP CPartsCatalogue::SetItem(LONG itemID, BSTR itemDescription)
{
    WCHAR buffer[1024];

    if (!AuthorizedUser(FALSE))
    {
        wsprintfW(buffer,
                L"Failed to SetItem %ld, '%s': user not authorized",
                itemID, itemDescription);
        Audit(buffer);
        return E_FAIL;
    }

    if (m_pList->Insert(itemID, itemDescription))
    {
        wsprintfW(buffer, L"SetItem %ld, '%s'", itemID, itemDescription);
        Audit(buffer);
        return S_OK;
    }
    else
    {
        wsprintfW(buffer,
                L"Failed to SetItem %ld, '%s': cannot Insert item",
                itemID, itemDescription);
        Audit(buffer);
        return E_OUTOFMEMORY;
    }
}
```

Both **CSecurePartsCatalogue** and **CPartsCatalogue** implement an **Audit()** method. Whenever an event occurs, **Audit()** is called to add a message to the audit log. This method adds the date, the time, the currently logged on user's name, and the message to the audit file **Parts.log** held in the root directory.

```
void CPartsCatalogue::Audit(LPWSTR msg)
{
    USES_CONVERSION;

    HANDLE hfile;
    hfile = CreateFile(_T("\\parts.log"), GENERIC_WRITE, 0, NULL,
                        OPEN_ALWAYS, 0, 0);

    if (INVALID_HANDLE_VALUE == hfile)
        return;
```

```
    SetFilePointer(hfile, 0, NULL, FILE_END);

    SYSTEMTIME st;
    GetLocalTime(&st);

    // Do it all in wide chars
    WCHAR buffer[1024] = {0};
    DWORD towrite;
    towrite = 2 * wsprintfW(buffer,
        L"[%04d-%02d-%02d %02d:%02d:%02d]%s %s\r\n",
        st.wYear, st.wMonth, st.wDay, st.wHour, st.wMinute, st.wSecond,
        m_userName, msg);

    DWORD written;
    DWORD offset = 0;

    do
    {
        WriteFile(hfile, buffer + offset, towrite, &written, NULL);
        offset += written;
        towrite -= written;
    }
    while (written > 0);

    CloseHandle(hfile);
}
```

Client

The client is a simple Visual Basic application. When the user runs the client application, they see the following dialog box:

Catalogue Test

Logon	Username	
Get	Password	
Add	0	

The **Load** event of the form does a **CreateObject()** on the ProgID **"SecurePartsCatalogue.SecurePartsCatalogue.1"**. The **ISecurePartsCatalogue** interface is given as the default interface of the **coclass**, so we can call the **Logon()** method of this interface without any messing about. This is done when the user presses the Logon button. If the username and password are valid, the Logon button is disabled and the Add and Get buttons are enabled. The user can then type in an ID and press Get to get the description of the item, or type in an ID and a description and press Add to add it to the database. If an error occurs (the logon information is invalid, or the server cannot find an item, or add it to the database), a description of the error appears at the bottom of the dialog.

Catalogue Test

Logon	Username	Bill_Gates
Get	Password	xxxxxxxxxx
Add	456789	
Cannot Find Item		

326

Here the user has logged on successfully (the password is the same as the username), but the server cannot find part number 456789.

Now when we use the object, we can *authenticate* the user to make sure that they can use the interface. In this simple example, the authentication routine checks to see if the username and password are the same, but we could be a little more secure and use some database of usernames and passwords or a more sophisticated algorithm to validate the password.

When the user tries to read or write an item, we must check that the user is *authorized* to do it. This simple example just checks to see if their username begins with `'R'`, but an alternative scheme could be used.

Finally, whenever an event occurs, we *audit* the action by logging it to a file.

So we have fulfilled most of the requirements for our security system: we can authenticate users, authorize them, and audit their actions. But look at the code that was required to do it. If we write another application that needs similar security then all that code will be replicated. If we have a persistent store of users, we would need a method of specifying which user had which permissions on what program and the auditing is particularly troublesome since it requires the programmer to explicitly place **Audit()** calls in the code, and there is no way of turning off auditing wholly or partially.

We haven't even considered the case of large-scale networks with many thousands of users spread over large geographic areas and thus the problem of providing means for databases of permitted users to be managed in such a system.

In fact the major problem of this implementation is that the onus of security is placed upon the application. Usernames and passwords should be the responsibility of the operating system, only the security checks should be the responsibility of the object that is being accessed.

Imagine a C++ class that is the base class of all objects that are protected by security:

```
class SecureObject
{
public:
   SecureObject();
   virtual ~SecureObject();
   virtual BOOL Create(LPCTSTR userName, LPCTSTR password);
   virtual BOOL Delete();
   virtual DWORD DoWork(LPVOID param) = 0;
protected:
   void Audit(LPCTSTR msg);
};
```

This is an abstract base class. The object could be created by calling the **Create()** function which takes the username and password of the client wishing to use the object. The object implementor could write their own **Create()** function to call the base class version which would authenticate the user and then using the username and a central repository of audit information audit the action. Similarly, when the user has finished with the object, the **Delete()** method would be called. This would have code specific to the object type as well as calling the base class implementation to audit the action. Finally the actual work of the object would be carried out in the **DoWork()** function that the programmer *must* implement. Now the object manages its own security, using services provided to all objects.

This is essentially the situation with NT security. NT provides some basic executive object types that have security properties that you can use in your application. These object types use a centralized object security (user permissions and auditing) through a system process called the **Security Manager**. All accesses to these objects are checked against a list of users that can or cannot access the object and then the action is checked against a list of actions that should or should not be audited.

Furthermore, to enable users from across the network to use an object, NT security implements a domain model where many machines share a dynamic database of **trusted** users.

NT security applied to DCOM allows this idea to be extended further by allowing you to define new object types and then get the Security Manager to manage who can or cannot access objects of that type.

Now that we've seen why the operating system should help provide security, let's summarize the main reasons for applying security:

Protecting Servers from Users

Protecting servers from users is, perhaps, the main use for security. Servers provide functionality and will perform the specified tasks only if authenticated users are authorized for that task.

Protecting Users from Servers

Unsuspecting users could be tricked into providing personal or financial information to a server program acting like the server that the client application intended. If the spoof server is written well enough, it will look like the real server; providing appropriate responses to the clients' requests until its dastardly deed is done.

What is required is a mechanism where the client can be assured that the server is who it says it is. This is similar to the case of the client being able to prove that it is who it says it is and is another case of authentication.

Protecting Users from Themselves

Let's look at another example. Imagine you have a configuration file (like **System.ini** in 16-bit Windows), that contains system information about hardware configuration settings and software drivers. Normally a user would not want to change these settings, but the machine administrator would, especially when installing new hardware or software.

If a non-technical user does have access to this file, and decides to change some settings (maybe they are based in the UK and, in a spontaneous burst of jingoism, decide to change all references of '**Color**' to '**Colour**'), this could really mess up the machine, perhaps making it unusable. Such people need protecting from themselves.

The configuration file object should have a list of users who can access it, and the level of access those users have. The NT registry, for example, applies security to its keys, only allowing appropriate users to access them. This sort of protection is known as authorization.

Ringing Alarm Bells

Finally, if the user can get authorization to call server methods, it can then obtain information, and perhaps change the internal state of the server. The ability to audit these actions allows an administrator to keep an audit trail of who is using the server and the changes that are made. Audits should also keep information about unsuccessful as well as successful events.

The NT Security Model

The last section, I hope, has whetted your appetite for a description of how security is applied in NT. This section will explain the security model and describe how it works. I'll start by explaining the main terms and I'll show how these map to things that you, as an NT user, can see when you log on.

Accounts

The most important thing that you need when you log onto an NT machine is an account. On a standalone workstation the account is specific to the machine and is held in a database called the **Security Accounts Manager** (**SAM**). This database holds all the accounts and groups local to this machine. When a user logs on with an account, the logon is authorized by the **Local Security Authority** (**LSA**). LSA uses SAM to validate the account and password and once the user is validated, it gives the user access to the system.

An administrator creates accounts using the User Manager. When given the details of a new account, it will generate a unique ID that will identify the account whenever the account is used to access and secure resources (such as NT objects or remote resources).

The SAM is a secure part of the system registry. Normally you do not have direct access to the SAM. (There are some Win32 functions to access account information, as we will see later.) If you are interested, one place you can conveniently see the SAM is in the repair disk information that is made automatically when you install NT, or is made when you run the **rdisk.exe** utility (found in the **system32** folder).

This information is saved in the **repair** folder of your NT folder in a compressed format that can be saved to the repair disk. One of these files is the **sam._** file that contains the SAM database. You can use the **expand** utility to expand this file and use a hex file viewer to look at the information. Although you will see account names and descriptions, you will not see plain text passwords. These are saved in a doubly encrypted format.

When a user on another machine wants to use a resource on a remote machine, that user must have access to an account on the remote machine. If the user gives a valid account but an invalid password, SAM cannot validate the account and so the user cannot access the resource. However, if the user gives the name of an account that is not known by SAM, it will give the user access using the built in **Guest** account.

There are a number of built-in accounts that are used for various purposes:

Account	Description
Administrator	The highest level account that has full access to the system. On some machines the human administrator may have renamed this account to something not so obvious to hide make it less obvious to hackers. It cannot be deleted or disabled.
Guest	This is the 'default' account that gives restricted access to the system. Even though, by default, it has few permissions, you should review carefully whether you really do need it. Note that NT 4.0 Service Pack 2 allows the **Guest** account to launch a remote object.

Table Continued on Following Page

Account	Description
System	This is only used by the system, you cannot logon interactively as the system account, nor can you disable, delete or edit it. The system account has unlimited power on the local machine, but has no access to network resources. Typically this account is used by system services.

Workgroups

Single NT machines can be grouped together into administrative groups called **Workgroups**. These do not extend the security model beyond that of the single NT machines. Workgroups are a peer-to-peer model where a user on one machine gets access to remote resources by logging on with an account on that remote machine.

A more powerful security model is the one that is used when you introduce an NT Server into your network: the NT Domain Model.

Domains

Whereas Workgroups are peer to peer (each machine is equal), the Domain model has a hierarchy of clients and servers. To create an NT domain, you need at least one NT Server to manage **domain accounts**. This server is called the **Primary Domain Controller** (**PDC**). If there is more than one NT Server in a domain then these can be **Backup Domain Controllers** (**BDC**) or just members of the domain.

A PDC holds domain accounts, and these accounts are valid on *all* machines that are part of the domain (unlike local accounts, which are valid only on the local machine). The PDC maintains a database of domain accounts and authenticates users when they log onto the domain.

The BDCs hold copies of the domain accounts, and can also authenticate users. This reduces network traffic and the load on the PDC. As its name suggests, a BDC can backup the action of a PDC if it fails. However BDCs do not maintain accounts, instead they are updated periodically from the PDC.

The NT logon dialog has a dropdown list box marked Domain, which gives the names of any domains that you have access to, as well as the name of the local machine. If you select the local machine, the Local Security Authority of that machine is used to authenticate the account that you type in. If you select a domain, the account is authenticated on the domain server, whether it's the PDC or a BDC. Once the domain has authenticated the account, it logs you on to the local machine with this *domain account*.

Logging on with a domain account allows the user to access any machine on the network that allows access to domain users. The resource machine gets authentication from the domain, so it doesn't have to fill its own SAM with permitted user accounts.

Trusted Domains

If one domain **trusts** another, it allows access to its resources to members of the other domain. In the diagram below, you can see that the **LONDON** domain trusts the **PARIS** domain, so users with accounts in the **PARIS** domain can use resources controlled by machines in the **LONDON** domain. If a user in the **PARIS** domain wants access to a resource in the **LONDON** domain, **LONDON** asks **PARIS** to authenticate the user. If **PARIS** says that the user is valid, **LONDON** will trust this judgment.

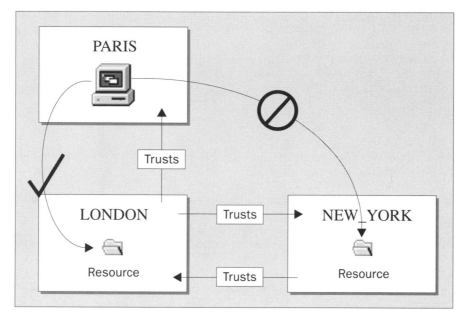

Trust relationships are one way unless explicitly set to be two way. Users in the **LONDON** domain can't access resources in **PARIS** because **PARIS** doesn't trust **LONDON**. **LONDON** and **NEW_YORK** have a two way trust relationship, so users in either domain can access resources in the other.

Trust relationships are not transitive, so users from **PARIS** can't access resources in **NEW_YORK**, despite the fact that **NEW_YORK** trusts **LONDON**, and **LONDON** trusts **PARIS**. **NEW_YORK** must trust **PARIS** directly if it wants to let **PARIS** accounts access its resources.

This process of one domain trusting another domain, and passing authentication of users to the trusted domain, is called **pass-through authentication**.

Domain Account != Local Account

Note that domain accounts and local (machine) accounts are completely distinct. Even if a local account has the same name and password as a domain account, the two accounts are different. If you log on to an NT 4.0 machine with a domain account, you will get a different desktop to the one used by the local account: any shortcuts that you make for the local account will not necessarily be visible on the desktop of the domain account.

Similarly, don't expect to get administrator privileges on the local machine if you log on with a domain account that just so happens to have the same name as a local administrator account. By default, any domain account will not be an administrator, so you will not have that access on the local machine. You can log on as a local administrator and then make the domain account an administrator of the local machine, but this illustrates the fact that the two accounts are separate even though they have the same name.

For this reason, you will often find an account prefixed with the security authority where it is valid. This can be the domain or the local machine, depending on whether it is a domain or local account. For example on the **ROUNCIL_DOMAIN** domain there may be an account called **RichardGrimes**, so this is often referred to as **ROUNCIL_DOMAIN\RichardGrimes**. There may be a machine in the **ROUNCIL_DOMAIN** domain called **Zeus** that also has an account called **RichardGrimes** and this is referred to as **Zeus\RichardGrimes**. This combination of a security authority and account is known as a **security principal**.

Groups

Groups are a convenient method of collecting accounts together so that their abilities (such as access to particular resources) can be more easily administrated.

For example, suppose you are a system administrator and you have a monochrome laser printer and a color laser printer available for your advertising department. You may decide that those people who design your adverts need to see color proofs of their ads, so they should be allowed access to the color printer. However, the people responsible for buying advertising space only need to print reports, so they can make do with black and white.

You would have a group, perhaps called **AdvertisingDesigners**, which would group together the accounts of the designers, and another group, **AdvertisingBuyers**, to group the accounts of the buyers. You would simply give access to the color printer to the **AdvertisingDesigners** group, and access to the monochrome printer to the **AdvertisingBuyers** group.

Once you've set up a sensible system of groups, administration becomes easy. When a new resource is obtained, the members of a group can be allowed use of the resource in a single stroke. This is considerably less work than going through all the users on the system and deciding who can use a particular resource.

This adds more flexibility to the administration of the system. As users are added to the system, they are also added to particular groups. The rights of the group can be defined at a particular point in time or can evolve over a length of time.

You can create a group and add users to a group using the NT User Manager. A group is identified internally using a security ID, like user accounts.

Don't be confused by groups and user accounts that have similar names. For example the **Administrators** group has particular rights to allow members of this group to administer the system (creating users and installing device drivers, for example). Any user can be made a member of this group, but obviously you will want to restrict its membership. The **Administrator** account is a built-in account that has administrator's rights but cannot be deleted or disabled (this is so that there is always at least one administrator). The two are different: one is a group, the other is a user account.

> NT 4.0 extends the terminology by introducing the term trustee. A trustee is an account to which the system can give rights and thus could be a user or a group. There is a new API built up around trustees and the TRUSTEE structure that acts on a higher programming level than the NT 3.51 security API.

Security IDs

As I've mentioned, **security IDs** (**SIDs**) are unique IDs used to identify users or groups of users. When a user is created on a machine or domain, a unique SID is created to identify that user.

A SID contains the following data:

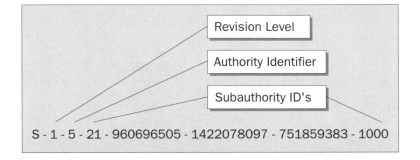

Here the SID **S-1-5-21-960696505-1422078097-751859383-1000** is broken into its constituent parts. The **S** identifies this as a SID. The first item is the revision level for the issuing authority, which depends on version of the security authority and the second item is the identifier for that authority (**SECURITY_NT_AUTHORITY**). After the authority are the **relative IDs** (**RIDs**) that describe sub-authority values, 32-bit values that uniquely identify the user or group. Security authorities only ever issue a RID once. This example has 5 subauthority values starting with **21**.

If you look up SID in the Win32 help, you'll not get much information since Microsoft does not intend you to manipulate SIDs directly, however the **Winnt.h** header defines **SID** as:

```
typedef struct _SID_IDENTIFIER_AUTHORITY
{
    BYTE   Value[6];
} SID_IDENTIFIER_AUTHORITY, *PSID_IDENTIFIER_AUTHORITY;


typedef struct _SID
{
  BYTE   Revision;
  BYTE   SubAuthorityCount;
  SID_IDENTIFIER_AUTHORITY IdentifierAuthority;
#ifdef MIDL_PASS
  [size_is(SubAuthorityCount)] DWORD SubAuthority[*];
#else // MIDL_PASS
  DWORD SubAuthority[ANYSIZE_ARRAY];
#endif // MIDL_PASS
} SID, *PISID;
```

The following table gives some of the authority values that can be used:

Authority Value	Description
SECURITY_NULL_SID_AUTHORITY	NULL authority: no members
SECURITY_WORLD_SID_AUTHORITY	All users

Authority Value	Description
`SECURITY_LOCAL_SID_AUTHORITY`	Local users
`SECURITY_CREATOR_SID_AUTHORITY`	Creator of objects
`SECURITY_NT_AUTHORITY`	The NT security authority

RIDs can be:

`SECURITY_NULL_RID`

`SECURITY_WORLD_RID`

`SECURITY_LOCAL_RID`

`SECURITY_CREATOR_OWNER_RID`

`SECURITY_CREATOR_GROUP_RID`

These RIDs can be combined with the authority values to produce well known SIDs (which also have constants in **Winnt.h**):

SID	Name	Description
`S-1-0-0`	Null SID	No one
`S-1-1-0`	World	Everyone
`S-1-2-0`	Local	Local users
`S-1-3-0`	Creator Owner ID	Creator of objects
`S-1-3-1`	Creator Group ID	Primary group ID of the object creator
`S-1-5-1`	Dialup	A user who dials up via a modem
`S-1-5-2`	Network	A user who logons on across a network
`S-1-5-3`	Batch	A user logging on via a batch queue facility
`S-1-5-4`	Interactive	Users logging on for interactive access
`S-1-5-6`	Service	An account authorized for security services
`S-1-5-5-X-Y`	Logon IDs	A logon session.
`S-1-5-0x12`	LocalSystem	The account used by the operating system
`S-1-5-0x15-...`	NT non-unique IDs	IDs for NT user accounts
`S-1-5-0x20`	Built-in domain	This is the built-in system domain

You can find the user SID in the system registry under **HKEY_USERS**:

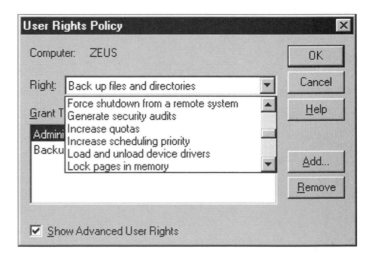

As you will see later, Win32 provides many functions to manipulate SIDs.

Privileges and User Rights

Up to this point we have seen how users are identified on a system or a domain, however we have not seen what those users can do and how the system enforces restrictions on that, so we'll start to look at that now.

The abilities of a user are split into **privileges** and **permissions**. Since permissions are granted on a per-object basis, we'll look at them after we've discussed precisely what an NT object is. For now, we'll just consider privileges.

Privileges are given out by the system administrator to allow particular users certain abilities. Privileges are settings that affect how a user or group can interact with the system, they don't affect how the user interacts with any particular object. You change the privileges for each user or group with the NT User Manager (where, confusingly, they are identified as User Rights).

You can bring up the dialog shown here to change the privileges for a user or group by selecting the Policies | User Rights... menu item:

You can see all the available privileges by checking the Show Advanced User Rights check box near the bottom of the dialog. Note that these privileges are tucked away in a dialog that is not used very often, because these are privileges that should be kept only for special users.

AccessTokens

When a user logs on, they get an access token, and this describes the privileges that the user holds. Each privilege is a 64-bit number called a **locally unique identifier** (**LUID**), which is unique on the local machine, but not necessarily across machines. To identify a privilege globally, each has a string representation, and in the Win32 API you can either use a LUID or the string:

Privilege Constant	Privilege
SE_ASSIGNPRIMARYTOKEN_NAME	Assign the primary token of a process.
SE_AUDIT_NAME	Generate audit-log entries.
SE_BACKUP_NAME	Perform backup operations.
SE_CHANGE_NOTIFY_NAME	Receive notifications of changes to files or directories.
SE_CREATE_PAGEFILE_NAME	Create a paging file.
SE_CREATE_PERMANENT_NAME	Create a permanent object.
SE_CREATE_TOKEN_NAME	Create a primary token.
SE_DEBUG_NAME	Debug a process.
SE_INC_BASE_PRIORITY_NAME	Increase the base priority of a process.
SE_INCREASE_QUOTA_NAME	Increase the quota assigned to a process.
SE_LOAD_DRIVER_NAME	Load or unload a device driver.
SE_LOCK_MEMORY_NAME	Lock physical pages in memory.
SE_PROF_SINGLE_PROCESS_NAME	Gather profiling information for a single process.
SE_REMOTE_SHUTDOWN_NAME	Shut down a system using a network request.
SE_RESTORE_NAME	Restore operations.
SE_SECURITY_NAME	Identifies its holder as a security operator.
SE_SHUTDOWN_NAME	Shut down a local system.
SE_SYSTEM_ENVIRONMENT_NAME	Modify the non-volatile RAM of systems.
SE_SYSTEM_PROFILE_NAME	Gather profiling information for the entire system.
SE_SYSTEMTIME_NAME	Modify the system time.
SE_TAKE_OWNERSHIP_NAME	Take ownership of an object without being granted discretionary access.
SE_TCB_NAME	Identifies its holder as part of the trusted computer base.
SE_UNSOLICITED_INPUT_NAME	Read unsolicited input from a terminal device.

Since a user can be a member of several groups, which are identified by SIDs, an access token also contains all the SIDs relevant to that user. If a SID is a driver's license that identifies a person, and the person's library card, video club card and supermarket loyalty club card are the equivalent to group SIDs, then an access token is the equivalent of a wallet containing the license and all these club cards. The wallet not only identifies the person, but also *describes* the person. The access token describes what the logged on user can do.

An access token is given to a user when they successfully log on to NT. When a user launches a process, the process will get this access token, indicating what the process can do. This combination of process and user access token is known as a **subject**. A subject is said to be running in the **security context** of the user.

We can identify two types of subject: **simple subjects**, where a process has the context of the user that started it; and **server subjects** where there may be several clients with different security settings using the process. This last type is important since it is the situation with NT services. Such a server will have its own security context (the **primary ID**) and when a client (with the **client ID**) contacts the server (through some inter-process communication method like RPC or named pipes), the server will try to ascertain if the client has the authority to perform the task. It does this through **client impersonation**, where the server will impersonate, and hence gain the security context of, the client.

Impersonation

A server program is created using its own access token and hence runs under a specific security context. When a client connects to the server, it will request a service, however, the server will not necessarily want the client to have the same access to objects as it has. For example, in the Catalogue program, some users have read-only access and others have read and write access.

So that the server can behave in the right manner, it can **impersonate** the client. The server can then use the Win32 API to determine what sort of accesses it has on the object and if they match those needed to perform the requested action, the process can continue. Otherwise, it can return an appropriate error back to the client. Although the server impersonates the client, it can still check the access token to find its actual identity. Auditing also shows that the server is impersonating a client.

NT Objects

The NT operating system is a client-server system based upon objects. The definition of an object is different from that used by languages like C++ and certainly different from what COM thinks is an object. An object is an instance of an NT system **object type** and an object type defines **object attributes** and **object services** for this type.

Under NT all objects are controlled by the **object manager,** which is part of the NT executive. The object manager is responsible for creating, deleting, protecting and tracking objects. By centralizing these actions to a single process, NT can monitor objects' resource usage and the access to these objects from one place.

An object's **attributes** define the state of the object much like data members define the state of a C++ object. The object **services** act upon these attributes, like C++ object methods. Note that, like COM, the attributes of an NT object cannot be accessed directly. They can only be accessed via an object service.

Object attributes are one of two types: they are either in the **object header**, which means that they are the stock attributes that all objects must have, or they are in the **object body**, which means that data is specific to this particular object type. The object manager acts upon the attributes in the object header in a type-independent way. The header contains those attributes that identify the object (its name and type for example) and define its current usage (a reference count of the object, and a database of the processes using the object).

The object manager provides several services that apply to all objects:

Service	Description
Close	Close the handle on an object
Duplicate	Duplicate an object's handle so that it can be used by another process
Query Object	Gets information about an object's header attributes
Query Security	Gets an object's security descriptor
Set Security	Changes the object's security descriptor
Wait for single object	Synchronizes a thread with a single object
Wait for multiple objects	Synchronizes a thread with multiple objects

These are the default services that objects implement, and two of these are specifically concerned with **security descriptors**. Security descriptors basically define who can access an object, what actions are audited, and who owns the object. We'll look in more detail at security descriptors shortly. In addition to these services, an object will have specific object type-dependent services.

NT provides several object types, implemented by the NT executive, which are accessible by the NT subsystems in user mode (in other words, your process). These are called **executive objects** and in general map to the objects of the same name provided by the Win32 API. Executive objects are based on lower level objects called **kernel objects** that are implemented in the NT kernel.

Here are some executive objects:

Object	Description
Process	A program. This holds information about the resources used by the program
Thread	A thread of execution within a process
File	An opened file of I/O device

These map to the Win32 entities of processes, threads and files. In addition, named pipes and mailslots are also based upon executive file objects. The significant thing about this table is that every process that you create, and every thread in that process, leads to the object manager creating an executive object, allocating the necessary resources, and giving that object a security descriptor. Like it or not, when you create a process in NT, there is security attached to that process.

Processes can either create or gain access to other objects. When a process requests that a new object is created, the object manager will allocate the resources for the object and create it, giving it a **security descriptor** and placing a reference to the object in the **object directory**. The object directory is part of the universal object namespace on an NT machine. This means objects can have names to allow them to be shared between processes.

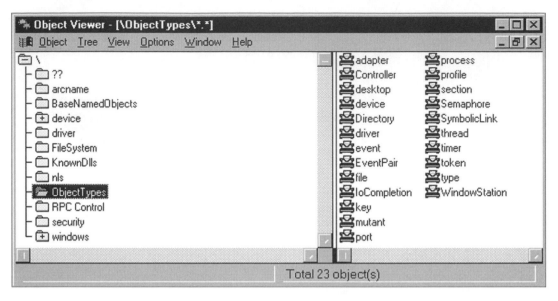

This picture shows the Object Viewer, which is a tool supplied with the Win32 SDK, the right hand pane shows the object types provided by NT.

Finally, when the object is created, the object manager will return a **handle**. All access to an object is via this handle; you cannot access an executive object without the object's handle. Handles, however, may be duplicated so that they can be passed around between processes and threads. If a process spawns another process, the new process may inherit handles from its creator.

This may sound a little too free and easy. You may be worried that if you can create a named object then another process could access that object using the object namespace and change it, perhaps in a way that you would not want. However, the security descriptor can prevent that.

Security Descriptors

Every NT object has a **security descriptor** as one of its attributes. This security descriptor is applied to the object when the object is created. The SD may be explicit, or it may be implicit, inherited from the process that created the object.

A security descriptor essentially defines the **permissions**, the **auditing**, and the **ownership** of an object. For example, files on an NTFS partition have a security descriptor. You can change this descriptor by using Explorer to bring up the property sheet for a file then selecting the Security tab. The buttons on this page give you access to dialogs that can alter the security descriptor for that file.

A security descriptor has four parts

Item	Description
Owner SID	The user or group that owns the object. This user can change the ACL for the object.
Group SID	Not used by Win32, but is used by POSIX.
Discretionary ACL	Identifies which users or groups that can be granted or denied particular access permissions. DACLs are controlled by the object's owner.
System ACL	Controls which auditing messages the system will generate. SACLs are controlled by security administrators.

Access control lists (**ACLs**) are lists of **access control entries** (**ACEs**). There are three types of ACE, **access-allowed**, **access-denied**, and **system-audit**. Access-allowed and access-denied ACEs are linked together in the **discretionary access control list** (**DACL**). System-audit ACEs are linked together in the **system access control list** (**SACL**). An ACE just relates an **access mask** to a particular user or group and determines whether the rights are to be allowed (access-allowed ACE), denied (access-denied ACE) or audited (system-audit ACE).

An access mask is simply a collection of access rights. An **access right** defines a particular set of abilities that can be granted or denied to a process when it attempts to use an object. There are generic, standard and specific rights. Generic rights are defined by NT as:

Right	Description
GENERIC_ALL	Read, write, and execute access
GENERIC_EXECUTE	Execute access
GENERIC_READ	Read access
GENERIC_WRITE	Write access

As these are so generic, it is up to the object what they mean. Some may even be meaningless for some objects.

Standard rights are more specific and affect access to the security descriptor of the object:

Right	Description
DELETE	Delete access.
READ_CONTROL	Read access to the security descriptor
STANDARD_RIGHTS_ALL	Combines **DELETE**, **READ_CONTROL**, **WRITE_DAC**, **WRITE_OWNER**, and **SYNCHRONIZE** access.
STANDARD_RIGHTS_EXECUTE	Currently defined to equal **READ_CONTROL**.
STANDARD_RIGHTS_READ	Currently defined to equal **READ_CONTROL**.
STANDARD_RIGHTS_REQUIRED	Combines **DELETE**, **READ_CONTROL**, **WRITE_DAC**, and **WRITE_OWNER** access.
STANDARD_RIGHTS_WRITE	Currently defined to equal **READ_CONTROL**.
SYNCHRONIZE	Synchronize access. Allows a thread to wait for the object.
WRITE_DAC	Write access to the DACL.
WRITE_OWNER	Write access to the owner.

Specific rights depend on the type of object.

Different object types have different types of permissions that can be set in an ACE. Also, some objects are containers of objects, and this means that the objects that they contain may inherit the permissions of the container (for example, the files in a directory may inherit the read permission of a directory, but the file owner can change this permission).

Note that an *empty* DACL means that no access is granted so access is implicitly denied. However an object that has *no* DACL, has no protection, so all access is granted.

The following is an example of a file object:

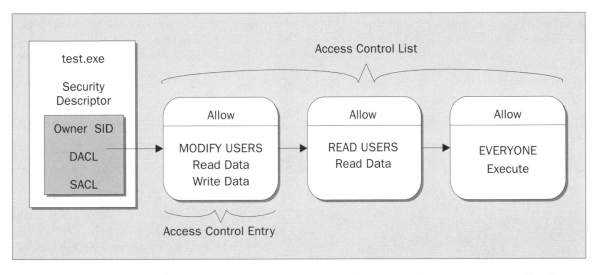

Here we have three groups, (**MODIFY_USERS**, **READ_USERS** and **EVERYONE**) given access to a file object, **Test.exe**. The groups are set up so that every user that has access to the machine is a member of the **EVERYONE** group, so these security settings mean that everyone can execute **Test.exe**. However, getting access to read the file, as binary data, is only granted to the **READ_USERS** and the **MODIFY_USERS** groups, and access to change the file is only granted to members of the **MODIFY_USERS** group.

Summary

The following diagram summarizes the various objects as structures used in NT security.

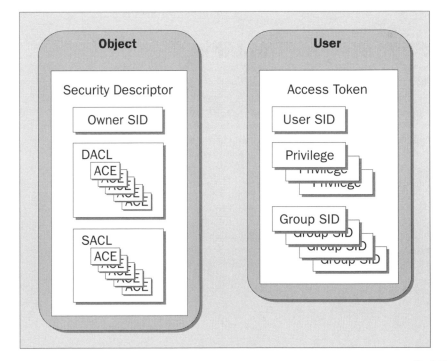

Accessing Objects

Now we have the two halves of the object interaction, the access token of the user, identifying the user and the groups that the user belongs to, and the object's security descriptor that identifies what particular users and groups can (or cannot) do to it. Accessing an object requires the user to specify the type of access that is required and then the system compares the DACL of the object's security descriptor with the values in the user's access token to see if the user has that permission. This can be quite a lengthy process; however, NT does optimize this by ordering access-denied ACEs before access-allowed ACEs.

The comparison process, performed by the system, is:

- ▲ The SID in the ACE is compared with the SIDs in the user's access token. If there is a mismatch, the next ACE is examined.

- ▲ If access is denied, the system checks to see if the desired access contained only a **READ_CONTROL** and/or a **WRITE_DAC**. If this is so, and the requestor is the owner of the object, access is granted.

- ▲ For an access-denied ACE, the desired access mask is compared with the accesses in the ACE. If any match, access is denied and processing stops. Otherwise processing continues with the next ACE.

- ▲ For an access-allowed ACE, the desired access mask is compared with the accesses in the ACE. If *all* accesses in the desired mask are matched, access is allowed and processing stops. Otherwise processing continues with the next ACE.

- ▲ If the end of the ACL is reached and the accesses in the desired mask have been check with no denies, access is given.

When a decision is made about the comparison, the SACL is used to determine whether the access request should be logged.

Security Programming

So far the discussion has described how the security system works. This next section explains how to use it through the Win32 API. Be warned though, Win32 is not the most friendly way of interacting with the security system, the API is rather obscure and in some respects appears quite arcane. NT 4.0 introduces some higher-level functions, and although these require less programming than the earlier security functions, they are rather eccentrically named.

Getting Information

There is no Win32 function to enumerate the users that have accounts on a particular system. Instead, you can ask the NT machine to find out information about a user based on the username or SID; the system will then return the SID or username and the domain on which the account was found. The two functions are:

Function	Description
`LookupAccountSid()`	Obtains the name of the user and the domain name on which the SID was found
`LookupAccountName()`	Obtains the SID of the user and the domain name on which the name was found

Both of these functions also return information as to what type of account was looked-up as part of the **SID_NAME_USE** enumeration:

Value	Description
`SidTypeUser`	User SID.
`SidTypeGroup`	Group SID.
`SidTypeDomain`	Domain SID.
`SidTypeAlias`	Alias SID.
`SidTypeWellKnownGroup`	A SID for a well-known group.
`SidTypeDeletedAccount`	A SID for a deleted account.
`SidTypeInvalid`	An invalid SID.
`SidTypeUnknown`	An unknown SID.

Typically you can obtain the owner of an object by looking at the security descriptor to get the SID, then using these APIs to get the actual account name.

SIDs

As we have already seen, SIDs aren't particularly user friendly. To a large extent, you really do not have to worry about SIDs. The User Manager will create users and allocate SIDs for you. However, if you intend to look at the security descriptors of objects, or the access tokens of a process, you may need to obtain and compare SIDs.

Basic SID creation and manipulation is carried out with the following API functions:

Function	Description
`AllocateAndInitializeSid()`	Creates a SID based on the information passed to the function. The SID must be freed with `FreeSid()`
`CopySid()`	Copies a SID to a pre-allocated buffer
`EqualPrefixSid()`	Checks two SIDs for equality except the last subauthority

Table Continued on Following Page

Function	Description
EqualSid()	Checks two SIDs for equality
FreeSid()	Frees a SID allocated by **AllocateAndInitializeSid**
InitializeSid()	Initializes a SID with the authority, but not the subauthorities
GetSidLengthRequired()	Returns the length of a buffer needed for a SID with the specified number of subauthorities
IsValidSid()	Checks that the SID is valid

Once a SID has been created (or obtained by some other means), you can use the following functions to obtain its constituent parts. Effectively they return the memory addresses of the members of the **SID** structure that Microsoft would prefer us not to mess with:

Function	Description
GetSidIdentifierAuthority()	Returns the identifier authority
GetLengthSid()	Gets the length of the SID
GetSidSubAuthority()	Returns a particular subauthority
GetSidSubAuthorityCount()	Returns the number of subauthorities

Trustees

Trustees are essentially accounts on a machine or domain. A trustee is described by a **TRUSTEE** structure:

```
typedef struct _TRUSTEE
{
    PTRUSTEE                    pMultipleTrustee;
    MULTIPLE_TRUSTEE_OPERATION  MultipleTrusteeOperation;
    TRUSTEE_FORM                TrusteeForm;
    TRUSTEE_TYPE                TrusteeType;
    LPTSTR                      ptstrName;
} TRUSTEE;
```

TrusteeForm determines if **ptstrName** is the trustee name or a SID. The trustee could be an individual user or a group, and this is determined by the **TrusteeType** member. In the future this structure can be used to identify a server account that can impersonate this user. This functionality is not available in NT 4.0, so the first member must be **NULL** and the second one **NO_MULTIPLE_TRUSTEE**.

A **TRUSTEE** is initialized with the **BuildTrusteeWithName()** and **BuildTrusteeWithSid()** API functions. Given a valid **TRUSTEE**, you can get the form, name and type with **GetTrusteeForm()**, **GetTrusteeName()** and **GetTrusteeType()**.

When manipulating ACLs of various kinds, you will find that the new NT 4.0 APIs are much easier to use than the NT 3.51 low-level security APIs. These new functions use the **TRUSTEE** structure.

Access Tokens

The access token for a process or thread can be obtained using the ID for that object. The access token that is obtained is the token for the user that launched the process.

Function	Description
`OpenThreadToken()`	Opens and returns a handle to the access token for this thread
`OpenProcessToken()`	Opens and returns a handle to the access token for this process

Both of these functions take a parameter that specifies the sort of access that you require on the access token. The DACL in the access token is consulted to see if the access can be allowed. Once a valid handle is returned, the token can be queried for the information it holds, and if the process has the right access, the token can be modified:

Function	Description
`AdjustTokenGroups()`	Changes the groups in an access token
`AdjustTokenPrivileges()`	Enables or disables privileges in the access token
`DuplicateToken()`	Duplicates an existing access token
`DuplicateTokenEx()`	Creates or duplicates a primary or impersonation access token
`GetTokenInformation()`	Gets the information in a token
`SetTokenInformation()`	Sets the information in a token
`SetThreadToken()`	Assigns an impersonation token to a thread

To query for a user's permissions is also fairly straightforward:

```cpp
// AdminCheck.cpp
#include <windows.h>
#include <iostream>

int main()
{

    HANDLE          hToken = NULL;
    HANDLE          hProcess = GetCurrentProcess();
    TOKEN_GROUPS*   pTokens = NULL;
    DWORD           dwNoGroups = 0;
    DWORD           dwGroup = 0;
    PSID            psidAdmin = NULL;
    BOOL            bAdmin = FALSE;

    OpenProcessToken(hProcess, TOKEN_QUERY, &hToken);

    GetTokenInformation(hToken, TokenGroups, NULL, 0, &dwNoGroups);
    pTokens = (TOKEN_GROUPS*)new BYTE[dwNoGroups];
    GetTokenInformation(hToken, TokenGroups, pTokens, dwNoGroups, &dwNoGroups);
```

```
        SID_IDENTIFIER_AUTHORITY SidAuth = SECURITY_NT_AUTHORITY;
        AllocateAndInitializeSid(&SidAuth, 2, SECURITY_BUILTIN_DOMAIN_RID,
                           DOMAIN_ALIAS_RID_ADMINS,0, 0, 0, 0, 0, 0, &psidAdmin);
        for (dwGroup = 0; dwGroup < pTokens->GroupCount;
                           dwGroup++)
        {
           if (EqualSid(pTokens->Groups[dwGroup].Sid, psidAdmin))
           {
              bAdmin = TRUE;
              break;
           }
        }
        delete [] pTokens;
        CloseHandle(hToken);
        FreeSid(psidAdmin);

        if (bAdmin)
           std::cout << "User is an Administrator\n";
        else
           std::cout << "User is not an Administrator\n";

        return 0;
    }
```

This code determines if the process is running under the context of an administrator. The first action is to open the access token for the process, since we are just looking at the access token, we use **TOKEN_QUERY** as the desired access on the access token. **OpenProcessToken()** will return a handle on the access token of the specified thread.

Next we need to allocate enough space to hold all the groups held in the access token. The subject may be a member of many groups, and so we cannot automatically assume the number of groups to allocate for. Hence the call to **GetTokenInformation()** with the pointer to the receiving buffer as **NULL** and the size of this buffer specified as zero. This indicates that we are querying for the size of the buffer and this is returned in the buffer pointed to by the last parameter.

We can now allocate enough memory for the buffer and call **GetTokenInformation()** again. This time the function fills the buffer with information about the subject's groups. The second parameter specifies what information is required and it can be one of these (from the **TOKEN_INFORMATION_CLASS** enumeration):

Enumeration	Description
TokenUser	Access token's users
TokenGroups	Access token's groups
TokenPrivileges	Get the privileges of the access token
TokenOwner	Get the SID of the token's owner
TokenPrimaryGroup	Get the primary group of the token
TokenDefaultDacl	Get the DACL
TokenSource	Get the source, i.e. who created the access token
TokenType	Is this a primary token or an impersonation?

Enumeration	Description
`TokenImpersonationLevel`	Indicates how the impersonation is carried out
`TokenStatistics`	Miscellaneous information, like the expiry time, how many groups and privileges are in the access token

Now we need to examine every group in the token to see if it is the **Administrators** group. To do this we create a SID for the **Administrators** group and compare this with the SID of every group in the token. **AllocateAndInitializeSid()** returns the SID for the group specified. We need to identify the security authority, which is the first parameter, how many subauthorities, and then give the values of the subauthorities. In this case the two subauthorities used are **SECURITY_BUILTIN_DOMAIN_RID** and **DOMAIN_ALIAS_RID_ADMINS**, which specifies domain administrators.

Finally a comparison of the created SID and the SID of the group is made and the verdict is displayed in the console window.

Privileges and Rights

The NT defined privileges identified previously, can be queried using the following functions:

Function	Description
`LookupPrivilegeValue()`	Returns the LUID for a given name
`LookupPrivilegeDisplayName()`	Returns a description of the privilege for a given name
`LookupPrivilegeName()`	Returns the name for a given LUID

An access token can be queried for particular privileges using the **PrivilegeCheck()** function. This is typically called by a server program when a client makes a connection. The server can pass the client token handle to this function along with an array of privileges and the function will set a user-defined flag to **TRUE** if the token has all the privileges. Thus a server can determine if a client has all the privileges necessary for the requested service.

Privileges are identified by locally unique IDs (LUIDs). A LUID is unique on the local machine for the current session and the 64-bit value can be obtained by calling **AllocateLocallyUniqueId()**, passing a pointer to a LUID structure. The privilege can be enabled or disabled with **AdjustTokenPrivileges()**. The Win32 documentation is a little contradictory about what this function does: under the entry for **AdjustTokenPrivileges()** it says that the function can only enable or disable a privilege, not add or remove them. However, the entry under **SetTokenInformation()** specifies that **AdjustTokenPrivileges()** should be used to add and remove privileges. Experience shows that the latter statement is true, **AdjustTokenPrivileges()** can be used to add a privilege.

As an example of privileges, look at the Privileges example, which you can download from the Wrox Press web site. This queries the privileges of the logged on user (or the user that the primary thread impersonates), and lists them in a list box

When a privilege has been selected, the display name is given in the lower static control. In the screenshot, I have logged on as an Administrator and hence I am a fairly privileged user. If I log on as a more plebeian user, my privileges are considerably curtailed.

The example is not terribly exciting. It is an MFC dialog based application and in the handler for **WM_INITDIALOG**, it calls the member function **GetProcessToken()** to get the process access token and then the member **DisplayPrivileges()** to add those privileges into the list box. To get the privileges, **GetProcessToken()** calls **OpenProcessToken()** with the requested access to adjust the privileges of the user:

```
HANDLE CPrivilegesDlg::GetProcessToken(void)
{
   DWORD dwError;
   HANDLE hProcess = NULL;
   HANDLE hToken = NULL;
   CString str;

   hProcess = OpenProcess(PROCESS_ALL_ACCESS, FALSE, GetCurrentProcessId());

   if (NULL == hProcess)
   {
      dwError = GetLastError();
```

```
                str.Format("Cannot get process handle: %ld (0x%x)\n",
                           dwError, dwError);
        Message(str);
        return NULL;
    }

    if (!OpenProcessToken(hProcess,
                TOKEN_ADJUST_PRIVILEGES | TOKEN_QUERY,
                &hToken))
    {
        dwError = GetLastError();
        str.Format("Cannot get process token: %ld (0x%x)\n",
                   dwError, dwError);
        Message(str);
        CloseHandle(hProcess);
        return NULL;
    }

    CloseHandle(hProcess);
    return hToken;
}
```

The **DisplayPrivileges()** function calls **GetTokenInformation()**, checking the returned required buffer size to see if a larger buffer needs to be allocated:

```
BOOL CPrivilegesDlg::DisplayPrivileges(HANDLE hToken)
{
    CListBox* pList = (CListBox*)GetDlgItem(IDC_PRIVILEGE);
    ASSERT(pList);

    DWORD dwSize = sizeof(TOKEN_PRIVILEGES);
    TOKEN_PRIVILEGES* tp =
                (TOKEN_PRIVILEGES*)new BYTE[dwSize];
    DWORD dwRequired = 0;
    if (!GetTokenInformation(hToken, TokenPrivileges,
                            (LPVOID)tp, dwSize,
                            &dwRequired))
    {
        delete [] tp;
        if (0 == dwRequired)
            return FALSE;
        // Reallocate the buffer and try again
        dwSize = dwRequired;
        dwRequired = 0;
        tp = (TOKEN_PRIVILEGES*)new BYTE[dwSize];
        if (!GetTokenInformation(hToken, TokenPrivileges,
                                (LPVOID)tp,
                                dwSize, &dwRequired))
        {
            delete [] tp;
            return FALSE;
        }
    }

    CWnd* pStatic = GetDlgItem(IDC_NUMBER);
    ASSERT(pStatic);
```

```
   CString msg;
   DWORD dwNameSize = 256;
   LPTSTR name = new TCHAR[dwNameSize + 1];
   GetUserName(name, &dwNameSize);
   msg.Format("%s has %ld privileges", name,
              tp->PrivilegeCount);
   pStatic->SetWindowText(msg);

   dwNameSize = 256;

   for (DWORD index = 0; index < tp->PrivilegeCount;
              index++)
   {
      DWORD dwRequiredSize = dwNameSize;
      if (LookupPrivilegeName(NULL,
              &tp->Privileges[index].Luid,
              name, &dwRequiredSize))
      {
         pList->AddString(name);
      }
      else
      {
         delete [] name;
         dwNameSize = dwRequiredSize;
         LPTSTR name = new TCHAR[dwNameSize + 1];
         if (!LookupPrivilegeName(NULL,
              &tp->Privileges[index].Luid,
              name, &dwRequiredSize))
            break;
         pList->AddString(name);
      }
   }

   delete [] name;
   delete [] tp;
   return TRUE;
}
```

Security Descriptors

When you create an object using the Win32 API, one of the parameters will be a security descriptor. You can specify **NULL** for this parameter, in which case the SD of the process (generated from the access token) will be used. Examples of Win32 functions to create secure objects are:

Function	Description
`CreateFile()`	Opens a handle on a file object
`CreateDirectoryEx()`	Creates a directory with a security context
`RegCreateKeyEx()`	Creates a key with a security context

Function	Description
`CreateEvent()`	Creates a synchronization object
`CreateSemaphore()`	Creates a synchronization object
`CreateMutex()`	Creates a synchronization object
`CreateFileMapping()`	Create a sharable piece of memory (a section)
`CreateMailslot()`	Creates a file-based object
`CreateNamedPipe()`	Creates a file-based object
`CreatePipe()`	Creates a file-based object
`CreateProcess()`	Create a process (or subject)
`CreateProcessAsUser()`	Create a process for a specified user
`CreateThread()`	Create a thread in a process
`CreatePrivateObjectSecurity()`	Creates a new security descriptor

The parameter that refers to the security descriptor is in fact a pointer to a **SECURITY_ATTRIBUTES** structure to specify the context that the new object will run under.

```
typedef struct _SECURITY_ATTRIBUTES
{
   DWORD  nLength;
   LPVOID lpSecurityDescriptor;
   BOOL   bInheritHandle;
} SECURITY_ATTRIBUTES;
```

The **lpSecurityDescriptor** member points to a **SECURITY_DESCRIPTOR** structure. This is defined in **Winnt.h** as:

```
typedef struct _SECURITY_DESCRIPTOR
{
   BYTE  Revision;
   BYTE  Sbz1;
   SECURITY_DESCRIPTOR_CONTROL Control;
   PSID Owner;
   PSID Group;
   PACL Sacl;
   PACL Dacl;
} SECURITY_DESCRIPTOR, *PISECURITY_DESCRIPTOR;
```

SECURITY_DESCRIPTOR_CONTROL is a **WORD** field that acts as a flag member of the structure. The **SECURITY_DESCRIPTOR** structure is another structure that Microsoft is reluctant to allow you to change, but there are two ways you can initialize this structure: before you create the object, using the low-level functions; and after you have created the object, using the new NT 4.0 functions.

The high-level NT 4.0 functions will be described in the next section, the low-level functions are:

Function	Description
InitializeSecurityDescriptor()	Initializes a new SD ready for its fields to be set
IsValidSecurityDescriptor()	Checks each member of the SD for validity
GetSecurityDescriptorLength()	Gets the length of the structure
GetSecurityDescriptorControl()	Gets the revision level and control members of the SD
GetSecurityDescriptorOwner()	Gets the owner SID
GetSecurityDescriptorGroup()	Gets the primary group SID
GetSecurityDescriptorDacl()	Gets the DACL in the SD
GetSecurityDescriptorSacl()	Gets the SACL in the SD

For each **Get** function, there is an equivalent **Set** function (except for
GetSecurityDescriptorLength()).

Building the security descriptor involves allocating and initializing it and then initializing the constituent parts using the functions given above. Of course, calling a function like **SetSecurityDescriptorDacl()** is only part of the story, the real work is to create the structure, in this case the DACL, which is inserted into the SD.

To construct a SD requires initializing it and then calling the functions to initialize the revision level, owner, primary group, SACL and DACL – five function calls. NT 4.0 defines a new function, **BuildSecurityDescriptor()**, which initializes the SD and all its parts in one step, assuming that the appropriate SIDs and ACLs have already been constructed.

Access Control Lists

An Access Control List is an **ACL** structure followed by an ordered list of zero or more ACEs. The **ACL** structure is defined as:

```
typedef struct _ACL
{
   BYTE AclRevision;
   BYTE Sbz1;
   WORD AclSize;
   WORD AceCount;
   WORD Sbz2;
} ACL;
```

As with the other structures used in security, there are Win32 functions to get and set members of an ACL:

Function	Description
InitializeAcl()	Initializes the ACL
IsValidAcl()	Checks the revision level of the ACL and that there is space for the ACEs

Function	Description
AddAce()	Adds one or more ACEs to the ACL
DeleteAce()	Deletes an ACE from the ACL
AddAccessAllowedAce()	Adds an access-allowed ACE to the ACL
AddAccessDeniedAce()	Adds an access-denied ACE to the ACL
AddAuditAccessAce()	Adds a system-audit ACE to the ACL
FindFirstFreeAce()	Gets a pointer to the first free byte in the ACL
GetAce()	Gets an ACE of a particular index in the ACL
GetAclInformation()	Gets information about the ACL
SetAclInformation()	Sets information about the ACL

If you think this looks rather involved, then you are right, but then I did say they were low-level functions. NT 4.0 introduces some new higher-level functions.

Function	Description
GetSecurityInfo()	Gets the ACLs from an object using a handle
GetNamedSecurityInfo()	Gets the ACLs from a named object
SetSecurityInfo()	Sets the ACLs of an object with a particular handle
SetNamedSecurityInfo()	Sets the ACLs of a named object
SetEntriesInAcl()	Initializes the ACL, or adds an ACE to an ACL
BuildExplicitAccessWithName()	Builds an ACE
GetEffectiveRightsFromAcl()	Gets the effective rights for a trustee
GetAuditedPermissionsFromAcl()	Gets the audited rights for a trustee
GetExplicitEntriesFromAcl()	Gets both the effective and audited rights for a trustee
GetAce()	Gets an ACE from a ACL

The process of adding (or changing) an object's security descriptor is now quite straightforward. You have to decide if you want to apply the security before or after creating the object. If you decide that before is the best course of action then follow this procedure:

 Build the **TRUSTEE**s structures to identify the owner and the primary group of the object (every object must have an owner).

 Define who can access the object by creating an array of **EXPLICIT_ACCESS** structures for the access and audit ACEs.

 Call the mammoth **BuildSecurityDescriptor()** to create a security descriptor. This SD must be released later with a call to **LocalFree()**.

If you decide to apply the security after creating the object then follow this recipe:

- Create the object with a **NULL** security descriptor

- Create an ACL and initialize it with **SetEntriesInAcl()**.

- Use the **BuildExplicitAccessWithName()** function to add an ACE to an **EXPLICIT_ACCESS** structure. Merge in the ACE with **SetEntriesInAcl()**. Do these for every ACE.

- Set the object's security descriptor with **SetNamedSecurityInfo()** or **SetSecurityInfo()**.

After creating a security descriptor you can get the constituent parts of it by calling **LookupSecurityDescriptorParts()**, but any returned pointers must be freed with **LocalFree()**.

Impersonation

To impersonate a client, the server must call **ImpersonateLoggedOnUser()**, with the handle to an access token, the handle can be obtained by **OpenProcessToken()** or **OpenThreadToken()**, or the server can log on as a particular user using **LogonUser()**. Once the server has finished impersonating the user, it can log off the user and act as itself again by calling **RevertToSelf()**.

Note that **LogonUser()** will not succeed for every user, in particular it will fail if the user does not have the **SE_TCB_NAME** ("SeTcbPrivilege"), privilege (meaning "act as part of the operating system"). Services have this privilege, but interactive users do not (unless explicitly granted it).

Services

Services, as far as COM is concerned, are covered in Chapter 8. However, it is worthwhile exploring a little about the security aspects of NT services in this section.

By default, services are run under the **System** account (also known as the **LocalSystem** account). This is a special account that is designed for use only by services, the account has the name **System** and no password. Even though there is no password, this is not a security risk because of the restrictions applied to this account. Note that the account is a special account, you do not see it listed in the User Manager, and you cannot logon under this account at the NT logon dialog.

A service that runs under the **System** account has the security context of the **service control manager** (**SCM**). The **System** account is restricted in the registry keys that it can access (for example it cannot access **HKEY_CURRENT_USER**), and it is restricted in the network resources that it can connect to. This last point is quite important, since if you wish to connect to a network share, or connect to another server via a named pipe, you will find that, by default, the **System** account has no access. However, the following key:

HKEY_LOCAL_MACHINE\SYSTEM\CurrentControlSet\Services\LanmanServer\Parameters

has two values, **NullSessionPipes** and **NullSessionShares** that lists the pipes and shares that NULL sessions (i.e. those that are not validated) from a remote machine can connect to on the local machine. Furthermore, if you add a new named value called **RestrictNullSessAccess** and give it a value of **0** (a DWORD value), any remote session can have access to shares and pipes on the local machine. This is a severe security breach and should not be done!

Moreover, objects created with the **System** account will have an empty DACL, which will expressly exclude any access to the object by other accounts. If a service needs to share an object, it will need either to impersonate a user that can share objects and use the security context of that user, or explicitly create a DACL for the object it wants to share (a NULL DACL will allow access to all users).

One other aspect of the **System** account is that, by default, it has complete access to all files on a local NTFS volume. This permission can be removed from a file, but it is not recommended because you may be restricting NTFS housekeeping.

You can configure a service to run under an account other than the **System** account using the Services applet in the Control Panel:

The scheduler, running under the **System** account is quite useful for experimenting with the privileges and rights of the **System** account. Try this: start the Schedule service and then start a command prompt using the **at** command:

```
at 12:00 /interactive cmd.exe
```

Change **12:00** to be a time a few minutes into your future. The **/interactive** ensures that the command prompt will appear on the interactive user's desktop.

At the specified time a command prompt will appear and you can determine that it is running under the **System** account by typing **set** and then checking the **USERNAME** environment variable. From this command prompt you can use the **start** command to start processes, for example running the Privileges example shows that the **System** account has 20 privileges (as opposed to 16 privileges held by my administrator account).

Window Stations and Desktops

When you logon as an interactive user, you get the NT desktop on which you can see all the GUI applications that you have started. Now imagine that a service is also running on your machine. As we have seen in the last section, a service can run under the **System** account or under an account that you specify.

Normally a service is a non-GUI application, but there may be cases when GUI elements are created: the most common situation is the generation of message boxes. (Yes, I *know* that a service should not require interactive user input, but programmers tend to develop services as console applications and then forget to remove the message boxes during the conversion to a service. Shame on them!)

If the service produces a standard message box, the interactive user won't see it because it's not shown on the user's desktop. Instead it remains invisible and, since the message box is modal, the current thread will be blocked. This may also block clients attached to the service.

> *I have come across this problem many times, most recently when I tried to access the OLE services of a well-known database vendor from an ISAPI module; my HTTP connection kept timing out due to a message box trying to tell me that the database connection was unsuccessful (due to a bad installation program omitting some registry values). I could only get to see the message box by running IIS under a debugger (IIS cannot be run under another account or interact with the desktop).*

To show a message box from a service, you can use the **MB_SERVICE_NOTIFICATION** flag to show the message box on the interactive user's desktop, assuming a user is logged on, of course. Alternatively, the service, logged on as the **System** account or as the interactive user, can access the interactive user's desktop.

The desktop is just one of the Windows objects that a user is given when they logon. To gather these other objects together, the Win32 API has an object called a **window station**. A window station is a secure object that contains the desktops, clipboard and global atoms that the logged-on user has access to. Every user logged onto a machine has a window station so that any process executed by the user can interact with a GUI desktop without affecting what the interactive user sees. (If you are wondering what a global atom is, then don't worry: these are strings of 256 bytes or less referenced by an index that a process can use to pass data to another process, 16-bit Windows uses them extensively, but they are virtually unused in 32-bit Windows.).

If the user is the interactive user, the window station will also contain the keyboard, mouse and the display device.

The following functions allow you to manipulate window stations:

Function	Description
`CreateWindowStation()`	Creates a new window station.
`OpenWindowStation()`	Opens a handle of an existing window station.
`GetProcessWindowStation()`	Returns the handle of the window station for the current process.
`SetProcessWindowStation()`	Assigns a window station to the current process.
`EnumWindowStations()`	Enumerates the window stations in the system.
`CloseWindowStation()`	Closes a window station.

EnumWindowStations() works like the **EnumWindows()** function: a user-defined callback function is called for every window station used by the current user. This callback is passed the name of the window station. The default window station for a logged on user is called **WinSta0**. To access the window station, you need to obtain a handle. This can be obtained by calling the **OpenWindowStation()** function.

OpenWindowStation() requires that the desired access is given, which can be a combination of one or more of the following flags:

Access	Description
WINSTA_ACCESSCLIPBOARD	Use the clipboard.
WINSTA_ACCESSGLOBALATOMS	Allow manipulation of global atoms.
WINSTA_CREATEDESKTOP	Allow creation of new desktop objects on the window station.
WINSTA_ENUMDESKTOPS	Allow enumeration of existing desktop objects.
WINSTA_ENUMERATE	Allow enumeration of window stations.
WINSTA_EXITWINDOWS	Allow calls to **ExitWindows()** and **ExitWindowsEx()**.
WINSTA_READATTRIBUTES	Read the attributes of a window station object.
WINSTA_READSCREEN	Access screen contents.
WINSTA_WRITEATTRIBUTES	Write the attributes of a window station object.

The process also needs the appropriate permissions to access the window station. If necessary, these can be attained by impersonating the creator of the window station. Once the handle to a window station has been obtained, the process can access the clipboard and global atoms of the window station user, or by calling **OpenDesktop()**, it can obtain a handle to a named desktop in the window station.

The Win32 functions associated with desktops are:

Function	Description
CreateDesktop()	Creates a new desktop.
OpenDesktop()	Opens a handle of an existing desktop.
GetThreadDesktop()	Returns the handle of the desktop for the current thread.
SetThreadDesktop()	Assigns a desktop to the current thread.
SwitchDesktops()	Switches to a specified desktop.
EnumDesktops()	Enumerates the desktops in a window station.
EnumDesktopWindows()	Enumerates the windows on a desktop.
CloseDesktop()	Closes the desktop.

Just as for window stations, opening a desktop requires you to specify the type of access you require. Possible choices are shown in the table below:

Access	Description
`DESKTOP_CREATEMENU`	Create menus on the desktop.
`DESKTOP_CREATEWINDOW`	Create windows on the desktop.
`DESKTOP_ENUMERATE`	Allow enumeration of desktops.
`DESKTOP_HOOKCONTROL`	Establish any of the window hooks.
`DESKTOP_JOURNALPLAYBACK`	Perform journal playback on the desktop.
`DESKTOP_JOURNALRECORD`	Perform journal recording on the desktop.
`DESKTOP_READOBJECTS`	Read objects on the desktop.
`DESKTOP_SWITCHDESKTOP`	Activate the desktop using `SwitchDesktop()`.
`DESKTOP_WRITEOBJECTS`	Write objects on the desktop.

Using Window Stations

So what does all this mean? Well window stations allow services to impersonate a user and use UI features of a desktop without affecting the desktop of the interactive user (indeed there may not be an interactive user at all). Looking at this from another perspective, the APIs also allow a service logged on as a user other than the interactive user to access the interactive desktop.

The first case is important if the service is a UI process and thus will need to paint to a window without interfering with the desktop that the interactive user is viewing. If this was not allowed, the service would crash. The second case is important because, by default, services don't paint to the interactive desktop, so if a service needs to present some information to the interactive user, it must be able to access that user's desktop.

With these functions, you could, for example, write a service that accesses the interactive desktops and "shadows" the windows via some IPC method to another machine on the network. It could then allow support staff to remotely administer the machine by capturing the keyboard and mouse clicks of the remote machine, and applying them to the interactive desktop.

I have already mentioned that you can set a service to run under the account of the interactive user (using the Services control panel applet). Services that run with this setting can have the best of both worlds (or desktops), because they receive the mouse, keyboard and other windows messages bound for both of the desktops (the interactive desktop and the desktop of the service's window station).

However, this can have a bizarre effect if you do not design the service to be aware of this. For example a recent process I had to debug was launched using `CreateProcess()` from a service set to interact with the desktop. When an interactive user logged on, the user saw the window of the process, but when that user logged off, the process stopped. In this case, when the user logged off, all the windows were sent the `WM_ENDSESSION` message. This message is only applicable to the interactive desktop, but because the server process received messages from the interactive desktop, it handled the message (in this case with a `PostQuitMessage()` to kill the process).

COM Security

You now know how NT security works and the API that is used to manipulate it. To a large extent, even as an NT programmer, you probably will not have had to manipulate security, usually the default security it sufficient. DCOM, however, allows objects to be accessed and *activated* remotely. The activation part of that last statement is important since by activating an object server, the remote client instructs the server machine to start up a new executable and to set up the server on a known endpoint.

Of course, not just anyone should be allowed to do this. After all, the client could run a server that could wreak havoc on the server machine. There are two approaches that could be used, the server machine (on which objects are run) could specify which executables can be activated, or it could specify the user accounts that have the rights to launch an object. In fact DCOM uses a combination of the two, as we will see shortly.

Before DCOM was released, COM had no specific security features. This meant that a client process, running under a particular security context, could access an object in a local (out-of-process) server, launching it if necessary, without having any security checks imposed by COM. This object would then take the security context of the client. Since DCOM extends the way that COM objects are activated, security-wise, this could have meant that any pre-DCOM legacy applications would not work as remote objects. Microsoft could not allow this, so mechanisms have been implemented to allow pre-DCOM clients to call remote objects and clients to remotely call pre-DCOM servers.

Registry

The system registry (unsurprisingly) has entries that affect how security is applied to COM objects launched by a remote client. Each object class has an **AppID**, and each of these has settings specific to the individual object server. These settings affect the launching of the object server and making method calls. The **AppID** key, as explained in Chapter 4, has a key (the **AppID**, normally the same as the class **CLSID**) for every object that can be launched on a remote machine. Under this key are entries that specify the name of the remote machine (on which the object will run) and the users and groups that can launch and access this object from a remote client.

To manipulate the security settings for a server, you can edit the registry with the Registry Editor. However, some of the settings are access control lists and are saved as binary data. There are two excellent tools available to manipulate these registry values, **DCOMCnfg** and **OLEView**. Which of these you use is personal preference.

DCOMCnfg

DCOMCnfg has been written to show just the servers with **AppID**s and so gives a slightly less cluttered view than **OLEView**:

Distributed COM Configuration Properties [?][X]

Applications | Default Properties | Default Security |

Applications:

Microsoft Schedu
Microsoft Word D
MSDEV.APPLICA
MTS Catalog 1.0
MultiServer Class
Netscape.Help.1
PartsCatalogue Cl
Remote Automatic
Remote Clipboard
Remote Debug M
RemoteAlarm Clas
RemoteTime Clas
Reverse Class
Sound (OLE2)
Transaction Conte
Transaction Conte
WinZip
WordMail Mail Me
WordPad Docume

Properties...

MultiServer Class Properties [?][X]

General | Location | Security | Identity |

The following settings allow DCOM to locate the correct computer for this application. If you make more than one selection, then DCOM uses the first applicable one. Client applications may override your selections.

[ ] Run application on the computer where the data is located

[✓] Run application on this computer

[ ] Run application on the following computer:

[   ]   Browse...

OK   Cancel   Apply

Usually objects with **AppID**s are EXE servers, however, using a surrogate, you can remotely activate an inproc object. You must add an **AppID** for the object for it to show in **DCOMCnfg**, but you cannot add an **AppID** with this tool. **DCOMCnfg** is also implemented as a dialog-based application and as such does not allow resizing of the windows. One property that I find particularly irritating is the lack of a minimize button.

The security information is quite easy to find. When you launch it, **DCOMCnfg** will search through the **AppID** key and put an entry in the list box for every entry in that key. Most of the items are ProgIDs; in the **AppID** key these ProgIDs just map to a GUID key elsewhere in the parent key (via a named value called, unsurprisingly, **AppID**), **DCOMCnfg** will list just the ProgID. Some objects do not register a ProgID and so **DCOMCnfg** will just show the GUID.

From this initial window, you can click on the Default Security tab to get to a page that allows you to alter the **DefaultLaunchPermission** and **DefaultAccessPermission** named values that are used when no security is expressly given. To alter the security on an object (i.e. determine who can launch and access the object), you need to double-click on an entry in the list box on the Applications tab. Note that every object has security. So if you are launching an object as a local object from a client on the same machine, security will still be applied.

The tabs allow you to specify where the object will be launched, what account will be used to launch it (either locally, or on the remote machine), and also specify who is allowed to launch and access the object on *this* machine.

OLEView

OLEView has a tree view of COM information in the left-hand pane and detailed information about the selected item in the right-hand pane. Although it does order COM objects, the ordering is not always useful. For example, one branch of the tree is marked Application IDs, which you would imagine would act like the list box in **DCOMCnfg**, however the information given in the right-hand pane for a selected named object is just the stringified **AppID** (as opposed to all the entries which are given by **DCOMCnfg**.)

OLEView presents far more information than **DCOMCnfg** and it offers more flexibility in the settings that you can change. In fact, if you open the tree below an object, **OLEView** will instantiate the object to get information from it by making successive calls to the object's **IUnknown::QueryInterface()** (**OLEView** will **QI()** for every interface it finds in the **Interface** key in the registry). This is quite a useful feature when developing an object, because it allows you to determine if the object class has been registered properly.

So, to find the security information for an object class, you need to search for the class name in the one of the other branches of the tree, most likely **Object Classes\All Objects**. This can involve much scrolling up and down the tree control, especially if you do not know the class name. However, these are minor gripes for what is a very useful tool (Oh, and the window can be resized and I can minimize it to the taskbar).

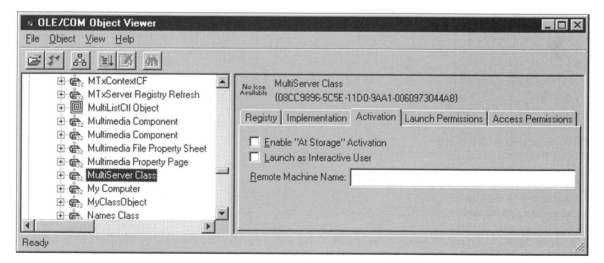

The next few sections explain in detail the registry items relevant to security.

EnableDCOM

This key is the granddaddy of them all. Without the permission of this key, no DCOM is possible. It can be found under `HKEY_LOCAL_MACHINE\Software\Microsoft\OLE` and has a value of '`Y`' or '`N`'. The value of this key affects globally whether any remote clients can launch, or connect to already running objects. If the value is '`Y`', remote clients can connect to objects as long as the launch or per-call permissions are correct. If this value is '`N`', COM objects can only be launched by local processes, but the individual launch permissions (`AppID\AppID\LaunchPermission` or `DefaultLaunchPermission`) still apply.

This value can be set directly using the registry editor or via the Default Properties tab of `Dcomcnfg`.

Activation Security

This determines the clients that can launch a server and obtain objects from it. The launch security can be changed by clicking on the Security tab of an object's properties:

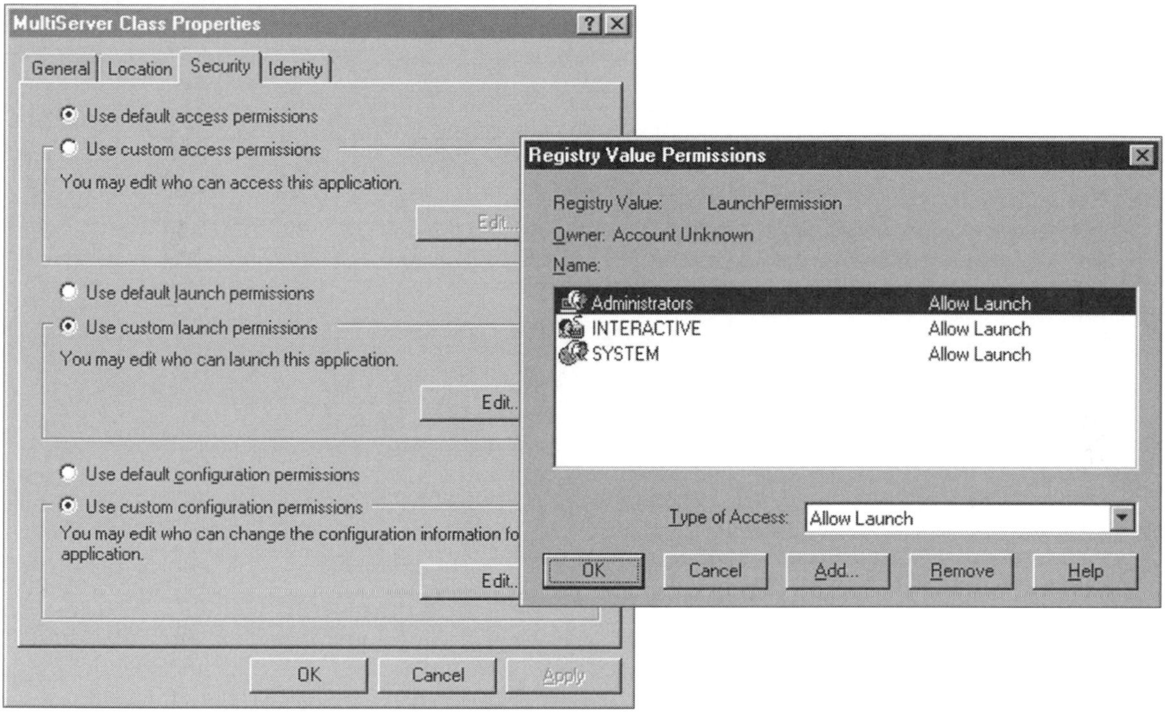

If the Use default launch permissions radio button is selected, the ACL saved under the **DefaultLaunchPermission** value in the **HKEY_LOCAL_MACHINE\Software\Microsoft\OLE** key is used. Otherwise, if the Use custom launch permissions is selected, you can create an ACL with the users that are able to launch the object. This ACL is then saved under the **LaunchPermission** value under the **AppID** UUID for the object server under **HKEY_LOCAL_MACHINE\Software\Classes\AppID**.

The equivalent view in **OLEView** is shown below. Clicking on Modify... will bring up the same standard system permissions dialog.

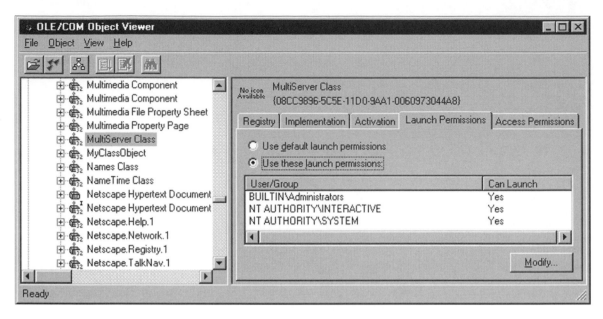

Whichever application is used will query the local system and the domain on which the current user is logged on for the SIDs of the groups and users they support. Using this dialog is welcome since the application will generate the appropriate ACL from the entered values and enter it into the registry.

If a remote client (or indeed a local client) attempts to create an object that would result in the object server being launched, the Service Control Manager will check for the **LaunchPermission** of that object's **AppID**. If it cannot find that key, it will use the ACL defined in the **DefaultLaunchPermission** instead. Once it has the ACL, it can compare the account of the client to those allowed in the ACL.

Note that on a newly installed machine, the ACL in this key defaults to allowing **Administrators**, the **SYSTEM** and **INTERACTIVE** groups to launch servers. It is unlikely that a client process on a remote machine will have such security and hence it is almost always necessary to change the **LaunchPermission** for an individual **AppID**. Note that it is possible to change the ACL of the default launch permissions via the Default Security tab of **DCOMCnfg**. However, you are cautioned against this if the same effect is possible via another method.

Call Security

Call-level security can be done in two ways, the programmer can use the COM API to apply security on a per-call basis, or registry values can be used to give an ACL that defines the access. The latter is the easiest to apply, but it does require some configuration to be performed when the object is installed.

If you do decide to use the registry values, the easiest way to carry out the configuration is to use **DCOMCnfg** or **OLEView**. However, you may decide to use a **.reg** file to add the appropriate values into the registry, and although binary data can be put in a **.reg** file it is not easy to maintain.

Here are the relevant registry values:

AccessPermission

This registry value is used to hold the ACL of the users that can access this object. Like the **LaunchPermission** value, this is altered via **Dcomcnfg** for a particular object class. If this value is not set then the COM system will look at the ACL in the **DefaultAccessPermission**.

DefaultAccessPermission

This binary value determines the ACL of the users and groups that can access an object when no other access permissions are given. It can be found under **HKEY_LOCAL_MACHINE\Software\Microsoft\OLE**.

The default value allows access to system administrators, **SYSTEM** and **INTERACTIVE** groups. A remote client's user is unlikely to be a member of any of these groups (certainly not **INTERACTIVE**), so unless specifically allowed via the object's **AccessPermission** registry value, it will be denied access.

Impersonation

As we have seen in the earlier part of this chapter, when a service is started, it is run under the **System** account which, though privileged, is not necessarily the account that the service should be run under. For services there were two solutions, either the service could be started impersonating a particular account, or the impersonation is carried out on a per-call basis where the thread for the client connection will call **LogonUser()** and **ImpersonateLoggedOnUser()**.

DCOM servers are launched by the Service Control Manager and it must know what account to use when launching the server. There are several keys in the registry that determine what account is used.

The **AppID** key, again, holds the necessary information. The value **RunAs** gives the username that will be used to launch the server and it can be either a local or domain account or it can be the string "**Interactive User**" to specify that the account of the logged on user should be used. If this value is missing, the SCM will use the "Launching User" i.e. the user that has requested the object (of course, only if the client allows this with the requested impersonation level).

The easiest way to set these values is in the Identity tab for the class in **DCOMCnfg**. **OLEView** doesn't seem to offer a way of setting an object to run as a particular user.

ObjLauncher Class Properties   ? X

General | Location | Security | Identity

Which user account do you want to use to run this application?

○ The interactive user

◉ The launching user

○ This user:

    User: [   ]   Browse...

    Password: [   ]

    Confirm Password: [   ]

○ The System Account (services only)

[OK]   [Cancel]   [Apply]

Notice that near the bottom of this dialog there is a radio button to use the **System** account. Although both DCOM object servers and services are launched by the SCM, the SCM treats them differently. Remember from Chapter 2, I mentioned about activation methods. In that chapter I said that, when set up to do so, a service is launched by the system when the machine reboots, and without any logged on user. This makes services very useful, especially if there is a possibility of the server machine needing a rebooted perodically.

Such a behavior could be useful for COM servers too since, as I mentioned in Chapter 3, COM servers can be marked as **REGCLS_MULTIPLEUSE** – n other words, many clients can create objects from the same server. If such a server had some complicated start up code, it may be prudent to do this once and to leave the server running waiting for connections from a client. Such a situation is the case for DCOM servers implemented in an NT Service as described in Chapter 8.

An object server that is running as an NT Service needs to have the **LocalService** value under the **AppId** key to give the service name (*not* the object ProgID, nor its path). If any command line parameters need to be passed to the service, these are specified in the **ServiceParameters** named value.

The following values apply to legacy code written before DCOM and exist under the **HKEY_LOCAL_MACHINE\Software\Microsoft\OLE\legacy** key. (In fact these are used by COM to determine what parameters to pass to **CoInitializeSecurity()** on the server's behalf.)

LegacyAuthenticationLevel

This determines the authentication level applied for all legacy servers. The values are

Name	Value	Description
RPC_C_AUTHN_LEVEL_NONE	1	No authentication
RPC_C_AUTHN_LEVEL_CONNECT	2	Authentication occurs when a connection is made to the server. Connectionless protocols do not use this, see **_PKT** below.
RPC_C_AUTHN_LEVEL_CALL	3	The authentication occurs when a RPC call is accepted by the server. Connectionless protocols do not use this, see **_PKT** below.
RPC_C_AUTHN_LEVEL_PKT	4	Authenticates the data on a per-packet basis. All data is authenticated
RPC_C_AUTHN_LEVEL_PKT_INTEGRITY	5	This authenticates that the data has come from the client, and it checks that the data has not been modified
RPC_C_AUTHN_LEVEL_PKT_PRIVACY	6	In addition to the checks made by the other authentication techniques, this encrypts the packet.

Note the distinction made between connection-based (stream) protocols and connectionless protocols. In the former case, once the connection is made, the server can assume that the user will remain the same. Once the connection is broken (the client releases the object, it dies or there is a network failure), the server knows that the user no longer requires access to the object.

However, for connectionless (datagram) protocols, the server does not know whether the client has released the object, or is just taking its time over requesting more services. The COM runtime can determine if the client has died by waiting for an appropriate ping period and if the ping has not occurred the client is dead. This explains why authentication has to be carried out on a packet-level.

Note that, by default, NT uses UDP (connectionless) but DCOM for Windows 95 and the beta version of DCOM for Solaris use TCP (connection-based). In addition, Windows 95 does not have security and although it can make calls as a client on any level, it can only accept calls on the **_NONE** and **_CONNECT** levels. The **RPC_C_AUTHN_LEVEL_CONNECT** level of authentication allows the client to pass an account name to be authenticated by a server.

LegacyImpersonationLevel

If the server uses security, it will need to use some security context. This value determines the default value that is used if none is specified on the object level. The possible values are:

Name	Value	Description
`RPC_C_IMP_LEVEL_ANONYMOUS`	1	The client is anonymous. This is equivalent to, say, an anonymous ftp session, and is not currently supported in DCOM.
`RPC_C_IMP_LEVEL_IDENTIFY`	2	The server can impersonate the client to check permissions in the ACL, but cannot access system objects.
`RPC_C_IMP_LEVEL_IMPERSONATE`	3	The server can impersonate the client, and access system objects on the client's behalf
`RPC_C_IMP_LEVEL_DELEGATE`	4	In addition to the `_IMPERSONATE` level, this level can impersonate the client on calls to other servers. This is not supported in the current release.

The default value is `_IDENTIFY`.

LegacySecureReferences

This determines whether client calls to **AddRef()** and **Release()** are secure for objects that do not call **CoInitializeSecurity()**. A value of '**Y**' will mean that COM will apply security on these object reference calls, however, it will slow down COM.

Experiments

Let's experiment with these values. The Launcher example is an ATL server that has the following interface:

```
interface IObjLauncher : IDispatch
{
    [id(1)] HRESULT UserName([out, retval] BSTR* userName);
    [id(2)] HRESULT AccountName([out, retval] BSTR* accountName);
    [id(3)] HRESULT BlanketInfo([out, retval] BSTR* clientName);
};
```

For the first few experiments, the first two methods will be used. The third, **BlanketInfo()**, will be used later.

The server is straightforward to create following the recipes from earlier chapters, but here are the main points:

- Create an ATL project for an EXE server.
- Use the ATL COM ObjectWizard add a simple object called **ObjLauncher**
- Right-click on the **IObjLauncher** interface in the ClassView and add the three methods.

You can now implement the methods. **UserName()** calls the Win32 **GetUserName()**, to get the name of the account that launched the object. This is typically the API you would call in your processes to get the current logged on user. The implementation of the **UserName()** method is shown next:

```
STDMETHODIMP CObjLauncher::UserName(BSTR * userName)
{
    // Make ATL do the conversion
    USES_CONVERSION;

    // Start with a 128 character buffer and increase it
    // until the call succeeds
    DWORD dwSize = 0;
    BOOL bSuccess = TRUE;
    LPTSTR pstrName = NULL;

    do
    {
        dwSize += 128;
        if (pstrName)
            delete [] pstrName;
        pstrName = new TCHAR [dwSize];
        bSuccess = ::GetUserName(pstrName, &dwSize);
    } while (!bSuccess);

    LPWSTR wname = T2W(pstrName);
    *userName = SysAllocString(wname);

    delete [] pstrName;

    return S_OK;
}
```

AccountName() uses the security API to call **LookupAccountSid()**.

```
STDMETHODIMP CObjLauncher::AccountName(BSTR * accountName)
{
    // Enable ATL to do the string conversion
    USES_CONVERSION;

    HANDLE hProcess;
    HANDLE hToken;

    // Pseudohandle so don't need to close it
    hProcess = GetCurrentProcess();

    if (!OpenProcessToken(hProcess, TOKEN_QUERY, &hToken))
    {
        return E_HANDLE;
    }

    DWORD tusize = 0;
    TOKEN_USER* ptu;

    // Get the required size
    GetTokenInformation(hToken, TokenUser, NULL, 0,
                        &tusize);
    ptu = (TOKEN_USER*)new BYTE[tusize];

    if (!GetTokenInformation(hToken, TokenUser,
                        (LPVOID)ptu, tusize, &tusize))
```

```
   {
      CloseHandle(hToken);
      delete [] ptu;
      return E_HANDLE;
   }

   CloseHandle(hToken);

   // Get the buffer sizes needed
   LPTSTR pstrName;
   LPTSTR pstrDomain;
   DWORD dwNameSize = 0;
   DWORD dwDomainSize = 0;
   SID_NAME_USE snu;

   LookupAccountSid(NULL, ptu->User.Sid, NULL, &dwNameSize,
                    NULL, &dwDomainSize, &snu);

   pstrName = new TCHAR[dwNameSize + 1];
   pstrDomain = new TCHAR[dwDomainSize + 1];

   if (!LookupAccountSid(NULL, ptu->User.Sid, pstrName,
                         &dwNameSize, pstrDomain,
                         &dwDomainSize, &snu))
   {
      delete [] ptu;
      delete [] pstrName;
      delete [] pstrDomain;

      return E_FAIL;
   }

   // Create the return buffer
   LPTSTR retval;
   retval = new TCHAR[dwNameSize + dwDomainSize + 2];
   wsprintf(retval, "%s\\%s", pstrDomain, pstrName);

   delete [] ptu;
   delete [] pstrName;
   delete [] pstrDomain;

   LPWSTR wname = T2W(retval);

   *accountName = SysAllocString(wname);

   delete [] retval;
   return S_OK;
}
```

To get hold of the SID of the account used to launch the object, we need to get hold of the process' access token. To do this, the method gets the process' handle and calls **OpenProcessToken()**. The information in the token is obtained by calling **GetTokenInformation()** twice, the first time to see how big a buffer needs to be allocated. The code can extract the owner SID from the token and call **LookupAccountSid()** to get the name of the account. After that the account name is converted to a **BSTR** and sent back to the client.

The last method of the interface is used later in the chapter, when we'll carry out experiments on the DCOM blanket security APIs. For now just get it to return an **E_NOTIMPL** value.

For this experiment, the client is a VB application. To create the VB client, you should have a form with two edit boxes, two buttons and a label. The edit boxes will return the user and account names and the label will print out any errors. One button is used to fill the edit boxes, the other to exit the application:

The object is created by using a global object variable declared in the (General)(Declarations) section.

```
Dim obj As New ObjLauncher
```

For this code to work, you must select the type library for the ObjLauncher in the References dialog box since the code activates the object using type information.

The GetInfo button calls both **UserName()** and **AccountName()** on the object and puts the returned information in the edit boxes, any errors are reported in the static control at the bottom of the form. The GetInfo button handler is implemented as:

```
Private Sub cmdLaunch_Click()
   lblError.Caption = ""

   On Error GoTo err_UserName
   UserName.Text = obj.UserName

   On Error GoTo err_AccountName
   AccountName.Text = obj.AccountName

   Exit Sub

err_UserName:
   lblError.Caption = "User name error: " & _
                  Hex$(Err) & " "
   Resume Next

err_AccountName:
   lblError.Caption = lblError.Caption &_
                  "Account name error: " & Hex$(Err)
End Sub
```

The handler for the Exit button is simple:

```
Private Sub cmdExit_Click()
    Set obj = Nothing
    Unload Me
End Sub
```

Since this uses a VB client, there are a few things that need to be done on the client machine.

- ▲ Copy **LaunchTest.exe** (the VB client) to the client machine.
- ▲ Compile the proxy, **Launcherps.dll** and copy it to the client machine
- ▲ Register **Launcherps.dll** on the client with **RegSvr32**. This makes sure that the **IObjLauncher** interface is registered on the client machine.

  Run RegEdit on the client
- ▲ Add the key **{31386223-9625-11D0-BBCF-002018349816}** under **CLSID** and under this key, add the named value **AppID** with the string value of this CLSID.
- ▲ Under the root in **HKEY_CLASSES_ROOT** add **Launcher.ObjLauncher.1**, since this is the ProgID used by the VB program. Under this, add a key **CLSID** and give the default value of this key the CLSID of the object.
- ▲ Under **AppID** add the key **{31386223-9625-11D0-BBCF-002018349816}** and make the default value **"Launcher"**.
- ▲ Run **DCOMCnfg**, select Launcher and under the Location tab check Run application on the following Computer and add the server name. Click on Apply.

Now when you run the LaunchTest client, it will attempt to start a copy of the server on the remote server machine.

One thing to notice about this example is that the client is written with VB and thus knows nothing about DCOM. This is why we used **DCOMCnfg** to add the remote server name into the registry. The other information, the launch permissions, access permissions and the authorization and impersonation levels are taken from the default values held in the registry.

With a server machine using the default DCOM settings, the tests would fail. This is because the default authentication is set to Connect. To make the tests succeed, use **DCOMCnfg** to set the default authentication level to None. Otherwise, a VB error number **70** (**0x46**) would be returned: "Permission Denied".

For the tests that follow, I added some extra users to my machines. On the server machine I have two new users, **ObjectUser** and **AnotherUser**, which are members of the **Users** group. On the client machine, I have two new users, **ObjectUser** and **OrdinaryUser**, both members of the **Users** group. In addition to these, both machines have a **RichardGrimes** account that is a member of the **Administrators** group. These are all local accounts, but remember as far as NT security is concerned an NT workstation, in the absence of an NT Server Domain, is effectively the only member of its own domain.

The tests were carried out by logging onto the server machine with an administrator's account, altering the values in the Identity tab for the **ObjLauncher** class to interactive user, launching user, or the specific user, **AnotherUser**. Always at this point I was careful to check the Task Manager to see if the object server (**Launcher.exe**) was running, and if so wait for it to end (i.e. when the server has timed out) or stop it, either with the Task Manager or with the **kill** utility from the NT 3.5 Resource Kit (available on the Developer's Network CDs).

The first test used the administrator's account, **RichardGrimes**, on both machines:

Identity	Returned User Name
Interactive User	**RichardGrimes**
Launching User	**RichardGrimes**
This User	**AnotherUser**

This is not surprising, since the interactive user on the server machine is **RichardGrimes**. The reason that this works is that the server machine has accounts with the same name as the accounts used on the client machines. Now when I use the **OrdinaryUser** account on the client, all accesses fail whatever identity is used. The error code that VB returns is **70** (**0x46**). This is because the **OrdinaryUser** account is only on the client, there is no account called **OrdinaryUser** on the server.

When the server is logged on as **ObjectUser**, and the client is logged on as the administrator's account, **RichardGrimes**, we have the following results:

Identity	Returned User Name
Interactive User	**ObjectUser**
Launching User	**RichardGrimes**
This User	**AnotherUser**

For any other client user, the VB error **70** is returned.

Now for the interesting bit, when the server has no logged on user, the client can *still* access the object server. Whatever user is logged on to the client when the server identity is set to interactive user, an error of **429** (**0x1AD**) is returned: "OLE automation server cannot create object". There is no surprise here since there is no user logged on the server machine, and so no interactive user. When the identity is set to launching user or a specified user, the access fails (with an error of **70**) for all users on the client except for the administrator, **RichardGrimes**.

Note that in all the above tests, the object server uses the *default* access and launching permissions. For the access permission this is a NULL DACL, giving access to all. By default only the **System**, **Administrators** and the **Interactive User** can launch the object. **DCOMCnfg** can be used to change these permissions. If the launch permissions are changed so that the **Everyone** group is added to the DACL, we can now access the server object using the **OrdinaryUser** account on the client. Adding the **Everyone** group will remove the "Permission Denied" error previously obtained.

So, in summary, for a legacy application like our VB client, the administrator must adjust the default permissions on the server machine so that the authentication level is None and, so that users other than **Administrators** can access the object. The **Everyone** group (or some appropriate domain group or user) must be added to the launch permissions of the object server.

Coding Security

The previous sections have shown that if you ignore security in the client and server code, the machine administrator can still control who can launch and access the object by changing values in the registry, using **DCOMCnfg**.

For better control, the programmer can code in the security information that will be used. The downside to encoded security is that your code now becomes NT specific: it will fail on cross platform Windows 95 DCOM systems, since DCOM 95 has no security.

In the first part of this section, we will go over the various methods of specifying security information, and in the last part of the section, we will test these out using a test application.

Initializing Security

During the earlier chapters of this book we have come across one method of specifying security information. In the earlier chapters we ignored the security and made sure that the client machine was logged on with a suitable account to give access to the object.

When you wish to change security information for an object, you have an initial choice of whether you want to apply these values on a process-wide basis, or on an interface or method call basis. These are not mutually exclusive, an application can have COM carry out process-wide security checks, and then make security checks on an interface or per-method level.

Process-wide Basis

We have already seen the process-wide method of changing the security context. The **pServerInfo** parameter in the **CoGetClassObject()** function is a pointer to a **COAUTHINFO** structure that holds information about the authentication, authorization and impersonation used in the object launch. This structure has these members:

```
typedef struct _COAUTHINFO
{
    DWORD               dwAuthnSvc;
    DWORD               dwAuthzSvc;
    WCHAR*              pwszServerPrincName;
    DWORD               dwAuthnLevel;
    DWORD               dwImpersonationLevel;
    AUTH_IDENTITY*      pAuthIdentityData;
    DWORD               dwCapabilities;
} COAUTHINFO;
```

The first member is the authentication service to use and is one of the values in the following table. There are five values (other than none), but currently the choice is simple: only **RPC_C_AUTHN_WINNT** is supported by NT 4.0. Others may be supported by third party add-ons, or may even be supplied in future versions of NT.

Value	Description
RPC_C_AUTHN_NONE	No authentication is used
RPC_C_AUTHN_DCE_PRIVATE	Use DCE private key authentication.

Value	Description
`RPC_C_AUTHN_DCE_PUBLIC`	Use DEC public key authentication (reserved for future use).
`RPC_C_AUTHN_WINNT`	Use NTLMSSP (NT Security Service).
`RPC_C_AUTHN_DEFAULT`	The system default authentication service. Windows NT 4.0 defaults to DCE private key authentication.

The third member, **`pwszServerPrincName`**, is the name used for the authentication server, and for NT authentication it should be **`NULL`**.

Once the authentication service has been chosen, the level must then be specified. This is the reason for the fourth parameter, which can be one of:

Name	Description
`RPC_C_AUTHN_LEVEL_NONE`	No authentication
`RPC_C_AUTHN_LEVEL_CONNECT`	Authentication occurs when a connection is made to the server. Connectionless protocols do not use this, see **`_PKT`** below.
`RPC_C_AUTHN_LEVEL_CALL`	The authentication occurs when a RPC call is accepted by the server. Connectionless protocols do not use this, see **`_PKT`** below.
`RPC_C_AUTHN_LEVEL_PKT`	Authenticates the data on a per-packet basis, all data is authenticated
`RPC_C_AUTHN_LEVEL_PKT_INTEGRITY`	This authenticates that the data has come from the client, and it checks that the data has not been modified
`RPC_C_AUTHN_LEVEL_PKT_PRIVACY`	In addition to the checks made by the other authentication techniques, this encrypts the packet.

Recognize these? These are the levels of authentication that can be specified for legacy applications and held under the **`HKEY_LOCAL_MACHINE\Software\Microsoft\OLE\legacy`** key.

The authentication service will need additional information about the client to be able to authenticate the call. This is the purpose of the sixth parameter which has data specific to the particular authentication service used. For **`RPC_C_AUTHN_WINNT`** it is in the form of Windows NT's **`SEC_WINNT_AUTH_IDENTITY`**:

```
typedef struct _AUTH_IDENTITY
{
   USHORT*   User;
   ULONG     UserLength;
   USHORT*   Domain;
   ULONG     DomainLength;
   USHORT*   Password;
   ULONG     PasswordLength;
   ULONG     Flags;
} AUTH_IDENTITY;
```

The **USHORT*** members are pointers to null terminated strings holding the names of the user, the domain and the user password, each of these is followed by a member indicating the length of these strings. If the **Flags** parameter is 1, the strings are ANSI, otherwise they are Unicode. These values provide all the information needed to authenticate the user.

The second member of the **COAUTHINFO** structure, **dwAuthzSvc**, is the authorization of the call. This can be one of the values in the following table, for calls to an NT (or Windows 95) server, the value should be **RPC_C_AUTHZ_NONE** because the others are not supported yet.

Value	Description
RPC_C_AUTHZ_NONE	The server will perform no authorization.
RPC_C_AUTHZ_NAME	The server uses the client's principal name as a basis for the authorization.
RPC_C_AUTHZ_DCE	The server uses the client's DCE privilege attribute certificate (PAC) information. This is sent to the server, with each remote procedure call using the binding handle, access is checked against DCE access control lists (ACLs).

Finally, since we have provided authentication (the client is who it says it is) and authorization (the client has the authority to carry out this action), the server is now reassured that the client is real and can do the action. However, the server may not be able to perform the action 'in its own name', since the server may have been activated as an NT service and hence may not have all the necessary permissions to carry out the task.

Furthermore, for auditing purposes the server should use a user name relevant to the client, so that the audit trail in the event log more accurately reflects that the action was performed on behalf of a client and not the server. This is done by the server *impersonating* a user.

Impersonation is controlled by the fifth parameter of the **COAUTHINFO** structure, **dwImpersonationLevel**, which has one of the following values:

Name	Description
RPC_C_IMP_LEVEL_ANONYMOUS	The client is anonymous. This is equivalent to, say an anonymous ftp session, but is not currently supported in DCOM.
RPC_C_IMP_LEVEL_IDENTIFY	The server can impersonate the client to check permissions in the ACL, but cannot access system objects.
RPC_C_IMP_LEVEL_IMPERSONATE	The server can impersonate the client, and access system objects on the client's behalf
RPC_C_IMP_LEVEL_DELEGATE	In addition to the **_IMPERSONATE** level, this level can impersonate the client on calls to other servers. This is not supported in the current release.

NT 4.0 only supports the **_IDENTIFY** and **_IMPERSONATE** levels. In other words the server can impersonate the user to determine if the user has the correct permissions to perform the action or it can impersonate the user to actually do the action.

If a legacy client is remotely launching an object, the impersonation level from the
`HKEY_LOCAL_MACHINE\Software\Microsoft\OLE\legacy` key is used. The value can be set using
`DCOMCnfg`.

The final parameter determines the capabilities of the proxy used to remote the call. This flag is not used
at present, so it should be set to zero.

Once the values have been set and `CoGetClassObject()` called, these security values are applied
whenever the client makes an access to the server. When COM on the server machine gets the launching
or method access request, it queries the registry for the appropriate class security value or drops to the
default value if a per-class value cannot be found.

The other way to specify security information is to call `CoInitializeSecurity()`. This can be used on
both the client and server side and acts as a process-wide setting of security attributes. The parameters are
given in the following table, and although they mirror some of the values passed in **COAUTHINFO**, there
are also parameters to pass the DACL of allowed or denied users:

Parameter	Parameter Type	Description
pVoid	PSECURITY_DESCRIPTOR	The security descriptor that has the DACL of granted or denied users. The SACL must be NULL
cAuthSvc	DWORD	The number of authentication and authorization services to use, a value of -1 tells COM to choose one
asAuthSvc	SOLE_AUTHENTICATION_SERVICE*	An array of the authentication and authorization services to register.
pReserved1	void*	Should be **NULL**
dwAuthnLevel	DWORD	Authentication level
dwImpLevel	DWORD	Impersonation level
pAuthInfo	RPC_AUTH_IDENTITY_HANDLE	Should be **NULL**
dwCapabilities	DWORD	Additional capabilities
pvReserved2	void*	Should be **NULL**

Note that if the security descriptor passed as the first parameter is **NULL**, DCOM will construct one that
will allow access from the current user and the Local System.

Interface-Wide Client-Side

Security is applied on the client-side through the `IClientSecurity` interface. It is implemented by the
interface remoting layer. Thus the client process can `QueryInterface()` the object's `IUnknown` interface
for the `IClientSecurity` interface. You can actually see this interface when you instantiate an object
with `OLEView`.

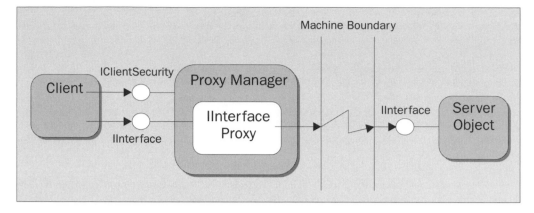

This interface has the following methods:

Method	Description
QueryBlanket()	Retrieves authentication information.
SetBlanket()	Sets the authentication information that will be used to make calls on the specified proxy.
CopyProxy()	Makes a copy of the specified proxy.

QueryBlanket() gets security information about the proxy that is used to marshal the method calls to the server. This function essentially obtains the same authentication information as is passed to the **CoInitializeSecurity()** function described above.

To indicate the proxy that is queried, the caller passes a pointer to the interface in the first parameter of **QueryBlanket()**. Normally, the caller would pass the interface that it is using on the server, but any interface on the object will do (the salient point is that the interface does not have the **[local]** attribute, which indicates that the interface can only be used on objects on the local machine). This parameter also acts as an **[out]** pointer, pointing to the authentication level used.

This function is designed to be used in conjunction with a call to **SetBlanket()**. The sixth parameter of **QueryBlanket()** is an **[out]** parameter that points to a structure that indicates the identity of the client. This pointer is passed in a later call to **SetBlanket()**. This parameter is rather odd in terms of COM calls because this is not a copy of the identity information, it is a pointer to the actual information and as such you should not attempt to free the memory pointed to by this pointer.

If you wish to change the authentication used when you call a method on a particular interface (through a particular proxy object), you call the **SetBlanket()** method. This method changes the security information for this proxy object and hence any other clients using this proxy will also be affected. You pass the proxy pointer, as well as the **RPC_AUTH_IDENTITY_HANDLE** obtained from the call to **QueryBlanket()**, to **SetBlanket()**.

Finally the interface has a method called **CopyProxy()**. A call to **SetBlanket()** will affect all users of the proxy, which may not be what you want. To make a private copy of the proxy you call

CopyProxy() passing the proxy pointer. The function returns a pointer to the copy of the proxy and this can then be passed to **SetBlanket()**. Of course, you must follow COM rules and call **Release()** on this interface once you are finished with it.

These copies are private, thus if you change the security of a copy and then **QI()** for another interface on the pointer, you will get an interface pointer for that interface which has the *original* security context.

IUnknown is a special case, since it cannot be copied. Instead a call to **SetBlanket()** on an **IUnknown** interface will nominally affect all users, however calls to **QueryInterface()** are often cached and so the proxy call would probably not be made (another problem is that if an object is **QI()**ed for an interface, it *must* reply **S_OK** even if the client does not have the security to access the interface). Calls to **AddRef()** and **Release()** *always* use the security set with **CoInitializeSecurity()** (or if this is not explicitly called, they use default values held in the registry). Remember the **LegacySecureReferences** registry value mentioned earlier? This is used to control this object reference security for legacy objects.

Querying for and altering the proxy security requires that you obtain a pointer to **IClientSecurity**, call the method and then release the interface. To make your life easier, such a sequence of calls is wrapped up in each of the following helper functions:

```
CoQueryProxyBlanket()
CoSetProxyBlanket()
CoCopyProxy()
```

Interface-Wide Server-Side

Server-side security is managed through the **IServerSecurity** interface. The server may call this interface's methods to alter how impersonation is handled.

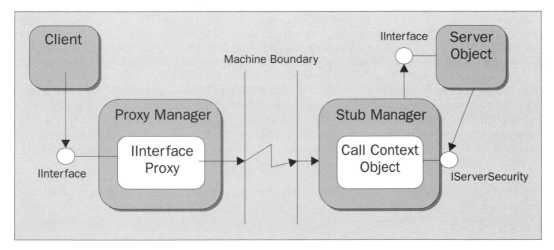

To obtain a pointer to this interface, the server calls **CoGetCallContext()**. Once an interface pointer has been returned, the server can call **QueryBlanket()** to obtain the authentication and authorization level of the client. This method returns the principal name and a string identifying the client. In terms of implementation, the principal name is allocated from system memory and must be released with a call to **CoTaskMemFree()**, whereas the client identifier is a pointer to the actual value and thus must not be freed.

Method	Description
QueryBlanket()	Called to find out about the client that invoked one of its methods.
ImpersonateClient()	Allows a server to impersonate a client for the duration of a call.
RevertToSelf()	Restores the authentication information on a thread to the process's identity.
IsImpersonating()	Indicates whether the server is currently impersonating the client.

The main use for this interface is to allow the server to impersonate the client. This is done by calling the **ImpersonateClient()** method. Once the call has been completed, the server can call **RevertToSelf()**.

There are several helper methods that wrap up **IServerSecurity** calls:

```
CoQueryClientBlanket()
CoImpersonateClient()
CoRevertToSelf()
```

So what would you use these for? The **CoQueryClientBlanket()** can be used to obtain information about the client from the server, we will see how to use this function in the **LauncherClient** example that follows. In that example, we use this function to obtain the client identity; in a real application this could be used to check against a database of permitted users. However, we have seen the folly of this approach in the **Catalogue** example earlier in the chapter since it would mean that we would have to maintain the database of user names and the permissions that they have.

A better approach would be to use the client identity to log on as a user on the server machine and then attempt to perform the requested task under the user's access token. The main problem with this approach is that although you can get the client identity in terms of the user and domain name, from **CoQueryClientBlanket()**, to use **LogonUser()**, we also need the user's password.

But hang on, the password has been specified in the **COAUTHINFO** member of the **COSERVERINFO** parameter of the **CoCreateInstanceEx()** call (and in the **CoSetProxyBlanket()**). So the security context knows about the user and his password. There is no way that COM will tell you the password (of course), but if you ask it to it will use this information to impersonate the client. This is the reason for the **ImpersonateClient()** method of **IServerSecurity**. Server code can call this method through an interface pointer or call the helper function **CoImpersonateClient()**.

Now the server thread can try to access various objects and the system will check if the impersonated user has the correct security context for that action. This combination of **IClientSecurity** and **IServerSecurity** allows the security context to be remoted, in effect, from the client to the server.

Experiments

We will now experiment a little with these security settings. This example will extend the last example by implementing the **BlanketInfo()** method of the **IObjLauncher** interface, To remind you here is the interface IDL:

```
interface IObjLauncher : IDispatch
{
    [id(1)] HRESULT UserName([out, retval] BSTR* userName);
```

```
    [id(2)] HRESULT AccountName([out, retval] BSTR* accountName);
    [id(3)] HRESULT BlanketInfo([out, retval] BSTR* clientName);
};
```

We have already seen the first two methods: the **LauncherTest** example used these. In the following tests, we will query the security blanket for the name of the client that is attempting a connection. The implementation of this code is:

```
STDMETHODIMP CObjLauncher::BlanketInfo(BSTR * clientName)
{
   LPWSTR pPrivs;
   HRESULT hRes;
   *clientName = NULL;
   hRes = CoQueryClientBlanket(NULL, NULL, NULL, NULL,
                       NULL, (LPVOID*)&pPrivs, NULL);
   if (FAILED(hRes))
      return hRes;
   *clientName = ::SysAllocString(pPrivs);
   return S_OK;
}
```

This makes a call to **CoQueryClientBlanket()** to see what security settings are being used. Note that all the parameters are **NULL** except for **pPrivs**. This is because in this example we are not interested in the authentication and authorization services and levels that are used, we are only interested in the client name which is passed in the **pPrivs** parameter. (Since we are using the NTLMSSP, the principal name will be **NULL** anyway and the impersonation level is not returned by this function even though a parameter is present to do so.)

The client software is more sophisticated than the **LauncherTest** shown before. This time the client is written with DCOM in mind and hence it provides information about the security that will be used. The client will then query the server as to the username used on the server and present these in a dialog.

You can download the complete code from the Wrox web site. When you run the client, you will get a logon dialog:

I have restricted the combo boxes to show the values relevant to NTLMSSP. The Identity frame allows you to determine what username to use. If you select Use Process Token, COM will use the current process access token, otherwise the three edit boxes are enabled and the user can enter an account name.

Once you have entered the values that you want to test, the code then calls **CreateServer()**, which is implemented like this:

```
void CLaunchClientDlg::CreateServer()
{
   CServer dlg;

   dlg.m_strServerName = m_strServerName;
   dlg.m_strUserName = m_strUserName;
   dlg.m_strDomain = m_strDomain;
   dlg.m_strPassword = m_strPassword;
   dlg.m_dwAuthnService = m_dwAuthnService;
   dlg.m_dwAuthnLevel = m_dwAuthnLevel;
   dlg.m_dwAuthzService = m_dwAuthzService;
   dlg.m_dwImpLevel = m_dwImpLevel;

   if (m_bUseVals)
      dlg.m_nIdentity = 1;
   else
      dlg.m_nIdentity = 0;

   if (m_pLaunchServer)
   {
      m_pLaunchServer->Release();
      m_pLaunchServer = NULL;
   }

   // Get the name of the server to use
   if (dlg.DoModal() == IDOK)
   {
      m_strServerName = dlg.m_strServerName;
      m_strUserName = dlg.m_strUserName;
      m_strDomain = dlg.m_strDomain;
      m_strPassword = dlg.m_strPassword;
      m_dwAuthnService = dlg.m_dwAuthnService;
      m_dwAuthnLevel = dlg.m_dwAuthnLevel;
      m_dwAuthzService = dlg.m_dwAuthzService;
      m_dwImpLevel = dlg.m_dwImpLevel;
      m_bUseVals = (dlg.m_nIdentity == 1);
   }

   // Let's create the server
   HRESULT hr;
   COSERVERINFO serverinfo;
   COSERVERINFO* pServerInfo;
   COAUTHINFO athn;

   if (NULL == m_pIdn)
      m_pIdn = new SEC_WINNT_AUTH_IDENTITY;
   else
   {
      // Clean up the strings
      delete [] m_pIdn->User;
```

```
      delete [] m_pIdn->Domain;
      delete [] m_pIdn->Password;
   }

   // Create the server info, note that we use the
   // CString to convert to wide chars
   serverinfo.dwReserved1 = 0;
   serverinfo.dwReserved2 = 0;
   serverinfo.pwszName = m_strServerName.AllocSysString();
   serverinfo.pAuthInfo = &athn;

   athn.dwAuthnSvc = m_dwAuthnService;
   athn.dwAuthzSvc = m_dwAuthzService;
   athn.pwszServerPrincName = NULL;
   athn.dwAuthnLevel = m_dwAuthnLevel;
   athn.dwImpersonationLevel = m_dwImpLevel;
   athn.pAuthIdentityData = (COAUTHIDENTITY*)m_pIdn;
   athn.dwCapabilities = EOAC_NONE;

   m_pIdn->UserLength = m_strUserName.GetLength();
   m_pIdn->DomainLength = m_strDomain.GetLength();
   m_pIdn->PasswordLength = m_strPassword.GetLength();

#ifdef UNICODE
   m_pIdn->User = new TCHAR[m_strUserName.GetLength() + 1];
   m_pIdn->Domain = new TCHAR[m_strDomain.GetLength() + 1];
   m_pIdn->Password = new TCHAR[m_strPassword.GetLength()
                      + 1];
   m_pIdn->Flags = SEC_WINNT_AUTH_IDENTITY_UNICODE;
#else
   m_pIdn->User =
                  (unsigned char*) new
                     TCHAR[m_strUserName.GetLength() + 1];
   m_pIdn->Domain = (unsigned char*)new
                     TCHAR[m_strDomain.GetLength() + 1];
   m_pIdn->Password = (unsigned char*)new
                     TCHAR[m_strPassword.GetLength() + 1];

   m_pIdn->Flags = SEC_WINNT_AUTH_IDENTITY_ANSI;
#endif
   lstrcpy((LPTSTR)m_pIdn->User, (LPCTSTR)m_strUserName);
   lstrcpy((LPTSTR)m_pIdn->Domain, (LPCTSTR)m_strDomain);
   lstrcpy((LPTSTR)m_pIdn->Password,
                              (LPCTSTR)m_strPassword);
   if (m_strServerName.IsEmpty())
      pServerInfo = NULL;
   else
      pServerInfo = &serverinfo;

   MULTI_QI qi = {&IID_IObjLauncher, NULL, 0};

   hr = CoCreateInstanceEx(CLSID_ObjLauncher,
               NULL,
               CLSCTX_LOCAL_SERVER | CLSCTX_REMOTE_SERVER,
               pServerInfo, 1, &qi);

   if (SUCCEEDED(hr) && SUCCEEDED(qi.hr))
   {
```

```
        // Now get the interface
        m_pLaunchServer = (IObjLauncher*)qi.pItf;
        hr = CoSetProxyBlanket(m_pLaunchServer,
                serverinfo.pAuthInfo->dwAuthnSvc,
                serverinfo.pAuthInfo->dwAuthzSvc,
                serverinfo.pAuthInfo->pwszServerPrincName,
                serverinfo.pAuthInfo->dwAuthnLevel,
                serverinfo.pAuthInfo->dwImpersonationLevel,
                m_bUseVals
                    ? serverinfo.pAuthInfo->pAuthIdentityData
                    : NULL,
                serverinfo.pAuthInfo->dwCapabilities);
        if (FAILED(hr))
        {
            CString str;
            str.Format("CoSetProxyBlanket failed: 0x%x", hr);
            Message(str);
            m_pLaunchServer->Release();
            m_pLaunchServer = NULL;
            Message("Released object");
        }
    }
    else
    {
        m_pLaunchServer = NULL;
        CString str;
        str.Format("Cannot get object: 0x%x and QI: 0x%x",
                    hr, qi.hr);
        Message(str);
    }

    CWnd* pgetinfo = GetDlgItem(IDC_GETINFO);
    ASSERT(pgetinfo);

    pgetinfo->EnableWindow(SUCCEEDED(hr));

    CWnd* pkillobj = GetDlgItem(IDC_KILLOBJECT);
    ASSERT(pkillobj);

    pkillobj->EnableWindow(SUCCEEDED(hr));

    // Free the buffer previous allocated
    ::SysFreeString(serverinfo.pwszName);
}
```

This function creates the **COSERVERINFO** parameter required by **CoCreateInstanceEx()**. If this is successful, the information is used in a call to **CoSetProxyBlanket()** to set the security settings for the current proxy.

The Win32 documentation specifies that COM will keep a pointer to your identity information until COM is uninitialized or a new value is used. Because of this, I have created the buffer used by these structures on the heap.

If the server creation is successful, the main dialog is shown:

The Get Info button calls **UserName()**, **AccountName()** and **BlanketInfo()** on the server, placing the results in the edit boxes and adding any errors into the list box. The New User button will release the server and bring up the Server Details dialog so that you can change the settings that you want for the server. Finally the Kill Object button will release the object immediately. I found this useful when I wanted to change the settings on the server with **DCOMCnfg**.

The client code, as mentioned above, calls **CoSetProxyBlanket()** to set the security context for the proxy. The server code uses the default settings in the registry and can be conveniently altered with **DCOMCnfg**. I could have called **CoInitializeSecurity()** on the server to set the context there, however, there was no convenient way to change the settings used in the function call. I couldn't send them from a client because they affect client connections!

The best method, perhaps, would be to save the values in some shared area and then use a utility to alter the saved values. However, there is no need to write a new utility since the security settings saved under **AppId** in the registry is used by DCOM as the values for **CoInitializeSecurity()** and the utility, **DCOMCnfg**, is supplied specifically to alter these values.

There are several interesting aspects arising from this test application. You will need to set up the access permissions on the server to allow access from the client; if you use an administrator's name in the client, you will get access, but this is obviously not the best course of action. Instead add appropriate users to the Custom Access Permissions on the Security tab, or better still create a group and add that group to the list of users with access. That way you can add new users to the group when you want to give them access to the object.

The next point that you need to be aware of is that both the client side and the server side (through the call to **CoInitializeSecurity()**) can be used to give a level of authentication through registry settings. DCOM will use the higher of the two, so if you set the server to a higher level via **DCOMCnfg** than you choose on the client side, the server side value will be used. This is a prudent security measure and applies to the impersonation level.

The example shows quite nicely the use of the client identity. In the following picture, the server has been set to give the object the interactive user's identity and the logged on user is **RichardGrimes**. However, on the client side, the identity offered in the call to **CoSetProxyBlanket()** is **AnotherUser**. The dialog shows that the server has launched the user under the context of **RichardGrimes** but fully knows who the client is. Although this example does not demonstrate this, the server could call **CoImpersonateClient()** to take the client's token rather than the token of **RichardGrimes**.

The converse of this is to set the server impersonation to use the user **AnotherUser** with **DCOMCnfg** and then call the client using the specified account **RichardGrimes**. In this case the client name reverts to **zeus\RichardGrimes** and the other names to **AnotherUser**.

Note that the client can determine the domain. This is really only useful if the machines are part of a domain, in which case the domain security database would be used. In my tests I have used local accounts. The domain portion can be used to specify the machine on which the account lies, so in the above two cases I specified, using the domain edit box on the client, that the two users were on **zeus**.

What happens if I log on to the server with, say, **zeus\AnotherUser** and then attempt to use a user name that exists on **hera**, for example **hera\ObjectUser**? In this case, NT security will go into "fallback" mode. The remote machine, **zeus**, will not know about **hera\ObjectUser** but it does know about **ObjectUser** on **zeus** (because I set up this account on **zeus**), so it falls back to checking just the username part. **zeus** attempts to connect to **ObjectUser** on **zeus**, and since the password is valid (the two are the same), the connection succeeds.

What if the client uses an account that has no corresponding account on the server? In this case there is an automatic fallback to the **Guest** account.

Summary

Security is extremely important, especially when you are using distributed objects. Look at it two ways:

If you're the client, you are activating code on another machine, getting those objects to do some action, and then acting upon the results of that action. You have to know that the object can be trusted. For a start if a spoof object changes some network resource on your behalf, will you take the responsibility? If the spoof object returns a result, it may return a completely random value or even a malicious one. The client must be sure that the server is who it says it is (this is carried out by the authentication level), and it should only let the object carry out tasks on its behalf when it is sure that the server will not abuse the trust. This is the impersonation level that the user specifies.

Now look at it from the server. Since remote clients want to run code on your machine, the first thing you have to check is the identity of the client. Once that is established, you have to determine if the client has the right permissions to launch the object. When the object is running the client will make method calls on the object so there must be checks to make sure that the client can call the object methods. Finally when the object does some action, it will need to use an account to do that, and the logical account to use is the client account.

All these things and more are carried out by COM.

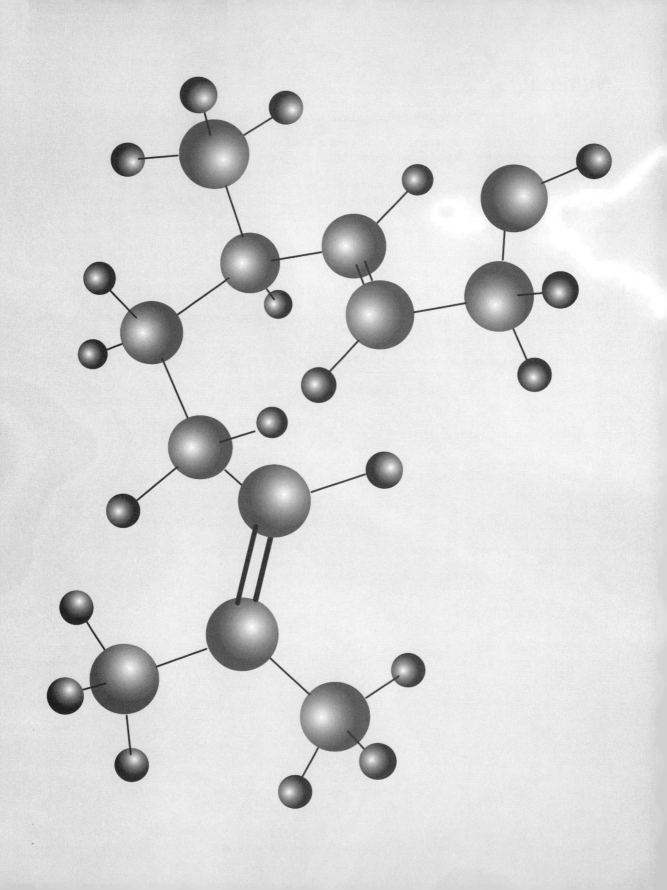

DCOM Servers as NT Services

Introduction

When you boot up your NT machine, you will see a lot of disk activity while the software loads. After selecting NT from the boot options, the machine devices will be identified and then the HAL (Hardware Abstraction Layer) and the kernel are loaded. After that some device drivers are loaded and you will get the graphical screen. At this point, even before you've logged in, you will still hear your disk whirring. There are obviously many processes that need to be loaded before the machine can be truly counted as started. The key to that disk activity is NT services.

Services are an integral part of NT, they provide a service for clients, whether those clients are the interactive user or remote users. Services do not even require that the machine has an interactive user and this means that if the machine should be rebooted for some reason (a cleaner removing the power cable to use the socket for the vacuum cleaner, for example), the service will be restarted once the machine restarts.

Services don't have any visual output: they are not GUI applications, nor are they console applications providing text output, neither do they take any direct interactive input.

Services are special NT processes that require different treatment than other NT processes. They are started by the system rather than by an interactive user and this means that the startup code in a service is a little more complicated than usual. However, to a large extent this is boilerplate code that is common to all services.

This chapter is divided into two. In the first half, I'll describe what NT services are and go through the code required to start a service and provide communications with the system and to clients. In the second half, I'll show you how to package a DCOM server as an NT service. The example in this chapter revisits the window enumeration example from Chapter 2, providing this as a service. The chapter closes with an explanation and example of how to use the NT Event Log, the only consistent way for a service to log administrative messages.

NT Services

A service EXE can be thought of as a collection of services in one file. The EXE has a single **main()** or **WinMain()** entry point, but the function of this code is just to register one or more **ServiceMain()** functions with the **Service Control Manager** (SCM). The SCM then calls a **ServiceMain()** function when it wishes to start a service. However, the startup procedure does not end here; a service will serve a client, but it must also be controlled by the system, so the **ServiceMain()** function will register a control function with the SCM and it is at this point that the service can be started.

If this sounds a little confusing think of how a Windows GUI application is arranged. **WinMain()** is the entry point, but this is not the main code for the application. **WinMain()** sets up the infrastructure to allow communications between the application and the system. It is the system, through Windows messages, that tells the application to start up.

Work in a GUI application is carried out in windows, it is the responsibility of the **WinMain()** function to create the initial windows and to tell the system how to communicate with those windows, it does this by registering a window procedure for each window type (a window's 'class'). The window procedure is called by the system when the system needs to inform the window of some action. This may be immediate (the creation of the window) or the window procedure may not be called for a long time. When the system has a message for the window, it calls the window procedure passing it the message. (This, of course, is not the full story since the **WinMain()** function actually polls the system for messages in its *message loop*, but part of this loop is a call to **DispatchMessage()** where the system sends the extracted message to the window's window procedure.)

Since a service EXE is a *collection* of services it has an extra level. A service is a Win32 process, but it does not matter whether its entry point is **main()** or **WinMain()** since there is no interactive input and so it has no visual component (however, this does not means that it does not have any windows, since a service could implement a COM server and, as we saw in Chapter 6, a COM server that uses a Single Threaded Apartment has a window to synchronize access). The entry point, **main()** or **WinMain()**, gives the SCM an array of **ServiceMain()** pointers, one for each service. These entry point functions are equivalent to the GUI process' **WinMain()**. The system (in this case the SCM) calls these registered **ServiceMain()** functions when it wants to inform the service of some action. This is shown in the following diagram:

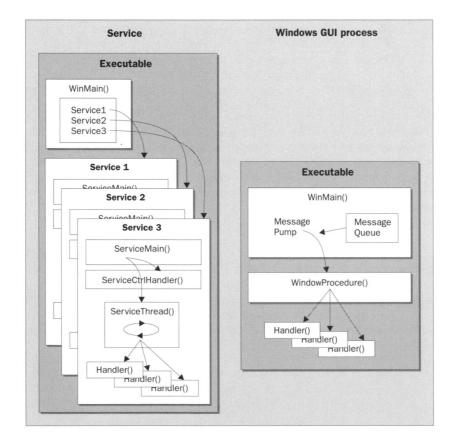

It is here that the analogy starts to disappear. In a GUI application most of the interaction with the process is done through the process' Windows message queue (although GUI applications can create a named pipe end point, or a Winsock socket for client communications). In the case of a service, *no* interaction is expected from the interactive user. In fact, I should be more assertive here: not only shouldn't you expect any interaction from the currently logged on user, you should not even expect there to be a logged on user.

So, to get commands to do some work, the service must create some inter-process communication mechanism. The following table lists some of the IPC mechanisms that can be used:

IPC Mechanism	Inter-machine?
Named Pipes	Yes
Mailslot	Yes
MAPI	Yes
TCP or UDP sockets	Yes
Memory Mapped File based message queue	No
Windows message queue via a hidden window	No
DDE	Yes (with NetDDE)
Microsoft RPC	Yes
COM	Yes (with DCOM)

Some of these are low-level (like TCP/UDP sockets), and hence require code to initialize and maintain the communications. Others, like named pipes and RPC have well defined APIs to set up the end points and handle facilities like security. To set up the IPC mechanism, the service should start up a new thread in the **ServiceMain()** to initialize the mechanism and then wait for a client connection. The rough analogy here to the GUI application is the call to **GetMessage()** in the application's **WinMain()** that will create a message queue (if one doesn't exist) and then wait for a message.

Utilities

NT needs services, just about all the underlying work in NT is carried out by services. There are four common ways of finding out what services are available or running.

 Control Panel

WinMsd

SC

Registry

Control Panel

The most common way of configuring services is to use the Services applet in the control panel. This allows you to view all the currently registered services, their start up parameters and also to determine if the service has already started.

Services

An example of the view of the applet is:

Service	Status	Startup	
Remote Procedure Call (RPC) Service	Started	Automatic	Close
Schedule		Manual	Start
Server	Started	Automatic	
SNMP	Started	Automatic	Stop
SNMP Trap Service		Manual	
Spooler	Started	Automatic	Pause
TCP/IP NetBIOS Helper	Started	Automatic	Continue
Telephony Service		Manual	
UPS		Manual	Startup...
Workstation	Started	Automatic	HW Profiles...

Startup Parameters:

Help

You will become quite adept at using this applet during your time developing services. Briefly, here is a description of what each part of the dialog is for:

The list box shows the currently registered services and whether each has been started; it also gives details of how the service is started (Automatic - at boot time; Manual - with user intervention; Disabled - the service cannot be started).

Although the system will start a service (if instructed) at boot up, you can start and stop services using the SCM, and this is the reason for the Start, Stop, Pause and Continue buttons. If you start a service, you will get a dialog like this:

Service Control

Attempting to Start the Schedule service on ZEUS

When you attempt to stop a service, a similar dialog is shown:

Service Control

Attempting to Stop the Schedule service on ZEUS

These dialogs show an animated stopwatch to keep you informed about the progress of the action. You will see later how the dialog determines if the service has started (or stopped) successfully and what feedback is used to make the stopwatch hand move. (The Pause and Continue buttons produce similar dialogs.)

If the service requires information to be passed to it on the command line at start up, this data can be entered in the edit box near the bottom of the main dialog, this data is sent to the **ServiceMain()** function of the selected service. You can think of this as analogous to the command line passed to the entry point (**main()** or **WinMain()**) of a normal Win32 process.

Some services require more start up information than this and so these parameters are usually obtained from the user via a Control Panel applet for the service. This applet could then start the service and pass the startup information, or it could store the service parameters in some kind of persistent storage. The most appropriate persistent storage is usually the registry. A service applet like this provides initialization parameters, it is not a GUI front end to a service.

The HW Profiles... button determines the hardware profiles for which the currently selected service is enabled or disabled. For example, you may have a portable computer, which you use on the road and in the office with a docking station. This docking station gives you access to a LAN. Since you only have access to the LAN when the computer is docked, you may decide that some services (for example, the Network Monitoring Agent used by NetMon) can only be used when the machine is docked.

> **Remember that services are processes and they take up system resources when they are running. If you are running low on available memory, it may be useful to stop any unnecessary services (assuming you know which are necessary and which are not!).**

Finally the Startup... button allows you to determine how the service is started. This is the source of the data in the third column of the list box. We looked briefly at this in the last chapter, but for completeness here it is again:

The top frame determines how the service is started. The lower frame determines the security context that will be used. This allows you to determine the account that will be used when the service is started. Selecting the first option uses the **System** account as we discussed in Chapter 7. This account is quite privileged in some respects, but not in others.

Since this account is a built-in account you cannot log on as **System** and configure it. On the other hand, if you specify a specific account (local or domain), you can log on to that account and set up the network shares that the account has access to. Indeed the **System** is a **null session account** so other machines will reject any attempt to access them using this account, even if the machine has granted access to **Everyone**.

If the service must access some other network resource, there are two solutions. Either the network administrator can change the remote machines so that they allow connections from null sessions (either on directory shares or via named pipes) or impersonation can be used. The first solution is a desperate action and shouldn't really be considered as a viable option because it reduces the security of your machines across the board; the second one requires that the service can determine the identity of the client and use that identity.

I said that the **System** account is privileged. You may remember from Chapter 7 that we showed that it has 20 privileges, compared with the 16 privileges held by a standard administrator account. You can see the privileges listed in the table below:

Privilege	System	Administrator
SeAssignPrmaryTokenPrivilege	✓	
SeAuditPivilege	✓	
SeBackupPrivilege	✓	✓
SeChangeNotifyPrivilege	✓	✓
SeCreatePagefilePrivilege	✓	✓
SeCreatePermanentPrivilege	✓	
SeCreateTokenPrivilege	✓	
SeDebugPrivilege	✓	✓
SeIncreaseBasePriorityPrivilege	✓	✓
SeIncreaseQuotaPrivilege	✓	✓
SeLoadDriverPrivilege	✓	✓
SeLockMemoryPrivilege	✓	
SeProfileSingleProcessPrivilege	✓	✓
SeRemoteShutdownPrivilege		✓
SeRestorePrivilege	✓	✓
SeSecurityPrivilege	✓	✓
SeShutdownPrivilege	✓	✓
SeSystemEnvironmentPrivilege	✓	✓
SeSystemtimePrivilege	✓	✓
SeSystemProfilePrivilege		✓

Privilege	System	Administrator
SeTakeOwnershipPrivilege	✓	✓
SeTcbPrivilege	✓	

The two privileges that the administrator has that **System** doesn't have are **SeRemoteShutdownPrivilege** and **SeSystemProfilePrivilege**. These two allow the account to remotely shutdown a machine and to use the NT profiler, neither of which is appropriate to an account that normally has no interaction with the desktop.

However, the 6 privileges that **System** has that an Administrator doesn't have are quite significant:

Privilege	Description
SeAssignPrmaryTokenPrivilege	Allowed to modify a process security access token.
SeAuditPivilege	Allowed to generate security audits.
SeCreatePermanentPrivilege	Allowed to create special NT permanent objects.
SeCreateTokenPrivilege	Allowed to create security access tokens.
SeLockMemoryPrivilege	Allows this user to lock pages in memory.
SeTcbPrivilege	Allows the user to perform as part of the operating system.

By possessing these privileges, this account can create and manipulate access tokens; it can generate audits; it can lock pages in memory (which is quite antisocial since this will make physical memory more scarce and make other processes more reliant on paged virtual memory) and it marks the user as 'part of the operating system'.

One other property of the **System** account is that if your file system is NTFS, by default the **System** account has access to all files (of course, if the file system is FAT or FAT32 every account has access to all files). You can select files and remove **System** from the DACL, but it is generally not recommended. The **System** account, is a useful account, as long as it does not need to access remote resources.

Winmsd

A little known NT utility is **WinMsd**, which can be found in the **System32** directory. This utility has been revamped in NT 4.0 and it lists all the currently installed services and their status in a more compact form than the Control Panel applet.

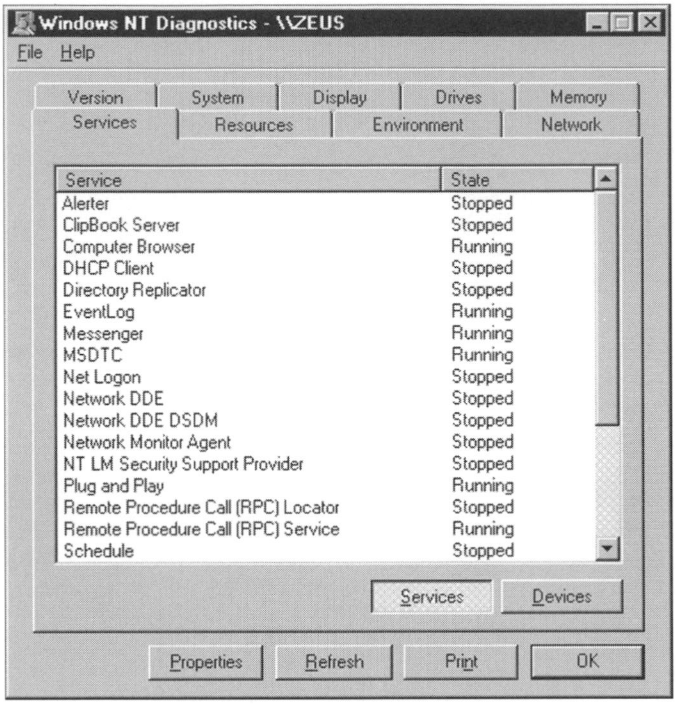

SC

SC.exe is a command line utility, provided with the Win32 SDK, that does more than just list the running services. The following screenshot shows the command line switches that can be used with SC.

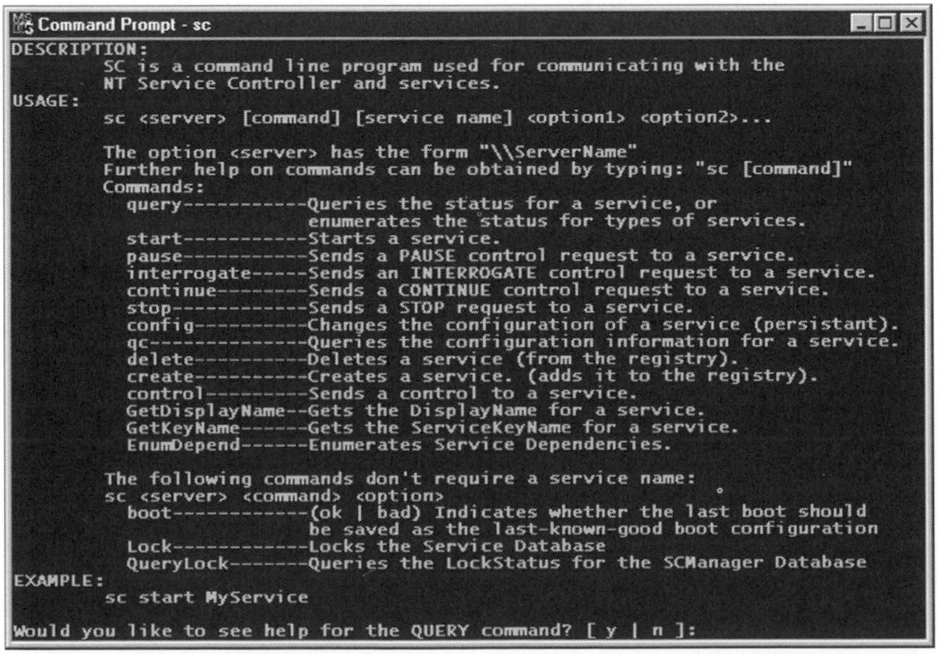

The significant difference between this utility and, say, **Winmsd** is that the latter is concerned only with the *local* machine. **SC** will allow you to query a remote machine for the running services and perform other administrative tasks.

This utility is invaluable for developing services, but note that many of its features require the user to have Administrator privileges.

Registry

All information about services is held in the registry. Later on in this chapter (and throughout the Win32 documentation), you will see the term *the services database*. Well, that's the registry. The information about installed services and device drivers can be found under

HKEY_LOCAL_MACHINE\SYSTEM\CurrentControlSet\Services

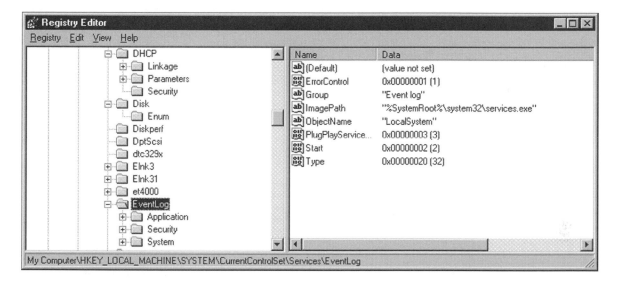

Every entry has the name of the service and under that key are other keys or named values that define how the service behaves. For example the startup options for a service appear in the registry under the **Start** named value. When you install a service, you must add entries into the registry, otherwise the Service Control Manager does not have enough information to locate and start the service. In particular, the **ImagePath** of a service points to the executable that contains the service. If you browse through these settings you will see that the **ImagePath** of many of the services points to the same file (**Services.exe**), this reinforces the description above of a service executable as being a container for one or more services.

Writing an NT Service

There are essentially three stages of initialization required in the implementation of a service executable. These are:

- An executable entrypoint (**main()** or **WinMain()**)
- **ServiceMain()**
- **ServiceCtrlHandler()**

The following is a simple code example:

```
VOID WINAPI FirstServiceMain(DWORD argc, LPTSTR* argv);
VOID WINAPI SecondServiceMain(DWORD argc, LPTSTR* argv);

VOID WINAPI main()
{
   SERVICE_TABLE_ENTRY ServiceDispatchTable[]=
   {
      { _T("FirstService") , FirstServiceMain  },
      { _T("SecondService"), SecondServiceMain },
      { NULL               , NULL              }
   };

   if (!StartServiceCtrlDispatcher(ServiceDispatchTable))
   {
      OutputDebugString(_T("StartServiceCtrlDispatcher() error\n"));
   }
}
```

Executable Entry Point

The executable entry point has three main uses. The first is that it registers with the SCM the **ServiceMain()** function(s) for the service(s) that the executable contains. In this scenario the entry point function is called by the SCM which expects prompt action. Within about 30 seconds of the call, this function must call **StartServiceCtrlDispatcher()**, otherwise the service is terminated. This function has a single parameter that is a pointer to an array of **SERVICE_TABLE_ENTRY** structures:

```
typedef struct _SERVICE_TABLE_ENTRY
{
   LPTSTR                   lpServiceName;
   LPSERVICE_MAIN_FUNCTION  lpServiceProc;
} SERVICE_TABLE_ENTRY, *LPSERVICE_TABLE_ENTRY;
```

The last entry in the array has **NULL** values for each of these fields, to mark the end of the array, much as you do with a string.

The **SERVICE_TABLE_ENTRY struct** associates a service name with a **ServiceMain()** function in the executable. If there is just one service in the process then the name is not used, it is ignored. The **StartServiceCtrlDispatcher()** function will return a value indicating whether the registration is successful. If it isn't successful, the SCM will not call the services in this executable and so the executable should stop, by returning.

The second use of the entry point function is for global initialization. There are several places where initialization is appropriate. This is where you should initialize data that is global to all services in the executable. However, it must be done before the call to **StartServiceCtrlDispatcher()** and it must not take more than 30 seconds. Another method is to create a thread to do the initializations before this call. However, this then brings in issues of synchronization, in particular ensuring that the services do not access the data before it has been initialized.

The final use of the entry point is for installation and uninstallation. Normally, a service should not be called by the interactive user from the command line, and you should catch any such calls either by writing an error message (to the event log), or by running the service function without any calls to the SCM. This last action still allows the service to initialize any IPC endpoint and hence accept client connections, but since the process is run under the security context of the interactive user, it will not have the privileges expected under the **System** account and as such it may not run as expected. Also running a service this way means that the SCM will not be able to control the service.

The other thing that could be done when a service executable is started at the command line is to check for command line switches to install or uninstall the service. We will see later how to do this (or at least how ATL does this). This is quite a convenient place to put this code, as it keeps all the installation code together with the service.

ServiceMain()

The developer chooses what to call this function, but the prototype is:

```
VOID WINAPI ServiceMain(DWORD dwArgc, LPTSTR *lpszArgv);
```

This has a remarkable resemblance to the C **main()** function. In fact it has the same purpose. The SCM creates a new thread and calls this function when it is starting the service, and it will pass any command line parameters through to the service via the **lpszArgv** parameter (the number of parameters is passed in via **dwArgc**). As with **main()** the first argument string is always the name of the service, so **dwArgc** is always at least 1.

```
SERVICE_STATUS          FirstServiceStatus;
SERVICE_STATUS_HANDLE   FirstServiceStatusHandle;

VOID WINAPI FirstServiceMain (DWORD argc, LPTSTR* argv)
{
  DWORD status;
  DWORD specificError;

  FirstServiceStatus.dwServiceType    = SERVICE_WIN32;
  FirstServiceStatus.dwCurrentState   = SERVICE_START_PENDING;
  FirstServiceStatus.dwControlsAccepted =
                    SERVICE_ACCEPT_STOP |
                    SERVICE_ACCEPT_PAUSE_CONTINUE;
  FirstServiceStatus.dwWin32ExitCode = 0;
  FirstServiceStatus.dwServiceSpecificExitCode = 0;
  FirstServiceStatus.dwCheckPoint    = 0;
  FirstServiceStatus.dwWaitHint      = 0;

  FirstServiceStatusHandle = RegisterServiceCtrlHandler(
                    _T("FirstService"),
                    FirstServiceCtrlHandler);
```

```
    if (FirstServiceStatusHandle == (SERVICE_STATUS_HANDLE)0)
    {
       OutputDebugString(_T("RegisterServiceCtrlHandler() error\n"));
       return;
    }

    // Initialize the service
    status = FirstServiceInitialization(argc, argv, &specificError);

    // Check for errors
    if (status != NO_ERROR)
    {
       // Found an error so set the status to inform SCM
       // and return
       FirstServiceStatus.dwCurrentState  = SERVICE_STOPPED;
       FirstServiceStatus.dwCheckPoint     = 0;
       FirstServiceStatus.dwWaitHint       = 0;
       FirstServiceStatus.dwWin32ExitCode = status;
       FirstServiceStatus.dwServiceSpecificExitCode =
                       specificError;

       SetServiceStatus (FirstServiceStatusHandle,
                       &FirstServiceStatus);
       return;
    }

    // Now that we've initialized the service, we need to
    // report service status
    FirstServiceStatus.dwCurrentState = SERVICE_RUNNING;
    FirstServiceStatus.dwCheckPoint   = 0;
    FirstServiceStatus.dwWaitHint     = 0;

    if (!SetServiceStatus(FirstServiceStatusHandle,
                       &FirstServiceStatus))
    {
       OutputDebugString(_T("SetServiceStatus() error\n"));
       return;
    }

    // ... This is where your service does its work

    OutputDebugString(_T("Returning from FirstServiceMain()\n"));
    return;
}

// Initialization function.
DWORD FirstServiceInitialization(DWORD argc, LPTSTR* argv,
                                 DWORD* specificError)
{

    //... Do the initialization here

    return 0;
}
```

This function should call **RegisterServiceCtrlHandler()** to register the **ServiceCtrlHandler()** for this service and then let the SCM know what is happening with a call to **SetServiceStatus()**.

This first function has two parameters: the first is the name of the service and the second is a pointer to the **ServiceCtrlHandler()** for this particular service. This handler function will only ever be called by the SCM, although another process can get access to the SCM and ask it to send the **ServiceCtrlHandler()** a message.

To keep the SCM informed at all times, the service must call **SetServiceStatus()**. This function has two parameters, the first is a handle returned by the previous call to **RegisterServiceCtrlHandler()** and the second is a pointer to a **SERVICE_STATUS** structure that indicates the current status of the service.

```
typedef struct _SERVICE_STATUS
{
    DWORD dwServiceType;
    DWORD dwCurrentState;
    DWORD dwControlsAccepted;
    DWORD dwWin32ExitCode;
    DWORD dwServiceSpecificExitCode;
    DWORD dwCheckPoint;
    DWORD dwWaitHint;
} SERVICE_STATUS, *LPSERVICE_STATUS;
```

This structure contains information about the sort of service that is starting and what stage it is at in the startup process. It has more uses than just passing back status codes to the SCM! The service calls **SetServiceStatus()** at strategic points during the service's startup and it is the source of the clock ticks on the stopwatch that is shown by the Services applet.

The **dwServiceType** is one of:

Flag	Description
SERVICE_WIN32_OWN_PROCESS	There is only one service in this process.
SERVICE_WIN32_SHARE_PROCESS	There is more than one service in this process.
SERVICE_KERNEL_DRIVER	This is an NT device driver.
SERVICE_FILE_SYSTEM_DRIVER	This is an NT file system driver.
SERVICE_INTERACTIVE_PROCESS	This service can interact with the desktop.

The last one is interesting. This specifies that the service can create windows on the default desktop of the currently logged on user, this may sound tempting, but it should be avoided if possible, since you cannot guarantee that there will be an interactive user.

However, it can be useful during the development process, since it allows message boxes (intentional or due to assertions or exceptions) to be shown on the interactive desktop. You should be careful with message boxes, as we discussed in the last chapter.

dwCurrentState specifies whether the service has initialized or not. It can be one of:

Flag	Description
SERVICE_STOPPED	The service is not running.
SERVICE_START_PENDING	The service is starting.
SERVICE_STOP_PENDING	The service is stopping.
SERVICE_RUNNING	The service is running.
SERVICE_CONTINUE_PENDING	The service continue is pending.
SERVICE_PAUSE_PENDING	The service pause is pending.
SERVICE_PAUSED	The service is paused.

The function should specify **SERVICE_START_PENDING** until the initialization is complete, in which case **SetServiceStatus()** should give **SERVICE_RUNNING**.

To inform the SCM as to what control signals the service can accept, the **dwControlsAccepted** member specifies a combination of:

Flag	Meaning
SERVICE_ACCEPT_STOP	The service can be stopped.
SERVICE_ACCEPT_PAUSE_CONTINUE	The service can be paused and continued.
SERVICE_ACCEPT_SHUTDOWN	The service is notified when the system shuts down.

These determine the access that other processes have to the service through SCM, and specify which messages the service will accept. A service could decide that these control messages are only acceptable at particular times. For example, if the service is doing some critical database transaction, it could disable all messages until the transaction is complete, and then it could call **SetServiceStatus()** to enable them again. These messages are handled in the **ServiceCtrlHandler()** function, and are listed later.

If the service fails to initialize properly, it can send back an error code through the **dwWin32ExitCode** and **dwServiceSpecificCode** fields. The former passes a Win32 error code, but if you want to determine your own code, pass a value of **ERROR_SERVICE_SPECIFIC_ERROR** in **dwWin32ExitCode** and pass the code in **dwServiceSpecificCode**.

Finally, the last two members of the **struct**, **dwCheckPoint** and **dwWaitHint**, give an indication of how far into the initialization or shutdown operation the service is and how much more there is to come. The first, **dwCheckPoint** should be incremented in the service code every time the **SetServiceStatus()** function is called. The last parameter gives an indication of how long, in milliseconds, it will be before the **SetServiceStatus()** function will be called again. If **dwCheckPoint** is not incremented before this time expires, or there has not been a change in **dwCurrentState**, the SCM will assume that the service has died.

The **ServiceMain()** function for a service should perform any initialization required by the service and, at each stage of the process, inform the SCM how it is doing. This is important, because the service may be started before any user has logged on, so it should be able to start up without any user interaction. To enable this, the SCM errs on the side of caution, so that if the service looks like it is not starting up properly, the SCM will stop the process and treat the service as unstartable.

If the purpose of your service is to wait upon some event or perhaps a client IPC connection, the **ServiceMain()** function should be used to kick off the initialization of this mechanism and then go into the waiting state. However, prior to going into a waiting state, the service should indicate that it is ready for action by sending a **SetServiceStatus()** with **SERVICE_RUNNING**.

When an application's **main()** function returns, the application has finished. This is the same with a service, except that it is the **ServiceMain()** function returning that indicates that the service has finished. So to prevent the service shutting down prematurely, the **ServiceMain()** must wait for some indication from the service code that it should terminate. One implementation is to create an event and wait for it to become signaled, another (which is used by ATL because COM requires a message queue) is to implement a Windows message loop, returning from the **ServiceMain()** when the **WM_QUIT** message is received.

It is up to the service code (either the code used to service client requests or the **ServiceCtrlHandler()**) to tell the **ServiceMain()** function to end. This code should signal the event, or post the message to the main thread, to indicate that the service should stop.

ServiceCtrlHandler

Once the handler is registered with the SCM, it will be called when the SCM wants the service to do something. Note that this is the *SCM* wanting some action from the service and not a *client*. The handler function is only concerned with requests from (or *via*) the SCM.

```
VOID WINAPI FirstServiceCtrlHandler(DWORD FwdControl)
{
   DWORD status;

   switch(FwdControl)
   {
     case SERVICE_CONTROL_PAUSE:

       // ... Add your code to make the sure the service
       // pauses

         FirstServiceStatus.dwCurrentState = SERVICE_PAUSED;
         break;

     case SERVICE_CONTROL_CONTINUE:

       // ... Add your code to make the sure the service
       // continues to run

         FirstServiceStatus.dwCurrentState = SERVICE_RUNNING;
         break;

     case SERVICE_CONTROL_STOP:

       // ...Add your code to make the sure the service
       // stops

         FirstServiceStatus.dwWin32ExitCode = 0;
         FirstServiceStatus.dwCurrentState =
                          SERVICE_STOP_PENDING;
         FirstServiceStatus.dwCheckPoint   = 0;
```

```
            FirstServiceStatus.dwWaitHint      = 0;

            if (!SetServiceStatus(FirstServiceStatusHandle,
                                  &FirstServiceStatus))
            {
              OutputDebugString(_T("SetServiceStatus() ")
                                _T("error\n"));
            }

            return;

          case SERVICE_CONTROL_INTERROGATE:
            // Proceed to set the status
            break;

          default:
            OutputDebugString(_T("Illegal operation code \n"));
             return;
        }

        // Send current status.
        if (!SetServiceStatus(FirstServiceStatusHandle,
                              &FirstServiceStatus))
        {
          OutputDebugString(_T("SetServiceStatus() error\n"));
        }
        return;
    }
```

As with all other interaction between the service and SCM, the service must call **SetServiceStatus()** in the handler whether the handler does any work or not. The **ServiceCtrlHandler()** function can have whatever name seems appropriate, but it must have the following prototype:

```
  VOID WINAPI ServiceCtrlHandler(DWORD fdwControl);
```

The **fdwControl** parameter is one of:

Message	Meaning
SERVICE_CONTROL_STOP	Requests a service to stop.
SERVICE_CONTROL_PAUSE	Requests the service to pause.
SERVICE_CONTROL_CONTINUE	Continues the service after a pause.
SERVICE_CONTROL_SHUTDOWN	Indicates that the system is shutting down.
SERVICE_CONTROL_INTERROGATE	Requests that the service updates its status held by the SCM.
128 – 256	User defined code.

The first five parameters are NT predefined; however, the service can also accept values in the range 128 - 256, which are interpreted as user defined messages. To be able to accept user-defined values, the service must be started with **SERVICE_USER_DEFINED_CONTROL** access. This means that a client can send requests to the service via the SCM using these codes. However, note that no other data can be sent and that the only reply back from the service is from the **SERVICE_STATUS** returned in **SetServiceStatus()**, so it is not the most ideal way to communicate with the service.

A service *must* handle **SERVICE_CONTROL_INTERROGATE**, but it can choose whether it wishes to handle the other control messages by setting a value in the **dwControlsAccepted** member sent via **SetServiceStatus()**. When handling the control message, the function must return within 30 seconds of starting. Thus if the handler will take longer than this, it must create a secondary thread and return the appropriate **SERVICE_*xxx*_PENDING** value.

Logging Errors

We know that a service, by default, runs in the **System** account and that, running under this account, the service can be configured to interact with the default desktop. We also know that a service can be configured to run under a particular account, or it can impersonate a user, and if it has the necessary security access, it can access the interactive desktop.

If something catastrophic happens in the service, it may be necessary to interact with the desktop, but remember that a service should not expect there to be an interactive user and accessing the default desktop will be pointless since there will be no one to interact with? If this is the case, what should a service do if there are some diagnostic messages that need to be logged?

One possibility would be to write the message to a private log file, but there are many problems with this idea. The first problem is that you will need to have some convention as to where these log files are kept. If such a convention existed and every service complied with it, the number of log files could be quite large. In fact, individual files could also get quite large if the services' logging routines did not provide some code to counteract it.

Another problem is that one service may rely on another service and so diagnostic messages from one service may be pertinent to another log file. Finally, if the server machine is in a locked cupboard, the log files must be shared across the network to allow an administrator to view them. There must be some way to wrap up all the functionality together.

There is—NT provides a service called the **EventLog** (you can find it in the control panel Services applet). This allows any process to register itself as a source for event log messages and once the process has done this, it can report messages to the Event Log. The **EventLog** service handles its own log files and also handles any synchronization issues of several processes trying to report to or read from the event log at any time.

NT has been designed to be multilingual, and so should your processes. Because of this, the API used to add a message to the event log, **ReportEvent()**, passes the message as an identifier for a format string and an array of strings to insert into the format string. The format string is a bit like a **printf()** format string, providing insert parameter placeholders like **%s**.

Part of the registration of an event log source requires a message resource file to be specified. This file could be any file from which a **HMODULE** can be obtained, which means it could be an EXE or a DLL (usually it is a resource-only DLL). This resource file contains the format message strings bound in as a resource created by the message compiler (**Mc.exe**). These strings can be marked as being for a particular language ID, and there can be many language ID strings for a single message ID. This means that when a process reads the event log, it can pass a language ID and the system will make sure that the correct format string is used.

The NT utility, **Eventvwr.exe**, does just this for you: if your machine has been installed with the French version of NT, the French format strings will be used and if the US version is installed, the English format strings will be used. If a language-specific format string is not available, the Event Viewer will use the language neutral string (in international English) or state that the format string cannot be found.

If you want to know more about the event log, you can look in the Win32 SDK documentation, but be warned that the API is a little obscure and there are several places where it can catch you out. The following code is taken from the ATL code for a service:

```
void CServiceModule::LogEvent(LPCTSTR pFormat, ...)
{
   TCHAR   chMsg[256];
   HANDLE  hEventSource;
   LPTSTR  lpszStrings[1];
   va_list pArg;

   va_start(pArg, pFormat);
   _vstprintf(chMsg, pFormat, pArg);
   va_end(pArg);

   lpszStrings[0] = chMsg;

   if (m_bService)
   {
      /* Get a handle to use with ReportEvent(). */
      hEventSource = RegisterEventSource(NULL,
                                         m_szServiceName);
      if (hEventSource != NULL)
      {
         /* Write to event log. */
         ReportEvent(hEventSource,
                     EVENTLOG_INFORMATION_TYPE,
                     0, 0, NULL, 1, 0,
                     (LPCTSTR*) &lpszStrings[0],
                     NULL);
         DeregisterEventSource(hEventSource);
      }
   }
   else
   {
      // As we are not running as a service, just write
      // the error to the console.
      _putts(chMsg);
   }
}
```

This code really does not do justice to what you can do with the API. The code actually behaves like **printf()**, taking a format string and insert parameters, it then creates a string from that and then uses **ReportEvent()** to report this with message ID of 0, *whatever the message is*. Since it creates the fully formatted string with a call to **_vstprintf()**, this means that the language used in the message is defined by the process and not the event log reader. You really should not do this in professional software, as it is rather presumptive to assume that all your customers speak the same language as you do.

The ATL code must be able to log an event message, and this is the simplest way to do this using the **EventLog**. However, for a complete application you should create a message resource file, and register this and the event source. I will show you how to do this later in the chapter.

Communication with SCM

Thus far the only process talking to the service is the SCM via the **ServiceCtrlHandler()**. Other processes can start and stop the service as well as send the service control messages, but they must do it via the SCM.

To do this, the process first calls **OpenSCManager()** to get a handle to the SCM. Once the process has the SCM handle, it can then call **OpenService()** or **CreateService()** to get a handle to the service. If **OpenService()** is used, the service is not started, the API just returns a handle. You can start the service with this handle by calling **StartService()**. The function takes an array of strings that are passed as parameters to the **ServiceMain()** function of the service.

If the service has not been installed, the process can call **CreateService()** which will add the service to the SCM Database (the registry) and then start it. Both **OpenService()** and **CreateService()** will return a handle which can be used in a call to **ControlService()** to send a control message to the service.

The messages that can be sent to the service have been identified in the section above for **ServiceCtrlHandler()**. If you specify **SERVICE_USER_DEFINED_CONTROL** as the **dwDesiredAccess** parameter for **OpenService()** or **CreateService()** then you can send a user defined control message in the range 128-256. The service can respond to the message, but the only return value will be in the **SERVICE_STATUS** that was passed to the service from the calling process. This structure has one 32-bit value, **dwServiceSpecificExitCode**, that can be used to return a value.

This is rather restrictive, and for better control, a service should use some other IPC mechanism as mentioned before. Note that **OpenSCManager()** takes a machine name as a parameter. If you have the correct security, you can open a handle to the SCM on a remote machine and no setting up of the remote connection is required.

To determine whether the service can accept a control message, you can either call **QueryServiceStatus()** or call **ControlService()** with a message of **SERVICE_CONTROL_INTERROGATE**.

Service Database

The installed services are held in the Service Control Manager Database. This is, in fact, a key in the registry and although you could install and configure services by manipulating the registry directly, the SCM API is easier to use and provides checks on the parameters passed.

To create a service, add it to the SCM Database and start the service, you call **CreateService()**. This is quite a complex function and has the following parameters:

Parameter	Type	Description
hSCManager	SC_HANDLE	Handle to the SCM.
lpServiceName	LPCTSTR	The name of the service.
lpDisplayName	LPCTSTR	The name used in the control panel for the service.
dwDesiredAccess	DWORD	The access that the calling process has to the service.
dwServiceType	DWORD	Determines the type of the service.
dwStartType	DWORD	Determines how the service is started.
dwErrorControl	DWORD	The severity of the failure code.
lpBinaryPathName	LPCTSTR	Path to the executable that contains the service.
lpLoadOrderGroup	LPCTSTR	Defines a group of services and the order they are started.
lpdwTagId	LPDWORD	A tag used to identify this service in the previous parameter.
lpDependencies	LPCTSTR	Gives the names of the services that must be started before this service can start.
lpServiceStartName	LPCTSTR	A username to use when starting the process.
lpPassword	LPCTSTR	The password of the account specified previously.

The **lpdwTagID** and **lpLoadOrderGroup** are used by kernel device drivers to specify groups of services and the order that they should be loaded. For Win32 services these are ignored.

Most of the other parameters have been explained earlier, but several are of interest. The last two determine the account under which the service is run. The account name is either a domain (or local) account or is **NULL**, which specifies that the **System** account should be used. The **dwErrorControl** parameter determines the severity of the failure of the service to start. These severities are:

Value	Description
SERVICE_ERROR_IGNORE	The startup program logs the error but continues the startup operation.
SERVICE_ERROR_NORMAL	The startup program logs the error and displays a message but continues the startup operation.
SERVICE_ERROR_SEVERE	The startup program logs the error. If the last-known-good configuration is being started, the startup operation continues. Otherwise, the system is restarted with the last-known-good configuration.
SERVICE_ERROR_CRITICAL	The startup program logs the error, if possible. If the last-known-good configuration is being started, the startup operation fails. Otherwise, the system is restarted with the last-known-good configuration.

To add the service to the Service Control Manager Database, **CreateService()** uses the **lpServiceName** to add a key under the following key in the registry:

```
HKEY_LOCAL_MACHINE\System\CurrentControlSet\Services
```

It then adds the values specified in the function call as named values in this new key. If the service needs persistent start up information, it can store this in the registry as subkeys in this key.

The call to **CreateService()** returns a handle which can be used to identify the service when accessing the other SCM database API functions. When the calling process has finished with the handle, it can call **CloseServiceHandle()**. Note that the handle is closed with this API and not **CloseHandle()**, and that closing the handle does not stop the service or affect the service entry in the SCM database.

To stop a service, a process must call **ControlService()** with **SERVICE_CONTROL_STOP** and to mark the service for removal from the SCM Database, it can then call **DeleteService()**. The actual keys and subkeys for the service are only deleted when all the handles on the service are closed.

Finally, the parameters inserted into the SCM Database by **CreateService()** can be changed with a call to **ChangeServiceConfig()**.

Multithreading

If your service will allow multiple connections from clients, you must create some mechanism to handle this. You may immediately say "threads!" but while they are undoubtedly useful, using multiple threads can introduce subtle bugs in your program. The next chapter covers multithreading in depth, but it is worthwhile mentioning a couple of ways of using multiple threads in a service.

Worker Threads

The simplest model is to have a worker thread for every client connection. The thread lives as long as the connection remains. For example, your service listens on a TCP port in its service thread. When a connection is made, the service creates a new thread and passes the connection's socket to this thread which it uses to handle the request. The listening thread can now continue to listen for client connections. Such a simple scheme may look fine on the surface, but it is far from ideal.

The major problem is that if the service creates many threads, the machine will grind to a halt context switching between all of them. There is a simple illustrative example of this in the next chapter.

IO Completion Ports

Windows NT 3.5 introduced a new kernel object called an **IO Completion Port**. The idea here is to create a pool of a small number of worker threads that can service client requests. If a great number of client requests are made at any time, the requests exceeding the number of worker threads are blocked until a thread becomes free and only then can another request be allocated a thread.

IO completion ports use overlapped IO and so are restricted to those APIs that use file semantics, e.g. file operations, named pipes and sockets communications. The IO completion port API is quite badly documented, but once you get over the steep learning curve they do offer a more efficient thread model.

IO completion ports are covered briefly in the next chapter.

Registry Settings

A service's registry entries can be found under

`HKEY_LOCAL_MACHINE\System\CurrentControlSet\Services\`*`service`*

where *`service`* is the name of the service as given by the Services control panel applet (and is the `lpServiceName` parameter passed to `CreateService()`). The standard named values under this key are:

Value	Meaning
ErrorCode	The severity of the error code if the service fails to start.
Group	Gives the name of the group of which the service belongs (if it is a member of a group).
DependOnGroup	One or more groups of services that must be started before this service.
DependOnService	One or more services that must be started before this service.
ImagePath	The name of the service executable.
ObjectName	The account name under which the service is started.
Start	Specifies whether the service is loaded automatically, manually or is disabled.
Tag	A name that specifies this service in the load order of a group of services.
Type	The type of the service, either own process or shared process.

In addition to these, the service can add subkeys for its own use.

Global Settings

There are two important registry settings that affect all services: `NoInteractiveServices` and `WaitToKillServiceTimeout`:

You can specify that a service has access to the default desktop by marking it as an interactive service. You either do this in the control panel, if SCM will start the service, or if you will use `CreateService()`, you specify the `SERVICE_INTERACTIVE_PROCESS` in the `dwServiceType` parameter. There is a global value called `NoInteractiveServices` in the following registry key:

`HKEY_LOCAL_MACHINE\SYSTEM\CurrentControlSet\Control\Windows`

If `NoInteractiveServices` has a nonzero value then no service will run interactively, whatever value is used for `dwServiceType`.

Throughout the discussion above we have seen that the `ServiceMain()` and `ServiceCtrlhandler()` functions must be rather prompt in their actions. In particular, if the system is shutting down, a service will get the `SERVICE_CONTROL_SHUTDOWN` notification and will have 20 seconds to clean up any resources it has. This timeout can be changed by adding the named value, and the timeout in `WaitToKillServiceTimeout` under the key:

`HKEY_LOCAL_MACHINE\SYSTEM\CurrentControlSet\Control`

Security

As mentioned earlier, the service is likely to be started in the context of the **System** account, and to allow auditing to be attributed to the client, or even to allow the service to access resources only accessible to the client, the service must impersonate that client. To do this the service IPC mechanism must either have built-in security, thus allowing the service to use built-in IPC calls to impersonate the client (e.g. **ImpersonateNamedPipeClient()** or **RpcImpersonateClient()**) or the IPC must pass the necessary information for the service to log on (**LogonUser()**) as the user and then impersonate that user (**ImpersonateLoggedOnUser()**).

There are two functions that allow a process to get or set the security descriptor of a service. Such a process should get a handle to the service with a call to **OpenService()** or **CreateService()** and then it can pass this handle to **QueryServiceObjectSecurity()** to get the service security descriptor or to **SetServiceObjectSecurity()** to set it. Although a helper application could change the security descriptor of a service, normally a service would use the impersonation API to handle security in the security context of the client.

Debugging Services

The main problem with a service is that it runs under a different security context than the interactive user, since it usually runs under the **System** account. As such, it will more than likely act differently if you try and debug it under the context of the interactive user.

There are ways to get round this. One way is to start the service as usual and then run the Windows NT Task Manager. The Processes tab will list all active processes including any executables containing services. You can select a process and then right-click on it to get the context menu. This will allow you to start the currently registered debugger and attach it to the service:

If your favorite debugger is not registered as the default debugger, it may be invoked with a command line switch to attach it to a running process. The Win32 Knowledge Base gives full details of how to do this. Developer Studio for example, can be started with the **/P** switch to give the process ID of the debugee.

Another option could be to start the service from your debugger. However, the problem here is that the debugger has the security context of the interactive user. To get round this you can start the debugger from a command box that is running under the appropriate account. The easiest way to do this is to get the Scheduler service to start a command line with the **at** command.

If the current time is 12:00 type the following at the command line:

```
at 12:01 /interactive cmd.exe
```

This will start a command box in one minute's time, and this box will be running under whatever account the scheduler was configured to use (probably the **System** account), you can then use this to start your debugger. This will give you access to the service from an appropriate account. However, the service *process* must be written in such a way that allows the *service* to start when run from the command line. ATL code does allow this.

Normally a service is started and stopped by messages from the SCM. If the service is started from the command line and not started by SCM, it will not get messages from the service manager, so you won't be able to debug the handlers for control messages.

DCOM Services

When considering writing a DCOM server as a service, there are two things you need to consider: what you will lose and what you will gain. Let's consider each of these in turn.

Cons

The chief disadvantage of writing your DCOM server as an NT service is the loss of portability. You may not want to run your server solely on Windows NT. Windows 95 has no notion of an NT service. Although Windows 95 does allow for pseudo-services, as we discussed in Chapter 2, all this means is that the process is automatically started by the system when a user logs on. The other advantages of services, those of running under a privileged account and running without an interactive user, are not applicable to pseudo-services.

Of course, Windows 95 is a special case since to a large extent the Win32 code written for NT will work on Windows 95. Your server machine may be a Unix machine or a Mac. COM is, or will be, available on most Unix variations and the MacOS. This means that DCOM code can be written for these platforms that allow them to be clients and servers for DCOM, widening the interconnectivity options. If you write your server as an NT service, you are limiting its use to that platform.

To stress this point, the beta version of DCOM for Solaris comes with ATL, which is the same as ATL for Windows (with only a few minor differences). This means that most server code can be simply recompiled to create a DCOM server on Solaris. An NT service would need to be completely rewritten to convert it to a Solaris daemon.

Pros

Of course, dependence on NT may not be a problem for your particular server if it already has dependencies, but why bother to write your server as a service when even standard DCOM servers can be remotely activated? The two main reasons are performance and recovery from failure.

DCOM is ideal in terms of allowing you to provide methods on objects that can be called remotely. However, a DCOM object may have some complex initialization. For example, it might need to connect to some remote database, or maybe the DCOM server handles input and output to some hardware device.

There are obvious performance issues here. If the initialization is a once-only affair, and the initialized resource is shared by all subsequent DCOM objects, it makes sense to do this initialization at some point when there are not expected to be any client connections. Such a situation would be when the system starts and the processes that are automatically started when a system starts are services. (If the initialization takes more than 30 seconds, it needs to be done in a separate thread.)

Another case could be a server that obtains data from one source and then allows a client to connect to get the data. For example, a point of sale server could poll a central server every hour to get up to date catalogue and pricing information. By making the server a service and running it under the `System` account, no logged on user is required. If the machine needs to be rebooted, the server will restart and continue getting up to date information, without any extra human intervention.

Code

We have already seen that a service can be started either using the security context of the `System` account or under the context of a user account specified either in the control panel applet or as a parameter to `CreateProcess()`. The security context is important since the COM client will have a security context as well as the server, and if the two are different, there may be problems.

Indeed in NT 3.51, if the client and server contexts were different, the interaction was not possible. The only way to connect a client and server was to ensure that the two had the same security context. Normally, in NT 3.51, when your process activates a COM object, COM ensures that the object is activated with the right context. However, if the object class factory is in a service, COM does not have control over the security context of the object, which will take the context of the service. This meant that effectively the service had to be started with a particular account and could only service clients impersonating the same account. This was extremely restrictive.

NT 4.0 has added new COM security APIs that allow you to define the security blanket for the client-server interaction. This is a great innovation since now the server need not be started with a particular account and, similarly, the client does not have to log on as a particular account.

ATL Support for Services

In this section, we'll look at the code generated by the ATL COM AppWizard for a service and we'll use this as the basis for our own service that enumerates the windows on the desktop, just like the example from Chapter 2.

Start by creating an ATL project called **EnumWinSvr**, selecting Service (EXE) for the type of server that you want.

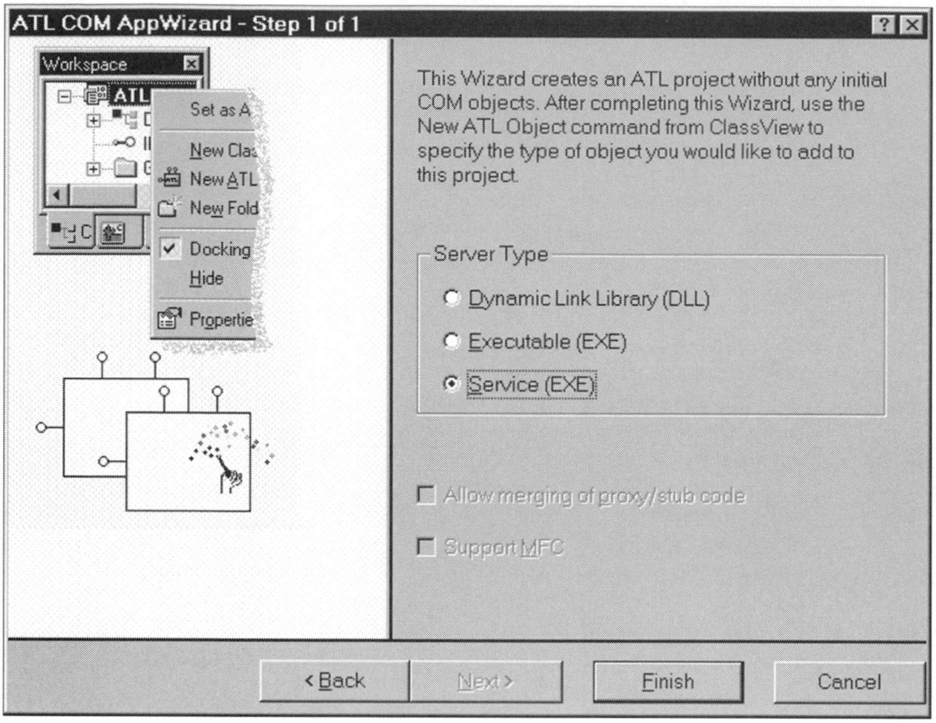

When you press the Finish button, the AppWizard will generate the new project and you'll be able to see the main classes for the service in the ClassView of the project workspace window.

For now, let's look at how ATL manages the service side of the code. The service's **WinMain()** is shown here:

```
extern "C" int WINAPI _tWinMain(HINSTANCE hInstance,
   HINSTANCE /*hPrevInstance*/, LPTSTR lpCmdLine,
   int /*nShowCmd*/)
{
   //this line necessary for _ATL_MIN_CRT
   lpCmdLine = GetCommandLine();
   _Module.Init(ObjectMap, hInstance, IDS_SERVICENAME);
   _Module.m_bService = TRUE;

   TCHAR szTokens[] = _T("-/");

   LPCTSTR lpszToken = FindOneOf(lpCmdLine, szTokens);
   while (lpszToken != NULL)
   {
      if (lstrcmpi(lpszToken, _T("UnregServer"))==0)
         return _Module.UnregisterServer();

      // Register as Local Server
      if (lstrcmpi(lpszToken, _T("RegServer"))==0)
         return _Module.RegisterServer(TRUE, FALSE);
```

```
      // Register as Service
      if (lstrcmpi(lpszToken, _T("Service"))==0)
         return _Module.RegisterServer(TRUE, TRUE);

      lpszToken = FindOneOf(lpszToken, szTokens);
   }

   // Are we Service or Local Server
   CRegKey keyAppID;
   LONG lRes = keyAppID.Open(HKEY_CLASSES_ROOT,
                             _T("AppID"));
   if (lRes != ERROR_SUCCESS)
      return lRes;

   CRegKey key;
   lRes = key.Open(keyAppID,
           _T("{DE524C41-A619-11D0-9B49-0060973044A8}"));
   if (lRes != ERROR_SUCCESS)
      return lRes;

   TCHAR szValue[_MAX_PATH];
   DWORD dwLen = _MAX_PATH;
   lRes = key.QueryValue(szValue, _T("LocalService"),
                         &dwLen);

   _Module.m_bService = FALSE;
   if (lRes == ERROR_SUCCESS)
      _Module.m_bService = TRUE;

   _Module.Start();

   // When we get here, the service has been stopped
   return _Module.m_status.dwWin32ExitCode;
}
```

The service starts by calling the **Init()** method. This sets up the COM infrastructure through a call to the base class **CComModule::Init()**, and then it obtains the service name from the application's resources, for registration purposes.

The next task is to see if the service has been started from the command line and if so if there are any command line parameters. This allows the user to install the service merely by running it with the command line switch **-Service**, eliminating any separate installation procedure. If the user wants to install the server the necessary changes are made to the registry and the process is terminated.

Note that **RegisterServer()** is called in two situations: when the process is being registered as a COM *server* (with the **-RegServer** switch) and when it is being registered as a *service* (with the **-Service** switch). In the former case, the necessary COM entries are added into the registry for a local server, but in the latter case the object is registered with the **LocalService** value allowing it to be used as a service. A function called **Install()** is called to add the service entries into the registry.

This is a nice touch, since it allows you to write a COM server and use the installation script to determine if the server should be used as a DCOM server (and hence objects are activated when needed) or as a service.

If the reason for running the process was for installing the server, then the process finishes at this point. Otherwise, the process has to determine if it was started as a COM server or as a service. It does this by looking for the **LocalService** value in the registry. The rules of activation order for COM are that if the server has a **LocalService** entry then this is used in preference to the **LocalServer32** entry. Once the process knows how it was started, it stores this information in an instance variable for later use.

Finally, the **WinMain()** function calls **_Module.Start()**. This function registers the service with a call to **StartServiceCtrlDispatcher()** as we would expect. This function specifies that its **ServiceMain()** function is the **static** member of the class called **_ServiceMain()** (a **static** is used here, and later on for the control handler function, because **static** members do not have an implicit **this** pointer in the function signature).

It then checks to see if the server is being run as a local server and, if so, calls the **Run()** method. Calling **Run()** like this means that the service's functionality is available, but not under the control of SCM via the normal services API.

If the server is run as a service, the SCM must be told this. When the service registers itself with the SCM with the call to **StartServiceCtrlDispatcher()** it is doing just this. The **CServiceModule::ServiceMain()** method starts the control dispatcher with a call to **StartServiceCtrlHandler()** passing the address of the **static** member **Handler()**, and then it runs the service by calling the class method **Run()**. **Run()** does all the COM stuff, registering the objects in the server and going into a message loop.

First, let's look at the handler code. Just as the **static() _ServiceMain()** calls the non-**static()** **ServiceMain()**, so the **_Handler()** method calls the non-**static Handler()**. This should handle messages sent from the SCM, but in this case only one of the standard control messages is handled with any code: **SERVICE_CONTROL_STOP**. It does this by posting a message to the current thread to quit. This breaks out of the message pump in the **Run()** method to allow it to return and thus allows the **ServiceMain()** to return and the service to stop.

The **Run()** function deserves better study:

```
void CServiceModule::Run()
{
    HRESULT hr;

    _Module.dwThreadID = GetCurrentThreadId();

    HRESULT hRes = CoInitialize(NULL);
    // If you are running on NT 4.0 or higher you can use
    // the following call
    //    instead to make the EXE free threaded.
    //  This means that calls come in on a random RPC thread
    //    HRESULT hRes = CoInitializeEx(NULL, COINIT_MULTITHREADED);

    _ASSERTE(SUCCEEDED(hr));

    // This provides a NULL DACL which will allow access
    // to everyone.
    CSecurityDescriptor sd;
    sd.InitializeFromThreadToken();
    hr = CoInitializeSecurity(sd, -1, NULL, NULL,
        RPC_C_AUTHN_LEVEL_PKT, RPC_C_IMP_LEVEL_IMPERSONATE,
        NULL, EOAC_NONE, NULL);
```

```
        _ASSERTE(SUCCEEDED(hr));

        hr = _Module.RegisterClassObjects(CLSCTX_LOCAL_SERVER |
                CLSCTX_REMOTE_SERVER, REGCLS_MULTIPLEUSE);
        _ASSERTE(SUCCEEDED(hr));

        LogEvent(_T("Service started"));
        SetServiceStatus(SERVICE_RUNNING);

        MSG msg;
        while (GetMessage(&msg, 0, 0, 0))
            DispatchMessage(&msg);

        _Module.RevokeClassObjects();

        CoUninitialize();
    }
```

Notice the use of the global object **_Module**. This is initialized at the top of the file with:

CServiceModule _Module;

The static data members of the *class* are assigned through the global *object's* data members. This odd C++ device is used to ensure that only one object of the type **CServiceModule** is created. If the programmer is tempted to create another one, it won't work because the data members manipulated will always be those of **_Module**.

The first task of this method is to save the thread ID, which is used in the handler function to post a **WM_QUIT** message as mentioned above. Next **CoInitialize()** is called (or **CoInitializeEx()** if you want a free threaded service). Then security is initialized, giving packet level authentication (**RPC_C_AUTHN_LEVEL_PKT**) and **RPC_C_IMP_LEVEL_IMPERSONATE** for the impersonation level. You may decide to change this if you want greater control over who can use the service, or if you want to provide encryption on the packets sent across the network. In particular, you may want to reduce the authentication to none if you want this code to run on Windows 95 as a DCOM server.

Next the COM class is registered and the main thread message loop is entered. This message loop will handle all the COM connections allowing the SCM to create objects and call methods on those objects (more details in the next chapter). This message pump is broken when the thread receives a **WM_QUIT** message, and this is sent when the control message **SERVICE_CONTROL_STOP** is received. When the message loop is broken, the service should clean up and quit. It does this by revoking the class object, uninitializing COM, and then returning.

EnumWinSvr

Now that we've seen how ATL handles the service side of things for us, it's up to us to finish implementing the server. The server will return data about the currently open windows on a desktop on the server machine. The client specifies the impersonation to use to get a desktop and the server returns the window names using a standard string enumeration interface.

First we need to add a new COM class to the project. This class will implement two interfaces, one that the client can call to get the enumeration interface and the other will be the enumeration interface itself.

We could implement the enumeration interface as a separate object, but it's easier in this example not to. However, the interfaces will be exposed in such a way that it would be relatively easy to split off the enumeration interface into a separate object, if we decided to.

Add a new ATL class to the project using the Insert | New class... menu item, filling in the dialogs as shown:

Note that we specify *custom* rather than *dual* interfaces here. You will also need to set the filename used by this class to be the one shown in the screenshot. The default, **EnumWinSvr.cpp**, won't work because that file already exists. Press the Change... button and change the source and header files to **EnumWinSvrClass**.

You will need to use the Edit... button to bring up the Edit Interface Information dialog to change the names of the interfaces to **IGetEnumWindows** and **IEnumString**:

Once you've added this class to the project, you can right-click on the interfaces in ClassView and add their methods. The IDL is shown below:

```
interface IGetEnumWindows : IUnknown
{
   HRESULT GetEnumWindows([in] ServerImp impersonate,
                          [out, retval] IEnumString** ppretval);
};

interface IEnumString : IUnknown
{
   HRESULT Next([in] ULONG celt, [out, string] LPOLESTR* rgelt,
                [out] ULONG* pceltFetched);
   HRESULT Skip([in] ULONG celt);
   HRESULT Reset();
   HRESULT Clone ([out] IEnumString** ppenum);
}
```

Using ClassView to add the methods means that you get the function declarations and stubs added to **CEnumWinSvr** for free, but since **IEnumString** is a standard interface, we don't actually need its definition in the IDL file. You should delete the references to **IEnumString**, both its **interface** definition and its mention in the **coclass**. It's not necessary for the client to know that the **IEnumString** interface is implemented by the same object as **IGetEnumWindows**.

Now there is just one more change to make to the IDL: you need to add an **enum** to the top of the file. This enumeration is used for the single **[in]** parameter of **GetEnumWindows()**, which determines the type of impersonation that the client requires. This can be one of three levels:

IMP_NONE   The server uses its own security context.

IMP_CLIENT   The server impersonates the client.

IMP_INTERACTIVE   The server attempts to access the interactive user.

After this, your IDL file should look similar to that given below:

```
typedef enum ServerImp_tag
   {IMP_NONE, IMP_CLIENT, IMP_INTERACTIVE} ServerImp;

   [
     object,
     uuid(3AD1AF1E-A3A4-11D0-974B-98AA04000000),
     helpstring("IGetEnumWindows Interface"),
     pointer_default(unique)
   ]
   interface IGetEnumWindows : IUnknown
   {
     [helpstring("method GetEnumWindows")]
     HRESULT GetEnumWindows([in] ServerImp impersonate,
                            [out, retval] IEnumString** ppretval);
   };


[
   uuid(3AD1AF11-A3A4-11D0-974B-98AA04000000),
   version(1.0),
```

```
      helpstring("EnumWinSvr 1.0 Type Library")
   ]
   library ENUMWINSVRLib
   {
      importlib("stdole32.tlb");
      importlib("stdole2.tlb");
      [
         uuid(3AD1AF20-A3A4-11D0-974B-98AA04000000),
         helpstring("EnumWinSvr Class")
      ]
      coclass EnumWinSvr
      {
         [default] interface IGetEnumWindows;
      };

   };
```

Now if you open the **EnumWinSvrClass.h** header file, you will find that the wizards have added the method declarations that you need. You just need to add two private data members (one a pointer to an enumeration object, which we'll define shortly, and the other for the impersonation level) and an override for **FinalRelease()**.

```
// Data members
private:
    CEnumData* m_pEnumeration;
    ServerImp m_impersonate;

// CComObjectRoot overrrides
public:
   void FinalRelease();
```

You need to initialize the pointer to **NULL** in the class constructor and **delete** it in **FinalRelease()**.

```
CEnumWinSvr() : m_pEnumeration(NULL) {}
```

```
void CEnumWinSvr::FinalRelease()
{
   delete m_pEnumeration;
   m_pEnumeration = NULL;
   CComObjectRoot::FinalRelease();
}
```

The actual enumeration is carried out with the help of a class called **CEnumData** in a similar fashion to how it is done in Chapter 2. **CEnumData** merely implements a linked list. To add this class use the Insert | New class... menu item and create a new generic class called **CEnumData**. Once the class is added, you will need to remove the following line from the top of the new source file to get it to compile:

```
#define new DEBUG_NEW
```

Now you can define and implement the class as shown below:

```
class CEnumData
{
public:
```

```
   CEnumData();
   virtual ~CEnumData();

   void Add(LPWSTR name);
   BOOL GetNext(LPWSTR* pname);
   void Reset();

private:
   // Implementation Detail: windows titles are held as a
   // linked list of CHwndNode structures
   struct CHwndNode
   {
      CHwndNode* pNext;
      WCHAR* wstrName;
      CHwndNode(LPWSTR name) : pNext(NULL)
      {
         wstrName = new WCHAR [(lstrlenW(name) + 1)];
         lstrcpyW(wstrName, name);
      }
   };

   CHwndNode* m_pPosition;
   CHwndNode* m_pHead;
};
```

```
CEnumData::CEnumData() : m_pPosition(NULL), m_pHead(NULL)
{ }

CEnumData::~CEnumData()
{
   // Walk linked list and delete data
   while (m_pHead)
   {
      m_pPosition = m_pHead->pNext;
      delete [] m_pHead->wstrName;
      delete m_pHead;
      m_pHead = m_pPosition;
   }
}

void CEnumData::Add(LPWSTR name)
{
   CHwndNode* new_node = new CHwndNode(name);

   if (m_pHead == NULL)
   {
      m_pHead = new_node;
      m_pPosition = new_node;
   }
   else
   {
      m_pPosition->pNext = new_node;
      m_pPosition = new_node;
   }
}
```

```
BOOL CEnumData::GetNext(LPWSTR* pname)
{
    if (pname == 0)
        return FALSE;

    if (m_pPosition == NULL)
    {
        pname[0] = 0;
        return FALSE;
    }

    *pname = m_pPosition->wstrName;
    m_pPosition = m_pPosition->pNext;
    return TRUE;
}

void CEnumData::Reset()
{
    m_pPosition = m_pHead;
}
```

Since this class is used in **CEnumWinSvr**, you should include **EnumData.h** at the top of
EnumWinSvr.cpp and **EnumWinSvrClass.cpp**, before the include for **EnumWinSvrClass.h**.

The list of windows names is generated and returned using the string enumeration interface when a client
calls **GetEnumWindows()**. This means that I can set the security context in response to the impersonation
level specified by the client *before* getting hold of the list of windows.

The **GetEnumWindows()** function deserves some study.

```
STDMETHODIMP CEnumWinSvr::GetEnumWindows(ServerImp impersonate,
                                         IEnumString * * ppretval)
{
    HRESULT hr;

    m_impersonate = impersonate;

    *ppretval = (IEnumString*)this;
    (*ppretval)->AddRef();
    // Initialize the windows list
    if (m_pEnumeration)
        delete m_pEnumeration;
    m_pEnumeration = new CEnumData;

    // Create the list of windows
    switch (m_impersonate)
    {
    case IMP_INTERACTIVE:
        {
            HWINSTA hwinstaSave = GetProcessWindowStation();
            HDESK hdeskSave = GetThreadDesktop(GetCurrentThreadId());

            HWINSTA hwinstaUser = OpenWindowStation(_T("WinSta0"),
                                        FALSE, MAXIMUM_ALLOWED);
            SetProcessWindowStation(hwinstaUser);
            HDESK hdeskUser = OpenDesktop(_T("Default"), 0, FALSE,
                                        MAXIMUM_ALLOWED);
```

```
                if (hdeskUser == NULL)
                    EnumWindows((WNDENUMPROC)AddToList,
                            (LPARAM)m_pEnumeration);
                else
                    EnumDesktopWindows(hdeskUser,
                            (WNDENUMPROC)AddToList, (LPARAM)m_pEnumeration);

                SetThreadDesktop(hdeskSave);
                SetProcessWindowStation(hwinstaSave);
                CloseDesktop(hdeskUser);
                CloseWindowStation(hwinstaUser);
                break;
        }
    case IMP_CLIENT:
        {
            hr = CoImpersonateClient();
            EnumWindows((WNDENUMPROC)AddToList,
                        (LPARAM)m_pEnumeration);
            hr = CoRevertToSelf();
            break;
        }
    case IMP_NONE:
        EnumWindows((WNDENUMPROC)AddToList, (LPARAM)m_pEnumeration);
    }

    return S_OK;
}
```

I get the **IEnumString** interface by using a simple cast; this is one place where multiple inheritance is wonderful. Then I create a new **CEnumData** object, this will be used to hold the linked list of window names. Next I check for the required impersonation level. If **IMP_NONE** is specified I call the Win32 **EnumWindows()** function using the callback function **AddToList()** (which we'll look at a little later) and a pointer to the enumeration object. **AddToList()** will be called for every window that the function finds. If **IMP_CLIENT** is specified, I take the added step of impersonating the client.

If **IMP_INTERACTIVE** is specified, I attempt to obtain access to the interactive user's desktop. The first code saves the current window station and desktop, and then opens the window station called **WinSta0**, which is the standard window station for the interactive user. Then I set this to be my window station and attempt to access the **Default** desktop of the interactive user.

Next I test to see if I have a valid desktop handle and if so, I call **EnumDesktopWindows()**. This is essentially the same as the Win32 **EnumWindows()** except it allows you to specify which desktop you want to access. If I couldn't get the desktop, I just do another **EnumWindows()** call.

The function that is passed to these enumeration functions is called **AddToList()** and should be defined at the top of **EnumWinSvrClass.cpp**.

```
BOOL CALLBACK AddToList(HWND hwnd, LPARAM penum)
{
    CEnumData* pEnumeration = (CEnumData*)penum;

    HRESULT hr;
    LPWSTR pPrivs;
    hr = CoQueryClientBlanket(NULL, NULL, NULL, NULL, NULL,
                            (LPVOID*)&pPrivs, NULL);
```

```
    // Make the buffer bigger just in case it has no name
    int size = GetWindowTextLengthW(hwnd) + lstrlenW(pPrivs) + 4;
    LPWSTR wndname = new WCHAR [size + 11];

    lstrcpyW(wndname, L"[");
    lstrcatW(wndname, pPrivs);
    lstrcatW(wndname, L"] ");

    if (0 == ::GetWindowTextW(hwnd, wndname + lstrlenW(pPrivs) + 3,
                              size + 1))
    {
        wsprintfW(wndname + lstrlenW(pPrivs) + 3, L"[%08x]", hwnd);
    }

    pEnumeration->Add(wndname);
    delete [] wndname;

    return TRUE;
}
```

The first thing to do is to take the **LPARAM** and cast it to a **CEnumData** class pointer so that we can save the data. Next I call **CoQueryClientBlanket()** to get the client name. The window name that I will return back will be a combination of the window title and the client name.

I query for the size of the window title, and allocate a buffer slightly larger so that if the window has no title, I can add the window handle into the saved string. The **CEnumData** object holds all the strings as wide chars, so I only use the wide char versions of the API functions. I then call **GetWindowTextW()** to get the window name and if this is not successful, I add the window handle to the text buffer. Finally I add this to the linked list with a call to **Add()** and then clean up any allocated memory.

Once the client's got hold of the enumeration interface, it needs to call the methods to get the window titles. The most used function is **Next()** which attempts to return the required number of window names. The actual number is returned in the **[out]** parameter **pceltFetched** and the strings are copied as server allocated **LPOLESTR** string pointers, which are put in the **[out]** parameter **rgelt**.

```
STDMETHODIMP CEnumWinSvr::Next(ULONG celt, LPOLESTR * rgelt,
                               ULONG * pceltFetched)
{
    ULONG ulNumReturned = 0;

    if (pceltFetched == NULL)
    {
        if (celt != 1)
            return S_FALSE;
    }
    else
        *pceltFetched = 0;

    if (NULL == rgelt)
        return E_POINTER;

    LPOLESTR* ppcopy = new LPOLESTR [celt];

    ULONG total = celt;
```

```
    while (celt > 0)
    {
      if (m_pEnumeration->GetNext(&ppcopy[total - celt]))
         ulNumReturned++;
      else
         break;

      celt--;
    }

    // Copy the data into the array
    celt = 0;
    while (celt < ulNumReturned)
    {
      rgelt[celt] = (LPWSTR)CoTaskMemAlloc(
                    (lstrlenW(ppcopy[celt]) + 1) * sizeof(WCHAR));
      lstrcpyW(rgelt[celt], ppcopy[celt]);
      celt++;
    }

    delete [] ppcopy;

    if (pceltFetched != NULL)
       *pceltFetched = ulNumReturned;

    if (ulNumReturned == 0)
       return S_FALSE;

    return S_OK;
}
```

The remaining methods are either extremely simple or not implemented.

```
STDMETHODIMP CEnumWinSvr::Skip(ULONG celt)
{
   LPOLESTR name;
   while (celt > 0 && m_pEnumeration->GetNext(&name))
   {
      celt--;
   }

   return S_OK;
}

STDMETHODIMP CEnumWinSvr::Reset()
{
   m_pEnumeration->Reset();
   return S_OK;
}

STDMETHODIMP CEnumWinSvr::Clone(IEnumString * * ppenum)
{
   return E_NOTIMPL;
}
```

Before you can compile the project, you must make sure that **_WIN32_DCOM** symbol is defined. Once you have done that, compile the project and you will find that the server will register itself as a COM server, because the ATL Wizard adds the custom build step to run the process with the **/RegServer** switch. To make it register itself as a service you need to run the process with the **/Service** switch (you could add this to the custom build settings). Once this is done, you can check that the service is registered by looking in Regedit:

Note that the service is dependent upon another service, this is **Rpcss.exe**, which is the service that implements the SCM. This entry is added by the ATL code when the service is registered.

If you run **WinMsd** and double-click on the entry for **EnumWinSvr** you will get the same information formatted in a more readable fashion.

You can now use the control panel (or **SC**) to start the service, but to access the COM server, you will need a client.

Client

The client is quite straightforward. It uses code mostly from the **LaunchClient** project in the last chapter. When you start the application, you will get a dialog box like this:

This allows you to specify the name of the server and the client account to use, if the Domain edit box is left empty then the current domain (".") is used. The Impersonation group of radio buttons allow you to decide what level of impersonation to pass when the client calls **GetEnumWindows()**. Pressing OK gives the next dialog, which gives the names of the windows for the specified account on the specified machine:

This states that there are 76 windows each of which are listed in the list box. To refresh the display click on the Refresh button. The items in the list box have the account name followed by the window name. If the window does not have a title, the **HWND** is given instead.

Creation

This client is created like most of the previous MFC-based clients: create a new project called **EnumWinClient** using MFC AppWizard (exe), select a Dialog based application in the first page of the wizard, then accept the defaults in the rest of them.

You will need to initialize the COM libraries in **CEnumWinClientApp::InitInstance()** by adding the following code (plus a string resource for **IDP_OLE_INIT_FAILED**):

```
// Initialize OLE libraries
if (!AfxOleInit())
{
   AfxMessageBox(IDP_OLE_INIT_FAILED);
   return FALSE;
}
```

While you have got the application object's implementation file open add the following line just above the include for the dialog class:

```
#include "stdafx.h"
#include "EnumWinClient.h"
#include "EnumWinSvr.h"
#include "EnumWinClientDlg.h"
```

You'll also need to add this include to **EnumWinClientDlg.cpp**. **EnumWinSvr.h** is the header file created by MIDL in the server project. You should copy this and **EnumWinSvr_i.c** from the server directory into the current project directory. Add this last file to the project and make sure that you turn off precompiled headers for it in the project settings.

Now create a new dialog resource called **IDD_SERVERNAME**. This will be the first window that appears when the application starts. You'll need to add three edit boxes for logon information, an edit box for the server machine name and a group of radio buttons for the impersonation level. (The OK and Cancel buttons will be on the dialog box resource when its created, so need not be added.)

Use ClassWizard to create a new class for this dialog called **CServerName**, then add member variables for the major controls: **CString**s for the server name and the user account details (**m_strServerName**, **m_strUserName**, **m_strDomain**, **m_strPassword**) and an **int** for the radio button group (**m_nImpersonation**).

Now add the following members to the main dialog class, **CEnumWinClientDlg**.

```
// Implementation
protected:
    CString m_strServerName;
    CString m_strUserName;
    CString m_strDomain;
    CString m_strPassword;
    ServerImp m_nImpersonation;

    IGetEnumWindows* m_pGetEnumInterface;

    void Message(const CString& strMessage);
```

This **CServerName** dialog is created in the **OnInitDialog()** handler for the main dialog, **CEnumWinClientDlg**:

```
BOOL CEnumWinClientDlg::OnInitDialog()
{
    // ... Standard initialization

    CServerName dlg;

    // Get the name of the server to use
    if (dlg.DoModal() == IDOK)
    {
        m_strServerName = dlg.m_strServerName;
        m_strUserName = dlg.m_strUserName;
        m_strDomain = dlg.m_strDomain;
        m_strPassword = dlg.m_strPassword;
        switch (dlg.m_nImpersonation)
```

```
         {
         default:
         case 0:
            m_nImpersonation = IMP_NONE;
            break;
         case 1:
            m_nImpersonation = IMP_CLIENT;
            break;
         case 2:
            m_nImpersonation = IMP_INTERACTIVE;
            break;
         }
      }
      else
      {
         m_strServerName.Empty();
         m_nImpersonation = IMP_NONE;
      }

      // Let's create the server
      m_pGetEnumInterface = NULL;

      HRESULT hr;
      COSERVERINFO serverinfo;
      COSERVERINFO* pServerInfo;
      COAUTHINFO athn;
      SEC_WINNT_AUTH_IDENTITY idn;

      // Create the server info, note that we use the CString
      // to convert to wide chars
      serverinfo.dwReserved1 = 0;
      serverinfo.dwReserved2 = 0;
      serverinfo.pwszName = m_strServerName.AllocSysString();
      serverinfo.pAuthInfo = &athn;;

      athn.dwAuthnSvc = RPC_C_AUTHN_WINNT;
      athn.dwAuthzSvc = RPC_C_AUTHZ_NONE;
      athn.pwszServerPrincName = NULL;
      athn.dwAuthnLevel = RPC_C_AUTHN_LEVEL_CONNECT;
      athn.dwImpersonationLevel = RPC_C_IMP_LEVEL_IMPERSONATE;
      athn.pAuthIdentityData = (COAUTHIDENTITY*)&idn;
      athn.dwCapabilities = EOAC_NONE;

      idn.UserLength = m_strUserName.GetLength();
      idn.DomainLength = m_strDomain.GetLength();
      idn.PasswordLength = m_strPassword.GetLength();

#ifdef UNICODE
      idn.User = new TCHAR[m_strUserName.GetLength() + 1];
      idn.Domain = new TCHAR[m_strDomain.GetLength() + 1];
      idn.Password = new TCHAR[m_strPassword.GetLength() + 1];

      idn.Flags = SEC_WINNT_AUTH_IDENTITY_UNICODE;
#else
      idn.User = (unsigned char*)new
                     TCHAR[m_strUserName.GetLength() + 1];
      idn.Domain = (unsigned char*)new
```

```
                              TCHAR[m_strDomain.GetLength() + 1];
      idn.Password = (unsigned char*)new
                              TCHAR[m_strPassword.GetLength() + 1];

      idn.Flags = SEC_WINNT_AUTH_IDENTITY_ANSI;
   #endif

      lstrcpy((LPTSTR)idn.User, (LPCTSTR)m_strUserName);
      lstrcpy((LPTSTR)idn.Domain, (LPCTSTR)m_strDomain);
      lstrcpy((LPTSTR)idn.Password, (LPCTSTR)m_strPassword);

      if (m_strServerName.IsEmpty())
         pServerInfo = NULL;
      else
         pServerInfo = &serverinfo;

      MULTI_QI qi = {&IID_IGetEnumWindows, NULL, 0};

      hr = CoCreateInstanceEx(CLSID_EnumWinSvr, NULL,
                  CLSCTX_LOCAL_SERVER | CLSCTX_REMOTE_SERVER,
                  pServerInfo, 1, &qi);

      if (SUCCEEDED(hr) && SUCCEEDED(qi.hr))
      {
         // Now get the interface
         m_pGetEnumInterface = (IGetEnumWindows*)qi.pItf;
      }
      else
      {
         m_pGetEnumInterface = NULL;
         CString str;
         str.Format("Cannot get object: 0x%x and QI: 0x%x",
                     hr, qi.hr);
         Message(str);
      }

      // Free the buffer previous allocated
      ::SysFreeString(serverinfo.pwszName);
      delete [] idn.User;
      delete [] idn.Domain;
      delete [] idn.Password;

      OnRefresh();

   return TRUE;  // return TRUE  unless you set the focus
                 // to a control
}
```

From the first dialog box, the instance variables are initialized, and these are used to initialize the **COSERVERINFO** structure that is sent to the call to **CoCreateInstanceEx()**. Note the initialization of the **SEC_WINNT_AUTH_IDENTITY** structure, which has pointers to the username, domain and password strings. These can be either ANSI or wide char; the **Flags** member indicates which is used.

When the **CoCreateInstanceEx()** is successful, the instance variable **m_pGetEnumInterface** is initialized with the interface pointer and the member function **OnRefresh()** is called; this is the handler for the refresh button click event, which is given here:

```
void CEnumWinClientDlg::OnRefresh()
{
    CListBox* pList = (CListBox*)GetDlgItem(IDC_WINDOWS);
    ASSERT(pList);

    pList->ResetContent();

    if (NULL == m_pGetEnumInterface)
            return;

    DWORD dwFetched;
    LPOLESTR array[10];
    UINT uCount = 0;

    HRESULT hRes;
    IEnumString* pEnum;
    hRes = m_pGetEnumInterface->GetEnumWindows(
            m_nImpersonation, &pEnum);
    if (FAILED(hRes))
            return;

    pEnum->Reset();

    do
    {
            hRes = pEnum->Next(10, array, &dwFetched);
            if (FAILED(hRes) || hRes == S_FALSE)
                    break;

            uCount += dwFetched;

            for (DWORD dwIndex = 0; dwIndex < dwFetched;
               dwIndex++)
            {
                    CString str(array[dwIndex]);
                    pList->AddString(str);
                    CoTaskMemFree(array[dwIndex]);
            }
    }
    while (dwFetched > 0);

    pEnum->Release();

    CWnd* pCount = GetDlgItem(IDC_COUNT);
    ASSERT(pCount);

    CString szCount;
    szCount.Format("%ld windows", uCount);

    pCount->SetWindowText(szCount);
}
```

The **OnRefresh()** code calls the **GetEnumWindows()** function on the remote object to obtain the **IEnumString** interface. As we have seen, this method initializes an internal list in the object with the windows names of the account specified by the impersonation parameter, this list is accessed through the **IEnumString** interface pointer passed back as an **[out]** parameter.

The client code first calls **IEnumString::Reset()** to ensure that the enumeration starts at the beginning and then it calls **IEnumString::Next()** until the method either returns **S_FALSE** or zero entries. The parameters passed to this method are the number of entries required (hard coded to 10), an array of **LPOLESTR** pointers that will be filled by the remote object, and an **[out]** parameter which returns the actual number of pointers returned.

The returned strings are converted to the appropriate type (ANSI or wide char), by initializing a **CString** with the string, then added to the list box. Finally the remote string must be freed via a call to **CoTaskMemFree()**.

As usual, the interface is released in response to **WM_DESTROY**, and to compile this client, you need to define the preprocessor symbol **_WIN32_DCOM**.

The final step of all is to make sure that you compile the proxy-stub DLL generated by ATL for the server project and register this on the client so that the interface is properly registered and then start the service on the server machine.

Tests

Let's have a look at a few examples of running the client on a networked machine. In all these examples the **DCOMCnfg** settings specify that the server has the identity of the **System** account. In the first example, the client and server are logged in on the account **RichardGrimes**, but the client specifies that no impersonation is used.

Here is the result:

The server tells the client that there are only two windows on the server desktop. This is the same result as using **IMP_CLIENT** for the impersonation level.

The user account that the server is reporting is not surprising since **CoQueryClientBlanket()** is used to get the client identity. However, the fact that the dialog shows that in these two cases the window station has only two windows may seem odd. Why is this? Well, in both cases we get access to the window station of the **System** account in which COM creates a window to serialize the COM messages. This is the window that we saw was used in Chapter 6; the fact that the thread was told to impersonate the client is irrelevant.

The big surprise comes when the client asks to impersonate the interactive user. In this case when the account **RichardGrimes** is logged on the server we get:

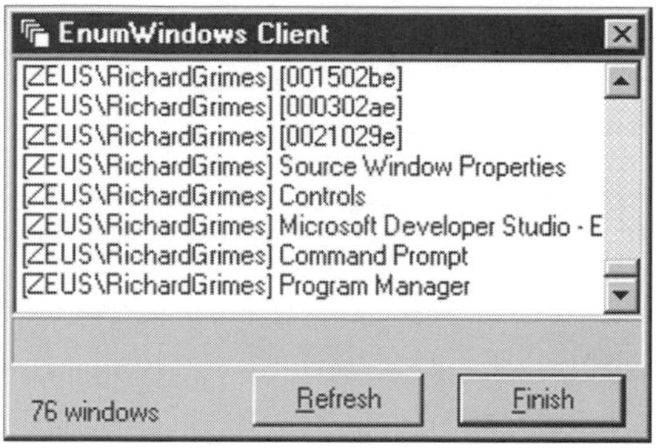

Whoa, 76 windows! When I scroll through the list box, I can see that all the windows I can see on my server machine's desktop are in the list box shown on the client. This is quite powerful. The service now has access to the desktop of the interactive user, which means that the service can get a window's handle and from that, the window's device context. The service can thus send back a view of the desktop, or an individual window back to the client.

If you have access to a window's device context, you could also write to the window. This means that a service like **EnumWinSvr** could be altered to provide remote CBT (computer based training), allowing an instructor to write on the student's desktop or lead the student through a complex procedure, for example. Since the DCOM server is implemented as a service there is minimal amount of server initialization and the service can be set up to run automatically on the student's machine, the student does not have to interact at all with this software to start it up.

But what happens if there is no interactive user?

The screen shot shows what the client sees if there is no user logged on the server machine:

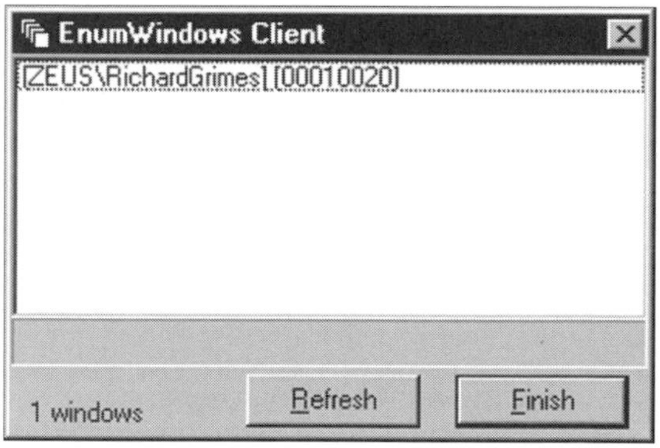

This time we get just one window. The server will still run even if there is no interactive user.

Event Log

The final part of this chapter is not completely COM based, but it is pertinent here. This section is about the NT Event Log. This is a vital diagnostic tool, but is poorly understood. We have seen earlier on in this chapter that ATL doesn't really use the event log, it makes a feeble attempt to log an event, but the effect is disappointing. This section will show that with a small amount of effort the Event Log can be used to more effect.

The first exposure I had to the NT event log was when I was asked to change the project I was working on to log messages to the NT event log instead of to application maintained files. Looking through the documentation and examples of event logging showed that the area was seriously lacking. Of the examples in the Windows SDK one was particularly telling: the example was of a service, that logged an event when the service ended, however the message was rather obscure. The NT implementation of the flagship product of one of the world's largest database companies also logged this rather obscure event, which just went to show that their NT developers didn't understand the Win32 documentation either!

So, to make sure you do not make the same error, I'll cover NT event logging in a few pages.

Before we start, let me reiterate why the event log is so useful. The event log is an NT system service that handles calls from a client to log an event. It writes these events into a few files in the `%systemroot%\system32\config` directory. Many event sources will log events to the same file so the `EventLog` service has to make sure that the calls to read from and write to these files are serialized.

The event log is particularly useful for services because these processes do not have an interactive user and so any diagnostic messages displayed on a modeless window for example will have no audience and would not be read. The event log provides a persistent store for these messages that can be viewed by the machine administrator at a convenient time.

One other important aspect about the event log API is that even though it predates DCOM, it has distribution built in. The API to read from the event log allows you to specify the remote machine that you want to read.

The Event Viewer

NT comes with a tool to read the event log. This is called the event viewer and you can find it in NT's Administrative Tools folder (or in the `system32` directory). Here is a view from my PC:

Date	Time	Source	Category	Event	User	Computer
1/17/97	7:47:07 PM	Srv	None	2013	N/A	ZEUS
1/17/97	7:42:05 PM	SNMP	None	1001	N/A	ZEUS
1/17/97	7:41:53 PM	EventLog	None	6005	N/A	ZEUS
1/17/97	1:29:15 AM	BROWSER	None	8033	N/A	ZEUS
1/17/97	1:29:15 AM	BROWSER	None	8033	N/A	ZEUS
1/16/97	10:04:44 PM	Service Control Mar	None	7000	N/A	ZEUS
1/16/97	10:04:44 PM	Service Control Mar	None	7013	N/A	ZEUS
1/16/97	10:04:10 PM	Service Control Mar None		7000	N/A	ZEUS

This is a view of the Application log on my PC. Event Viewer recognizes three logs: the `Application`, `System` and `Security` logs. You can select which log you are viewing from the File menu:

`Application`   This is used by user mode services and processes.

`System`   This is used by kernel mode services and device drivers.

`Security`   This is used by the security system.

This menu will also allow you to save the events either in event log format, comma separated format, or as plain text. The second format is particularly useful for loading an event log into a spreadsheet to perform analysis.

By default, the view shows all the events in the specified log, but from the View menu you can filter for particular events:

This is pretty much self-explanatory, but two items deserve more explanation: the Source specifies the process that generated the event. In the first screenshot, for example, we have an event from the **EventLog** service stating that it has started.

The item below that allows you to filter on the Category of the event. When an event is logged, the process can specify what category the event is; an event can have any category that you have defined. Categories are defined by the source and can be used for whatever purpose that you wish to use them for. I use categories in my applications to group together the messages from a particular object type (class), so it allows me to quickly filter the event log for messages from a particular object.

Note that categories are independent of the *severity* of the message, they are just a convenient way of grouping messages of a particular type. Let's go back to the first screenshot again. In the extreme left hand column there is an icon for the severity of the message; this can be one of information, warning, error, audit success or audit fail. Next are the time and date that the event was logged, and then the source and category.

After that comes the message ID, which gives an ID for a format string in the source's format string resource. The resource for each source must be registered in the registry, as we will see later. The last two fields give the user, under whose account the process was running, and the machine that generated the event. Of these fields, only the source, category and message ID are under the control of the programmer – NT provides the rest.

If you double-click on an entry,
you will get a dialog with details of
the event:

This example shows that the system knows that my **D:** drive is more than 90% full. The message is event **2013** of the **SVR** service; the registry shows that this source uses the message file **netevent.dll**.

If I use **dumpbin** on **netevent.dll**, we can see the format string for message **2013**.

```
net.txt - Notepad
File  Edit  Search  Help
00001160  64 2E 0D 0A 00 00 00 00 | 50 00 00 00 54 68 65 20   d.......|P...The
00001170  25 32 20 64 69 73 6B 20 | 69 73 20 61 74 20 6F 72   %2 disk |is at or
00001180  20 6E 65 61 72 20 63 61 | 70 61 63 69 74 79 2E 20    near ca|pacity.
00001190  20 59 6F 75 20 6D 61 79 | 20 6E 65 65 64 20 74 6F    You may| need to
000011A0  20 64 65 6C 65 74 65 20 | 73 6F 6D 65 20 66 69 6C    delete |some fil
000011B0  65 73 2E 0D 0A 00 00 00 | 58 00 00 00 54 68 65 20   es......|X...The
```

Reformatted, the string is

The %2 disk is at or near capacity. You may need to delete some files

The **%2** here is an insert string that the caller will fill with the drive name.

Normally the format strings that you write will either use **%s** for all of the insert strings or will number them from **%1**. This string has the insert strings start at **%2** because the message originated from a system service, **SVR**, the server driver. System services and device drivers use a different API to log events than used by applications and user services, they use a function called **IoWriteErrorLogEntry()**. This function uses the first insert string passed in the buffer to identify the name of the device and hence this takes up parameter **%1** (this buffer is created with **IoAllocateErrorLogEntry()**).

Now look back at the detailed view of the event in event viewer again. The lower half of the dialog gives an edit box with some hex data. When you record an event you can specify some raw data that will help in diagnosing the problem.

Before we leave the event viewer, there is one menu item that you should look at: the Log Settings... item in the Log menu:

```
Event Log Settings
Change Settings for  Application ▼  Log          OK
                                               Cancel
Maximum Log Size: 512 ▲ Kilobytes (64K Increments)  Default
Event Log Wrapping                                  Help
  ○ Overwrite Events as Needed
  ● Overwrite Events Older than  7  ▲ Days
  ○ Do Not Overwrite Events (Clear Log Manually)
```

This allows you to configure how the **EventLog** service handles the three default event logs: how big the event log file can grow, and what happens when the event log file reaches that limit. These are saved as values in the registry, but this is a convenient place to alter them.

439

Event Sources

Event Log Sources are processes that create event messages. Any process can create event messages, but to do so they have to call the Event Log API as explained below. The event log functions require an event log handle and this can be obtained by calling either `RegisterEventSource()` or `OpenEventLog()`. (The two functions appear to do the same thing and it's not clear why there are two functions with different names that do the same thing.) These functions take the name of the machine on which the event log will be accessed, and the name of the source that will be used.

This source name is found in the registry under one of the keys in the

`HKEY_LOCAL_MACHINE\SYSTEM\CurrentControlSet\Services\EventLog`

key. This key will have three keys, one each for the `Application`, `System` and `Security` logs; under these keys are the keys for the event log sources. Note that these three event logs are recognized by the NT event log viewer, but if you really must, you can create your own event log, a process that will be described at the end of the chapter.

The handle that is returned from these functions must be passed to the `EventLog` functions to access the specified event log. When you are finished with the event log, you can call either `DeregisterEventSource()` or `CloseEventLog()` to close the handle – do not call `CloseHandle()`.

If the source name that you pass to open the event log cannot be found in the registry, the system will log the events in the `Application` event log. Otherwise, if the source name is under the `System` or `Security` key (or in your own event log file) then logged messages will be placed in that event log.

The following code shows how ATL logs an event. ATL does not add any keys into the registry for your service, so when it opens the event log with this code (from `CServiceModule::LogEvent()`), the `EventLog` service will open the `Application` log.

```
hEventSource = RegisterEventSource(NULL, m_szServiceName);
if (hEventSource != NULL)
{
   ReportEvent(hEventSource, EVENTLOG_INFORMATION_TYPE,
                 0, 0, NULL, 1, 0,
                   (LPCTSTR*) &lpszStrings[0], NULL);
   DeregisterEventSource(hEventSource);
}
```

Unfortunately, this code is a bit weak, because the ATL COM AppWizard doesn't create a message resource. If you do nothing else with the event log, you should at least create a message resource with a format string for the message ID number 0, and register it in the registry for your service. If you do *not* then when the ATL service logs an event, the event viewer will give the following text for the event:

The description for Event ID (0) in Source (EnumWinSvr) could not be found. It contains the following insertion string(s): Service started.

This is hardly the result expected from professionally authored software. If you create a format string resource and register it, it could simply have the format string `%1` for event ID number 0. The NT event log viewer will then give the following description for the same event:

Service started.

This looks far more professional and the example at the end of this chapter shows you how to do this.

Message Resource Files

When you add an event into an event log, you will specify the message ID and some insert strings. An event log viewer will read the event log to get that message ID and insert strings. This means that although the event log is an efficient way to save messages, it is dependent upon the resource file. Once the event log reader has the name of the source, it can find its resource file, open it, and then pass the handle of the file to the **FormatMessage()** API with the data read from the event log. This function will read the format message for the message ID (and specified language) and insert the insert strings into the replacement parameters in the format string.

This format string can have three types of replaceable parameters

Parameter	Example	Description
%s	**The file %s cannot be found on drive %s**	String
%n	**The file %1 cannot be found on drive %2**	Numbered Parameter
%%n	**The file %s cannot be found on drive %%1**	Replacement Parameter

The first type is the most common, and is just a specific version of the second type. The second type allows you to specify up to 99 replaceable parameter that can be strings or integer types. This is done by adding a **printf** style format specifier enclosed in exclamation marks (e.g. **%2!x!**). If the specifier is omitted, it defaults to **!s!**. The **FormatMessage()** function is passed either a **va_list** pointer or a pointer to an array of 32-bit values, and it will fill the parameters with the data these pointers point to.

The third type is a little different and is used mainly by device drivers that try to restrict their use of memory. These replaceable parameters are language independent strings that are held in a resource file called a parameter message file (it could be the same file that holds the format strings). This resource file is also registered for the source and when the event log viewer application gets a string back from **FormatMessage()** with a **%%n** parameter, it must load the parameter message file and use **FormatMessage()** with the specified ID (i.e. **n**) to get the string and then use **FormatMessage()** one more time to insert the parameter into the original string.

So what are these resource files. Well, they can be a DLL or an EXE, usually the file is a separate DLL, but as our example shows later, it can be the same EXE as the service. The format strings are bound in as resources and these resources are created by the SDK message compiler **MC.EXE**. This tool is a little arcane, and although it is provided with Visual C++, it is not integrated into the IDE. This means that if you want to create a message resource file, you need to add the message compiler step as a custom build step into the Visual C++ makefile.

The message compiler uses **.MC** files as its input, and it creates three files as its output: a binary resource, a resource script and a header file. If you are creating a resource-only DLL then the **MC**-created resource script can be used to add the binary resource to the DLL, otherwise the binary resource can be added to your EXE's or DLL's resources. The header file gives **#define**'d symbols that can be used in your code when you call **ReportEvent()**.

The **.MC** files have two sections, the header section and the message definition section. Each section has entries of the general form **keyword=value**.

The header section has these entries:

Keyword	Description
MessageIdTypedef	Defines the type that will be used for messages in the generated header.
SeverityNames	Lists the severity names that will be used.
FacilityNames	Lists the facility names that will be used.
LanguageNames	Lists the any private languages that will be used.

Most of these you can leave out of your **.MC** file, in which case the message compiler will use adequate default values.

The only one that you should be aware of is the **LanguageNames** keyword. This allows you to use more than one language in a **.MC** file. If you leave out the **LanguageNames** keyword, the messages in the file are International English and the **Language** for the message should be specified as **English**. If you specify the **LanguageNames** keyword then you are committing yourself to give at least two format strings per message, **English** and the language you specify.

The value of this keyword is of the form:

LanguageNames=(language=langid:res_file)

Where **language** is the name that you will use in the **Language** keyword of the message definition, **langid** is the language identifier that will be used in the resource file and **res_file** is the name of the output binary resource file. If you want to use many languages then you can have many **LanguageNames** lines:

LanguageNames=(British=0x809:MSG00809)

LanguageNames=(French=0x40c:MSG0040c)

This specifies that the file has message definitions for international English (implicit), UK English and French. The international English resource will be saved in the resource file **MSG00001.BIN** and the UK English and French definitions are saved in the files **MSG00809.BIN** and **MSG0040C.BIN**.

In the message definition section, you can use the following keywords for each message:

Keyword	Description
MessageId	Bits 0 - 15 of the format string ID.
Severity	Bits 30 and 31 of the format string ID.
Facility	Bits 16 - 27 of the format string ID.
SymbolicName	The symbol defined in the **MC** generated header.
Language	The language resource generated.

Every message entry starts with the **MessageId** keyword and ends with the format string given after the **Language** keyword and therefore each entry must have these two. The other keywords are optional.

The **MessageId** can have a value and if it does, this defines part of the format string ID. If this value is omitted, the message compiler will increment the value after the last one used. This does assume, however, that the first message definition has a specified value.

If the **Severity** or **Facility** keywords are used, these are combined with the **MessageId** to generate the format string ID. If neither are specified, a severity of **Success** and a facility of **Application** are used (both are zero, the SDK documentation erroneously gives **Application** as **0xFFF**). For all but the most specialist of cases, use the default values.

The **Language** value is important. This string is mapped via the **LanguageNames** keyword to a language ID and it is also used to specify which resource file will be used for the output.

The format string is given on the line after the **Language** keyword; it can cover many lines and is terminated by a single period on its own line. The string may contain escape characters, and, in particular, it should contain placeholders for the insert strings.

Finally, comments can be added in by preceding them with "**;**", these will be added to the header file that **MC** creates.

As an example, here is a message file:

```
LanguageNames=(British=0x809:MSG00809)
LanguageNames=(French=0x40c:MSG0040c)

MessageId=1
Language=English
Hello! %s
.
Language=British
Alright! %s
.
Language=French
Salut! %s
.
```

There are three versions of the message and each one will be put in the specified language-dependent file. Running the message compiler on this file will create a header, three **.BIN** files (one for each language), and a resource script, shown here:

```
LANGUAGE 0xc,0x1
1 11 MSG0040c.bin
LANGUAGE 0x9,0x1
1 11 MSG00001.bin
LANGUAGE 0x9,0x2
1 11 MSG00809.bin
```

I mentioned previously that when reporting an event, you could specify a category. Well, categories are just strings in the message resource file, so if you have a process that has three objects, **knife**, **fork** and **spoon**, and you wish to log events for each one under a different category, you can specify these in the **.MC** file as:

```
MessageID=10
SymbolicName=CAT_KNIFE
Language=English
Knife
.
MessageID=
SymbolicName=CAT_FORK
Language=English
Fork
.
MessageID=
SymbolicName=CAT_SPOON
Language=English
Spoon
.
```

The header file will have three symbols:

```
#define CAT_KNIFE                    0x0000000AL
#define CAT_FORK                     0x0000000BL
#define CAT_SPOON                    0x0000000CL
```

These can be used as the category in the **ReportEvent()** call, and the event viewer will give the string declared in the resource when displaying a message of one of these categories. Note that this function treats categories as **WORD** values, so you will either have to cast these symbols or use the **MessageIdTypedef**.

Registry Entries

To enable event log viewers to obtain information about the resource file used for a particular event source, there are entries under that source's name in the registry. These values are:

Named Value	Description
TypesSupported	The types of messages that can be logged, these are OR'ed together.
EventMessageFile	The path to the file that has the message format strings.
CategoryCount	The number of categories used.
CategoryMessageFile	The path to the file that has the category strings.
ParameterMessageFile	The path to the file that has the parameter strings.

If **EventMessageFile** (or **ParameterMessageFile**, if only **%%n** strings are logged) is missing, you get the horrible message from event viewer shown previously. As already mentioned, you can store the messages in the resources of the source's executable, in which case you would give the path to the executable here.

Within the general event log file key (e.g. **Application**, **Security** and **System**) are values that determine how the event log file is handled:

Named Value	Description
File	Path to the actual file that holds the data.
MaxSize	The maximum size of the file in bytes.
Retention	What happens when the file size exceeds **MaxSize**.
Sources	The sources that use this event log.

The **Sources** key is maintained automatically by the **EventLog** service.

Reporting Events

Reporting events is quite straightforward. Once you have a handle on an open event log, you can call **ReportEvent()**. The parameters are:

Parameter	Type	Description
hEventLog	HANDLE	Handle to an open event log.
wType	WORD	The type of event.
wCategory	WORD	Specifies the category of this event.
dwEventID	DWORD	The ID used to get the format string in the resource file.
lpUserSid	PSID	The SID of the logging user (or **NULL**).
wNumStrings	WORD	The number of insert strings.
dwDataSize	DWORD	The size of raw data logged.
lpStrings	LPCTSTR*	The insert strings.
lpRawData	LPVOID	The raw data.

lpRawData points to a buffer that holds raw data that will be added to the event log. This could be additional data that cannot be easily rendered as a string. The format string insert strings are held in the array **lpStrings**. Note that although the message compiler and **FormatMessage()** can handle integer values, **ReportEvent()** can only handle strings. The function adds this data to the event log.

wType can be one of:

Icon	Value	Description
	EVENTLOG_ERROR_TYPE	Error event.
	EVENTLOG_WARNING_TYPE	Warning event.
	EVENTLOG_INFORMATION_TYPE	Information event.
	EVENTLOG_AUDIT_SUCCESS	Success Audit event.
	EVENTLOG_AUDIT_FAILURE	Failure Audit event.

The first three are the values you are most likely to use: Error, Warning and Information. The other two are security events and specify whether a security event was a success or failure.

In addition to these values, the function adds other data. Firstly, since you have already opened the event log with a source name, the **Eventlog** will add this, but also it will add the time and date that the message was generated (i.e. when the API was called) and the time when it was actually written to the event log file. Finally, the API will read the name of the computer and will add this to the event log.

Reading Events

A process can read from the event log. To do this, it must open an event log and call **ReadEventLog()**. The source name used to open the event log can be a particular source (which then filters for events generated by only this source), or it can be one of the event log names (**Application**, **System** or **Security**) to get all the events in that log.

Here is where the API gets a little complicated. **ReadEventLog()** has these parameters:

Parameter	Type	Description
hEventLog	HANDLE	A handle to an open event log.
dwReadFlags	DWORD	How to read from the event log.
dwRecordOffset	DWORD	Where to start reading from.
lpBuffer	LPVOID	Buffer to take the read data.
nNumberOfBytesToRead	DWORD	Size of the buffer.
pnBytesRead	DWORD*	Returns the actual number of bytes read.
pnMinNumberOfBytesNeeded	DWORD*	Number of bytes required for the next record.

The function returns data in variable-sized **EVENTLOGRECORD** structures, which are put in the **lpBuffer** that is passed in. The function can read the event log record from a particular record number (which is a field in the **EVENTLOGRECORD** structure) or forwards or backwards from the last record read. This direction is specified in the **dwReadFlags** parameter:

Value	Meaning
EVENTLOG_FORWARDS_READ	The log is read in forward chronological order.
EVENTLOG_BACKWARDS_READ	The log is read in reverse chronological order.
EVENTLOG_SEEK_READ	The read operation starts from the record specified.
EVENTLOG_SEQUENTIAL_READ	The read operation proceeds sequentially from the last call.

If the read is from a particular record number then that record must be specified in the **dwRecordOffset** parameter and the direction of the read must also be given.

If the buffer passed is too small to take the data then the function fails, but if the buffer is too big, the function will fill it with as many whole records as it can. This odd behavior can complicate enumerating the messages in the event log.

The data is returned in an **EVENTLOGRECORD** structure, whose size depends on the number and size of the insert strings, the size of the raw data, and whether a user SID was logged.

Example: Adding an Event Resource File

As an example of how to use the event log, we will add the resource for our service so that when the service logs message ID **0**, the event viewer will give a properly formatted message rather than the message that it cannot find the resource file.

The message file, **MsgFile.mc** is simple:

```
;// EnumWinSvr Event Messages
MessageID=0
Language=English
%1
.
```

You can then compile it from a command line with the message compiler:

mc MsgFile.mc

The resource file, **msg00001.bin** can be added to the resources of the server using the Visual C++ resource editor. To do this, select Resource Includes... from the View menu. You can now add the binary resource into the Compile-time directives box:

Now all you need to do is build the project and the format string is bound in.

The next step is to make sure that the registry has information about the resource file. Although you can edit the registry by hand, or provide a **.REG** script, it is better to do it in the service code. To do this we will use the ATL **CRegKey** class to add a new key under the **EventLog** key. The best place to do this is when the service is registered in the **CServiceModule::RegisterServer()** method.

Here is the code:

```
inline HRESULT CServiceModule::RegisterServer(
        BOOL bRegTypeLib, BOOL bService)
{
    HRESULT hr = CoInitialize(NULL);

    // ... Standard Wizard-supplied code

    CoUninitialize();

    // ** Code to register the message resource ** //
    if (bService)
    {
        // Add event log information
        CRegKey event_log;
        TCHAR newkey[_MAX_PATH];
        lstrcpy(newkey,
                    _T("SYSTEM\\CurrentControlSet\\Services"
                    "\\EventLog\\Application\\"));
        TCHAR szModule[_MAX_PATH];
        GetModuleFileName(_Module.GetModuleInstance(),
                        szModule, _MAX_PATH);
        TCHAR szName[_MAX_FNAME];
        _tsplitpath(szModule, NULL, NULL, szName, NULL);
        lstrcat(newkey, szName);

        LONG ret;
        ret = event_log.Create(HKEY_LOCAL_MACHINE, newkey);
        if (ERROR_SUCCESS != ret)
            return ret;

        // Now add the values
        ret = event_log.SetValue(szModule,
                            _T("EventMessageFile"));
        if (ERROR_SUCCESS != ret)
            return ret;

        DWORD dwtypes =  EVENTLOG_ERROR_TYPE |
                        EVENTLOG_WARNING_TYPE |
                        EVENTLOG_INFORMATION_TYPE;
        ret = event_log.SetValue(dwtypes,
                            _T("TypesSupported"));
        if (ERROR_SUCCESS != ret)
            return ret;
    }

    return hr;
}
```

This just adds the key with the same name as the service into the **EventLog** key and adds the
EventMessageFile and **TypesSupported** named values.

Adding a New Event Log

Finally, you may decide to use your own event log. To do this, add a new key in the **EventLog** key using **RegEdit**. When you create this key, you will find that the system will create a named value in that key called **Sources** and will automatically fill this with the name of the new event log. When you add a new key under this new event log key, it will be automatically added to the **Sources** value. The **EventLog** service will check this value when an event log is opened to find the registry values for that source.

Here, I have added the new event log called **MyEventLog** and added a source called **evLog**. These have been added automatically into the **Sources** key. I have also added the value **File** to specify where the event log information is saved.

Now you can use **RegisterEventSource()** or **OpenEventLog()** to open the event log passing the event name source (here, **evLog**). The **EventLog** service will search the **Sources** values in all the keys in the **EventLog** key until it finds the source name, and it will then open the appropriate file.

Just as with the default event logs, you can then write to your event log with **ReportEvent()** or read events from it with **ReadEventLog()** using the handle to the event log. Once you have finished with your event log, you can close it with **DeregisterEventSource()** or **CloseEventLog()**.

The main problem with doing this is that the NT event log viewer, **EventVwr.exe**, will not recognize your event log. However, you could always read the event log with the **ReadEventLog()** function, so the data is available. It means, therefore, that if you wish, you can use the **EventLog** API to log private messages that can only be accessed with your own viewer.

Summary

In this chapter, we've examined implementing a DCOM server in an NT service. The first half of the chapter explained what a service is and how to create one, and the second half dealt with the DCOM-specific issues of putting code in a service.

NT services are the way that NT provides functionality to remote (as well as local) clients, in processes that are started up automatically when the machine boots. DCOM, of course, allows objects to be activated by the client (and thus the server process is started if necessary). Services can reduce the start up time compared with just in time activation.

One of the issues that was briefly mentioned in this chapter is multithreading. This is the subject of the next chapter.

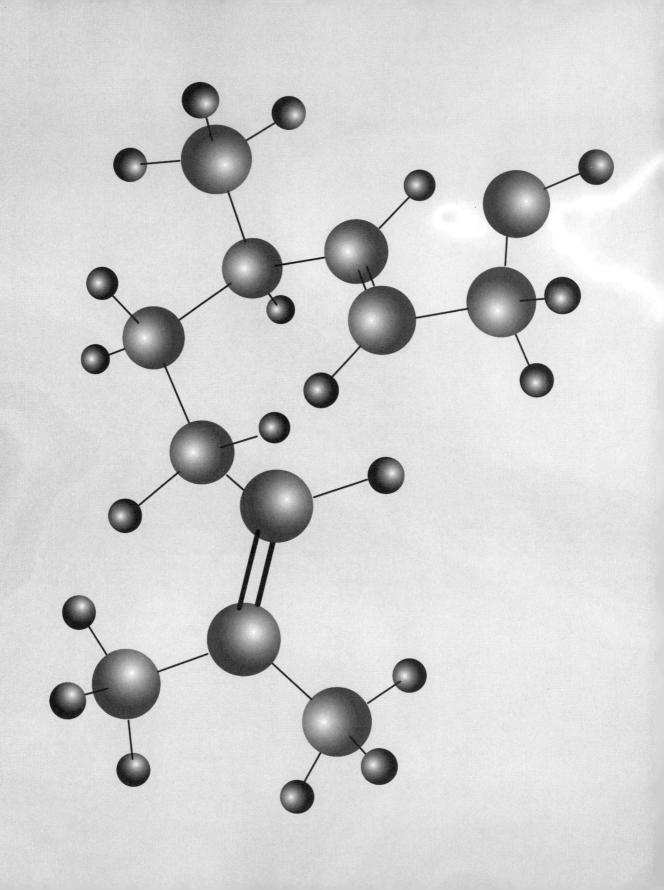

Multithreading

Multithreaded Win32 Applications

Threads have a strange effect on new Win32 programmers. They come to threads after writing procedural applications that have a single path of execution. In such a program it's usually straightforward to determine, at any point in time, what part of the code is being executed. Threads seem to complicate the application, especially if these threads have access to the same global data.

When the new developer gets more accustomed to threads, learning how to create them and synchronizing data access between them, they're often tempted to spin many threads to perform many small concurrent tasks. The more experienced programmer will look at this code and strip away many of the threads and amalgamate the tasks, or perhaps suspend some threads in preference of others.

Although threads are useful, and simplify code in some cases, they still need to be scheduled by the system and this will use up system resources. If you have a single CPU and many threads, the system has to switch between each thread and it must change the CPU registers and stack to match the code about to be executed as it does so. If you have a task, and then split it between two threads, the total time taken to perform the task will be more than if a single thread performed the whole task, because of the context switching.

Threads will not increase the performance of your application unless you have a corresponding increase in the number of processors in your computer, so they should be used with caution. However, creating extra threads in your application can make it more responsive, and can allow you to code the application more efficiently.

This chapter starts by explaining how to use threads in Win32 and shows some code to implement two thread models. The second part of the chapter shows how to use threads in COM servers and also looks at the issues of passing interface pointers between threads. The example that is developed at the end of the chapter demonstrates Win32 thread synchronization as well as illustrating the differences between the COM threading models.

Before we can look at multithreading in COM we need to get a grounding in multithreading in Win32. The following sections show how to create threads, how to communicate between them, and how to synchronize thread access to global data.

Thread Handling Functions

Lifetime of a Thread

The following diagram shows the lifetime of a thread and the Win32 functions that affect it. Briefly, here is a description of states that a thread can be in and how that state is obtained.

A thread is created using **CreateThread()**, this specifies the controlling function that the thread will use. The caller can create a thread in one of two states: suspended or running. If the thread is suspended, it can be made to run by another thread calling **ResumeThread()** conversely, another thread can suspend a thread by calling **SuspendThread()**. Threads are kernel objects and as such they have a security context. This means that only users that have the correct rights can get a handle to a thread, and you need the thread's handle to suspend or resume a thread.

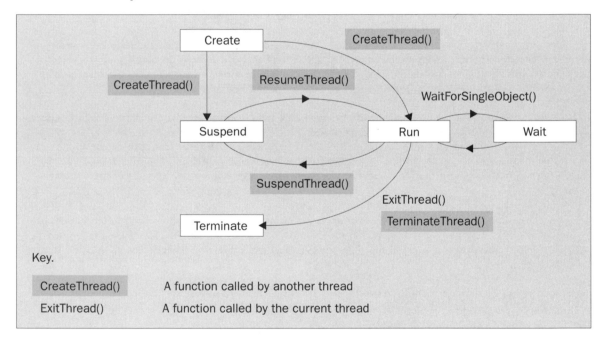

Once the thread is running, it will execute whatever code is in the controlling function. The thread may depend on an object created, or in use, by another thread. To allow for synchronization between the two threads, the current thread can voluntarily go into an efficient waiting state by calling **WaitForSingleObject()** (or the corresponding API **WaitForMultipleObjects()**).
These functions allow a thread to be suspended while taking up few CPU cycles (an *inefficient* way for a thread to wait is to go into a **for** loop). The thread specifies what object it is waiting for and gives a timeout value. The thread comes out of the wait state when either the object is available or the timeout has expired.

The thread can die in one of three ways:

- ▲ Naturally - which means that the controlling function returns (a bit like a process' **main()** function returning)
- ▲ Commit suicide - with a call to **ExitThread()**(a bit like a process calling **exit()**)
- ▲ Another thread explicitly kills the thread with a call to **TerminateThread()**

In just about all cases, it's best to tell a thread that it must die rather than killing it. A call to **TerminateThread()** will not allow a thread to clean up any resources to which it has access.

This just shows one thread in isolation, but on a system there will be more than one thread running at any one time. If there are fewer processors in your machine than there are threads, the system will have to context switch between the running threads. I will leave the full details of this process to other books, but, put simply, the code running in one thread will run for a timeslice and then the thread will be suspended by the system and another thread will run.

The system does not care about the language used to write the thread code and thus has no respect for any functions or language operations that are performed.

Thus a C statement like

```
x = x * 10.0;
```

will take many machine operations and the scheduler could suspend the thread on any of these machine operations.

Imagine a situation where one thread runs a function that alters a global variable and is suspended halfway through that code. Now a second thread runs the same function to change the same variable. Because the first thread has been suspended with the variable in an inconsistent state, the second thread will get invalid data, and change it using this invalid data. When the first thread is resumed, it will try to complete its operation on data that has changed since it was suspended. This has the real potential of corrupting the global variable.

What is needed is a mechanism that will mark a section of code to say that it can only be executed by one thread at a time, and if a thread is suspended whilst executing in this code, no other thread will be able to run the code. Such code is called a **critical section** and is one of the synchronization methods possible with Win32. This, and the other methods, are described later.

Creating Threads

Creating threads in Win32 is easy: just call the Win32 **CreateThread()** function.

```
HANDLE CreateThread(
            LPSECURITY_ATTRIBUTES lpThreadAttributes,
            DWORD dwStackSize,
            LPTHREAD_START_ROUTINE lpStartAddress,
            LPVOID lpParameter,
            DWORD dwCreationFlags,
            LPDWORD lpThreadId
              );
```

This function has six parameters. It creates a kernel object and so it's natural that one of the parameters is a pointer to the security attributes that the current thread uses to create the new thread. If the creation is successful, the function returns a handle to the thread object.

The second parameter determines the size of stack to be used by the thread because each thread has its own stack. If you do not specify a size for the thread, the size of the primary thread's stack will be used and by default this will be 1Mb. (The primary thread is the main thread of the process, the one that was created for the process to run in.) Of course, the 1Mb stack is not committed memory or your machine would rapidly run out of virtual memory! What it does mean is that the thread *could* have a thread of 1Mb, before a stack overrun occurs.

A thread is a unit of execution and this implies that it's created to run some code. Therefore we need to indicate what code should be run, this is the reason for the third parameter, **lpStartAddress**. The function must have the prototype:

```
DWORD WINAPI ThreadFunc(LPVOID lpParameter);
```

Typically this is a function in the same source file, but it need not be. The parameter is a pointer to some data that you want to pass to the thread. You can pass whatever you like and this is done by supplying a pointer in the fourth parameter of **CreateThread()**.

> *Notice that the thread function returns a value. When this function returns the thread has died, the return value can be used to indicate the reason for the thread death*

You can get this return value by calling **GetExitCodeThread()**, passing the thread handle, and a pointer to a **DWORD**. If the thread hasn't finished then it will not have a return value, instead the function returns a value of **STILL_ACTIVE** (**0x103**). For this reason, a thread should never return a value of **STILL_ACTIVE** when it finishes.

If you decide that the thread function is naturally part of an object you are using it in, you may be tempted to add it as a method to the class. Indeed, if you want your thread function to access private data in an object, this would be the only way to implement the function. However, there is one problem, class methods have an implicit parameter that is a pointer to the object: the **this** pointer. Passing this pointer to the method allows the method to call other class methods and access data members, but it also means that the prototype of the method now has two parameters. **CreateThread()** requires a function pointer with a single **LPVOID** parameter.

To prevent this, you can make the thread function **static**. Now, the compiler will not pass it a **this** pointer because a **static** function is part of the class and isn't called through a specific object. Unfortunately this means that the function can only access **static** variables, so one of the reasons for making the method part of the class in the first place (encapsulation of object data and methods) is no longer valid. To get round this you could employ some mechanism like passing the thread function the **this** pointer of the creating object. It's messy, but it works.

The fifth parameter to **CreateThread()** determines whether the thread is created running or suspended. If it is created suspended then you can set it running it at a later stage with a call to **ResumeThread()**.

The final parameter is pointer to a variable that will take the new thread's ID. This is unique for every thread and is the value given against each thread in programs like **PView**. Note that although you can identify a thread with this value, threads are accessed (and hence identified to the system) by using the thread handle. Handles can be inherited by child processes and hence used outside of the process that creates them. If a handle is not created this way, the thread handle *value* will only be specific to this thread and so not unique across the machine. Win32 API will allow you access to the thread through the handle and this can obviate the need for a unique thread ID. If we need to actually message to the thread, from another context, then the ID is, of course, imperative. We'll be utilizing this property in an example later in the chapter.

As I've already indicated, the handle is to a kernel object, so you need to release it when the thread has died. Since the thread handle remains valid even when a thread has died, it means that you can use the handle to test whether the thread has died with **GetExitCodeThread()**. If the thread has died, you can use this same function to test for the return value.

Since the handle is valid after the thread has died, the thread object must still be taking up system resources. Once you have finished with this object, you must free it by closing the thread handle. This may sound easy to do, but quite often it complicates your code.

Consider the following fragment:

```
HANDLE hThread;
DWORD dwThreadID;
hThread = CreateThread(NULL, 0, DoTask, NULL, 0,
                       &dwThreadID);
WaitForSingleObject(hThread, INFINITE);
CloseHandle(hThread);
```

This creates a thread, tells it to perform some action, and waits for the thread to finish then releases the thread handle. This is completely unnecessary, since the thread that called **CreateThread()** is waiting for the created thread to finish and so is not doing any work. So why create the new thread? It may look obvious, but this is the sort of code that some texts give as an example of multithreading.

Another way to carry out the same task is to create two threads - now the creating thread is used to manage other threads rather than do work itself. To test whether more than one thread has finished you can use **WaitForMultipleObjects()**:

```
HANDLE hThreads[2];
DWORD dwThreadIDs[2];
hThreads[0] = CreateThread(NULL, 0, DoTask, NULL, 0,
                       &dwThreadIDs[0]);
hThreads[1] = CreateThread(NULL, 0, DoOtherTask, NULL, 0,
                       &dwThreadIDs[1]);
WaitForMultipleObjects(2, hThreads, TRUE, INFINITE);
CloseHandle(hThreads[0]);
CloseHandle(hThreads[1]);
```

WaitForMultipleObjects() has four parameters, the first specifies how many threads to wait for and the second is an array of handles to those threads. The third specifies if the function should wait for all the threads to die before returning, or if just one thread dying will make the function to return. If the second option is selected, the return value of the function will identify which thread died.

The code above waits for all the threads to die and then closes the thread handles. Writing code that'll maintain thread handles, and close them, when the associated thread dies, can be a headache.

Terminating a Thread

A thread can die in three ways as outlined above. Since a thread may be using resources that require cleanup before the thread can die (an open file for example), it's best not to call **TerminateThread()** from another thread. This will not allow for an orderly closedown of the thread. Instead, if one thread wants to close another one, it should tell that thread to die (a bit like sending someone a piece of paper with a black spot on it).

One way to do this is for the controlled thread to be created with an **event object**. The controlling thread can use this event to indicate that the controlled thread should die. Events are kernel **synchronization** objects that can be in one of two states: signaled or non-signaled. (Synchronization is explained later.)

Events are created by a call to **CreateEvent()** which can indicate whether the event is created in the signaled or non-signaled state. This function will return a handle that can be sent to calls to **WaitForSingleObject()** or **WaitForMultipleObjects()**. These functions will return when the event is signaled. You can signal an event by calling **SetEvent()** and unsignal it with a call to **ResetEvent()**.

So, to manage the controlled thread, the controlling thread should call **SetEvent()** to set the event object and indicate that the other thread should die. The controlled thread can then test the state of the event object at strategic points using **WaitForSingleObject()** with a zero timeout. If the event becomes signaled, it can either immediately call **ExitThread()** or it can branch to the terminating code and return from the controlling function.

Threads and Windows

Every process has at least one thread known as the primary thread. A Windows GUI application will have a message queue and it will use a message pump to obtain messages from the queue and dispatch them to the appropriate window. Typically the **WinMain()** of the application will have a message pump implemented like this:

```
MSG msg;
while (GetMessage(&msg, hWnd, 0, 0))
   DispatchMessage(&msg);
```

This will look into the message queue for messages destined for the window with the handle **hWnd**. Since this window must have been registered to have been created, the registration will specify a windows procedure and this is called in response to calling the **DispatchMessage()**.

In reality, you don't need a window to use a message queue. Any thread can have a message queue, and calling **GetMessage()** in a thread will ensure that a queue is created for the current thread. You don't need to know how this happens – Win32 will do it for you. The thread can then implement a message pump.

First though, the above code needs changing. There's no window handle, since there's no window, so the call to **GetMessage()** should pass a **NULL** for this parameter. Then, there's no registered window procedure and hence **DispatchMessage()** will not work.
Instead you must provide your own message handling procedure and call it explicitly:

```
LRESULT DispatchThreadMessage(HWND, UINT, WPARAM, LPARAM);

DWORD ThreadFn(LPVOID)
```

```
    {
        MSG msg;
        while (GetMessage(&msg, NULL, 0, 0))
            DispatchThreadMessage(NULL, msg.message, msg.wParam,
                                  msg.lParam);

        return msg.message;
    }

    LRESULT DispatchThreadMessage(HWND/*not used*/,
            UINT message, WPARAM wParam, LPARAM lParam)
    {
        switch (message)
        {
            // ... do the message handling here
        }
        return 0;
    }
```

I have coded this to look like a window procedure, but you can see that there's little difference between the two. It does beg the question of how a message gets into a thread's message queue.

There's one Win32 function to do this, **PostThreadMessage()**.

```
    BOOL PostThreadMessage(DWORD idThread, UINT Msg, WPARAM wParam, LPARAM lParam);
```

This is like **PostMessage()** except it takes a thread ID (you knew there was a reason to hang onto that value, didn't you?) and like the window version it returns immediately. There is no equivalent to **SendMessage()**. This makes sense since **SendMessage()** blocks until the window procedure of the target window has returned. The system does not know about any procedure used to handle thread messages. There is little point in a hypothetical **SendThreadMessage()** returning the value returned from a thread procedure because this would mean that the thread would have to die!

Thread message queues are quite useful in controlling threads since two threads can communicate via messages with simpler code than events, for example. The thread pool example implemented later in this chapter will illustrate this.

Fibers

This is a convenient point to talk about **fibers**, which were introduced in service pack 3 of NT 3.51 for the benefit of developers porting Unix code to NT. As the name suggests a fiber is a lightweight thread, and there may be many fibers in a thread. The lightweight description refers to the fact that fibers are scheduled by your process and not the system. The NT thread scheduler is efficient and so you shouldn't need to use fibers to implement your own version.

Thread Data

Thread code will need to operate on data. When a thread is created with **CreateThread()** you can pass a **void** pointer to some data and the thread controlling function is given this pointer as its only parameter. Since this is a void pointer it could be a pointer to a primitive type, or to a structure or object. The thread controlling function will have to cast the pointer to the appropriate type.

Since the thread code is just another part of your process, it can access the global variables you have declared in your code modules, and can also use any functions used by other code in your process, including code that uses **static** data.

The problem here is that when you have more than one thread, more than one thread could be accessing these global and **static** variables, and thus you have to be careful how this occurs.

Synchronization

What happens if two threads want to change the same resource?
For example, here's some code where two threads are trying to access the same variable:

```
DWORD AddFn(LPVOID);
DWORD MinusFn(LPVOID);
DWORD x;

VOID SomeFunction()
{
   CreateThread(..., AddFn, ...);
   CreateThread(..., MinusFn, ...);
}

DWORD AddFn(LPVOID)
{
   for (x = 0; x < 1000; x++);
   return 0;
}

DWORD MinusFn(LPVOID)
{
   for (x = 0; x > -1000; x--);
   return 0;
}
```

The code in **SomeFunction()** will probably never return since **x** is a used by both thread functions. The obvious problem is **AddFn()** adding some value on to **x** in its **for** loop in one timeslice and then **MinusFn()** subtracting some value in the next. The less obvious problem is that most C statements are not atomic and a thread could be rescheduled half way through an action like **x++**.

If you think in terms of the actual machine code executed in this statement, it may help to make you more wary about synchronization issues. When you say **x++** the machine code will retrieve the value of **x** from memory, increment it and the put the result back into memory. If the thread is suspended after it has retrieved the value, it will carry out the rest of the operation when it is resumed at a later stage. If in this time between suspension and resumption another thread completes the whole operation of incrementing this variable, when the suspended thread resumes, it will increment an out of date value. The value that it writes back to memory will be invalid.

Here **x** is an integral value, if **x** was a more complex value, or a member of an object or **struct**, then the operation to retrieve it from memory may involve many steps, perhaps involving multiple indirections. There is potential for many places for the thread to be interrupted during a seemingly simple operation.

In this code you would have to rethink why the thread functions are accessing a global variable and whether it is really necessary. If two threads must access the same data then they should be synchronized to use it.

In the case of a single object, you can protect it by creating a **mutex**. This kernel object provides mutual exclusive access to a resource:

```
DWORD AddFn(LPVOID);
DWORD MinusFn(LPVOID);
HANDLE hmutex;
DWORD x;

VOID SomeFunction()
{
    HANDLE hthreads[2];
    hmutex = CreateMutex(NULL, FALSE, NULL);
    hthreads[0] = CreateThread(..., AddFn, ...);
    hthreads[1] = CreateThread(..., MinusFn, ...);
    WaitForMultipleObjects(2, hthreads, TRUE, INFINITE);
    Closehandle(hthreads[0]);
    Closehandle(hthreads[1]);
    Closehandle(hmutex);
}

DWORD AddFn(LPVOID)
{
    WaitForSingleObject(hmutex, INFINITE);
    for (x = 0; x < 1000; x++);
    ReleaseMutex(hmutex);
    return 0;
}

DWORD MinusFn(LPVOID)
{
    WaitForSingleObject(hmutex, INFINITE);
    for (x = 0; x > -1000; x--);
    ReleaseMutex(hmutex);
    return 0;
}
```

This rather pointless code will create two threads, one to increment a global variable, and another to decrement it. To control access to the variable, we also create a mutex. The thread functions must obtain ownership of the mutex before accessing it, and ownership is obtained when **WAIT_OBJECT_0** is returned from **WaitForSingleObject()** (since this code has a timeout of **INFINITE**, it cannot return **WAIT_TIMEOUT**). When a thread uses a global variable guarded in this way, it can assume that it will have exclusive access to the variable as long as it owns the mutex. To allow another thread to own the mutex, a thread must call **ReleaseMutex()**.

Using mutexes like this to guard a global variable requires discipline from the programmer, if the **WaitForSingleObject()** was missed out of **MinusFn()**, we would be in the same situation as before, with two threads accessing the same global data non-exclusively.

Mutexes are just one of many objects that can be in a signaled or unsignaled state and hence can be waited upon. These other objects include events, threads, processes and semaphores. The Win32 documentation gives the complete list. If your code requires several objects to become signaled then you can call **WaitForMultipleObjects()**. You should pass an array of object handles and a flag, indicating, if you want one or all of the objects to be signaled (as was used in **SomeFunction()** above).

In the first case, if an object becomes signaled, the return value of this function indicates which object it was. There are constants defined starting at **WAIT_OBJECT_0** to specify the object index. If all objects must become signaled, a value of **WAIT_OBJECT_0** is returned when they do.

If the code that is waiting implements a message pump then you may also want the wait to finish when the message queue receives a message. You can do this by calling **MsgWaitForMultipleObjects()**. This is essentially the same as **WaitForMultipleObjects()** but it takes an additional parameter that specifies the type of message that will make the function return. The function treats the message queue as another waited-upon object, so if the function returns because of a Windows message, the reply value is **WAIT_OBJECT_0 + nCount** where **nCount** is the number of objects waited upon. (Because of zero-indexing, this makes the message queue the **nCount + 1** object.)

Note that if you object to accessing the mutex via a global handle, you can create a named mutex by passing a name as the last parameter to **CreateMutex()** and then open a local handle to the mutex with **OpenMutex()**:

```
VOID SomeFunction()
{
   HANDLE hmutex;
   hmutex = CreateMutex(NULL, FALSE, "X_MUTEX");
   // ... Create threads and wait
   Closehandle(hmutex);
}

DWORD AddFn(LPVOID)
{
   HANDLE hmutex;
   OpenMutex(MUTEX_ALL_ACCESS, FALSE, "X_MUTEX");
   WaitForSingleObject(hmutex, INFINITE);
   for (x = 0; x < 1000; x++);
   ReleaseMutex(hmutex);
   CloseHandle(hmutex);
   return 0;
}
```

Named mutexes are particularly useful when you want to share a mutex between processes. Note that the call to **CloseHandle()** in **AddFn()** does not destroy the mutex since there will be an outstanding handle already open on the mutex from **SomeFunction()**.

Reentrancy

The previous example had two threads using two different thread functions handling a global variable, but what if you have just one thread function and create several threads to use it? Consider this code for a thread controlling function:

```
DWORD FileData(LPVOID param)
{
   // ... Do something
   HANDLE hfile;
   hfile = CreateFile("test.log", ...,
           FILE_SHARE_READ | FILE_SHARE_WRITE, ...);
   DWORD written;
   WriteFile(hfile, param, lstrlen((LPCTSTR)param),
           &written, NULL);
   CloseHandle(hfile);
```

```
   // ... Now do something else
   return 0;
}
```

If two threads are created and both have this as their controlling function, we could have the situation where one thread is preempted by the system while it still has a handle open on the file. When the other thread is scheduled to run, it would then open the file and write to it.

The file could be protected by a mutex, but another way to protect this code is to define a **critical section**. You do this by declaring a global critical section object. Then, before you start the guarded code, tell the system that you are entering a critical section. After the guarded code has finished, tell the system that you are leaving the critical section. The critical section object must be global so that all threads can access it.

```
CRITICAL_SECTION g_cs;

void main()
{
   InitializeCriticalSection(&g_cs);

   CreateThread(..., FileData, (LPVOID)"First Thread",
               ...);
   CreateThread(..., FileData, (LPVOID)"Second Thread",
               ...);

   // ... Wait for threads to end and clean up
   DeleteCriticalSection(&g_cs);
}

DWORD FileData(LPVOID param)
{
   // ... Do something
   EnterCriticalSection(&g_cs);
   HANDLE hfile;
   hfile = CreateFile("test.log", ...,
           FILE_SHARE_READ | FILE_SHARE_WRITE, ...);
   DWORD written;
   WriteFile(hfile, param, lstrlen((LPCTSTR)param),
           &written, NULL);
   CloseHandle(hfile);
   LeaveCriticalSection(&g_cs);

   // ... Now do something else
   return 0;
}
```

The **main()** function creates a critical section object and two threads. When the thread function needs to access the shared resource, it calls **EnterCriticalSection()**, and when it has finished with the resource, it must call **LeaveCriticalSection()**. If a second thread attempts to execute the guarded code when our first thread is in the critical section, the second thread will be put to sleep. The second thread is only awoken when the first thread has left the section.

Notice how this works, you use a global variable and specify when the critical section starts and when it ends. Because it uses a global variable, it's important that **LeaveCriticalSection()** is called, otherwise no other thread could run the code. Critical sections cannot be named and are valid only in a single process. If you use a mutex to guard a code section, you could name it and use it to protect an associated code section in another process. Another difference between critical sections and the other synchronization objects is that you cannot wait on a critical section. This makes sense because they are used to guard a section of code, i.e. they have a specific task, whereas the synchronization objects are more general.

Synchronizing Thread Actions

We can now allow a thread to access global data in a safe way, ensuring that the data is only accessed by one thread at a time.

What happens if you have one thread writing to a global object, but many threads wanting to read it?

In such a situation, if the object is guarded by a mutex, only one thread can access the object, so once the writing thread has finished with the object and released the mutex, the reading threads will only have access to the object one-by-one by having to obtain and then release the mutex.

Event Object

To enable all the reading threads to know when the writing thread has finished with it, the code could use an **event** object. This object is either set or reset (signaled or unsignaled), and when it is set, a wait on the event handle with **WaitForSingleObject()** will return immediately. The writing thread could reset an event object, write to the global object, then set the event once it's finished its writing action. The reading threads, however, will wait on the event handle and once the event is set, the wait will return and the reading threads can assume that the object is fully initialized and so they can safely access it.

Of course, such a scheme should also guard against the possibility of the writing thread pre-empting the reading threads before they have finished reading the object. If it didn't, a reading thread could be half way through reading the object, when the writing thread preempts the reading thread, changes the object and then allows the reading thread to resume, reading changed data.

You create an event with a call to **CreateEvent()** and set or reset it with **SetEvent()** and **ResetEvent()** as explained above. This action of setting and resetting an event is quite useful, and so there's a Win32 function, **PulseEvent()** to do just that. **PulseEvent()** sets (to signaled) the state of the specified event object and then resets it (to nonsignaled) after releasing one or all the threads that are waiting on the event. When you create an event you specify if the event is a manual reset event or an auto-reset event. In the second case, when a single thread has been released, the event is reset automatically, thus a single thread is released when **PulseEvent()** is called.

Thread Local Storage

So far we have seen how to allow threads to use global resources. Now let's look at threads having their own data.

First of all, there are local, stack variables. Every thread is created with its own stack. This must be the case since if threads shared a stack, there would be clashes between them when the controlling function is called, since the parameter of the function and the address for the function to return to is passed on the stack.

Since every thread has its own stack, any local variables in a function (**auto** variables) are local to just that one thread. So you can create local variables and be assured that there will be no problems when the function is executed by more than one thread.

Also, if you are careful, you can create objects on the heap and use them exclusively by particular threads. You must make sure that if synchronization objects are not used, the object pointer is only used by a single thread:

```
void main()
{
    CAnObject* pobj1 = new CAnObject;
    CAnObject* pobj2 = new CAnObject;
    CreateThread(..., UseObject, (LPVOID)pobj1, ...);
    CreateThread(..., UseObject, (LPVOID)pobj2, ...);
    // Wait for the threads to finish
    // using the objects
    delete pobj1;
    delete pobj2;
}

DWORD UseObject(LPVOID param);
{
    CAnObject* pobj = (CAnObject*)param;
    // Use the object
    return 0;
}
```

The **UseObject()** function is passed a pointer to a separate object for both of the threads. Of course, the object is not really local since it is created before the thread function is used, but this is one technique that allows threads to manipulate objects safely.

> *Note also that the thread controlling function could pass the object pointer to other functions and these can use the object knowing that the data is specific to this particular thread. This technique is a little cumbersome and does not encapsulate the data with the thread that uses it*

First though, let's look at another problem. When an object is created as an **auto** variable in a function, the object is created on the stack. Quite often the object could be large and could take time to initialize, so C programmers often get round this by creating a **static** variable:

```
DWORD AddFn(LPVOID);
void PrintData(DWORD);

VOID SomeFunction()
{
    CreateThread(..., AddFn, ...);
    CreateThread(..., AddFn, ...);
}

DWORD AddFn(LPVOID)
{
    DWORD x;
    for (x = 0; x < 100; x++)
        PrintData(x);
    return 0;
}

void PrintData(DWORD x)
```

```
{
    static char buffer[1024];
    wsprintf(buffer, "The value is: %ld\n", x);
    puts(buffer);
}
```

Here, a **static char** buffer is created just once, when the process is initialized. When the **PrintData()** function is called, the function has access to **buffer** and although this variable can only be accessed from this function, and thus it is not a global variable, it behaves like a global variable in that it is only created and initialized once.

This is not good thread code. The problem is that there is only *one* buffer, so in this code both threads have access to this single buffer. A thread running **PrintData()** could be preempted by another thread between the calls to **wsprintf()** and **puts()**, for example, corrupting the output of that thread.

To make this thread-safe, you have to mark the buffer as being **thread static**. When you do this, the compiler ensures that a separate buffer is created for every thread. This is done by using the storage class attribute **__declspec(thread)**. So the **PrintData()** function could be rewritten as:

```
void PrintData(DWORD x)
{
    __declspec(thread) static char buffer[1024];
    wsprintf(buffer, "The value is: %ld\n", x);
    puts(buffer);
}
```

Of course your compiler must support this type of attribute. This is the syntax for Microsoft compilers.

The other problem is that since the compiler allocates the thread static buffers, the buffers must be known at compile time. If you put a function like **PrintData()** in a DLL and link your process to the import library of the DLL, there are no problems since the compiler will know about the thread static buffers in the DLL and can make sure that when the function is called outside of the DLL, a buffer specific to the thread is used.

If the DLL is loaded dynamically using **LoadLibrary()**, the compiler doesn't know about the internal implementation of the DLL functions and will not allocate any thread static buffers. The effect is worse than having many threads accessing a global variable, the symptom of this problem is that the DLL functions will appear to use memory allocated to other variables. The compiler basically makes no attempt to handle the buffers – thus, using **__declspec(thread)** in a DLL function is usually not a good idea!

Thread Local Storage

The way to get round this is to use the Win32 thread local storage (TLS) functions. TLS was covered briefly in Chapter 2, but here is a recap. You start using TLS by calling **TlsAlloc()** to obtain an index into an array of 32-bit values, this is done at some point in a controlling thread. The array that you have access to is then allocated specifically for each thread, so when a thread is created, it can use the index to save data to memory that is specific to this thread. Since the index is created in the controlling thread, every thread will have the same value.

More than one call to **TlsAlloc()** can be made and the indexes returned will be unique. However, there are a limited number of indexes. The system DLLs and the CRT use TLS indexes, so it's best to use just one index. When you have finished with the index, you can free it with a call to **TlsFree()** from the controlling thread when all other threads have finished. You can store any data in the array using

TlsSetValue() and read it with **TlsGetValue()** and the usual method is to allocate a buffer on the heap and save the pointer in the array.

The TLS API does require extra coding to use, but it can be useful.

Thread Models

Lets look at a few examples of using threads, this is by no means an exhaustive list, as there are many thread models that you can use. This section covers two thread models that fit in with the later discussion on multithreaded COM servers, worker threads and thread pools.

Worker Threads

The idea here is that a main thread (usually, but not necessarily, the primary thread of the application) will spin a new thread to perform a task. This main thread then continues with its work while the worker thread runs concurrent with it.

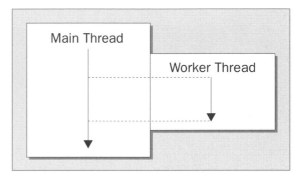

Since the main thread is running concurrent with the worker thread, any data generated by the worker thread should only be used by the main thread *after* the worker thread has finished with the data.

This model is probably best suited to user applications (such as a web browser downloading images asynchronously) rather than for servers. A common scenario is an application starting a complex process (a recalculation of a spreadsheet, or maybe a search on the Internet).
The task will take a great deal of time and thus, if it was handled by the main thread, the user would see the Windows hourglass and the UI of the application would be effectively frozen (after all, in a single threaded application, the same thread will handle the UI elements and any calculations the user requests).

To get round this problem, the application will create a new thread and allow that to handle the lengthy task, while the application's primary thread responds to messages from the application's message queue. As stressed before, this will only give a speed advantage if the application is running on a multiprocessor machine - and even then only if there are sufficient processors for all the other threads currently running. This does *not* mean that you cannot create more threads than there are processors, such a suggestion is absurd, but it does mean that creating more threads will not make your process run faster. It will result in a *longer* total execution time.

What you gain here is *responsiveness*. In the single threaded case, if the user wants to cancel the task, it's not usually possible. If it were to be possible, the code handling the task would have to constantly poll for user interruptions (as is done in 16-bit windows to handle the Cancel button on a print dialog, for example). In addition, the user would not have the opportunity to start another task, that would be asking *too* much.

A multithreaded application using worker threads can improve on this. In this case when the user wants to perform a task, a new thread is created. This thread is only concerned with the specified task (say, a recalculation of a spreadsheet). Another thread, the UI thread and usually the application's primary thread, carries out the task of accepting, and handling messages from the message queue.

Now if the user decides to stop the recalculation before it is finished, by clicking on a toolbar button or a menu item, then the message will be accepted immediately since the UI thread is only concerned with polling the message queue. In fact, the message will be accepted *almost* immediately because the UI thread may be sleeping while another thread is running. The UI thread could then handle the message without any intervention from the worker thread (although stopping the worker thread does require some inter-thread communication).

Furthermore, if the user decides to perform a second calculation whilst the first one is still being performed, the UI thread would just start a new worker thread.

So, with the reservations about synchronization, this seems to be a perfect solution: one thread handles requests for action and upon each request it creates a new thread and then goes back to waiting for a new request. The sort of code you could expect to see is:

```
static HANDLE hThread;
static DWORD dwThreadID;

switch (uMsg)
{
   case WM_COMMAND:
   {
      WORD wID;
      switch (wID)
      {
         case IDM_CALCULATE:
            hThread = CreateThread(NULL, 0, DoTask,
                        NULL, 0, &dwThreadID);
            break;
      }
      break;
   }

   // ... etc.
}
```

Here the UI thread of the process handles the dispatched messages from the message pump, and when the user wants to perform a complex calculation, it creates a new thread. Since this thread is not created as suspended it will start the calculation immediately, and when the calculation has finished, the thread will die all on its own. If a **WaitForSingleObject()** call was made in the message handler for **IDM_CALCULATE**, the UI would be frozen until the calculation had completed, defeating the point of creating the calculation thread.

The thread is created with the Win32 API **CreateThread()**. This is fine if the application does not use the C runtime library. However, if you use the CRT, you should use the CRT function **_beginthreadex()** to ensure that the correct CRT thread static buffers are used by the new thread. If **CreateThread()** is used instead, there is a small memory leak (80 bytes) when the thread ends.

In the above code, I am using a **static** variable to hold the thread handle. This is the typical solution used for saving persistent values in the windows procedure of a Win 3.1 application, which did not have threads, but is dangerous code for multithreaded Win32 code. For example, what would happen if the user selected the Calculate menu item twice? This would be handled correctly in terms of creating more threads to handle the requests, but using a **static** variable would mean that the previous thread handle would be overwritten and hence lost.

Before you suggest *thread local storage* as a solution, think again. It is inappropriate here since it's the UI thread that is running and handling the dispatched messages and hence the thread local storage used would only be for this thread; you gain nothing in using TLS here. This is important because it highlights one aspect about multithreading that confuses novices: you really must be sure about which thread is executing a section of code and make an informed choice on how to handle the data in the code.

What is needed is a list of the currently active threads, which can be updated whenever a new thread is created, dies, or is destroyed. The trick is to know when a thread has died. You could wait on a thread handle with `WaitForSingleObject()` but this blocks the waiting thread, and is exactly the sort of situation that we are trying to avoid.

Another possibility is to periodically test a thread handle to see if the thread is still active, the following code does this with `GetExitCodeThread()`:

```
// Some global list created on the heap
CHandleLinkedList* g_phlist;

switch (uMsg)
{
   // ... etc
   case WM_COMMAND:
   {
      WORD wID;
      switch (wID)
      {
         case IDM_CALCULATE:
            HANDLE hThread = CreateThread(NULL, 0, DoTask,
                     NULL, 0, &dwThreadID);
            g_phlist->AddTail(hThread);
            break;
      }
      break;
   }
   case WM_TIMER:
   {
      POSITION pos;
      pos = g_phlist->GetHeadPosition();
      while (pos)
      {
         POSITION rempos = pos;
         DWORD dwExitcode;
         HANDLE hThread = g_phlist->GetNext(pos);
         GetExitCodeThread(hThread, &dwExitcode);
         if (dwExitCode != STILL_ACTIVE)
         {
            CloseHandle(hThread);
            g_phlist->RemoveAt(rempos);
         }
      }
      break;
   }
   // ... etc.
   case WM_DESTROY:
   {
      POSITION pos;
      pos = g_phlist->GetHeadPosition();
      while (pos)
```

```
    {
        DWORD dwExitcode;
        HANDLE hThread = g_phlist->GetNext(pos);
        TerminateThread(hThread, &dwExitcode);
        CloseHandle(hThread);
    }
    g_phlist->RemoveAll();
    delete g_phlist;
    break;
}
}
```

Of course, if you were writing this code, you could use the ClassWizard to add message handlers. I have used a **switch** here as it shows the technique more succinctly.

Here we have some class, **CHandleLinkedList**, derived from the MFC **CList** class that holds a list of thread handles. The list is created on the heap, perhaps in the **WM_CREATE** handler, and is destroyed when the window closes.

When a new thread is created, in the **WM_COMAND** handler for the menu item, its handle is added to the list. To check whether a thread died, the code checks the thread handles in the list when a timer message is received. This requires the code to move through the list and check each thread handle to see if the thread is still alive and if not, close the handle and remove the item from the list.

This code is still very messy but it serves the point that using threads is not as simple as it may first appear. In this code, we are taking great pains to clear up after the thread and in a user application this may not seem to be of any great importance. After all, most user applications are only run for a few hours and are usually shutdown at the end of the working day, so the application is likely to only leak a few thread handles. Once the application closes, the Win32 subsystem will perform cleanup on resources that a user application has been careless to release.

In the case of server applications, we have a different situation. A server application could be run for months before any user intervention, let alone a machine reboot. In such a situation, the process must be robust. A handle leak in a server application would build up, over a few days, or weeks, into a serious resource problem. Thus a server will have to make sure that all server thread handles are always closed. On the other hand, the code to check for dead threads takes extra time to execute and this affects the server's overall performance. The next section looks at another model better suited to servers.

I am certainly *not* encouraging you to write user application code that leaks resources, I am stressing the importance of ensuring that your server code is leak-free! A small resource leak in a user application is not likely to bring down the application during the time it is used, and if the application does die, the interactive user can restart the application. A server application should not have any user intervention, and if a server dies, you are likely to annoy many clients!

Improving the Server Model

The problem with the code above is that a routine must be run periodically to test for dead threads. What we really need is some code to be run implicitly whenever a thread dies. One technique that could be used is to implement a DLL to handle the thread management. The advantage of this approach is that every DLL loaded by the process gets a notification when a new thread is created and when the thread is destroyed (although such a notification can be disabled with a call to **DisableThreadLibraryCalls()**). Such a DLL could keep hold of a list of thread handles, adding to the list when a new thread attaches and deleting from the list (and closing the handle) when a thread detaches.

The disadvantage of this approach is that threads may be created when you are unaware. For example, I wrote an ISAPI module that, in the initial design, created some uninitialized resources in the **DllMain()** function when a thread attached and stored a pointer to the resources in thread local storage. When the thread died, the ISAPI DLL was informed with a call to **DllMain()**, which I handled by releasing the resource. The actual resource was initialized and used in the ISAPI code called in response to a call to **HttpExtensionProc()**.

This code worked fine until I started to use COM objects in the ISAPI functions and found that I was getting regular access violations. When I did a **CoCreateInstance()** to create a COM object, the COM runtime created a new thread, so my **DllMain()** function would be called, forcing a new, uninitialized, resource to be created. However, this resource would never be initialized, so when I released the object, COM would finish the thread and **DllMain()** would attempt to release the uninitialized resource causing the access violation.

I assumed that only my code would be creating threads. After I sat down and thought about it, I realized that I was being rather naïve. COM has its own reasons for creating the extra thread, and you can see the creation and destruction of COM threads by looking at the output window of Visual C++ when running an application under the debugger. Also IIS could create threads for its own use and this would cause my ISAPI extension's **DllMain()** to be called, so such a strategy was flawed from the start. I redesigned my ISAPI extension to create the object by another mechanism.

Threads In MFC

Before moving on, it is worthwhile looking at how MFC handles threads. The application class **CWinApp** is derived from a **CWinThread**. This class is appropriately named since it wraps up most of the functionality required to handle UI threads. Indeed, it is quite clear looking through the code that this class is preoccupied with providing support for a thread that will have its own message queue, and allowing interaction with the MFC UI classes.

You can create a worker thread from **CWinThread**, but I think that it's just too much effort. A **CWinThread**-derived worker thread is created in a different way to how you would create a UI thread, and the code is implemented in the object in different methods in the two types of threads. You gain very little from deriving a worker thread from **CWinThread** and the code is much clearer using the Win32 API directly.

Another method of creating a worker thread is to call **AfxBeginThread()**, this takes parameters similar to **CreateThread()** and returns a pointer to a **CWinThread** object that MFC creates for you. This has some advantages over using the Win32 API directly as it encapsulates the Win32 thread API. Remember, there's a certain overhead involved in constructing a **CWinThread** object, and personally I prefer in this situation to talk directly with Win32.

As for general thread handling in MFC, well, there are many internal structures used to hold thread specific state information and much of the initialization of MFC applications (and in the **DllMain()** of MFC DLLs) is devoted to initializing these structures. Remember that MFC was designed as a lightweight wrapper around the Win16 API (I remember when I started using MFC 1.0 with Microsoft C/C++ v7 that the documentation went to great lengths to stress this point). Looking through the code you may get a feeling that multithreading has been tacked on to make what was essentially a single threaded architecture into a multithreaded one.

MFC does well what it is designed for: handling the UI elements of Windows. But for any serious work you should consider a client-server approach, with the server devoted, more than that, *obsessed*, with serving the client's request. Such a server needs no UI and needs little (or no) message handling. While MFC could be used in this situation, you should be cautious. If you use sockets to connect to the server, there may be messy problems with MFC's handling of **CWnd** objects with multithreaded applications. If you decide to use COM to create your server objects then MFC is not a good choice if you want to implement custom or dual interfaces; the obvious choice here is ATL.

ATL and MFC can coexist, you can use MFC in ATL code and vice versa. However, if you find that all you need to use it is for the convenience of **CString** and the list and array classes, you're probably better off looking at the Standard Library instead. Another situation where you may decide to use MFC in a server could be if that server handles windows messages (for example, in the last chapter I described a service that could catch window messages from a window station's desktop and transmit them to a another machine). You could use the MFC message maps to handle this, but another, more efficient way to do the same thing would to use the windows message crackers (a series of macros in **windowsx.h**).

Thread Pool

The last example was great for UI applications that need to create extra threads to maintain their responsiveness to user interactions, but what about server applications?

A server application could take a worker thread approach: implementing a listening thread to accept client requests and then spin a worker thread to handle that request. The code required would be quite straightforward since once the worker thread has started, it would have the responsibility of doing the work and talking back to its client. Once the worker thread has finished, it would close the connection with the client and die. Nice and neat. (Except, of course for the Windows thread handle cleanup, but you could easily create a thread devoted to checking a thread handle list for 'dead' threads.)

However, creating and destroying threads is not free. It takes resources, both time and memory, to create a thread, and you may feel nervous about writing code that could result in a potentially infinite number of threads being created. If a thousand requests come in, should the server really create a thousand threads to handle them? If you're feeling reckless, try this simple application:

```cpp
// Danger.cpp
// Are you sure you want to run this? Read on.
#include <Windows.h>
#include <Stdio.h>

DWORD WINAPI ThrdFn(LPVOID);

int main()
{
    for (short i = 0; i < 150000; i++)
    {
        DWORD dwthreadID;
        printf("Creating thread #%d\n", i);
        CreateThread(NULL, 0, ThrdFn, NULL, 0, &dwthreadID);
    }
    return 0;
}

DWORD WINAPI ThrdFn(LPVOID)
{
    Sleep(10000);
    return 0;
}
```

I have made no attempt to save the thread handle or close it, there is no point because the application will crash before it finishes. Why? Well, on my machine by the time the code had created around 4500 threads, there was so much disk swapping, as it swapped thread contexts and the committed pages of the thread stacks, that my machine became unworkable. You may find a different number of threads makes your machine slow to an unacceptable rate. Use Task Manager to monitor and kill off the example. This many threads is plainly silly, but I have seen 'production' software that creates a thousand threads and the developers have wondered why the software was so slow (and why the hard disk life seemed to be shorter than most).

A solution to this is to restrict the number of threads that will be used. One way to do this is to create a pool of threads when the application starts and use these threads to handle the requests for work. The threads will be suspended when they complete their work and then wait for further work. When the application finishes, it can finally destroy all the worker threads and clean up their resources.

This solution is best used when a server program is running all the time, probably as a service, handling requests from clients. These clients could be remote, using some IPC mechanism to attach to the server; or they could be on the same machine as the server and use a local IPC mechanism. When a client makes a request, the server tests to see if there is a worker thread available and if so, wakes it up and gives it the task. If no thread is available, the client request can be rejected or, better still, queued until a worker thread becomes available. The NT system works like this; it holds a pool of threads to carry out its tasks, boosting this number only if absolutely necessary.

The advantage of this is that the overhead of creating and destroying the threads occurs when the application starts and finishes, when client connections would either be impossible or disallowed. It also limits the number of threads that the process uses, ensuring that the process doesn't unnecessarily consume resources.

A thread pool is not a trivial piece of code, however. The following code shows one way to do it:

```
// EvtThreadPool.h

#define TIMEOUT   1000

//////////////////////////////////////////////////////////////// CEvtThreadData

class CEvtThreadData
{
public:
   CEvtThreadData()
      : m_hthread(NULL), m_data(0)
   {
      m_dowork = CreateEvent(NULL, TRUE, FALSE, NULL);
      m_available = CreateEvent(NULL, TRUE, TRUE, NULL);
      m_die = CreateEvent(NULL, TRUE, FALSE, NULL);
   }

   ~CEvtThreadData()
   {
      SetEvent(m_dowork);
      SetEvent(m_die);
      Sleep(0);
      if (WAIT_TIMEOUT == WaitForSingleObject(m_hthread, TIMEOUT * 2))
```

```
        {
          printf("[%ld] murdering thread\n", m_ID);
          TerminateThread(m_hthread, 0);
        }
      CloseHandle(m_hthread);
      CloseHandle(m_dowork);
      CloseHandle(m_available);
      CloseHandle(m_die);
    }

    HANDLE m_dowork;
    HANDLE m_available;
    HANDLE m_die;
    HANDLE m_hthread;
    DWORD m_data;
    DWORD m_ID;
};

///////////////////////////////////////////////////////////////// CEvtThreadPool

class CEvtThreadPool
{
public:
  CEvtThreadPool(UINT noThreads) : m_noThreads(noThreads)
  {
    m_data = new CEvtThreadData[m_noThreads];
    DWORD dwThreadID;
    for (UINT i = 0; i < m_noThreads; i++)
    {
      m_data[i].m_hthread = CreateThread(NULL, 0,
                   ThreadFn, (LPVOID)&m_data[i],
                   0, &dwThreadID);
      m_data[i].m_ID = i;
    }
  }

  ~CEvtThreadPool()
  {
    delete [] m_data;
  }

  BOOL DoWork(DWORD dwData)
  {
    for (UINT i = 0; i < m_noThreads; i++)
    {
      if (WAIT_OBJECT_0 == WaitForSingleObject(
                   m_data[i].m_available, 0))
      {
        printf("<%ld> handled by thread [%ld]\n",
                   dwData, i);
        m_data[i].m_data = dwData;
        SetEvent(m_data[i].m_dowork);
        Sleep(0);
        return TRUE;
      }
    }
```

```
        return FALSE;
    }

    static DWORD WINAPI ThreadFn(LPVOID lparam)
    {
        CEvtThreadData* pdata = (CEvtThreadData*)lparam;

        printf("\t[%ld] initialized\n", pdata->m_ID);
        while (TRUE)
        {
            WaitForSingleObject(pdata->m_dowork, INFINITE);
            if (WAIT_OBJECT_0 == WaitForSingleObject(
                            pdata->m_die, 0))
                break;
            ResetEvent(pdata->m_available);
            printf("\t[%ld] handled request <%ld>\n",
                            pdata->m_ID, pdata->m_data);

            // Do work here
            Sleep(TIMEOUT);
            printf("\t[%ld] done work for request <%ld>\n",
                            pdata->m_ID, pdata->m_data);

            if (WAIT_OBJECT_0 == WaitForSingleObject(
                            pdata->m_die, 0))
                break;
            ResetEvent(pdata->m_dowork);
            SetEvent(pdata->m_available);
            Sleep(0);
        }
        printf("[%ld] died\n", pdata->m_ID);
        return ERROR_SUCCESS;
    }

private:
    CEvtThreadData* m_data;
    UINT m_noThreads;
};
```

This code is shown as **inline** functions to emphasize their relationships. This code uses event objects to schedule the work between the threads in the pool. Basically the **CEvtThreadPool** class creates **m_noThreads** threads in its constructor. Each one has data represented by **CEvtThreadData**. Objects of this class have three event objects, one becomes signaled to indicate that the thread should die, and the other two allow the calling object to determine if the thread is available or working. For good measure, the thread ID is also held.

When a client makes a request, the listening thread (the primary thread of the process) checks all the threads in the pool to see if the **m_available** event is signaled.

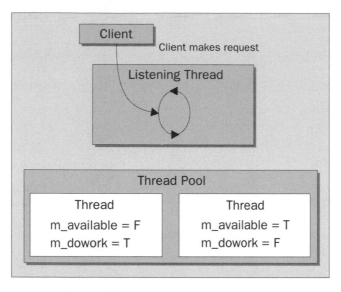

Then when a thread is found, the thread's **m_dowork** event is set.

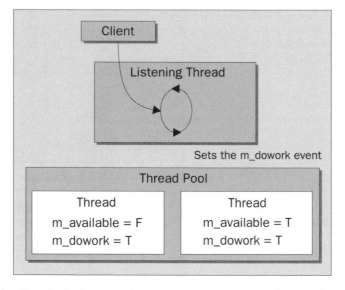

This wakes up the thread which resets it's **m_available** event and starts doing its work. Since **m_available** is set, the thread will not be asked to do any other work.

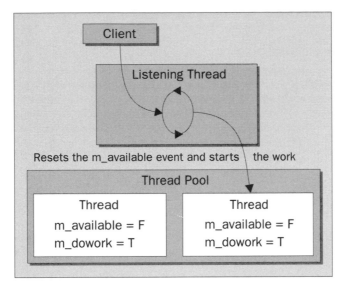

When the thread has finished, it sets the **m_available** event and resets **m_dowork** and waits until it is asked to do some work.

When the thread pool is being destroyed, it must tell all the threads to die. This is done by setting the **m_die** event. However, this will not necessarily be enough since the thread function may be waiting on the **m_dowork** event ready to do some work. The destructor must set both the **m_dowork** and the **m_die** events to give the thread function a chance to get the message.

The threads test for a request to die with a call to **WaitForSingleObject(pdata->m_die, 0)**. By expressing a timeout of **0**, I am using this function to read the current state of the event: if the event is set, a value of **WAIT_OBJECT_0** is obtained and the thread therefore knows that it can die.

This test is done twice. The first time is before the work will start, in case the thread was idle and then told to die. The second time this test is done is just after the work has been done; this is just in case the thread was told to die before the thread function resets the **m_dowork** event. If this test did not happen then when the destructor tells the thread to die, the **m_dowork** and **m_die** events would be set and thus the **m_dowork** event would be reset and the loop continued. This would mean that the thread would continue to wait and will refuse to die.

Finally, if a thread refuses to die when told to (perhaps **DoWork()** was taking a long time to execute), the **CEvtThreadData** destructor waits for a time out period and then explicitly kills the thread.

Notice the sprinkling of **Sleep(0)** in the code. This tells the system that it would be switch to another thread. If one thread sets an event that another thread is waiting on, the waiting thread only wakes up when the system schedules it to do so. If the first thread still has time in its time slice left, it will happily go on working until the system reschedules it. A call to **Sleep(0)** tells the system that the time slice for this thread has finished, allowing the other threads to be scheduled.

Calling this code is easy:

```
// Main.cpp
#include <windows.h>
#include <stdio.h>
#include "EvtThreadPool.h"

int main()
{
   CEvtThreadPool thrds(5);

   for (DWORD x = 0; x < 10; x++)
   {
      Sleep(100);
      printf("<%ld> Making request\n", x);
      while (!thrds.DoWork(x));
   }
   return 0;
}
```

The nature of this implementation is that the threads are reused in the order that they were created. A more intelligent implementation would have a last-in first-out list of available threads to optimize on thread resource page swapping.

Just to show that it is possible, let's see the same code but using a message queue to tell the threads when to work and when they should die:

```
// MsgThreadPool.h

#define TIMEOUT        1000
#define THRD_DOWORK   (WM_USER + 1000)


///////////////////////////////////////////////////////////// CMsgThreadData

class CMsgThreadData
{
public:
   CMsgThreadData()
      : m_hthread(NULL), m_threadID(0)
   {
      m_died = CreateEvent(NULL, TRUE, FALSE, NULL);
      m_available = CreateEvent(NULL, TRUE, TRUE, NULL);
   }

   ~CMsgThreadData()
   {
      Sleep(0);
      PostThreadMessage(m_threadID, WM_QUIT, 0, 0);
      if (WAIT_TIMEOUT == WaitForSingleObject(m_died,
                                      TIMEOUT * 2))
      {
         printf("[%ld] murdering thread\n", m_ID);
         TerminateThread(m_hthread, 0);
      }
      CloseHandle(m_hthread);
      CloseHandle(m_available);
```

```
            CloseHandle(m_died);
    }

    HANDLE m_died;
    HANDLE m_available;
    HANDLE m_hthread;
    DWORD m_threadID;
    DWORD m_ID;
};


///////////////////////////////////////////////////////////// CMsgThreadPool

class CMsgThreadPool
{
public:
    CMsgThreadPool(UINT noThreads) : m_noThreads(noThreads)
    {
        m_data = new CMsgThreadData[m_noThreads];
        for (UINT i = 0; i < m_noThreads; i++)
        {
            m_data[i].m_hthread = CreateThread(NULL, 0,
                        ThreadFn, (LPVOID)&m_data[i],
                        0, &m_data[i].m_threadID);
            m_data[i].m_ID = i;
        }
    }

    ~CMsgThreadPool()
    {
        delete [] m_data;
    }

    BOOL DoWork(DWORD dwData)
    {
        for (UINT i = 0; i < m_noThreads; i++)
        {
            if (WAIT_OBJECT_0 == WaitForSingleObject(
                            m_data[i].m_available, 0))
            {
                printf("<%ld> handled by thread [%ld]\n",
                            dwData, i);
                PostThreadMessage(m_data[i].m_threadID,
                            THRD_DOWORK, (WPARAM)dwData, 0);
                Sleep(0);
                return TRUE;
            }
        }

        return FALSE;
    }

    static DWORD WINAPI ThreadFn(LPVOID lparam)
    {
        CMsgThreadData* pdata = (CMsgThreadData*)lparam;

        printf("\t[%ld] initialized\n", pdata->m_ID);
```

```
        MSG msg;
        while (GetMessage(&msg, NULL, 0, 0))
        {
           switch (msg.message)
           {
           case THRD_DOWORK:
               // Do work here
               ResetEvent(pdata->m_available);
               Sleep(TIMEOUT);
               printf("\t[%ld] done work for request <%ld>\n",
                       pdata->m_ID, msg.wParam);
               SetEvent(pdata->m_available);
           }
        }
        printf("[%ld] died\n", pdata->m_ID);
        SetEvent(pdata->m_died);
        return ERROR_SUCCESS;
    }

private:
    CMsgThreadData* m_data;
    UINT m_noThreads;
};
```

Again we have two events, one to indicate if a thread is available for work, but the second one now indicates if a thread is dead, not that it should die. The request that a thread should carry out the work is made by posting a message to the queue of the thread, the thread will get the message, **THRD_DOWORK** and then carry out the requested work. To tell a thread to die, another thread posts the **WM_QUIT** message, this makes **GetMessage()** return **FALSE** so the thread function returns.

As an aside, it is interesting to change the implementation of the **DoWork()** method so that it does not wait on the **m_available** event, but assigns the requests on an equal basis to the threads with something like this:

```
BOOL DoWork(DWORD dwData)
{
   // m_curthread is a class variable

   printf("<%ld> handled by thread %ld\n", dwData,
          m_curthread);
   PostThreadMessage(m_data[m_curthread].m_threadID,
          THRD_DOWORK, (WPARAM)dwData, 0);
   m_curthread = (m_curthread + 1) % m_noThreads;
   Sleep(0);
   return TRUE;
}
```

m_available is not used at all here, and the thread message queue is used to hold requests, so **DoWork()** always succeeds. The disadvantage of this approach is that if a thread dies for some reason, any outstanding requests in its message queue are lost.

IO Completion Ports

Windows NT 3.5 introduced a new kernel object called an **IO completion port**. The idea here is to create a pool of a small number of worker threads that can service client requests. If a great number of client requests are made at any time, the requests exceeding the number of worker threads are blocked until a thread becomes free and only then can another request be allocated a thread.

The programmer creates a completion port with **CreateIoCompletionPort()**, which allows you to associate the completion port with a file handle. This handle is to any object that you can open with **CreateFile()** including files, named pipes, and mailslots. You specify in the call the number of threads that will be used. Next you can create the pool of threads and these can go into a waiting state by calling **GetQueuedCompletionStatus()**. If this function returns then a queued IO operation has been passed to this thread.

One of the parameters of this function returns a pointer to an **OVERLAPPED** structure from the **CreateFile()** call. The thread can then perform the task and set the event in the **OVERLAPPED** structure and then call **GetQueuedCompletionStatus()** again to sleep until another request is made.

If you are writing a server that handles connections through named pipes, for example, an IO completion port is a good way to handle these through a thread pool. But notice that the API makes use of **OVERLAPPED** structures and is not appropriate for mechanisms that do not use this structure. However, you will, of course, be using DCOM for your servers and DCOM handles all the client connections for you.

Multithreaded DCOM Servers

Now you have had a grounding in Win32 threads, it is time to see how this applies to COM. In Chapter 6, you saw how COM uses thread message queues to handle requests to a COM object. This section will now explain in more detail how and why these queues are used, and it will cover the issues involved in handling multiple threads in both a client and a server.

Apartment Models

The previous sections on threading should have impressed upon you that when more than one thread has access to some piece of data, there is a possibility of simultaneous access that could corrupt the data or even crash the threads. In a multithreaded environment, writing thread safe code is extremely important. But what happens if you have some legacy code that is not thread-safe? One answer is to rewrite the code, but this is not always possible, it lengthens development time and it has the potential of adding new bugs into previously bug-free code.

Furthermore, you may not have access to the source code. The only way to get round this problem is to make sure that the code can be accessed by only one thread at a time. This is a problem that COM faced, and it is the reason behind the different threading models that are available.

COM was originally released on 16-bit Windows 3.1, which was single-threaded. Objects in 16-bit windows could be accessed by only one thread. However, COM on 16-bit Windows did require a mechanism to handle multiple connections. For example, an object server in 16-bit Windows could have two or more client applications create an object each and so there could be calls from each client on the objects' methods. The server had to be able to handle requests from each client.

Looking at this from another perspective, a client application may create an object and pass it an **IAdviseSink** interface pointer so that when the object data changes, the object will inform the client. The client is likely to be performing some task when the object makes this call, so in a single threaded operating system, there must be some mechanism to periodically suspend the current code and check for requests from other programs. There is such a mechanism in 16-bit Windows, it is a mechanism used to cooperatively multitask: the window message queue!

In 16-bit COM, object requests were made using LRPC (Local RPC) calls that are handled by hidden windows created for the server. If there was more than one client and each made a method request on the object, the request would end up as a message in the server's COM message queue. The server could then take an individual message out of the message queue, process it and return the result, then go back to the queue for the next request. Since the server gets the message out of the queue, it decides when to handle a request and thus multiple requests are *serialized*. The server developer did not need to worry about this serialization since it was provided by the COM runtime. This meant that 16-bit COM servers could be assured that there were no synchronization problems.

*NT supports threads, so when 32-bit COM appeared on NT, there was the danger that unthread-safe code would be run in a multithreaded environment. For this reason, Microsoft developed the concept of **apartments**. An apartment can be thought of as isolated as far as COM is concerned. Interactions between objects within a single apartment are not restricted, but calls between objects in different apartments must be marshaled.*

The first version of 32-bit COM (on NT 3.51 and later on Windows 95) allowed a single thread in an apartment, but would allow many apartments in a process. This is the so-called **Apartment Model**, and each apartment is known as a **Single Threaded Apartment** (STA).

This essentially allows clients to create multiple threads, but these threads are separate. As far as COM is concerned, the interaction with COM within each apartment is as if it is from a single thread in a process. This means that COM has to be initialized in each apartment and any interaction between objects in other apartments, even apartments in the same process, has to be marshaled through a proxy.

The reason for this restriction is that if one thread creates an object, this thread can call an object's methods to change its internal state. If a second thread had direct access to the same object, it could also call on the same object's methods to change its state, so there would have to be synchronization code in the object to guard its data. Creating an object in an STA ensures that even though the object doesn't have synchronization, there is no danger of synchronization problems: the model handles that.

In the apartment model, COM serializes calls through a message queue. Since messages are taken from a message queue one by one, it ensures that only one call to the object is active at any time. The restriction of marshaling objects to other threads ensures that the calls are serialized even when there is more than one thread in a single process accessing an object. When an object is marshaled, a proxy is created and the proxy will handle the synchronization issues.

This makes life easier for developers. Just as proxies provide call transparency, which means that the client does not care whether the server is inproc, local or remote; proxies also insulate the client from the thread model of the server and vice versa.

With NT 4.0 (and Windows 95 with DCOM '95) a new threading model was introduced. This is the **Free Threading Model**. With free threading, COM no longer synchronizes object calls through a message queue. Instead, the programmer is expected to handle synchronization. When a client creates multiple threads that use free threaded objects, the threads are part of the same apartment. This is because code in one thread can safely access objects in another thread since those objects handle synchronization. Since there are many threads in this type of apartment, it is called a **Multi Threaded Apartment**. It does put more responsibilities on the object developer, but it also allows the object to be more efficient, as we will see later.

Note that any out-of-process object always requires a proxy, so the issues of marshaling interface pointers is only relevant when in-process objects are created, either by the process itself or via a DLL inproc server. Also, an apartment can create (or, for a server, implement) several objects.

So to recap, each STA has only one thread but a process can have many STAs. A thread that uses free threading lives in the process' MTA and although a process can have, at most, just one MTA, it can have both a MTA and one or more STAs. In this last situation, the process is known as having a mixed model.

Single Threaded Apartment

The reason for the single threaded apartment is to isolate COM code in such a way that threading issues like synchronization and reentrancy are handled by COM and not by the object designer. The STA model covers both the cases of older, single threaded COM processes and of newer, multithreaded COM processes that leaves synchronization to COM. Note, however, this is not the whole story.

To mark a thread as running in an STA the thread calls **CoInitializeEx(NULL, COINIT_APARTMENTTHREADED)**. This is the same as calling **CoInitialize(NULL)**. However, although this is fine for client and EXE servers, it does not work in inproc servers. This is because inproc servers are DLLs loaded into the address space of the client that uses it. An object that should be loaded must indicate its threading model with a named value under its CLSID key called **ThreadingModel**, and this should have the string **Apartment**. This is where the slight problem with legacy inproc servers occurs. Such servers will not mark their threading model and COM will refuse to load the object with a very unhelpful **REGDB_E_NOTREG**. Adding the **ThreadingModel** value solves the problem.

A schematic of a COM process looks like this:

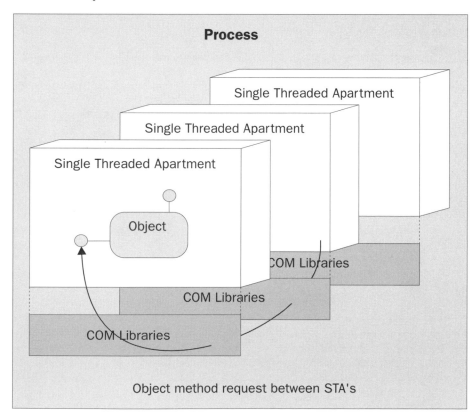

Here the process is multithreaded, but each thread is isolated from one another as far as COM is concerned. The arrow represents a method call on an object in one STA from another STA. This method call requires the intervention of the COM libraries.

The most important rule for the apartment model is that a COM object lives in exactly one apartment, and so its methods can only be called directly (without the intervention of a proxy) by a thread that belongs to the same apartment. In terms of an STA, there is only one thread in the same apartment as the object, and this thread is obviously the one that manages the object.

An object isolated in a single thread is not as useful as one that can be accessed from another thread. The STA model handles this by using proxies. This is why the diagram shows the method request going through the COM libraries, to make this request, a proxy must be created and it handles the method call.

So, the proxy sits between an object client in one STA and the object in another. But why are STAs isolated like this? Creating a proxy creates the hidden window as part of the LRPC mechanism to transmit method calls between processes. The hidden window on the server implements a message queue, and method requests on the object come into the server as Windows messages in this queue. (We saw these messages in great detail back in Chapter 6.)

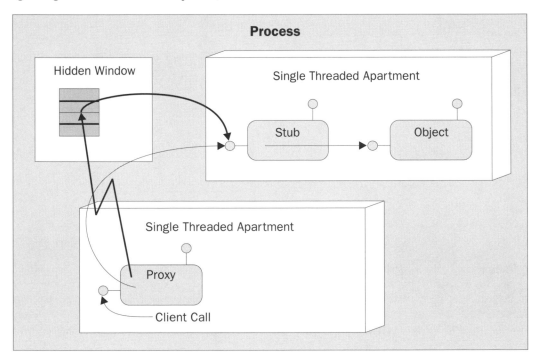

By placing COM requests into a message queue, the COM designers have serialized the call. The COM library on the server handles the requests one by one from the message queue. This is like the behavior that we saw earlier on in this chapter with the implementation of a thread pool using a thread message queue, except the original COM designers were only using a single thread of execution.

As with the inter-process situation, the proxy exists to marshal data and requests. In the case of STAs in a process, this means to marshal requests in a manner to ensure thread synchronization. By using the proxy in this way, the COM libraries can utilize the message queue of each thread to synchronize the object method calls.

There are some rules that must be applied when writing an STA:

- Each STA must initialize COM to obtain access to its own initialized copy of the COM libraries.
- All interface pointers must be marshaled when passing them between apartments.
- Each single-threaded apartment must have a message loop to handle calls from other processes and apartments within the same process.

Although each STA initializes COM with a call to `CoInitialize(NULL)` or `CoInitializeEx(NULL, COINIT_APARTMENTTHREADED)`, the first apartment to do this initialization is a little special and is called the main apartment. This STA is singled out because when a client calls an inproc server, with a different threading model, COM will need to create a proxy and it needs to know in which STA to do this. So if I call `CoCreateInstance()` from multiple threads in an MTA on an inproc server that does not support free threading, COM will not allow the MTA to access the object without the use of a proxy. Since the object server is Apartment model, the proxy must be created in an STA, but the client has not created an STA for this access, so instead COM uses the main STA.

So what are the mechanics of marshaling calls between STAs? In fact, most of the time COM will do it for you. If you pass an interface pointer as a parameter to a COM method, COM will use a proxy to do this. However if you need to pass an interface pointer to another thread without using COM then the interface pointer must be marshaled.

The thread that has the interface pointer calls `CoMarshalInterThreadInterfaceInStream()` which marshals an interface pointer into a stream (along with any other parameters that you wish to pass to the other STA in a thread safe manner). The stream is then passed to the other thread, via a global variable or a function call. The second thread then calls `CoGetInterfaceAndReleaseStream()` to unmarshal the interface pointer and release the stream. You'll see these calls in use in the example a little later in the chapter.

Passing interface pointers back and forth like this is a little tiresome, but since interface pointers which are parameters of object method calls are automatically marshaled by COM, this means that you can set up inter thread communications by creating a COM object that passes interface pointers to and from a thread. However, this object must be created in one thread so at least one call to `CoMarshalInterThreadInterfaceInStream()` must be made to marshal it to another thread.

Note that these interface marshaling functions are wrappers for a call to `CoMarshalInterface()` on the server-side and a call to `CoUnmarshalInterface()` on the client-side. These two functions themselves are wrappers for calls to `IMarshal`. This interface could be implemented by the object or, if standard marshaling is used, by the system.

The wrapper functions obtain the CLSID of the proxy object and write it into a stream. This stream is then marshaled to the client. `IStorage` and `IStream` have been written to allow them to be remoted; a stream, of course, is just a buffer of data. Since the marshaling is between two threads, the free-threaded marshaler is used. When the client receives the stream, it can obtain the CLSID and thus is able to instantiate a proxy object. You, as the client programmer, do not need to know how to do this since the wrapper functions will do it for you.

Since inter-STA calls are handled using a message queue, it means that they are particularly useful for applications that have a user interface and hence use Windows messaging, since the object calls will be serialized with the UI calls.

485

The handling of method calls from an out-of-process object to an object in an STA is just the same as the inter STA calls: the call comes into the server as a message posted to the COM message queue and the message pump of the COM window passes the message on to the stub that unmarshals the data and calls the object.

Multithreaded Apartment

Multithreaded apartments allow you to implement more than one thread and to have direct access between the objects in those threads. The up-side of an MTA is that inter thread access is direct, requiring no proxy intervention, however, this is also the down-side, since it requires the object designer to handle synchronization to ensure that two threads do not have access to an object's resources at the same time.

The following picture shows a schematic of an MTA process. The apartment has many threads and each of these may implement one or more objects. Because the threads are all in the same apartment, they have direct access to each other. This is shown in the following picture, a thread can make a call directly to an object in another thread.

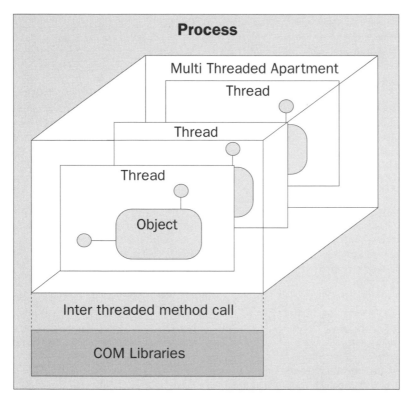

Since an MTA does not serialize the COM calls using a window's message queue, the object method must be implemented in such a way as to allow for multithreaded access. This is quite a burden on the programmer, but it does allow for more efficient code, since synchronization code is only applied where it is needed. In an STA, only one method call can be active at a time.

A process can only have at most one MTA, but it can also have one or more STAs, and inter-apartment method calls are handled just as they are in the multi STA case: through proxies in the calling apartment.

When an out-of process client calls the server, the client creates a proxy and this, using the COM runtime RPC Channel, calls the MTA server. This request is accepted by a listening thread, which picks a thread from a pool to handle the call. This handling thread then calls the stub, which unmarshals the request and calls the method on the object. Contrast this with the STA method - the MTA does not use the message queue to accept the incoming messages.

We saw this in Chapter 6 when we turned **ReverseDCOM** from an STA application into a free-threaded application. **ReverseDCOM** printed out the messages received in the primary thread message queue. When the process was an STA, there were many messages received during DCOM method calls. When the application was converted to a free threaded application, the number of messages reduced to zero.

Choosing Between STA and MTA Models

So what are the issues involved in choosing between the two models?
Well, the initial difference between the two is:

- In single threaded model, every thread that uses COM must initialize it by a call to **CoInitialize(NULL)** (or **CoInitializeEx(NULL, COINIT_APARTMENTTHREADED)**)

- In a multithreaded apartment the COM libraries will have been loaded when the first thread entered the MTA. Subsequent threads, however still need to call **CoInitializeEx(NULL, COINIT_MULTITHREADED)** before they enter the MTA.

With a mixed model, there must be one or more calls with **COINIT_APARTMENTTHREADED** and one or more calls with **COINIT_MULTITHREADED**, the order does not matter.

Each STA can implement one or more objects (as can an MTA), but if code in an STA requires access to an object in another STA, or in an MTA, and this apartment is still in the same process, the interface pointer has to be marshaled via a proxy. The STA implements a message queue and incoming method calls are synchronized in this queue. In this way, the multithreading issues of object synchronization can be addressed, as we have seen in the last few sections.

If the application uses an MTA then the interface pointers can be copied between threads with no marshaling problems. However, since there is more than one thread of execution, more than one thread could be running the same piece of code and so any global data must be protected.

Thus it is a case of six-of-one and half-a-dozen-of-the-other. One has synchronization built in, but requires interface pointers to be marshaled, and the other requires you to implement synchronization, but frees you from marshaling interface pointers between threads.

One main criterion to bear in mind is compatibility. Providing different threading models like this ensures that code is compatible with earlier versions of COM, while allowing for multithreading to improve on the performance of the COM calls. Remember that COM is inherently synchronous and a client call to an object from a single threaded client will block on the object method call. However, a multithreaded client can devote one thread to the COM object calls while still handling other application tasks through the process' other threads.

The other main criterion for choosing between the two is performance. If you write an interface that has no global data, and no other issues that require synchronization then when you implement it in an MTA, you need not use any synchronization, and multiple clients from other threads in the process can access the object at the same time.

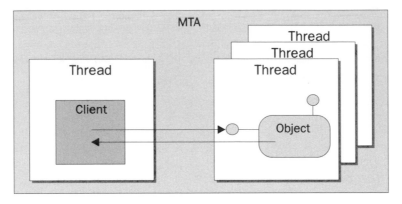

However, when you implement this object in an STA, COM will serialize all calls from objects in other STAs (or an MTA) in the same process though the message queue and via proxies.

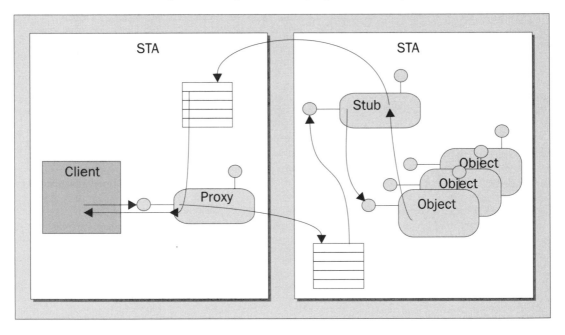

This means that there are several levels of indirection required for the STA object and only one proxied client can access the interface at any one time.

As a final point, if you are developing a new object that will be used on NT 4.0 (or with DCOM 95) you should make it free threaded, and likewise the client should have an MTA. Remember if either is of a different threading model, COM will compensate with a proxy.

Mixed Model

The mixed model means that a process has a single MTA and has one or more STAs. In fact, this model is just an extension of the multiple STA process we saw earlier. It's just that one of the apartments is multithreaded.

Why would you have this situation? As mentioned earlier, some objects, written before multithreading was introduced in COM, are thread unsafe, so should be used in an STA to ensure that the object state remains consistent between object calls. You may have an object that is thread safe and uses multiple threads, one of which wants to use the thread unsafe object. In this situation the thread unsafe object is run in an STA and the other thread safe code is run within an MTA.

Another case when you will see the mixed model used is when objects are implemented in in-process servers (DLLs).

InProc Servers

As mentioned above, an inproc server does not call **CoInitializeEx()**, so does not indicate the thread model to use. This could be a problem since one inproc server could be thread safe and so could be used via a direct interface pointer in a thread in an MTA. Another object could be thread unsafe and thus must be run in an STA.

Since the object does not say what thread model to use, there must be another method to specify the model. The way that this is done is to store the thread model in the registry. Every class has a **CLSID** key and an inproc server has a key called **InProcServer32**. Under this is a value called **ThreadingModel** which can be **Apartment**, **Free**, or **Both** (or not there at all).

The goal of COM is to allow *any* client to access *any* object regardless of location (in-process, out-of-process or remote) or the threading model of either. This then presents a problem when (for example) an inproc object using the apartment model (and hence thread unsafe) is accessed from a multithreaded client that uses an MTA (and thus implements thread synchronization).

What should COM do in this case? It knows that the object would be unsafe, so should it reject the activation? Well, COM handles this by sandboxing the object in an STA. Here are the various combinations of client and inproc server that arise.

Single Threaded Server and Multiple-STA Client

The client has more than one thread and each is running in an STA. One or more of these STAs call the server, which is implemented as **Apartment** (STA). Neither the client nor the server code is thread safe hence the code runs in multiple STAs. COM will create the object in the client's *main* apartment. This gives direct access to the object for the thread in this STA but requires that all other client thread accesses be via a proxy. This ensures that some form of synchronization is applied to the object.

The 'main' apartment is arbitrary: it is just the one that was created first.

Single Threaded Server and MTA Client

In this situation, the server is still single threaded and the client multithreaded, but now the client has all the threads running in an MTA. As mentioned above, COM cannot activate the object in a thread in the MTA because the object does not synchronize access to global resources. So COM creates an STA host thread in the client, this host will create the object and marshal the interface to the MTA in the client. Again, COM provides the synchronization to the object.

MTA Server and STA client

Now we turn the situation around and make the server multithreaded, but thread safe (i.e. all threads in an MTA) and the client is now using an STA. When asked to create the object, COM creates an MTA host thread in the client. The object can be accessed via this STA and the client code can access the object via a proxy.

The other case not mentioned is MTA client and MTA server, but there is no problem here since all the code is thread safe.

Examples

LoggerSvr

Let's create and develop a DCOM server and look at some of the multithreading issues identified earlier in the chapter. The application will be an ATL server and its sole purpose will be to log diagnostic messages to file as the COM object is created, accessed and destroyed. The server will have a single interface with a single method:

```
interface ILogger : IDispatch
{
   [id(1)] HRESULT LogMessage([in]DATE date, [in]BSTR message);
};
```

First create a new project for a standard EXE server using the ATL COM AppWizard and call it **LoggerSvr**. The Wizard-produced code creates a single apartment for the server initialized in **_tWinMain()**:

```
extern "C" int WINAPI _tWinMain(HINSTANCE hInstance, HINSTANCE /*hPrevInstance*/,
LPTSTR lpCmdLine, int /*nShowCmd*/)
{
//this line necessary for _ATL_MIN_CRT
    lpCmdLine = GetCommandLine();
    HRESULT hRes = CoInitialize(NULL);
// If you are running on NT 4.0 or higher you can use the
// following call instead to make the EXE free threaded.
// This means that calls come in on a random RPC thread
// HRESULT hRes = CoInitializeEx(NULL, COINIT_MULTITHREADED);
    _ASSERTE(SUCCEEDED(hRes));
    _Module.Init(ObjectMap, hInstance);
    _Module.dwThreadID = GetCurrentThreadId();
    TCHAR szTokens[] = _T("-/");

    int nRet = 0;
    BOOL bRun = TRUE;
    LPCTSTR lpszToken = FindOneOf(lpCmdLine, szTokens);
    while (lpszToken != NULL)
    {
      if (lstrcmpi(lpszToken, _T("UnregServer"))==0)
      {
        _Module.UpdateRegistryFromResource(IDR_LoggerSvr, FALSE);
        nRet = _Module.UnregisterServer();
        bRun = FALSE;
        break;
      }
      if (lstrcmpi(lpszToken, _T("RegServer"))==0)
      {
        _Module.UpdateRegistryFromResource(IDR_LoggerSvr,TRUE);
        nRet = _Module.RegisterServer(TRUE);
        bRun = FALSE;
        break;
      }
```

```
        lpszToken = FindOneOf(lpszToken, szTokens);
    }

    if (bRun)
    {
        hRes = _Module.RegisterClassObjects(
                            CLSCTX_LOCAL_SERVER,
                            REGCLS_MULTIPLEUSE);
        _ASSERTE(SUCCEEDED(hRes));

        MSG msg;
        while (GetMessage(&msg, 0, 0, 0))
            DispatchMessage(&msg);

        _Module.RevokeClassObjects();
    }

    CoUninitialize();
    return nRet;
}
```

This is pretty straightforward, with the relevant COM code highlighted. The code first initializes the COM libraries and then it initializes the C++ object, **_Module**, that represents the process (or DLL if this was an inproc server).

Stdafx.h defines the **CExeModule** class from which the global object, **_Module**, is created. This class declares a **public** data member **dwThreadId**. The sole purpose of this member is to allow the class' **Un-lock()** method to post a **WM_QUIT** message to the thread message loop and hence finish the **WinMain()** function and stop the process. The **Unlock()** method determines how many clients are using the server and thus whether it can be unloaded.

> Note that in the version of ATL 1.1 distributed with the DCOM SDK for Solaris, this code does not work. This is because the NT daemon created by Software AG does not handle Win32 Windows messaging, but it does handle Win32 kernel service, file IO, registry and COM services. For Solaris the code that uses Windows messages to handle server lifetime should use an event kernel object instead.

As the comments near the top of **_tWinMain()** indicate, we can change the type of apartment created from an STA to an MTA by using the call to **CoInitializeEx()** that is currently commented out.

Further on in **_tWinMain()** is a message loop. Whichever threading model is used, the process needs a message loop. It provides a thread safe way to indicate that there are no more clients and so the server can close down. The other reason is that it is used by the LRPC mechanism for STA model to call methods on the objects created by the server. As we saw in Chapter 6, this inter-process communication comes in via the single, hidden COM window.

Finally, at the bottom of **_tWinMain()**, we have the cleanup code provided by ATL. When the server closes down, the class factory can be revoked and the COM libraries uninitialized.

ATL Threading Models

ATL supports different threading models for your server. The ATL AppWizard will, by default, define **_ATL_APARTMENT_THREADED** in **Stdafx.h**. This follows since the implementation of **_tWinMain()** calls **CoInitialize()** and hence uses apartment threading. There are three possible threading models:

```
_ATL_SINGLE_THREADED
_ATL_APARTMENT_THREADED
_ATL_FREE_THREADED
```

If none is defined, **Atlbase.h** will define **_ATL_FREE_THREADED** for you. Using the thread model symbol, ATL **typedef**s the following classes for you in **Atlbase.h**:

```
#if defined(_ATL_SINGLE_THREADED)
   typedef CComSingleThreadModel CComObjectThreadModel;
   typedef CComSingleThreadModel CComGlobalsThreadModel;
#elif defined(_ATL_APARTMENT_THREADED)
   typedef CComSingleThreadModel CComObjectThreadModel;
   typedef CComMultiThreadModel CComGlobalsThreadModel;
#else
   typedef CComMultiThreadModel CComObjectThreadModel;
   typedef CComMultiThreadModel CComGlobalsThreadModel;
#endif
```

These classes provide a method to allow ATL to provide thread safe code for increments and decrements and for critical sections. These **typedef**ed classes are used if your ATL object uses **CComObjectRoot**. This class is used in code originally created with ATL 1.1, it is implemented by using a **typedef** to **CComObjectRootEx<>**.

An ATL 2.1 object is derived directly from **CComObjectRootEx<>**. This class **typedef**s a class called **_ThreadModel** to the class passed as a parameter to the template, and a class called **_CritSec** **typedef**ed to the critical section class of this parameter:

```
template <class ThreadModel>
class CComObjectRootEx : public CComObjectRootBase
{
public:
   typedef ThreadModel _ThreadModel;
   typedef _ThreadModel::AutoCriticalSection _CritSec;

// ...

   void Lock() {m_critsec.Lock();}
   void Unlock() {m_critsec.Unlock();}
private:
   _CritSec m_critsec;
};
```

_ThreadModel is used whenever the class wants to increment or decrement a value (which this class will do since it handles reference counting for the object). **_CritSec** is used for a member variable that handles code locking.

This parameter to **CComObjectRootEx<>** can be **CComSingleThreadModel** or **CComMultiThreadModel**. The first uses normal C++ **++** and **--** operators for the increment and decrement methods, whereas the other class uses the thread safe APIs **InterlockedIncrement()** and **InterlockedDecrement()**.

```
class CComMultiThreadModel
{
public:
```

```
   static ULONG WINAPI Increment(LPLONG p)
      {return InterlockedIncrement(p);}
   static ULONG WINAPI Decrement(LPLONG p)
      {return InterlockedDecrement(p);}
   typedef CComAutoCriticalSection AutoCriticalSection;
   typedef CComCriticalSection CriticalSection;
   typedef CComMultiThreadModelNoCS ThreadModelNoCS;
};

class CComSingleThreadModel
{
public:
   static ULONG WINAPI Increment(LPLONG p) {return ++(*p);}
   static ULONG WINAPI Decrement(LPLONG p) {return --(*p);}
   typedef CComFakeCriticalSection AutoCriticalSection;
   typedef CComFakeCriticalSection CriticalSection;
   typedef CComSingleThreadModel ThreadModelNoCS;
};
```

As for the critical section **typedef**: the first class uses **CComFakeCriticalSection** that has empty implementations for the method calls that lock code sections. In the multithreaded case, **CComCriticalSection** is used that is implemented with the critical section API. The difference between **CComCriticalSection** and **CComAutoCriticalSection** is that the former uses **Init()** and **Term()** methods to initialize and cleanup for the object, whereas the latter uses the class constructor and destructor.

Using all this code, ATL can make sure that your code is as thread safe as it needs to be. For ATL 2.1 code, this is determined by the parameter passed to the **CComObjectRootEx<>** template that is the base class for your object. For ATL 1.1 code, it is determined by the **#define**d symbol in **Stdafx.h**.

CLogger

Now we need to create the coclass that will implement the **ILogger** interface we saw earlier. Use the Insert | New ATL Object... menu item to create a new Simple Object with a Short name of Logger. You can leave the other items with their default settings. If you click on the Attributes tab you will see that, by default, the Apartment threading model is selected, leave it so. (Note that if you select one of the other options, the Wizard just changes the parameter to the **CComObjectRootEx< >** base class).

Now use ClassView to add the single method to the **ILogger** interface (right-click on the interface and select Add Method...) and add in the method **LogMessage()**. Now open the header file for the **CLogger** class and add the code shown highlighted below.

```
class ATL_NO_VTABLE CLogger :
   public CComObjectRootEx<CComSingleThreadModel>,
   public CComCoClass<CLogger, &CLSID_Logger>,
   public IDispatchImpl<ILogger, &IID_ILogger, &LIBID_LOGGERSVRLib>
{
public:
   CLogger()
   {
   }

DECLARE_REGISTRY_RESOURCEID(IDR_LOGGER)
```

```
BEGIN_COM_MAP(CLogger)
   COM_INTERFACE_ENTRY(ILogger)
   COM_INTERFACE_ENTRY(IDispatch)
END_COM_MAP()

// Statics
public:
   static HANDLE s_mutex;
   static void Message(LPCTSTR msg, LPVOID _this);

// CComObjectRootEx<> overrides
   HRESULT FinalConstruct();
   HRESULT FinalRelease();

// ILogger
public:
   STDMETHOD(LogMessage)(/*[in]*/ DATE date,
                         /*[in]*/ BSTR message);
};
```

As we've discussed, the wizard has generated code to derive your class from
CComObjectRootEx<CComSingleThreadModel>. If we want to change the threading model, there are
two places where we have to change code to reflect this. The first is the parameter to
CComObjectRootEx<>:

Model	**CComObjectRootEx<> Parameter**
Single	**CComSingleThreadModel**
Apartment	**CComSingleThreadModel**
Free	**CComMultiThreadModel**
Both	**CComMultiThreadModel**

The other place is in **_tWinMain()** in the **LoggerSvr.cpp** file. The ObjectWizard seems to be a little
negligent with this file, if you create a free or both threading model object the wizard does not change this
file, so you have to do it by hand. If you are using free threading (or both), all you need to do is to
uncomment the line with **CoInitializeEx()** and comment the line with **CoInitialize()**. Similarly,
if you are using single or apartment threading model then you need to use **CoInitialize()**.

s_mutex

This example logs messages to a file. To prevent more than one thread accessing the file at any one time,
we use a mutex whose handle we keep as a **static** member of **CLogger** called **s_mutex**. The mutex is
created in **_tWinMain()** after COM is initialized – if a call to **OpenMutex()** fails, we assume that the
mutex doesn't exist, so we create it with a call to **CreateMutex()**. The mutex is destroyed when the
server closes down:

```
extern "C" int WINAPI _tWinMain(HINSTANCE hInstance,
   HINSTANCE /*hPrevInstance*/, LPTSTR lpCmdLine, int /*nShowCmd*/)
{
   lpCmdLine = GetCommandLine(); //this line necessary for _ATL_MIN_CRT

   HRESULT hRes = CoInitialize(NULL);
```

```
// HRESULT hRes = CoInitializeEx(NULL,
//                                COINIT_MULTITHREADED);
   _ASSERTE(SUCCEEDED(hRes));
```

```
   CLogger::s_mutex = OpenMutex(MUTEX_ALL_ACCESS, FALSE,
                           _T("LOGGER_MESS_MUTEX"));
   if (NULL == CLogger::s_mutex)
     CLogger::s_mutex = CreateMutex(NULL,
                           FALSE,_T("LOGGER_MESS_MUTEX"));
   _ASSERTE(SUCCEEDED(CLogger::s_mutex));
```

```
   _Module.Init(ObjectMap, hInstance);
   _Module.dwThreadID = GetCurrentThreadId();
   TCHAR szTokens[] = _T("-/");

   // ... Standard Wizard-supplied registration code

   if (bRun)
   {
     // ... Standard Wizard-suplied code
   }
```

```
   if (CLogger::s_mutex)
     CloseHandle(CLogger::s_mutex);
```

```
   CoUninitialize();
   return nRet;
}
```

Since it is a **static** variable **s_mutex** needs to be initialized in **Logger.cpp**:

```
   HANDLE CLogger::s_mutex = NULL;
```

Message()

Message() is a helper function that actually saves data to the log file. This is made a **static** function so that it can be called without an instantiated object. **LoggerSvr** does not use it this way, but the next example, which is based on **LoggerSvr**, will. To identify whether the function was called from an instantiated object, and which particular object, the **this** pointer is passed to the method (if no instantiated object was used, **NULL** is passed).

The **this** pointer is logged because it is the only reliable identifier that we have for the object: when COM creates the object, any method call from the client to the object is always to the object that COM created when the client called **CoGetClassObject()**. In addition to the **this** pointer, a message is also passed. Both items are saved to a file. **Message()** is called from **LogMessage()** where we pass the **this** pointer of the C++ object.

```
   void CLogger::Message(LPCTSTR msg, LPVOID _this)
   {
     // Write to the logging file
     FILE* f;

     WaitForSingleObject(CLogger::s_mutex, INFINITE);
```

```
    f = _tfopen(_T("\\logger.log"), _T("a"));
    _ftprintf(f, _T("%08x, %08x, %s\n"),
                  _this, GetCurrentThreadId(), msg);
    fclose(f);

    ReleaseMutex(CLogger::s_mutex);
}
```

This logs the current thread ID, the pointer and the string. The thread ID is given here so that we can see how COM uses its thread pool to make method calls.

FinalConstruct()/FinalRelease()

The **CLogger** class overrides the **FinalConstruct()** and **FinalRelease()** methods, the former is called during the **CreateInstance()** of the class factory of the object and the latter method is called before the object is destroyed. In these methods we have code to indicate what is going on. All they need to do at present is call the **static** function **Message()** to indicate that the object has been created or destroyed.

```
HRESULT CLogger::FinalConstruct()
{
    HRESULT hRes = S_OK;

    Message(_T("Created object"), this);
    return hRes;
}

HRESULT CLogger::FinalRelease()
{
    Message(_T("Destroying object"), this);

    return S_OK;
}
```

LogMessage()

The interface method **LogMessage()** is called via COM from the client. It has two parameters: a message string and an automation-compatible **DATE** type:

```
STDMETHODIMP CLogger::LogMessage(DATE date, BSTR message)
{
    SYSTEMTIME st;
    VariantTimeToSystemTime(date, &st);
    HRESULT hRes = S_OK;
    LPTSTR szMsg;

    int nMsgLength = lstrlenW(message) + 1;
    LPSTR mbcsMsg = new char [nMsgLength];
    WideCharToMultiByte(CP_ACP, 0, message, -1, mbcsMsg,
                        nMsgLength, NULL, NULL);

#ifdef _UNICODE
    szMsg = message;
#else
    szMsg = mbcsMsg;
#endif
```

```
    LPTSTR buffer = new TCHAR [(lstrlen(szMsg) + 22 + 1)];
    wsprintf(buffer, _T("%04d-%02d-%02d %02d:%02d:%02d %s"),
          st.wYear, st.wMonth, st.wDay,
          st.wHour, st.wMinute, st.wSecond, szMsg);

    Message(buffer, this);

    delete [] buffer;
    delete [] mbcsMsg;
    return hRes;
}
```

This method basically takes the message and data and reformats them into a readable form before calling
Message() to log the files to disk.

VB Client

The client in these tests is a
Visual Basic client, which uses
the following form:

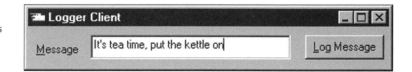

The code behind the form is simplicity itself:

```
Dim obj As New Logger

Private Sub Log_Click()
    obj.LogMessage Now, Message.Text
End Sub

Private Sub Form_Unload(Cancel As Integer)
    Set obj = Nothing
End Sub
```

If we run three instances of this client, for an STA server (make sure that the class is derived from
CComObjectRootEx<CComSingleThreadModel> and that **CoInitialize()** is used in
_tWinMain()), the log file will have values something like this:

```
this       ThreadID  Message
00800930, 0000009e, Created object
00800930, 0000009e, 1997-03-28 11:23:29 client1
008009e0, 0000009e, Created object
008009e0, 0000009e, 1997-03-28 11:23:39 client2
00800a90, 0000009e, Created object
00800a90, 0000009e, 1997-03-28 11:23:45 client3
00800930, 0000009e, 1997-03-28 11:23:51 client1-2
008009e0, 0000009e, 1997-03-28 11:23:54 client2-2
00800a90, 0000009e, 1997-03-28 11:23:59 client3-2
00800930, 0000009e, Destroying object
008009e0, 0000009e, Destroying object
00800a90, 0000009e, Destroying object
```

What does this mean? Three objects are created and the strings **client1**, **client2**, **client3** are logged.
Then the strings **client1-2**, **client2-2**, **client3-2** are logged and finally all three objects are

destroyed. Note that the **this** pointer is the same for all interactions with a particular client and that the thread ID is the same for all the actions, regardless of client. This is not surprising since the object is running under the STA model, and there is just one STA.

Now change **_tWinMain()** so that we are using an MTA (uncomment the **CoInitializeEx()** and comment out **CoInitialize()**), and change the base class of **CLogger** to **CComObjectRootEx<CComMultiThreadModel>**:

```
this       ThreadID  Message
00800930,  00000090, Created object
00800930,  00000090, 1997-03-28 11:15:57 client1
008009e0,  0000007b, Created object
008009e0,  0000007b, 1997-03-28 11:16:04 client2
00800a90,  00000090, Created object
00800a90,  00000090, 1997-03-28 11:16:10 client3
00800930,  0000007b, 1997-03-28 11:16:15 client1-2
008009e0,  00000090, 1997-03-28 11:16:18 client2-2
00800a90,  0000007b, 1997-03-28 11:16:23 client3-2
00800930,  00000090, Destroying object
008009e0,  0000007b, Destroying object
00800a90,  00000090, Destroying object
```

The significant difference between these results and those for the STA is that the ID of the threads used is not the same for all the actions. Furthermore, **client1** connects via thread **0x90** initially, and on the second call connects with thread **0x7b**. This is because COM maintains a pool of threads to connect to the objects in the server and any one of these threads may be used for any object. It highlights the rule that in an MTA, you should *not* assume that an object will be accessed with the same thread on each call, hence you should *not* save any state information in thread local storage.

ReverseLoggerSvr

The example is fine as far as it goes, but it uses just one object. Let's change it so that it uses another object. The application will use the **Reverse** object defined in the **ReverseDCOM** example from Chapter 6, so that when a message is sent to this server, it will log the message and the reverse of the message string.

We could create a **Reverse** object in **CLogger::FinalConstruct()**, however this would mean that every **Logger** object would have its own **Reverse** object. This may be fine in some situations, but in this example, we want just one **Reverse** object to service all the **Logger** objects. To do this, we will create a thread and create the **Reverse** object in this thread. Now, using various synchronization and marshaling hocus-pocus, each **Logger** object will be able to get an interface pointer to the single **Reverse** object.

First, we need to copy the files **ReverseDCOM.h** and **ReverseDCOM_i.c** from the **ReverseDCOM** project directory into the current project directory. As usual, add the **ReverseDCOM_i.c** file to the project and alter its settings so that it doesn't use precompiled headers, then add **#include**s for the header file to **Logger.h**.

Now we change the **CLogger** class to:

```
class ATL_NO_VTABLE CLogger :
   public CComObjectRootEx<CComSingleThreadModel>,
   public CComCoClass<CLogger, &CLSID_Logger>,
   public IDispatchImpl<ILogger, &IID_ILogger,
                        &LIBID_LOGGERSVRLib>
```

```
{
public:
   CLogger()
   {
   }

DECLARE_REGISTRY_RESOURCEID(IDR_LOGGER)

BEGIN_COM_MAP(CLogger)
   COM_INTERFACE_ENTRY(ILogger)
   COM_INTERFACE_ENTRY(IDispatch)
END_COM_MAP()

// Statics
public:
   static void Message(LPCTSTR msg, LPVOID _this);
   static HANDLE s_mutex;

// CComObjectRootEx<> overrides
   HRESULT FinalConstruct();
   HRESULT FinalRelease();

// Reverse Thread members
   static DWORD WINAPI ReverseThread(LPVOID lparam);
   static IReverse* s_pReverse;
   static DWORD s_dwThreadID;
   static BOOL s_bSTA;

private:
   IReverse* m_pReverse;

// ILogger
public:
   STDMETHOD(LogMessage)(/*[in]*/ DATE date,
                         /*[in]*/ BSTR message);
};
```

In this example we will need to have different code for the STA and MTA cases. To enable us to switch between the two, the class has a **static** variable **s_bSTA** that has a value of **TRUE** for the STA case and **FALSE** for MTA. Using this variable we can just change the value of it in one place and then change the derivation of **CLogger** (as before). Change **_tWinMain()** to use this boolean as shown:

```
extern "C" int WINAPI _tWinMain(HINSTANCE hInstance,
   HINSTANCE /*hPrevInstance*/, LPTSTR lpCmdLine,
   int /*nShowCmd*/)
{
// this line necessary for _ATL_MIN_CRT
   lpCmdLine = GetCommandLine();

   HRESULT hRes;
   CLogger::s_bSTA = TRUE;

   if (CLogger::s_bSTA)
      hRes = CoInitialize(NULL);
   else
      hRes = CoInitializeEx(NULL, COINIT_MULTITHREADED);
   _ASSERTE(SUCCEEDED(hRes));
```

This **static** also needs to be initialized in an implementation file, as shown in a moment. But first, back to the definition of **CLogger**. The **static s_pReverse** is a pointer to the **IReverse** interface on the **Reverse** object, remember that there should only be one **Reverse** object, so when it is created its interface should be accessed by all object instances, hence the reason for a **static** variable.

There is also an instance variable **m_pReverse**. The reason for this variable is that it is this that is used to access the actual object. But doesn't **s_pReverse** point to the **Reverse** object? Yes it does, but if an STA is used, we cannot access the interface pointer directly, instead we have to create a proxy and access it through that. The **m_pReverse** instance variable is used whether the object is created in an STA or an MTA, the code will determine (through the **s_bSTA** variable) whether **m_pReverse** has the same value as **s_pReverse** or whether it is a pointer to a proxy that accesses the object.

The actual **Reverse** object is created in the **ReverseThread()** thread controlling function, and the thread created to run this code has its ID saved in **s_dwThreadID**. Since the server only has one version of the thread running at any time, it is safe to hold this in a class **static** member.

Of course the **static** data members need to be initialized in **Logger.cpp**:

```
// Statics
HANDLE CLogger::s_mutex = NULL;
BOOL CLogger::s_bSTA = TRUE;
IReverse* CLogger::s_pReverse = NULL;
DWORD CLogger::s_dwThreadID = 0;
```

_tWinMain()

Before we look at the methods of this class, let's look at the changes to **_tWinMain()**. This function needs to create a new thread before it registers the **LoggerSvr** class factory and then destroy the thread after the class factory is revoked. Here is the code:

```
extern "C" int WINAPI _tWinMain(HINSTANCE hInstance,
   HINSTANCE /*hPrevInstance*/, LPTSTR lpCmdLine,
   int /*nShowCmd*/)
{
   // ... Code as before

   if (bRun)
   {
      // Create a new thread
      HANDLE evmade = CreateEvent(NULL, TRUE, FALSE, NULL);
      HANDLE hworker = CreateThread(NULL, 0,
                         CLogger::ReverseThread,
                         (LPVOID)evmade, 0,
                         &CLogger::s_dwThreadID);
      // Wait for the thread to create the object
      WaitForSingleObject(evmade, INFINITE);
      CloseHandle(evmade);

      hRes = _Module.RegisterClassObjects(
               CLSCTX_LOCAL_SERVER, REGCLS_MULTIPLEUSE);
      _ASSERTE(SUCCEEDED(hRes));

      MSG msg;
      while (GetMessage(&msg, 0, 0, 0))
         DispatchMessage(&msg);
```

```
      _Module.RevokeClassObjects();

      PostThreadMessage(CLogger::s_dwThreadID, WM_QUIT,
                        0, 0);
      WaitForSingleObject(hworker, INFINITE);
      CloseHandle(hworker);
   }

   if (CLogger::s_mutex)
      CloseHandle(CLogger::s_mutex);

   CoUninitialize();
   return nRet;
}
```

The code creates an event and then calls **CreateThread()** passing the event handle as the thread function parameter. It then waits on this event. When the thread function has finished initializing, it will set the event and the wait will finish. At this point, we do not need the event any more, so it is destroyed by calling **CloseHandle()**.

When the process message loop finishes, we know that no more clients are attached, so we can close down the process. Before we can do this, we must stop the thread, which we do by sending the thread a **WM_QUIT** message with a call to **PostThreadMessage()**. This is why we kept the thread ID. Since the thread must shut down the **Reverse** object, we wait patiently for the thread to finish by waiting on the thread's handle using **WaitForSingleObject()**. Once we are sure that the thread has finished, we can tidy up and leave.

ReverseThread()

The thread function looks like this:

```
DWORD WINAPI CLogger::ReverseThread(LPVOID lparam)
{
   HRESULT hRes = S_OK;
   HANDLE evmade = (HANDLE)lparam;

   // If we are using multiple STAs, we need to initialize
   // the COM libraries to put this thread in its own
   // apartment. If not, we don't need to initialize COM
   // again and this thread will go in the process' MTA
   if (CLogger::s_bSTA)
   {
      hRes = CoInitialize(NULL);
      _ASSERTE(SUCCEEDED(hRes));
   }

   hRes = CoCreateInstance(CLSID_Reverse, NULL,
                  CLSCTX_SERVER, IID_IReverse,
                  (LPVOID*)&CLogger::s_pReverse);
   _ASSERTE(SUCCEEDED(hRes));

   TCHAR buffer[256];
   wsprintf(buffer,
      _T("Created interface pointer: 0x%08x, ")
      _T("hRes = 0x%08x"),
      CLogger::s_pReverse, hRes);
   CLogger::Message(buffer, NULL);
```

```
        SetEvent(evmade);

        MSG msg;
        while (GetMessage(&msg, 0, 0, 0))
        {
           if (msg.message == WM_USER && CLogger::s_bSTA)
           {
              // Need to marshal interface?
              hRes = CoMarshalInterThreadInterfaceInStream(
                        IID_IReverse, CLogger::s_pReverse,
                        (IStream**)msg.wParam);
              SetEvent((HANDLE)msg.lParam);
           }
           else
              DispatchMessage(&msg);
        }

        if (CLogger::s_pReverse)
           CLogger::s_pReverse->Release();

        // If we're in an STA, we initialized COM, so we also
        // need to uninitialize it
        if (CLogger::s_bSTA)
           CoUninitialize();

        return 0;
    }
```

It looks like there's quite a lot going on here, but it's quite simple really. At the beginning and end of the function we check to see if the thread is part of an STA or an MTA. If it's the only thread in an STA then the COM libraries must be initialized and uninitialized. Also, if the thread is in an STA then it *must* have a message loop to handle the messages sent by COM. In this case, we also use the loop for some messaging of our own (to tell the thread to shut down), so the MTA thread needs the message loop too.

After initializing COM (if necessary), the code then creates the **Reverse** object with a call to **CoCreateInstance()**. The interface pointer is saved in the **static CLogger::s_pReverse**. As mentioned above, this is a once only initialization and the **static** variable just holds the value, the class should not call methods on it. After creating the object, a message is logged. This uses the **static Message()** function in **CLogger**, notice that **NULL** is passed as the second parameter, this is because at this stage there is no object. It is for this reason that the method was made **static**. The reason for its use here is to print the value of the interface pointer.

The thread function has now initialized so the event is set to indicate to the primary thread that **_tWinMain()** can continue running. **ReverseThread()** then goes into a message loop. This loop will be broken when a **WM_QUIT** message is received, at which point the **Reverse** object is released.

Let's look at the message loop in more detail:

```
        while (GetMessage(&msg, 0, 0, 0))
        {
           if (msg.message == WM_USER && CLogger::s_bSTA)
           {
              // Need to marshal interface?
              hRes = CoMarshalInterThreadInterfaceInStream(
                        IID_IReverse, CLogger::s_pReverse,
                        (IStream**)msg.wParam);
```

```
        SetEvent((HANDLE)msg.lParam);
    }
    else
        DispatchMessage(&msg);
}
```

In addition to **GetMessage()/DispatchMessage()**, which are required to handle the COM synchronization messages, this loop handles the **WM_USER** message. When running in an STA, we send this message to the thread from code in **CLogger::FinalConstruct()** so that we can marshal the interface pointer from the apartment containing the **Reverse** object into the apartment of the newly created **Logger** object.

We'll only send this message in the STA case when a new **LoggerSvr** object is created, but just to be on the safe side, we also check the value of **CLogger::s_bSTA**. If we are sure this came from the creation of an object in an STA, we marshal the interface to that object. The **wParam** of the message is a pointer to an **IStream** pointer to use to marshal the interface data, and the **lParam** is an event handle, which this code uses to indicate that the interface has been marshaled. We have to use an event to ensure that the code in **FinalConstruct()** doesn't continue executing before the interface has been marshaled. Remember that thread message loops do not respond to **SendMessage()** which would have been useful here.

At this point, you may be wondering why we need to marshal the interface from the **Reverse** apartment each time a **Logger** object is created. Surely we could marshal the **IReverse** interface to a global stream just once, then leave each client to unmarshal the interface from that global stream. Unfortunately, we are using **CoGetInterfaceAndReleaseStream()** to unmarshal the interface. Using this function means that the first client would just release the global stream, making it unavailable for future use.

The Win32 documentation states that **CoGetInterfaceAndReleaseStream()** calls **CoUnmarshalInterface()** then does a **Release()** on the stream pointer, so it may seem that there's a solution to our problem: call **CoMarshalInterThreadInterfaceInStream()** just once and save the **IStream** pointer in a global variable. You could then call **CoUnmarshalInterface()** on this stream when a new object is created and only release the stream when the server dies. However, **CoUnmarshalInterface()** calls **IMarshal::ReleaseMarshalData()** on the marshaler used in the process and so the stream becomes invalid, even though the stream's still there. We could unmarshal the interface pointer ourselves from the stream and ensure that the stream stays valid, but this would involve more code than we're currently using, so we'll stick with the code that we've got.

FinalConstruct()/FinalRelease()

Let's look at the object code. **FinalConstruct()** has been changed to check the thread model and then marshal the interface if necessary:

```
HRESULT CLogger::FinalConstruct()
{
    HRESULT hRes = S_OK;

    // Need to marshal the interface?
    if (CLogger::s_bSTA)
    {
        // Ask thread to marshal interface
        IStream* pStream;
        HANDLE evInt = CreateEvent(NULL, TRUE, FALSE, NULL);
        PostThreadMessage(s_dwThreadID, WM_USER,
                    (WPARAM)&pStream, (LPARAM)evInt);
```

```
            WaitForSingleObject(evInt, INFINITE);
            CloseHandle(evInt);
            hRes = CoGetInterfaceAndReleaseStream(pStream,
                        IID_IReverse, (LPVOID*)&m_pReverse);
        }
        else
        {
            m_pReverse = CLogger::s_pReverse;
            m_pReverse->AddRef();
        }

    Message(_T("Created object"), this);
    return hRes;
}
```

Here, we check to see if the object is in an STA. If it is *not* then we can use the **IReverse** interface
pointer directly. Otherwise we create an event and pass its handle and a pointer to an **IStream** pointer to
the thread function using **PostThreadMessage()**. The code waits on the event, and when the event is
set, it indicates that the marshaling stream has been returned. This is then used to unmarshal the interface
with a call to **CoGetInterfaceAndReleaseStream()**.

After all this **m_pReverse** has a valid pointer to an **IReverse** interface. The **FinalRelease()** is quite
simple:

```
HRESULT CLogger::FinalRelease()
{
    Message(_T("Destroying object"), this);

        m_pReverse->Release();

    return S_OK;
}
```

All it does is decrement the reference count on the interface.

LogMessage()

The **IReverse** interface is actually used in the **LogMessage()** method:

```
STDMETHODIMP CLogger::LogMessage(DATE date, BSTR message)
{
    SYSTEMTIME st;
    VariantTimeToSystemTime(date, &st);
    HRESULT hRes = S_OK;
    LPTSTR szMsg;
    LPSTR  revstr;

    int nMsgLength = lstrlenW(message) + 1;
    LPSTR mbcsMsg = new char [nMsgLength];
    WideCharToMultiByte(CP_ACP, 0, message, -1, mbcsMsg,
                        nMsgLength, NULL, NULL);

#ifdef _UNICODE
    szMsg = message;
#else
```

```
        szMsg = mbcsMsg;
#endif

    LPTSTR buffer = new TCHAR [(lstrlen(szMsg) + 22 + 1)];
    wsprintf(buffer, _T("%04d-%02d-%02d %02d:%02d:%02d %s"),
            st.wYear, st.wMonth, st.wDay,
            st.wHour, st.wMinute, st.wSecond, szMsg);

    Message(buffer, this);
```

```
    // Save the interface pointer
    TCHAR szInterfaceMsg[40];
    wsprintf(szInterfaceMsg, _T("Reverse interface is ")
            _T("0x%08x"), m_pReverse);
    Message(szInterfaceMsg, this);

    // Now reverse the string
    if (m_pReverse)
      hRes = m_pReverse->Reverse((unsigned char*)mbcsMsg,
                                 (unsigned char**)&revstr);
    else
      hRes = E_POINTER;

    if (FAILED(hRes))
    {
      wsprintf(buffer, _T("Error with Reverse 0x%08x"),
               hRes);
      szMsg = buffer;
    }
    else
    {
#ifdef _UNICODE
      // If UNICODE we need to convert to wide char
      MultiByteToWideChar(CP_ACP, 0, revstr, -1,
                          szMsg, nMsgLength);
#else
      szMsg = revstr;
#endif
    }

    Message(szMsg, this);

    CoTaskMemFree(revstr);
```

```
    delete [] buffer;
    delete [] mbcsMsg;
    return hRes;
}
```

The additional parts to this function are to log the address of the interface pointer, and then to call the **Reverse()** method on the **Reverse** object and log the result. Because the object is returning an **[out]** parameter, the memory must be freed with a call to **CoTaskMemFree()**. Also note that the interface passes **unsigned char*** pointers and so there is some casting required to keep the compiler happy.

Running the code

Now what about running the code? Well the first thing to do is to make sure that the **Reverse** object is registered. You can refer to the **ReverseDCOM** example in Chapter 6 to see how to do this. This object will create a console to log progress, which is quite useful in this example; the console is destroyed when the object is destroyed.

Now, let's test the **Logger** object using the STA model, (make sure that **CLogger::s_bSTA = TRUE** in **_tWinMain()** and the class derives from **CComObjectRootEx<CComSingleThreadModel>**). You can use the same VB client as before. The following results are obtained from three client instances, mirroring the first set of tests we carried out.

```
00000000, 0000009c, Created interface pointer: 0x00147334, hRes = 0x00000000
00800940, 00000084, Created object
00800940, 00000084, 1997-03-28 11:08:14 client1
00800940, 00000084, Reverse interface is 0x001471fc
00800940, 00000084, 1tneilc
008009f0, 00000084, Created object
008009f0, 00000084, 1997-03-28 11:08:28 client2
008009f0, 00000084, Reverse interface is 0x001471fc
008009f0, 00000084, 2tneilc
00800aa0, 00000084, Created object
00800aa0, 00000084, 1997-03-28 11:08:35 client3
00800aa0, 00000084, Reverse interface is 0x001471fc
00800aa0, 00000084, 3tneilc
00800940, 00000084, 1997-03-28 11:08:41 client1-2
00800940, 00000084, Reverse interface is 0x001471fc
00800940, 00000084, 2-1tneilc
008009f0, 00000084, 1997-03-28 11:08:42 client2-2
008009f0, 00000084, Reverse interface is 0x001471fc
008009f0, 00000084, 2-2tneilc
00800aa0, 00000084, 1997-03-28 11:08:44 client3-2
00800aa0, 00000084, Reverse interface is 0x001471fc
00800aa0, 00000084, 2-3tneilc
00800940, 00000084, Destroying object
008009f0, 00000084, Destroying object
00800aa0, 00000084, Destroying object
```

Since this is an STA, there are only two threads identified. The first, **0x9c**, creates the **Reverse** object, and the other one, **0x84**, is the main thread of the application. Look at the pointer used for the interface. The creator thread says that it is **0x00147334**, but all the objects reckon it is **0x001471fc**. Of course, the latter pointer is to a proxy, but it is worth noting that the same proxy is used for all the clients.

(As you do these tests watch the console window for the **Reverse** object. You will see the requests come in from the client and be handled. If we had implemented **LoggerSvr** to have a separate **Reverse** object for each client, you would have had a new console for each of the clients.)

Now let's recompile the server to create an MTA and repeat the test:

```
00000000, 00000098, Created interface pointer: 0x001471a4, hRes = 0x00000000
00800940, 00000056, Created object
00800940, 00000056, 1997-03-28 10:59:22 client1
00800940, 00000056, Reverse interface is 0x001471a4
00800940, 00000056, 1tneilc
008009f0, 0000008a, Created object
008009f0, 0000008a, 1997-03-28 10:59:35 client2
008009f0, 0000008a, Reverse interface is 0x001471a4
008009f0, 0000008a, 2tneilc
00800aa0, 00000056, Created object
00800aa0, 00000056, 1997-03-28 10:59:43 client3
00800aa0, 00000056, Reverse interface is 0x001471a4
00800aa0, 00000056, 3tneilc
00800940, 0000008a, 1997-03-28 11:00:11 client1-2
00800940, 0000008a, Reverse interface is 0x001471a4
00800940, 0000008a, 2-1tneilc
008009f0, 00000060, 1997-03-28 11:00:14 client2-2
008009f0, 00000060, Reverse interface is 0x001471a4
008009f0, 00000060, 2-2tneilc
00800aa0, 0000008a, 1997-03-28 11:00:18 client3-2
00800aa0, 0000008a, Reverse interface is 0x001471a4
00800aa0, 0000008a, 2-3tneilc
00800940, 00000060, Destroying object
008009f0, 0000008a, Destroying object
00800aa0, 00000060, Destroying object
```

This is just as we would expect. The client calls are coming in on different threads, and even calls from the same client are not necessarily coming in on the same thread each time. Look at the calls from **client1**, first it uses **0x56** and then it uses **0x8a**. Now look at the reported interface pointer. Each object reports the same interface as the creator thread, **0x001471a4**. Given that no marshaling is necessary in this case, this should not be a surprise.

Summary

This chapter has introduced you to the pleasures of multithreading. In the first half of the chapter I gave dire warnings about multithreading citing problems with reentrancy and synchronization, but I hope that I've shown you that these aren't insurmountable. You can use the Win32 synchronization objects to guard data or blocks of code. The use of these objects makes sure that only one thread can access the protected data or code.Remember that if you replace a piece of code run in one thread with several pieces of code running concurrently in multiple threads on a single processor machine, the multithreaded version will never run faster than the single threaded case. This is because there is always an overhead involved in the context switching between the threads. If you are lucky enough to have a multiprocessor machine, you may find that the multithreaded version will run faster, because the CPUs won't need to switch contexts between threads. What multithreading gives you in a Win32 process is better *responsiveness*, which is important to UI threads.

COM allows you to create object servers that are single, apartment or free threaded. Most objects you write should be free threaded, but you may decide to use apartment threading if you cannot guarantee the thread safety of the code you use.

The single and apartment threaded objects are run in a Single Threaded Apartment. STAs only have one thread. Free threaded objects are run in a Multi Threaded Apartment. MTAs, as the name suggests, can have many threads. A process can have many STAs, but it can have at most one MTA. Objects in apartments can communicate with objects in other apartments, but only through a proxy. Communications between objects within an apartment do not need proxies, so an object in one STA can talk to another object in the same STA, but more significantly an object in one thread in an MTA can talk directly to an object in another thread in the MTA. This has obvious synchronization issues and it is the developer's responsibility to apply the appropriate synchronization objects.

Wouldn't it be nice if COM handled all these threading issues for you, and allowed you to create an object that could create and talk directly to other objects? Well this is one facility of the Microsoft Transaction Server. MTS handles concurrency issues as well as providing transaction semantics around the access to an object. MTS is the subject of the next, and last, chapter of this book.

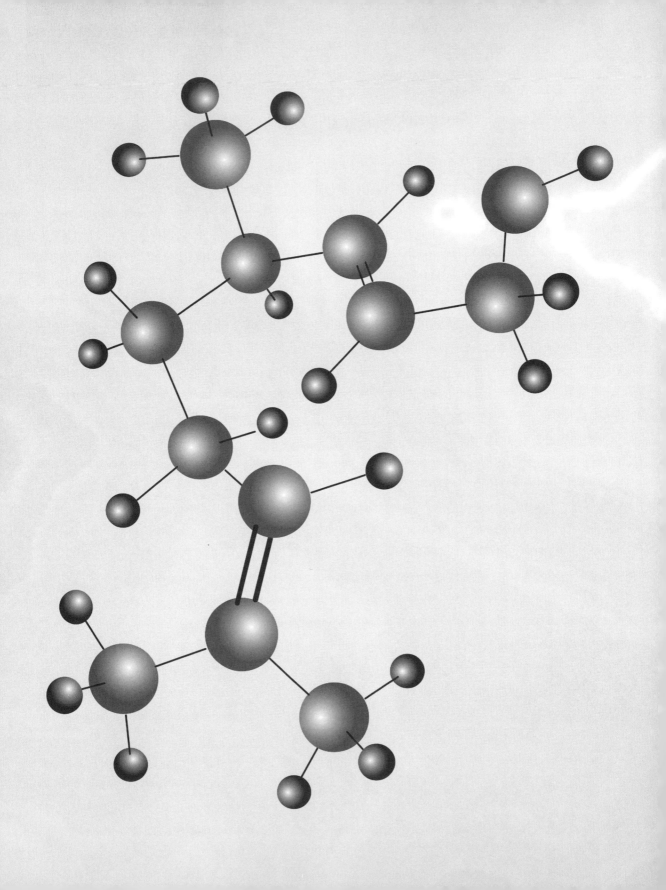

Microsoft Transaction Server

Introduction

In this chapter, we're going to take a look at **Microsoft Transaction Server** (**MTS**). MTS provides a coherent infrastructure for component based distributed applications, using DCOM as its communication mechanism. MTS provides the following benefits to component developers:

- Provides support for transactions
- Eases threading concerns
- Simplifies security
- Makes installation easier
- Provides scalability through optimizations such as JIT activation and instance pooling

Transactions

Anyone who has ever programmed a database application will understand the need for transactions. Transactions are essential to ensuring the integrity of data by composing a series of actions into a single, atomic unit. The actions will either succeed as a whole (in which case the transaction is **committed**) or fail as a whole (in which case the transaction must **rollback**).

The classic example of a transaction is the case of updating one bank account with funds from another. For example, suppose I want to pay a utility bill. If the bank debits my account first then fails the communication link before updating the utility company's account, I lose money and the bill still isn't paid. If the bank credits the utility's account first and then fails before debiting my account, my bill is paid and I keep my money (I like failures like this!), but the bank ultimately loses out.

If the two actions are covered by a transaction, then it doesn't matter what action happens first – if the transaction fails, the rollback mechanism ensures that activity up to the point of failure is reversed.

With components in mind, Microsoft Transaction Server allows you to define and use transactions within COM objects. Applications will coordinate their state across multiple machines.

Threading

Threading is a problem for component developers because it introduces difficult synchronization issues. MTS handles this for you by creating threads when needed and discouraging you from creating threads of your own from within Transaction Server components. MTS also provides you with a single logical thread of execution across multiple machines, known as an **activity**, by preventing more than one thread calling into an activity at one time.

Security

MTS simplifies security by taking a high level view. It introduces the concept of **roles** that define a logical group of users, and separates the application's security requirements from the operating system's underlying security model. This makes it easy to administer access to an application and use security programmatically. MTS security is further simplified by **packages**, which are collections of components that make up an application. You define the security for the whole package rather than its individual components.

Installation

Packages also make installation easier. Once you have defined the components in a package and set various security options, you can export the whole lot to a **.pak** file so that it can be imported to another Transaction Server. When you do this, all of the necessary server DLLs, type-libraries and proxy-stubs will be copied to the export directory.

JIT Activation and Object Pooling

Just-in-time (**JIT**) **activation** allows clients to hold references to MTS components for long periods of time with limited consumption of server resources. Components are only created when they need to do some useful work and they are released as soon as they have finished.

Object pooling increases the efficiency of activating and deactivating objects by calling methods on one of the object's interfaces to tell it when to obtain and free resources. This is instead of creating and destroying the whole object each time it needs to do some work.

These techniques allow MTS to work well with clients holding references to many objects that need to work infrequently and to objects that are being used more often. This allows MTS to scale well.

Sounds good, doesn't it? In this chapter, we'll take a look at each of these items and I'll show how MTS can simplify or solve problems associated with writing DCOM-based applications.

What is MTS?

The major goal of MTS is to provide the entire infrastructure for distributed applications so that the developer need only worry about their business problems and not the problems involved in distribution, threading, scalability, security and transaction processing.

MTS started life as the Distributed Transaction Coordinator in SQL Server 6.5, which was developed to maintain transactions across several SQL Server installations. With Transaction Server, Microsoft have provided the functionality of MS DTC for the COM developer, while extending its security and installation facilities.

There are three main parts to MTS:

- ▲ A surrogate process, **MTS.exe**
- ▲ An NT service, the **Microsoft Distributed Transaction Coordinator** (**MS DTC**)
- ▲ An administrative tool, the **MTS Explorer**

Of course, these three items represent just the infrastructure provided by MTS. The real functionality of a distributed application running under the control of MTS is provided by components. Your COM objects work with **resource managers** and **resource dispensers**, which provide access to resources that can be controlled by the DTC.

Surrogate Exe

The secret to the power of MTS is that it provides a surrogate process for the components that it manages. This means that MTS can wrap components to provide a single thread of execution, context information, and transaction abilities without forcing you to write your components specifically for MTS.

MTS acts as an object dispenser as well as a transaction server. Once a component is registered as an MTS object, calls to **CoCreateInstance()** for that component will be handled by the MTS server process. **MTS.exe** will create a wrapper class factory for the class, then call the component's class factory to create the object. We'll look at the changes that are made in the registry to allow this 'magic' a little later.

The wrapper class factory creates a wrapper for the component and a **context object** through COM containment. The stub object that communicates with the proxy in the client is for this wrapper object rather than your component. This means that whenever you make a call on the component, MTS can intercept the call.

This allows MTS to provide its facilities without either the client or the component having to be written specifically for MTS. Wrapping up a component in an extra object like this will have a slight performance hit on accessing object methods, but this is far outweighed by the facilities that the context object supplies.

The following figure shows this architecture. The Server Process Executive is the runtime needed to communicate with DTC to handle transactions.

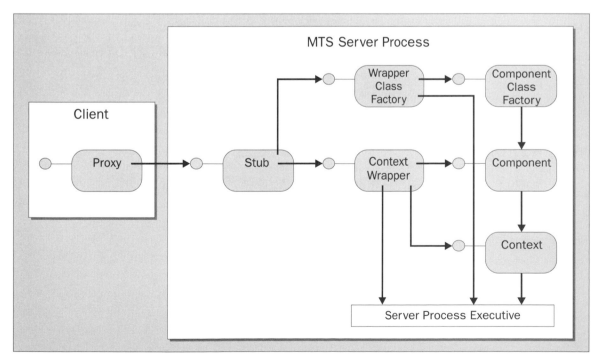

There is one context object per interface for the object. The context wrapper is used to receive and dispatch calls. Since MTS always sits between the client and its object, MTS can do things to enable transactions and to optimize these calls. One responsibility of the context object is to cache type libraries, this means that when an object is deactivated and reactivated at a later stage (we will see how this happens later), the context will still have the type library. This will lead to a performance gain, especially if there are many client calls.

Distributed Transaction Coordinator

When you install MTS, a service called MS DTC will be installed. This is configured to run automatically at boot up and provides the **transaction context objects** that are used in the component context objects. DTC allows for *distributed* transactions, so if an MTS object fails during a transaction, all the other objects in the transaction are aborted regardless of what machine they are running on.

This is extremely powerful: whereas DCOM provides the communications infrastructure, DTC provides the services that allow for scaleable, fail-safe, distributed applications. DTC is provided as part of MTS and SQL Server 6.5, and should become part of the operating system in WindowsNT Server 5.0.

Resource Provision

Transactions are used to protect data or resources. The DTC coordinates transactions, but it relies on resource providers to understand particular types of data and know how to commit or rollback changes on those resources. Resource providers are COM processes that must be written to understand MTS transactions. MTS distinguishes between two sorts of resource providers: **resource managers** and **resource dispensers**.

Resource managers handle durable data - data that is not lost should the system fail. Resource dispensers are for non-durable data – if the system should fail, the state of the dispenser is not maintained.

This separation of resource management from transaction coordination means that MTS uses an extensible system. Transactions can be applied to different types of resource if an appropriate resource manager or dispenser is available.

There is currently only one resource manager available for MTS, SQL Server 6.5. MTS comes with two resource dispensers, the ODBC Resource Dispenser and the Shared Property Manager. We'll look at transactions, resource managers and resource dispensers in more depth later in the chapter.

MTS Explorer

The visible part of MTS, to the system administrator, is the MTS Explorer. This tool has two main roles, the first is to manage the objects that MTS can use, and to allow the administrator to monitor the state of running objects.

The following screenshot shows the MTS Explorer running on my machine:

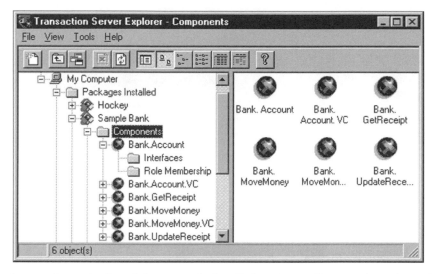

The left-hand pane shows the list of the currently installed packages. Every package is made up of components, where each component is a COM object, exposing functionality through COM interfaces.

The other function of the Explorer is to allow the administrator to monitor object usage and this is accessed via a branch further down in the left-hand pane's tree:

Through these items, you can determine statistics about the number of objects and information about a selected object:

Branch	Context
Transaction List	The current transactions in which this server participates
Transaction Statistics	Statistics about a selected transaction
Trace Messages	Allows you to monitor trace messages generated by MTS about the object

You can also monitor an individual component's usage by selecting a component in the Packages Installed*package*\Components list and selecting Status from the View menu. This gives information about the number of objects, how many are activated and how many are currently handling a method call:

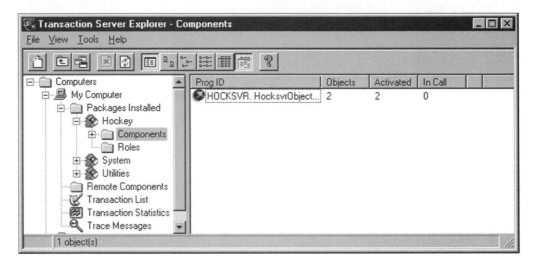

The Remote Components branch identifies the remote objects that can be used in transactions run on this server. An implicit attribute of a remote component is the remote server machine on which the object will be created. You identify a server by adding it to the top level Computers branch. Then when adding a remote component to this copy of MTS, the Explorer will query the remote machine and present you with the available remoted packages. Of course, this assumes that the remote machine is also running MTS.

MTS Components

Before we continue, let's define precisely what an MTS component is. I've already mentioned that MTS components are COM components, and that's exactly what they are. However, there are a few restrictions placed on the type of component that can be managed by MTS, the most important of which is that they must be in-process servers (i.e. DLLs). The complete list is shown below. The conditions are not too restrictive and you will probably find that most of the inproc objects you have already written comply with most of these requirements:

- The component can only be in-process (DLL)

- The component must have a standard class factory that is exposed through **DllGetClassObject()** and implements **IClassFactory**

- The component must only export interfaces that can be standard marshaled (either type library marshaling or **MIDL**-produced proxy-stub).

- If the component does not use type library marshaling, the proxy-stub DLL must be linked to **Mtxih.lib**. The proxy-stub DLL should be generated with **MIDL** version 3.00.44 or later using **- Oicf** on the command line and **Mtxih.lib** must be the first file that you link.

Since the component is inproc, it means that MTS can load it in the appropriate server context. The class factory requirement gives MTS control over how the component is made and the last two requirements allow marshaling to occur with the component instantiated as a local or remote object.

You cannot use the licensing facilities provided by **IClassFactory2**

Registration

I've mentioned that MTS creates a context object for the components it creates and also that neither the client nor the component needs to be specially written to create this context, so how's this done? Let's look into the component installation and activation in a little more depth.

When you register a COM object, you need to register its **ProgID** and **CLSID** and, if you want the object to be a remote object with DCOM, you also need to register its **AppID**. Finally, so that the object can actually do some work, you need to register its interfaces and any proxy-stub objects that they'll use. ATL inproc objects export standard **DllRegisterServer()** (and **DllUnregisterServer()**) to carry out most of this server registration.

The **CLSID** key has an **InprocServer32** key that indicates the name of the DLL that contains the server code. Now, if you register the **HockSvr** object, which is provided as an MTS example, with:

```
regsvr32 hocksvr.dll
```

You'll get the following entry in the registry:

If a client should call **CoCreateInstance()** (or **CoGetClassObject()**) this will ultimately lead to the system reading this value in the registry to determine what DLL to load.

Now create a package called **Hockey** in MTS and add this component to it:

When you look at the **CLSID** for this, you'll see:

The **InprocServer32** key is now empty and we have an entry in the **LocalServer32** key: our inproc object has now changed to a local object! Well, not completely, the object is handled by the **Mts.exe** server, which is launched with the command line:

/p:{F30E0C8C-8746-11D0-9B14-0060973044A8}

This is very similar to the UUIDs that we've created before (for example the CLSID for the **RemoteTime** class was **{FE725172-8453-11D0-9B07-0060973044A8}**). This coincidence is not too surprising since these UUIDs were created on the same machine. We know this because the DCE UUID algorithm uses a machine identifier for the last 6 bytes of the UUID and in Chapter 6 we saw that my machine's MAC address (the network card identifier) is **00-60-97-30-44-A8**. The other bytes in the UUID essentially give the time that the UUID was created.

OK, so this UUID was created on my machine and we can guess that the MTS Explorer created it, but what exactly does it identify?

The clue is further on in the registry under **HKEY_LOCAL_MACHINE** in the key, **SOFTWARE\Microsoft\Transaction Server\Packages**:

The UUID refers to the package, **Hockey**, that we created for the component. MTS can then use this entry to discover which components are installed. In the **Components** key (above the **Packages** key) there's an entry for the **CLSID** which finally identifies the DLL that has the class factory for the **HockSvr** inproc server.

So now when we create an object through a call to `CoCreateInstance()`, COM will start up **Mts.exe** and tell it that we want to use the **Hockey** package. MTS will read the registry to find out the **CLSID** of the component and launch it along with a context object. We'll then be returned an interface pointer to the **HockSvr** object, none the wiser that MTS is handling it. If the object is created on a remote machine, the same process occurs, but **Mts.exe** will be running on the remote machine.

In MTS terminology, the registry is called the **Transaction Server Catalog**.

The Context Object

Now we've seen precisely what an MTS component is and how MTS registers the component so that it can provide a surrogate process. We also know that one of the major reasons for this is so that MTS can provide a context object for the component. Now let's see precisely how this context object benefits us.

First the component writer needs to get access to the object's context which it can do by calling `GetObjectContext()`.

```
HRESULT GetObjectContext ( /* [out] */ IObjectContext** ppInstanceContext);
```

`IObjectContext` has the following methods:

IObjectContext method	Description
`CreateInstance()`	Creates an MTS object
`DisableCommit()`	Disables all attempts to commit the object
`EnableCommit()`	Re-enables the permission to commit the object
`IsCalledInRole()`	Called to determine if the caller is in the specified role
`IsInTransaction()`	Called to determine if the object is part of a transaction
`IsSecurityEnabled()`	Determines if security is enabled

Table Continued on Following Page

519

IObjectContext method	Description
SetAbort()	Specifies that the transaction should ultimately be aborted
SetComplete()	Specifies that the object's transaction can be committed and that the object should be deactivated

Of these methods the most important are **CreateInstance()**, which is used to create another MTS object in the same context; and **SetAbort()** and **SetComplete()** which are used to indicate whether the transaction should be committed or aborted.

The three parameters of **CreateInstance()** are the same as three of the five parameters used in **CoCreateInstance()**. These are:

- The CLSID of the object
- The IID of the interface to be used
- An **[out]** pointer to the returned interface

The other two parameters of **CoCreateInstance()** are irrelevant. These are the server location parameter (which is unnecessary because this is defined by the MTS settings) and the **IUnknown** of the controlling object for aggregation (which isn't allowed because aggregation can only be used in-process and MTS strives for location transparency).

Passing Interface Pointers

MTS does impose one more restriction, in the way that interface pointers are passed through methods. This is because MTS needs to provide the context object and lifetime management.

With 'straight' COM, you can pass interface pointers as **[out]** parameters to method calls. If the method call crosses a machine boundary or an apartment boundary, COM will create a proxy to the interface. But beware, the proxy that is created is for the interface that is returned as defined by the IDL. COM is not clever, it won't guess what you 'mean' to call rather than what you actually do. For example, let's say you've a dual interface and return a pointer as an **LPDISPATCH [out]** parameter. If this is marshaled, the proxy will only handle the **IDispatch** methods, not the methods in the vtable.

If you're determined to pass a pointer to one of your component's interfaces as an **[out]** parameter, COM will happily create a proxy for you, in the client. Here's the catch - the proxy will not connect to the context wrapper object and so you will lose all that the context provides. In this situation you should call the **SafeRef()** function provided in the MTS runtime, passing the interface pointer that you want to return. The function will return a proper object reference that includes the context.

> *This problem does not exist for pointers passed via* **QueryInterface()** *since that is already handled by the context wrapper*

Component Location

MTS upholds the COM principle of *location transparency*. This means that the client can access an object without having to care where the object is. COM distinguishes between in-process servers, local server and remote servers. MTS has a similar distinction, but now MTS will 'get in the way' wherever the component is activated.

Objects are created with the standard COM API functions (`CoGetClassObject()` or the wrapper function `CoCreateInstanceEx()`) or `IObjectContext::CreateInstance()`, and you can then use the object as if it were created in an object server other than MTS.

The administrator can determine where an MTS object is created, by setting a property on the component in the MTS Explorer:

The Location frame has three options:

- ▲ The object can be run inproc in the address space of the creator (the client)
- ▲ Run as a part of the MTS server process
- ▲ Run as a remote object in the MTS server process

In the first case, the client process thinks it's loading an inproc server. However, MTS loads a wrapper DLL that then loads your inproc server DLL. This wrapper DLL provides the class factory wrapper and context wrapper objects as discussed above.

In the second case, the component is loaded into the MTS server process on the same machine as the client. This is loosely like a COM client loading a local server but, of course, our component was and always is, developed as an inproc server. The MTS server process provides all the required wrapper objects.

Finally, the administrator could decide that the component is on another machine, in which case this dialog allows them to specify that the component will run under the MTS server process on that machine. This is like marking an object as remote in `DCOMCnfg`.

Packages

Anyone who has developed a multi-object project spread across several DLLs and EXEs will recognize the non trivial task of ensuring all the classes, interfaces and type libraries are correctly registered.

MTS tackles this problem of multiple objects by using **packages**. Packages allow the developer to group together the components needed for an application. By putting two components into the same package, you indicate that the two components can be loaded into the same process space. The implication of this is that when one activated component in a package calls another one in the same package, the security credentials are not checked. This is very useful, but is also a security risk and so you should carefully choose how you group components into packages. Security in MTS is configured using the MTS Explorer, as described later.

MTS Packages

There are two packages installed by default with MTS, the **System** and the **Utils** packages. The **System** package has two components, **MtxCatEx.CatalogServer** and **MtxExTrk.MtxExecutiveTracker**. The first, not surprisingly, gives information about the installed components and packages, while the other tracks application server processes (ASP).

The **Utils** package also has two components, **TxCTx.TransactionContext** and the imaginatively named **TxCTx.TransactionContextEx**. These components have interfaces with the same name as the object (prefixed with an **I**) and the methods are used to control the transaction context. These components provide the **IObjectContext**, that we've already seen, which allows a client to create an MTS object within its own context or, for it to commit or, abort a transaction.

Creating Packages

You can create packages for your own server applications and use these packages to install the application on other machines. Packages contain all the information that is needed to run the components in a package: the server DLLs, proxy stub DLLs, type libraries, security and context information. Normally you use the MTS explorer to create a package and then you export the package to a **.pak** file that can be imported in another copy of MTS running on another machine.

Base Clients and Activities

So how do you actually use an MTS component? Well, you start with a client that calls **CoCreateInstance()** (or equivalent) on an MTS component. Such a client is known as a **base client**. This client may be a server itself, but that is largely irrelevant. As far as the base client is concerned, there's no difference between creating an MTS object and creating any other sort of COM object. The base client calls **CoGetClassObject()** or **CoCreateInstance()** and it's the registry entry for the class that determines that the object should be run under the **Mts.exe** surrogate.

When a base client uses **CoCreateInstance()** to create an MTS component, a new **activity** is created, which is recorded in the MTS object's context. An activity is simply the set of objects that is executing on behalf of a base client. When one MTS object creates another using a context object or transaction context object, the second object is created in the same activity as its creator. MTS tracks the activity of the running components and uses it to prevent synchronization problems.

MTS can check for any cases of parallelism – that is, two objects carrying out the same task – and ensure that there is a single logical thread of execution *even across machine boundaries*. Such a facility is important because if there are several MTS objects attempting to carry out the same task, they could attempt to access a resource and corrupt it.

MTS does this by assigning the MTS objects an activity ID that identifies the base client's activity. When the base client calls an object (in the activity), any other request on the object is blocked. The activity ID is also used to track errors that occur in the activity so they can be associated with the base client that started the activity.

Note the difference, for an MTS component, between calling **CoCreateInstance()** and **IObjectContext::CreateInstance()** through its own context. In the first case, the existing MTS object is creating a new context for that object. Since a transaction is part of the context, this new object will be run under another transaction. In the second case, the MTS object creates the new object as part of that same context, so any transactions that are performed on the present object will apply to the created one.

Say you are creating a web page that allows a user to buy products from an online catalogue. The catalogue information could be handled by an object from a distributed database and the user's account information could be represented with another object. When the user attempts to pay for a product, the application could create an object representing the online store's account and then debit the user's account and credit the store's account. Naturally, this should be run within the context of a standard transaction. In this case the store's account object should be created with **IObjectContext::CreateInstance()**.

However, the catalogue object really does not belong as part of the payment transaction, so it's unnecessary to create it within the context of the user's and store's account objects. It could be created using the usual COM **CoCreateInstance()**.

Remember then: you can create several objects within a base client and these objects can be created separately or within the same transaction context. It's clear that the objects that are created under the same context are closely associated and these objects are said to be created within a single activity.

Transactions

Without a transaction mechanism, a failure, part of the way through a task could be disastrous. Most commercial databases provide transactions, and those that provide stored procedures can hide the transaction semantics from the client by placing commands (begin trans/end trans or whatever) within the stored procedure. The user should not know that a transaction is used; the stored procedure just returns a success or failure to the client.

Let's start by defining the properties of a transaction. Transactions should be able to pass the so-called "ACID" test. They should have:

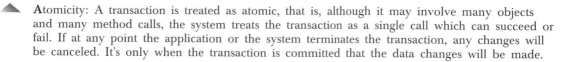

- **A**tomicity: A transaction is treated as atomic, that is, although it may involve many objects and many method calls, the system treats the transaction as a single call which can succeed or fail. If at any point the application or the system terminates the transaction, any changes will be canceled. It's only when the transaction is committed that the data changes will be made.

- **C**onsistency: When there are data (or state) changes, they're done in a consistent manner. That is, the object is changed from one valid state to another valid state.

- **I**solation: Concurrent transactions are isolated from each other. When one transaction is writing some data, this change is isolated from any other transaction. Therefore a second transaction will see the data in its state before the change, or after the change is committed.

- **D**urability: Committed transactions are permanent even if the system fails.

The atomicity property of transactions is provided by MTS through the DTC, whereas the other attributes are provided by the resource managers that handle and modify the data.

Resource Managers

Resource managers are the services that provide the resources to be used in transactions. When the resource manager is first called by an object, it tells MTS that it is being used; this is called **enlistment**. When a resource manager enlists with MTS, it ensures that it'll receive any messages from MTS to indicate that the transaction has been committed or aborted. If the transaction is aborted, the resource manager must rollback to the initial state. How it does this is up to the particular resource manager and could involve maintaining a log of any changes to the resource.

When the application commits the transaction, MTS uses a two-phase commit protocol to get all the enlisted resource managers to commit. Two-phase means that MTS ensures that either all or none of the resource managers commit. The first phase sends a message to each resource manager to see if it is *prepared* to commit and if MTS gets affirmative answers from all the enlisted resource managers. It then goes into the second phase where it tells each one to commit. If any part of this process fails then the transaction in total has failed (this is the idea of atomicity, again).

What if MTS itself should fail, or the machine on which it's running crashes? A transaction may be pending and the objects in the transactions may still be viable, so how is this handled? Well, MTS keeps a log of all transactions and persists this on disk, recording the start of a transaction, the resource managers that have enlisted and any decisions made on the transaction. If MTS does fail, then when it restarts, it can read the log to obtain the state of every transaction that it's monitoring, thus the transaction is durable.

SQL Server 6.5

At the moment there is just one available resource manager: SQL Server 6.5. Microsoft doesn't currently provide an SDK to write your own resource manager. This is partly because writing one would be quite a difficult task, but the main reason is that at the moment MTS uses OLE Transactions, which is specific to Microsoft. The industry standard is XA and MTS should have a service pack ready soon to upgrade MTS to be XA compliant. This will allow it to use transactions that are compatible with existing systems, certainly this'll widen the choice of resource managers you can use with MTS.

Resource Dispensers

MTS provides two resource dispensers, the **ODBC Resource Dispenser** and the **Shared Property Manager**. Resource dispensers manage non-durable data, in other words, if the system should fail, the data that the dispenser maintains is lost. This shouldn't be a great loss because the prime reason for dispensers is to share existing data dynamically.

A separate copy of a dispenser is created in each process that runs a package

ODBC Resource Dispenser

The ODBC Resource Dispenser manages a pool of connections to an OBDC database. This means that when a client wants access to the database, there is no overhead in opening the connection. In addition to this, the dispenser can automatically reclaim connections for use by other clients. When a client gets a connection from the dispenser, it's automatically enlisted in the object's transaction.

Shared Property Manager

Shared Properties are properties global to the server. They are defined by the server designer, and could be some item of data or a shared object (such as the DCOMReverse object used in the LogServer example in the previous chapter). Since these properties are shared with all clients, there's a distinct problem of synchronization. This is the reason for the Shared Property Manager – it exists to manage synchronized access to shared properties.

If a component uses a shared property, then it must register this fact with the Shared Property Manager Resource Dispenser. To do this, the component first creates a **SharedPropertyGroupManager** and then **QI()**s for the **ISharedPropertyGroupManager** interface which provides the following methods:

ISharedPropertyGroupManager Method	Description
CreatePropertyGroup()	Creates a new property group with a particular name
get_Group()	Returns an interface pointer to a specific property group
get__NewEnum()	Creates an enumerator

The first method creates a property group. This gives the group a name and a locking method, i.e. it determines how long the current object has a lock on the property, and thus how 'sharable' it is. The possible values are:

- ▲ **LockSetGet**, which specifies that locking is only applied when a property in the group is accessed
- ▲ **LockMethod**, which applies the lock on the entire group during this method call. This call will return a pointer to the **ISharedPropertyGroup** created

A component can get a pointer to an already created property group by calling either **get_Group()** with the name of the group, or **get__NewEnum()** which returns an **IEnumVARIANT** enumerator.

Once you have created a property group and got an interface on it, you can then create and access properties through the methods of the **ISharedPropertyGroup** interface:

ISharedPropertyGroup Method	Description
CreateProperty()	Creates a new, named property
CreatePropertyByPosition()	Create a new property accessed by an index
get_Property()	Access the name property
get_PropertyByPosition()	Access the indexed property

This allows you to create properties in two ways, either with a name, or with an index and then return a pointer to the property. In both cases, if the property already exists, the pointer returned is the original property. Although named properties are easier to manage (certainly in terms of reading your code), indexed properties are more efficient. If you create one type of property, you cannot change it to the other type, however there are no restrictions about mixing named and indexed properties in a group, and indexes need not be sequential.

Finally, once you have created and accessed a property, you get hold of its data through the
`ISharedProperty` interface:

ISharedProperty Method	Description
get_Value()	Returns the property's value as a **VARIANT**
put_Value()	Sets the property's value

The property can have any value that can be held in a **VARIANT**.

Transaction Requirements

You've already seen that the transaction context of an MTS object is part of its MTS context and can be
committed or rolled back using the methods of the **IObjectContext** interface. You've also seen that the
context of an object can be passed to other MTS objects by creating them with
IObjectContext::CreateInstance(). What you haven't yet seen is how you define transactional
requirements. What if a particular component should never run as part of a transaction? What if a
component requires a new transaction to be started?

The main way of determining transactional requirements for a component is to set its transaction attribute
using MTS Explorer. When a client activates an MTS object, MTS looks at this attribute to determine if a
new transaction context object should be created. If it should, one is created. Neither the object, nor the
client need call any API to start a transaction as it is created automatically when required.

An object that runs under a transaction can always get hold of its transaction context object. The client can
call methods on this object to create more objects that run under the same context or to complete/abort
the context. If the application or one of the resource managers fail, MTS will abort the transaction.

Every MTS component has a transaction attribute that indicates whether transactions are used and how the
requirement is enforced. The four options are:

Transaction Attribute	Description
Does not support transactions	When an object is run, it is not run within the context of a transaction, but it does have a context object
Supports transactions	The object is run within the context of the client's transaction. (If the client does not have a transaction then neither does the object.)
Requires a transaction	The object *must* execute in the context of a transaction. If the client does not have a transaction, one will be created.
Requires a new transaction	The object must execute in the context of its own transaction, and so a new transaction context will always be created

The transaction attribute can be set
as one of the properties of a
component in the MTS Explorer:

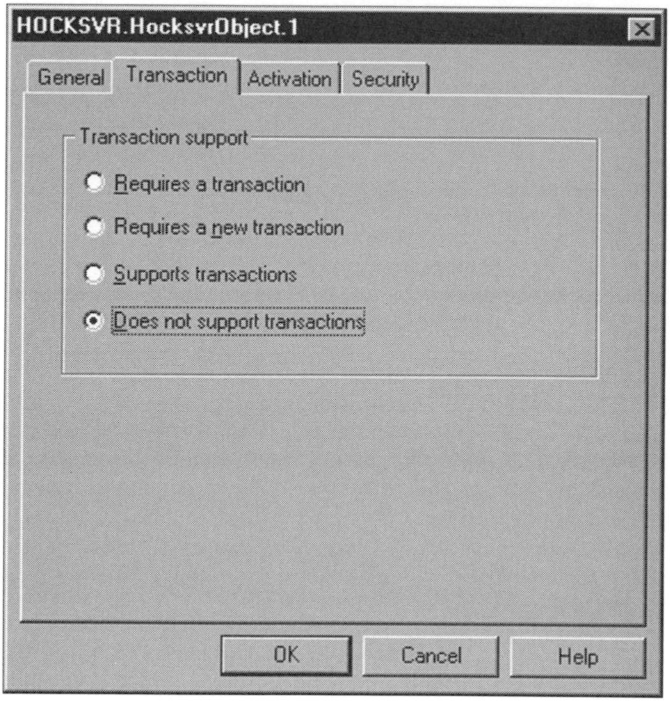

This allows you to turn off transactions for components where transactions are not relevant, and thus
disable the (small) overhead that would have been endured. The screenshot above shows the settings for
the **Hockey** example, supplied with MTS. This example demonstrates shared properties and so transactions
are turned off.

Remember, to utilize the other advantages of MTS (such as: concurrency control and object dispensers)
the object still needs a context. MTS will create the object context, including security, but not a transaction
context.

> *In future releases of MTS, the type library of a component could be used to give this transaction
> requirement. This would require a change in the type library format, so it remains a future enhancement:
> the present release uses manual intervention.*

A base client doesn't need to know about MTS, although it can get access to MTS interfaces if it wishes.
The base client just creates objects and if these have been installed as MTS components, they will be run
as part of MTS under a security context and, if necessary, under a transaction context.

If a base client knows that an object it created runs under a transaction, it can get a hold of the object's
transaction interface by calling **QI()** for **ITransactionContext**. This interface has these methods:

ITransactionContext Method	Description
`CreateInstance()`	Creates an MTS object in the context of the transaction
`Abort()`	The transaction should be aborted
`Commit()`	The transaction should be committed

A client can force the creation of a new transaction by creating a `TransactionContextEx` object. This is just a simple component provided with MTS whose transaction attribute has been set to Requires a new transaction. It implements the `ITransactionContextEx` interface to allow the client to control the outcome of the transaction.

Distributed Transactions

So far I've described MTS handling transaction objects on a single machine. Now, if many machines on a network are running MTS then these can cooperate in transactions that involve distributed objects: distributed transactions.

When a client makes a request for a component that resides on a remote machine, the client makes this request through a **global commit coordinator**. The client can specify the machine that has the coordinator or, if it's omitted, then the default specified in the DTC Client Configuration applet is used. This coordinator then establishes a relationship with MTS on the remote machine that has the component. The coordinator has an **outgoing** relationship, whereas the remote MTS has an **incoming** relationship. The combinations of outgoing and incoming form a **commit tree** that is used as part of the two phase commit.

Each MTS handles the commits to the resource managers enlisted in the transaction. The commit is triggered by the MTS at the root of the commit tree, which is of course, the global commit coordinator. A remote MTS can be in doubt about a transaction, but the global commit coordinator cannot be.

If a computer fails, the MTS on that machine can regain its state from the log that it keeps. If an MTS is a global commit coordinator for a particular transaction, it can then use the log to determine the relationships that it had with other machines and then make a decision about the transaction. If the failed machine's MTS had an incoming relationship with another machine, it can query that global commit coordinator as to the outcome of the transaction. At the same time, of course, the enlisted resource managers are restarted and if any are in doubt, they can query their local MTS.

When a transaction is in doubt, the resources used in the transaction are locked from other clients. This is problematic in the single machine case since the 'in doubt' state may last for some time. A failure causing an in doubt condition should be rare in this situation. When distributed systems are used, there are many more causes for failures (a network error for example), so there's a greater change of a transaction becoming in doubt.

DTC and Transactions

So far, the term *transaction* has been bandied around a lot, but we haven't really said how they're created, and where. The simple reply is that you don't need to worry about where and when they're created, since MTS will do it for you. To satisfy your curiosity, here's a brief description of the internals. Bear in mind that DTC started life in SQL Server. When DTC appears as part of the operating system in NT Server, you can expect the file system and other parts of the OS to be resource managers and thus be able to take part in transactions.

DTC uses a protocol called OLE Transactions to talk to the resource managers that are part of a transaction (the industry standard is XA). Since DTC allows for distributed transactions, there may be many copies of DTC running on many servers and each will have one or more resource managers. When a client creates components across this network, the same transaction has to be propagated across the various machines. This is done using a transaction object.

The client creates a component and MTS creates a context object for this component. This context object has information about the object security, threading model and its transaction. In fact, when the context object is created, it creates a transaction object.

In SQL Server, you had to do this explicitly with a call to **DtcGetTransactionDispenser()** to get the Dispenser and then call **BeginTransaction()** on this object to get hold of a transaction object. The ODBC driver could be told about this transaction object with a call to **SQLSetConnectOption()**, and subsequent ODBC calls would be done under the context of this object.

Now, when a application makes a call on a resource manager (for example SQL Server), the local DTC tells the remote DTC about the transaction, and this DTC will create a transaction object local to itself. It returns back to the application DTC a unique identifier (commonly known as a cookie) to identify the transaction. The ODBC driver on the application server will then send this cookie to SQL server on the remote machine, which can enlist itself in the transaction. Now the application and the resource manager have associated transaction objects.

Threading

So far, we've agreed that MTS objects are run single threaded. We've also introduced the concept of a logical thread – that is, there is just one logical thread of execution within an activity, even if that activity has objects distributed over many machines. However, we've also noted that objects written prior to MTS could be MTS objects and, as we saw in the last chapter, these inproc objects will be marked with a threading model. How is this handled by MTS?

The first point to make is that MTS handles all threading issues for a component. In fact, a component should *not* create or terminate any threads. This should be a great relief after the last chapter, since you've no responsibility to provide synchronization or ensure that objects are created and released in the right order, MTS does it all. It does though, put responsibility on the object developer, to steer away from creating any threads. If an object does thread, MTS will suspend that thread and so any advantages of creating that addition will be lost.

Don't forget, an MTS component does have a concept of a threading model, and there are varying degrees of 'single-threadedness'. So a component (as an inproc server) must declare a threading model in the **ThreadingModel** value in the registry. There are three to choose from: **main, apartment** and **rental.** (These are sometimes called *single threaded,* apartment and *worker.*) If the component does not express a preference, the main threading model will be assumed.

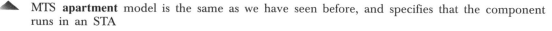 **Main** model is equivalent to a single threaded pre-apartment model. In other words, it is non-reentrant

▲ MTS **apartment** model is the same as we have seen before, and specifies that the component runs in an STA

▲ **Rental** model is a free threaded version and is not used in the current version of MTS

Main

If a component is single threaded (main), every instance of the class runs in the same thread, this model must be used if multiple instances of a component use global data - this is the case if the component was written in VB4.

This model can cause deadlocks. For example imagine two clients which create an object of the same class running under the main model. The first client calls a method that locks a database record and then carries out some work, but before it can call **SetComplete()** (which would have the effect of releasing the lock), the second client calls the same method. Since this is the main threading model, both objects are running in the same thread, so the second object preempts the first one. This means that when the second object attempts to lock the database record, it cannot (since it is already locked) and the thread will be blocked while the second object waits for the record to be unlocked. This is a deadlock, and there is no way out of it.

To prevent this situation occurring the component should call **SetComplete()** when it gets the resource, indicating that the transaction can be committed to release the lock on the resource. This only works if the object is not stateful (holds state between method calls), and it does not allow for effective use of transactions.

Apartment

In the apartment model each instance of the component runs in its own thread, therefore when the client makes successive method calls to the object, the calls will always be on the same thread. Thread local storage can be used (but only if it's absolutely necessary). Different instances of the same class run on different threads. Components written with VB5 use this model. To indicate that the component is using the apartment model, its registry **ThreadingModel** should be **Apartment**.

Rental

Components that use the rental model, mark themselves in the registry with the DCOM models **free** or **both**. Each instance of the component class can run on a different thread each time a method is called. For this model, MTS should (in a later release) keep a pool of threads for method calls. When a thread is executing a component method, and that method creates a new object, MTS will suspend the current thread and then create a new thread to handle the new object.

This may seem a little odd, but remember back to the last chapter. Each thread is run for a time slice before being put to sleep to allow other threads to execute. When NT switches between threads it needs to switch the thread context, and this includes the stack of the thread. If a thread has been running for a while and is at the bottom of a complicated call stack with many auto variables defined, the stack could get quite large. By suspending this thread and creating a new, clean thread, the context switches are quicker. MTS components assume that they are single threaded, and this is not violated since there is only one thread running and anyway this thread is calling out, not calling in.

Security

Security in DCOM can get a little complicated. You only have to browse through Chapter 7 to realize this. The reason for the complexity is that the NT security model is built to be as flexible as possible, and security in DCOM (which uses NT security by default) is designed to be replaceable. "Flexible and replaceable" means "complicated" to any developer, and this is so with DCOM.

MTS takes a higher level view of security. Someone in Redmond has sat down and thought about security and decided that security means defining *who* can use an object and *what* they can do to it. So how can this be applied in the simplest way?

Security is closely linked to packages. All the components in a package run in the same process and this means that all components in a package have access to each other *without any security checks*. Since packages of components are run in a process, it's natural for you to want to determine what NT security is used in that process. Remember that for most packages the server process is **Mts.exe** and so there must be a way for different packages to use this process launched under different NT accounts.

The way to do this is to specify the account during installation, or at a later stage, by looking at the package's properties:

This is similar to the Identity tab in **DCOMCnfg**. The identity specified here is the one that will be used when launching the server process, and if the components make some call to access resources outside of the package (access a file for example), its NT security context is derived from this ID.

Components in a package can use NT impersonation, however this is discouraged (because it uses that nasty, complicated NT security model), and the preferred method is to use an MTS **role**. Roles are groups of users and roughly map to NT groups (indeed NT groups may be added to roles). However, I said *roughly* because MTS is designed to separate between development and deployment. (In other words, it could be used on a system that does not use NT the security model.)

Roles are defined during development time: basically you say a member of a role can do *this* but not *that* and a component checks for membership of a role when a client makes a call. At deployment time an administrator determines which users (and groups of users) belong to which role.

There are two ways to apply this security model on components:

declarative access control – is administered using the MTS Explorer and requires no programming
programmatic access control - accesses the security of a component at runtime using the **IObjectContext** interface

Declarative Access Control

This defines two attributes, **roles** and **permissions**. Roles describe who can have access to the component. In this picture my friend, OrdinaryUser, and I are Clerks that can access the components in the Bank package.

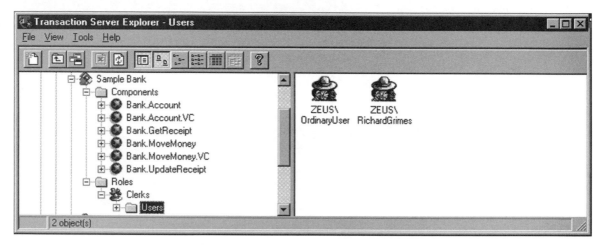

Permissions determine what each Role can do, under NT this maps to a DACL. MTS implements security in this fashion to abstract security from the operating system.

Programmatic Access Control

The component can get information about its security context through the **IObjectContext** and **ISecurityProperty** interfaces on the associated context object. The former allows the component to determine if security is enabled (**IsSecurityEnabled()**) or if the client application's security context is in a particular role (**IsCallerInRole()**). The **ISecurityProperty** interface is used to get the identity of the client that created, or is calling, the component.

The **ISecurityProperty** interface is provided by the context object (just **QI()** for it) and provides information about who originally created the object and who is presently calling the object. It has the following methods:

ISecurityProperty Method	Description
`GetDirectCallerSID()`	Returns the SID of the process that called the current object
`GetDirectCreatorSID()`	Returns the SID of the process that created the current object
`GetOriginalCallerSID()`	Gets the SID of the base client that initiated the call into the object
`GetOriginalCreatorSID()`	Gets the SID of the base client that initiated the creation of the object
`ReleaseSID()`	Releases any returned SIDs

These methods distinguish between the **Direct** and **Original** caller and creator. The **OriginalCreator** is defined as the base client that created an MTS object, which may be the current object or it may have created the current object. The **DirectCreator** is the role that actually created the current object.

Once you have a SID, you can use this in NT security operations as described in Chapter 7. In particular, to get the username you can call **LookupAccountSid()**.
SIDs are variable length data structures, so these methods take a pointer to a **PSID** pointer. The interface will make a copy of the creator/caller SID and return a pointer to it in the **PSID [out]** parameter. As with all **[out]** parameters, the client must make sure that the memory of the parameter is released, but this is one of the few interfaces where you do this by calling a method on the interface, **ReleaseSID()**.

Activating Objects

As we have seen throughout this book, when you create a COM object, the object retains its state until it's released. This means that if the object has a database connection open and the client goes to sleep for some reason, that connection is open until another method call closes it or the object is released (and hopefully releases its resources). On a single machine with a single client, this may not be too bad, but imagine an intranet with hundreds of connections.

If you still cannot grasp the problem, imagine this situation: a COM object that dials a number and keeps the telephone line off the hook until you release it. Such resource usage (your telephone bill) is wasteful. MTS has a solution, using just in time activation.

Note that these facilities are not present in the current release of MTS but will become available when MTS is updated.

Just in Time Activation

With **just in time activation** an MTS object is activated (and its state is reset) when a method call is made on the object. When the object code calls **SetComplete()** or **SetAbort()** on its **IObjectContext** interface, to end a transaction, the object is deactivated and its resources are released. It is this method call that releases the resources, and not the client. Indeed, the client *still* has a reference on the object (through an interface pointer to an MTS wrapper).

The deactivated object is only a 'ghost' object and not a 'real' object because it does not have any internal state - it's been released. However, the object's context object has not been released and the client will actually have a reference to this object. When the client makes a method call, the context object can create the 'real' object and the method can be called: just in time.

Let's reiterate this. When the object is first created, the MTS server just holds a context object, the underlying object is uninitialized and has no state. When a client makes the first method call, it is activated, initialized and thus has a state. If the method call returns without calling **SetComplete()** or **SetAbort()** then the object is left in an activated state. It's only when there's another method call that calls **SetComplete()** or **SetAbort()** on the context, that the object will be deactivated and thus lose its state.

MTS encourages the use of **stateless** objects. These are objects that can be deactivated after every method call. All you need to do to create a stateless object is to call **IObjectContext::SetComplete()** during each method call.

Instance Pooling

Instance pools allow MTS to be more efficient in handling objects. An object that supports instance pooling must implement the **IObjectControl** method and return **TRUE** when MTS calls **IObjectControl::CanBePooled()**. When MTS creates an object, it will **QueryInterface()** for the **IObjectControl** interface, which has the following methods:

IObjectControl Method	Description
Activate()	Carries out initialization of the object specific to this activity and before any object methods are called
Deactivate()	Carries out any clean up required before the object is released or recycled
CanBePooled()	Indicates if MTS can recycle objects through an instance pool

The **IObjectControl** interface is useful for any object that needs to perform MTS context-dependent initialization or cleanup. The **IObjectContext** interface cannot be called in the class factory, **AddRef()** or **Release()** methods, so any context-specific initialization (or any context-specific clean up) that needs to be done for a specific instance of an object must be done in the methods of the **IObjectControl** interface. The **Activate()** and **Deactivate()** methods will always be called when the object is activated and deactivated.

If the **IObjectControl** interface is not present, or if it is and **IObjectControl::CanBePooled()** returns **FALSE**, instance pooling is disabled. In the present release of MTS, a class cannot take part in instance pooling, but it's a feature to expect in later releases.

When a component can be pooled, it indicates that when the object is released, it's not totally destroyed. Instead, it's put in the instance pool where it can be used later when another client creates a new object. To the client a new object and a *recycled* one are exactly the same, but to MTS a recycled object is using resources more efficiently. MTS will use objects in the instance pool, and will only create a new object when there are no more recycled objects.

There is a threading issue with pooling when used for components that use the apartment model. In this model an instance is run in an STA, so it cannot be reused on a different thread. The implication of this is that if more than one thread is used (as is the case), there has to be a separate pool for each thread. This is clearly impractical and provides no benefits, so components in an STA should not be instance pooled.

ATL Components

You may have noticed that there is an object type in the ATL Object Wizard in Visual C++ 5.0 for MS Transaction Server objects. If you insert one of these into your project, you will see that the wizard enables you to name the component as usual, but the second tab, labeled MTX, features some new options.

Essentially the wizard makes it very easy to add to your component support for the **IObjectControl** interface. If you select support for **IObjectControl**, the wizard will add that interface to the generated class and provide code that gets the context object in **IObjectControl::Activate()** and releases it in **IObjectControl::Deactivate()**:

```
HRESULT CMTSComp::Activate()
{
    HRESULT hr = GetObjectContext(&m_spObjectContext);
    if (SUCCEEDED(hr))
            return S_OK;
    return hr;
}

BOOL CMTSComp::CanBePooled()
{
    return TRUE;
}

void CMTSComp::Deactivate()
{
    m_spObjectContext->Release();
}
```

If you decide not to add support for that interface, the wizard can still benefit you in three ways: it declares that your component isn't aggregatable, it selects the apartment threading model, and it includes the Transaction Server header.

Note that since the MTS objects are inproc and run under the **Mts.exe** surrogate, you must use the surrogate as the application to launch when debugging the object. To do this select the Project | Settings menu item and then the Debug tab and in the edit box for the Executable for debug session type in the path to **Mts.exe** and for Program arguments type **/p:{GUID}** where **{GUID}** is the GUID of the package as registered in:

HKEY_LOCAL_MACHINE\SOFTWARE\Microsoft\Transaction Server\Packages

Programming Paradigm

Over the last few years there have been many changes in how programmers have coded their projects, another change is required when writing components for MTS.

Initially, programmers used procedural techniques with a single thread of execution and a defined path of execution, modularization split these programs into functions and code modules.

Then OO languages (and languages with OO extensions) appeared and programmers took an object approach. Analysts talked about objects sending messages to other objects. The reason for this is quite clear to anyone trying to debug an object based project: it's difficult to define an execution path through all the objects. It's simpler (and more natural) to let objects manage their own state and make calls on, and return the calls from, other objects. Objects were created, manipulated and then destroyed, and throughout this time the objects had some state (data in instance variables) that defined the object.

Then multithreading came along. This allowed the system to maintain multiple threads of execution and the programmer could run objects in different threads to allow for some concurrency. However, this did produce problems with synchronization.

Now with MTS we take a step back. An object in MTS is run in a single thread. In fact an *activity*, which can contain many objects, is run in a single logical thread. This means that an object need not worry about synchronization with static data or reentrancy problems, MTS guarantees isolation.

In the old object model (multi- or single-threaded) servers typically created many objects, each with its own state. These objects may not be active (i.e. processing a client call), but held in memory for their clients to use at some later stage. In most cases the object state is just a small amount of data, but in some cases it could be an important resource. A database object could hold a connection to a database. Since creating this connection is quite time consuming, the object client may decide to keep the object alive for a considerable amount of time, just in case it needs to access the data again. Such a model is wasteful.

MTS encourages a different approach. MTS encourages the use of stateless objects which are created as deactivated and are only activated when a method call is made on the object. At this point the object can get its resources and initialize its internal state, the method can even return, so the object retains the state. The neat part is that a method can call **SetComplete()** to indicate that it has finished, and the state is released, along with any resources. The object is deactivated, but the client still has a reference on it.

The advantage of this approach is that the client need not go through the process of creating the object and it can call upon it again at any time in the future, at which point just-in-time activation occurs and the object gets its state again. However, during the time the object was deactivated, it uses few server resources.

The change in programming practices required is that clients can hold onto objects as long as they wish. 'Good' clients, that previously had to create, use, and delete objects as quickly as possible, can now hang onto object references for as long as they wish. They do have to be aware of what methods change the state and which will deactivate the object.

Server programmers have to be more disciplined. Components should acquire resources as late as possible and call **SetComplete()** as early as possible. The shift, if you like, is moving this responsibility from the client to the server developer.

MTS does, however, allow objects to be used that were written before MTS, and this is apparent in the various types of threading model supported. This means that you can write an MTS application that uses a mixture of MTS-aware and MTS-unaware objects, but the real power lies in writing specifically for MTS.

MTS and DCOM

So where does DCOM fit into all of this? In this chapter, it has been mentioned many times that MTS (through MS DTC) allows for activities to contain remote objects and to have distributed transactions covering those objects. These objects are accessed with COM and the transaction mechanism uses COM, thus to distribute all of this requires DCOM.

However, the reason for this chapter is not just to show an application that uses DCOM as its plumbing (although MTS is a good example of how DCOM is used transparently). The real reason is to show the way forward in object development.

DCOM allows objects to be distributed across a network and through NT's distributed security model, the entire application can run under the same security context. But DCOM forces a developer to think about the mechanics of security, threading and scalability rather than application-specific issues.

MTS gives the framework to produce applications that contain distributed objects, but keeps a tight control on these objects. Although your application can access and manipulate the object it creates, MTS is always there in the shadows if something goes wrong. Although transactions are essentially confined to a single database at the moment, the future promises some other exciting resource managers, the file system is one resource that should be covered by transactions in the next release of NT.

MTS handles concurrency for you! You write your objects to be single threaded, safe in the knowledge that MTS will not allow any thread to preempt the current thread. Finally, MTS offers a security model that is consistent throughout the transaction, relieving you of the onerous task of making sure that the security contexts of all your objects are run under the correct user.

Summary

Microsoft Transaction Server is in a state of change. At the moment it provides distributed transactions using OLE Transactions, but the only resource manager that uses this method is SQL Server 6.5. This will be remedied soon when the MTS service pack 1 is released and XA compliance will be supported. At this point MTS will become very important because it will allow you, the developer, the facility of accessing many different resources from your application under the same transaction context, all complying to the same ACID attributes. This, combined with the scalability that MTS offers, will trigger a new wave of internet and intranet applications that are safe and scaleable.

The next wave of applications will arrive when the new Windows NT Server is released. The functionality of MTS should be part of the operating system allowing for transactions to occur without a separate process. Indeed, the system itself should apply transactions over its access to resources like the file system.

The final piece of the puzzle will be in place when Falcon, the Microsoft Message Queue, is released. The combination of MTS and DCOM running over Falcon will mean that not only will object interactions be performed under transactions, but they will be *guaranteed* to be carried out – Falcon will continue to call on an object until the method is called. This will give functionality to NT machines that is currently only available to large mainframes.

The gauntlet is about to be thrown down, as a server developer you're entering some of the real challenges of computing in the new century.

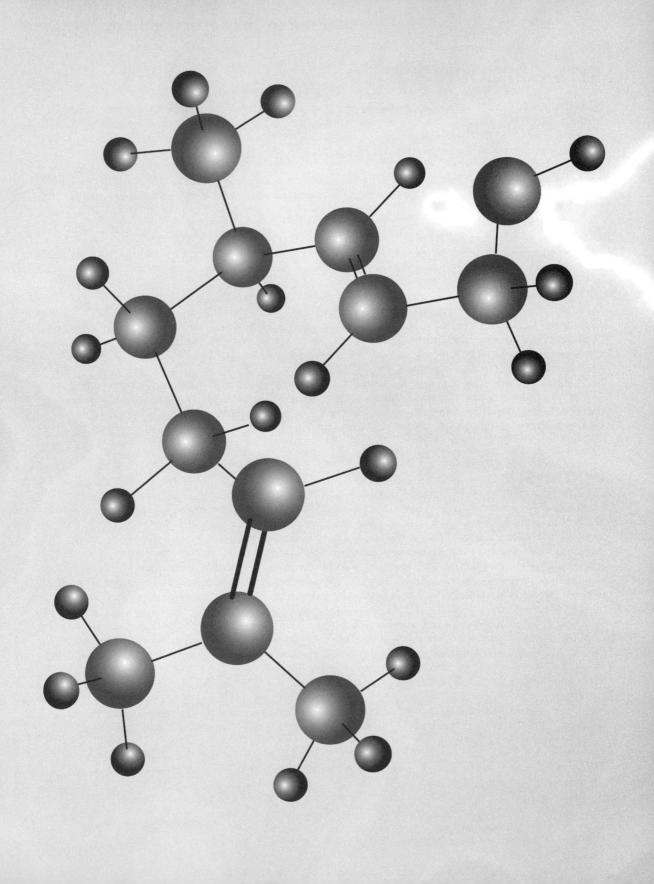

Debugging Tips

Debugging DCOM Servers

There are several ways that you can debug a DCOM server. You can start a server and set breakpoints that are tripped when a client connects, or you can debug the server once it is running. Let's take a quick look at each of these methods.

Starting a Server from Developer Studio

If you are debugging an EXE server that registers the class factories of the classes that it supports, and effectively waits for a client connection when it's run, then you can start the server from Developer Studio. ATL and MFC EXE servers fall into this category.

As soon as a client requests an object, whether the client is local or remote, the server will be used and it will stop when a breakpoint is reached.

If you try this technique and find that the breakpoints are not reached, the most likely reason is that there's a copy of this process already running. Use the NT Task Manager to find this server and stop it.

Attaching to a Running Server

Being able to debug your server by setting it running from Developer Studio is useful, but may not be appropriate if it needs to run under a particular account. This is also true if it's a service, which must be started by the SCM to ensure that its **ServiceMain()** and **ServiceCtrlHandler()** are called.

Fortunately, it's easy to debug a server that's already running, by using the NT Task Manager – just right-click on a running process and select <u>D</u>ebug from the context menu. If your account has the **SeTcbDebug** privilege then NT will attach the debugger to the process. If the process does not have debug information then you will not be able to step through the code.

```
┌─────────────────────────────────────────────────────────┐
│ 💻 Windows NT Task Manager              [_][□][X]         │
├─────────────────────────────────────────────────────────┤
│ File  Options  View  Help                                │
├─────────────────────────────────────────────────────────┤
│ ┌──────────┐ ┌──────────┐ ┌────────────┐                 │
│ │Applications│ Processes │ Performance │                 │
│                                                          │
│  ┌─────────────────────────────────────────────────────┐│
│  │ Image Name       │ PID │ CPU │ CPU Time │ Mem Usage  ││
│  │ System Idle Process│  0 │ 00  │ 0:16:35  │     16 K   ││
│  │ System            │  2 │ 00  │ 0:00:24  │    120 K   ││
│  │ smss.exe          │ 18 │ 00  │ 0:00:00  │    120 K   ││
│  │ csrss.exe         │ 30 │ 00  │ 0:00:00  │    416 K   ││
│  │ winlogon.exe      │ 32 │ 00  │ 0:00:00  │      0 K   ││
│  │ services.exe      │ 38 │ 00  │ 0:00:01  │    940 K   ││
│  │ spoolss  End Process│ 40 │ 00 │ 0:00:00 │    596 K   ││
│  │ lsass.e  Debug     │ 41 │ 00  │ 0:00:00 │    136 K   ││
│  │ msdtc.e           │ 63 │ 00  │ 0:00:00  │   1264 K   ││
│  │ RpcSs.   Set Priority ▶│ 70 │ 00 │ 0:00:00│  396 K   ││
│  │ snmp.exe          │ 93 │ 00  │ 0:00:00  │    188 K   ││
│  │ Explorer.exe      │101 │ 00  │ 0:00:04  │   1732 K   ││
│  │ nddeagnt.exe      │103 │ 00  │ 0:00:00  │      0 K   ││
│  │ MSDEV.EXE         │117 │ 00  │ 0:00:16  │   1496 K   ││
│  │ SysTray.Exe       │132 │ 00  │ 0:00:00  │     20 K   ││
│  │ MSOFFICE.EXE      │134 │ 00  │ 0:00:00  │    504 K   ││
│  │ FINDFAST.EXE      │136 │ 00  │ 0:00:46  │   2060 K   ││
│  │ WINWORD.EXE       │139 │ 96  │ 2:09:26  │   7056 K   ││
│  │ taskmgr.exe       │147 │ 01  │ 0:00:01  │   1348 K   ││
│  │ Psp.exe           │150 │ 03  │ 0:00:01  │    596 K   ││
│  │                                                      ││
│  └──────────────────────────────────────────────────────┘│
│                                          ┌─────────────┐ │
│                                          │ End Process │ │
│                                          └─────────────┘ │
├─────────────────────────────────────────────────────────┤
│ Processes: 20 │ CPU Usage: 100% │ Mem Usage: 37652K / 67796K │
└─────────────────────────────────────────────────────────┘
```

It's also possible to do the same thing right from Developer Studio, by selecting the Build | Start Debug | Attach to process... menu item.

Starting the Debugger from a Command Line

If picking an item from a menu sounds too easy, you could start the debugger from a command line. This technique requires you to note the process ID from the Task Manager and then run Developer Studio using this command line:

```
msdev /p process_id
```

Developer Studio will start and will break at the point in the code that you ran the debugger. You can then set breakpoints and run the code to stop at those places.

Debugging an Object Server from the Client

Perhaps the most convenient way of debugging servers, and a method that works for both local and inproc servers (but not remote servers), is to set breakpoints in the client and step into the server code from there.

For this to be possible, you have to make sure that OLE debugging is enabled by selecting the Options... item of the Tools menu. If you select the Debug tab, you'll see the following dialog:

Make sure that the boxes (at the bottom-right of the dialog) for Just-in-time debugging and OLE RPC debugging are both checked. If Just-in-time debugging is unchecked, the second box will be disabled. The second box is the important one here because it allows you to debug COM servers across process boundaries.

Once this is enabled, you can set breakpoints in your client on calls to your server's methods. When the debugger stops on such a breakpoint, you can select Debug | Step Into (usually bound to the *F11* key) and the debugger will step into your server code. If the object is inproc, then all this means is that you will step into code that is already in your process' address space.

If the object is a local server, the debugger will start a new debugger for the server process. The client thread will be blocked at this point (COM calls are synchronous). You may find that the new debugger will stop in some machine code, but don't worry, just single step through. When you get to a point where the debugger reaches some debug code, the relevant source file will be opened and you will be able to step through as usual.

Once you have debugged the code and got to the end of the method, you can continue to step through until you step out of the object and back into the client code.

Running an Object under an Appropriate Account

One problem with debugging objects is making sure that they are activated under the correct account, and one way to do this is to start a command prompt under the appropriate account and then start the debugger from the command line. The simplest way to do this is to start a command prompt using the NT Scheduler.

Using the Services applet in the control panel, you can specify the account used by the Scheduler service (use the Startup... button). You can then start a command line with the **at** command. For example, if the current time is 12:00, type the following at the command line:

```
at 12:01 /interactive cmd.exe
```

This will start a command box in a minute's time, and this box will be running under whatever account you set the Scheduler to use. You can then use this to start your debugger. This will give you access to the server from an appropriate account.

This is the best way to start a process under the **System** account.

COM Tips

Now we'll look at a few miscellaneous items to help you avoid some common mistakes and track down frequent problems.

CoCreateInstance() Fails

If **CoCreateInstance()** or **CoCreateInstanceEx()** fails to create your requested object, you may find that the returned **HRESULT** is not particularly helpful. The Win32 documentation says that **CoCreateInstance** can return:

Constant	Meaning
S_OK	Success
REGDB_E_CLASSNOTREG	The class is not registered
CLASS_E_NOAGGREGATION	The class cannot be created as part of an aggregate

And **CoCreateInstanceEx()** can return:

Constant	Meaning
S_OK	Success
CO_S_NOTALLINTERFACES	At least one, but not all, of the interfaces was returned. The **MULTI_QI** structures have values of **S_OK** and **E_NOINTERFACE** against the successful and failed interfaces
E_NOINTERFACE	None of the requested interfaces was returned

If you need more information, you may find it useful to expand these helper functions and find out exactly where the failure occurs. So for **CoCreateInstance()** use the following code:

```
HRESULT hRes;
IClassFactory* pCF = NULL;
hRes = CoGetClassObject(rclsid, dwClsContext, pServerInfo, IID_IClassFactory, &pCF);
if (SUCCEEDED(hRes))
{
   hRes = pCF->CreateInstance(pUnkOuter, riid, &pInt);
   pCf->Release();
}
```

where **rclsid** is the CLSID of the server, **riid** is the IID of the required interface, **dwClsContext** is the class context (inproc, local, remote etc), **pServerInfo** gives the server machine to query or is **NULL**, and **pInt** returns the obtained interface pointer.

Although these functions do not return any more information than the wrappers, you can tell if the call failed on the creation of the object, or the request for the interface. You can replace **CoCreateInstanceEx()** with similar code that attempts to obtain pointers for all the interfaces in the array.

Typically, the reason that **CoCreateInstance()** or **CoCreateInstanceEx()** fails for an out-of-process object is that the proxy stub DLL has not been registered. In this case, the call to **CoGetClassObject()** will succeed, but the call to **CreateInstance()** will fail.

You may also find that the server instantiation will return **RPC_S_SERVER_UNAVAILABLE** (0x800706ba)

Method Calls Fail

If the server throws an exception then a method call will fail. You will find that COM will take over the call and return a value of **RPC_E_SERVERFAULT** (0x80010105). The only way of finding out the source of the problem is to run the server in a separate copy of Developer Studio and put a breakpoint at the start of the method.

Casting Interface Pointers

Imagine you have an interface method that returns an interface pointer; both interfaces are dual, so they can be called from VB. The IDL looks something like this:

```
interface IChocolateChip : IDispatch
{
   [id(0)] HRESULT Eat();
};

interface IIceCreamPalour : IDispatch
{
   [id(0)] HRESULT GetChocolateChip([out, retval] IDispatch** ppCC);
};
```

You may be tempted to implement **GetChocolateChip()** like this (where **m_pCCInterface** is a pointer to the **IChocolateChip** interface):

```
HRESULT CIcecreamParlour::GetChocolateChip(IDispatch** ppCC)
{
    *ppCC = (IDispatch*) m_pCCInterface;
    return S_OK;
}
```

And use the returned pointer like this:

```
IChocolateChip* pCC = NULL;
m_pIcecreamParlour->GetChocolateChip((IDispatch**)&pCC);
pCC->Eat();
```

Don't do it! This code will only work if you are calling this code on an inproc server in the same apartment. If that's the case then the pointer returned by **GetChocolateChip()** will point to the actual vtable of the **IChocolateChip** interface, so the call to **Eat()** will succeed.

As soon as proxies get involved, whether between apartments or processes, you'll get an access violation because you will be using an invalid memory address as a function pointer. This is because when the interface is returned from the method in the **IIcecreamParlour** interface, COM will create a proxy for the interface according to the type of the parameter that is returned. In this case an **IDispatch** proxy is generated, so the client will only get a vtable to an **IDispatch**. It won't (and can't) assume that you want a vtable for all the functions in **IChocolateChip**.

The correct code is to pass back the actual **IDispatch** interface from the server and **QI()** for the required interface in the client. The server code shown above will return an **IDispatch** pointer, but the client code should be changed to:

```
IChocolateChip* pCC = NULL;
IDispatch* pDisp = NULL;
m_pIcecreamParlour->GetChocolateChip(&pDisp);
pDisp->QueryInterface(IID_IChocolateChip,(LPVOID*)&pCC);
pDisp->Release();
pCC->Eat();
```

Using OLEView

OLEView is an invaluable tool when developing COM servers. What's more, it's constantly kept up to date with every new facility that's added to COM. You can find the most up-to-date version of this tool on Microsoft's web site at

http://www.microsoft.com/oledev

When I develop a COM server, I use **OLEView** throughout the development, but I find it particularly useful during the development of the IDL and finally when the object has been written.

When you create an object with ATL, the type library will be bound into the code module as a resource. To check if the type library has been compiled into the resources, you can use the type library viewer of **OLEView**. This can also check that the changes you made in the IDL are reflected in the type library bound into the object. Make sure though, that you view the object's code module (EXE or DLL) and not the type library created by MIDL.

OLEView is also useful if my clients fail to create the object with a **CoCreateInstance()** call. In this case, I use **OLEView** to check that the object has been registered properly, checking to see if the object's ProgID is in the All Objects branch and that the object is also mentioned in the Application ID branch.

If you are having problems getting a particular interface then it is worth using **OLEView** to list the interfaces on the object. Select the object in the All Objects branch and click on the + next to the object name to open the branch. **OLEView** will instantiate the object and **QI()** it for every interface registered in the registry. You will then get a list of the interfaces the object supports.

If your interface is not listed then you ought to check your IDL file to see if the interface was defined. If the object has dispatch interfaces (dual or not), you can also view them by double-clicking on the **IDispatch** interface. **OLEView** will give you a dialog asking if you want to view the type library – just click on the View TypeInfo... button and you will be able to see what interfaces the object thinks it supports.

Remember that if you are viewing the type library or the interfaces supported by an object, **OLEView** has activated the object, so you must release the object before you try to build the object's code module. For the type library view, close the window. For the interface list, release the object by selecting Release Instance from the Object menu; just collapsing the branch (clicking on the -) will not do.

*You will find **OLEView** most useful if you select Expert Mode from the View menu so that you can see all the objects available on your system*

Writing VB Clients

VB is excellent as a test environment for objects that implement dual interfaces. There are several ways that you can get an interface on an object, but the first thing you need to do is to make sure that VB knows about the interface by selecting the object's type library in the references dialog (Project | References...):

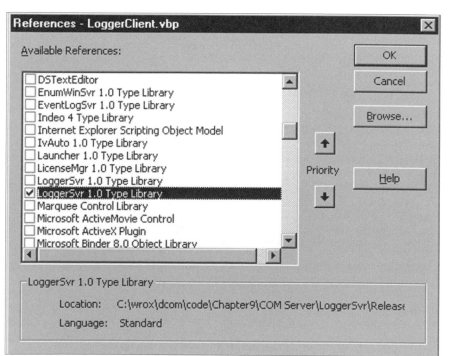

When you select one of the
references in this list, VB will load
the relevant type library. ATL will
bind a server's type library into the
server code module (DLL or EXE),
so VB will load this module to get
hold of the type library. It will keep
a reference on this module as long as
VB is open. The advantage of this is
that you will be able to browse the
type library at any time using the
VB Object Browser (View | Object
Browser):

There is one problem with this. If you are developing a server with Visual C++ and using a VB client to
test it, you will have both development tools open at the same time. This means that Visual C++ will not
be able to delete the server code module during builds, because VB will have a reference on the file. You
will have to shut down VB to release the reference, before rebuilding the project.

Creating Objects in VB

Activating an object in VB is very easy and you have a choice of several methods. The simplest way is
with the following syntax:

```
Dim LoggerObj As New Logger
```

Here the variable **LoggerObj** is declared as being of type **Logger**, which is the name of the **coclass**
declared in the type library. Using the **New** keyword here means that VB will automatically create the
object the first time that the **LoggerObj** variable is used. If you miss out this keyword, you will need to
create the object yourself, as shown:

```
Dim LoggerObj As Logger
Set LoggerObj = New Logger
```

To be able to use the **coclass** name as a data type, VB must have a type library reference for the class.
If you do not provide this reference, you can still create the object using the **CreateObject()** method
and the object's ProgID.

```
Dim Obj As Object
Set Obj = CreateObject("LoggerSvr.Logger.1")
Obj.LogMessage Now, "Hello"
```

When any of these variables go out of scope, the object will be released. You can also force the object to
be released by setting the object variable to **Nothing**.

```
Set Obj = Nothing
```

Visual Basic is pretty flexible in the way that it lets you call your COM objects. If you declare a variable
of type **Object**, the method calls through this variable will be **late bound**. This means that VB will

determine method dispIDs at runtime before calling the method via **Invoke()**. This slows the method call considerably and prevents VB from checking your code at compile time since VB can't know what methods the object supports. So, you could call a non-existent method on the object reference, but it has the advantage of not requiring a type library for the object.

If you use a specific object type, declared as a **coclass** in a type library, the VB compiler can check that the methods do exist and that the types of the parameters that you're passing are valid. VB can also gather all the necessary dispIDs at compile time, so your code will execute faster. This is known as **early binding**.

If your objects support dual interfaces, VB will use the vtable methods in preference to **Invoke()**. This makes the method calls even faster and is known as **very early**, or **vtable**, **binding**. There is no difference in the Visual Basic code that you write for early bound or vtable bound code. So, where possible, use a specific object type:

```
Dim Obj As Logger
Set Obj = CreateObject("LoggerSvr.Logger.1")
Obj.LogMessage Now, "Hello"
```

Note that for objects with multiple dual interfaces, VB will carry out all the required **QueryInterface()** calls with a minimum of fuss. Imagine you have an object that implements two interfaces, **IReadEvents** and **IWriteEvents**:

```
Dim EventLog As New EventLogSvr
Dim EVRead As IReadEvents
Dim EVWrite As IWriteEvents

Set EVRead = EventLog
Set EVWrite = EventLog
```

Here a new **EventLogSvr** object is created and the **EventLog** variable has a pointer to the object's **[default]** interface (as described in the **coclass** definition in the type library). The next two lines declare two variables for the two interfaces we are interested in. These are assigned on the last two lines. This syntax causes a **QI()** on the object for the requested interface.

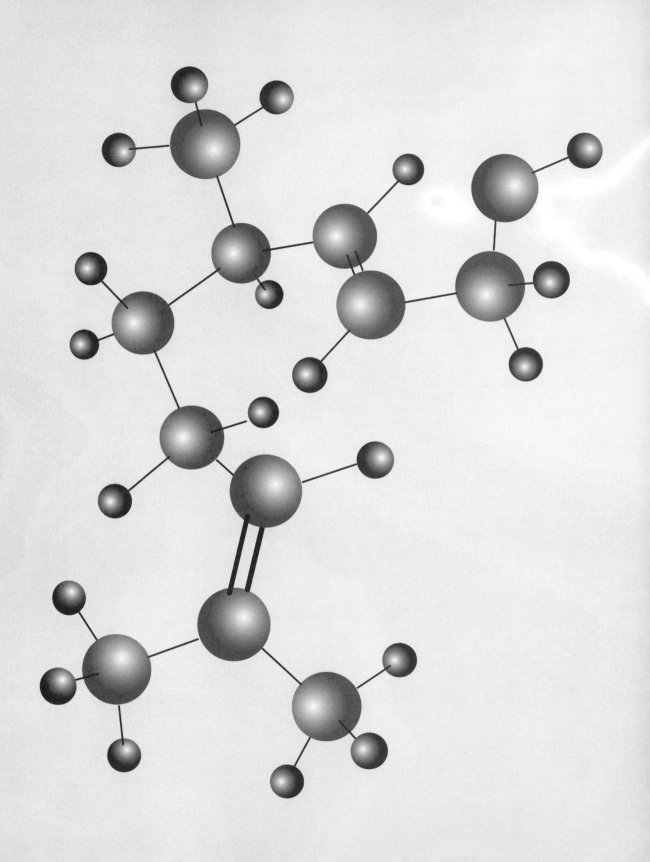

INDEX

Symbols

.bss data segment 67
.def files 52, 67
.mc files 442
.reg files
  marshaling example 221
.wav files, fun with 94
.xls files 104
[in] parameter, COM 98
[out] parameter, COM 98, 102
_beginthreadex() 468
_bind() 28
_declspec (dllexport) 52, 113
_declspec (dllimport) 52, 53
_declspec (thread)
  thread local storage, comparison 61
_lread() 75
_lwrite() 75
_rundown() 24
16-bit OLE 1.0 92
  editing objects 93
16-bit OLE 2.0 94
  advances 95
  UI features 95
32-bit OLE 95

A

accept() 34, 77, 82
access rights, Windows NT 342
  generic, listed 342
  specific 342
  standard, listed 342
access tokens 347
  Windows NT 337
AccessPermission 367
accounts, NT security 329

ACEs (Access Control Entries)
342
  Win32 API functions 354
ACLs (Access Control Lists) 342
  DCE RPC 22
  Microsoft NT 22
  Win32 API functions 354
ActivateAtStorage 154
activation security, COM 365
Active Template Library. see ATL
ActiveX Controls 96
activities, MTS 522
AddAccessAllowedAce() 355
AddAccessDeniedAce() 355
AddAce() 355
AddAuditAccessAce() 355
AddRef(), IUnknown 99
AdjustTokenGroups() 347
AdjustTokenPrivileges() 347, 349
Administration account, Windows NT 329
  privileges 397
Advise() 224
AfxBeginThread() 471
AfxOleInit() 215
aggregation 109
  COM 141
AllocateAndInitializeSid() 345
AllocateLocallyUniqueId() 349
ANSI DLLs 65
apartment model, threading
274, 481
AppIDs (Application IDs)
105, 110, 152
  AppIDs, what are they? 152, 153
  values 153
AppWizard 167
  Automation interfaces, creating 167
  COM servers, creating 168
arrays, MIDL 192
  conformant 194

  enumerators 196
  fixed 193
  open 196
  varying 195
asynchronous communications
15
ATL (Active Template Library)
122
  ATL 2.1 168
  CComBSTR 130
  COM servers, writing with 168
  DCOM services, support for 415
  MFC, comparison 168
  MFC projects, accessing ATL from
245
  tear-off interfaces 124
  threading models 491
AtlModuleRegisterTypeLib() 213
attributes
  IDL 186
  objects 140
authentication 320
  Kerberos Version 5 22
authority 320
  DCE RPC 22
  Microsoft 22
Automation
  Automation types, MIDL 189
  COM 126
  interface, writing 167
  MIDL Automation types 189
  ODL (Object Description Language)
127
    Automation, using 133
    binding 132, 133
    BSTR 118, 130
    data type coercion 132
  oleautomation 205
  remote automation 46
    DCOM, comparison 46
    Remote Automation Manager 46

B

base clients, MTS522
base types, MIDL 188
Basic Object Adapter. *see* BOA
BDC (Backup Domain Controller) 330
Bell Labs 17
bind() 35
binding
  early 132, 204
    early vs. late 133
  late 132
  monikers 138
  very early 133, 205
BindMoniker() 138
BindToObject() 138, 154
Black Widow, Java class library 35
BOA (Basic Object Adapter), CORBA 31
broker, distributed objects 9
BSD 4.3 sockets standard 77
BSTR 118, 130
  converting 130
  creating 130
  MIDL variable type 198
BuildExplicitAccessWithName() 355, 356
BuildSecurityDescriptor() 354, 355
BuildTrusteeWithName() 346
BuildTrusteeWithSid() 346
bytecode 33

C

C/C++ 53
  DLLs, implementing 53
  functions
    exporting, through DLLs 53
    name decoration, with DLLs 53
Cairo, Windows NT 96
call security, COM 366
callback, COM servers 114
CArchive class 76
CAsyncSocket class 74

Catalogue Project, security example 322
  client, creating 326
  servers, protecting from users 328
  user protection 328
CComBSTR, ATL 130
CDS (Cell Directory Service), DCE RPC 20
CDS Clerk, DCE RPC 21, 23
  clearinghouses 21
ChangeServiceConfig() 411
class factories, COM 107
  class factories, what do they do?
  IClassFactory 107
  IClassFactory2 107
class information, OLE 92
classes
  COM 97, 140
  defining, in MIDL
  exporting, through DLLs 55
  nested 122
ClassWizard 133, 177
clearinghouses, DCE RPC 21
clients, creating
  DCOM 160
    optimizations 161
    security 163
    servers, locating 160
    writing 185
      files required 187
  VB. *see* Appendix A
clipboard 91
CloseDesktop() 359
CloseEventLog() 440, 449
CloseHandle() 411, 440
CloseServiceHandle() 411
CloseWindowStation() 358
CLSIDs (Class IDs) 103
COAUTHINFO structure 161, 376
coclass, IDL 206
CoCreateGuid() 103
CoCreateInstance() 109, 288
  debugging. *see* Appendix A
  parameters 109
CoCreateInstanceEx() 160
  debugging. *see* Appendix A
code
  fixups, DLLs 53
  sharing, through DLLs 50

CoFreeLibrary() 112
CoFreeUnusedLibraries() 112, 159
CoGetCallContext() 381
CoGetClassObject() 111, 114, 152, 159, 376
  parameters 52, 108
  prototype 160
CoGetInterfaceAndReleaseStream() 485, 503
CoImpersonateClient() 382
COINIT_APARTMENT-THREADED 106
CoInitialize() 106
CoInitializeEx() 106, 485, 487
CoInitializeSecurity() 381, 387
  parameters 163
COleDispatchDriver class 133
CoLoadLibrary() 111, 112
COM 43, 76, 89-141
  see also DCOM; distributed systems.
  aggregation 109, 141
  alternatives to COM 49
  architecture 43
  Automation 126
    ODL, using with 133
  basics 97
  callbacks 114
  class factories 107
    what do they do? 107
  classes 97, 140
    defining, in MIDL 206
  COM, what is it?
  containment 141
  CORBA, comparison 144
  creating objects 107
  debugging. *see* Appendix A
  delegation 141
  DLLs 106
    comparison 98
  dual interfaces 134
  dynamic invocation 44
  encapsulation 140
  error reporting 102
  functions, return values 102
  history of COM 91
  identifiers 103
    CLSIDs (Class IDs) 103
    GUIDs (Globally Unique IDs) 103, 105
    IIDs (Interface IDs) 103

ProgIDs 104
UUIDs (Universally Unique IDs) 103
inheritance 140
implementation inheritance 141
interface inheritance 140
initializing 106
inproc handlers 116
inproc servers 111
creation 111
DLL management 113
interfaces
see also **interfaces**
Automation 127
CLSIDs (Class IDs) 103
custom 134, 251
dispinterfaces 127, 133, 189, 202, 211
dual interfaces 133, 189, 201
E_NOINTERFACE 101
enumeration 101, 196, 226
GUIDs (Globally Unique IDs) 103, 105
IIDs (Interface IDs) 103
implementing interfaces 120, 122, 124
incoming interfaces 223
marshaling 134-136
multiple inheritances 120
nested classess 122
object server lifetimes 124
outgoing interfaces 223
parameters 98
pointers 100
ProgIDs 104
tear-off interfaces 124
type information 227
type library marshaling 189
UUIDs (Universally Unique IDs) 103
introduction 89
language support 97
listening methods 76
local servers 113
marshaling 114
custom 116
interface marshaling 134-136
standard 116
memory allocation 98
MallocSpy 99
milestones 92-95
objects 97, 140
creating 107, 108, 109
defining, in MIDL 206
object orientation, COM 139
uninitialized 98
protocols recognised 76

proxy code 114
Time example 172
registry 104
see also **system registry**
file extensions 104
GUIDs 105
keys 105
ProgIDs 104
Regedit 104
remote servers 116
security 361
see also **security**
code, writing 376
context 376, 379, 381
experiments 382
initializing 376
registry 361-370
server activation 45
servers 110
see also **DCOM servers**
acknowledgement 291
inproc handlers 116
inproc servers 111, 113
local servers 113
locating, with DCOM 160
problems 54
remote servers 116
security 328
see also **security**
starting 73
standards, COM 96
static invocation 44
status codes, COM 102
stub code 114, 116
stub DLLs
type libraries 44
format, NT 4.0 v. NT 3.51 127
marshaling 45
MIDL definition 206
type library marshaling 45, 136, 210
data types supported 189
environment client 215
environment server 211
example 211
reg files 221
testing 219, 220
unmarshaling 114
CoMarshalInterface() 485
CoMarshalInterThread-
InterfaceInStream() 485, 503
CoMarshalnterface() 137
ComplexPing() 300

compound documents, OLE 93
conformant arrays, MIDL 194
connection points, COM 222
Alarm example
client 237
server 230
sink interface 244
testing 246
enumeration interfaces 226
implementing 228
making connections 223
type information 227
connection-based protocols
13, 17
problems 13
state persistence 15
connectionless protocols 13, 17
pros and cons 13
state persistence 15
constants, MIDL 190
containment, COM 141
context handle, RPC
multithreading 24
Control Panel utility, NT
Services 394
ControlService() 409
CopyProxy() 380
CopySid() 345
CoQueryClientBlanket()
382, 426
CoQueryProxyBlanket() 381
CORBA 25
BOA (Basic Object Adapter) 31
object activation modes 31
CORBAfacilities, OMA 31
CORBAservices, OMA 31
DCOM, comparison 28, 47, 144
DSOM (Distributed System Object
Model) 32
exceptions 27
fault tolerance 16
IDL 26
implementation inheritance 28
Implementation Repository 31
interfaces 15
DII (dynamic interface invocation) 30
Interface Repository 30
invocation 30
static interface invocation 30
Java, compatibility 40

multithreading 33

see also **multithreading; thread handling**.

objects

   object adapters 31

   Object class 28

OMA (Object Management Architecture) 31

ORB (Object Request Broker) 26

   interoperability 32

Orbix 32

platforms 32

security 32

   see also **security**

server activation 33

skeleton code 26

SOM (System Object Model) 32

stub code 26

CORBAservices, OMA 31

**CoRegisterClassObject()
114, 159, 179, 300**

CoRegisterSurrogate() 159

CoRevertToSelf() 382

**COSERVERINFO structure
160, 432**

CoSetProxyBlanket() 381, 386

CoTaskMemFree() 381, 434, 505

CoUnInitialize() 112

**CoUnmarshalInterface()
485, 503**

cpp_quote() 186

CreateDesktop() 359

CreateDirectoryEx() 352

CreateEvent() 353, 458, 464

CreateFile() 69, 352

CreateFileMapping() 69, 353

   parameters 69

CreateFileMoniker() 138, 154

CreateInstance() 108, 112, 159

CreateIOCompletionPort() 481

CreateMailslot() 353

CreateMutex() 353, 462, 494

CreateNamedPipe() 353

CreateObject() 206

CreatePipe() 353

CreateProcess() 107, 353, 415

CreateSemaphore() 353

CreateService() 409, 411

   parameters 409

CreateStdDispatch() 133

**CreateThread() 454-
457, 459, 468, 471, 501**

CreateWindowStation() 358

**critical section
455, 463, 464, 492**

CSocket class 74

CString, MFC 130

custom interfaces 134

custom marshaling 116, 136

D

**DACLs (Discretionary Access
Control Lists) 342**

data

   distributed 9

   dynamic 93

   formats 84

   native, OLE 92

   presentation, OLE 92

   representation 15

   static 66

data sections, DLLs 67

data sharing 66, 93

   COM

      advantages 98

      using 76

   DCE RPC, using 75

      what is RPC? 76

   DDE, using 75

   DLLs, using 66

   exporting data 67, 68

   listening executables 72-76

   listening methods 73-76

   Memory Mapped Files (MMFs) 68

   named pipes, using 75

   shared data sections, DLLs 67

   TCP, using 74

   UDP, using 74

data types

   automation 189

   BSTR 118, 130

      converting 130

      creating 130

   MIDL variable type 198

   dual interfaces 189

   SAFEARRAY 130

   type library marshaling 189

VARIANT 128, 132

data typing 14

   coercion, ODL 132

**data_seg pragma, shared data
sections 67**

datagram protocols. *see*
connectionless protocols

DCE IDL

   MIDL, comparison 20

DCE RPC 19, 75, 143

   see also **RPC; MS-RPC.**

   ACLs (Access Control Lists) 22

   authentication 22

   authority 22

   C++ compatibility 25

   CDS (Cell Directory Service) 20

      CDS Clerk 21, 23

   DCOM, relation to 143

   delta-pinging 149

   facilities 19

   Global Directory Agent, CDS 21

   IDL (Interface Definition Language)
19

      see also **IDL; MIDL.**

   interfaces 19

      IOXIDResolver interface 299

      IRemoteActivation interface 301

      UUIDs (Universally Unique IDs) 19

   Limbo, comparison 19

   Microsoft RPC

      see also **MS-RPC**

      comparison 20

   multithreading 24

      see also **thread handling;
      multithreading.**

   object support 24, 143

   OODCE, Hewlett Packard 25

   pinging 149

   Privilege Attribute Certificate 22

   resource objects, support 25

   SCM (Service Control Manager) 300

   security 22, 143

      see also **security**

   server activation 25

   stub code 19

   threading details 20

   tickets 22

   UUIDs (Universally Unique IDs) 19

DCE security 143

DCOM 143

see also COM
alternatives 49
classes, defining, in MIDL 206
client code 160
    optimizations 161
    security 163
    servers, locating 160
communication mechanisms 15
CORBA, comparison 28, 47
DCE RPC, relation to 143
DCOMCnfg 150, 156
debugging. see Appendix A
future developments 97
history 10
interfaces
    see also interfaces
    inheritance 28
introduction 143
legacy components 150
    ActivateAtStorage 154
    limitations of DCOM 159
    registry settings 152
    surrogates 156, 157, 158
MS-RPC, relation to 143
objects 146
    defining, in MIDL 206
    delta-pinging 148
    pinging 146
    reference counting 146
    releasing objects 149
ORPC (Object RPC) 143
protocols 145
remote automation, comparison 46
security 16
    see also security
    client code 163
    security model 321
    server code 167
    SSPI (Security Support Provider Interface) 321
servers 185
    acknowledgement 291
    as NT Services 391
    debugging. see Appendix A
    locating 160
    writing 165, 167, 185
        security 167
        threading issues 165
services 414
    see also NT Services
    ATL support 415
    client creation 429

EnumWinSvr example 419
    writing 414-416, 429, 434
Solaris version 97
TCP server, comparison 86
type library marshaling 210
    environment client 215
    environment server 211
    example 211
    reg files 221
    testing 219, 220
UDP, preferred protocol 74
what is DCOM? 43, 143
Windows, support 144
writing servers 167
DCOMCnfg 361
DDE (Dynamic Data Exchange) 75, 92
    listening methods 75
    Mosaic DDE 92
    Network DDE 94
    NT IPC mechanism 393
debugging. see Appendix A
DEF files 52
DefaultAccessPermission 367
delegation, COM 141
DeleteAce() 355
DeleteService() 411
delta-pinging 148
    OXID (object exporter IDs) 149
    OXID Resolver 149
    ping-set 148
DeRegisterEventSource() 440, 449
Developer Studio, debugging. see Appendix A
DII (Dynamic Interface Invocation) 15, 30
    CORBA 30
    pros and cons 30
Dis, Inferno 17
DisableThreadLibraryCalls() 470
Discretionary Access Control Lists. see DACLs
discriminated unions, MIDL 191
DispatchMessage() 392, 458
dispinterfaces 127, 211
    calling 133
    data types supported 189
    dual 134
    MIDL definition 202

DisplayPrivileges() 350
DISPPARAMS structure 128
distributed data 9, 10
    see also data; distributed systems.
    history 10
    introduction 9
    uses 12
distributed objects 9, 11
    see also objects; distributed systems.
    broker 9
    choosing a system 13
    introduction 9
    uses 12
    with Windows 49
distributed systems 13
    see also distributed data; distributed objects.
    availability 16
    choosing a system 13
    COM 43-45
        see also COM
    communication 14-15
    CORBA 25-32
        see also CORBA
    DCE RPC 19, 24
        see also DCE RPC
    Inferno 17, 18
    Java 33, 35, 40, 43
    load balancing 16
    Microsoft RPC 20
        see also MS-RPC
    network protocols 13
    object locator 14
    reliability 16
    RPC mechanism 19, 20
        see also RPC
    security 15
        see also security
    Sockets 17
Distributed Transaction Coordinator 514
DllCanUnloadNow() 112, 125, 126
DLLDATA_ROUTINES(), macro 187
DllGetClassObject() 111
DllRegisterServer() 136
DLLs (Dynamic Link Libraries) 50
    ANSI 65

C++, implementing in 53
code
fixups 53
sharing 50
COM, comparison 98
data sections 67, 68
DEF files 52
dynamic data sharing 66
dynamic linking 50
interfaces 51, 52
exception handling 65
explicit linking 53
pros and cons 54
exporting
classes 55
functions 52
header files 57
implicit linking 53
pros and cons 54
import libraries 53
inproc servers 113
interfaces 51
defining 56
linking
dynamic 50-52
explicit 53, 54
implicit 53, 54
runtime 55
loading 54
memory management 65
problems 52, 54, 65
register, using 57
resource-only DLLs 66
runtime linking 55
advantages 55
shared data sections 67
static data sharing 66
thread local storage (TLS) 60
_declspec(thread), comparison 61
UNICODE 65
DllSurrogate 157
DllUnregisterServer() 136
domains, NT 21
domains, NT security 330, 331
trusted domains 330
DOMCnfg 150
Door ORB, SUN 40
implementation 42
DSOM (Distributed System Object Model) 32
see also SOM

DTC. *see* Distributed Transaction Coordinator
dual interfaces 133, 205
data types supported 189
MIDL definition 201, 204
dual interfaces, COM 45
DuplicateToken() 347
DuplicateTokenEx() 347
dwClsContext 108, 152
flags 109
dynamic data
see also data; data sharing.
DDE 93
Mosaic DDE 92
sharing, through DLLs 66
dynamic data exchange (DDE) 92, 93, 96
Mosaic DDE 92
Network DDE 94
dynamic interface invocation. *see* DII
dynamic linking, through DLLs 50

E

E_NOINTERFACE 101
early binding 204
embedded objects (OLE) 92, 94, 95
EnableDCOM 364
encapsulated unions, MIDL 191
encapsulation 24
COM 140
RPC support 24
EnterCriticalSection() 463
entities, IDL 186
EnumDesktops() 359
EnumDesktopWindows() 359
enumeration
arrays, MIDL 196
interfaces, COM 196, 226
enumerations, MIDL 190
EnumWindows() 54
EnumWindowStations() 358
EnumWinSvr, DCOM Services example 419
environment client 215

environment server 211
EqualPrefixSid() 345
EqualSid() 346
error reporting, COM 102
Event Log, NT 435
.mc files 442
adding log entries 449
event resource file, reading 447
Event Sources 440
Event Viewer 436
events
reading 446
reporting 445
example 447
Message Resource Files 441
registry entries 444
event objects 458, 464
Event Viewer, NT 436
Eventvwr utility, NT Services 408
exceptions
CORBA 27
handling exceptions, DLLs 65
ExitThread() 455, 458
explicit linking, DLLs 53
pros and cons 54
exporting data 67
exporting functions, through DLLs 52
EXPORTS, DEF files 52

F

fault tolerance. *see* reliability
fibers 459
file extensions, registry 104
FindClose() 196
FindConnectionPoint() 229
FindFirstFile() 196
FindFirstFreeAce() 355
FindNextFile() 196
fixed arrays, MIDL 193
fixups, DLLs 53
FormatMessage() 441
fread() 75
free threading model 278, 482, 486, 487, 488, 494, 508
FreeSid() 346

FreeSurrogate() 159
fwrite() 75

G

GetAce() 355
GetAclInformation() 355
GetAuditedPermissionsFromAcl() 355
getClientHost() 38
GetComputerName() 175
GetDocumentation() 199
GetEffectiveRightsFromAcl() 355
GetEnvironmentVariable() 212
GetExitCodeThread() 456, 457, 469
GetExplicitEntriesFromAcl() 355
GetFuncDesc() 200
GetIDsOfNames() 128, 133
getInputStream() 34
GetLengthSid() 346
GetlongArray() 197
GetMessage() 458
GetNamedSecurityInfo() 355
getOutputStream() 34
GetProcAddress() 54, 135
GetProcessToken() 350
GetProcessWindowStation() 358
GetQueuedCompletionStatus() 481
GetSecurityDescriptorControl() 354
GetSecurityDescriptorDacl() 354
GetSecurityDescriptorGroup() 354
GetSecurityDescriptorLength() 354
GetSecurityDescriptorOwner() 354
GetSecurityDescriptorSacl() 354
GetSecurityInfo() 355
GetSidIdentifierAuthority() 346
GetSidLengthRequired() 346
GetSidSubAuthority() 346
GetSidSubAuthorityCount() 346
GetThreadDesktop() 359
GetTokenInformation() 347
GetTrusteeForm() 346

GetTrusteeName() 346
GetTrusteeType() 346
GetTypeAttr() 228
GetTypeInfo() 128
GetTypeInfoCount() 128
Global Directory Agent, CDS 21
global variables, in DLL data sections 67
groups, NT security 332
Guest account, Windows NT 329
Guidgen 103
GUIDs (Globally Unique IDs) 103, 105

H

HAL (Hardware Abstraction Layer), NT 391
help file support, MIDL 198
heterogenous systems, handling 12
HKEY_CLASSES_ROOT 104, 136, 152
Horb, Java class library 35
host order, Sockets 17
htonl() 85
htons() 85

I

IAdviseSink 481
IClassFactory interface 107
IClassFactory2 interface 107, 206
IClientSecurity interface 160, 379
IConnectionPoint interface 223
IConnectionPointContainer interface 223, 225
IDataObject() 201
identifiers 103
    AppIDs (Application IDs) 152
    CLSIDs (Class IDs) 103
    GUIDs (Globally Unique IDs) 103, 105
        creating 103

IIDs (Interface IDs) 103
    ProgIDs 104
    UUIDs (Universally Unique IDs) 103
IDispatch interface 44, 128, 211
    data types 129
    IID 103
    type information 128
IDL (Interface Definition Language) 117, 185
    see also MIDL
    attributes 186
    Automation, using 133
    binding
        early 132, 204
        early vs. late 133
        late 132
        monikers 138
        very early 133, 205
    coclasses 206
    compiler 76
    entities 186
    help file support 198
    IDL compiler 76
    statements 187
    structure 186
idlgen, SUN 35, 40
IDropTarget() 201
IEnumConnectionPoints interface 227
IEnumConnections interface 227
IEnumXXXX interfaces 197, 226, 227
IExternalConnection 272
IIDs (Interface IDs) 103
    IDispatch interface, specific 103
    IUnknown interface, specific 103
IMarshal interface 136, 159, 485, 503
IMoniker interface 154
ImpersonateClient() 382
ImpersonateLoggedOnUser() 356, 367
impersonation
    client impersonation 338
    COM security 367
    impersonation level 320
    Windows NT 338
        Win32 API functions 356
implementation inheritance 28
Implementation Repository, CORBA 31

implicit linking, DLLs 53
    pros and cons 54
import library, DLLs 53
incoming interfaces 223
Inferno 17
inheritance 28
    COM 140
    implementation inheritance 28, 141
    interface inheritance 28, 140
    virtual 28
InitializeAcl() 354
InitializeSecurityDescriptor()
354
InitializeSid() 346
inproc handlers 116
inproc servers 111
    creation 111
    DLL management 113
    surrogates 156
        inproc objects, activating 157
instance pooling. see object
pooling
interface inheritance 28
interface marshaling 134
    custom 136
    standard 135
    type library 136
Interface Repository, CORBA
30
interface-wide security context
    client-side 379
    server-side 381
interfaces 14
    ATL and interfaces 168
    Automation 127
        MIDL definition 201
    COM interfaces 97, 117
        CLSIDs (Class IDs) 103
        custom interfaces 134, 251
        dispinterfaces
        127, 133, 134, 189, 202, 211
        dual interfaces
        45, 133, 189, 201, 204, 205
        E_NOINTERFACE 101
        enumeration interfaces 101, 196, 226
        example, test interface 251
        GUIDs (Globally Unique IDs) 103, 105
        IClassFactory 107
        IClassFactory2 107, 206
        IClientSecurity 160, 379
        IConnectionPoint 223

IConnectionPointContainer 223, 225
IDispatch 44, 103, 128, 211
IEnumConnectionPoints 227
IEnumConnections 227
IEnumXXXX 197, 226
IExternalConnection 272
IIDs (Interface IDs) 103
IMarshal 136, 159
IMoniker 154
implementing 120, 122, 124
incoming 223
IProvideClassInfo 228
IRemUnknown 300
IServerSecurity 160, 382
IStdIdentity 272
ISurrogate 159
ITypeInfo 102, 128, 198, 228
IUnknown 43, 98, 99, 103, 117
marshaling 134, 135, 136
multiple inheritance 120
nested classes 122
object server lifetime 124
outgoing interfaces 223
parameters 98
ProgIDs 104
tear-off interfaces 124
type information 227
type library marshaling 189
UUIDs (Universally Unique IDs) 103
CORBA interfaces 15
    defining 27
    DII (Dynamic Interface Invocation) 30
    Interface Repository 30
    static interface invocation 30
custom interfaces
    MIDL definition 201
    test interface, example 251
DCOM interfaces
    see interfaces, COM.
DII (Dynamic Interface Invocation)
15
    CORBA 30
    pros and cons 30
dispinterfaces 127, 211
    calling 133
    data types supported 189
    dual 134
    MIDL definition 202
dual interfaces 45, 133, 205
    data types supported 189
    MIDL definition 201, 204
enumeration interfaces 227
format, MIDL 201

IAdviseSink 481
IDL (Interface Definition Language)
19, 117
incoming interfaces 223
inheritance 28, 140
interface pointers 100
invocation, CORBA 30
marshaling 134, 485
    custom 136
    IMarshal 485, 503
    standard 135
    type library 136
MFC and interfaces 168
Microsoft Transaction Server
    IObjectContext 519
    IObjectControl 534, 535
    ISecurityProperty 532
    ISharedProperty 526
    ISharedPropertyGroup 525
    ISharedPropertyGroupManager 525
    ITransactionContext 527
    ITransactionContextEx 528
outgoing interfaces 223
pointers 100
    debugging. see Appendix A
tear-off interfaces 124
    pros and cons 124
test interface, example 251
type library marshaling
    data types supported 189
UUIDs (Universally Unique IDs) 19
viewing, OLEView 151
InterlockedDecrement() 492
InterlockedIncrement() 492
Internet Protocol (IP) 17
Invoke() 128
IO completion ports 411, 480
IOAllocateErrorLogEntry() 439
IObjectContext 519
IObjectControl 534, 535
IOCompletionPort() 73
IOWriteErrorLogEntry() 439
IOXIDResolver interface 299
IPC (Inter-Process Communica-
tion) mechanisms 393
IProvideClassInfo interface 228
IProxyInterface 187
IRemoteActivation interface 301
IRemUnknown interface 300
ISecurityProperty 532

IServerSecurity interface 160, 382
ISharedProperty 526
ISharedPropertyGroup 525
ISharedPropertyGroupManager 525
IsImpersonating() 382
Isis RDO 16
IStdIdentity 272
IStorage 485
IStream 485
IStubInterface 187
ISurrogate interface 159
IsValidAcl() 354
IsValidSecurityDescriptor() 354
IsValidSid() 346
ITransactionContext 527
ITransactionContextEx 528
ITypeInfo interface 102, 128, 198, 228
IUnknown interface 43, 98, 99
  AddRef() 99
  functions 117
  IID 103
  implementing 117
  QueryInterface() 101
    example 101
  reference counting 99
  Release() 99

J

Java 33
  bytecode 33
  CORBA, compatibility 40
  IDL (Interface Definition Language) 40
  Microsoft Java VM 33
  problems with 40
  remote objects, naming 35
  RMI (Remote Method Activation) 35
  Servant interface 41
  server activation 40, 43
  sockets 34
  VM (virtual machine) 33
JIT activation 512, 533

K

Kerberos 5, 22, 143

L

last_is() 196
LaunchPermissions 161
LeaveCriticalSection() 463
legacy components
  ActivateAtStorage 154
  DCOM 150
  registry settings 152
  surrogates 156
    inproc objects, activating 157
    registry entries 157
    writing 158
LegacyAuthenticationLevel 369
LegacyImpersonationLevel 369
LegacySecureReferences 370
length_is() 196
Limbo, Inferno 17
  bytecode 33
  DCE RPC, comparison 19
linking
  dynamic 50
  explicit 53
    pros and cons 54
  implicit 53
    pros and cons 54
  import library 53
  objects (OLE) 92, 94, 95
  runtime 55
load balancing, distributed systems 16
LoadDllServer() 159
LoadLibrary() 107, 113
LoadLibrary(), DLLs 54
local reference counting 146
  remote reference counting, comparison 146
Local Security Authority. *see* LSA
local servers 113
LocalFree() 355
LocalServer32 key 106, 113
LocalService 110
location transparency 116

locator, MS-RPC 21
Lock() 68
LockServer() 125
LogonUser() 356
LookupAccountName() 345
LookupAccountSid() 345
LookupPrivilegeDisplayName() 349
LookupPrivilegeName() 349
LookupPrivilegeValue() 349
LPTSTR 65
LSA (Local Security Authority) 329
lstrlen() 197
Lucent Technologies 17
LUIDs (Locally Unique IDs) 337

M

Mailslot, NT IPC mechanism 393
MallocSpy 99
MAPI, NT IPC mechanism 393
MapViewOfFile() 69, 71
MapViewOfFileEx() 71
marshaling 45, 114
  between apartments 485, 503
  custom 116, 136
  standard 116, 135
  type library marshaling 45, 136, 210
    environment client 215
    environment server 211
    example 211
    reg files 221
    testing 219, 220
MC.EXE 441
memory allocation, COM 98
memory management, DLLs 65
Memory Mapped Files (MMFs) 68
  example 69
  NT IPC mechanism 393
  problems 70
  UNICODE applications, compatibility 71
  what are MMFs? 69
  Windows NT, using MMFs with 69
Memphis, Windows 97 33

message resource files, Event Log 441
methods, of objects 140
MFC
   ATL
     accessing 245
     comparison 168
   COM servers, writing with MFC 167
   non-multithreaded, discussion 68
Microsoft Directory Services 21
MicrosoftJava VM 33
Microsoft Directory Services 21
Microsoft Transaction Server
16, 156, 511, 522
   activities 522
   base clients 522
   catalog 519
   components 516
     ATL 534
     passing interface pointers 520
     registration 517
     requirements 516
   context objects 514, 517, 519-523, 527
     GetObjectContext() 519
     IObjectContext 519
   JIT activation 512, 533
   MTS Explorer 514
   object locator 14
   object pooling 512, 534
   packages 521
   resource dispensers 514
   resource managers 514
   security 512, 530
     see also **security**
     permissions 532
     roles 532
   SQL Server 514
   surrogates 513
   threading 511, 529
     see also **thread handling**
     apartment model 530
     main model 530
     rental model 530
   transaction context objects 514, 523, 526, 527
   transactions 511, 523
     attributes 526
     commit tree 528
     Distributed Transaction Coordinator 514, 528

     global commit coordinator 528
     ITransactionContext 527, 528
     requirements 526
     the ACID test 523
MIDL compiler
76, 118, 185, 186
   see also **IDL**
   classes, defining 206
   coclasses 206
   DCE IDL, comparison 20
   files created 187
   help file support 198
   interface definitions 120, 200
     see also **interfaces**
     format 201
     library blocks, within 207
     outgoing interfaces 223
   language mappings 210
   marshaling, standard 136
   modules 209
   objects, defining 206
   ODL (Object Description Language) 127
     see **ODL**
   outgoing interfaces 223
   proxy-stub code 187
   type libraries 206
   variable types 187
     arrays 192-196
     automation types 189
     base types 188
     constants 190
     enumerations 190
     exceptions 198
     strings 197, 198
     structs 190
     typedefs 189
     unions 191
MkTypeLib 127, 186
modules, MIDL definition 209
monikers 138
   binding 138
   persistent state 138
   running object table 138
Mosaic DDE 92
MS-RPC 75
   C++ compatibility 25
   COM infrastructure 96
   DCE RPC
     comparison 20
     mixed 23

   DCOM, relation to 143
   locator 21
   mixed
     with DCE RPC 23
     with Microsoft RPC 23
   multithreading 24
     see also **thread handling**
   nsid (name service interface demon) 23
   NT IPC mechanism 393
   object support 24
   OODCE, Hewlett Packard 25
   resource objects, support 25
   Rpcss.exe, bug 179
   RPC, what is it? 76
   security 22
     see also **security**
   server activation 25
   test application 279
     client creation 283
     local testing 284
     network tests 285
     remote testing 285
   what is RPC? 76
MsgWaitForMultipleObjects() 462
MTA. *see* **multithreaded apartment**
MTS. *see* **Microsoft Transaction Server**
MULTI_QI structure 162
multiple inheritance 120
multithreaded apartment 482, 483, 486, 487, 489, 502
multithreading 453
   see also **thread handling**
   COM 45
   context handles 24
   CORBA 33
   DCE RPC 24
   functions 454
   IO completion ports 411
   Java 43
   MS-RPC 24
   NT Services, writing 411
     IO completion ports 411
     worker threads 411
   TCP server example 84
   worker threads 411
mutex 67, 461-464, 494

synchronization, in shared data
sections 67

N

name service interface demon.
see nsid
named pipes 22, 75
  listening methods 75
  NT IPC mechanism 393
  restrictions 75
native data, OLE 92
NEO ORB, SUN 40
nested classes 122
NetClip 94
NetMon utility 285
NetWare networks 74
Network DDE 94
Network OLE 96
network protocols 13
  connection-based protocols 13, 17
  connectionless protocols 13, 17
  datagram protocols. *see* connectionless
  protocols
  DCOM 145
  stream protocols
    see connection-based protocols
Next() 197
non-encapsulated unions, MIDL
192
nsid (name service interface
demon) 23
NT Services 25, 391
  see also DCOM Services
  Control Panel utility 394
  DCOM servers, using 391
  downloading 144
  Eventvwr utility 408
  IPC mechanisms 393
  NT Services, what are they? 391
  registry settings 412
  Registry utility 399
  SC utility 398
  security 413
    see also security
    Win32 API functions 356
  servers, starting 73
  service manager 25

utilities 393
  Control Panel utility 394
  Eventvwr utility 408
  Registry utility 399
  SC utility 398
  Winmsd utility 397
  which services are available? 393
  Winmsd utility 397
  writing an NT Service 400
    database 409
    debugging services 413
    errors, logging 407
    executable entry point 400
    intialization 400
    multithreading 411
      see also thread handling
    registry settings 412
    SCM, communication with 409
    security 413
    see also security
    ServiceCtrlHandler 405
    ServiceMain() 401
ntohl() 85
ntohs() 85

O

Object class, CORBA 28
Object Linking and Embedding
(OLE) 90
  32-bit OLE 95
  Network OLE 96
  OCXs (OLE Controls) 95
  OLE 1.0 92
    editing objects 93
  OLE 2.0 94
    advances 95
    COM 94
    UI features 95
  oleautomation 205
  OLE Controls (OCXs) 95
  OLEView 102
object orientation, and COM 89-
141
object pooling 512, 534
object server lifetime 124
object_to_string() 27
objects
  aggregation 141

attributes 140
COM 97, 140
  class factories 107
  creating 107, 108, 109
containment 141
CORBA
  object adapters 31
  object bus 26
    delta-pinging 148
    pinging 146
    reference counting 146
DCOM
  delta-pinging 148
  object lifetimes 146
  pinging 146
  reference counting 146
  releasing objects 149
defining in MIDL 206
delegation 141
distributed 9, 11
  broker 9
  history 10, 11
  introduction 9
  methods of distribution 16
  see also distributed systems
  uses 12
embedded 92, 94, 95
encapsulation 140
inheritance 140
  implementation inheritance 141
  interface inheritance 140
linked 92, 94, 95
methods 140
MIDL, defining in 206
object activation modes, BOA 31
object locator, distributed systems 14
  CORBA 2 14
  Microsoft Transaction Server 14
  object orientation
  history 11
object references, CORBA 26
OLE 90
  32-bit OLE 95
  activating, OLE 1.0 93
  OLE 1.0, 16-bit 92
  OLE 2.0, 16-bit 94
  viewing with OLEView 102
polymorphism 141
proxy 12
  history 12
resource
  RPC support 25

RPC
handling 25
support 24
uninitialized objects 98
viewing, with OLEView 102
Visual Basic
creating. see Appendix A
Windows 49
Windows NT 338
accessing 344
attributes 338
directory 339
object manager 338
services 338
OCXs (OLE Controls) 95
ODL *see* Object Description
Language
OLE *see* Object Linking and
Embedding
OleInitialize() 106, 166
OMA (Object Management
Architecture), CORBA 31
OMG Transaction Service 16
OODCE, Hewlett Packard 25
open arrays, MIDL 196
Open Group, The 75
OpenDesktop() 359
OpenEventLog() 440, 449
OpenMutex() 462, 494
OpenProcessToken()
347, 350, 356
OpenSCManager() 409
OpenService() 409
OpenThreadToken() 347, 356
OpenWindowStation() 358
flags 359
optimizations, DCOM 301
multiple calling 302
multiple clients 307
test results 313
ORB (Object Request Broker),
CORBA 26
interoperability 32
Orbix 28, 32
ORPC (Object RPC), DCOM
143
OSF DCE RPC 19, 75
see also RPC; DCE RPC; MS-RPC.
Microsoft implementation 75
UUIDs 103

outgoing interfaces 223
OXID (object exporter IDs),
DCE ping 149
OXID Resolver 299

P

packages, Microsoft Transaction
Server 521
PDC (Primary Domain
Controller) 330
permissions, Windows NT 336
persistent state monikers 138
pinging 86, 146, 300
DCOM 146
delta-pinging 148
OXID (object exporter IDs) 149
OXID Resolver 149
ping-set 148
example 147
polymorphism 24
COM 141
RPC support 24
pong. *see* pinging
PostMessage() 459
PostThreadMessage()
459, 501, 504
ppvObject 108
presentation data, OLE 92
Privilege Attribute Certificate,
DCE RPC 22
PrivilegeCheck() 349
privileges, Windows NT 336
Win32 API functions 349
process-wide security context
376
ProgIDs 104
protocols
connection-based protocols 13, 17
connectionless protocols 13, 17
datagram protocols. *see* connectionless
protocols
DCOM 145
SPX 13
stream protocols. *see* connection-based
protocols
TCP 13
proxy DLLs, COM

IProxyInterface 187
MIDL, creating with 187
proxy object 12, 44
history 12
see also pinging
ProxyStubClsid32 136
pServerInfo 108, 376
PulseEvent() 464

Q

QueryBlanket() 380, 382
QueryInterface(), IUnknown 101
QueryServiceStatus() 409

R

Randomize() 200
ReadEventLog() 446, 449
parameters 446
ReadFile() 75
rebind() 35
recv() 77
reference counting 99, 146
RegCreateKeyEx() 352
Regedit 104
RegisterEventSource() 440, 449
RegisterServer() 213, 417
RegisterServiceCtrlHandler()
402
RegisterTypeLib() 214
registry
COM
file extensions 104
GUIDs 105
HKEY_CLASSES_ROOT 104
keys 105
LocalServer32 113
ProgIDs 104
Regedit 104
security 361
activation security 365
call security 366
DCOMCnfg 361
EnableDCOM 364
experiments 370

impersonation 367
OLEView, using 363
Event Log, registry entries 444
keys 145, 161, 412
Registry utility, NT Services 399
settings 412
surrogate registry entries 157
Registry utility, NT Services 399
RegQueryValue() 193
RegSetValue() 193
RegSvr32 136
relative IDs. *see* **RIDs**
Release() 99, 112, 124, 125
ReleaseMutex() 461
reliability, distributed systems 16
remote automation 46
DCOM, comparison 46
Remote Automation Manager 46
remote reference counting 146
local reference counting, comparison 146
remote servers 116
ReportEvent() 407, 408, 441, 449
parameters 445
ResetEvent() 464
resource dispensers 514, 524
ODBC Resource Dispenser 514, 524
Shared Property Manager 514, 525
resource managers 514, 524
SQL Server 514, 524
resource objects
RPC support 25
resource-only DLLs 66
ResumeThread() 454, 456
RevertToSelf() 356, 382
RIDs (relative IDs), NT security 334
RMISecurityManager class 39
ROT (Runinng Object Table) 138
RPC
see also **DCE RPC**; **MS-RPC**.
C++ compatibility 25
IOXIDResolver interface 299
IRemoteActivation interface 301
multithreading 24
context handle 24
object support 24
OODCE, Hewlett Packard 25

resource objects, support 25
RPC mechanism 19, 20
RPC, what is it?
Rpcss.exe, bug 179
SCM (Service Control Manager) 300
server activation 25
pros and cons 25
stub code 19
test application 279
client creation 283
local testing 284
network tests 285
remote testing 285
test interface 252
threading details 20
what is RPC? 76
rpc_server_listen() 25
RPC_S_SERVER_UNAVAILABLE 102
rpc_server_listen() 24
RpcImpersonateClient() 23
RpcRevertToSelf() 23
RpcServerListen() 24, 25
running object table monikers 138
runtime linking, DLLs 55

S

SACLs. *see* **System Access Control Lists**
SAFEARRAY 130
fFeatures 131
SafeRef() 520
SAM. *see* **Security Accounts Manager**
SC utility, NT Services 398
SCM. *see* **Service Control Manager**
NT Services, communicating with 409
SDK, writing COM servers with 167
security 319-389
access tokens 347
ACLs (Access Control Lists)
authority 22
Win32 API functions 354
authentication 320

Kerberos Version 5 22, 143
authority 22, 320
Catalogue Project, example 322-328
client impersonation 338
COM 361-389
code, writing 376
experiments 382
initializing 376
registry 361-367, 370
context
interface-wide 379, 381
process-wide 376
CORBA 32
DCE 143
MS-RPC, comparison 22
DCOM 163, 361
client code 163
client security context 290
context, security 376, 379, 381
server code 167
server identification 290
descriptors 339, 340
Win32 API functions 352
distributed systems 15
impersonation 338
client impersonation 338
impersonation level 320
Win32 API functions 356
introduction to security 319
Kerberos Version 5
authentication system 22
Kerberos Version 5 143
Microsoft Transaction Server 512, 530
NT Services 413
Win32 API functions 356
programming security 344
RIDs (relative IDs) 334
security descriptors 339, 340
Win32 API functions 352
security, why do we need it? 321
SIDs (Security IDs) 334
Win32 API functions 345
Win32 API and security 344
window stations, Win32 API functions 358
Windows NT 321, 329
access rights 342
access tokens 337, 347
accounts 329
ACLs 354
authority 334

domains *330, 331*
groups *332*
impersonation *338, 356*
LSA (Local Security Authority) *329*
NT Services *356*
objects *338*
    accessing *344*
privileges *336, 337, 349*
RIDs (relative IDs) *334*
SAM (Security Accounts Manager) *329*
security descriptors *339, 340, 352*
SIDs (Security IDs) *334, 345*
subjects *338*
trusted domains *330*
user rights *336, 349*
window stations *358, 359*
workgroups *330*
Security Accounts Manager (SAM) 329
send() 77
SendMessage() 459
Servant interface, Java 41
servers
activation
    CORBA *33*
    Java *43*
    COM *45*
    Java *40*
    RPC *25*
code, DCOM *165*
    security *167*
    threading issues *165*
COM *110*
    inproc handlers *116*
    inproc servers *111*
        creation *111*
        DLL management *113*
        surrogates *156, 157*
    local servers *113*
    locating, with DCOM *160*
    problems *54*
    remote servers *116*
    security *328*
    starting *73*
DCOM *185*
    acknowledgement *291*
    as NT Services *391*
    debugging. see Appendix A
    writing *185*
        files required *187*
starting servers *72*
    COM servers *73*
    interactive users *72*

NT services *73*
startup file *72*
Windows 95 PseudoServices *73*
Service Control Manager (SCM) 300
service manager, NT services 25
SERVICE_TABLE_ENTRY structure 400
ServiceCtrlHandler() 400, 402, 405, 409
parameters *406*
ServiceMain() 391, 400, 401
services, DCOM 414
ATL support *415*
client creation *429*
EnumWinSvr example *419*
writing *414, 415*
    client creation *429*
    code *415*
    cons *414*
    example *416*
    pros *415*
    tests *434*
services, NT 25, 391-452
Control Panel utility *394*
DCOM servers, using *391-452*
Eventvwr utility *408*
IPC mechanisms *393*
NT Services, what are they? *391*
Registry utility *399*
SC utility *398*
service manager *25*
utilities *393*
    Control Panel utility *394*
    Eventvwr utility *408*
    Registry utility *399*
    SC utility *398*
    Winmsd utility *397*
which services are available? *393*
Winmsd utility *397*
writing an NT Service *400*
    database *409*
    debugging services *413*
    errors, logging *407*
    executable entry point *400*
    initialization *400*
    registry settings, NT Services *412*
    SCM, communication with *409*
    security *413*
    ServiceCtrlHandler *405*
    ServiceMain() *401*

SetAclInformation() 355
SetBlanket() 380
SetEntriesInAcl() 355, 356
SetEvent() 458, 464
SetNamedSecurityInfo() 355
SetProcessWindowStation() 358
SetSecurityDescriptorDacl() 354
SetSecurityInfo() 355
SetServiceStatus() 403
SetThreadDesktop() 359
SetThreadToken() 347
SetTokenInformation() 347, 349
shared data sections, DLLs 67
    see also DLLs; data sharing.
    access, controlling *67*
    data-seg pragma *67*
    example *68*
    exporting data *67*
    global variables *67*
    naming conventions *67*
    synchronization, of data access *67*
SIDs (Security IDs), NT security 22, 334
    Win32 API functions *345*
simple subjects, Windows NT 338
SimplePing() 300
single threaded apartment 482-489, 491, 502
sink interfaces 223
sizeis() 197
skeleton code, CORBA 26
Sleep() 477
Sockets 17
    Java *34*
Solaris DCOM 97
SOM. see **System Object Model**
    see also DSOM
SPX protocol 13, 74
Spy++ 64
SQL Server 514
STA. see **single threaded apartment**
standard marshaling 116, 135
StartService() 409
StartServiceCtrlDispatcher() 400
startup file, starting a server 72
state persistence, distributed systems 15

static data 66
 see also **data**; **DLLs.**
static interface invocation,
CORBA 30
static invocation, COM 44
status codes, COM 102
STDMETHOD(), macro 121
stream protocols. *see* **connection-based protocols**
string_to_object() 27
strings, MIDL 197
 BSTRs 198
 methods returning strings, example
 197
structs, MIDL 190
stub code
 CORBA 26
 DCE RPC 19
 COM 114, 116
  MIDL, creating with 187
Styx, Inferno 17
subjects, Windows NT 338
SUCCEEDED(), macro 101
SUN
 Door ORB 40
 IDL (Interface Definition Language)
 35
 NEO ORB 40
surrogates 156
 inproc objects, activating 157
 Microsoft Transaction Server 513
 registry entries 157
 writing 158
SuspendThread() 454
SwitchDesktops() 359
synchronization 67, 68
 critical sections 455, 463, 464, 492
 events 458, 464
 mutexes 461-464, 494
synchronous communications 15
SysAllocString() 130
SysFreeString() 130, 218
System Access Control Lists
(SACLs) 342
System account, Windows NT
329
 privileges 396
System Object Model 32
 see also **DSOM**
system registry

COM
 file extensions 104
 GUIDs 105
 HKEY_CLASSES_ROOT 104
 keys 105
 LocalServer32 113
 ProgIDs 104
 Regedit 104
 security 361
  activation security 365
  call security 366
  DCOMCnfg 361
  EnableDCOM 364
  experiments 370
  impersonation 367
  OLEView 363
Event Log, registry entries 444
keys 145
 LaunchPermissions 161
 NT Services 412
Registry utility, NT Services 399
settings, NT Services 412
surrogate registry entries 157

T

TCHAR 65
TCP
 advantages 74
 listening methods 74
 NT IPC mechanism 393
 server example 76
  ClientSocket 83
  connection objects 82
  data formats 84
  data transmission 84
  DCOM, comparison 86
  exceptions 86
  functions, calling 85
  initializing the server 81
  multithreading 84
  pinging 86
  protocol 77
  putting it together 83
  TCPClient 77
  TCPServer 77
  thread handling 81
  WinSock 77
TCP/IP 13, 17, 22

 data sharing 74
TCPClient 77
TCPServer 77
tear-off interfaces 124
 pros and cons 124
TerminateThread() 455, 458
test applications
 DCOM 252
  network tests 285, 287
 MS-RPC 279
  client creation 283
  local testing 284
  network tests 285
  remote testing 285
thread handling 453
 Alarm example 233
 apartment 482
  main 489
 apartment model 274
 context handle 24
 CWnd* pointers, problems with 82
 DCOM server code 165
 fibers 459
 free threading model 278
 functions 454
 IO completion ports 411, 480
 limitations 453
 lifetime, threads 454
 MFC 471
  CWinApp 471
  CWinThread 471
 Microsoft Transaction Server 511
  see also **Microsoft Transaction Server**
  apartment model 530
  main model 530
  rental model 530
 models
  apartment 481, 482
  ATL 491
  free threading 482, 486-488, 494, 508
  mixed 488
  Windows 95 166
  Windows NT 166
 multithreaded apartment 482-483, 486-489, 502
 multithreading 453
  COM 45
  CORBA 33
  Java 43

NT Services, writing 411
RPC 24
server code, DCOM 165
single threaded apartment 482-489, 491, 502
synchronization objects 460
critical sections 455, 463-464, 492
events 458, 464
mutexes 461-464, 494
TCP server example 81, 84
techniques
thread pools 472, 475, 480
worker threads 467
thread local storage (TLS) 60, 464, 466
__declspec (thread), comparison 61
thread static data 466
Windows 95 166
Windows NT 166
worker threads 411
thread local storage (TLS) 60
_declspec (thread), comparison 61
ThreadingModel 166
tickets, DCE RPC 22
TlsAlloc() 60, 466
TlsFree() 61, 466
TlsGetValue() 61, 467
TlsSetValue() 61, 467
transaction context objects 514, 523, 526-527
transaction monitor, reliability 16
Microsoft Transaction Server 16
OMG Transaction Service 16
Transaction Server. *see* **Microsoft Transaction Server**
transactions, the ACID test 523
trusted domains, NT security 330
trustees 346
type information 128, 227
type libraries, COM 44
format, NT 4.0 v. NT 3.51 127
marshaling 45
MIDL definition 206
type library marshaling 45, 136, 210
data types supported 189
environment client 215
environment server 211

example 211
reg files 221
testing 219, 220
TYPEATTR structure 228
typedefs, MIDL 189

U

UDP/IP 17, 74
listening methods 74
NT IPC mechanism 393
Unadvise() 224
UNC 21
CDS, comparison 21
future 21
UNICODE DLLs 65
unions, MIDL 191
Unlock() 68
UnMapViewOfFile() 71
unmarshaling 114
UuidCreate() 103
UUIDs (Universally Unique IDs) 19, 103

V

variable types, MIDL 187
arrays 192
conformant 194
enumerators 196
fixed 193
open 196
varying 195
automation types 189
base types 188
BSTRs 198
constants 190
enumerations 190
exceptions 198
strings 197
BSTRs 198
methods returning strings 197
structs 190
typedefs 189
unions 191
VariantChangeType() 132

VARIANTs 128, 132
varying arrays, MIDL 195
VBXs 95
VDM (Virtual DOS Machine) 95
very early binding 205
virtual functions 118
virtual inheritance 28
VM (virtual machine), Java 33
vtables, C++ 117, 118, 120

W

WaitForMultipleObjects() 454, 457-458, 461-462
WaitForSingleObject() 454, 458, 461, 464, 468-469, 477, 501
Window Enumerator Library, DLL example 59
interface 62
enhancing 64
window stations 139
DCOM support 144
using 360
Win32 API functions 358
Windows and distributed objects 49-88
Windows 95. 95
DCOM support 144
PseudoServices 73
released 95
Rpcss.exe, bug 179
security 319
threading model 166
Windows 97. 33
Windows NT
boot sequence 391
DCOM support 144
domains 21
Event Log 435
.mc files 442
adding to 449
event resource file, reading 447
Event Sources 440
Event Viewer 436
events 445, 446
example 447
Message Resource Files 441

registry entries 444
LUIDs (Locally Unique IDs) 337
Memory Mapped Files, using 69
mixed DCE RPC/MS-RPC 23
NT Services 25, 391
   Control Panel utility 394
   DCOM servers, using 391
   downloading 144
   Eventvwr utility 408
   IPC mechanisms 393
   NT Services, what are they? 391
   registry settings 412
   Registry utility 399
   SC utility 398
   security 413
      see also **security**
      Win32 API functions 356
   servers, starting 73
   service manager 25
   utilities 393
      Control Panel utility 394
      Eventvwr utility 408
      Registry utility 399
      SC utility 398
      Winmsd utility 397
   which services are available? 393
   Winmsd utility 397
   writing an NT Service 400
      database 409
      debugging services 413
      errors, logging 407
   executable entry point 400
   intialization 400
   multithreading 411
      see also **thread handling**
   registry settings 412
   SCM, communication with 409
   security 413
      see also **security**
   ServiceCtrlHandler 405
   ServiceMain() 401
objects 338
   accessing 344
   attributes 338
   body 338
   directory 339
   header 338
   services 338
privileges
   listed 396
security 319, 329
   see also **security**
   access

   rights 342
   tokens 337, 347
   accounts 329, 396, 397
   ACLs 354
   descriptors 339, 340, 352
   domains 330, 331
   groups 332
   impersonation 338, 356
   LSA (Local Security Authority) 329
   NT objects 338
   NT Services 356
   NTLMSSP 321
   objects, accessing 344
   privileges 336, 337, 349
   RIDs (relative IDs) 334
   Security Accounts Manager (SAM) 329
   security descriptors 339, 340, 352
   SIDs (Security IDs) 334, 345
   subjects 338
   trusted domains 330
   user rights 336, 349
   window stations 358
   workgroups 330
servers, starting 73
services 25
   see also **NT Services**
   downloading 144
   service manager 25
   services, what are they? 392
subjects 338
UNC
   CDS, comparison 21
   future 21
Windows NT 3.1 94
Windows NT 3.51 207, 415
   threading model 166
Windows NT 4.0 207, 415
   security
      see also **security**
      functions, high-level 355
      functions, low-level 353
   threading model 166
Winerror.h, error codes 102
WinHelp() 199
WinMain() 391
Winmsd utility, NT Services 397
WinSock API, programming 76, 77
workgroups, NT security 330
World Wide Web
   Microsoft web site 151
   NT Services, downloading 144

Wrox web site 6
WOW (Windows on Windows) 95
WriteFile() 75
Wrox Press web site 6, 60

X

X/Open 75

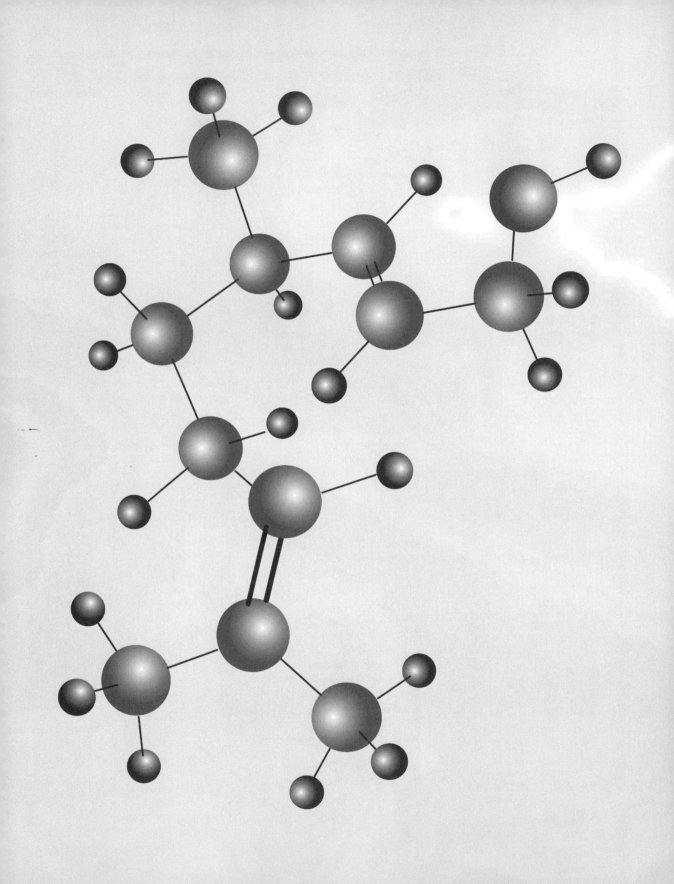

Professional Visual C++ 5 ActiveX/COM Control Programming

Authors: Sing Li and
Panos Economopolous
ISBN: 1861000375
Price: $40.00 C$56.00 £36.99

"We believe that we can show you how to crack open COM and produce robust ActiveX controls to use now. It's our aim to show you the efficient route past all the pitfalls and dead-ends we've encountered and to help you succeed with the best methods. We've grappled with this technology since its inception and we know we can help you put solutions into practice. For some, it'll be the first time you've seen these new programming tools in action, but by the end of the book, you'll be using them to relieve some of your major development headaches"

Sing and Panos

This book is for anyone taking up the challenge of programming in the COM environment, using Visual C++, to produce industry-strength ActiveX controls. You should be familiar with fundamental Windows development and using MFC. You will get the full benefit of learning how to develop professional controls for Win32 with the Active Template Library (ATL) included in Visual C++ 5

Professional Visual C++ ISAPI Programming

Author: Michael Tracy
ISBN: 1861000664
Price: $40.00 C$56.00 £36.99

This is a working developer's guide to customizing Microsoft's Internet Information Server, which is now an integrated and free addition to the NT4.0 platform. This is essential reading for real-world web site development and expects readers to already be competent C++ and C programmers. Although all techniques in the book are workable under various C++ compilers, users of Visual C++ 4.1 will benefit from the ISAPI extensions supplied in its AppWizard.

This book covers extension and filter programming in depth. There is a walk through the API structure but not a reference to endless calls. Instead, we illustrate the key specifications with example programs.

HTTP and HTML instructions are issued as an appendix. We introduce extensions by mimicking popular CGI scripts and there's a specific chapter on controlling cookies. With filters we are not just re-running generic web code - these are leading-edge filter methods specifically designed for the IIS API.

Instant ActiveX Web Database Programming

Authors: Alex Homer, Stephen Jakab
and Darren Gill
ISBN: 1861000464
Price: $29.95 C$41.95 £27.99

This book describes practical techniques for publishing database information on the web or intranet. Aimed at web developers who want to improve their sites by adding live data, and at programmers who want to create functional business applications for the Internet or intranet, the book covers IDC, OLEISAPI, dbWeb, Index Server and Active Server Pages. It also takes a look at the security issues you need to consider when publishing database information on the Internet.

Visual C++ 4 MasterClass

Authors: Various   ISBN: 1874416443
Price: $49.95 C$69.95 £46.99

The book starts by covering software design issues related to programming with MFC, providing tips and techniques for creating great MFC extensions. This is followed by an analysis of porting issues when moving your applications from 16 to 32 bits.

The next section shows how you can use COM/OLE in the real world. This begins with an examination of COM technologies and the foundations of OLE (aggregation, uniform data transfer, drag and drop and so on) and is followed by a look at extending standard MFC OLE Document clients and servers to make use of database storage.

The third section of the book concentrates on making use of, and extending, the features that Windows 95 first brought to the public, including the 32-bit common controls, and the new style shell. You'll see how to make use of all the new features including appbars, file viewers, shortcuts, and property sheets.

The fourth section of the book provides a detailed look at multimedia and games programming, making use of Windows multimedia services and the facilities provided by the Game SDK (DirectX).

The final section covers 'net programming, whether it's for the Internet or the intranet. You'll see how to make the most of named pipes, mailslots, NetBIOS and WinSock before seeing how to create the corporate intranet system of your dreams using WinINet and ActiveX technology.

Beginning Java 1.1

Author: Ivor Horton
ISBN: 1861000278
Price: $36.00 C$50.40 £32.99
Available May 97

If you've enjoyed this book, you'll get a lot from Ivor's new book, Beginning Java.

Beginning Java teaches Java 1.1 from scratch, taking in all the fundamental features of the Java language, along with practical applications of Java's extensive class libraries. While it assumes some little familiarity with general programming concepts, Ivor takes time to cover the basics of the language in depth. He assumes no knowledge of object-oriented programming.

Ivor first introduces the essential bits of Java without which no program will run. Then he covers how Java handles data, and the syntax it uses to make decisions and control program flow. The essentials of object-oriented programming with Java are covered, and these concepts are reinforced throughout the book. Chapters on exceptions, threads and I/O follow, before Ivor turns to Java's graphics support and applet ability. Finally the book looks at JDBC and RMI, two additions to the Java 1.1 language which allow Java programs to communicate with databases and other Java programs.

Beginning Visual C++ 5

Author: Ivor Horton   ISBN: 1861000081
Price: $39.95 C$55.95 £36.99

Visual Basic is a great tool for generating applications quickly and easily, but if you really want to create fast, tight programs using the latest technologies, Visual C++ is the only way to go.

Ivor Horton's Beginning Visual C++ 5 is for anyone who wants to learn C++ and Windows programming with Visual C++ 5 and MFC, and the combination of the programming discipline you've learned from this book and Ivor's relaxed and informal teaching style will make it even easier for you to succeed in taming structured programming and writing real Windows applications.

The book begins with a fast-paced but comprehensive tutorial to the C++ language. You'll then go on to learn about object orientation with C++ and how this relates to Windows programming, culminating with the design and implementation of a sizable class-based C++ application. The next part of the book walks you through creating Windows applications using MFC, including sections on output to the screen and printer, how to program menus, toolbars and dialogs, and how to respond to a user's actions. The final few chapters comprise an introduction COM and examples of how to create ActiveX controls using both MFC and the Active Template Library (ATL).

Parallax is a leading provider of application development and consultancy services in the distributed object technology arena. We help major blue-chip companies within the financial, manufacturing and retail market sectors, to realise the business benefits of object technology.

The key to our approach is to apply the right technology for the problem. Our solutions are leading edge; we design complete distributed systems, integrate with existing legacy systems and provide considerable expertise in migration strategies.

Our skills set is based on vanguard technologies. We make them commercially viable using the latest tools and techniques. Key areas include:

- Java, Web and Distributed Object Technologies (including DCOM and CORBA)
- Object-Oriented Methodologies and Technologies
- Open Systems and Client-Server Architectures
- Relational, Distributed and Object-Oriented Databases
- Multimedia Applications and GUIs
- UNIX, Windows and Windows NT
- Internet and Intranet Solutions
- C++, Visual Basic, 4GLs, Delphi, Perl

In all aspects of our work, innovation and creativity are hallmarks of the Parallax company culture and this has resulted in a number of accolades including:

- Becoming Sun's Object Reality Centre in the UK
- Being awarded Java Centre Status
- Member of the Iona Orbix Team
- IS9000 TickIt Certification
- Winning numerous awards including:
    - Infomatics Award for Best Use of Object Technology within an Enterprise or Large Systems Environment
    - Best ObjectStore Deployment of the Year
    - SMART Award for Research and Technology.

Parallax Solutions Limited, Stonecourt, Siskin Drive, Coventry CV3 4FJ

Telephone: **01203 514400**   *Fax:* **01203 514401**   *Email:* **info@parallax.co.uk**

http://www.parallax.co.uk

Supporting you on the web
http://www.wrox.com/

Fast download the source code to your book and collect updates on any errata

Preview forthcoming titles and test out some sample chapters

Get the full, detailed lowdown on any of our books - and read the reviews!

Sign-up for our free newspaper: "Developers' Journal" for Wrox activity, sample chapters and hot info on the industry

Drop into our mirror site at
http://www.wrox.co.uk